# LEGAL HOMICIDE

# William J. Bowers

with Glenn L. Pierce and John F. McDevitt

Foreword by Henry Schwarzschild

# Legal
# Homicide

DEATH AS PUNISHMENT
IN AMERICA, 1864–1982

NORTHEASTERN UNIVERSITY PRESS
BOSTON

Northeastern University Press

Copyright © 1974, 1984 William J. Bowers

Chapters 7 and 8 were originally published in *Crime &
Delinquency*, Vol. 26, No. 4 (October 1980), and are reprinted here with permission. Portions of Chapter 9 were
originally published in the *Yale Law Journal* (December
1975) and are reprinted here with permission.

Library of Congress Cataloging in Publication Data

Bowers, William J.
    Legal Homicide.
    Previous ed. published as: Executions in America.
1974.
    Bibliography: p.
    Includes index.
    1. Capital punishment—United States. 2. Executions
and executioners—United States. 3. Race discrimination—
United States. I. Pierce, Glenn L. II. McDevitt, John F.
III. Title.
HV8699.U5B68   1981     364.6'6'0973     81-11309
ISBN 0-930350-25-1

Printed in the United States of America
88  87  86  85  84     5  4  3  2  1

This book was composed in Trump Medieval by Crane
Typesetting Service, Barnstable, Mass. It was printed and
bound by The Murray Printing Co., Westford, Mass. The
paper is Warren's 1854, an acid-free sheet.

In the hope that this work will improve the quality of justice in America, I dedicate this book to those whose inspiration and encouragement have meant the most to me:

Steven
Michael
Paul
Deborah

# CONTENTS

# LIST OF TABLES

# LIST OF FIGURES

# FOREWORD

*Legal Homicide* is both the offspring and the embodiment of an underground classic entitled *Executions in America*. The earlier book (incorporated in Part One of this volume) has been the principal source of detailed sociological data about the manner in which our society employed the death penalty during the century when executions became the province of state government: namely, arbitrarily, discriminatorily, and frequently. In *The Death Penalty on Trial* (Part Two of this volume), Dr. Bowers has now added a devastating appraisal of our society's contemporary struggle to retain the death penalty by pretending to purge from it the elements declared unconstitutionally "cruel and unusual" by the Supreme Court in its 1972 *Furman* decision. This volume makes it clear that the death penalty is still guilty as charged in *Furman*. It is the institution of capital punishment that should be condemned to die.

In our times, governments have shed rivers of blood—in wars and "police actions," in extermination camps and forced labor camps, in revolutions and counterrevolutions, at the hands of sheriffs and death squads. Auschwitz and Hiroshima should have established for all time that the power of governments to kill is a menacing arrogation of both godlike wisdom and totalitarian ruthlessness. Those states that assert and use that power always cite benefits accruing to society to justify the selection of those they propose to kill. But homicide, even when called execution, and however lawful or ceremonious, remains the most destructive and brutalizing event in the life of a society.

In a perfect (and therefore entirely hypothetical) society, the death penalty could perhaps be imposed with infallibly accurate judgment and without a trace of discrimination on grounds of race, class, or sex. Even then the death penalty would corrupt the perfect society by continuing to teach that killing a human being is an acceptable solution to a social problem. But a perfect society would not need the death penalty; and in our own imperfect one, people who would not think of trusting the political institutions to tell them whom to marry or what newspaper to read are so frightened by crime and violence that they permit the state to say who shall live and who shall die. They make themselves believe that official acts of ultimate violence, called executions, will make their society safer. It is a fallacy that Dr. Bowers' data conclusively dispel.

On the issue of capital punishment, the United States seems intent upon marching in a direction opposite that of the rest of the world. Most countries with whom we share social, cultural, and legal values have abolished the death penalty in law or in practice (without, incidentally, suffering any known harmful effects). The major countries that continue to use capital punishment in the ordinary course of their criminal justice systems in such large numbers as ours are oppressive, racist, or irrational ones: the Soviet Union, the Republic of South Africa, the Ayatollah's Iran. Eventually, our return to so useless and brutalizing a criminal sanction as the electric chair, the gas chamber, the gallows, lethal injection, or the firing squad will also be recognized by us as oppressive, racist, and uncivilized.

As this book appears, there are over a thousand people on death row in the United States, and we are sentencing defendants to death at a rate of about two hundred a year (and the rate is rising). Executions themselves have not as yet resumed on a scale comparable to death sentencing, but only because the complex rulings of the U.S. Supreme Court have left many constitutional and legal issues to be resolved before that process can fully begin. There is now reason to fear that by 1984 the legal remedies for the death-row inmates who have been appealing their cases the longest will become exhausted. The process of ceremonious, lawful, premeditated state homicide will recommence in earnest and by then we are likely to be sentencing to death about one defendant per day. Will we really substitute a national bloodbath for a more thoughtful way of dealing with crime, for a more rational system of criminal justice, for a more humane penology?

If we bethink ourselves as a civilized people and choose a different course, Dr. Bowers' persistent contributions to knowledge rather than myth, his dedication to scientific scholarship rather than incantations about retribution, will have played a significant role in establishing those "evolving standards of decency that mark the progress of a maturing society."

*Summer 1983*                                  Henry Schwarzschild
                                               *Director*
                                               *Capital Punishment Project*
                                               *American Civil Liberties Union*

# PREFACE

This book seeks to answer the question: is death an acceptable punishment? People passionately disagree over the death penalty and advance their arguments as self-evident and morally compelling—as they did over slavery a century ago. Yet the death penalty's acceptability is very much an empirical question. This is so because the Eighth Amendment to our Constitution prohibits "cruel and unusual" punishment, and because the courts have translated this general standard into three specific tests: its fairness of application, its utility as a deterrent, and its compatibility with contemporary values—all tests that lend themselves to empirical evaluation.

In its now historic 1972 *Furman* decision, the United States Supreme Court applied these tests to capital punishment as it was administered under existing statutes. A majority of the judges found that the death penalty was unconstitutionally "cruel and unusual" punishment, specifically because it failed the test of fairness; its use, in the words of the various justices, was "arbitrary," "capricious," "freakish," "rare," and "discriminatory." To be sure, several justices, though not a majority, also held that the death penalty failed the test of utility because it "serve[d] no penal purpose more effectively than a less severe punishment" and the test of contemporary values because it was "morally unacceptable to the people of the United States at this time in their history." Notably, the justices did not agree about the empirical evidence. Several cited the findings of studies in support of their opinions, particularly evidence of the presence of racial discrimination and ions, particularly evidence of the presence of racial discrimination and of the absence of deterrence. Others challenged these studies as insufficient and outdated. Chief Justice Burger, for example, felt that the evidence did not warrant the majority's finding that the death penalty's use violated standards of "evenhanded justice." He called for evidence of "recent vintage" that would bear on the issues raised in the *Furman* case. "The case against capital punishment," he observed, "is not the product of legal dialectic, but rests primarily on factual claims."

While other nations—Great Britain, Canada, France, and Spain—abolished capital punishment altogether, the *Furman* decision launched an experiment unique to America. The United States has tested the fairness of capital punishment by trying to make its use conform to constitutional standards of evenhanded justice. State legislatures drafted new capital statutes designed to remedy the pre-*Furman* ills, trial courts began imposing death sentences under these new statutes, and the new death-row inmates began challenging these statutes in the appellate courts. Four years after *Furman*, the High Court reviewed the progress of this experiment in *Gregg* and companion cases. It ruled that the mandatory death penalty as a solution to the pre-*Furman* ills failed the contemporary values test. It examined further evidence on utility but found that the death penalty's alleged deterrent advantage had not been convincingly disproven. It did not, however, consider the fairness of post-*Furman* capital statutes, as applied. Indeed, the Supreme Court was not ready to apply the fairness test in 1978 when John Spinkelink asked it to review his death sentence on the grounds that the Florida statute was being administered unfairly. Subsequent Supreme Court decisions have narrowed the scope and applicability of the death penalty, for example by holding that its use for rape violates contemporary values. But the Court has been reluctant to apply the test of fairness, so critical in the *Furman* decision.

This volume is a response to the call for factual evidence of "recent vintage" on the issues of fairness, utility, and contemporary values. Part One (Chapters 1–5) examines America's experience with capital punishment for the century prior to the *Furman* decision. This work was conceived in response to *Furman* and originally published in 1974 as part of *Executions in America*. For this volume, I have incorporated newly available information on executions imposed over the past century, but Part One remains an account of capital punishment in America up to the *Furman* decision of 1972. It begins with a review of the historical struggle over the availability and use of capital punishment in our society (Chapter 1). For a picture of the actual use of the death penalty over time and across regions of the country during the century prior to *Furman*, we examine the historical record of the more than 5,700 executions imposed under state authority (Chapter 2). On the fairness of its application, we turn to this inventory of executions for information on race, age at execution, appeals prior to execution, and the crimes for which offenders were executed (Chapter 3). On the question of utility, we examine how homicide rates were affected by the movement of states from the mandatory to the discretionary imposition of death sentences and by the unprecedented national moratorium on executions that began in 1967 (Chapter 4). We end Part One with a review of historical and cross-national data that suggests the death penalty exists essentially for the extralegal functions it serves—a conclusion that challenges the Supreme Court's judgment that the unfairness it found unconstitutional in *Furman* might be remedied by statutory reforms (Chapter 5).

Part Two (Chapters 6–11) evaluates America's efforts to impose the death penalty fairly in the decade after *Furman* and adds to the evidence of the death penalty's effect on the incidence of homicides. This work took shape in response to the *Gregg* finding that some newly enacted capital statutes appeared "on their face" to remedy the pre-*Furman* ills, and to the appearance of research that purported to demonstrate the deterrent efficacy of capital punishment, contrary to all previous studies. Part Two opens with a review of the history of capital punishment since *Furman*; it traces the enactment and alterations of new capital statutes and the imposition of death sentences by state through 1982 (Chapter 6). We then consider the question of fairness with data from the states responsible for most of the death sentences handed down in the first five years after *Furman* (Chapter 7). In the next two chapters we turn to the question of deterrent utility. First, we examine the short-term effects of executions with data on the incidence of homicides in the months immediately following an execution (Chapter 8). Second, we take a close look at the study heralded as a breakthrough in deterrence research and cited prominently in *Gregg*; we test its dependence on restrictive analytic assumptions, and then introduce more reliable data on homicide rates into the analysis (Chapter 9). Next we turn our attention back to the question of fairness, this time with data on the successive stages in the handling of potentially capital cases, to see whether unfairness is concentrated in sentencing, as the *Gregg* Court assumed, or pervades the entire process, as suggested by the theory that capital punishment exists for its extralegal functions (Chapter 10). In the conclusion to this volume (Chapter 11) we review the findings of the earlier chapters in light of the tests of fairness, utility, and contemporary values and consider the meaning of death as punishment at this critical point in the history of capital punishment in America.

The record of more than 5,700 executions imposed under state authority after 1864 was originally compiled by Negley K. Teeters with the assistance of Charles J. Zibulka and is now updated with some 2900 corrections and additions supplied by M. Watt Espy, Jr., and extended through 1982. It is included as Appendix A of this volume. An inventory of the legislative enactments and reforms and the judicial invalidations and revisions of capital statutes since the *Furman* decision, prepared by Carla Bregman, with citations to legislative actions and judicial decisions in each state, is included as Appendix B. A comprehensive bibliography on capital punishment, originally compiled by Douglas B. Lyons with references through September 1973 and updated through December 1982 by Carla Bregman, Susan Laws, and Jeanne Winner, appears as Appendix C.

## Acknowledgments

Two people have played a crucial role in the form and existence of this book. Glenn Pierce has been a partner in many aspects of my work on capital punishment from the very beginning, when he enabled me to pursue this work by eagerly assuming various research responsibilities, including portions of the work originally published in *Executions in America*, especially what is now Chapter 4 of this book. Since that time he has been my co-author on the previously published versions of Chapters 7, 8, and 9, and he has aided me in the statistical analysis in Chapter 10. This volume owes much to his energies and insights and I owe him a deep debt of gratitude for his commitment and contribution to this work. Jack McDevitt has made this book possible by managing the preparation and updating of the various appendices, and by conducting the reanalysis of the revised data for Chapters 2 and 3. He has also collaborated with me in the analysis of data on the Georgia appellate review process reported in Chapter 10. And critically, by ably assisting me with a wide range of other administrative and research responsibilities, he has given me the time I have needed for the preparation of Chapters 6, 10, and 11 and the revision of Chapters 1, 2, 3, and 9. Hence, I have written this volume *with* Glenn and Jack as major contributors and collaborators.

Three other people deserve special mention for the help they have given me. Carla Bregman assisted me in a variety of ways that included reviewing many federal court decisions for Chapter 10 and preparing the inventory of legislative and judicial actions presented in Appendix B. Jeanne Winner has devoted much care and attention to the manuscript, especially the readability of Chapters 10 and 11. Susan Laws has typed and proofread the manuscript with painstaking care. And all three helped update the bibliography in Appendix C. I want to express my thanks to all of them for the exceptional quality of their work and for the many improvements they have made to this book.

Others I wish to thank for their help in the preparation of this volume include Jean Stethem, Sandra Mack, Dawn Cambra, Tracy Mayors, Augusto Diana, Carol Schaffer, and Baron and Elaine Briggs.

I am also glad for this opportunity to thank Bill Frohlich, Director of the Northeastern University Press, for his encouragement in this work, and especially Deborah Kops and Ann Twombly for their editorial sensibilities and patient good humor.

I cannot name all those who have contributed to this ongoing project. In the opening footnotes to Chapters 3, 4, 7, 8, and 9 I have mentioned some who helped me in the development of these specific analyses, and I acknowledged in *Executions in America* still others who helped early in this project. Three people deserve to be mentioned for their contributions to the forerunner of the present volume: Marvin Wolfgang and Ezzat Fattah who contributed chapters to *Executions in America*, and Andrea Carr whose help in the analyses and preparation of that book was indispensable. The work in Part One was conducted solely with the resources and the charter provided me by Northeastern University; the work of Part Two was carried out with additional support for data collection from the Southern Poverty Law Center and the NAACP Legal Defense and Educational Fund, Inc., and with support for the analysis of deterrent effects from the National Science Foundation and the National Institute of Justice; and the final preparation of this manuscript was aided by a grant from the Chicago Resource Center. To all those who have supported or contributed to this project, I reiterate my thanks.

This volume draws on published works as well as unpublished works recently completed or in progress. For my own published research included here, I gratefully acknowledge the National Council on Crime and Delinquency for permission to reprint the articles from the October 1980 *Crime and Delinquency* included in Chapters 7 and 8, and the Yale Law Journal Association for permission to reprint portions of the December 1975 *Yale Law Journal* included in Chapter 9.

For the material I have drawn from the published works of others, I wish to thank the following: Doubleday & Company, Inc. (Anchor Books), for permission to quote from *The Death Penalty in America*, copyright 1967 by Hugo A. Bedau; Alfred A. Knopf, Inc., for permission to quote from *Resistance, Rebellion, and Death* by Albert Camus, copyright 1960 by Alfred A. Knopf, Inc., translated by Justin O'Brien; Doubleday & Company, Inc., and the Sterling Lord Agency for permission to quote from *Eighty-eight Men and Two Women*, copyright

1962 by Clinton T. Duffy and Al Hirshberg; Sweet and Maxwell, Ltd., for permission to quote from *A History of the English Common Law from 1750* (volumes 1 and 4), copyright 1948 and 1968 by Leon Radzinowicz, published by Stevens and Sons, Ltd.; Harper & Row, Publishers, Inc., for permission to quote from *Capital Punishment* by Thorsten Sellin, copyright 1967 by Harper & Row; the *Harvard Law Review* for permission to quote from "The Supreme Court, 1971 Term, Cruel and Unusual Punishment," copyright 1972 by the Harvard Law Review Association; and *The Nation* for permission to quote from "Rush to Death: Spenkelink's Last Appeal," by Ramsey Clark, copyright 1979 by *The Nation*.

I wish also to thank the following authors of unpublished works: David C. Baldus, George Pulaski, and George Woodworth for permission to use the tabulations from their "Impact of Procedural Reform on Excessiveness, Differential Treatment along Racial Lines and Arbitrariness in Death Sentencing: The Georgia Experience before and after *Furman* v. *Georgia*" (draft report to the National Institute of Justice), Center for Interdisciplinary Studies, College of Law, Syracuse University, 1982; Mary Brennan for permission to use interview materials from her "Capital Representation in the State of Florida" (draft report prepared for the Florida Justice Institute), Miami, 1982; Samuel Gross and Robert Mauro for permission to quote from their manuscript "Patterns of Death," Stanford University Law School, 1983; Thomas Whitehead, head of Special Collections, Temple University Libraries, for permission to reproduce "Executions under State Authority: 1864–1967," compiled by Negley K. Teeters and Charles J. Zibulka in 1968; and M. Watt Espy, Jr., for his many additions and corrections to the Teeters-Zibulka inventory. The discovery of the inventory of state-imposed execution in February 1972 was the critical starting point of my work on capital punishment. I am therefore greatly indebted to those who compiled it and have helped me revise and update it.

# Execution in America

## THE CENTURY BEFORE *FURMAN*

## ONE

# 1

## CAPITAL PUNISHMENT UNDER ATTACK

That men kill one another is an inevitable consequence of their living together in society. They do so mostly by accident, sometimes out of momentary madness, and occasionally with premeditation and malice. When accident or passion is the cause, the killer experiences intense guilt and regret; when his action is willful, deliberate, and premeditated, those around him are horrified and outraged.

Notably, self-defense or the protection of another's life is about the only justification in modern society for taking a life. And to claim the legal protection it affords, the killer must demonstrate that he, or someone else he was acting to protect, faced an immediate life-threat, that he had no realistic alternative to violence, and that he acted not as a provocateur but in response to the threat, without premeditation or malice.[1]

Yet, there are limits to this apparent abhorrence of willful human killing. Warfare transforms some human beings into "the enemy"— an immediate threat to the security of the nation and to the lives of its citizens. To kill the enemy becomes a corporate act of self-defense: the killer becomes a patriot. Even so, he may be ambivalent or reluctant

---

1. At some times and places, an insult to honor has served as a legally acceptable justification for killing, if the homicide is performed according to strict conventions established for dueling. There may also have been times when killing was justified in the name of sport or as a demonstration of one's skill or bravery in combat, as in the Roman Colosseum.

unless the enemy has been "dehumanized" with propaganda about his demonic qualities, and the act of killing "impersonalized" with weapons that make it possible without its being seen. And once the enemy is no longer a threat—as a prisoner of war—the conventions of warfare forbid killing him.

Crimes like murder and treason are also a justification for killing in many nations of the world (Patrick 1965). They transform the perpetrator into "a public enemy"—perceived as dangerous to society and its citizens (Mead 1918). Yet, unlike the enemy soldier who is an agent of evil, the public enemy actually embodies the evil. The murderer is killed not so much for what he might do as for what he has done. His life is the debt he owes society for his crime; his death is intended to inhibit others from emulating his behavior. Thus, his execution is conceived as a corporate act of justice whose purpose is to reaffirm commitment to the laws that protect the lives and rights of citizens (Durkheim 1938, especially Chapter 2).

But, ironically, the punishment has much in common with the crime. It takes a form that would qualify it as a murder if it were perpetrated by one citizen against another. Unlike all other legally justifiable killings, the execution is a purposeful and prearranged homicide. The victim, the executioner, the state officials, and the spectators—all know ahead of time that they will be involved in killing. Moreover, at the time of the execution, the victim is a helpless captive. Were he a prisoner of war, his execution would be a crime.

Perhaps the fact that the execution resembles a murder accounts for the ambivalence displayed by spectators and participants when executions were public ceremonies. Observers often reported heavy drinking and unruly crowd behavior at public hangings. Onlookers were outraged both by bungled hangings and last minute reprieves. The executioner, in particular, was an object of scorn and hostility. In pre-Revolutionary America, executioners were often drawn from outside the community and sometimes masked or disguised to remain anonymous (Teeters and Hedblom 1967, 15 ff). More recently, mechanical contrivances such as the "triple switch" have been used to conceal the identity of the person who actually performs the killing. As for the victim, he has typically been hooded and often enclosed in an airtight, soundproof chamber.

Many partisans of the death penalty admit that the execution is a grotesque event and in that sense an evil. They argue, however, that it is a *lesser* evil than the crime for which it is imposed and a *necessary* evil for the protection of society. As Gabriel Tarde observed:

> . . . it is necessary, no doubt, to take into account the horror which the scaffold inspires in the condemned, the mental tortures of the unfortu-

nate who is dragged bare-necked like a woman at a ball to the legal butchery. This horror, these tortures are an evil to be avoided *unless they serve to prevent a greater evil* (Tarde 1912, 549, emphasis added).

And what is this greater evil?

... the danger which otherwise many honest and useful lives will incur and also the indignation, the moral suffering which the honest crowd and the family of the victim feel when a guilty man does not receive the punishment, which, as they think, his crime merits according to the ideas which they have formed and which they value very highly (Tarde 1912, 549–550).

Thus, capital punishment is said to be a double-edged sword— providing deterrence against future offenses and satisfying the demand for retribution in society. The protection it affords is not so much against the condemned offender, who could be incarcerated for life with the same effect, as against those who would otherwise follow in his footsteps. His execution is a warning to would-be offenders that the price they will have to pay is greater than the value such crimes can possibly have for them. And it is a notice to upright citizens that the criminal has paid for his crime in full measure, that the wrong has been avenged, that justice has been done.

The critics of capital punishment do not deny that punishment will have an impact on society at large, but they dispute the nature of this impact when punishment is death. They argue that the fundamental impact of the death penalty is to reduce respect for human life in society, rather than to increase abhorrence for murder and like offenses. The lesson that capital punishment teaches, according to its critics, is not restraint in the use of violence, but rather an acceptance of violence as an inevitable aspect of relations among men. The execution is a calculated use of death as an instrument of public policy, not a renunciation of killing. Instead of rejecting the method of the criminal, the state simply turns it against him. The consequence is, at least in the minds of some opponents, that this use of death as a punishment actually breeds more violence and killing than it deters.

Abolitionists add that the execution is not an act of justice, but a grave injustice. In practice, they say, it is imposed in response to momentary passions and enduring prejudices of the community, not as a consistent or equitable instrument of the law. And, inevitably, it denies the guilty victim the right of rehabilitation, and the innocent one the right of restitution. According to Albert Camus, the capital judgment that denies these rights and inflicts the most severe torture on the one who awaits his execution compromises the humanity of both the vic-

tim who suffers it and the society that sanctions it (Camus 1957). In
the words of Arthur Koestler, "the Gallows is the oldest and most
obscene symbol of that tendency in mankind which drives it toward
moral self-destruction" (Koestler 1957, xxii).


## The Legislative Assault: Repeal and Reform

The Italian jurist Cesare di Beccaria opened the assault on the death
penalty in the modern world with his treatise *On Crime and Punishment* in 1764.[2] Beccaria proclaimed the supreme value and sanctity of
human life. He argued that the right men claim to kill one another as
a punishment for crime is surely not the one from which law and
sovereignty arise. "Nothing in the social contract gives the state the
right to take human life." He argued that imprisonment is, in any case,
more effective than death in gaining atonement. "The mind that can
resist momentary violence will be touched by perpetual servitude." He
also argued that, as a deterrent, the atrocity of the execution is useless,
at best.

> If passion or the necessity for war has taught the spilling of human blood,
> laws designed to temper human conduct should not enhance a savage
> example which is all the more baneful when the legally sanctioned death
> is inflicted deliberately and ceremoniously. To me it is an absurdity that
> the law which expresses the common will and detests and punishes
> homicide should itself commit one and, in order to keep citizens from
> committing murder, order a public one committed (from Sellin 1967a,
> 43).

He also observed the public's ambivalence toward executions and commented on its effects:

> For most people the death penalty becomes a spectacle and for some an
> object of compassion mixed with abhorrence. Both of these sentiments
> dominate the minds of the spectators more than the salutary terror which
> the law wishes to inspire (from Sellin 1967a, 41).

2. No doubt the controversy over capital punishment has raged for as long as the death
penalty has been used and inspired ambivalence in those who used it. (For an ancient
debate on capital punishment, between Caesar and Cato, see Green 1929; reprinted
in Sellin 1967a.) Others in the modern world who spoke out against capital punishment earlier, but with less effect, include George Fox, Thomas More, and the dram-
atist Middleton, Shakespeare's contemporary (Ancel 1967; footnote 8 in Sellin 1967a).

And he saw this ambivalence manifested in attitudes toward the executioner:

> What are people's ideas on the death penalty? We note them in the acts of indignation or scorn with which people look on the executioner who is merely the innocent performer of the common will, the good citizen who contributes to the common welfare, the necessary instrument for public safety at home just as brave soldiers are elsewhere (from Sellin 1967a, 43).

Beccaria's arguments were inspired by the spirit of rationalism and reform that was afoot prior to the French Revolution. The iconoclastic mood of intellectuals such as Voltaire and Rousseau had subjected most established institutions to attack. But Beccaria's voice was the first to be heard on the subject of capital punishment. And his words struck not only at the brutality and doubtful effectiveness of the death penalty, but at its very legitimacy as an instrument of the state. Commenting on the impact of Beccaria's arguments in Europe, Ancel has written:

> Success was prompt and considerable, not among philosophers alone (Voltaire attached a celebrated commentary to the French translation of Beccaria's little book) but among sovereigns who prided themselves on being practitioners of an enlightened despotism. In 1767 Catharine II ordered the commission that she appointed to draft a new code to exclude the death penalty. In 1786 and 1787, respectively, Leopold II of Tuscany and Joseph II of Austria removed the death penalty from their Corpus Juris Criminalis. In France, early in its deliberations, the National Convention decided on its suppression "the moment peace would be re-established." Soon, in England, Sir Samuel Romilly began his famous campaign for reducing capital crimes, which at the time numbered over 200, and in 1829 the first association for the abolition of the death penalty was formed in London (from Sellin 1967a, 6).

In America, Beccaria's influence was first felt in the reform of Pennsylvania's capital statutes in 1794 when the death penalty was abolished for all crimes except "first degree" murder. This reform came about primarily through the efforts of Dr. Benjamin Rush, a Philadelphia physician and signer of the Declaration of Independence, who had become involved in prison reform activities and was deeply influenced by Beccaria's arguments. Dr. Rush first spoke out publicly against capital punishment in a lecture to influential citizens at the home of Benjamin Franklin in 1787, and later expanded his arguments, drawing heavily on Beccaria's work, in an essay, *Considerations on the Injustice and Impolity of Punishing Murder by Death*, published in 1792. Rush won the support of Benjamin Franklin and then-State Attorney General William Bradford in an effort to repeal Pennsylvania's capital statutes that resulted in the reform of 1794.[3]

The experience of Rush, Franklin, and Bradford in Pennsylvania might have served as a forewarning that reform would come more easily than abolition. The effect of the change they had won was to permit the jury to find a defendant guilty of murder (in the second degree) without requiring him to pay the maximum penalty. This distinction between "first degree" and other crimes, with the death penalty reserved only for offenses of the first degree, was adopted by Virginia in 1796, by Ohio in 1815, and by most other states in the next generation (Bedau 1967b, 24).

Early efforts at abolition met with disappointment. In 1821, Edward Livingston, the distinguished lawyer and future secretary of state, under a commission from the Louisiana state legislature, prepared a radical revision of the state's criminal code altogether eliminating the death penalty. This aspect of his proposed revision was rejected by the state legislature, but his report became one of the most prominent and influential statements against capital punishment in America (Filler 1952, in Sellin 1967a, 109).

In the 1830s the abolition movement gathered momentum. Petitions to abolish capital punishment were filed yearly in a number of state legislatures, special legislative commissions were established to consider the issue, and antigallows societies were organized in every eastern seaboard state (Bedau 1967b, 9).

Again, reform succeeded more easily than repeal. During the 1830s state legislatures began to remove executions from public view and to require that they be performed within jail house or penitentiary walls, open only to a small number of designated officials and relatives of the condemned. Pennsylvania was first to make executions private in 1834, followed by New Jersey, New York, and Massachusetts in 1835, and by many other states in the next couple decades (Teeters and Hedblom 1967, 152–153). Lawmakers were apparently willing to forego whatever deterrent effects executions might have on spectators in favor of preventing the often disorderly and sometimes violent conduct of crowds stirred up by anticipation of the executions and by the spectacle itself.

Finally, half a century after Rush and his colleagues had reformed

3. Under the "Great Act" of William Penn in 1682 the death penalty had been limited to premeditated murder only, until 1718 when Pennsylvania adopted a harsher code that included thirteen capital offenses. The precedent, together with active Quaker interest in prison reform during the Revolutionary period, undoubtedly aided the cause of Rush and his associates.

the capital statutes of Pennsylvania, the first abolition came, as shown in Table 1-1. In 1846, the Territory of Michigan voted to abolish capital punishment effective March 1, 1847, and thus became the first jurisdiction in the English-speaking world to abolish the death penalty for all crimes except treason. In 1852 and 1853, Rhode Island and Wisconsin, respectively, followed suit for all crimes including treason. In seven other states capital punishment was replaced by life imprison-

**Table 1-1.** *Abolition of the Death Penalty by Jurisdiction in the United States*

| Jurisdiction[a] | Period of Abolition | Jurisdiction | Period of Abolition |
|---|---|---|---|
| Michigan[b] | 1846– | Tennessee[g] | 1915–1916 |
| Rhode Island[c] | 1852– | Arizona | 1916–1918 |
| Wisconsin | 1853– | Missouri | 1917–1919 |
| Iowa | 1872–1878 | Alaska | 1957– |
| Maine[d] | 1876–1883 | Hawaii | 1957– |
| Maine | 1887– | Delaware | 1958–1961 |
| Colorado | 1897–1901 | Oregon | 1964– |
| Kansas[c] | 1907–1935 | Iowa | 1965– |
| Minnesota | 1911– | West Virginia | 1965– |
| Washington | 1913–1919 | Vermont[h] | 1965– |
| Oregon | 1914–1920 | New York[i] | 1965– |
| North Dakota[f] | 1915– | New Mexico[j] | 1969– |
| South Dakota | 1915–1939 | New Jersey[k] | 1972– |
| | | California[k] | 1972– |

*Source*: "Capital Punishment 1930–1970," *National Prisoner Statistics* (1971, Table 16), except for the judicial abolitions in New Jersey and California.

*Note*: The table includes all legislative and judicial abolitions until June 29, 1972, when the U.S. Supreme Court invalidated existing discretionary capital statutes in Furman v. Georgia.

[a] Iowa, Maine, and Oregon appear twice in the list because each has had two distinct periods of abolition.

[b] Death penalty retained for treason until 1963.

[c] Death penalty restored in 1882 for any life term convict who commits murder.

[d] In 1837 a law was passed to provide that no condemned person could be executed until one year after his sentencing and then only upon a warrant from the governor.

[e] In 1872 a law was passed similar to the 1837 Maine statute (see note d above).

[f] Death penalty retained for murder by a prisoner serving a life term for murder.

[g] Death penalty retained for rape.

[h] Death penalty retained for murder of a police officer on duty or guard or by a prisoner guilty of a prior murder, kidnapping for ransom, and killing or destruction of vital property by a group during wartime.

[i] Death penalty retained for murder of a police officer on duty, or of anyone by a prisoner under life sentence.

[j] Death penalty retained for the crime of killing a police officer or prison or jail guard while in the performance of his duties, and in cases where the jury recommends the death penalty and the defendant commits a second capital felony after time for due deliberation following commission of the first capital felony.

[k] Death penalty abolished by state supreme court decision.

ment for many lesser crimes (Bedau 1967b, 9–10). Yet, this movement toward abolition ended abruptly with the emerging struggle over slavery that culminated in the Civil War.

The abolition movement had little sustained success with legislative repeal after the Civil War. Between the war and the turn of the century, three more states—Iowa, Maine, and Colorado—abolished the death penalty, but all three reinstated it within a few years. Only Maine repealed it a second time to remain abolitionist from 1887 on.

Then, between the turn of the century and the First World War— in a progressive era of increasing support for feminism, prohibition, and prison reform—the pace of abolition quickened. In fact, between 1907 and 1917, nine states abolished capital punishment. However, the changing mood that accompanied America's entry into the war brought the death penalty back in six of these states by 1920. Abolition lasted until 1935 in Kansas. Only Minnesota and North Dakota resisted pressures to restore the death penalty, bringing the number of abolitionist states to just six by mid-twentieth century.

Indeed, four decades elapsed without a repeal between 1917 and the short-lived abolition in Delaware from 1958 to 1961. In 1960 Alaska and Hawaii gained statehood as abolitionist jurisdictions, both having repealed the death penalty as territories in 1957. Beginning in 1964 with Oregon, six more states repealed the death penalty; in 1972, two states nullified existing capital statutes by state supreme court action. But by the mid-1960s America had all but abandoned the use of capital punishment. The last execution was performed in 1967.

Again, after the Civil War as before it, reform succeeded where repeal had failed. Further discretion in the application of the death penalty was provided by statutes that permitted the jury to decide whether convicted first degree offenders deserved death or an alternative punishment, usually life imprisonment. There is some indication that the jury may have exercised such discretion in rape cases under the "Capital Laws" of Massachusetts as early as 1636, and that the death penalty became optional for all capital offenses except murder in Maryland in 1809 (Bedau 1967b, 28). But the first state to make all capital crimes, including all "degrees" of murder, optionally punished by death was Tennessee in 1838, followed by Alabama in 1841 and Louisiana in 1846.

Some twenty jurisdictions moved from mandatory to discretionary capital punishment between the Civil War and the turn of the century, when efforts at abolition were few and conspicuously unsuccessful. Table 1-2 shows the date at which capital punishment became discretionary for murder in the various jurisdictions, in some cases after a period of abolition.

The move to discretionary capital punishment in the twentieth century paralleled, to some degree, the pattern of abolitions. Fourteen states made the death penalty discretionary from the turn of the century until the First World War. Between the First and Second World Wars only four states turned to discretionary capital punishment, and two of these—Oregon and Kansas—were returning to the death penalty after periods of abolition, and in the latter case after a form of executive discretion. Finally, between 1949 and 1963, when the number of executions in America was declining markedly, the last seven jurisdictions to make the move—including Vermont for the second time—turned to the discretionary use of capital punishment.

**Table 1-2.** *Discretionary Capital Punishment for Murder by Jurisdiction in the United States*

| Jurisdiction[a] | Dates of Discretion[b] | Jurisdiction[a] | Dates of Discretion[b] |
|---|---|---|---|
| Tennessee[c] | 1838, 1917 | Colorado[c] | 1901, 1965 [b9] |
| Alabama | 1841 | New Hampshire[d] | 1903, 1915 [b5] |
| Louisiana | 1846 | Missouri[c] | 1907 |
| Georgia | 1861 [b1], 1969 [b2] | Montana | 1907 [b3] |
| Illinois | 1867 [b6] | Maryland | 1908 [b9], 1916 [b8] |
| Minnesota | 1868 [b2], 1883 [b9] | Washington[c] | 1909 [b2], 1919 [b2] |
| West Virginia | 1870 [b1] | Idaho | 1911 |
| Florida | 1872 [b3] | Vermont [c] | 1911, 1957 |
| Mississippi | 1872 [b1] | Nevada | 1912 |
| Kentucky | 1873 | Virginia | 1914 |
| California[d] | 1874 [b3] | Arkansas | 1915 [b1] |
| Utah | 1876 [b8] | Wyoming | 1915 [b1] |
| Iowa[c] | 1878, 1880 [b3] | New Jersey | 1916 [b1] |
| Texas[d] | 1879 | Delaware[c] | 1917 [b8], 1961 [b8] |
| Indiana | 1881 | Oregon[c] | 1920 [b1] |
| North Dakota | 1883 | Pennsylvania | 1925 [b3] |
| South Dakota[c] | 1883, 1939 [b8] | Kansas[c] | 1935 |
| Arizona[c] | 1885 [b2], 1918 [b3] | New Mexico | 1939 [b1] |
| Oklahoma | 1890 [b3] | North Carolina | 1949 [b1] |
| Nebraska | 1893 [b3] | Connecticut[d] | 1951 [b1], 1971 [b8] |
| South Carolina | 1894 [b1] | Massachusetts[f] | 1951 |
| U.S. Federal | 1897 [b1] | Hawaii | 1955 |
| Ohio | 1898 [b1] | District of | |
| Alaska | 1899 [b1] | Columbia | 1962 [b3] |
| | | New York[d,g] | 1963 [b7] |

*Source*: Memorandum on mandatory and discretionary capital statutes, prepared by Nick Garin under the direction of Jack Himmelstein, NAACP Legal Defense and Educational Fund, Inc., 1973.

[a] Michigan, Rhode Island, Wisconsin, and Maine are excluded from this table because they abolished capital punishment without first making it discretionary.

[b] The dates refer to years in which discretionary capital statutes for murder were enacted or revised. The statutes provided for unqualified jury discretion within sentencing bounds, unless otherwise noted as follows:

There were also changes in the method of execution designed to make it painless and swift. In 1888 the New York legislature approved the construction of an "electric chair" on the grounds that its use would make the execution more humane, and two years later the first electrocution was performed. Despite considerable doubt about the superiority of electrocution after the first attempt, it soon became the preferred method of execution in America. Ohio followed New York in 1897; three states turned to electrocution in the 1900s; nine more did so in the 1910s; and by the end of the 1920s more than half the death penalty jurisdictions were using the electric chair.

Not to be outdone, however, the Nevada legislature in 1921 provided that the condemned person be executed by means of lethal gas "without warning and while asleep in his cell." Three years later the first execution by asphyxiation was performed, though it had to be carried out in an especially constructed chamber instead of the prisoner's cell. Asphyxiation attracted seven states during the 1930s, and three more states that adopted lethal gas had previously employed the electric chair.

Two states—Nevada and Utah—made shooting a method of execution during the twentieth century. And Kentucky, which had moved to electrocution in 1911, returned to public hanging for rapists between 1920 and 1938, presumably as a less humane method of execution. The dates at which the various jurisdictions moved to electrocution and lethal gas are shown in Table 1-3.

These moves toward greater discretion in sentencing to death and

---

*Binding jury recommendation:*
[b1] The sentence was death unless the jury failed to concur or recommended otherwise.
[b2] The sentence was life unless the jury recommended death.
*Mixed jury-court discretion:*
[b3] The court had discretion if the jury failed to fix sentence by a unanimous or majority vote.
[b4] The court had discretion in case of a court trial or guilty plea.
[b5] In case of a guilty plea, the court could impose a life sentence or sumit the issue of punishment to a jury.
[b6] The jury could make a binding recommendation against death or a nonbinding recommendation of death.
[b7] The court could rule out death or submit the issue of punishment to a jury whose recommendation was binding if unanimous.
*Court discretion:*
[b8] The jury could make a non-binding recommendation of life or death.
[b9] The court had unqualified discretion, except for statutory bounds on sentencing.
[c] Discretion was preceded or interrupted by a period of abolition as indicated in Table 1-1.
[d] Guilt and punishment were decided in separate hearing or by a split verdict procedure.
[e] This is the only jurisdiction in which discretion was interrupted by a return to mandatory capital punishment, from 1913 to 1957.
[f] The mandatory death sentence was retained for murder that occurred in the course of rape or attempted rape.
[g] The death penalty for felony murder became discretionary in 1937.

**Table 1-3.** *Execution by (A) Electrocution, (B) Lethal Gas, and (C) Shooting, by Jurisdiction in the United States*

| Jurisdiction[a] | Period of Execution[b] | Jurisdiction[a] | Period of Execution[b] |
|---|---|---|---|
| **A. Periods of Electrocution** | | | |
| New York | 1890–1963 | Vermont | 1919–1954 |
| Ohio | 1897–1963 | Nebraska | 1920–1959 |
| Massachusetts | 1901–1947 | Florida | 1924–1964 |
| New Jersey | 1907–1963 | Texas | 1924–1964 |
| Virginia | 1908–1962 | Georgia | 1924–1964 |
| North Carolina | 1910–1936 | Alabama | 1927–1965 |
| Kentucky[c] | 1911–1962 | District of Columbia | 1928–1957 |
| South Carolina | 1912–1962 | Illinois | 1929–1962 |
| Arkansas | 1913–1964 | New Mexico | 1933–1956 |
| Indiana | 1914–1961 | Connecticut | 1937–1960 |
| Oklahoma[d] | 1915–1966 | Louisiana[e] | 1940–1961 |
| Pennsylvania | 1915–1962 | South Dakota[f] | 1947 |
| Tennessee | 1909–1960 | West Virginia | 1951–1959 |
| **B. Periods of Lethal Gas** | | | |
| Nevada | 1924–1961 | Missouri | 1938–1965 |
| Arizona | 1934–1963 | Oregon | 1939–1962 |
| Colorado | 1934–1964 | Mississippi | 1955–1964 |
| North Carolina[g] | 1936–1961 | Maryland | 1957–1961 |
| California[g] | 1937–1965 | New Mexico[f] | 1960 |
| Wyoming | 1938–1963 | | |
| **C. Periods of Shooting** | | | |
| Utah[h] | 1903–1960 | Nevada[f] | 1913 |

*Source:* This information was drawn from the Teeters-Zibulka inventory of executions under state authority included as an appendix to this volume.

[a] Delaware, Idaho, Iowa, Kansas, Maine, Michigan, Minnesota, Montana, New Hampshire, North Dakota, Rhode Island, Washington, and Wisconsin are excluded from this table because hanging was the only method ever used in these states. Executions under federal authority were carried out by the method of the state in which they were performed.

[b] Periods of execution indicate when the first and last executions by the specified method were performed, not the period for which a given method was provided by statute.

[c] In 1920 a statute specifically requiring public hangings for condemned rapists was enacted after a particulary heinous child rape. In 1938 the last public hanging for rape was performed and the statute was repealed.

[d] One federal prisoner convicted of kidnapping with bodily harm was hanged rather than electrocuted in 1936 by order of a federal marshal.

[e] From 1940 through 1956 executions were performed by means of a portable electric chair taken on a truck with a generator to the various county jails.

[f] Only one execution was performed by the specified method.

[g] Prisoners sentenced to death by another method prior to the adoption of lethal gas were executed according to their original sentences after the use of gas had begun.

[h] The condemned person was given a choice between shooting and hanging; two men chose hanging, one in 1912 and the other in 1958.

newer methods of execution occurred within a broader trend toward the "delocalization" of executions. With the growth of state penal institutions and the centralization of penal authority after the Civil

War, states began to require that all executions within their boundaries
be performed under state authority at a single state facility. This movement toward state-imposed executions began in 1864 when Vermont
and Maine imposed the first executions under state authority; it was
still in progress in 1955 and 1957 when Mississippi and Louisiana
brought their executions under state authority; and it was never fully
completed, with Delaware and Montana continuing to execute under
local authority until the de facto cessation of executions in these states.
(The specific dates at which the various jurisdictions moved executions
from local to state authority are presented in Table 2-1 in the next
chapter.)

The period of greatest movement to state-imposed executions—
from the 1890s through the 1920s, when some thirty-two jurisdictions
made the change—corresponds to the period in which most states turned
to electrocution as their method of execution. And the development
of a single central location for executions undoubtedly facilitated the
use of the electric chair and the gas chamber, which could not easily
be maintained at the local level.[4] We shall have more to say about the
nature and effects of this move from local to state-imposed executions
in the next chapter. For the moment, we simply note that the number
of legally imposed executions in America appears to have declined each
decade from the 1890s through the 1920s, perhaps as a function of this
delocalization process.

Thus, by mid-twentieth century, the application of the death penalty was narrowed to first degree offenses and made discretionary even
for these offenses in all but a handful of states. The execution itself
was first removed from the view of the local community and then from
the hands of local authorities. In effect, the execution was transformed
from a public ceremony, conceived to achieve retribution and deterrence in the community where the crime occurred, into a private ritual,
designed to maximize the certainty and speed of death and to minimize
the pain and agony to the victim. Moreover, this transformation of the
institution of capital punishment in America had occurred within the
context of a social movement that failed to achieve its avowed goal of
nationwide statutory repeal—which had, in fact, achieved abolition in
only six of fifty jurisdictions by mid-twentieth century.

Indeed, as Professor Hugo Bedau has observed, it seems likely that

... the very reforms in the administration of capital punishment, the
hard-won results of the struggle for abolition during the last century,

4. From 1940 through 1956, Louisiana did manage to make electrocution available
locally by means of a portable electric chair which was taken with a generator on a
truck from the penitentiary to the various county jails.

have paradoxically become the major obstacles to further statutory repeal. They have mitigated the rigidity and brutality of this form of punishment to a point where the average citizen no longer regards it as an affront to his moral sensibilities. As a consequence, he has no strong motive to press for further reduction, much less complete abolition, of the death penalty. The reforms referred to here are several, but four of them are particularly important: the disappearance of violent and repulsive modes of carrying out the sentence; the protection of the general public from exposure to executions; the limitation of the death penalty to the highest degree of murder; and the extension of authority to the trial jury in capital cases to grant imprisonment rather than death as the punishment (Bedau 1967b, 14–15).

## The Judicial Assault: Appeal and Abolition

After more than a century of legislative struggle had won enduring abolition in only six of fifty jurisdictions, the United States began to abandon the use of capital punishment. Without significant abolitionist activity or legislative action, executions declined from a highpoint of 199 in 1935 to a point of cessation in 1967 (see Table 1-4, given later).

Judges and juries became increasingly reluctant to impose the death sentence. There were fewer admissions to death row in the 1960s than executions in the 1930s, despite a comparable absolute number of homicides in these two decades. There were 106 admissions to death row per year on the average from 1961 through 1970 (according to Federal Bureau of Prisons 1971, Table 2) and 167 executions per year on the average during the 1930s (see Table 1-4, given later). And, of course, the latter figure excludes commutations.

Even more pronounced was the reluctance of state authorities to schedule and perform executions, particularly toward the end of this period. Despite abolition in five states during the 1960s, the number of prisoners under sentence of death grew from 219 at the end of 1960 to 608 at the end of 1970 (Federal Bureau of Prisons 1971, Table 2).

Significantly, this was the time when the United States Supreme Court became sensitive to defendants' rights in capital cases and responsive to appeals under the "due process" clause of the Fourteenth Amendment. In the 1930s, the Court insisted that counsel be provided for capital defendants in *Powell* v. *Alabama* (1932), saying that the accused in a capital case "requires the guiding hand of counsel at every step in the proceedings against him." In subsequent decisions, the Court ruled against racial discrimination in jury selection in *Patton* v. *Mississippi* (1947) and provided protection against coerced confessions in *Fikes* v. *Alabama* (1957). These later decisions gave specific grounds for appeals and demonstrated the Court's willingness to reverse capital convictions on various grounds. The earlier *Powell* decision had assured defendants of the legal expertise needed to recognize grounds for appeals and to carry such appeals forward.

In the 1950s and 1960s, the NAACP Legal Defense and Educational Fund, Inc., and the American Civil Liberties Union came to the aid of a number of persons who had been sentenced to death, and many condemned men had their convictions reversed. Further decisions by the Court, notably in *Shepherd* v. *Florida* (1951) and *Hamilton* v. *Alabama* (1961), clarified and extended the earlier rulings on jury discrimination and right to counsel. These and the earlier cases typically involved the rights of black defendants in southern trial courts, and it was particularly on behalf of such defendants that the NAACP Legal Defense Fund concentrated its efforts.

Although we lack data on appeals among the condemned who escaped execution, we do know that for those whose death sentences were carried out the proportion with appeals to federal courts grew tenfold—from 3.2 percent to 32.6 percent—between the 1930s and the 1960s (according to the data in Appendix A).[5]

No doubt, the courts' increasing willingness to review capital cases and to reverse lower court decisions made state authorities more reluctant to schedule and to perform executions. The result in the 1960s was mounting death row populations and increasing pressure on the Supreme Court to decide the constitutionality of capital punishment per se. In effect, the openness of higher courts to appeals in capital cases during this period appears to have contributed to the declining number of executions and the increasing numbers on death row. And these conditions, in turn, appear to have invited a direct assault on the constitutionality of capital punishment.

In 1966, the NAACP Legal Defense Fund mounted such a direct judicial assault on capital punishment (Meltsner 1973b). The fund's strategy included three important features: (1) bringing cases to the Supreme Court that would challenge the use of the death penalty under provisions of the Eighth and Fourteenth Amendments, (2) developing and employing social science evidence in support of petitioners' claims, and (3) attempting to block all further executions throughout the country while this litigation was in progress.

The fund's commitment to bring about a judicial moratorium on executions soon involved a large number of suits requiring a nation-

---

5. These figures undoubtedly reflect increasing concern for the rights of condemned offenders among lawyers as well as increasing receptivity to appeals on the part of the higher courts, since they include all appeals filed, not just those heard by the courts. (See Appendix A.)

wide effort to enlist the help of lawyers in the various states and to supply them with legal materials for use in appeals. This commitment also led to class action suits for the first time on behalf of death row prisoners in Florida and California where Governors Kirk and Reagan threatened to reinstate executions.

The fund had in 1965 helped design and sponsor a systematic study of some three thousand rape cases in the South to determine how race of defendant and victim affected sentencing (Wolfgang 1972, Wolfgang and Riedel 1973, 1975). The research pointed unmistakably to discrimination against black defendants whose victims were white. These findings were submitted as evidence in a number of appeals made to state and federal courts in the South, but the appellate courts were reluctant to find these data relevant to the specific cases under review (*Virginia Law Review* 1972: 136 ff). However, the precedent established in the historic school desegregation decision, *Brown* v. *Board of Education* in 1954, suggested that the Supreme Court might be more receptive to the findings of social scientists, particularly in matters of racial discrimination. An effort was therefore made to bring these data to the attention of the Supreme Court.

The fund attorneys began their attack on Fourteenth Amendment grounds in the case of William Witherspoon, and supplied research evidence in support of his argument that the practice of excluding persons who opposed the death penalty from the jury deprived the defendant of the right to a jury that was representative of the community. In *Witherspoon* v. *Illinois* (1968) the Court sustained this challenge ruling that the "death qualified jury" was unconstitutional.

The next year, fund attorneys attacked the death penalty on Eighth Amendment grounds in the case of Edward Boykin, who had received five separate death sentences for five robberies in Alabama. Fund attorneys submitted that the infrequent, arbitrary, and discriminatory use of the death penalty for the crime of robbery was "cruel and unusual" punishment. In *Boykin* v. *Alabama* (1969), however, the Court passed over the Eighth Amendment issues and returned the case to the state trial court on the grounds that Boykin's guilty pleas had been improperly accepted.

The fund then challenged the practice of having both guilt and punishment decided in a single trial proceeding. They argued that this practice in Arkansas had prevented William Maxwell from furnishing information that might mitigate his punishment. In the *Maxwell* case the High Court chose not to consider the evidence of racial discrimination developed in the research on some three thousand rape cases in the South.

The fund again brought to the High Court the issue of standards and practices in sentencing before the Court in the cases of Dennis

McGautha and James Crampton. This time, in the *McGautha* v. *California* (1971) decision, the Court upheld the constitutionality of existing practices. The Court held that the "due process" guarantee of the Fourteenth Amendment did not require states to establish standards or guidelines that juries must follow in sentencing nor to hold separate proceedings for the determination of guilt and punishment.

Then, in the fall of 1971, the fund brought the cases of Earnest Aikens, William Furman, and Lucious Jackson, two murderers and a rapist, before the Supreme Court on grounds similar to those developed in the *Boykin* case: namely, that their death sentences were "cruel and unusual" because of the rare, arbitrary, and discriminatory way in which the death penalty had been imposed for these crimes. Aiken's death sentence was nullified during the course of the Court's deliberations when the California Supreme Court declared that state's death penalty unconstitutional under the state prohibition against cruel and unusual punishment in *People* v. *Anderson* (1972); thus *Furman* v. *Georgia* became the lead case before the U.S. Supreme Court.

There came a turning point in the struggle against capital punishment in America. On June 29, 1972, the U.S. Supreme Court, in *Furman* v. *Georgia* and related cases, held by a 5–4 margin "that the imposition and carrying out of the death penalty in these cases constituted cruel and unusual punishment in violation of the Eighth and Fourteenth Amendments" (*Furman* v. *Georgia* 1972, 239–240). The Court made it clear, by also reversing the death sentences in some 120 other cases, that jury discretion in imposing the death penalty was unconstitutional. Each of the nine justices filed a separate opinion. The opinions of the majority, as reported by the *Harvard Law Review*, were as follows:

> Justice Douglas argued that the statutes before the Court allowed judges or jurors to apply the death penalty selectively against poor defendants who lack "political clout" or against members of a "suspect or unpopular minority, . . . saving those who by social position may be in a more protected position. The death penalty statutes were therefore "pregnant with discrimination . . . [,] an ingredient not compatible with the idea of equal protection of the laws that is implicit in the ban on 'cruel and unusual' punishments." Justice Douglas found this mandate of equal treatment by resort to the English history that led to the adoption of the cruel and unusual punishments clause of the English Bill of Rights, the source of the American version. Historically, he argued, the clause was a reaction not only to barbaric punishments, but also to the selective and irregular imposition of penalties upon persons disfavored by the British Crown. The clause is similarly applicable, the Justice argued, to the selective and irregular imposition of the death penalty upon socially disfavored persons in America today.

Justice Stewart, while agreeing that the discretionary nature of the death penalty statutes before the Court rendered them cruel and unusual punishments, did not rely on a notion of equal protection for this conclusion. Rather, he argued that since the legislature did not call for a mandatory death sentence, it had not made the judgment that death was a "necessary" punishment for the crime. The death sentences in these cases were therefore " 'cruel' in the sense that they excessively go beyond, not in degree but in kind, the punishments that the state legislatures [had] determined to be necessary." He also felt that death sentences left to the discretion of a judge or jury were imposed so infrequently that they were "unusual." Moreover, he argued in the alternative that such sentences were "cruel and unusual in the same way that being struck by lightning is cruel and unusual," concluding that "the Eighth and Fourteenth Amendments cannot tolerate the infliction of a sentence of death under legal systems that permit this unique penalty to be so wantonly and so freakishly imposed."

Justice White argued that when juries exercise discretion in sentencing, there is no meaningful distinction between cases in which the death sentence is imposed and those in which it is not, and that its imposition is therefore arbitrary. He also reasoned that the penalty is imposed so infrequently that it does not effectively contribute to the deterrence of crime or any other goal of criminal justice. He concluded that under these circumstances the imposition of the death penalty is a "pointless and needless extinction of life with only marginal contributions to any discernible social or public purposes" and is therefore cruel and unusual.

. . . Justice Brennan divined from previous Supreme Court decisions under the Eighth Amendment the general principle that it proscribes punishments which do "not comport with human dignity," and he set forth four tests calculated to guide judicial application of the amendment: (1) "a punishment must not be so severe as to be degrading to the dignity of human beings," (2) "the State must not arbitrarily inflict a severe punishment," (3) "a severe punishment must not be unacceptable to contemporary society," and (4) "a severe punishment must not be excessive," a punishment being "excessive under this principle if it is unnecessary." He found the death penalty as then administered offensive to all four tests and therefore concluded that it was cruel and unusual. Although Justice Brennan placed particular emphasis on the arbitrariness of the death penalty owing to its infrequent imposition by juries unguided by any standards, nowhere did he indicate that the absence of arbitrariness would have altered his decision. Unlike Justices Douglas, Stewart, and White, he did not explicitly limit his opinion to death penalties imposed at the discretion of a judge or jury.

Justice Marshall wrote the opinion which most unequivocally condemned capital punishment. Placing no reliance on the discretionary nature of the sentences, he argued that "a punishment may be deemed cruel and unusual for any one of four distinct reasons": (1) if the punishment involves "so much physical pain and suffering that civilized people cannot tolerate [it]"; (2) if the punishment has previously been unknown for a particular offense; (3) if the punishment "is excessive and serves no valid legislative purpose"; or (4) if popular sentiment abhors the punishment. Assuming that capital punishment did not involve severe physical pain and recognizing that it was not a novel punishment for rape and murder, Justice Marshall found both that it was excessive and unnecessary and that it offended contemporary moral values (*Harvard Law Review* 1972, 77–80).

By way of summary, the *Harvard Law Review* observed:

Each of the five concurring Justices filed a separate opinion, and none joined in the opinion of any other. Justices Douglas, Stewart, and White each relied on the fact that the death sentences in these cases were not mandatorily imposed by the legislature for the particular crime, but were imposed at the discretion of the jury. They explicitly refrained from deciding whether a mandatory death penalty for a particular crime would be constitutional. Justices Brennan and Marshall did not expressly limit their concurrences to capital punishment imposed at the discretion of a jury, although Justice Brennan did rely in part on the discretionary nature of the death penalty in reaching the conclusion that it is cruel and unusual (*Harvard Law Review* 1972, 77).

The Court's decision, by a one-vote margin, in *Furman* v. *Georgia* appears to have blocked the further use of capital punishment under statutes providing for the imposition of the death penalty at the discretion of the jury. Moreover, it prevented the sacrifice of some six hundred prisoners on death row at the time of the decision, and it did so without necessarily implying that the thousands of previous executions in America were unconstitutional. That is to say, the Court did not rule that capital punishment per se was unconstitutional, but only that it had *become* unconstitutional—cruel and unusual—as a result of the rare and arbitrary way in which it had recently been imposed.

By the same token, the Court's decision did not preclude the subsequent use of the death penalty if statutes could be formulated to meet the objections of the *Furman* majority. In fact, in view of the Court's concern about the discretionary character of the death penalty, a number of states shortly began considering and formulating capital statutes designed to limit jury discretion by specifying standards and procedures to be followed in determining punishment, or to remove jury discretion altogether by making the death penalty mandatory upon conviction (Bedau 1973a).

Although the Court's decision has had a decisive impact on the present status of capital punishment in America, its future effect is less certain in view of current efforts to reformulate capital statutes to meet the Court's objections and the possibility that future appointments to the Court, given the one-man majority in *Furman*, could tip the balance back in favor of the death penalty.

It is certain, however, that the direction of future Court decisions extending or further restricting the availability of the death penalty will depend heavily on developing scientific evidence of the sort that has played an important part in the series of cases leading up to and including *Furman*. Indeed, Chief Justice Burger in his dissenting opinion complained of the insufficiency of empirical data in support of the majority's claim "... that the present system of discretionary sentencing in capital cases has failed to provide evenhanded justice ..." (*Furman* v. *Georgia* 1972, 399). In this vein, he called for more extensive research, saying, in particular, that "data of more recent vintage is essential" (*Furman* v. *Georgia* 1972, 390 n.).

We shall turn in subsequent chapters to research of "recent vintage," most of it developed since Chief Justice Burger issued his request. But first let us briefly examine the scientific research on capital punishment of "earlier vintage," which represents an assault on the death penalty in its own right and will serve as a background for the upcoming analyses.

## The Scientific Assault: Discrimination and Deterrence

For the past several decades—roughly corresponding to the period of decline in executions in America—systematic scientific research on the institution of capital punishment has been accumulating. In particular, the long-debated issues of discrimination in the application of the death penalty and of the deterrent power of capital punishment have attracted scientific attention. And although the courts have only recently taken the findings of this research into account, the broader community of social scientists and administrators concerned with criminology and penology have for some time contributed to and been influenced by this growing body of evidence on the application and effects of capital punishment.

Certainly one of the most important developments from a scientific standpoint was the collection and publication of national statistics on executions. Beginning in 1930, the Bureau of the Census included executions as one of the "causes of death" for all states and the District of Columbia in its *Mortality Statistics*. (For information on unofficial execution figures before 1930, see Chapter 2.)

Beginning in 1950, these national execution statistics were more widely circulated in bulletins published annually by the Federal Bureau of Prisons as a regular part of its *National Prisoner Statistics* series.

These reports tabulated the number of executions yearly for each jurisdiction and broke down the cumulative total back to 1930 by type of offense leading to execution and race of those executed. The first of these reports immediately and unequivocally documented the fact that for the preceding twenty years the black man had been the principal victim of the death penalty in America and almost the exclusive victim of executions for rape. More than half of those executed were blacks, and nine out of ten executed for rape were blacks (Hartung 1952).

The 1940s marked the beginning of an accumulation of systematic scientific research on racial discrimination in capital punishment in America, although there was earlier evidence of such discrimination. (See references in Hartung 1952.) Charles Mangum (1940) found that among those sentenced to death in nine southern and border states, blacks were more likely than whites to have their death sentences carried out in every state. Guy Johnson (1941) found for selected jurisdictions in Virginia, North Carolina, and Georgia, that in murder cases the death sentence was disproportionately imposed when the defendant was black and his victim was white. Harold Garfinkel (1949) refined and extended Johnson's findings with data from ten counties in North Carolina, and showed that this tendency to impose the death sentence disproportionately in black offender–white victim murders was the cumulative result of differential treatment at each of several stages—indictment, charge, and conviction—of the judicial process. The findings of these studies together with the national execution statistics prompted Gunnar Myrdal's (1944, 554) conclusion in *An American Dilemma*: "The South makes the widest application of the death penalty, and Negro criminals come in for much more than their share of executions."

Additional evidence that blacks on death row were less likely than whites to receive commutations followed in the 1950s and 1960s for various states both inside and outside the South—North Carolina (Johnson 1957), Pennsylvania (Wolfgang et al. 1962), Ohio (Ohio Legislative Service Commission 1961), New Jersey (Bedau 1964), and Texas (Koeninger 1969). Moreover, these later studies began to take account of factors other than race, such as the nature of the crime (felonious vs. other murders), the type of defense counsel (private vs. court appointed), and other personal characteristics of the defendant (age, nationality, etc.), to determine whether the observed racial differences in commutations could be explained by such factors.

Further evidence of racial discrimination in the judicial process leading to execution was developed in a study of some three thousand rape cases in eleven southern states planned in collaboration with the NAACP Legal Defense Fund and conducted by Professor Marvin

Wolfgang (1972; Wolfgang and Riedel 1973, 1975). Begun in 1965, this research took account of a great many characteristics of the defendant, the victim, the crime, and the trial proceedings, factors that could conceivably account for the greater likelihood that blacks would receive the death sentence. These later investigations confirmed and broadened the earlier evidence that racial discrimination has played a major role in the administration of the death penalty in America.

With respect to the possible deterrent effects of the death penalty, the 1950s saw an impressive accumulation of research. In 1953, after an exhaustive four-year examination of data from many nations on capital punishment and its effects, the British Royal Commission on Capital Punishment (England, Royal Commission on Capital Punishment 1953, 23), in its highly respected and influential report concluded that ". . . there is no clear evidence in any of the figures we have examined that the abolition of capital punishment has led to an increase in the homicide rate, or that its reintroduction has led to a fall." In the United States, Thorsten Sellin, who pioneered in empirical research on the death penalty and worked closely with the British Royal Commission, showed that homicide rates were no higher in abolition than in contiguous death penalty states, that such rates were unaffected by the abolition or reintroduction of capital punishment in states that had made such changes, and that neither the killing of policemen nor killing in prison was more common in abolition than in death penalty states (Sellin 1955; 1959; 1967a).

Still further evidence against deterrence was developed during the 1950s. Karl Schuessler (1952), in a time series analysis of annual data on executions and homicides from eleven states, found no consistent evidence that certainty of execution affected subsequent levels of homicide. William Graves (1956), in a study of homicides in the days immediately before and after executions in California, found an increase in the incidence of homicide immediately before executions, suggesting that the anticipation of executions had a "brutalizing" effect on the population that more than offset any deterrent effects. Robert Dann (1935) had found, some twenty years earlier, that there were more homicides in the sixty days after well-publicized executions in Philadelphia than in the sixty days before executions, suggesting, in somewhat different terms, that the overall impact of the executions might actually be to increase the incidence of homicide. Leonard Savitz (1958b), in a study of homicide during the weeks before and after the death sentence was handed down in Philadelphia—conducted as a follow-up and refinement of Dann's work—found no reduced levels of homicide after the death sentence was imposed. Indeed, Savitz's data show that the highest incidence of homicide occurred in the couple of weeks immediately prior to sentencing, suggesting that the decision to impose the death penalty may, in fact, be a "repressive response" to increased levels of homicide just before sentencing (Bowers 1972; Bowers and Salem 1972).

Critics have claimed that the evidence against deterrence is "inconclusive" (Gibbs 1968), that deterrence has not been "disproved" (van den Haag 1969) in the case of capital punishment. They have complained (1) that gross homicide rates are not sensitive enough to pick up deterrent effects, specifically that the proportion of capital to noncapital homicides could be varying even when the overall homicide rate remains unaffected by abolition; (2) that the use of contiguous jurisdictions and before and after comparisons does not fully control for all other factors that could conceivably be masking deterrent effects; and (3) that deterrent effects may not be "jurisdictionally specific," that people may not be responsive to the presence of, or changes in, capital statutes in the particular state where they reside, as distinct from neighboring states.

Yet, the weight of the evidence has undoubtedly forced advocates of the death penalty to restrict their claims of its deterrent power and to adopt arguments that conflict as little as possible with the existing data. Thus, some have contended that deterrent effects may be relatively indirect, occurring through the power of the death penalty to buttress the "moral climate" of the community (van den Haag 1969) and to reinforce the community's "condemnation of criminality" (Gibbs 1968). The implication is that deterrent effects cannot be expected within days, weeks, or even years, but only decades or generations after a significant change in the institution of capital punishment in the nation as a whole. But this argument appears to ignore the experiences of other nations, which have been documented for relatively long periods before and after abolition. In this respect, it is also noteworthy that recent advocates of the death penalty have acknowledged its doubtful power as a general deterrent (see, for example, Barzun 1962).

The evidence of discrimination in the administration of the death penalty has been less subject to challenge. Appellate courts have been reluctant to grant its applicability in specific cases under review, but they have not directly disputed the statistical evidence itself. Questions do remain, however, about the extent and depth of such discrimination, whether it has been confined primarily to the South or has prevailed throughout the country, and to what extent social class, as well as race, has served as a basis for discrimination. Some believe that the proper approach to such discrimination by race is "to remedy the defect, not to abolish the system" (Hochkammer 1969, reprinted in McCafferty 1972b, 69). But this proposition makes a questionable assumption about the depth and tenacity of discrimination in the judicial process—one to be considered further in subsequent chapters.

## The Demise of Executions in America

Up to this point we have referred generally to the period of decline of executions in America from 1935, when legally imposed executions reached a historical highpoint for the nation as a whole, to 1967 when the last executions were carried out in California and Colorado. At this point, we shall examine this period of decline more closely to determine, insofar as possible, when and where executions began to decline and to what extent the decline was a result of changing patterns or practices within the justice system.

### When Did the Demise of Executions Begin?

The trend in executions after 1935 was not a consistent year-by-year decline, but rather a pattern with considerable annual fluctuation and with discrete points at which the level of executions dropped off substantially. Table 1-4 presents the number of executions annually from 1930 through 1967. Because there are considerable year-to-year variations, we have also indicated the average for five-year intervals from 1930 through 1964.

**Table 1-4.** *Executions, Homicides, and Execution Rates by Year for the United States from 1930 to 1967*

| Years | Number of Executions | Number of Homicides[a] | Executions per 100 Homicides the Year Before[b] |
|---|---|---|---|
| 1930 | 155 | 10,617 | 1.63 |
| 1931 | 153 | 11,160 | 1.44 |
| 1932 | 140 | 11,035 | 1.24 |
| 1933 | 160 | 12,124 | 1.45 |
| 1934 | 168 | 12,055 | 1.45 |
| *Average 1930–1934* | *155* | *11,398* | *1.44* |
| 1935 | 199 | 10,587 | 1.73 |
| 1936 | 195 | 10,232 | 1.92 |
| 1937 | 147 | 9,811 | 1.49 |
| 1938 | 190 | 8,799 | 2.01 |
| 1939 | 160 | 8,394 | 1.88 |
| *Average 1935–1939* | *178* | *9,565* | *1.81* |
| 1940 | 124 | 8,208 | 1.53 |
| 1941 | 123 | 7,929 | 1.55 |
| 1942 | 147 | 7,743 | 1.92 |
| 1943 | 131 | 6,690 | 1.76 |
| 1944 | 120 | 6,553 | 1.87 |
| *Average 1940–1944* | *129* | *7,425* | *1.73* |

**Table 1-4.** *(continued)*

| Years | Number of Executions | Number of Homicides[a] | Executions per 100 Homicides the Year Before[b] |
|-------|----------------------|------------------------|-------------------------------------------------|
| 1945 | 117 | 7,412 | 1.86 |
| 1946 | 131 | 8,784 | 1.85 |
| 1947 | 153 | 8,555 | 1.82 |
| 1948 | 119 | 8,536 | 1.45 |
| 1949 | 119 | 8,033 | 1.45 |
| *Average 1945–1949* | *128* | *8,264* | *1.69* |
| 1950 | 82 | 7,942 | 1.06 |
| 1951 | 105 | 7,495 | 1.38 |
| 1952 | 83 | 8,054 | 1.16 |
| 1953 | 62 | 7,640 | 0.80 |
| 1954 | 81 | 7,735 | 1.11 |
| *Average 1950–1954* | *83* | *7,773* | *1.10* |
| 1955 | 76 | 7,418 | 1.03 |
| 1956 | 65 | 7,629 | 0.92 |
| 1957 | 65 | 7,641 | 0.89 |
| 1958 | 49 | 7,815 | 0.68 |
| 1959 | 49 | 8,159 | 0.66 |
| *Average 1955–1959* | *61* | *7,727* | *0.84* |
| 1960 | 56 | 8,421 | 0.72 |
| 1961 | 42 | 8,543 | 0.53 |
| 1962 | 47 | 8,987 | 0.58 |
| 1963 | 21 | 9,192 | 0.24 |
| 1964 | 15 | 9,771 | 0.17 |
| *Average 1960–1964* | *36* | *8,983* | *0.45* |
| 1965 | 7 | 10,663 | 0.08 |
| 1966 | 1 | 11,560 | 0.01 |
| 1967 | 2 | 13,381 | 0.02 |

*Sources:* "Capital Punishment 1930–1960," *National Prisoner Statistics* (1971, Table 1); *Vital Statistics of the United States* (U.S. Bureau of the Census, for the respective years).
[a] These figures pertain only to the contiguous United States, excluding Alaska, Hawaii, and other territories and possessions. The annual number of homicides for Texas was not included in the *Vital Statistics* until 1933 when Texas reported 965 homicides. Thus, the national totals from 1930 through 1932 underestimate the actual number of homicides in the country by as much as 1,000 per year.
[b] The execution rate for a given year is based on the previous year's homicides *in death penalty jurisdictions only.* Specifically, for all abolitionist jurisdictions in the designated year, homicides committed the year before were subtracted from the national total in the preceding year. (See Table 1-1 for the abolitionist states and their periods of abolition.) Since the number of homicides is unavailable for Texas prior to 1933, executions performed by Texas from 1930 through 1933 were excluded in the calculations of the execution rates for these years.

These five-year averages reveal that the most substantial drop in executions during this period occurred between the late 1930s and the early 1940s when the yearly average dropped by almost fifty executions.

Between the early and late 1940s there was virtually no change in the yearly average. Then another substantial drop of some forty-five executions per year occurred between the late 1940s and the early 1950s. Thereafter, the average number of executions for each five-year interval declined at a steady pace.

The figures for specific years seem to pinpoint further the beginning of the 1940s and the beginning of the 1950s as the two most decisive points of reduction in executions throughout this period. During 1940 and 1941, in particular, the number of executions dropped well below those of any year during the 1930s. And in 1950, for the first time, the number of executions fell below 100 and, with the exception of 1951, remained below this level from then on. Thus it would appear that there were two distinct points—between the late 1930s and the early 1940s and between the late 1940s and the early 1950s—at which the number of executions in America dropped off markedly.

Were these both points at which the nation became decidedly more reluctant to execute? Table 1-4, column 3, shows the annual number of homicides from 1930 to 1967 as reported by the Bureau of the Census in its *Vital Statistics*. Notably, there was a substantial decline in homicides from more than 12,000 in 1933 and 1934 to some 6,500 in 1943 and 1944, as social tensions associated with the economic depression of the 1930s subsided and America's involvement in the Second World War sent many young Americans in the "high homicide" age brackets overseas. Parenthetically, in 1945 and 1946 when these soldiers returned to civilian society, the number of homicides in America climbed markedly—a 34 percent rise between 1944 and 1946, which is greater than for any two-year span throughout the entire period represented in the table. Note also that the number of executions in 1946 and 1947 likewise rose considerably, apparently in response to the rising incidence of homicide in the immediately preceding years.

The reduction in homicides from the mid-1930s to the mid-1940s, of course, suggests that the drop in executions over this period may not reflect any increasing reluctance to execute, but simply a declining number of candidates for execution. To determine when and to what extent executions may have declined apart from variations in the incidence of homicides, we show in Table 1-4, column 4, the number of executions per 100 homicides the year before.[6]

6. The time that elapses between the homicide and the execution of the offender is highly variable and has undoubtedly increased in recent years. We know that the median elapsed time between sentencing and execution was sixteen months in 1960 (McCafferty 1962, in Bedau 1967b, 95). Unfortunately, national data on the interval between sentencing and execution were not available before 1960 and have never been available on the interval between the crime and execution. Our one-year lag is therefore only a rough identification of the pool of homicides for which the executions in a given year are imposed.

Interestingly enough, between 1935 and 1947 the number of executions per 100 homicides remained relatively constant. All values over this thirteen-year period fell within the limits 1.49 to 2.01 set by the years 1937 and 1938. In 1948 and 1949 the execution rate dropped below the level for any of the preceding thirteen years to 1.45, but it was still on a par with the rate for the early 1930s which averaged 1.44 executions per 100 homicides.

Thus, it would appear that the turning point in the *willingness to execute* in America occurred primarily and most decisively between the late 1940s and the early 1950s. The earlier decline in executions between the late 1930s and the early 1940s appears to have been largely a function of changing levels of homicide as America moved from the Great Depression into the Second World War.

It should be noted that only a tiny fraction of the homicides resulted in executions—only between 1 and 2 in 100 before 1950 and less than 1 in 100 thereafter. Of course, not all the homicides were capital offenses and therefore not all of them were punishable by death. In fact, previous research (Wolfgang 1958; Bensing and Schroeder 1960) has suggested that capital homicides comprise from about 15 to 25 percent of all homicides and therefore that executions have been imposed for, at most, about 10 to 15 percent of the capital homicides in recent times.

*Where Did the Demise Begin?*

While we have been able to locate the historical point at which the nation as a whole, or at least the capital jurisdictions as a group, became considerably more reluctant to execute, it would be a mistake to suppose that this change came about at precisely the same time in all death penalty states throughout the country. Certainly the change took hold in most states, or in the states that imposed the most executions, around 1950. It is quite possible, however, that some death penalty states took the lead in refusing to execute and others followed suit.

To determine whether the growing reluctance to execute occurred uniformly throughout the nation or began in some areas and spread to others, we have tabulated the number of executions and the execution rate in five-year intervals for four geographical regions of the United States in Table 1-5.

It is immediately evident in Table 1-5 that the southern states performed more executions than the other three regions put together. In fact, they imposed about three out of every five executions in America after 1930. This means that the pattern of change in the execution rate for the South will dominate the picture for the nation as a whole. And the table shows that it was between the late 1940s and the early 1950s that the South experienced the most sizable drop in the number

**Table 1-5.** *Executions and Execution Rates in Five-Year Intervals for Four Regions of the United States from 1930 to 1964*

| Five-year Intervals | Northeast | | North Central | | South | | West | |
|---|---|---|---|---|---|---|---|---|
| | Number | Rate | Number | Rate | Number | Rate | Number | Rate |
| 1930–1934 | 155 | 1.97 | 106 | 1.02 | 419 | 1.38 | 96 | 2.24 |
| 1935–1939 | 145 | 2.98 | 119 | 1.34 | 525 | 1.69 | 102 | 2.65 |
| 1940–1944 | 110 | 2.66 | 42 | 0.74 | 420 | 1.72 | 73 | 2.13 |
| 1945–1949 | 74 | 1.63 | 64 | 1.03 | 420 | 1.82 | 81 | 1.96 |
| 1950–1954 | 59 | 1.26 | 44 | 0.72 | 244 | 1.09 | 66 | 1.66 |
| 1955–1959 | 51 | 1.10 | 17 | 0.28 | 185 | 0.89 | 51 | 1.15 |
| 1960–1964 | 17 | 0.28 | 17 | 0.25 | 102 | 0.46 | 45 | 0.79 |

Sources: "Capital Punishment 1930–1960," *National Prisoner Statistics* (1971, Table 3); *Vital Statistics of the United States* (U.S. Bureau of the Census, for the respective periods).
Note: The execution rate is the number of executions in the specified five year interval divided by the number of homicides *in death penalty jurisdictions* for the five year interval ending one year earlier in a given region. (For further details, see Table 1-4, note b.)

of executions and in the execution rate. Note that the decline in the execution rate from 1.82 to 1.09 between these two intervals was greater than for the nation as a whole at that time.

The other regions show different patterns, however. The north central states experienced a definite decline in the rate of execution between the late 1930s and the early 1940s, but because the states in this region performed relatively few executions, this change had little impact on the execution rate for the nation as a whole (as shown in Table 1-4). The northeastern states experienced an even more substantial decline in rate of execution between the early 1940s and the late 1940s, but this too was obscured by the fact that southern states actually had a slightly increased execution rate during this postwar period. The western states showed a slow but consistent reduction in the willingness to execute beginning in the 1940s, but again, because of the relatively small number of executions imposed, the pattern in the West had little effect on the national figures.

In effect, the data in Table 1-5 indicate that there was a reduced willingness to execute in the early 1940s in the north central states and in the late 1940s in the northeastern states, prior to the massive change in the southern states in the early 1950s. Because the South was responsible for the great bulk of executions in America, however, these earlier moves to reduce the rate of execution were not apparent in the national pattern shown earlier in Table 1-4.

It is noteworthy that the South, with more executions than the rest of the country during this period, had a relatively low execution rate. Indeed, of the four regions in Table 1-5, its execution rate ranks third in six of the seven five-year intervals represented in the table. In fact, the relative ranking of the four regions in execution rates is remarkably consistent over time. Thus, in most five-year periods the highest rate was in the West, followed by the Northeast, the South, and the North Central region, in that order, despite the dramatic decline in the number of executions over this period and the fact that the decline began at somewhat different points in the several regions. Obviously, though it is not explicitly shown in Table 1-5, the South accounted for more criminal homicides than the rest of the country throughout this period.

These regional variations in execution patterns are not, of course, perfectly reflected in all the states from a given region; indeed, some states depart substantially from the characteristic pattern for their region. Table 1-6 shows the number of executions in five-year intervals for the ten states that have imposed the most executions since 1930. Each state has performed at least 150 executions since that time, and together they account for some 2,357 executions, 62 percent of the total for that period. These states are arranged roughly according to the timing of their major decline in executions.

The dominant pattern for the southern region is exemplified by North Carolina, with executions dropping from sixty-one in the late 1940s to fourteen in the early 1950s. Similarly, South Carolina and Georgia also showed the steepest decline in the early 1950s. For Florida and Mississippi, however, the point of sharpest decline actually came a decade later, between the late 1950s and the early 1960s. Georgia also shows a sizable decline at this second point.

Texas, the other nominally southern state, appears to follow the pattern of California, and the western states in general, with a relatively constant level of executions after a drop in the early 1940s. In fact, in

**Table 1-6.** *Executions in Five-year Intervals for the Ten States Performing the Most Executions in the United States from 1930 to 1964*

|                | 1930–1934 | 1935–1939 | 1940–1944 | 1945–1949 | 1950–1954 | 1955–1959 | 1960–1964 |
|----------------|-----------|-----------|-----------|-----------|-----------|-----------|-----------|
| Ohio           | 43        | 39        | 15        | 36        | 20        | 12        | 7         |
| Pennsylvania   | 41        | 41        | 15        | 21        | 19        | 12        | 3         |
| New York       | 80        | 73        | 78        | 36        | 27        | 25        | 10        |
| North Carolina | 51        | 80        | 50        | 62        | 14        | 5         | 1         |
| South Carolina | 37        | 30        | 32        | 29        | 16        | 10        | 8         |
| Georgia        | 64        | 73        | 58        | 72        | 51        | 34        | 14        |
| Florida        | 15        | 29        | 38        | 27        | 22        | 27        | 12        |
| Mississippi    | 26        | 22        | 24        | 26        | 15        | 21        | 10        |
| Texas          | 48        | 72        | 38        | 36        | 49        | 25        | 29        |
| California     | 51        | 57        | 35        | 45        | 39        | 35        | 29        |

*Source*: "Capital Punishment 1930–1970," *National Prisoner Statistics* (1971, Table 3).

both Texas and California the pace of executions held up well into the 1960s, at which time these two states accounted for almost as many executions as the other eight leading states combined. Pennsylvania, although nominally a northeastern state, followed the pattern of Ohio and the other north central states, showing a substantial drop in executions during the Second World War years. New York, which accounted for more than half of the executions among the northeastern states, epitomizes the pattern of this region, with a distinct drop in executions in the late 1940s.

Information on states not included among the top ten and for specific years within the five-year intervals shown in Table 1-6 is available in the Teeters-Zibulka inventory of executions included as Appendix A to this volume. A further examination of these data reveals, for example, that New York and Pennsylvania, which together accounted for more than twenty executions per year throughout the 1930s, actually performed no executions in 1945, suggesting a period of intense reluctance to execute in the northeastern region. These data also show that in Indiana executions dropped from twenty in the late 1930s to two in the early 1940s, suggesting that this state may have played an influential role during the early period of increased reluctance to execute in the north central region.

In our discussion of the judicial assault on capital punishment in America, we suggested that growing receptivity of higher courts to appeals in capital cases may have played a crucial role in the demise of executions by encouraging death row prisoners to appeal their cases and by discouraging penal authorities from scheduling and performing executions. The increased reluctance to execute in the southern states in the early 1950s would seem to fit this explanation. The NAACP Legal Defense Fund had become active at about this time in appealing the cases of condemned offenders, particularly black rapists, in southern states and, by implication, of challenging the law enforcement and judicial practices that resulted in the death sentence for such offenders.

But the earlier reductions in the number and rate of executions— in the north central states during the Second World War and in the northeastern states in the immediate postwar years—suggest that other factors were at work to stem the tide of executions in these regions. Perhaps the war itself, and particularly the atrocities attributed to the  Nazis, produced a climate of heightened sensitivity about the use of capital punishment, especially in the north central states with sizable groups of German extraction. Perhaps the emerging scientific evidence, which at this time pointed to the discriminatory manner in which the death penalty had been imposed, raised questions about its use in the minds of informed authorities.

Certainly the abruptness of the suspension of executions, as noted for New York and Pennsylvania in 1945, and the magnitude of the decline in executions, as noted for Indiana during the war years, suggest that state officials were involved in bringing executions to a virtual standstill in some states. The fact that virtually all the states in the north central region showed a similar pattern of reduced willingness to execute during the war implies that there was a climate of caution and reluctance in the use of the death penalty that was shared and perhaps transmitted by influential officials and authorities throughout this region. And the fact that such a reduction in executions or execution rates was altogether absent in the South prior to the 1950s suggests that whatever emerging climate of unwillingness to execute there may have been was not a national phenomenon, but a historical development at the regional level during the war years.

A great deal more would be learned by examining the handling of capital cases at selected times and places for evidence of changes in the sentencing practices of juries, in the stays and commutations granted by governors, and in the numbers and success of appeals in the higher courts. In this way, it should be possible to piece together the story of the decline in the use of the death penalty from the mid-1930s on. For the present, we will have to be satisfied with this descriptive effort to narrow and sharpen the focus on points at which changes in the pattern of executions occurred. This emerging picture will, it is hoped, stimulate a more comprehensive and detailed historical analysis of the demise of executions in America.

## Capital Offenses: De Jure and De Facto

At this point we turn from the numbers executed over various periods of time and in various regions of the country to the kinds of crimes for which people could be and have been put to death. In a pluralistic, changing society like our own, a given crime may be a capital offense in one state and not in another, or at one point in time and not at another, suggesting regional and historical variations in social values or perceived threats to society. And, within a given jurisdiction, the death penalty may be optional for some offenses and mandatory for others, suggesting gradations of seriousness even among the most condemned forms of human conduct.

What, then, are the capital offenses in America—or what were they before the U.S. Supreme Court's *Furman* decision of June 1972 effectively abolished existing capital statutes? For fifty-five jurisdictions including the fifty states, District of Columbia, Puerto Rico, Virgin Islands, and federal civil and military law, Professor Hugo Bedau (1967b, 46) has tabulated (1) the number in which the death penalty was available for various offenses as of January 1967; (2) the number in which the death penalty was mandatory upon conviction for these offenses; (3) the number in which the death penalty has actually been used for these offenses since 1930. His figures are reproduced in Table 1-7.

Criminal homicide was punishable by death in forty-four of fifty-five jurisdictions in America as of 1967. Murder, referring generally to

**Table 1-7.** *Numbers of Jurisdictions in America in which Capital Punishment Was Available, Mandatory, and Actually Imposed*

| Type of Offense | Number of Capital Jurisdictions[a] | Number of Mandatory Jurisdictions | Number of Executing Jurisdictions[b] |
|---|---|---|---|
| Capitally punishable homicide | 44 | 9 | 44 |
| Murder | 40 | 0 | d |
| Other homicide[c] | 20 | 8 | d |
| Kidnapping[e] | 34 | 1 | 6 |
| Treason | 21 | 11 | 0 |
| Rape[f] | 19 | 0 | 18 |
| Carnal knowledge[g] | 15 | 0 | d |
| Robbery[h] | 10 | 0 | 7 |
| Perjury in a capital case[i] | 10 | 6 | 0 |
| Bombing[j] | 7 | 0 | 0 |
| Assault life term prisoner[k] | 5 | 3 | 1 |
| Burglary[l] | 4 | 0 | 2 |
| Arson | 4 | 0 | 0 |
| Train wrecking | 2 | 0 | 0 |
| Train robbery | 2 | 0 | 0 |
| Espionage[m] | 2 | 0 | 1 |
| Other[n] | 17 | 5 | 0 |
| *Total* [o] | *44* | *22* | *45* |

*Source*: Bedau (1967b, 46).

[a] Fifty-five jurisdictions: Fifty states, District of Columbia, Puerto Rico, Virgin Islands, Federal Civil and Military.

[b] Data from National Prisoner Statistics, "Executions 1961." Alaska and Hawaii excluded. Executions in years prior to 1930 excluded.

[c] Includes sixteen special capital homicide statutes.

[d] Information not available; see note b.

[e] Includes kidnapping, kidnapping for ransom, kidnapping with bodily harm, kidnapping for ransom and with bodily harm, taking a hostage.

[f] Includes rape, attempted rape, assault with intent to rape, drugging with intent to rape.

[g] Includes carnal knowledge of a minor and of a mentally deficient or mentally ill person.

[h] Includes robbery, aggravated robbery, armed robbery, bank robbery.

[i] Includes perjury and subornation leading to the death of a guilty person or to the death of an innocent person.

[j] Includes bombing, dynamiting, and bomb throwing.

[k] Includes assault and assault with a deadly weapon.

[l] Includes burglary and armed burglary.

[m] Includes gathering or giving information to an enemy or foreign power during wartime.

[n] Includes twenty-one special capital statutes.

[o] Because of duplications, the totals are less than the sum of the numbers in each column.

the willful, premeditated, and malicious killing of another person, was a capital offense in forty of these jurisdictions. Other forms of homicide, such as the unintended killing of someone in the course of some other crime, were defined as capital offenses in half as many jurisdictions.

Kidnapping, elevated to a capital offense in some two dozen states in the 1930s following the death of the kidnapped Lindbergh baby in 1932, was a capital crime in most American jurisdictions as of 1967. Forcible rape and carnal knowledge, which also involve violence or harm to relatively vulnerable or defenseless persons, were defined as capital offenses in a substantial minority of the jurisdictions.

Treason is the only other offense for which a sizable number of jurisdictions provided the death penalty. Since treason is generally a crime against the nation as a whole, it need not have been defined as a capital offense except in federal jurisdictions. Yet, unlike espionage, which may also be classified as a threat to national security or the political integrity of the nation, treason was punishable by death in twenty-one jurisdictions.

Moreover, those jurisdictions that punished treason by death tended to make the punishment mandatory, suggesting that it is more serious than most capital crimes. In fact, a number of states that have retained the death penalty for treason have specifically disallowed executive clemency for those under sentence of death for treason. No doubt the desire for protection against threats to political authority explains the fact that most other countries that have capital punishment define treason as a capital crime, often requiring the death penalty (Patrick 1965).

Where serious threats to law enforcement and the administration of justice have been defined as capital offenses, the death penalty also tends to be mandatory. Thus, assault by a life term prisoner and perjury in a capital case carry mandatory death penalties in more than half the jurisdictions where they are capital crimes.

When we turn to the number of jurisdictions that have actually administered the death penalty for the specific offenses in Table 1-7, it becomes evident that since 1930 capital punishment has been widely used only for homicide and rape: every one of the forty-four jurisdictions in which criminal homicide was a capital offense has used the death penalty for this crime, and eighteen of the nineteen death penalty jurisdictions for rape have executed rapists. By contrast, very few jurisdictions have actually executed offenders for any of the remaining crimes. For example, treason has not been punished by death since 1930 in any of the twenty-one jurisdictions in which it is available.[7]

7. The Federal Bureau of Prisons records 70 executions for crimes other than rape or murder since 1930. Of these, only eight have been imposed for crimes against the state on national security—six were Nazi spies and saboteurs executed in 1942 and the other two were Ethel and Julius Rosenberg executed for espionage in 1953.

And how did the offenses defined as capital vary by jurisdiction within the United States at the time of the Court's *Furman* decision? In 1971, the NAACP Legal Defense and Educational Fund, Inc., prepared an inventory of all statutory provisions for the death penalty in the United States as part of their brief in *Furman* v. *Georgia* (originally filed as *Aikins* v. *California*, 1971: Appendix G). For each state and the federal jurisdictions are listed the specific offenses punishable by death in the fall of 1971, with citations to the effective criminal code provisions.[8] The information is summarized in Table 1-8, which shows for each death penalty jurisdiction the number of capital provisions in its criminal code for various categories of crime. For simplicity of presentation, we have grouped some of the offense categories distinguished in Table 1-7 (as indicated in the notes to Table 1-8), which are themselves composites of related offenses (as indicated in the notes to Table 1-7).

This table makes it clear that the proliferation and coverage of capital statutes varied considerably by jurisdiction. In sheer numbers, the federal jurisdictions and southern states had the most provisions for the death penalty. The five states with ten or more capital provisions in their criminal codes were Alabama (20), Arkansas (13), Kentucky (12), South Carolina (12), and Virginia (10). The mean number of such provisions is eight for the southern states, five for the western states, and three for the northern states. Notably, the number of such provisions was greatest among the southwestern and border states within the southern region and least among the northeastern, especially the New England states, within the northern region.

There were also regional disparities in the types of offenses covered by these capital provisions. All sixteen southern death penalty states had capital provisions for murder, and a majority of these had such provisions for other forms of homicide, kidnapping, treason, sex offenses, and other crimes of violence against the person. The southwestern and border states were more likely to have such provisions than those on the eastern seaboard for all these offense categories except murder. Moreover, for sex offenses, other violent crimes against the person, and offenses endangering the lives of others, southern states accounted for most of the capital provisions in the nation as a whole. This is most pronounced for sex offenses, chiefly rape; 14 of the 18 capital jurisdictions and 27 of the 33 capital provisions were in the South. All eight of the southwestern and border states had the death penalty for rape. The South also led other regions in providing capital punishment for killing in a duel or by lynching.

---

8. This inventory with the specific references to the criminal statutes of the various jurisdictions is reproduced in full in Bowers (1974), Table 2-4, pp. 44–52.

**Table 1-8.** *Number of Statutory Provisions for Capital Punishment by Offense Category for State and Federal Jurisdictions*[a]

| Jurisdictions | Murder (1st Degree) | Other Special Homicide | Kidnapping | Treason; Espionage; Sabotage[b] | Rape; Carnal Knowledge[c] | Robbery/Assault; Train Robbery; Burglary[d] | Bombing; Arson; Train Wrecking[c] | Capital Perjury; Assault by a Lifer[f] | Other |
|---|---|---|---|---|---|---|---|---|---|
| *Northern States* | | | | | | | | | |
| New Hampshire | 1 | — | — | — | — | — | — | — | — |
| Vermont | — | 1 | — | — | — | — | — | — | — |
| Massachusetts | 1 | 1[g] | — | — | — | — | — | — | — |
| Rhode Island | — | 1 | — | — | — | — | — | — | — |
| Connecticut[h] | 1 | 3[i] | — | — | — | — | — | — | — |
| New York[i] | — | 2 | 1 | — | — | — | — | — | — |
| New Jersey | 1 | — | 1 | 1 | — | 1 | — | — | — |
| Pennsylvania | 1 | 2[ik] | 1[l] | — | — | — | — | 1 | — |
| Ohio | 1 | 6[i] | 1[l] | 1 | — | — | — | — | — |
| Indiana | 1 | 4[ikm] | 1 | 1 | — | — | — | — | — |
| Illinois | 1 | — | 1 | 1 | — | — | — | — | — |
| Missouri | 1 | 1 | 1 | 1 | 1 | 1 | 1 | 1 | — |
| N. Dakota | — | — | — | — | — | — | — | — | — |
| S. Dakota | 1 | — | 1[l] | — | — | — | — | — | — |
| Nebraska | 1 | — | 1[l] | — | — | — | — | — | — |
| Kansas | 1 | — | 1[l] | 1 | — | — | — | — | 1 |
| *Southern States* | | | | | | | | | |
| Delaware | 1 | — | — | — | — | — | — | — | — |
| Maryland | 1 | 4[i] | 1 | — | 3 | 3 | — | — | — |
| D.C. | 1 | — | — | — | — | — | — | — | — |
| Virginia | 1 | 1[m] | 1 | 1 | 2 | 3 | 1 | — | 1 |
| N. Carolina | 1 | — | — | 2 | 1 | 1 | 1 | — | — |
| S. Carolina[n] | 1 | 4[km] | 1 | 1 | 3 | — | — | 1 | 1 |
| Georgia | 1 | — | 1 | 1 | 1 | 1 | — | 1 | 2 |
| Florida | 1 | 2[im] | 1 | 1 | 1 | — | 2 | — | — |

| | | | | | | | |
|---|---|---|---|---|---|---|---|
| Kentucky | 1 | 5[ik] | 1 | 2 | 1 | 1 | — |
| Tennessee | 1 | — | 1 | 4 | — | 2 | — |
| Alabama[o] | 2 | 4[km] | 2 | 3 | 3 | 3 | — |
| Mississippi | 1 | 2[m] | 1 | 1 | 1 | 1 | — |
| Arkansas | 1 | 6[m] | 1 | 2 | 1 | — | — |
| Louisiana | 1 | — | 1 | 1 | 1 | 1 | — |
| Oklahoma | 1 | — | 1 | 2 | 1 | 1 | — |
| Texas | 1 | 1 | 1 | — | 1 | — | — |
| *Western States* | | | | | | | |
| Montana | 1 | 1[i] | 1 | — | 1 | 1 | — |
| Idaho | 1 | 1[i] | — | 1 | — | 1 | — |
| Wyoming[p] | 1 | 2[im] | — | 1 | — | — | 1 |
| Colorado | 1 | 3 | — | — | — | 2 | — |
| New Mexico | 1 | — | — | — | — | — | — |
| Arizona | 1 | — | 1 | 1 | — | 2 | — |
| Utah | 1 | 1[m] | — | — | — | 1 | — |
| Nevada | 1 | 2[m] | 2 | — | 1 | 1 | 1 |
| Washington | 1 | 1[i] | 1 | — | — | — | — |
| California | 2 | 1 | — | — | 2 | 2 | — |
| *Federal* | | | | | | | |
| Military | 1 | — | 1 | 1 | — | — | 7 |
| Civil/Federal Aviation[q] | 1 | 8[i] | 1 | 2 | 1 | — | — |

*Source:* NAACP Legal Defense and Educational Fund, Inc., brief, *Aikins v. California* (1971, Appendix G).

a Some of these provisions were unconstitutional and inoperative under United States v. Jackson, 390 U.S. 570 (1968).
b Combines treason, espionage (as defined in Table 1-7, note m) and sabotage.
c Combines rape and carnal knowledge (as defined in Table 1-7, notes f and g).
d Combines robbery, burglary (as defined in Table 1-7, notes h and l), train robbery, assault with a deadly weapon and other forms of assault.
e Combines bombing (as defined in Table 1-7, note j), arson, and train wrecking.
f Includes perjury in a capital case and assault by a life-term prisoner, but not assault with a deadly weapon or other assault (contrary to Table 1-7, note k; see note d to this table).

g This was a felony rape murder statute omitted from the inventory and subsequently ruled unconstitutional by the Massachusetts Supreme Judicial Court in Commonwealth v. O'Neal (1975).
h One statutory provision contained four distinguishable offenses.
i Death caused by train wrecking.
j One statutory provision contained two distinguishable offenses.
k Death caused by lynching.
l Kidnapping with bodily harm.
m Killing in a duel.
n One statutory provision contained two distinguishable offenses.
o One statutory provision contained two distinguishable offenses.
p One statutory provision contained two distinguishable offenses.
q Two statutory provisions each containing two distinguishable offenses.

The western states were similar to those in the South in their treatment of murder, other forms of homicide, kidnapping, and treason, but notably different with respect to sex offenses and offenses against the criminal justice system and its agents. In the West, all death penalty states had capital provisions for murder, most had them for other forms of homicide and kidnapping, and half did so for treason. In contrast with the South, however, only one of the western states provided the death penalty for rape or related sex offenses. Among other forms of homicide covered by capital provisions in the West, death by train wrecking was most common, but several states also covered death by dueling, as in the South. The most notable difference between the West and the rest of the country is the fact that a majority of the western states had capital provisions for crimes against police officers, prison guards or inmates, or the criminal justice process itself. Indeed, the western states accounted for more than half of all capital provisions for such offenses in the nation as a whole.

The northern states, especially those in the northeastern region, generally had capital provisions for a more restricted range of offenses. All northern death penalty states had capital provisions for homicide, eleven for murder and nine for other forms of criminal homicide. Within this region, the north central states more often had the death penalty for murder than for other forms of homicide; the opposite was true for northeastern states where felony homicide, killing by train wrecking, or killing a police officer or prison guard were more likely to be punishable by death than was the traditional category of murder with malice and premeditation. The only other offenses covered by capital provisions to any notable extent in the northern states were kidnapping and treason, and these crimes were made capital offenses almost exclusively in the north central states.

Both federal jurisdictions made murder and rape punishable by death. The military code was responsible for the largest number of capital provisions in the "other" category of Table 1-8. These provisions generally covered crimes against military authority and offenses by military personnel during wartime. The federal civil code was responsible for the largest number of capital provisions for "other special homicides," including those associated with national security, those with government officials as victims, those carried out by means of the mails, and those committed in federally controlled transportation such as aviation.

Thus, the profile of capital offenses is different in the several regions of the country and in the federal jurisdictions. In the South, crimes of interpersonal violence not resulting in death, especially sex offenses, were much more likely than they were elsewhere to be capital offenses. In the West, killing in a train wreck, kidnapping, and especially offenses against the justice system and its agents were more often made punishable by death. In the North, only murder and selected forms of homicide were subject to capital punishment in a majority of the states. In the federal jurisdictions, most of the capital provisions applied to offenses peculiar to that level of government, including threats to national security and the welfare of federal officials, or offenses against military authority or the conduct of warfare.

While the differences between the federal and state capital codes correspond, at least in part, to the distinctive functions of these levels of government, the explanations for distinct regional patterns are less obvious. To some extent such regional patterns may reflect differences in cultural values or perceived threats to social order. Thus, the extension of capital provisions to crimes of violence not resulting in death in the South may reflect a response through law to apprehension over the threat of personal attack—in what some have labeled a "regional culture of violence" (Gastil 1971). Capital provisions for nonlethal crimes against the legal establishment and its agents in the West suggest a historical premium on maintaining respect for the law and lawmen. The relatively restricted application of capital statutes in the North, especially the northeast and particularly New England, may reflect the effects of legislative assaults on the death penalty which have fallen short of abolition but may have succeeded in narrowing the applicability of capital punishment.[9]

The more than 250 statutory provisions for capital punishment represented in Table 1-8 underscore the vast gulf between the dwindling use of the death penalty in the decade of the 1960s and its remaining availability in the criminal codes of various jurisdictions of America. Obviously, the legislation providing for capital punishment and the criminal process through which it is imposed were two very different realms—one reflecting political determination to keep the death penalty alive and available and the other reflecting judicial aversion to the use of this ultimate and irrevocable sanction.


## Conclusion

Between the American Revolution and the Second World War, capital punishment in America underwent a slow but thorough metamorphosis. Statutory reforms restricted the death penalty to "first

9. For historical developments in the capital statutes of the various states and federal jurisdictions, the interested reader may wish to refer to the following sources: Bye (1926), Deets (1948), McCafferty (1954), Reifsnyder (1955), Savitz (1955), and *The Congressional Record* (1962). These references are drawn from Bedau (1967b, 39).

degree" offenses and gave juries discretion in choosing between life and death for first degree offenders. The execution itself was taken from the hands of local authorities to be performed at a time and place far removed from the original crime. Electricity and gas were introduced to make the execution swift and painless, further insulating observers from the event by requiring it to be conducted behind glass or within airtight enclosures. Indeed, the execution took on the character of a medical operation performed in an antiseptic environment by dispassionate experts. And, as we shall see, when executions became more remote from the public's experience, they appear to have declined not so much in absolute numbers, but certainly in relation to the growing population of the nation (see Table 2-2).

Then, about the time of the Second World War, America began to abandon capital punishment. At first the decline in executions appears to have been primarily the result of falling levels of homicide, but by mid-century there were definite indications that the nation was becoming more reluctant to execute. The progressive decline in executions was accompanied by mounting scientific evidence that the death penalty was being administered in a discriminatory fashion and with little, if any, deterrent effect. We shall see that it was also accompanied by the abandonment of capital punishment in many other countries around the world. In fact, about half of the forty-five or so presently abolitionist nations became so since the Second World War (see Table 5-3).

This abandonment of executions in America has not been adequately explained from a historical standpoint. A number of factors operating within the judicial system appear to have played a part. These include increasing receptivity of federal courts to appeals in capital cases, growing concern among lawyers for the rights of criminal defendants, and mounting reluctance of juries to hand down the death sentence and of governors and state penal authorities to schedule and carry out executions. These changes, in turn, may have been stimulated by accumulating scientific evidence on the application and effectiveness of the death penalty and changing moral standards in this country and abroad. In any case, executions came to an end de facto if not de jure in 1967, and it was in the courts, not the legislatures, that the struggle against executions was succeeding.

After five years without an execution, the nation's highest court in 1972 declared that the death penalty was "cruel and unusual" punishment because it had been used in a rare, arbitrary, and discriminatory fashion. Yet the Court's decision in *Furman* v. *Georgia* was not definitive in character. While two of the justices—Brennan and Marshall—found these and other ills to be inherent in the use of the death penalty in modern society, the other three members of the majority—

Douglas, Stewart, and White—linked their objections to the imposition of the death sentence under existing statutes. In effect, the majority ruled out the death penalty not because of its essential nature as a punishment, but because of the way it was being applied under existing laws.

Thus, as of 1974, the struggle over capital punishment continues. State legislatures are now formulating capital statutes designed to meet the objections of the Court. Some of the newly drafted statutes draw on earlier forms of capital punishment, particularly its mandatory use, as a model. Indeed, the death penalty has already been handed down under some of these new statutes, condemned men once again face the prospect of execution, and the Court will soon be confronted with appeals that again raise questions of the constitutionality of capital punishment.

Let us now turn to some evidence of "recent vintage" that the Court may wish to take into account the next time it considers the constitutionality of capital punishment.

# 2

## THE MOVEMENT TO STATE-IMPOSED EXECUTIONS

Executions in America began as public events, sometimes attracting thousands of spectators and often accompanied by a carnival atmosphere. (For numerous accounts of such executions, see Teeters and Hedblom 1967.) These public spectacles were transformed into private ceremonies when, in the 1830s and 1840s, most states moved them within the confines of the county jails, partly for humane reasons and partly to avoid the difficulty of controlling unruly mobs which became outraged at bungled hangings and last minute reprieves.

Within several decades a second movement began. With the development of state penal institutions and the centralization of penal authority at the state level, states began to require that executions be performed under state rather than local authority, usually at a single state facility. The hanging of one Sandy Kavanagh at the Vermont State Prison on January 20, 1864, marked the beginning of this movement toward state-imposed executions. Some 103 years later, when executions had come to an end, at least temporarily, with the hanging of Louis Jose Monge at the Colorado State Prison on June 2, 1967, all but two of the states with the death penalty—Delaware and Montana—had transferred executions from local to state authority.

Dimensions of this phase in the history of capital punishment in America are revealed in an inventory of executions under state authority, compiled in 1968 by Professor Negley K. Teeters with the assistance of Charles J. Zibulka and now amended and corrected with information supplied by Mr. M. Watt Espy, Jr. The original Teeters-Zibulka inventory, first published in full in the previous edition of this volume (Bowers 1974, Appendix A)[1] listed 5,707 state-imposed executions between 1864 and 1967. For these executions, the inventory provided the names of the condemned persons, the states and counties in which they were prosecuted, the crimes for which they were sentenced to death, the judicial appeals they may have made prior to execution, and the dates of their executions. For most of the condemned persons, the listing also gave race of offender and age at execution.

Mr. Espy had, as of February 1982, verified forty additional executions imposed under state authority prior to *Furman*, and since *Furman* six more state-imposed executions have been performed to date. The original inventory of state-imposed executions has now been amended and updated to include information on 5,753 executions—the 5,707 originally identified by Teeters and Zibulka, the additional forty pre-*Furman* executions verified by Espy, and the six post-*Furman* executions performed to date—as well as a great many other additions and corrections based on information provided by Espy. All this information has been incorporated in the revised inventory of *Executions under State Authority: 1864–1982* now published as Appendix A in this volume.[2]

Most of the information in the original Teeters-Zibulka inventory was supplied by wardens from the records of the departments of corrections of the various states. The data on appeals came from the indices of the *Decennial Digest* (West Publishing Company). The accuracy and completeness of these data were naturally dependent on the record-keeping practices of the various states and upon the reliability of the indices of the *Decennial Digest*. In particular, information on race and age were simply not recorded for some periods in some states; data on race were missing for 13.9 percent and on age for 45.0 percent of the executions. In their introductions to the original inventory, Tweeters and Zibulka noted difficulties they encountered in compiling the information and possible sources of inaccuracies in the data (see Appendix A).

1. A portion of this inventory (Alabama through Kentucky, alphabetically) appeared in *Hearings Before the Subcommittee on Criminal Laws and Procedures of the U.S. Senate Committee on the Judiciary, 90th Congress, 2nd Session, on S 1760*, March 21 and 22 and July 2, 1968 (1970, 209–236).
2. This listing includes electrocutions at the Cook County Jail, Chicago, and county jail hangings in Kentucky for rape; in both instances, county authorities exercised concurrent jurisdiction with state authorities. It also includes executions under federal jurisdiction imposed at two state penal institutions and executions performed in the District of Columbia, counting two performed prior to 1864 in Washington, D.C.

In 1971, Mr. M. Watt Espy, Jr., now of the University of Alabama Law School, undertook a compilation of all executions imposed in America since colonial times. In this ambitious project, Espy had by November 1982 verified some 13,630 legal, non-military executions—most of them imposed under local jurisdiction. To confirm executions and verify demographic information, Espy cross-checked numerous data sources including published and unpublished county histories, scholarly works, contemporary newspaper and periodical accounts (available on microfilm), reported cases of state supreme courts, and the records of historical societies and museums. For a given execution, the "Espy File" contains a set of bibliographic citations to authenticate the execution and accompanying data.

Beyond the forty additional state-imposed executions not previously listed by Teeters and Zibulka, Espy's work has led to some 2,906 alterations in their original inventory. These alterations include changes of all kinds from the spelling of names to the provision of missing information. In particular, the missing data on race of offender have been reduced from 13.9 to 5.6 percent and the missing data on age at execution have dropped from 45.0 to 23.3 percent of the cases.

The tabulations and analyses here and in Chapter 3 of this volume include the additions and corrections of pre-*Furman* data supplied by Mr. Espy through January 1982 and the six post-*Furman* executions imposed through December 1982. In overall development and substantive findings, these two chapters correspond quite closely to their counterparts in the earlier edition of this volume. Some of the more specific findings, particularly the relative strength of some of the relationships, are altered, and the specific numbers and percentages in the tables of these two chapters are changed in nearly all instances.

In the following sections of this chapter, we first examine coverage and completeness of the updated information on state-imposed executions in more detail. We then turn to historical and regional patterns in the movement of executions to centralized facilities under state jurisdiction. And finally we examine the characteristics of those executed under state authority within historical and regional context. In Chapter 3 we shall examine these data for evidence of racial differences in the treatment of offenders.

## The Coverage and Completeness of the Data

Any such ambitious effort to compile an extensive inventory of historical data is bound to encounter problems of coverage and completeness of information. Our first step will be to summarize the in-

formation available for the forty-two states having performed executions
under centralized state authority and the District of Columbia.[3] For
each jurisdiction, Table 2-1 indicates (1) the date of the first and last
executions performed under state authority; (2) period(s) during which
capital punishment may have been abolished in the various states;
(3) the number of executions imposed under state authority; and (4)
the number of executions for which information on age and race is
available.

**Table 2-1.**  *Data Available on Executions under State Authority
for 42 States and the District of Columbia*

| State | Period of Executions | Period of Abolition | Number of Executions | Number of Cases with Data on Age | Number of Cases with Data on Race |
|-------|------------|-----------|-----------|-----------|-----------|
| Alabama | 1927–1965 ª | | 153 | 131 | 153 |
| Arizona | 1910–1963 | 1916–1918 | 64 | 17 | 64 |
| Arkansas | 1913–1964 | | 172 | 60 | 171 |
| California | 1893–1967 | | 502 | 468 | 400 |
| Colorado | 1890–1967 | 1897–1901 | 77 | 34 | 45 |
| Connecticut | 1894–1960 | | 73 | 73 | 73 |
| District of Columbia | 1853–1957 | | 113 | 87 | 113 |
| Florida | 1924–1979 | | 198 | 174 | 198 |
| Georgia | 1924–1964 | | 422 | 405 | 421 |
| Idaho | 1901–1957 | | 9 | 4 | 9 |
| Illinois | 1928–1962 | | 98 | 63 | 63 |
| Indiana | 1897–1981 | | 74 | 73 | 74 |
| Iowa | 1894–1963 | 1965–*Furman* | 31 | 27 | 31 |
| Kansas | 1944–1965 | | 15 | 15 | 15 |
| Kentucky | 1911–1962 | | 171 | 93 | 171 |
| Louisiana | 1957–1961 | | 11 | 11 | 11 |
| Maine | 1864–1885 | 1887–*Furman* | 7 | 4 | 7 |
| Maryland | 1923–1961 | | 79 | 78 | 79 |
| Massachusetts | 1901–1947 | | 65 | 65 | 65 |
| Mississippi | 1955–1964 | | 31 | 30 | 31 |
| Missouri | 1938–1965 | | 39 | 39 | 39 |
| Nebraska | 1903–1959 | | 20 | 20 | 20 |
| Nevada | 1905–1978 | | 42 | 36 | 18 |
| New Hampshire | 1869–1939 | | 12 | 9 | 11 |
| New Jersey | 1907–1963 | | 161 | 159 | 160 |

3. Eight states have never imposed executions under centralized jurisdiction: the traditionally abolitionist states of Michigan, Minnesota, and Wisconsin, which have
conducted no executions under state or local authority throughout all or most of this
period; Rhode Island, which retained the death penalty for homicide by a life term
prisoner but has performed no executions under this provision; Delaware and Montana, which have performed executions during this period under local but not state
authority; and Alaska and Hawaii, both of which abolished capital punishment in
1957 prior to statehood.

| State | Period of Executions | Period of Abolition | Number of Executions | Number of Cases with Data on Age | Number of Cases with Data on Race |
|---|---|---|---|---|---|
| New Mexico | 1933–1960 | 1969–Furman [b] | 8 | 1 | 5 |
| New York | 1890–1963 | 1965–Furman [c] | 695 | 672 | 679 |
| North Carolina | 1910–1961 | | 362 | 210 | 362 |
| North Dakota | 1905 | 1915–Furman [d] | 1 | 0 | 0 |
| Ohio | 1885–1963 [e] | | 344 | 344 | 344 |
| Oklahoma | 1915–1966 | | 83 | 83 | 83 |
| Oregon | 1904–1962 | 1914–1920 | 60 | 35 | 60 |
| Pennsylvania | 1915–1962 | | 351 | 117 | 307 |
| South Carolina | 1912–1962 | | 241 | 78 | 241 |
| South Dakota | 1947 | | 1 | 1 | 1 |
| Tennessee | 1916–1960 [f] | | 134 | 88 | 134 |
| Texas | 1924–1982 | | 362 | 209 | 362 |
| Utah | 1903–1977 | | 32 | 32 | 32 |
| Vermont | 1864–1954 | 1965–Furman [g] | 21 | 19 | 16 |
| Virginia | 1908–1982 | | 238 | 235 | 238 |
| Washington | 1904–1963 [h] | 1913–1919 | 73 | 73 | 73 |
| West Virginia | 1899–1959 | 1965–Furman | 94 | 29 | 94 |
| Wyoming | 1912–1965 | | 14 | 9 | 13 |
| TOTALS | | | 5,753 | 4,410 | 5,486 |

Source: Appendix A, as updated with information supplied by M. Watt Espy, Jr., through January 1982.

[a] Appeal automatic from 1943, applies to 53 cases.
[b] Abolition except for murder of police and prison guards or second unrelated murder.
[c] Abolition except for murder of police and prison guards or by a lifer.
[d] Abolition except for treason and murder by a lifer.
[e] Appeals were automatic at the county level; an appeal on state constitutional grounds was heard by the Ohio Supreme Court.
[f] Not all appeals were recorded in law books.
[g] Abolition except for murder of police and prison guards or second unrelated murder.
[h] Death penalty restored after 1919 only if jury specifically recommends it.

The starting dates for state-imposed executions span almost a century from 1864 when Vermont first imposed executions under state authority through 1957 when Louisiana finally brought executions under centralized authority. For six states the effective period of state-imposed executions extends beyond the 1967 nationwide moratorium on executions; these are the states that have carried out executions between 1977 and 1982 under post-Furman capital statutes. For eleven states, the effective period of state-imposed executions was interrupted prior to the 1967 moratorium by periods of abolition. For all states, the 1972 Furman decision represented a further interruption in the effective period of state-imposed executions. Since Furman, legislatures have enacted new capital statutes in most states and state and federal courts have invalidated them or limited their scope and applicability. The legal status of capital punishment by jurisdiction in the post-Furman era is outlined in Appendix B (see also Bedau 1982, esp. 32–38).

According to Table 2-1, the forty-three jurisdictions were responsible for 5,753 executions under centralized authority. The number of
state-imposed executions by jurisdiction range from a high of 695 performed in New York state to a low of one each in North and South
Dakota. Seven states accounted for more than half of these executions:
New York (695), California (502), Georgia (422), North Carolina (362),
Texas (362), Pennsylvania (351), and Ohio (344). Another three states
bring the coverage up to 65 percent: South Carolina (241), Virginia
(238), and Florida (198). Notably, there is a close correspondence between these ten states and the ten identified in Table 1-6 as performing
the most executions since 1930. The only discrepancy is that Virginia
in this group has replaced Mississippi in the earlier table, owing to the
fact that Mississippi imposed executions under local authority until
1955, 47 years later than Virginia.

The total of 5,753 state-imposed executions represents an increase
of 46 executions over the previously published figure (Bowers 1974,
31). The six post-*Furman* executions add to the totals of six states:
Utah, Nevada, Florida, Indiana, Virginia, and Texas. The forty additional pre-*Furman* executions supplied by Mr. Espy are responsible for
increases in the number of executions in nineteen states (also including
Nevada and Virginia). In most instances, the state totals have changed
by only one or two executions; changes exceeding two executions occurred for Tennessee (9), Nevada (8), Georgia (5), and Arkansas (4).

Information on race of the condemned offender is available for 95.4
percent of the cases. It is complete for 29 states and available on at
least 90 percent of the cases in another six states. Only five states fall
below 75 percent coverage on race: Illinois (64 percent), New Mexico
(63 percent), Colorado (58 percent), Nevada (43 percent), and North
Dakota (no data). Mr. Espy added race where it had not previously been
available for 419 executions, leaving 267 executions unclassified by
race. The principal additions occurred for California (158), Pennsylvania (61), Colorado (44), Utah (32), and Illinois (29), which account
for more than three quarters of the additions.

With respect to age at execution, the data are less complete; age
is available for 76.7 percent of the state-imposed executions. It is present for all executions in eleven states; for at least 75 percent of the
executions in 15 more states; for 50 to 74 percent of the executions in
another eight states; and all but two states had information on age for
at least 25 percent of their executions. Age is missing for the one
execution in North Dakota and all but one of the eight in New Mexico—both states with very few executions. Mr. Espy supplied information on age for 1,406 executions, leaving 1,343 unclassified by age.
The greatest increases in the information on age came for Texas (209),
California (164), Pennsylvania (116), Kentucky (93), and the District of

Columbia (87), which account for half of the additional information on age at execution.

And finally, the additions and corrections supplied by Mr. Espy have improved the correspondence between the Teeters-Zibulka inventory and official statistics on executions compiled since 1930 and published periodically by the Federal Bureau of Prisons. The original Teeters-Zibulka listing recorded six fewer executions under state authority than did the report *Capital Punishment: 1930–1970* of the Federal Bureau of Prisons (Bowers 1974, Table 2-9). Of the forty additional pre-*Furman* executions identified by Espy, seven were performed under state authority after 1930, thus reducing the discrepancy from six fewer to one more state-imposed execution since 1930 in the Teeters-Zibulka inventory compared with the official statistics on executions.[4]

The other notable improvement is that the additional information supplied by Mr. Espy has reduced the discrepancy in race of executed offenders between the two data sources from 3.9 to 1.1 percent more nonwhites in the Teeters-Zibulka inventory. The very slight discrepancy in offense leading to execution of 0.1 percent more offenders executed for murder as opposed to rape and other lesser offenses remains essentially unchanged in the Teeters-Zibulka inventory.

Thanks to the painstaking efforts of Mr. Espy, we have been able to improve the coverage and completeness of the inventory as well as its correspondence with aggregate information on executions available from the official records of the Federal Bureau of Prisons. By available indicators, the revised Teeters-Zibulka inventory would appear to be a virtually complete and highly accurate listing of executions under state authority.

## Historical and Regional Developments

There was little perceptible movement toward state-imposed executions for at least two decades after the first execution under state authority in 1864. Only eight executions were performed at state penal

---

4. The revised Teeters-Zibulka inventory lists some 3,584 executions performed under federal and state authority from 1930 through 1967. The total number of executions under civil authority, federal, state, and local auspices, as reported in *Capital Punishment: 1930–1970* (Federal Bureau of Prisons, 1971) for this period is 3,859—a difference of 275 executions. During this period, however, five states—Mississippi, Louisiana, Missouri, Delaware, and Montana—conducted at least some executions under local rather than state authority. To make these two data sources strictly comparable in terms of state-imposed executions, therefore, we must exclude these executions in these five states and those under federal authority from both sources. The result is a discrepancy of one state-imposed execution—3,468 in the revised Teeters-Zibulka inventory vs. 3,467 recorded by the Federal Bureau of Prisons.

institutions between 1864 and 1889. Another twenty-three were conducted in the District of Columbia between 1853 and 1889. Altogether, this is an average of only about two executions per year under state and federal authority prior to the 1890s.

Then, in the 1890s, the movement toward state-imposed executions gathered momentum. In that decade the level of executions rose to an average of 15 per year, and in the four succeeding decades it climbed to 29, 63, 104, and 152 per year. In effect, progressively increasing numbers of executions were performed under state authority in each successive decade from the 1890s through the 1930s.

As we have already seen in Table 1-4, the pace of executions declined markedly after the mid-1930s. The average number of executions annually dropped to 118 in the 1940s, to 68 in the 1950s, and to 19 for the eight years during which executions were imposed in the 1960s. This dramatic decline was accomplished in thirty-two years—the time that elapsed between the peak in 1935 and the last execution in 1967.

This pattern of growth and decline in state-imposed executions by decade is shown in Table 2-2. It may conveniently be divided into the following four phases or periods as indicated in the rightmost column of the table.

1.  a *dormancy* period from the beginning of state-imposed executions through the decade of the 1880s, a period during which only 1.1 percent of all executions under state authority were performed

**Table 2-2.** *Number and Percentage of Executions under State Authority by Decade from the 1880s*

| Decades | Number of Executions | Percentage | Developmental Period |
|---|---|---|---|
| 1870s and earlier[a] | 33 | 0.6 | Dormancy |
| 1880s | 30 | 0.5 | Period |
| 1890s | 155 | 2.7 | |
| 1900s | 291 | 5.1 | Growth |
| 1910s | 633 | 11.0 | Period |
| 1920s | 1,038 | 18.0 | |
| 1930s | 1,523 | 26.5 | Peak Period |
| 1940s | 1,178 | 20.5 | Period of |
| 1950s | 681 | 11.8 | Decline |
| 1960s and later | 191 | 3.3 | |
| Total | 5,753 | 100.0 | |

*Note*: The figures in this and subsequent tables on state-imposed executions are tabulated from the Teeters-Zibulka inventory of *Executions under State Authority: 1864–1982*, published as Appendix A to this volume.
[a] Includes two executions in the 1850s in the District of Columbia.

2. a *growth* period covering forty years from the 1890s through the 1920s, a period when the number of executions progressively increased each successive decade and 36.8 percent of all state-imposed executions were performed

3. a *peak* period during the 1930s covering ten years and accounting for 26.5 percent of all state-imposed executions

4. a period of *decline* from 1940 through 1967 when the last execution under state authority was imposed, a twenty-eight year period during which some 35.6 percent of all state-imposed executions were performed.

This relatively clear-cut national pattern of dormancy, growth, peaking, and decline in state-imposed executions is, of course, a composite picture; it may not accurately represent the developmental pattern in any specific section or region of the country. That this is so can be seen in Figure 2-1, which graphically depicts trends in the use of state-imposed executions for the North, the South, and the West of the United States.

The developmental patterns in the three sections of the country are alike in that state-imposed executions peaked in the 1930s in all three regions. Yet, the rise and fall were most pronounced in the South and least so in the West. Throughout most of the dormancy and growth periods more state executions were conducted in the North than in the South or the West. During the peak period and the period of decline the South led the other two regions by a substantial margin; in fact, a

**Figure 2-1.** *Executions Per Decade under State Authority to the 1960s by Region*

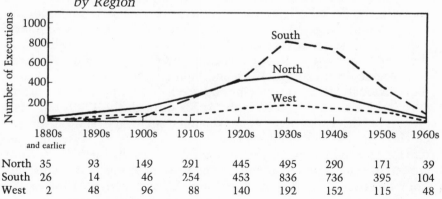

|        | 1880s and earlier | 1890s | 1900s | 1910s | 1920s | 1930s | 1940s | 1950s | 1960s |
|--------|-------------------|-------|-------|-------|-------|-------|-------|-------|-------|
| North  | 35                | 93    | 149   | 291   | 445   | 495   | 290   | 171   | 39    |
| South  | 26                | 14    | 46    | 254   | 453   | 836   | 736   | 395   | 104   |
| West   | 2                 | 48    | 96    | 88    | 140   | 192   | 152   | 115   | 48    |

*North* includes New England, Middle Atlantic, East North Central, and West North Central census regions.

*South* combines South Atlantic, East South Central, and West South Central census regions (including the District of Columbia).

*West* consists of Mountain and Pacific census regions.

majority of the state-imposed executions in each decade from the 1930s
on were conducted in the South. In effect, the South appears to have
lagged behind the rest of the country in bringing executions under state
authority and in abandoning them, but not in the numbers imposed.

Reference to the dates when states first began imposing the death
penalty in Table 2-1 sheds further light on the regional variation in
the growth of capital punishment under state authority. The long,
steady increase in state-imposed executions in the North, shown in
Figure 2-1, appears to reflect a relatively slow but continuous conversion to state-imposed executions among the states in that region. Among
twenty-one northern states, four first imposed execution under state
authority by the 1880s; four began in the 1890s; four more began in
the 1900s; and another five did so for the first time after the 1910s.
Four northern states never imposed the death penalty under state authority.

The movement to state-imposed executions in the South was clearly
more concentrated in time. Of seventeen southern jurisdictions (including the District of Columbia) ten imposed capital punishment for
the first time in the 1910s and the 1920s; West Virginia, Virginia,
Washington, D.C., and Tennessee had imposed the death penalty before
this time; Mississippi and Louisiana did not bring executions under
state authority until the 1950s; and Delaware never did so. Thus, there
was a concerted move toward state-imposed capital punishment in the
South during the twenty-year period from 1910 to 1929—about two
decades after a majority of the northern states that would do so had
adopted this practice.

Among the eleven western states (excluding, of course, Alaska and
Hawaii), the period of greatest movement toward state-imposed exe-
cutions came later than in the North but earlier than in the South.
Two western states first imposed executions under state authority in
the 1910s, four did so a decade earlier, and one did so a decade later.
New Mexico waited until 1933, and Montana never did so.

Obviously, then, the precipitous rise in state-imposed executions
during the growth period from the 1890s through the 1920s reflects a
process of "delocalization," or conversion from local to state authority.
Of the forty-two jurisdictions that eventually adopted state-administered capital punishment, thirty-one did so over this period. Yet this
growth in state-imposed executions may not have resulted exclusively
from the transfer of responsibility for the administration of capital
punishment from one level of authority to another; it may also have
resulted, in part, from an overall increase in the use of the death penalty
during this time.

To examine this possibility, we need to know the number of executions carried out under local as well as state auspices throughout

this period. Although reliable national statistics on all legally imposed executions under civil authority are available for the peak period and the period of decline in state-imposed executions (Federal Bureau of Prisons 1971), there are no official statistics on the total number of executions performed nationally during the growth period in state-imposed executions. There are, however, unofficial counts covering all but three years from 1890 through 1929. Although these unofficial figures cannot be an exact count, they provide reasonable estimates of the total number of executions performed annually during the forty years prior to 1930.

Figures for the period from 1890 through 1917 have been published by Bye (1919, 57–58) drawing chiefly on the yearbook of the *Chicago Tribune* as a source. He reports annual averages of executions for segments of this overall period as follows: 121 per year from 1890 through 1895; 122 per year from 1896 through 1900; 126 per year from 1901 through 1905; 106 per year from 1906 through 1910; 99 per year from 1911 through 1915; and 117 and 85 for 1916 and 1917, respectively.

For the period 1918 to 1920, no national figures have been reported. Bedau (1967b, 35), however, has provided an *estimate* of 114 per year for this period by averaging the number of executions for selected periods before and after this interval.[5]

For the period 1921 to 1926 a count is available from Barnes and Teeters (1942, 425) averaging 114 per annum, although no source is cited for the yearly counts.

Finally, for the years 1927 through 1929, Sellin (1950, 7) reports 139, 135, and 90 executions, respectively, and judges that they are very close to the actual numbers on the basis of his evaluation of their source, the Illinois Department of Welfare 1928.[6]

These data on legally imposed executions are included in Table 2-3. Column 1 shows the total number of executions under civil authority by decade from the 1890s through the 1960s, drawn from official records since 1930 and from unofficial counts prior to 1930. The number of executions under state authority is drawn from the Teeters-Zibulka inventory, and the number under local authority arrived at by taking the difference between all executions and state-imposed exe-

5. Bedau (1967b, 35) actually provided an estimate for the period 1918 through 1924 by taking the midpoint between the annual average for 1901 through 1917, i.e., 109.3, and the annual average for 1925 through 1929, i.e., 118.2. For the years 1921 through 1924, his result—114 executions per year—corresponds within one execution of the number reported by Barnes and Teeters (1942, 425) for the same four years (456 estimated by Bedau vs. 455 reported by Barnes and Teeters).

6. It should be noted that the figures from Barnes and Teeters for the years 1927 through 1929, i.e., 118, 132, and 87, respectively, fall below the count of the Illinois Welfare Department by an average of nine executions per year (owing primarily to the discrepancy for 1927).

**Table 2-3.** *Number of Executions in America by Decade from the 1890s through the 1960s*

| Decades | Legally Imposed Executions under: | | | Illegal Executions by Lynchings[c] | Total of Legal and Illegal Executions |
|---------|------------------------|-------------------|-------------------|---------------------|-------------------|
|         | All Civil Authority[b] | State Authority[a] | Local Authority   |                     |                   |
| 1890s   | 1,215                  | 155               | 1,060             | 1,540               | 2,755             |
| 1900s   | 1,192                  | 291               | 901               | 885                 | 2,077             |
| 1910s   | 1,039                  | 633               | 406               | 621                 | 1,660             |
| 1920s   | 1,169                  | 1,038             | 131               | 315                 | 1,484             |
| 1930s   | 1,670                  | 1,523             | 147               | 130                 | 1,800             |
| 1940s   | 1,288                  | 1,178             | 110               | 5                   | 1,293             |
| 1950s   | 716                    | 681               | 35                | 2[d]                | 718               |
| 1960s   | 191                    | 191               | 0                 | —[d]                | 191               |
| Total   | 8,480                  | 5,690             | 2,790             | 3,498               | 11,978            |

[a] Source: *Executions under State Authority* (Teeters and Zibulka 1968). Published as an appendix to this volume.
[b] *Sources*: For the 1930s and thereafter the figures are drawn from "Capital Punishment 1930–1970" (Federal Bureau of Prisons, *National Prisoner Statistics*, 1971). For the decades prior to 1930 estimates are drawn from the work of Bye (1919, 57–58) for the period 1890–1917; Bedau (1967b, 35) for 1918–1920; Barnes and Teeters (1942, 425) for 1921–1926; and Sellin (1950, 7) for 1927–1929.
[c] *Source*: *Historical Statistics of the United States, from Colonial Times to 1957* (Bureau of the Census 1960, 218).
[d] The published data on lynchings ended in 1956.

cutions for each decade. The table also includes data on illegal executions in the form of lynchings. For the moment, however, we shall concern ourselves only with the data on legally imposed executions under state and local authority.

The level of executions under civil authority remained remarkably constant during the growth period in state-imposed executions from the 1890s through the 1920s. There were slightly more than a thousand executions each decade; only 46 executions separate the first and last decades and the largest difference between any two decades is 176 executions. In view of the growing population of the country and the resulting increases in homicides over this period, the relatively constant number of legally imposed executions per decade actually represents a decline in the *rate* of executions in the population or among homicide offenders.

The data clearly indicate that the change during this period was not in the number of lawful executions performed but in the authority under which they were imposed. Locally imposed executions dropped from more than a thousand to less than two hundred per decade over this period, while state-administered executions showed a corresponding rise. Whereas locally imposed executions represented 87.2 percent of the total in the 1890s, by the 1920s state-imposed executions were

88.7 percent of the total. Clearly, then, this was a period of changeover or conversion from local auspices to state-administered executions, without any marked change in the number of executions performed under civil authority.

By contrast, the peak period and period of decline in state-imposed executions are also periods of peaking and decline in the total volume of executions conducted under civil authority (since more than 90 percent of all legal executions were state imposed during the 1930s and thereafter). It is interesting to note in Table 2-3 that during the peak period of the 1930s, the *proportion* of executions under local authority continued to decline from earlier levels, but the trend toward reduced *numbers* of local executions was temporarily reversed. Apparently the overall national trend toward increased levels of executions in the 1930s was experienced at both state and local levels.

The period of decline in executions saw the absolute number of executions in America drop off dramatically. Although it is true that some six states abolished capital punishment by law in the 1960s, there were no abolitions in the 1940s and only one—Delaware—in the late 1950s, when the total number of executions dropped by more than five hundred each decade. This progressive decline in executions was not, therefore, the result of any statutory change or transfer of authority as had occurred in the growth period of capital punishment under state authority. Instead, it was the result of increasing reluctance within the states to perform executions.

Our examination of state-imposed executions relative to all executions is not yet complete, for we still have to consider executions imposed without duly constituted legal authority, that is, lynchings. Some might argue that a lynching is not an execution but a murder, and, indeed, the laws of a number of states have defined lynching as a capital offense. Yet lynchings have much in common with legally imposed executions. The lynching is an action of the community against someone thought to have violated its most basic mores. It is intended as retribution for the alleged offender and as a deterrent to others who might be tempted to follow in his footsteps. It is performed by community representatives (albeit self-designated) who "take the *law* in their own hands in order to see to it that *justice* is done," to use the language of the lynch mob. The method of execution is typically the same as authorities have traditionally used to dispose of the legally condemned. And, indeed, the composition and behavior of the lynch mob may have no closer parallel than to the crowds at legally imposed public executions.

A documented count of the number of lynchings each year from the 1880s is available in the *Historical Statistics of the United States* (Bureau of the Census 1960; see also Raper 1933). Since there were unquestionably lynchings that never got recorded or documented, the existing record surely underrepresents the number of lynchings that actually took place, but this is likely to be a constant proportion of the number recorded. In Table 2-3 we also present the number of documented lynchings per decade from the 1890s to 1956, and in the last column of the table we show the combined number of legal and illegal executions per decade in America (the sum of those performed under state authority, under local authority, and by lynching).

Notably, in the 1890s there were more lynchings than legally imposed executions under both state and local jurisdiction. Indeed, during this decade almost three out of five executions in America were conducted outside any legal authority. In the 1900s the balance shifted to legally imposed executions, and locally imposed executions outnumbered those under state authority by more than three to one. In the 1910s executions under state authority became more common than either those under local authority or those outside the law. By the 1920s the majority of all executions were state imposed, and the proportion under state authority continued to increase each decade thereafter.

There is no telling how many of those who were lynched would have eventually met their doom at the hands of legal authorities were it not for the lynch mob. Since the sharpest decline in lynchings occurred a decade earlier than the most decisive decline in locally imposed executions, it may be that illicit executions were first brought under local authority before locally authorized executions were transferred to state auspices. The facts that lynchings were more common and persistent in the South and that the South was relatively late to transfer executions from local to state authority are consistent with this possibility.

Surely, requiring that alleged offenders be convicted and sentenced to death under the law removed the most blatant aspects of injustice and discrimination present in lynching. But whether legalization purged these faults altogether, or simply institutionalized them in muted form under official auspices, is another matter. In effect, during this period of growth in state-imposed executions, the states may have taken over the function of oppressor as well as that of executioner from local authorities, who in turn may have acquired both functions when locally imposed legal executions displaced illegal ones.

The final column of Table 2-3 shows that death as a reprisal for alleged violations of community mores has been declining in absolute terms (and even more so relative to the growth of population) since the late nineteenth century, with the exception of the 1930s when this overall trend was temporarily interrupted. Before the 1930s the decline was in extralegal, as opposed to legal, executions; after the 1930s the decline was in legal executions, by then conducted largely under state authority. Thus, the growth of state-imposed executions ran contrary to an overall long-term trend away from the use of death as a punishment in America. In fact, in light of the foregoing analysis, the increasing number of state-imposed executions during this period should be understood not so much as "growth" but as a "transfer" of executions from one locus of authority to another. And, indeed, this transfer of authority and responsibility for conducting executions from the local to state levels—the delocalization of execution—may have removed capital punishment from tenacious local sources of support, and thus set the stage for its eventual demise.

The overwhelming majority of executions under state authority have been imposed for murder.[7] One out of ten state executions has been imposed for rape, and one out of a hundred for all other offenses. We noted in our examination of Table 1-8 that southern and border states tended to have the most extensive capital statutes, that forcible rape was defined as a capital offense virtually throughout the South, and that other crimes such as robbery and burglary were punishable by death primarily in southern states. In view of these regional differences in the availability of capital punishment, we shall take region into account as we take a closer look at the de facto use of capital punishment in America since the early days of state-imposed executions. Figure 2-2 shows the number of executions for murder, rape, and all other offenses by region and by decade through the 1960s. Executions are plotted only for murder in both regions and for rape in the South; there were too few executions in the other categories to be represented in the figure.

The pattern for executions for murder in the South and in the rest of the country was relatively comparable over the history of state-imposed executions. In both regions executions for murder steadily rose to a peak in the 1930s and steadily declined thereafter. During the 1900s, 1910s, and 1920s, the South lagged behind the rest of the country by about two hundred executions per decade for murder; during the 1930s, 1940s, and 1950s, the number of executions for murder in the South actually rose somewhat above the level for the rest of the country, but only by an average of about fifty per decade. Thus, when we consider only state-imposed executions for murder, the difference

7. The Teeters-Zibulka inventory of state-imposed executions, like the data on executions published by the Federal Bureau of Prisons, does not distinguish among various forms of criminal homicide. Since the legal definition of criminal homicide varies from state to state, and since the great majority of executions in this category appear to have been imposed for first degree murder, we take the liberty of using the term "murder" interchangeably with "criminal homicide"—a practice also employed by the Federal Bureau of Prisons in its series on executions.

**Figure 2-2.** *Executions Per Decade under State Authority to the 1960s by Region and Type of Offense*

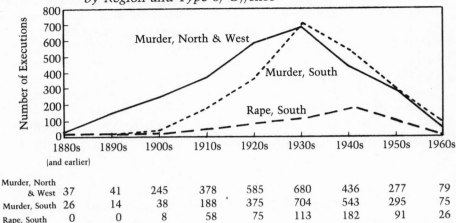

| | 1880s (and earlier) | 1890s | 1900s | 1910s | 1920s | 1930s | 1940s | 1950s | 1960s |
|---|---|---|---|---|---|---|---|---|---|
| Murder, North & West | 37 | 41 | 245 | 378 | 585 | 680 | 436 | 277 | 79 |
| Murder, South | 26 | 14 | 38 | 188 | 375 | 704 | 543 | 295 | 75 |
| Rape, South | 0 | 0 | 8 | 58 | 75 | 113 | 182 | 91 | 26 |

in patterns between the South and the rest of the country is certainly less pronounced than it was in Figure 2-1.

Executions for rape became relatively more prominent in later years, particularly during the period of decline in state-imposed executions. They reached a highpoint in the 1940s—a decade later than the peak in executions for murder both inside and outside of the South. For each decade from 1930 on very nearly one in four executions in the South was for rape, a decidedly more substantial proportion than in earlier decades. In effect, executions for murder began to decline earlier and declined more precipitously than they did for rape. It now appears that our earlier observation that the South was later than other regions to abandon executions is true in part, because the South was especially reluctant to abandon them for rape.

It is by now no secret that blacks have been the primary target of executions for rape—we shall see that more than 85 percent of those executed for rape by the states were black. It is not, therefore, premature to suggest that the reluctance to abandon executions for rape in the South may reflect something more than a desire for protection against this particular crime. It may also reflect a desire to maintain a social system that depends upon a social distance between the races. Perhaps this increased proportion of executions for rape was a response in the South to a feeling that the requisite social distance was not being adequately maintained in recent years.

## Characteristics of the Condemned

Now that we have seen the pattern of growth, peaking, and decline in state-imposed executions, we are ready to examine the characteristics of those who have been executed under state authority. We have noted that the Teeters-Zibulka inventory provides information on offense leading to execution, race of the offender, age at execution, and appeals prior to execution. With these data we can see whether the historical phases in the movement to state-imposed executions have been accompanied by changes in crimes, race, age, or appeals among those executed under state authority.

To avoid the confounding effects that would be introduced by differences in the movement to state-imposed executions between the South and the rest of the country and by the fact that execution for rape in the South became relatively more common in recent decades, we shall examine race, age, and appeals separately for murder and rape in the South and murder in the rest of the country.

Turning first to the race of those executed under state authority, as shown in Table 2-4, we find substantial differences by region and type of offense but relatively little variation within these categories over time. For rape in the South, about nine out of ten executions were imposed on blacks in each decade until the 1950s and 1960s when the figure drops a few points below the 90 percent mark. Moreover, as the table indicates, no information is missing on the race of those executed either for murder or for rape in the South—therefore the relatively high and uniform proportion of blacks executed for rape according to Table 2-4 is not the product of selective reporting in the South.

About two-thirds of those executed for murder in the South were black, and this figure remained quite constant over time. In every decade, at least 60 percent were black; in only two decades did the figure exceed 70 percent—71.3 in the 1940s and 78.7 in the 1910s. Over the last couple decades, as in the case of rape, there was also a slight decline in the percentage of blacks among those executed for murder

**Table 2-4.** *Percentage of Nonwhites among Those Executed under State Authority per Decade by Offense and Region*

|  | Murder | | Rape |
|---|---|---|---|
|  | South | North and West | South |
| 1890s and earlier | 60.0 (40) | 20.8 (149) | − (0) |
| 1900s | 68.4 (38) | 23.1 (208) | − (8) |
| 1910s | 78.7 (188) | 20.4 (353) | 98.3 (58) |
| 1920s | 68.5 (375) | 28.8 (538) | 89.3 (75) |
| 1930s | 69.0 (704) | 23.4 (603) | 90.3 (113) |
| 1940s | 71.3 (543) | 37.9 (383) | 89.6 (182) |
| 1950s | 63.4 (295) | 32.7 (254) | 86.8 (91) |
| 1960s and later | 61.3 (75) | 37.2 (78) | 84.6 (26) |
| All Years | 69.1 (2258) | 27.4 (2566) | 84.6 (553) |
| Missing cases | (0) | (314) | (0) |

in the South. Again, since there are no missing data on race for executions in the South, it is safe to say that at least two-thirds of those executed for murder in the South throughout the history of capital punishment under state authority were black.

Among those executed for murder in the North and West, blacks were consistently in the minority—representing only 27.4 percent of the total for this region, according to the figures in Table 2-4. And, in contrast with the pattern for murder and rape in the South, the figures for the North and West are somewhat less stable and the proportion of blacks among those executed appears to have risen slightly during the years of decline in capital punishment under state authority. Unfortunately, we are missing data on race for about an eighth of the executions performed outside of the South, which means that the figures on race for this region are only estimates of the true values; this may account for some of the instability in these figures over time.

It would appear that there was a slight decrease in the proportion of blacks executed in the South and a slight increase in the proportion executed outside the South during the period of decline in state-imposed executions, perhaps reflecting the migration of blacks from the South during and after the depression of the 1930s and the war of the 1940s. But apart from this relatively slight change accompanying the period of decline in executions, the racial composition of those executed for specific crimes inside and outside the South has remained remarkably constant throughout the history of capital punishment under state authority in the United States.

When we turn to age at execution, the pattern is equally uniform over time. Again, most of the variability occurs by type of offense and region of the country. As shown in Table 2-5, mean age at execution was highest for murderers in the North and West, next highest for murderers in the South, and lowest for rapists in the South, for every decade except the 1950s. We know from national crime statistics of the Federal Bureau of Investigation that age at arrest for rape is lower than for murder—that rape is a more "youthful" crime than murder—which could account for the lower mean age at execution among rapists. Why the mean age at execution should be lower, with only one exception, for murderers in the South than for those outside the South is more enigmatic. The evidence from the previous table that blacks were about twice as numerous among those executed for murder in the South as in the rest of the country provides a clue that we shall follow up in the next chapter.

With respect to the fluctuations in age at execution over the decades, it is interesting to note that age at execution for murder drops, especially for northern and western states, during the 1930s—a period of economic and social dislocation when the number of homicides, the

**Table 2-5.** *Mean Age at Execution among Those Executed under State Authority per Decade by Offense and Region*

|  | Murder | | Rape |
|---|---|---|---|
|  | South | North and West | South |
| 1890s and earlier | 34.7 (13) | 34.3 (150) | — |
| 1900s | 31.6 (28) | 31.6 (223) | 24.7 (6) |
| 1910s | 31.1 (93) | 31.5 (287) | 24.0 (26) |
| 1920s | 30.1 (200) | 31.3 (440) | 24.0 (45) |
| 1930s | 29.8 (508) | 30.8 (595) | 28.3 (90) |
| 1940s | 30.5 (405) | 31.7 (384) | 26.4 (144) |
| 1950s | 34.8 (243) | 33.2 (240) | 26.5 (74) |
| 1960s and later | 29.8 (69) | 31.9 (62) | 26.3 (15) |
| All Years | 30.6 (1559) | 31.7 (2381) | 26.6 (400) |
| Missing cases | (702) | (479) | (153) |

number of executions, and the execution rate all reached peaks (see Table 1-4). The relatively low age at execution in the 1920s and 1930s could reflect a shift toward criminal homicide among more youthful offenders or a greater willingness to impose the death penalty on youthful convicted murderers on the part of juries during this period. Curiously enough, this was also the time when the age at execution for rapists reached its highpoint.

In contrast with this period, the 1950s show a relatively high age at execution for murderers both inside and outside the South. Notably, this was a time of relative conformity and complacency in society when homicide rates were low and when the number and rate of executions were dropping off dramatically—especially in the South where the mean age at execution for murder climbed well above previous levels. Yet the exceptionally high mean age at execution in the South cannot be attributed to a generalized delay between sentencing and execution since rapists were, in fact, younger at execution than they had been in the previous two decades. Nor can the move of Louisiana and Mississippi to state-imposed executions for the first time in the 1950s account for this increase—the mean age at execution for murder was 31.8 in Louisiana and 31.1 in Mississippi during the 1950s. Indeed, a detailed examination of the Teeters-Zibulka inventory reveals that this pattern of increased age at execution for murder was replicated within the states—most notably, Georgia and Florida—that account for most executions in the South on which age data are available during the 1950s.

With respect to the missing data on age at execution, it is the South that has most conspicuously failed to provide such information; data on age are available for slightly more than two-thirds of the executions for both murder and rape in this region. The northern and western states have redeemed themselves somewhat in this respect: data on age are missing on less than one-fifth of their executions.

When we turn to appeals prior to execution—which reflect judicial practices rather than the social backgrounds and personal character-istics of the condemned—we find substantial changes over time. Be-cause the patterns differ for those having made any judicial appeal and those having made an appeal beyond the state appellate court level, Table 2-6 shows the percentage having "any appeals" and the per-centage having "higher appeals" by decade among those executed for murder and for rape in the South and for murder in the rest of the country. In the case of appeals, the data are nearly complete for the nation as a whole. Only Tennessee is missing data because "not all appeals in the state of Tennessee appear to be recorded in the law-books," according to the Teeters-Zibulka inventory. Thus, the missing data figures in Table 2-6 represent the 125 state-imposed executions in Tennessee. Since in most decades they represent only about 5 per-cent of the executions under state authority in the South, they cannot have much of a biasing effect on the appeals figures in Table 2-6.

Considering first the percentage having made any appeals, we find a close parallel with the patterns for race and age among the northern and western states and a distinct departure from these patterns in the southern states. Outside the South, there was virtually no change in the proportion having appeals prior to execution. In every decade, very nearly two-thirds of those executed for murder made some judicial appeal. In the South, on the other hand, appeals were quite uncommon

**Table 2-6.** *Percentage Having Appeals among Those Executed under State Authority by Offense and Region*

| | Murder | | | | Rape | |
|---|---|---|---|---|---|---|
| | South | | North and West | | South | |
| | Any Appeals | Higher Appeals | Any Appeals | Higher Appeals | Any Appeals | Higher Appeals |
| 1890s and earlier | 15.0 (40) | 7.5 | 62.4 (178) | 5.1 | – (0) | – |
| 1900s | 16.2 (37) | 0.0 | 62.4 (245) | 1.2 | – (7) | – |
| 1910s | 30.8 (185) | 0.0 | 64.3 (378) | 1.1 | 19.6 (51) | 0.0 |
| 1920s | 57.9 (354) | 2.5 | 65.8 (585) | 2.2 | 32.9 (70) | 1.4 |
| 1930s | 71.9 (666) | 3.3 | 66.6 (680) | 2.4 | 59.6 (104) | 1.9 |
| 1940s | 70.3 (518) | 5.8 | 65.7 (436) | 11.7 | 60.4 (169) | 6.5 |
| 1950s | 75.9 (291) | 12.4 | 68.2 (277) | 21.7 | 75.6 (90) | 22.2 |
| 1960s | 76.0 (75) | 25.3 | 68.4 (79) | 43.0 | 84.6 (26) | 11.5 |
| All years | 64.4 (2166) | 5.5 | 65.6 (2858) | 6.6 | 55.7 (517) | 7.2 |
| Missing cases | (94) | | (0) | | (36) | |

in the early days of state-imposed executions. For murder, the proportion with appeals began at 15 percent in the 1890s, and rose to above 70 percent in the 1930s and thereafter. For rape, the proportion with appeals rose from less than 20 percent in the 1910s to above 75 percent in the 1950s and 1960s.

Evidently, there was a dramatic rise in the level of appeals among those executed for capital offenses in the South between the beginning of state-imposed executions and the periods of peaking and decline in executions in America. In view of the patterns in Tables 2-4 and 2-5, it is clear that this change occurred without any substantial alteration in the race or age of those executed over this period. And considering the relatively small number of executions for which data on appeals are missing, this trend is obviously not the product of selective reporting.

Perhaps the rise in appeals among executed capital offenders in the South during the growth period in state-imposed executions was a response to the same forces that caused executions to be removed from the hands of local authorities. Indeed, this may have been a further step in the "delocalization" of executions, mentioned in our discussion of Table 2-3. There we noted that the movement of executions from local to state authority may have come only after illegal executions in the form of lynchings were first brought under local authority or, at least, displaced by locally authorized executions. In turn, the growth in appeals appears to have come only after executions were transferred to state authority. First, local authorities lost their responsibility for performing executions, and then the local community lost its power to prescribe death without the sanction of higher judicial authority. Even though few death sentences may have been reversed upon appeal, this increase in appeals obviously meant that the actions of the local trial courts were being subjected to scrutiny and that unfettered local autonomy in sentencing was beginning to fade.

Higher appeals—those to United States district courts, the United States Circuit Court of Appeal, and the United States Supreme Court—were seldom made prior to the period of decline in state-imposed executions. Indeed, 75.6 percent of all higher appeals occurred from 1940 on, when the number of executions was dropping off consistently and substantially. The increase in higher appeals between the 1930s and the 1960s was more than tenfold—from 2.8 to 31.1 percent. Table 2-6 shows that the pattern of rising higher appeals began about the same time for all three categories of offenders, but that it was more pronounced for murderers in the northern and western states.

We noted in Chapter 1 that in the 1930s the U.S. Supreme Court began to insist on certain procedural safeguards for defendants in capital cases under the "due process" clause of the Fourteenth Amend-

ment. In 1932, in *Powell* v. *Alabama*, the Court guaranteed the right
to counsel in capital cases, and in the 1940s and 1950s subsequent
decisions prohibited discrimination in jury selections and coerced
confessions and generally clarified the procedural rights of criminal
defendants. The Court's concern for the rights of the criminal defendant and its receptivity to appeals as manifested in these decisions undoubtedly contributed to the increase in higher appeals after the 1930s
(shown in Table 2-6). The Court's decisions established grounds for
appeals and provided defendants with the legal expertise to pursue such
appeals.

At the same time, it is equally evident that the earlier rise in the
proportion having any appeals among executed murderers and rapists
in the South during the growth period of state-imposed executions
occurred quite independently of the Court's concern for the procedural
rights of capital defendants. This earlier rise in appeals to state appellate
courts was apparently the result of processes and forces operating within
the states to limit local autonomy and abuses in the application of the
death penalty.

## Summary

With the development of state penal institutions and the centralization of penal authority within the various states, there was a movement from local to state administration of capital punishment in
America. This transition to state authority proceeded quite slowly from
the first state-imposed execution in 1864 through the 1880s. Most of
the change occurred during the period from the 1890s through the
1920s, when state-imposed executions grew from one out of ten to nine
out of ten legally performed executions in America. The South lagged
somewhat behind the rest of the country in bringing executions under
state authority and in abandoning them, but not in the numbers performed.

This movement toward state-imposed capital punishment did not
mark an increase in the volume of legally performed executions. Rather,
it represented a transfer of responsibility from local to state authority.
With the exception of the 1930s when legal executions did reach a
highpoint, the total number of executions under civil authority—both
state and local—remained relatively constant from the 1890s through
the 1940s. If we also include lynchings, however, the total number of
executions—both legal and illegal—has declined steadily since the 1890s,
again with the exception of the 1930s.

The statutes of the various state and federal jurisdictions in America have made the death penalty available for a wide variety of offenses.
These include actions that seriously threaten national security, that

seriously hamper law enforcement and the administration of justice, that endanger the lives of a great many people, that severely threaten or harm relatively vulnerable or defenseless persons, and of course, that take another person's life. In practice, however, murder and rape have accounted for almost all executions performed under state authority, and those for murder have outnumbered those for rape about nine to one.

While murder has been defined as a capital offense and punished by execution in virtually all death penalty jurisdictions, rape has been so defined and punished exclusively in southern and border states. Blacks have predominated as victims of the death penalty in the South and especially so in executions for rape. Consistently, from the beginning of state-imposed executions in the South, blacks have accounted for about two-thirds of the executions for murder and nine-tenths of those for rape. In the South, offenders have also been consistently younger at execution than in the rest of the country, and this was so for murderers as well as rapists. These consistent regional differences in offenses leading to execution, race of the condemned, and age at execution suggest that the death penalty may have been used as an instrument of discrimination or oppression against blacks in the South—an implication to be pursued in the next chapter.

Appeals prior to execution, unlike race and age, changed dramatically during the history of capital punishment under state authority. First, appeals to state appellate courts among offenders later executed in the South rose markedly to the level for the rest of the country during the growth period in state-imposed executions. Second, appeals to federal courts increased among offenders later executed both inside and outside the South during the period of decline in state-imposed executions. This increasing scrutiny of local trial courts, first by state judicial authorities and later by the federal judiciary, may indeed have been a response to increasingly evident and persistent abuses, particularly racial discrimination, in the administration of capital punishment at the local level. Whether this increasing scrutiny was effective in purging such abuses will also be considered in the upcoming analysis.

Finally, the Teeters-Zibulka inventory of executions under state authority, which will provide the data for the next chapter, has been checked against officially reported data on executions for its completeness, accuracy, and representativeness in the years since 1930. This evaluation indicates that the Teeters-Zibulka inventory is a virtually complete list of state-imposed executions since 1930 and one that is quite comparable to the aggregated official statistics with respect to the crimes for which executions have been performed and the race of the offender.

# 3

## RACIAL DISCRIMINATION IN STATE-IMPOSED EXECUTIONS

In the fall of 1971, attorneys for the NAACP Legal Defense and Educational Fund, Inc., went before the United States Supreme Court to argue that the death penalty violates the constitutional prohibition against "cruel and unusual" punishment. They contended that capital punishment does not comport with evolving standards of human decency, as revealed by the recent movement away from the death penalty among many countries of the world and by the moratorium on executions since 1967 in this country. In the language of the brief:

> In historical context, the world-wide abandonment of capital punishment marks an overwhelming repudiation of the death penalty as an atavistic barbarism. The penalty remains on the statute books only to be—and because it is—rarely and unusually inflicted. So inflicted, it is not a part of the regular machinery of the state for the control of crime and the punishment of criminals. It is an extreme and mindless act of savagery, practiced on an outcaste few. This is exactly the evil against which the Eighth Amendment stands (NAACP, Legal Defense Fund brief for *Aikens* 1971, 6).[1]

---

1. Aikens v. California was the lead death case before the United States Supreme Court until the Supreme Court of California declared that state's death penalty unconstitutional under the state prohibition against cruel or unusual punishment in People v. Anderson, 6 Cal. 3d 628, 100 Cal. Rptr. 152, 493 P. 2d 880 (1972). Accordingly, the Supreme Court of the United States then dismissed the petition for writ of certiorari in Aikens v. California, 406 U.S. 813 (1972) as the death penalty issue was moot, and Furman v. Georgia, O.T. 1971, No. 69-5003 became the lead case.

In particular, they attacked the discriminatory application of the death penalty:

> Those who are selected to die are the poor and powerless, personally ugly and socially unacceptable. In disproportionate percentages, they are also black. Racial discrimination is strongly suggested by the national execution figures. It has been borne out in a number of discrete and limited but carefully done studies, and it has seemed apparent to responsible commissions and individuals studying the administration of the death penalty in this country (NAACP, Legal Defense Fund brief for *Aikens* 1971, 51–52).

The "national execution figures" to which the brief refers show that since 1930 more blacks than whites have been executed under the law in our predominantly white society. In part, of course, this disparity reflects differential *offense rates* between blacks and whites for murder and rape, the two crimes most commonly punished by death. In turn, the National Commission on the Causes and Prevention of Violence has attributed the higher levels of violent crime among black than among white Americans to the effects of racism or racial discrimination in our society (Mulvihill and Tumin 1969, 426–431, 495–517; see also Wolfgang and Cohen 1970). These suggest, in effect, that a society that places and holds certain of its citizens in conditions of poverty and disadvantage with respect to occupation and education has itself created the circumstances that lead to criminal violence among members of its oppressed minority.

Yet the disproportionate execution of blacks may also reflect *differential application of the law*. Prior to the Civil War, capital statutes differed for blacks and whites in the South. After the war effectively abolished these "Black Codes," many southern states broadened their capital statutes to include crimes that had previously been capital offenses only for blacks. The acknowledged purpose was to provide a legal framework within which differential application of the death penalty could continue. As Johnson (1941, 95) notes, ". . . it is common knowledge that 'first degree burglary' is defined as a capital crime in several states as a threat to Negro offenders who enter a white residence after dark."

Moreover, there is, in practice, some leeway in deciding whether a capital offense has actually occurred. For instance, whether in the eyes of the law a rape, particularly an attempted rape, has been committed will depend largely on the word of the alleged victim. If she is white and the alleged offender black, the social climate may almost force an accusation of rape or attempted rape as an explanation of an interracial encounter. Or again, where felonious homicide is punishable by death, whites may be tempted to invent a felony to accompany the homicide committed by a black offender. And, of course, arrests and charges for capital offenses can occur through false testimony against blacks and through the police's extracting false confessions from blacks.

Still another source of the disproportionate execution of blacks may be *differential administration of justice*. The courtroom is a context in which evidence of guilt and innocence is weighed in light of social values as well as legal definitions. In fact, the jury system explicitly brings community sentiments into the judicial decision-making process. Although the law prohibits considerations of race in the determination of guilt and punishment, where race is an important aspect of social relations in the broader community it may become a factor in the judicial process as well. As Johnson (1941, 97) has observed, "When a Negro goes into court he goes with the consciousness that the whole courtroom process is in the hands of 'the other race'—white judges, white jurors, white attorneys, white guards, white everything, except perhaps some of the witnesses and spectators."

After conviction and sentencing the condemned offender may still escape execution through judicial appeal and, failing that, by executive clemency. Both in appeals and in commutations there is, of course, the possibility that the black offender will suffer discriminatory treatment at the hands of the judicial process. Thus, Johnson might have added, "When the condemned Negro offender seeks to escape execution it will be before white higher court justices and a white governor."

Differential offense rates for capital crimes between blacks and whites have been well documented in criminological research, but what about differential application of the law and differential administration of justice? After all, racial differentials in law enforcement and judicial administration refer to discriminatory treatment *under* the criminal justice system. To the extent that such differential treatment by race is present, it represents injustice perpetrated, paradoxically, by the very system whose aim it is to secure justice.

It is the "discrete and limited but carefully done studies" referred to in the passage from the brief for *Aikens* quoted above that provide explicit evidence that the disproportionate execution of blacks in America was not simply a function of differential offense rates but also a result of differential treatment *within* the criminal justice system. These studies vary considerably in the kinds of data they have examined, in the stages of the justice process on which they have focused, and in the scope and representativeness of their findings.

Two of the earliest systematic investigations (Johnson 1941; Garfinkel 1949) began with samples of capital offenses and traced the treatment of black and white alleged offenders over several stages in the justice process. These studies found that blacks were indicted,

charged, convicted, and sentenced to death in disproportionate numbers—indicating that the full extent of racial discrimination will not
be revealed in an analysis of any single stage in the justice process.
Also, by taking the victim's as well as the offender's race into account,
these investigations turned up consistent evidence that discrimination
throughout the justice process was especially concentrated against blacks
whose victims were whites. Unfortunately, investigations like these,
which span several stages in the justice process, have been confined
to selected jurisdictions within only a few southern states (Johnson
1941, for selected jurisdictions in Virginia, North Carolina, and Georgia; Garfinkel 1949, for ten counties in North Carolina).

More recently, two other investigations, one by Wolfgang (1972;
Wolfgang and Riedel 1973, 1975; and Chapter 4 of Bowers 1974), and
the other published in the *Stanford Law Review* (Judson et al. 1969)
have gathered extensive data from court records and trial transcripts
that would make it possible to determine whether racial differences
in sentencing were the result of discrimination or of relevant legal
considerations. The more ambitious of these investigations, directed
by Professor Wolfgang, sampled the case records of some three thousand convicted rapists in eleven southern states (although the analysis
has thus far been limited to data from representative counties in six
of these states). The study found that black offenders were disproportionately sentenced to death for rape, that this tendency was extraor-
dinarily pronounced when their victims were white, and that other
considerations such as the degree of force used by the offender, the
extent of injury suffered by the victim, the fact of some other contemporaneous felony, and the like, did not begin to account for the racial
differences in sentencing. A similarly designed investigation of the
imposition of the death sentence upon convicted murderers in California (*Stanford Law Review*, Judson et al. 1969) also showed that
blacks were disproportionately sentenced to death. But the California
investigation found that the social class of the convicted offender was
also a significant extralegal factor in sentencing and one that largely
accounted for the observed racial differences.

Studies of death row populations in various states have consistently found that blacks were less likely than whites to have their
death sentences commuted. The size of these racial differences in commutations varies from state to state with the largest differences tending
to occur in the South. But in virtually every state where meaningful
comparisons could be made, the condemned black man had less chance
of receiving a commutation than his white counterpart (Mangum 1940,
for selected periods in nine southern and border states; Johnson 1957,
for North Carolina; Ohio Legislative Service Commission 1961; Maryland Legislative Council 1962; Wolfgang, Kelly, and Nolde 1962, for

Pennsylvania; Bedau 1964, for New Jersey; Koeninger 1969, for Texas). The only exception is Oregon, where only nine nonwhites have been on death row since 1903 (Bedau 1965). Furthermore, in the few instances where this possibility has been examined, these racial differences in commutations could not be attributed to the fact that blacks have been disproportionately sentenced to death for felony murder (Wolfgang et al. 1962; Bedau 1964).

Studies have also examined the characteristics of those who have been executed and compared them with other relevant populations for evidence of racial discrimination in capital punishment. Thus, for Virginia, an investigation has compared the proportion of blacks among those executed with the proportion among those imprisoned for various capital offenses, and found that blacks were more apt to be executed than whites for each category of offense. In fact, blacks alone have been executed for rape in Virginia since 1908, whereas only 55 percent of those imprisoned for rape are black (*Virginia Law Review* 1972). For California, an investigation has compared blacks, whites, and Mexican-Americans executed since 1939 in terms of age at execution and delay between sentencing and execution, and, although it found no significant differences between blacks and whites, at least in these respects, the research did turn up indications of discrimination against Mexican-Americans (Carter and Smith 1969).

There are obvious shortcomings in this body of research. The studies are regionally and historically selective. Most states with the death penalty have not been included in any of these investigations, and for those that have, the analysis has often covered relatively brief and recent periods in their use of it. Furthermore, most of the existing investigations have focused on a single stage in the justice process, and most have failed to test the independence of the racial differences they have uncovered. Thus, while the existing research has gone a long way in developing a picture of the breadth and depth of racial discrimination in capital punishment, the picture is still incomplete, segmented, and possibly biased. We need research that will add representativeness and comprehensiveness to the picture of racial discrimination in capital punishment that has thus far emerged.

The investigation reported in this chapter attempts to provide a broader historical and regional perspective on racial discrimination in capital punishment. Using the data available in the Teeters-Zibulka inventory of *Executions under State Authority* (included in this volume as Appendix A), we examine evidence of differential treatment by race for all states that have imposed the death penalty under state authority for as long as they have done so, except where data on the race of those executed are missing (as indicated in Chapter 2). We focus on the relationship between race and various factors that may reflect differential treatment within the criminal justice system. Specifically, we compare whites and nonwhites who have been executed in terms of crimes leading to execution, appeals prior to execution, and age at execution. Differences between the races in these dimensions will suggest the presence and extent of discrimination that may operate throughout various stages of the law enforcement and criminal justice processes.

Differences between the races in age at execution will, of course, reflect social and economic processes leading to age at offense, as well as legal processes from arrest through execution. Within the legal system, differences in age at execution will reflect not simply the speed with which black and white offenders are processed, but perhaps more significantly differences in rates of arrest, indictment, conviction, sentencing, and execution for younger and older offenders of the two races. To the extent that racial differences in age at execution exceed those in age at offense, we can infer that discrimination is present within the criminal justice process.

Appeal prior to execution is obviously more specific with respect to the stage of the judicial process involved. However, racial differences in appeals among those who have been executed provide only a partial indication of discrimination that may have been present after the death sentence was handed down, because they do not directly take account of condemned offenders who escaped execution. Thus, if whites were more likely than blacks to have successful appeals and/or if commutations were more likely for whites than for blacks whose appeals were unsuccessful, racial differences in appeal prior to execution will be a conservative measure of discrimination in the appeals process; that is, black-white differences in appeals among those who were executed would be less than among those who faced execution.[2]

Thus, instead of having direct measures of, for example, conviction, sentencing, or appeals, for samples of people who faced each of these stages in the judicial process, we will be looking for differences that discrimination at these points would produce among those who reach the very final stage of the process. In this respect, our indicators of age and appeal are substitutes for more direct and precise measures of treatment within the judicial process at the various points where

2. Evidence on the final dispositions of death row inmates in selected states—North Carolina (Johnson 1957), Pennsylvania (Wolfgang et al. 1962), New Jersey (Bedau 1964), Oregon (Bedau 1965), and Texas (Koeninger 1969)—indicates that from two to four out of ten escaped execution primarily by having their death sentences commuted. Moreover, these studies generally show that whites were more likely than blacks to receive commutations. Successful appeals also account for some of those who have escaped execution—39 percent in New Jersey, 27 percent in Oregon, and 5 percent in Texas. But the existing research provides no data specifically on racial differences in successful appeals.

discrimination may actually have taken place. Our task will be to infer from the variations in these indirect and imperfect indicators the conditions under which discrimination has been more or less pronounced. In so doing, we rely not on a single test of discrimination but on a series of replications of racial differences within various subgroups of executed offenders, and on similarities in the patterns of racial differences in age and appeals.[3]

With the very large number of executions under investigation, it will be possible to examine variations in the dimensions relevant to discrimination within geographical regions and historical periods, and to control one dimension when we are examining racial differences in another. Naturally, we will be restricted by the number of dimensions on which comparisons can be made and by some missing data on race and age at execution, but these disadvantages are more than offset by the unique opportunity in these data to provide a comprehensive view of racial discrimination in capital punishment over an extended period of time for a nation as a whole.

## Racial Differences in Treatment

Most advocates of capital punishment would agree that the severity and finality of the death penalty require that it be used only for society's most serious crimes, only upon confirmed or incorrigible offenders, and only with assurance that there have been no mistakes in the administration of justice. To the extent that capital punishment has been used in a racially discriminatory or oppressive fashion in this country, we should expect to find that these canons of judicial responsibility do not apply equally to the members of both races; specifically, that nonwhites, when compared with whites, will have been executed (1) for less serious crimes and for crimes less commonly receiving the death penalty, (2) at a younger age on the average, and (3) more often without judicial appeals.

Table 3-1 shows the distribution of executions by (A) type of offense, (B) age at execution, and (C) level of appeal, for nonwhites, whites, and those unclassified by race. (We have included the "unclassified" group in this table to show how it compares. In subsequent tabulations we omit the "unclassified" category.)

3. Because of the very large number of executions available for analysis, there is a tendency for quite small percentage differences to qualify as "statistically significant." To avoid inferences where there are too few cases to yield stable statistics, however, we have omitted means and percentages that would be based on ten or fewer executions in the tables of this chapter. (For further discussions of the appropriateness of statistical significance tests in multivariate tabular analysis, see Lipset, Trow, and Coleman 1956, 427 ff; Hirschi and Selvin 1967, 216 ff; Morrison and Henkel 1970.)

**Table 3-1.** *Percentage Executed (A) for Various Offenses, (B) at
Various Ages, and (C) After Various Levels of Appeal for
Nonwhites, Whites, and Those Unclassified by Race*

|  | Nonwhite | White | Unclassified |
|---|---|---|---|
| A) Offenses Leading to Execution | | | |
| Murder | 80.7 | 96.5 | 100.0 |
| Rape | 17.9 | 2.2 | 0.0 |
| Other | 1.4 | 1.4 | 0.0 |
| Total (Number of Cases) | 100.0(2807) | 100.1(2653) | 100.0(283) |
| B) Age at Execution | | | |
| 19 years or less | 10.4 | 4.3 | 4.0 |
| 20–24 | 27.3 | 21.0 | 18.6 |
| 25–29 | 23.6 | 23.9 | 20.3 |
| 30–39 | 25.2 | 29.4 | 25.4 |
| 40 or older | 13.5 | 21.4 | 31.6 |
| Total (Number of Cases) | 100.0(2034) | 100.0(2207) | 99.9(169) |
| C) Appeals Prior to Execution | | | |
| None | 41.0 | 30.7 | 31.1 |
| State Appellate Court | 53.5 | 61.7 | 62.6 |
| Federal District or | | | |
| Supreme Court | 5.4 | 7.6 | 6.3 |
| Total (Number of Cases) | 99.9(2720) | 100.0(2610) | 100.0(293) |

Turning first to the offense for which capital punishment has been
imposed, we see that murder is by far the most common offense for
all three groupings by race. Rape is the only other offense for which a
substantial number of executions has been imposed. The table shows
that executions for rape were eight times as common among blacks as
among whites (17.9 as opposed to 2.2 percent, respectively) who have
been put to death under state authority. Indeed, the absolute numbers
reveal that the death penalty for rape has been imposed overwhelmingly on blacks—502 to 58—by a nine-to-one ratio.

By most standards, rape is a less serious offense than murder. It
has been judged less serious by various population subgroups (Sellin
and Wolfgang 1964); it has been less severely punished by length of
imprisonment (Tittle 1969; Chiricos and Waldo 1970); and it has been
punishable by death in far fewer jurisdictions both within the United
States (see Tables 1-7 and 1-8) and abroad (Patrick 1965). Clearly, then,
relative to whites, blacks have been executed for less serious crimes
and for crimes that less often receive the death penalty.

There is more to say about black-white differences in type of offense. Table 3-1, part A, shows that blacks do not exceed whites in the
proportion executed for crimes other than homicide and rape. It is
*primarily* rape that distinguishes blacks from whites who have been

executed.[4] Apparently, the disproportionate execution of blacks for rape is not simply a matter of greater readiness to impose the death penalty on blacks for lesser crimes.

Professor Wolfgang's research on rape (Wolfgang 1972; Wolfgang and Riedel 1973, 1975; Bowers 1974, Chapter 4) has indicated that blacks who raped whites have been the primary targets of the death penalty. His findings show that the death penalty was imposed in 35.6 percent of the black-offender–white-victim cases, as opposed to only 2.1 percent of cases with all other offender-victim racial combinations—a seventeen-to-one ratio. His data also indicate that black-offender–white-victim rapes represented about 40 percent of the convictions involving black defendants and about a quarter of all convictions for rape in the six southern states he has analyzed. On the basis of these estimates, it follows that 90 percent of the blacks executed for rape had white victims and that 85 percent of all executions for rape involved this offender-victim combination.

We have argued that rape is a less serious crime than murder by most standards, but in this particular offender-victim combination it would seem to be a very serious offense. Perhaps the dominant white majority under a caste-like system perceives this kind of rape as a challenge, at least symbolically, to its ability to regulate relations between the races and thus to maintain its position in the social order. In effect, the readiness to execute for black-offender–white-victim rape dramatizes the fact that it is not rape per se but the threat posed by a particular form of rape to established patterns of separation and social distance between the races that makes it a grave offense against the caste system itself. We shall return to this point for further elaboration.

When we turn to age at execution and appeals prior to execution (Table 3-1, parts B and C) distinct racial differences once again appear. In terms of age, nonwhites were clearly executed younger than were whites or those unclassified by race. Thus, 37.7 percent of the blacks were executed before age 25 as compared with 25.3 percent of the whites. The difference is quite pronounced in the youngest age category, 19 or younger, where, proportionately, nonwhites exceed whites by more than two to one. The mean age at execution for murder for nonwhites is 29.9 and for whites, 32.3—a difference of over two years.

Similarly, the data on appeals show that nonwhites were less likely to have appealed their cases prior to execution than whites or those

4. Among the "other offenses" for which executions have been imposed, blacks have more often been executed for burglary and robbery, and whites more often for kidnapping. Judging by the number of jurisdictions in which the death penalty has been available for such offenses (Table 1-7), it appears that blacks have been executed for the lesser offenses within this residual category.

unclassified by race. Six out of ten nonwhites made appeals before they were executed, as compared with more than seven out of ten whites. Nonwhites were also slightly less likely to have made appeals beyond the state appellate court level. Thus, like type of offense, appeals prior to execution and age at execution also suggest discrimination by race in the application of capital punishment.

Yet it could be that age at execution and appeal prior to execution are not really independent indicators of differential treatment. Non-whites may have been executed at a younger age than whites because of the differences in kinds of offenses for which they were executed. Rape is, after all, a more "youthful" crime than murder, in terms of the average age of offenders (see, for example, the data on age at arrest for criminal homicide and forcible rape in the *Uniform Crime Report* of the Federal Bureau of Investigation; also compare the figures in Wolfgang 1958 and Amir 1971). Perhaps, therefore, whites and non-whites who committed the same kinds of crimes were no different in age at execution.

Or, again, appeals may have been characteristically less common in rape cases. The fact that the victim is alive and able to testify in court may tend to remove uncertainty about the identity of the offender and the events surrounding the crime. If so, differences in level of appeal between the races might be attributable to the differences in the kinds of offenses for which executions were imposed, rather than standing as an independent indication of racial discrimination. The two parts of Table 3-2 permit us to examine these possibilities.

Table 3-2, part A, shows quite clearly, however, that nonwhites were executed younger than whites whether for murder or for rape. While it is true that rapists were younger at execution than murderers, this does not alter the fact that nonwhites were younger at execution than whites—about two and a half years younger for murder and three years younger for rape.

Table 3-2, part B, shows that appeals were less common for blacks

**Table 3-2.**   *Mean Age at Execution and Percentage Having Appeals by Type of Offense for Nonwhites and Whites*

|  | Murder | | Rape | |
|---|---|---|---|---|
|  | Nonwhites | Whites | Nonwhites | Whites |
| A) Mean Age at Execution | 29.9 | 32.3 | 26.4 | 29.4 |
| (Number of Cases) | (1640) | (2130) | (362) | (44) |
| B) Percentage Having an Appeal | 60.0 | 69.1 | 54.4 | 69.8 |
| (Number of Cases) | (2204) | (2521) | (471) | (53) |

than for whites, apart from the nature of their offenses. While it is true that appeals were less common among those executed for rape than for murder, this does not account for the differences in the levels of appeals between the races, where a difference of 10 to 15 percentage points remains for both kinds of offenses.

The data in Table 3-2, then, make it clear that differences between the races in age at execution and likelihood of appeal cannot be attributed to differences in the types of offenses for which whites and nonwhites have been executed. Thus, racial inequity in age at execution and level of appeal are independent of the offense leading to execution. But are they independent of one another?

Execution must await the outcome of judicial appeals. The lower level of appeals among nonwhites may, therefore, have brought their executions on with less delay and thus caused them to be younger at execution on the average than their white counterparts. It seems doubtful that the review process would account for a difference of two and a half to three years in age at execution between the races, but it could be responsible for some of the difference. Table 3-3 bears on this point.

The table shows age at execution for both races, within categories of appeal and type of offense. Again, regardless either of whether an appeal was made prior to execution or of the nature of the offense, nonwhites have a lower mean age at execution than whites. For murder the difference is approximately two years (1.4 years with no appeal versus 2.9 years with an appeal) while for rape nonwhites are executed approximately three years younger than whites (3.7 years without an appeal versus 3.0 years with an appeal).

It could be that blacks were, on the average, younger than whites when they committed the same offenses. Unfortunately, national data on age at arrest for criminal homicide and rape are not broken down by race in the Federal Bureau of Investigation's *Uniform Crime Reports*. Studies of selected samples of offenders have, however, shown that

**Table 3-3.** *Mean Age at Execution by Level of Appeal and Type of Offense for Nonwhites and Whites*

|  | Murder | | Rape | |
| --- | --- | --- | --- | --- |
|  | Nonwhites | Whites | Nonwhites | Whites |
| No Appeal | 30.9 | 32.3 | 25.8 | 29.5 |
| (Number of Cases) | (621) | (640) | (153) | (12) |
| Appeal | 29.4 | 32.3 | 26.8 | 29.8 |
| (Number of Cases) | (1983) | (1461) | (193) | (27) |

blacks tend to be younger at arrest than whites for both of these offenses, but in no case do they indicate that the age differences at arrest
are as large as those at execution shown in Table 3-3. The difference
in mean or median age at arrest for homicide is typically less than two
years (Wolfgang 1958; Brearly 1932).

Evidently, then, at least some of the age difference between blacks
and whites at execution reflects differential treatment within the criminal justice system. It did not appear in Table 3-3 that the appeal process
was responsible for much, if any, of the differences in age at execution
between the races. Perhaps, instead, these differences reflect a tendency
for *young* black offenders to have been singled out as targets of discrimination in the application of capital punishment.

The implication that young blacks may have been subjected to
particularly discriminatory treatment within the judicial process can
be followed up if we shift our focus from age at execution to level of
appeal. If discrimination has been concentrated against younger blacks,
we might expect to see it reflected in the appeals process. That is,
young blacks should have particularly low levels of appeal and the
difference in appeals between blacks and whites should be more pronounced at the younger age levels. Table 3-4 shows the level of appeals
in murder and rape cases for blacks and whites executed at various
ages.

There is evidence of discriminatory treatment against young black
rapists. Black rape offenders executed before age twenty were definitely
less likely to have had an appeal than older black rapists. In fact, this
is the only category in Table 3-4 for which less than half (43.1 percent)
of the condemned had appeals prior to execution. Because no whites
under age 20 have been executed for rape, we cannot say whether any
such tendency to be executed without appeals also holds for young
white rapists.

The data on murder show no comparable tendency; there is little
variation in level of appeals by age for either blacks or whites. The
racial disparity in appeals is consistent by age. Apparently then, only

**Table 3-4.** *Percentage Having an Appeal by Type of Offense and
Age at Execution for Nonwhites and Whites*

|  | Murder | | Rape | |
|---|---|---|---|---|
|  | Nonwhites | Whites | Nonwhites | Whites |
| 19 years or younger | 159.2 (147) | 60.0 (90) | 43.1 (51) | (0) |
| 20–24 | 67.4 (408) | 72.0 (441) | 60.3 (121) | 60.0 (10) |
| 25–29 | 60.4 (376) | 68.4 (494) | 55.7 (79) | 75.0 (12) |
| 30–39 | 60.1 (421) | 70.2 (621) | 57.1 (77) | 76.9 (13) |
| 40 years or older | 56.0 (252) | 69.5 (455) | 55.6 (18) | 50.0 (4) |

young black rapists suffer *greater* discrimination although blacks as a group suffered consistent discrimination in terms of appeals within the judicial process.

At this point in the analysis we have substantial indications of racial discrimination in the application of capital punishment. We have seen that among those put to death under state authority, nonwhites were disproportionately executed for rape, were younger at execution, and less often had an appeal prior to execution than whites. We have also seen that each difference is independent of the others. Separately, each of these findings might be subject to alternative interpretation, but together they seem to point in the same direction—to a general *pattern* of racial discrimination in capital punishment.

In the next section, we examine how these racial differences in the application of capital punishment vary by region of the country and historical period. If the differences we have uncovered thus far do indeed reflect the presence of racial discrimination, we might expect them to be especially pronounced where such discrimination has been most thoroughly institutionalized—in the South. We might also expect these relationships to have diminished somewhat in recent years with the decline in strict racial segregation in the South and with the growing tolerance in racial attitudes throughout the country over the last three decades (Skolnick 1969, 182). We shall try, then, to determine whether regionally institutionalized patterns of relations between the races and recent changes in public sentiment about race are reflected in the application of capital punishment.

## Regional and Historical Perspectives

Racial segregation became a way of life in the South with the importation of black slaves and the development of a plantation economy. In response to the disruptions in this way of life produced by the Civil War and Reconstruction, the white majority displayed intense hostility toward the black minority and took oppressive actions to regain and reaffirm its position of dominance in southern society. Thus, as we noted in the preceding chapter, lynchings became a conspicuous feature of race relations in the South in the post-Reconstruction era.

In more recent years state-imposed executions for rape may have become the counterpart to lynching. We saw in Figure 2-2 that executions for rape have been almost exclusively a southern phenomenon. Of the 560 executions for rape recorded in the Teeters-Zibulka compilation, all but 7 were conducted in the South. Moreover, executions for rape were a relatively recent development in the history of capital punishment under state authority. Some 304, or 54 percent, of state-imposed executions for rape were conducted after 1940; about 25 percent of all executions performed in the South since 1940 were for rape. We have already established that executions for rape have been imposed overwhelmingly upon blacks (Table 3-1, part A), selectively upon younger blacks without appeals (Table 3-4), and primarily upon blacks whose victims were white (Wolfgang 1972; Wolfgang and Riedel 1973, 1975; Bowers 1974, Chapter 4). Thus, like lynchings, executions for rape have been largely a southern phenomenon and one directed primarily against blacks.

Since executions for rape were performed almost exclusively in the South, our investigation of regional variations in the indicators of racial discrimination must be restricted to executions for murder. (Tables 3-5 and 3-6 will therefore include only executions for murder.) We turn first to age at execution for murder among nonwhites and whites, both with and without appeals and inside and outside the South, as shown in Table 3-5.

Note that the difference in age at execution between blacks and whites has been much greater in the South than in the rest of the country. In the South, black murderers were three to four years younger at execution than whites, depending on appeals. This is close to the difference in age between blacks and whites executed for rape as shown in Table 3-2, part A. Since almost all the executions for rape occurred in the South, it would appear that the three- to four-year age differential at execution between blacks and whites is independent of the offense leading to execution in the South.

In the rest of the country, on the other hand, age difference at execution between blacks and whites was relatively small. Among the minority who had no appeal, blacks were about one-half year younger than whites at execution; among the majority who did have an appeal, blacks were about two years younger. Even for those who had appeals, however, the difference in age at execution was not much greater than

**Table 3-5.** *Mean Age at Execution for Murder by Region of the Country and Level of Appeal for Nonwhites and Whites*

|  | South | | North and West | |
|---|---|---|---|---|
|  | Nonwhites | Whites | Nonwhites | Whites |
| No Appeal | 30.3 | 33.2 | 31.7 | 32.1 |
| (Number of Cases) | (368) | (124) | (253) | (516) |
| Appeal | 29.4 | 33.7 | 29.5 | 31.8 |
| (Number of Cases) | (643) | (359) | (340) | (1102) |

reported differences in age at arrest for criminal homicide between blacks and whites (Wolfgang 1958; Brearly 1932).

When we turn to appeals in Table 3-6, a similar pattern emerges. In the South at every age level, black murderers were less likely to have had their cases appealed prior to execution than whites—a difference of roughly 10 percentage points for four of the five age categories. For the rest of the country there was a consistent difference between black and white murderers in the percentage having had an appeal prior to execution. Young blacks below age twenty-five actually had appeals nearly as often as young whites. Overall, the differences in appeals between the races outside the South tend to be small but consistent.

And so our regional specification reveals a difference of degree between the South and the rest of the country. In the South, differential treatment of whites and nonwhites in terms of appeals prior to execution and age at execution is substantial and consistent. Among those executed for murder, southern blacks were about three to four years younger at execution and roughly 10 to 15 percentage points less likely to have had an appeal prior to execution than southern whites. Outside the South, such differences of treatment by race were consistent but less pronounced. At this point, then, both regions display evidence of racial discrimination in capital punishment under state authority.

Perhaps these patterns of differential treatment have diminished or even disappeared in recent years in response to pressures toward universalism and equality before the law, and especially with the increasing review of capital cases in higher courts. To examine this possibility we must turn to a historical breakdown of the evidence on discrimination in capital punishment.

We shall examine three periods—the growth period, the peak period, and the period of decline—in capital punishment under state authority for evidence of change in the extent of racial discrimination. We turn first to historical variations in age at execution in Table 3-7.

**Table 3-6.** *Percentage Having an Appeal Prior to Execution for Murder by Region of the Country and Age at Execution for Nonwhites and Whites*

| Age at Execution | South | | North and West | |
|---|---|---|---|---|
| | Nonwhites | Whites | Nonwhites | Whites |
| 19 years or younger | 61.5 (104) | 70.6 (17) | 53.5 (43) | 57.5 (73) |
| 20–24 | 66.7 (264) | 69.5 (95) | 68.8 (144) | 72.5 (346) |
| 25–29 | 63.8 (240) | 75.3 (93) | 54.4 (136) | 66.8 (401) |
| 30–39 | 61.8 (249) | 75.3 (150) | 57.6 (172) | 68.6 (471) |
| 40 years or older | 67.3 (154) | 76.6 (128) | 45.9 (98) | 66.7 (327) |

**Table 3-7.**  *Mean Age at Execution for Murder and Rape by Historical Period and Region of the Country for Nonwhites and Whites*

| Historical Period | Murder | | | | Rape |
|---|---|---|---|---|---|
| | South | | North and West | | South |
| | Nonwhites | Whites | Nonwhites | Whites | Nonwhites |
| The 1920s and earlier— the Growth Period | 29.2 (214) | 33.3 (120) | 30.8 (229) | 31.7 (777) | 24.8 (72) |
| The 1930s— the Peak Period | 28.2 (349) | 33.4 (159) | 29.8 (124) | 30.8 (424) | 28.5 (81) |
| The 1940s and later— the Period of Decline | 30.9 (484) | 34.0 (233) | 30.3 (240) | 33.3 (417) | 26.0 (205) |

In contrast to Table 3-5, we make no attempt to control for appeals when examining variations in age at execution. From the previous analysis (Tables 3-3 and 3-5) it is evident that appeals account for little of the variation in age at execution (and the relatively small numbers having had no appeals in recent years make it virtually impossible to examine age at execution within this category). Also, in contrast with Table 3-5, we include rape offenders to permit historical comparisons in age at execution for this group. Thus, we present mean age at execution by historical period, region of the country, type of offenses, and race of the offender (with rape confined to nonwhites in the South) in Table 3-7.

Black-white differences in age at execution for murder in the South did diminish during the period of decline in capital punishment. During the growth period, the difference in mean age was about four years. The difference in age increased during the peak period to 5.2 years, then fell to 3.1 during the period of decline.

In the rest of the country black-white differences in age at execution were relatively small during the growth and peak periods of state-imposed executions: blacks were only about one year younger at execution than whites on the average. However, in the period of decline the difference between the races increased markedly in the northern and western states; blacks were three years younger than whites for executions imposed from 1940 on.

As we have noted in Table 2-4, the 1940s also marked an abrupt and decisive increase in the proportion of blacks among those executed outside the South—from 23.4 percent in the 1930s to 37.9 percent in the 1940s. This was, of course, a period when the nonwhite population in northern and western states grew substantially as a result of the migration of blacks to urban centers in the North after the Great Depression and World War II. The increased racial difference in age at execution after 1940 may, then, be a reflection in the criminal justice process of growing tensions between the races as blacks became more numerous and visible in the North. In effect, discrimination that appears to have been quite substantial in the South throughout the history of state-imposed executions may have begun to surface in the North as racial tensions mounted with the increasing influx of blacks.

Furthermore, the changes that have occurred in age at execution in the South are dwarfed by the persistent historical continuities. Thus, the black-white differences among those executed for murder were more than twice as great in the South as outside of it until the period of decline. Or again, until the most recent period, southern blacks were younger and southern whites were older at execution than their counterparts outside the South. And even in the period of decline in capital punishment, the closing gap between the South and the rest of the country in black-white differences is not so much a result of decreasing differences in the South as it is the result of increasing differences in the North and West.

Appeal prior to execution pertains specifically to treatment within the judicial system after the death sentence has been handed down. Unlike age at execution, it is analytically independent of economic and social conditions affecting age at offense and of selectivity in arrest, conviction, and sentencing. As a relatively visible and discrete aspect of the judicial system, the appeal process may be especially both subject to and responsive to efforts to eliminate discrimination. To pursue this possibility, we present appeals prior to execution by historical period, regions of the country, type of offense, age at execution, and race of offender in Table 3-8. (Again, rape is confined to nonwhites in the South.) We have included age at execution in the breakdown to permit comparisons that may reflect differential treatment of blacks and whites that may be specific to the younger age categories.

Looking first at those executed for murder in the South, we find that there has been a decline in differences between the races over time. Thus, before 1930, nonwhites, both young and old, were about 20 percentage points lower in appeals than whites. But during the 1930s these differences averaged about 15 percentage points; by the 1940s and later they were reduced to an average of less than ten points. In the rest of the country, differences in level of appeal between blacks and whites were somewhat smaller and less consistent on the average.

Young black rapists executed in the South prior to 1930 had the fewest appeals of all. The table shows that only 20.4 percent of young black rapists had appeals during the early growth period. This is well below the level of appeals for black murderers executed in the South during the same period. The situation improved for southern black rapists (as it did for southern black murderers) during and after the

**Table 3-8.**  *Percentage Having an Appeal Prior to Execution for*
*Murder and Rape by Historical Period, Region of the*
*Country, and Age at Execution for Nonwhites and*
*Whites*

| Age at Execution | Murder | | | | Rape |
|---|---|---|---|---|---|
| | South | | North and West | | South |
| | Nonwhites | Whites | Nonwhites | Whites | Nonwhites |
| *The 1920s and earlier* | | | | | |
| 29 years or younger | 35.9 | 58.2 | 52.9 | 67.3 | 20.4 |
| | (131) | (55) | (121) | (397) | (54) |
| 30 years or older | 36.4 | 56.4 | 46.3 | 66.8 | 31.3 |
| | (77) | (55) | (108) | (380) | (16) |
| *The 1930s* | | | | | |
| 29 years or younger | 70.5 | 82.1 | 55.4 | 70.7 | 64.0 |
| | (210) | (67) | (65) | (242) | (50) |
| 30 years or older | 65.0 | 85.5 | 59.3 | 67.0 | 64.0 |
| | (120) | (83) | (59) | (182) | (25) |
| *The 1940s and later* | | | | | |
| 29 years or younger | 74.2 | 73.5 | 70.1 | 68.0 | 65.5 |
| | (267) | (83) | (137) | (181) | (145) |
| 30 years or older | 69.9 | 77.9 | 57.3 | 69.9 | 59.6 |
| | (206) | (140) | (103) | (236) | (52) |

1930s when appeals were made by about two-thirds of the blacks executed in the South, whatever their ages or offenses.

A point relating to age and appeal should be noted. We observed in Table 3-4 that executed young black rape offenders were especially likely not to have had appeals. It now appears from Table 3-8 that judicial practices in the early period of state-imposed executions are largely responsible for the lower level of appeals among young black rapists as a group. By 1940 and thereafter, they were actually more likely than their older counterparts to have had appeals prior to execution.

The spectre of declining racial differences in appeals over time raises the possibility that such differences may have altogether vanished at some point after 1940 but before executions ended in 1967. Has the judicial system managed to purge itself of racial difference in appeals in recent years? Let us carry our analysis one step further to examine this possibility.

In Table 3-9 we examine in more detail the period of decline in capital punishment from 1940 on. The overall period has been divided into five intervals. With this refined breakdown we have too few cases to control for age at execution. The table presents two values for each category of offenders and time interval: the first is the percentage hav-

**Table 3-9.** *Percentage Having Any Appeals and Higher Appeals Prior to Execution by Type of Offense, Region of the Country, and Race for Five Intervals from 1940 to 1967*

| | Murder | | | | Rape |
|---|---|---|---|---|---|
| | South | | North and West | | South |
| | Nonwhites | Whites | Nonwhites | Whites | Nonwhites |
| *1940–1944* | | | | | |
| % having any appeals | 63.6 | 69.7 | 65.5 | 74.2 | 64.1 |
| % having higher appeals | 6.3 | 1.3 | 0.0 | 4.7 | 9.0 |
| | (176) | (76) | (58) | (128) | (78) |
| *1945–1949* | | | | | |
| % having any appeal | 73.1 | 79.7 | 65.5 | 59.1 | 57.9 |
| % having higher appeals | 5.1 | 11.6 | 21.8 | 19.1 | 5.3 |
| | (197) | (69) | (87) | (110) | (76) |
| *1950–1954* | | | | | |
| % having any appeals | 76.2 | 86.4 | 57.4 | 69.4 | 77.5 |
| % having higher appeals | 9.9 | 16.9 | 10.6 | 21.4 | 35.0 |
| | (101) | (59) | (47) | (98) | (40) |
| *1955–1959* | | | | | |
| % having any appeals | 69.0 | 74.5 | 66.7 | 71.2 | 65.8 |
| % having higher appeals | 6.0 | 23.4 | 13.9 | 32.9 | 7.9 |
| | (84) | (47) | (36) | (73) | (38) |
| *1960–1967* | | | | | |
| % having any appeals | 71.7 | 82.8 | 62.1 | 71.4 | 81.8 |
| % having higher appeals | 17.4 | 37.9 | 24.1 | 53.1 | 4.5 |
| | (46) | (29) | (29) | (49) | (22) |

ing had an appeal (that is, any appeal) prior to execution—the value used in previous tables; the second is the percentage having had an appeal beyond the state appellate court level—the U.S. District Court, the U.S. Circuit Court of Appeals, or the U.S. Supreme Court (that is, higher appeals). (Because this is a subgroup of those having had any appeals, it will always be a smaller percentage of the number executed.)

Higher appeals have been relatively infrequent among those who have been executed (as shown in Table 3-1). They were made by only 5.4 percent of the nonwhites and 7.6 percent of the whites in the Teeters-Zibulka listing. It turns out, however, that higher appeals became considerably more common during the period of decline in capital punishment. In fact, three-quarters of all higher appeals occurred after 1940, making them a prominent aspect of the judicial review process in this late period in capital punishment—and an additional area of possible discrimination in the administration of capital punishment.

Looking first at the percentage having an appeal of any sort prior to execution, we find in the South that black murderers and rapists were less likely than white murderers to have had appeals in each of the five time intervals from 1940 on. Despite the fact that in many cases the percentages are based on relatively small numbers of executions, the disparity between southern blacks and southern whites is quite consistent throughout the entire period. The racial difference is by no means eliminated as we move from the beginning to the end of this period—or from the South to the North and West.

In the case of higher appeals, there is actually a pattern of *growing* differentiation between the races both inside and outside the South. In the early 1940s all five categories of executed offenders were relatively unlikely to have had higher appeals; less than 10 percent of any group had such appeals. In the late 1940s and early 1950s the percentage having had higher appeals began to rise for most categories of offenders, and a difference began to emerge between blacks and whites in the extent of such appeals.[5]

In the late 1950s and the 1960s the difference between the races in higher appeals became more exaggerated. Among those executed for murder in both regions, it rose from an average of about 12 percentage points in the late 1940s and early 1950s to about 20 points in the late 1950s and the 1960s in the South. In the rest of the country the differences continued growing into the 1960s to 30 percentage points. Furthermore, much of this increasing difference between the races is attributable to the rising level of higher appeals among whites, without much change in the extent of higher appeals among blacks. Thus, among southern white murderers, higher appeals climbed from 16.9 percent in the early 1950s to 23.4 percent in the late 1950s and 37.9 percent in the 1960s; among white murderers in the rest of the country, the corresponding figures are 21.4 percent, 32.9 percent, and 53.1 percent respectively.

Thus, toward the end of the period of decline in capital punishment, we find a pattern of growing differentiation between the races in higher appeals both inside and outside the South. Perhaps the increasing readiness of higher courts to hear appeals provided a context in which whites under sentence of death were able to marshal greater resources and sympathy than nonwhites in efforts to escape their execution.

Clearly, discrimination with respect to the relatively visible appeals process has not disappeared in recent years. Indeed, during the

5. The level of higher appeals in the early 1950s among those executed for rape was distinctly higher than the levels in rape cases before and after this five-year interval. An examination of the Teeters-Zibulka inventory for the years 1950 to 1954 reveals that the executions of seven blacks from Martinsville City, Virginia, who had appeals before the United States Supreme Court in a multiple offender rape case, account for much of the deviation of this particular period from the level of higher appeals in rape cases from 1940 on.

last ten to fifteen years of capital punishment it seems to have taken on a new dimension. In terms of the data in Table 3-9, blacks executed in the South, whatever their offense, continued to have fewer appeals of any sort throughout the period of decline in capital punishment, and blacks in both regions of the country became relatively deprived of higher appeals as executions in the United States came to an end.

## Discrimination under the Mandatory Death Sentence

It might be argued that the foregoing evidence of differential treatment of blacks and whites in the administration of capital punishment is historically interesting but irrelevant to the future of the death penalty in America because it pertains largely to a form of capital punishment that the Supreme Court has now ruled unconstitutional. If the death penalty is to be reinstated in America, its administration will have to take a different form. The principal alternative that advocates have recommended is to make the death sentence mandatory upon conviction for clearly defined capital crimes. This, they argue, will remove the arbitrariness and discrimination that the Court objected to under discretionary sentencing in capital cases.

This approach, of course, assumes that the discrimination we have thus far uncovered is primarily attributable to the sentencing process. But there is also empirical evidence of discrimination at other stages in the judicial process leading to execution: specifically, at indictment and conviction before sentencing and in appeals and commutations afterwards. Indeed, the evidence of differential appeals between blacks and whites developed in the preceding section points to discrimination in the judicial process quite apart from sentencing.

Making the death penalty mandatory upon conviction would, by definition, eliminate discrimination in sentencing. Whether it would substantially reduce the overall level of discrimination in capital punishment, however, depends on how extensive discrimination is at the point of sentencing and to what extent it might be displaced to other stages of the judicial process under mandatory sentencing. Indeed, the failure of the mandatory death sentence to reduce the overall level of racial discrimination in capital punishment would lend support to the notions that such discrimination is a reflection of community sentiments that will inevitably find their expression in the institution of capital punishment, and that it is not simply the function of a defect in the judicial process that can be remedied by statutory reforms.

Our best indication of what might be expected from the mandatory death sentence lies in what its effect has been in the past. Between 1838 and 1963, some forty-eight capital jurisdictions in the United

States moved from mandatory to discretionary sentencing for first degree murder (Table 1-2). Of these, nineteen made the move after bringing executions under state authority, and sixteen actually imposed state executions under both forms of sentencing,[6] as shown in Table 3-10.

The table indicates when each state moved to discretionary capital punishment for murder, how long executions under state authority were performed before and after the year of the change, how many executions were imposed before and after the change year, and how

**Table 3-10.** *States Imposing Executions under Both Mandatory and Discretionary Capital Punishment*

| States | Year of Change to Discretion | Period of Executions | | Number of Executions[a] | | Number of Executions for Comparable Periods[b] | |
|---|---|---|---|---|---|---|---|
| | | Before Change (Yr/Mo) | After Change (Yr/Mo) | Before Change | After Change | Before Change | After Change |
| Ohio | 1898 | 12/6 | 53/6 | 33 | 309 | 33 | 39 |
| Colorado | 1901 | 5/8 | 45/10 | 12 | 65 | 12 | 5 |
| New Hampshire | 1903 | 33/10 | 35/7 | 9 | 3 | 9 | 2 |
| Washington | 1909 | 4/8 | 42/6 | 9 | 61 | 12 | 3 |
| Idaho | 1911 | 9/2 | 35/10 | 5 | 5 | 5 | 0 |
| Vermont[c] | 1911 | 47/0 | 0/1 | 14 | 1 | 0 | 1 |
| Nevada | 1912 | 6/4 | 48/8 | 10 | 31 | 9 | 1 |
| Virginia | 1914 | 5/3 | 47/3 | 59 | 171 | 59 | 34 |
| Arkansas | 1915 | 1/4 | 48/1 | 9 | 161 | 9 | 4 |
| Wyoming | 1915 | 2/8 | 50/0 | 2 | 12 | 2 | 3 |
| New Jersey | 1916 | 8/1 | 46/1 | 39 | 117 | 43 | 32 |
| Oregon | 1920 | 10/0 | 41/8 | 26 | 33 | 11 | 14 |
| Pennsylvania | 1925 | 9/11 | 36/4 | 136 | 195 | 136 | 94 |
| New Mexico | 1939 | 5/6 | 20/2 | 2 | 6 | 2 | 0 |
| North Carolina | 1949 | 38/10 | 11/10 | 331 | 19 | 148 | 19 |
| Connecticut | 1951 | 56/1 | 8/5 | 67 | 6 | 8 | 6 |

[a] The sum of the figures in these two columns will not always equal the total number of executions under state authority for a given state, since those conducted in the year of the change have been omitted.

[b] For a given state, executions for periods before and after the change are equivalent to the shorter period in columns 2 and 3.

[c] Vermont returned to mandatory sentencing in 1913 and to discretionary sentencing again in 1957, three years after its last execution under state authority. Since there were no executions after Vermont's second move to discretion, the table records information only through Vermont's first change, from 1864 through 1912.

6. Massachusetts and Washington, D.C., performed their last executions under state authority before moving to discretionary sentencing; New York performed two executions in the year of the change, but it is likely that the offenders were sentenced under the mandatory statute. (See also footnote c in Table 3-10.)

many were imposed in equal time periods before and after the move. The table shows that most of the changes to discretionary sentencing occurred during the growth period in state-imposed executions, prior to 1930. In fact, most of them came within a decade after the move to state-imposed executions (see Table 2-1). Thus, for most states there were fewer executions under state authority before than after the change.

To compare the pace of executions under mandatory and discretionary sentencing, we must, therefore, count executions for equal periods before and after the change in each state. Since the mandatory period is shorter than the discretionary in thirteen of the sixteen states, we have counted executions for equivalent time periods after the change to discretionary sentencing in these states. For three states, however, the discretionary period is shorter—in Vermont because the state returned to mandatory sentencing after a one-year interlude of discretion, and in North Carolina and Connecticut because the change to discretion came not long before the end of executions in these states—and thus establishes the period for counting the number of executions under the mandatory death penalty.

Notably, when we compare the number of executions in equivalent periods before and after the move to discretionary sentencing (the last two columns in Table 3-10), it becomes evident that the change was typically followed by a marked decline in executions. As a group, for the states with fifteen or fewer executions before the change, there were only about half as many in comparable periods after the change. For most of the remaining states, the number of executions dropped more than 30 percent after the change. Moreover, the decline in Pennsylvania of 30.9 percent came when executions were rising by roughly the same amount in the nation as a whole. The much greater decline in North Carolina of 87.2 percent undoubtedly reflects the fact that the change came when executions were declining nationally by about 50 percent between the 1940s and the 1950s (see Table 2-2). For most of the states in Table 3-10, however, the change to discretionary sentencing came during a period when the level of legally imposed executions in America was remarkably constant. (The growth in state-imposed executions during this period reflected a state-by-state transfer of the executions' function from local to state authority, without much change in the absolute number of executions imposed.) Finally, the only two states that did not show a decline in executions after the change to discretionary sentencing—Vermont and Wyoming—together account for only two executions before and four after the change, too few to provide a meaningful assessment of its effect.

These data leave little doubt about the fact that executions were less common under discretionary capital punishment. It appears that juries exercising discretion recommended imprisonment for a number of offenders who would have been put to death under the mandatory death penalty. And it is the exercise of such discretion, according to advocates of the mandatory death sentence, that enables the jury to send a convicted white murderer to jail and to call for the death of a black man convicted of the same crime. If this interpretation is correct, we should find, for states that moved from mandatory to discretionary capital punishment, that as the pace of executions dropped, the proportion of blacks among those executed increased sharply.

Our analysis of racial discrimination under mandatory and discretionary sentencing cannot proceed exactly as it did in the previous section. Specifically, we cannot simply pool all executions imposed under mandatory and all those under discretionary sentencing for the change states, in the way that we previously pooled executions by region and historical period. To do so would be to end up largely with a comparison between the few states with many executions under mandatory sentencing (particularly North Carolina and Pennsylvania) and most of the rest (especially Ohio) with a relatively large number under discretion. Even if we were to take equal numbers or periods of executions before and after the change in each state and pool them, the pattern would be dominated by a state like Pennsylvania, which has many more executions on *both* sides of the change than any of the other change states in Table 3-10.

Instead, our approach in this particular analysis will be to compare the periods of mandatory and discretionary capital punishment separately for selected change states. As shown in Table 3-10, there were only five states—Ohio, Virginia, New Jersey, Pennsylvania, and North Carolina—that performed as many as nineteen executions under state authority *both* before and after the change to discretionary sentencing. In effect, these are the only states that performed enough executions on both sides of the change to permit reliable comparisons. For the purpose of this analysis we have included all executions performed under state authority within ten years on either side of the change date and, in the cases of Ohio and North Carolina, where executions under state authority were performed for longer than ten years on *both* sides of the change, we have extended the boundaries to twelve years, six months and eleven years, ten months, respectively.

Now, to the extent that the reduction in executions under discretionary sentencing, evident in Table 3-10, was a product of the tendency of juries to be more lenient with white than with black convicted murderers, we should find an increased percentage of blacks among those executed in the discretionary, as compared with the mandatory, period in the states. Table 3-11, part A, shows the percentage of nonwhites among those executed for murder before and after the

**Table 3-11.** States under Mandatory and Discretionary Capital Punishment for Murder with Respect to (A) Percentage of Nonwhites among Those Executed, (B) Mean Age at Execution by Race, and (C) Percentage Having an Appeal Prior to Execution by Race

| | A) Percentage Nonwhite | | B) Mean Age at Execution | | | | C) Percent Having an Appeal | | | |
| --- | --- | --- | --- | --- | --- | --- | --- | --- | --- | --- |
| | Mandatory | Discretionary | Mandatory | | Discretionary | | Mandatory | | Discretionary | |
| | | | Nonwhite | White | Nonwhite | White | Nonwhite | White | Nonwhite | White |
| Ohio[a] | 9.1 (33) | 36.4 (33) | — (3) | 31.1 (30) | 27.2 (12) | 35.5 (21) | NA | NA | NA | NA |
| Virginia | 73.3 (45) | 95.0 (40) | 26.6 (31) | 32.3 (12) | 26.8 (37) | — (2) | — (33) | 16.7 (12) | 31.6 (38) | — (2) |
| New Jersey | 38.1 (42) | 12.1 (33) | 29.3 (16) | 34.1 (26) | — (4) | 32.5 (29) | 18.8 (16) | 38.5 (26) | — (4) | 51.7 (29) |
| Pennsylvania | 38.5 (130) | 32.3 (93) | — (4) | 30.7 (15) | — (8) | 27.7 (22) | 42.0 (50) | 51.3 (80) | 60.0 (30) | 74.6 (63) |
| North Carolina | 75.7 (107) | 75.0 (12) | 28.8 (55) | 34.5 (20) | — (6) | — (1) | 86.4 (81) | 92.3 (26) | — (9) | — (3) |

[a] All death sentences were automatically reviewed at the county level in Ohio, according to the Teeters-Zibulka inventory.

change to discretionary sentencing for each of the five states under investigation.

The first two states to make this move—Ohio and Virginia—did, indeed, experience an increase in the proportion of blacks among those executed when they changed from mandatory to discretionary capital punishment. A closer examination of the pattern for Ohio reveals, however, that the increased proportion of nonwhites during the discretionary period is not fully attributable to the change in sentencing practices. Discretionary sentencing per se can only be expected to reduce the number of executions imposed for a given category of convicted offenders. But in Ohio the absolute number of blacks rose from three in the mandatory period to twelve in the discretionary period—a change that must be attributed to other factors. In Virginia, on the other hand, there was an evident decline in the number of whites executed, from twelve in the five years and three months prior to the change to just two in the ten years subsequent to it. This is consistent with the claim that discretionary sentencing promotes discrimination by permitting juries to withhold the death penalty for convicted white murderers while imposing upon their black counterparts.

By contrast, the other three states—New Jersey, Pennsylvania, and North Carolina—all experienced a decline in the percentage of nonwhites after moving to discretionary sentencing. In the case of New Jersey the difference was substantial, and due almost exclusively to a decline in the number of blacks executed under discretionary sentencing. Black executions dropped from sixteen in the eight years and one month prior to the change to just four in the ten years after the change, while the number of white executions changed little. Thus, there were more states in which the proportion of blacks decreased than increased between the mandatory and discretionary periods, and for the one state where the change may have been accompanied by increased discrimination against blacks there was also one in which such discrimination may have subsided as a result of the change.

As a group, then, these five states yield no consistent evidence of greater racial discrimination under discretionary than under mandatory sentencing, at least in terms of the proportion of nonwhites among those executed before and after the change. Because we are dealing with relatively small numbers of cases in individual states, we might expect to observe some inconsistency simply as a result of random or idiosyncratic fluctuations in the data. And in one instance discretionary sentencing may have facilitated racial discrimination, but this is not to say that discretionary sentencing was wholly or primarily responsible for it or that the mandatory death penalty would prevent it. To the contrary, the fact that these five states, as a group, displayed no consistent effect of the move from mandatory to discretionary capital punishment suggests that discretionary sentencing alone bears only marginal responsibility for the arbitrariness and discrimination that has characterized the administration of capital punishment in recent years.

With the data developed earlier in this chapter we are in a position to pursue the question of racial discrimination under mandatory and discretionary sentencing further. We have previously observed racial differences in age at execution and suggested that they reflect discriminatory treatment within the criminal justice system, especially a punitive approach toward youthful black offenders. To the extent that discretion in sentencing is responsible for differences in age at execution, we might expect to find that whites were older and blacks younger at execution under discretionary than under mandatory sentencing. The prejudiced jury can be expected to be relatively lenient with young white offenders and especially hard on young blacks when choosing between life and death.

Unfortunately, our analysis of variations in age at execution will be restricted by the need to distinguish between blacks and whites in the mandatory and discretionary periods and by the fact that data on age are not altogether complete for the states that supplied such information. In fact, for no state do we have enough data to yield reliable means for blacks and whites under mandatory and discretionary sentencing—where there are ten or fewer executions, we regard the data as insufficient for analysis. Despite these difficulties, however, the available data on age at execution, presented in Table 3-11, part B, add an important dimension to the analysis of discrimination under mandatory and discretionary capital punishment.

Between the mandatory and discretionary periods we can make four comparisons—the difference in age at execution for blacks in Virginia and for whites in Ohio, Pennsylvania, and New Jersey. The changes in Virginia and New Jersey were small and not indicative of discrimination. Blacks were only slightly older at execution on the average after the change to discretionary sentencing in Virginia and whites were about one and a half years younger after the change in New Jersey. The changes in Pennsylvania and Ohio were more substantial but in opposing directions. In Ohio the fact that whites were four years older at execution in the discretionary than the mandatory period does suggest that juries may have been relatively lenient with young white murderers when they could exercise sentencing discretion. On the other hand, in Pennsylvania whites executed in the discretionary period were three years younger on the average than their counterparts in the mandatory period, suggesting the opposite. On balance, these limited comparisons are not consistent with the hypothesis of greater discrimination under discretionary than mandatory sentencing.

These data also permit comparisons between blacks and whites in age at execution within mandatory, though not discretionary, periods, and the results are quite enlightening. In all three cases where such comparisons are possible, the difference between blacks and whites in age at execution under the mandatory death penalty are quite substantial. In fact, they are in every case greater than would be expected for states in the same region at the time of the change (according to Table 3-7). In Virginia, blacks were 5.7 years younger at execution than whites, whereas the difference was 4.1 years for southern states during the growth period in state-imposed executions. For New Jersey, blacks were 4.8 years younger at execution under mandatory sentencing, although the difference was only .8 years for northern and western states during the growth period. And for North Carolina blacks were actually 5.7 years younger at execution, while the difference for southern states in the period of decline in executions was 3.1 years. In effect, in all three cases, there were greater than average racial differences in age at execution under the mandatory death sentence, and in one of the three, the difference was six times the average for the region and time period of the change.

While these comparisons do not bear directly on the change from mandatory to discretionary sentencing within specific states, they do speak quite directly and dramatically to the issue of the mandatory death sentence as a solution to discrimination in the administration of capital punishment. They consistently indicate that discrimination, at least in terms of age at execution, has been more, not less, pronounced in states with the mandatory death sentence. Although it seems doubtful that the mandatory form of sentencing itself promoted such discrimination, it appears that this approach to the institution of capital punishment has been more characteristic where the climate of community sentiments supports the racially oppressive use of the death penalty. Clearly, in these three states, the mandatory death penalty did not eliminate racial differences in age at execution.

And finally, let us consider appeals prior to execution. We have noted earlier that under the mandatory death sentence discrimination might be displaced from the sentencing phase to other points in the judicial process, including the appeals stage. Appeals prior to execution do not, however, indicate the extent to which the appeals process may have served to spare whites and to seal the fate of blacks convicted of the same crimes. To assess this filtering function, we would need information on successful as well as unsuccessful appeals. Instead, our measure of appeals prior to execution, as a reflection of unsuccessful appeals only, will serve to indicate the extent to which legal advice and aid was available to condemned offenders, and the extent to which those in the criminal justice system encouraged and assisted offenders in their efforts to postpone and to escape execution.

We present the percentage having had an appeal prior to execution by race under mandatory and discretionary capital punishment in Table 3-11, part C. Again, one state—Ohio—affords no comparisons because, according to the Teeters-Zibulka inventory, all death sentences in Ohio were routinely reviewed at the county level. The fact that data on appeals are complete for the other four states under investigation means that we can make a few more systematic comparisons than we could with age at execution.

In every instance where comparisons can be made, we find that appeals were consistently and substantially more available after the move from mandatory to discretionary sentencing. In Pennsylvania, where comparisons are possible for both blacks and whites, appeals were about 20 percentage points higher under discretionary than under mandatory sentencing. After the change to discretion, appeals were up 31.6 points for blacks in Virginia and 13.2 points for whites in New Jersey. (While the increase in Virginia might have been the result of a regional trend, the increases in New Jersey and Pennsylvania occurred when northern and western states displayed a constant level of appeals over time; see Table 2-6.) Furthermore, with the exception of North Carolina,[7] there were generally fewer appeals for both blacks and whites under the mandatory death penalty in these states than in neighboring jurisdictions that typically employed discretionary capital punishment at about the same time (again see Table 2-6).

The apparently increased levels of appeals under discretionary sentencing may have reflected the addition of a new phase to the judicial process and hence a new basis or opportunity for appeals. However, the generally lower levels of appeals (except for those to state appellate courts in North Carolina) during the periods of mandatory sentencing in the change states also suggest that there was little assistance or encouragement for convicted capital offenders in seeking to reverse their dispositions and that the decision of local trial courts was more typically accepted as final and irreversible. In view of the extraordinary differences in age at execution between blacks and whites under the mandatory death penalty, those lower levels of appeals certainly did not indicate that there was less cause for appeals under mandatory capital punishment. Indeed, taken together, the reduced

7. However, with respect to higher appeals, which began to increase in numbers during this time, North Carolina (with higher appeals for only two of eighty-nine executed murderers in the eleven years and ten months before the change to discretionary sentencing) fell below the level of southern states in the 1940s, which is shown in Table 3-9.

levels of appeals and the increased racial differences in age at execution give the impression that mandatory sentencing has typically been associated with a climate of intolerance against racial minorities and a lack of concern for the rights and interests of capital offenders.

Finally, when we look at differences between blacks and whites in appeals under mandatory sentencing in Table 3-11, part C, we find that comparisons are possible in four of the change states during their mandatory periods, and all four show that whites were more likely than blacks to have had appeals prior to execution. By comparison with their surrounding states at the time of their changes, racial differences in appeals were greater than average in Pennsylvania and particularly in New Jersey, about average in North Carolina, and somewhat less than average in Virginia. And, it is actually conceivable that these differences are a more conservative measure of discrimination under mandatory than under discretionary systems of capital punishment.[8] The quite evident racial differences in appeals under the mandatory death sentence strongly suggest that statutory reforms that apply to sentencing cannot be expected to eliminate discrimination at other points in the judicial process. And, the tendency for discrimination to persist in spite of judicial reform is consistent with our contention that prejudice and discrimination in the community will manifest itself in the administration of capital punishment—if not in sentencing, then in other phases of the judicial process leading to execution.

If our analysis is correct, then we would expect to find the historical changes in the extent of discrimination occurring in states with discretionary capital punishment equally evident among states with the mandatory death penalty. We have noted that among northern and western states there was little indication of discrimination in capital punishment before World War II. Then, during the period of decline in capital punishment in America, when blacks migrated in increasing numbers to northern and western states and racial tensions became more apparent outside the South, black-white differences in age at execution and higher appeals emerged.

New York state, which has imposed more executions under state authority than any other jurisdiction, did so under mandatory sentencing from 1890 until 1963, when it became the last state to give up the mandatory death penalty. In effect, New York imposed executions

8. We have observed earlier that racial differences in appeals prior to execution will be a conservative measure of discrimination in the availability of appeals to the extent that whites are more likely than blacks to have successful appeals or commutations. If any of the discrimination in commutations or in the success of appeals that took place under the mandatory death sentence was displaced to the sentencing process under the discretionary death penalty, comparable racial differences in appeals prior to execution under the two systems will actually mean greater discrimination under mandatory than under discretionary capital punishment.

under mandatory sentencing throughout the period when northern and western states experienced an increase in racial discrimination. Was New York, with the mandatory death penalty, able to resist the regional trends toward increased racial differences in age at execution and in higher appeals? The answer is to be found in Table 3-12.

First of all, Part A of the table shows that blacks doubled as a proportion of those executed from the 1930s through the 1940s—a period during which the nonwhite population of New York more than doubled. Second, Part B shows that blacks were five and six years younger at execution than were whites in the 1940s and 1950s, whereas they had been much closer in age in the 1920s and 1930s. These racial differences in age at execution after 1940 clearly exceed those for northern and western states during this period (indeed, they are more than double the regional differences when New York is removed from the regional average). And finally, Part C shows that higher appeals, which had not been made by any executed offenders in New York during the 1920s and 1930s, began to be filed by whites in increasing numbers in the 1940s and 1950s but remained essentially unavailable to blacks even after 1940.

Because of the large number of executions in New York and its long history of mandatory sentencing, it makes an excellent test case for our proposition that discrimination in capital punishment is a product of community sentiments and tensions, quite apart from sentencing practices in capital cases. And New York's experience could hardly be a more clear-cut confirmation of this proposition. When discrimination and racial tension increased in the North, racial differences in age at execution and in higher appeals appeared in New York, with the mandatory death sentence, as much as or more than they did in the other northern and western states, which typically used discretionary capital punishment. Obviously, the mandatory death penalty in New York was of little help in overcoming racial discrimination in capital punishment.

**Table 3-12.** *New York State under Mandatory Capital Punishment from 1920 to 1962 with Respect to (A) Percentage of Nonwhites, (B) Mean Age at Execution by Race, and (C) Percentage Having Higher Appeals by Race*

|  | (A) Percentage Nonwhite | (B) Mean Age at Execution | | (C) Percentage Having Higher Appeals | |
|---|---|---|---|---|---|
|  |  | Nonwhite | White | Nonwhite | White |
| 1920s | 15.2 (125) | 26.2 (19) | 29.5 (106) | 0.0 (19) | 0.0 (106) |
| 1930s | 19.0 (153) | 30.0 (29) | 28.9 (124) | 0.0 (29) | 0.0 (124) |
| 1940s | 39.5 (114) | 25.7 (45) | 30.6 (69) | 4.4 (45) | 7.2 (69) |
| 1950–1962 | 36.5 (63) | 28.5 (23) | 34.6 (40) | 0.0 (23) | 20.0 (40) |

Historically, discretionary sentencing has been advocated as a reform designed to reduce arbitrariness and injustice within the judicial process. Where the death penalty was automatic, guilty offenders were believed to have gone free because juries were reluctant to see them executed despite convincing evidence of guilt. There was also a feeling that the nature of the crime and the personal circumstances of the offender should play a role in determining punishment, if not guilt. Indeed, some of the inequities and abuses under the mandatory system probably prompted the adoption of discretionary sentencing. It is paradoxical, then, that the mandatory death penalty is now being advanced as a means of eliminating the acknowledged inequities existing under discretionary capital punishment.

## Summary and Conclusion

The findings presented in the foregoing analysis point unmistakably to a pattern of racial discrimination in the administration of capital punishment in America—a pattern that appears to be deeply rooted in the fabric of our society. It was most evident in the South, where a caste system has characterized relations between blacks and whites and produced what Myrdal (1944) terms "an American dilemma." And it has persisted throughout the history of capital punishment under state authority, diminishing in some of its more obvious aspects in recent years only to reappear in subtler forms.

More specifically, we have seen that among some 5,753 persons executed under state authority over the past one hundred years, blacks were executed for less serious crimes and crimes less often receiving the death penalty—notably rape—than whites; that blacks were younger on the average than whites at execution, whatever their offenses and whether or not they had appeals; and that blacks were more often executed without appeals, whatever their offense or age at execution. In effect, each of these indicators—type of offense, age at execution, and appeal prior to execution—revealed independent evidence of racial discrimination in the administration of capital punishment.

Discrimination was concentrated in the South. Executions for rape were almost exclusively a southern phenomenon and nine out of ten persons executed for rape were blacks. Furthermore, black rapists were the youngest at execution and the least likely to have had appeals prior to execution of any group under investigation. Indeed, young black rapists (less than twenty years old at execution) were far less likely than other categories of offenders to have had appeals, suggesting that they were prime targets of discrimination within the judicial process leading to execution.

Among those executed for murder, differences in age at execution and appeals prior to execution between the races occurred primarily in the South until recent times. Blacks in the South were on the average three to four years younger at execution and 10 percentage points less likely to have had appeals prior to execution than whites. In the rest of the country there were smaller and less consistent differences in appeal between the races and, until recently, the differences in age at execution were about the same as those in age at arrest.

Discrimination against southern blacks was most pronounced during the period of growth in capital punishment under state authority. Prior to 1930, over five out of ten southern white murderers had appeals prior to execution as compared with only three or four out of ten southern black murderers and two out of ten southern black rapists. Differences in age at execution between black and white murderers in the South were greater than four years, and southern black rapists were more than four years younger at execution than southern black murderers. In fact, the previously noted intense discrimination against young black rapists in the South occurred primarily during the growth period in state-imposed executions.

The period of peak volume in executions during the 1930s witnessed two opposing trends in the South. Racial differences in appeals prior to execution were reduced from their highpoint in the growth period, but racial differences in age at execution climbed to a highpoint during this peak period. The pattern was one of growing age differences and more youthful executions (except for rape).

During the period of decline in executions, racial differences in both age and appeals dropped off in the South. For age at execution, the reduction was small relative to the remaining differential. Thus, southern black murderers were still three years younger at execution than their white counterparts. For appeals prior to execution, on the other hand, most of the earlier gap between the races had been closed, raising the possibility that by the end of this period it might have altogether vanished. However, a closer examination of the period of decline, subdivided into shorter time intervals, revealed that the gap between the races in appeals remained evident throughout and, in addition, that toward the end of it a new gap had emerged between blacks and whites in *higher* appeals (that is, beyond the state appellate court level).

Among northern and western states, on the other hand, there was less evidence of discrimination in the growth and peak periods of state-imposed capital punishment. Then, in the period of decline, racial differences in age at execution increased markedly—blacks were three years younger at execution than whites, whereas they had been only about one year younger in the earlier periods. Furthermore, the gap in higher appeals that emerged during the period of decline was even more pronounced in the northern and western states than it was in the South. Together, these growing differences in age at execution and in higher appeals provide a strong indication of mounting discrimination in capital punishment outside the South as executions began to decline in America. Indeed, as reflected in these indicators, racial discrimination in northern and western states began to rival that in the South (at least for this period).

There is no evidence in these data, then, that the discrimination we uncovered has vanished in recent years, nor do the characteristics of those on death row after the de facto abandonment of executions give any such indication. Indeed, executions for rape, where discrimination has been especially evident, have become relatively more common in the years since 1940. And, as we have just noted, since about 1955 a new and perhaps subtler form of discrimination in higher appeals has appeared.

On the assumption that such discrimination may be remedied by statutory reform, some have advocated making the death penalty mandatory upon conviction for certain offenses. But the experience of five states that have imposed executions under both mandatory and discretionary sentencing indicates that discrimination is no less pronounced under mandatory than under discretionary capital punishment. Despite changes within specific states, the disproportionate execution of blacks was, on balance, about the same under both forms of sentencing. Where the data were sufficient for comparisons, racial differences in age at execution and in appeals prior to execution were uniformly evident under the mandatory and discretionary death penalty. In fact, differences in age at execution appear to have been even greater under mandatory than under discretionary sentencing. The clearest difference between the two forms of sentencing, however, was in the number of executions imposed. In equal time periods before and after the change to discretion, there were considerably more executions under the mandatory death penalty.

These data strongly suggest that the particular form of sentencing has little to do with the extent of racial discrimination that will be present in the administration of capital punishment. And notably, New York state's experience with the mandatory death penalty over an extended period of time indicates that it afforded no protection against mounting pressures toward discrimination in capital punishment. Racial differences in age at execution and in higher appeals increased under the mandatory death sentence in New York after World War II just as they did in non-southern jurisdictions where discretionary sentencing was in effect.

Under the mandatory death sentence discrimination may, of course, be transferred to other points in the judicial process. For instance, discrimination before and after sentencing has been well documented for North Carolina in the 1930s when the death penalty was mandatory for first degree murder. During this period blacks were more likely to have been indicted, charged and convicted for murder than whites; indeed, blacks with white victims were four times as likely to have been convicted on this charge than others (Garfinkel 1949, Table 3). And among those sentenced to death in North Carolina over an extended period of time when the mandatory death penalty was in effect, blacks were consistently more likely than whites to have their death sentences carried out (Johnson 1957, Table 7).

Apparently the sentiments that supported the mandatory death penalty were also those that tolerated extensive discrimination in its application. What is important in view of the current debate over the mandatory death sentence is the consistent evidence of its failure to remove discrimination in capital punishment. By all the standards we have used to gauge such discrimination—racial composition of those executed, racial differences in age at execution, and racial differences in appeals prior to execution—the mandatory death penalty has displayed no advantage over discretionary capital punishment. Although further research is needed, the implications of the findings are unmistakable. They are certainly sufficient to shift the burden of proof to those who argue that the mandatory death sentence would be an effective remedy for racial discrimination in capital punishment. Claims to this effect will no longer do.

The data we have examined on offense, age, and appeals do not by any means encompass the full extent of racial discrimination that may have occurred in the administration of capital punishment. These are indicators of discriminatory treatment among those who have been executed; they do not necessarily reflect discriminatory treatment that may have resulted in escaping execution. To have a full view of the extent of discrimination in capital punishment, it would be important to examine and compare at each stage of the process that leads to execution those who go to the next stage and those who go no further.

Thus, where we found no racial difference in terms of these specific indicators, it does not mean that discrimination was not present; it could be simply that these indicators did not pick it up. Specifically, the fact that we found relatively small racial differences in appeals prior to execution for most periods of state-imposed executions outside of the South does not mean that discrimination was not present in the rest of the country. Indeed, racial differences in the execution of condemned offenders has been documented for both Pennsylvania (Wolfgang et al. 1962) and New Jersey (Bedau 1964). But since these studies report racial differences in the extent to which death row inmates have *escaped* execution, their findings are largely independent of ours, based as ours are on exclusively those who have been executed.

Of course, the racial differences we have uncovered here may, in some measure, be a reflection of discrimination by social class. To distinguish between racial and class discrimination in these data, we would need a measure of the social class backgrounds of those who have been executed. Such information could be drawn from trial court records, at least for subsamples of black and white offenders. But even if social class were to account for most of the disparity in treatment between the races, it would simply represent an additional or alternative basis of discrimination in capital punishment—one that would subject the death penalty to the same kind of constitutional challenge implicit in racial discrimination. And while social class discrimination may play some role, the patterning of racial differences revealed in these data leaves little doubt that broadly pervasive and deeply rooted racism in our society has bent the judicial process to its service, particularly in the South.

For some it may come as a rude shock to learn that the criminal justice system, like others of our institutions, has been susceptible to, and perhaps even an instrument of, prejudices and biases rooted in the fabric of our society. Nor has racial discrimination within the justice system been confined to the administration of capital punishment.[9] Although considerations such as the race of offenders and victims are irrelevant under the law, they are not thereby purged from the actions of those who apply the law. And where such factors are a salient aspect of the social milieu, they are more evident in the workings of the judicial process. Apparently the criminal justice system is responsive to the same forces that have caused racial disparities in education, occupation, and criminal behavior.

Not only does the criminal justice system itself perpetuate an injustice in the way it dispenses capital punishment, but the nature of the punishment makes the injustice irreparable. Death, unlike other punishments, is an ultimate and absolute denial of the right to restitution and compensation for injustices suffered at the hands of the justice system. In the face of existing evidence of racial discrimination under both discretionary and mandatory application of the death penalty, would not a return to capital punishment be an affirmation of irreparable injustice for some Americans, and a denial of a system free of a known and lasting injustice to all Americans?

9. Thus, differential treatment of blacks and whites has been well documented in studies of decisions by the police about the disposition of juveniles (Piliavin and Briar 1964), of provision of counsel to defendants (Sutherland and Cressey 1966), and of commitment to prison and length of sentence imposed (Korn and McCorkle 1959). (For additional recent evidence on differential handling and disposition by race, see Warren 1970; Arnold 1971; Marshall and Purdy 1972; Chiricos, Jackson, and Waldo 1972.)

# 4

## THE AMERICAN EXPERIENCE WITH THE MORATORIUM ON EXECUTIONS AND THE MANDATORY DEATH PENALTY

In the recently renewed debate over capital punishment, proponents of the death penalty have used two arguments relating to the presumed deterrent power of the death penalty to bolster their case. The first is that the nationwide judicial moratorium on executions in America in the 1960s was, in part, responsible for the recent rise in murder rates in this country. They assert that the growing awareness in the late 1960s that death would no longer be imposed as a punishment for criminal homicide removed an effective constraint on would-be murderers. Second, they claim that a return to mandatory capital punishment upon conviction for capital offenses would harness the deterrent power of the death penalty. The fact that as many as nine out of ten convicted murderers have escaped death under discretionary

Our analysis of the effects of the 1967 judicial moratorium on executions in the United States draws on the work of Marvin E. Wolfgang as reported in his testimony before Subcommittee No. 3 of the Committee on the Judiciary of the United States House of Representatives, on proposed legislation for a moratorium on capital punishment (Hart-Celler Hearings, March 16, 1972, pp. 181, 183–189). Our analysis of the effect of the mandatory death sentence was first suggested to me by Jack Himmelstein of the NAACP Legal Defense and Educational Fund, Inc. In the preparation and analysis of the data in this chapter Andréa Carr and Glenn Pierce made a substantial contribution. To each of these four, I wish to express my appreciation.

capital punishment in recent years, they argue, robbed the death penalty of its deterrent potential.

While previous research gives no indication that the death penalty has greater deterrent power than imprisonment, it is true that these investigations have typically examined the de jure existence of the death penalty rather than the extensiveness of its use. In particular, there are no investigations directed specifically at the effect of the de facto cessation of executions, as in the case of the 1967 moratorium on executions in America. It might be argued that existing studies of differential use of the death penalty (Schuessler 1952; Ohio Legislative Service Commission 1961), of the impact of discrete executions (Dann 1935; Graves 1956), and of sentencing to death (Savitz 1958) should show some evidence of deterrence if the actual application of the death penalty, apart from its existence, acts as a constraint on homicide. Admittedly, however, none of these investigations focuses directly on the cessation of executions. The impact of the nationwide moratorium on executions may, therefore, be regarded as an open question from the viewpoint of existing evidence on deterrence. And certainly it is an important issue for investigation in view of the claim that it has led to a precipitous rise in homicide in the United States.

Nor do any existing studies direct themselves specifically to the possible deterrent effects of the mandatory death sentence. Research has not been able to establish that increased risk or certainty of execution for capital crimes contributes to the deterrent value of the death penalty (Schuessler 1952; Ohio Legislative Service Commission 1961). It is conceivable, however, that the states under investigation imposed discretionary capital punishment, and that the certainty of execution under this alternative simply did not reach a high enough level to produce demonstrable deterrent effects. It might be argued that if the mandatory death penalty were a distinctly potent deterrent, this should have been reflected in at least some of the comparisons that have been made between abolition and death penalty states (Sellin 1959). But without knowing in which, if any, of the death penalty states its use was mandatory, we cannot be sure that it was associated with lower homicide rates. The possibility remains, therefore, that mandatory capital punishment may have a deterrent advantage over its discretionary use or imprisonment as alternatives.

Our purpose in this chapter is to make a direct assessment of these two claims—that the judicial moratorium on executions has contributed to increased homicide rates and that mandatory capital punishment would tend to reduce the incidence of homicide. We shall adopt the form of analysis used by Professor Thorsten Sellin in his pioneering work on the deterrent effects of capital punishment. Sellin has compared homicide rates for contiguous death penalty and abolition states and for a given state at varying points in time to determine whether its availability bears any relationship to the level of homicide in the state.

For such comparisions to be an adequate test of deterrence, it must be assumed (1) that the proportion of capital murders among all homicides remains reasonably constant over time and from one jurisdiction to the next; (2) that the effects are felt primarily within the jurisdiction in which the existence or imposition of the death penalty occurs; and (3) that the effect of other factors (i.e., population characteristics and sociocultural environment) known to influence murder rates in a serious manner are eliminated or taken into account or assumed to be constant across state lines. For this purpose, Sellin has used one or more *contiguous* states as controls. In the analysis that follows, we too rely heavily on this procedure of comparing states of primary interest with one or more contiguous states serving as controls.

The first empirical section of this chapter examines selected states before and after the judicial moratorium on executions in America. It reports data initially presented in 1972 by Professor Marvin E. Wolfgang in his testimony before the House Subcommittee on the Judiciary, then considering legislation for a continuation of the existing moratorium (Hart-Celler Hearings, March 16, 1972, 181, 183–189). Professor Wolfgang's analysis covered the eight-year period from 1963 through 1970 (four years before and three years after the nationwide moratorium in 1967) and included all states in which the death penalty was abolished throughout this eight-year period, together with contiguous death penalty states.

We have extended the scope of his analysis (1) by including additional states that abolished the death penalty within the four-year period prior to the nationwide moratorium on executions, and (2) by adding 1971 homicide rates, not available from the *Uniform Crime Reports* of the F.B.I. at the time of Wolfgang's analysis, to cover four-year periods both before and after the moratorium in 1967. As a result, our analysis will cover a nine-year period and include *every* state in which the death penalty was not legally available throughout the period of the moratorium, with at least one contiguous death penalty state as a control. (We exclude Alaska and Hawaii for lack of contiguous jurisdictions.)

In the second empirical section, we examine states that have made a change from mandatory to discretionary capital punishment for first degree murder. This move to discretionary use of the death penalty has occurred in all death penalty jurisdictions over the course of the last century or so (see Table 1-2). Until very recently, however, information on the timing of such changes was available only for states that made this move after the Second World War (Bedau 1967b, 27–

30; S. Ehrmann 1961). Our analysis was begun with this more restricted information on recent moves to discretionary capital punishment. Fortunately, a complete inventory of the changes from mandatory to discretionary capital punishment was recently compiled (Garin 1973) in time for us to extend the analysis to include states that made this move prior to World War II. The analysis as it now stands includes *every* state for which data on homicide rates can be obtained for a period of four years before and after the move to discretionary capital punishment. (The one exception to this rule is New Hampshire, for which data are available for three years before and four years after its move to discretionary capital punishment.) The homicide rates that serve as bases for the figures in this chapter are presented in Bowers (1974), Appendix C.

## The Effect of the Judicial Moratorium

As in the case of the Canadian experiment with abolition, the judicial moratorium on executions in the United States was also a nationwide phenomenon that can be given a specific beginning point. In the Canadian experiment, however, the change was relatively abrupt in the sense that according to legislative decree, no further executions (except for the killing of a law officer) could be performed. In the case of the judicial moratorium in the United States, the awareness that executions had come to an end was undoubtedly less immediate and widespread. Indeed, convicted offenders were still being sentenced to death after June 1967, and there was no legislative assurance that these sentences would not eventually be carried out. Thus, growing recognition that the death penalty would not be imposed might be expected to produce *gradually* increasing levels of homicide in death penalty states after the moratorium, *relative* to the levels of homicide in abolition states.

More specifically, if the death penalty exercises a greater deterrent effect on prospective murderers than does imprisonment, the following propositions ought to be true:

1. Death penalty states should show increased levels of homicide after the 1967 judicial moratorium. Growing public awareness that the death penalty was no longer being employed in practice should have resulted in progressively increasing homicide rates among states that previously imposed the death penalty.
2. There should be no noticeable change (upturn) in the level of homicides for abolition states subsequent to the cessation of executions.

Any changes in the homicide rates of abolition states should be the result of ongoing trends over time.

3. States that abolish capital punishment in the period immediately before the judicial moratorium should show increased levels of homicide relative to contiguous death penalty states prior to the moratorium, but death penalty states should tend to narrow any gap in homicide rates previously opened by recent abolition states after the cessation of executions.

Figures 4-1 through 4-8 present eight graphs comparing the homicide rates of abolition states and contiguous death penalty states for the four years prior to the judicial moratorium on capital punishment and the four years subsequent to it. The first four figures in our analysis compare death penalty states with states that were abolitionist for the entire nine-year period under investigation—1963 through 1971.

The homicide rates for Michigan, an abolition state, with its contiguous death penalty state, Illinois, are shown in Figure 4-1. The graph directly contradicts the argument that the death penalty is a uniquely effective deterrent. Prior to 1967 the homicide rates of abolitionist Michigan were consistently lower than those of Illinois. And after 1967 it is the abolitionist state and not the death penalty state, as the deterrence perspective would predict, that experiences the greater rise.

Figures 4-2 and 4-3 permit comparisions among the New England states of Maine, New Hampshire, Vermont, Massachusetts, Rhode Island, and Connecticut. Of these states, Maine and Rhode Island had no death penalty for the entire period under study, and Vermont abolished its death penalty in 1965. In Figure 4-2 we can see an obvious similarity of homicide rates and trends for Massachusetts, Connecticut, and Rhode Island. All three states, regardless of their punishment for murder, show a general and gradual increase in homicide throughout

**Figure 4-1.** *Annual Homicide Rates Before and After the Judicial Moratorium on Executions in Michigan and Illinois*

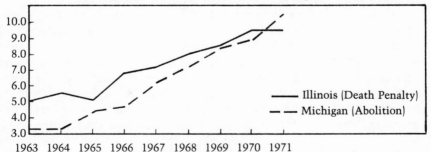

*Source*: Annual state homicide rates from Federal Bureau of Investigation, *Uniform Crime Reports* (Annual).

**Figure 4-2.** *Annual Homicide Rates Before and After the Judicial Moratorium on Executions in Rhode Island, Connecticut, and Massachusetts*

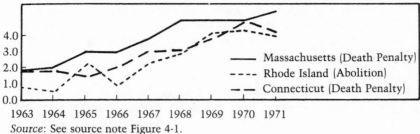

1963  1964  1965  1966  1967  1968  1969  1970  1971
*Source*: See source note Figure 4-1.

**Figure 4-3.** *Annual Homicide Rates Before and After the Judicial Moratorium on Executions in Maine, Vermont, and New Hampshire*

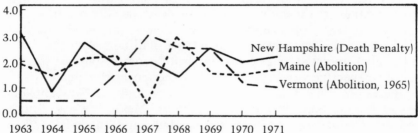

1963  1964  1965  1966  1967  1968  1969  1970  1971
*Source*: See source note Figure 4-1.

the period; the ranking of the three states in terms of homicide rate is the same in 1971 as it was in 1963.

The homicide rates for Maine, New Hampshire, and Vermont are shown in Figure 4-3. As might be expected, these states showed greater instability of rates from year to year than did their more populous New England counterparts. However, New Hampshire, with the death penalty, showed little overall increase in its homicide rate after 1967, while the abolitionist states of Maine and Vermont showed an increase and a decrease, respectively. The only evidence in the graph to suggest that the death penalty may be a more effective deterrent than imprisonment is the rise of Vermont's homicide rate in the two years following abolition of the death penalty. Yet further examination of the graph reveals that after 1967 Vermont's upward homicide trend is completely reversed and that by 1971 its homicide rate is almost back to the 1963 level.

Figure 4-4 presents the homicide rate for North Dakota, an abolition state, and two contiguous death penalty states, South Dakota and

**Figure 4-4.** *Annual Homicide Rates Before and After the Judicial Moratorium on Executions in North Dakota, Nebraska, and South Dakota*

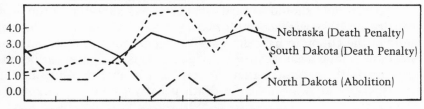

1963  1964  1965  1966  1967  1968  1969  1970  1971
*Source:* See source note Figure 4-1.

**Figure 4-5.** *Annual Homicide Rates Before and After the Judicial Moratorium on Executions in Oregon, Idaho, and Washington*

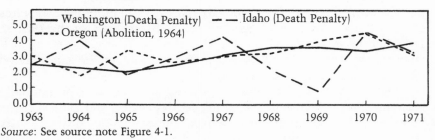

1963        1964        1965        1966        1967        1968        1969        1970        1971
*Source:* See source note Figure 4-1.

Nebraska. Like the less populous New England states, these three states show substantial fluctuations in homicide rates; but here again we find no evidence supporting the death penalty as a more effective deterrent. Note that during the period 1963 to 1967 the homicide rate for North Dakota dropped, while the corresponding rates of Nebraska and South Dakota increased. After the moratorium, however, North Dakota's homicide rate climbed gradually, while the rates for the two contiguous death penalty states display contrasting trends. Homicides in Nebraska rose slightly, while those in South Dakota generally, though irregularly, declined.

Figures 4-5 through 4-7 present three states that recently abolished the death penalty—Oregon (1964), New York (1965), and West Virginia (1965)—together with their respective contiguous death penalty states.

Figure 4-5 compares recently abolitionist Oregon with Washington and Idaho, both death penalty states. Comparison of these three states is difficult because of the relative instability of their homicide rates, but it does appear that all three states, irrespective of their mode of punishment, experienced similar homicide trends over the 1963–1971 period. The state showing the most stability in its trend, Washington, did experience a rising homicide rate after 1967, but this pattern clearly seems to have been established prior to the judicial moratorium.

Special note should be made that Oregon's abolition of the death penalty in 1964 was accomplished by public referendum—the only state in the Union to have done so—and consequently there was considerable public awareness of the change. This is significant because it bears on the argument that the residents in abolition jurisdictions are typically unaware that the death penalty cannot be imposed in their state.

With reference to Oregon's abolition of the death penalty, Figure 4-5 shows that homicide did increase in the year immediately after abolition but this rise was not much greater than the drop in homicide occurring the year before. Moreover, if the analysis is extended to include the three years prior to abolition (two of which do not appear in the graph), and the three years after (to the beginning of the judicial moratorium), Oregon's homicide rate increased no more than the rates of its two contiguous death penalty states. Its average for the 1961 to 1963 period was 2.9 and for 1965 to 1967, 3.1, an increase of 0.2; whereas the average for Washington and Idaho over the same period increased 0.2 and 0.6 respectively.

Figure 4-6 shows that West Virginia's homicide rate rose gradually between 1965 (when it abolished the death penalty) and 1967. Yet the increase was no greater than Virginia's, the contiguous death penalty state. After the judicial moratorium both states continued to show similar increases in homicide rates. In 1969 Virginia experienced a sharp drop in homicide; the following year Virginia's rate returned to its previous level. When the entire 1967 to 1971 period is considered, we find no evidence to suggest that Virginia's homicide rate had risen more than West Virginia's.

Figure 4-7 compares New York, which abolished the death penalty

**Figure 4-6.**  *Annual Homicide Rates Before and After the Judicial Moratorium on Executions in West Virginia and Virginia*

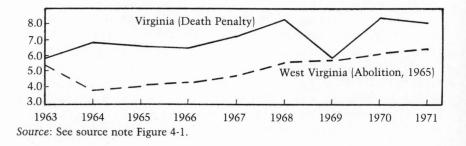

Source: See source note Figure 4-1.

**Figure 4-7.** *Annual Homicide Rates Before and After the Judicial Moratorium on Executions in New York, New Jersey, and Pennsylvania*

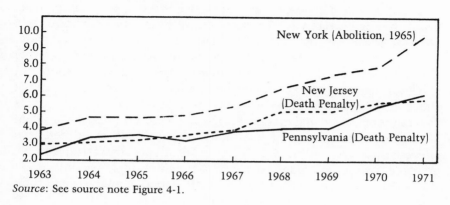

*Source*: See source note Figure 4-1.

**Figure 4-8.** *Annual Homicide Rates Before and After the Judicial Moratorium on Executions in Iowa, Minnesota, and Wisconsin*

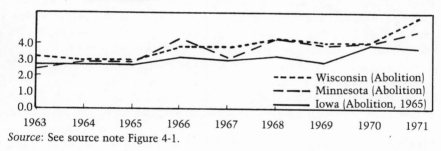

*Source*: See source note Figure 4-1.

in 1965, with Pennsylvania and New Jersey, both death penalty states. In the two years after New York's abolition, its homicide rate rose from 4.6 to 5.4, or a 17 percent increase, while the corresponding rates for New Jersey and Pennsylvania rose 22 percent and 9 percent respectively. This pattern continued in the year immediately after the moratorium. Starting in 1969, however, we find a more precipitous rise in New York's homicide rate than in either New Jersey's or Pennsylvania's—precisely the opposite of what we should expect if the death penalty were having a unique deterrent effect that was forfeited by the moratorium.

The final graph, Figure 4-8, contains the North Central states of Minnesota, Wisconsin, and Iowa. The first two are abolition states for the entire period, and the third, Iowa, abolished the death penalty in 1965. Since all three states had abolished the death penalty by 1967, we should not expect the moratorium to affect their homicide rates. However, we should expect Iowa, after its abolition in 1965, to exhibit an increase in homicide relative to Wisconsin and Minnesota (see proposition 3 above). The graph, however, reveals the opposite to be true. Iowa's homicide rate rose 0.5 between 1965 and 1971, whereas the rates for Wisconsin and Minnesota increased 1.3 and 1.0 respectively.

Our analysis to this point has uncovered no evidence suggesting that the death penalty is a more effective deterrent than imprisonment. However, chance fluctuations in the homicide rates of the individual states examined so far have, in some cases, made it difficult to assess the effects of the judicial moratorium. In order to minimize the problem of random instability and focus more specifically on the differential effect of the moratorium on abolition and death penalty states, we have prepared a summary graph in Figure 4-9, which includes only those states that were abolitionist for the entire period of analysis and their contiguous death penalty states (data from Figure 4-1 through 4-4 excluding Vermont in Figure 4-3).

The summary graph in Figure 4-9 shows the average homicide rates for states that abolished the death penalty for the entire 1963–1971 period and the average rates for their contiguous death penalty states. The graph supports our previous analysis of individual states. Notice that it is the abolition states that show a somewhat greater increase in homicide after the cessation of executions in 1967.

In summary, we can find no evidence to suggest that the death penalty is a uniquely deterrent form of punishment. With regard to the specific issue of the judicial moratorium, none of our findings supports the proposition that its de facto suspension in 1967 has been

**Figure 4-9.**  *Average Homicide Rates of Abolition States with Corresponding Contiguous Death Penalty States Examined in Figures 4-1 through 4-8*

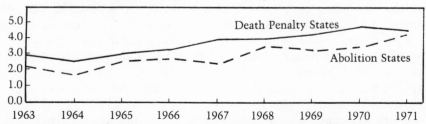

Note: Since each comparison of an abolition state with contiguous death penalty states was a unique test of the effect of the judicial moratorium, the average annual homicide rates in Figure 4-9 were not weighted according to state population. Where an abolition state had more than one contiguous death penalty state the homicide rates of the latter jurisdictions were averaged to provide single annual estimates. Finally, the values for Figures 4-5 through 4-8 and for Vermont from Figure 4-3 were omitted from this figure in order to avoid the possible confounding effects of recent abolition.

responsible for increasing homicide rates in those states which impose the death penalty.

One of the assumptions in the foregoing analysis, as we have noted, is that the effect of the death penalty will be felt primarily in the jurisdiction where it exists and is applied; hence, our inference that death penalty states would be more seriously affected than abolition states by the moratorium on executions. The various Canadian provinces all had the death penalty available prior to the nationwide experiment with abolition beginning in December 1967.

To show that rising homicide rates in the late 1960s in Canada were not a response to that nation's experiment with abolition, Professor E. A. Fattah (1972; Bowers 1974, Chapter 5) compared the trends in homicide with those for other serious crimes in Canada. The analysis revealed that in fact homicide rates increased at a slower pace than did the rates of other serious and violent crimes for which death was not an available punishment before the period of abolition began.

It is also instructive to turn briefly to national trends in homicide and other offenses in assessing the impact of the moratorium in the United States. Thus, in addition to comparing selected jurisdictions within the United States, Professor Wolfgang in his original analysis also examined the national pattern of homicide rates from 1963 to 1970 and compared it with the patterns for other major crimes over the same period. The following excerpt from his testimony before the House Subcommittee on the Judiciary summarizes his findings and presents his conclusions:

We have examined homicide rates in the United States four years prior to the judicial moratorium and four years subsequent to it. In general, during the past four years, the criminal homicide rate has increased at a slower pace than any of the seven major crimes in the crime index, according to the *Uniform Crime Reports* of the F.B.I. For all serious crimes (homicide, rape, robbery, aggravated assault and battery, burglary, larceny, auto theft) there was a 42.6 per cent increase between 1967–1970, but for criminal homicide there was only a 27.8 per cent increase. Moreover, the increase in the homicide rate from 1963 (4.5 per 100,000) to 1967 (6.1) was 35.5 per cent; while the increase from 1967 (6.1) to 1970 (7.8) was lower, or 27.8 per cent. In short, the rate of the incline of homicide was less in the four years since the judicial moratorium than before the judicial moratorium.

Wolfgang concludes his analysis:

In sum, there is no evidence to indicate that an additional two year moratorium by legislative enactment would have any untoward effect on the homicide rate . . . The absence of a moratorium would, however,

continue racially discriminatory and cruel and unusual sentencing and
application of the death penalty.

Thus, while it is true that Canada and the United States both
experienced rising homicide rates in the late 1960s, these rates increased at a slower pace than did the rates of other serious crimes for
which the death penalty was never available. It is also true that both
nations entered periods of reduced use and/or availability of the death
penalty in 1967, but it should be noted that a moratorium on executions
in Canada, comparable to the one in the United States, actually occurred with the last Canadian execution in 1962. If a moratorium on
executions were responsible for subsequently increasing levels of homicide, such increases should have occurred some five years earlier in
Canada than in the United States. The fact that increasing homicide
rates were closely associated with increasing levels of other major and
particularly violent crimes in Canada and the United States plainly
suggests that it is not the suspension or abolition of the death penalty,
but broader social forces contributing to violent criminal behavior that
account for the variations in criminal homicide rates in these two
contiguous nations.

## The Effect of Mandatory Capital Punishment

The Supreme Court's recent decisions in *Furman* v. *Georgia* and
related cases appear, at least to the advocates of capital punishment,
to leave the way open for the mandatory use of the death penalty.
Indeed, making the death penalty mandatory for selected offenses is
an approach now being advocated by proponents of a return to capital
punishment in America. Many see in the mandatory death sentence a
more powerful deterrent—one that, by contrast with discretionary capital punishment, ensures severe and certain punishment for convicted
offenders.

Our concern in this section is with the claim that the mandatory
death sentence has some deterrent advantage over the death penalty
applied at the discretion of judge or jury. If it does we should expect
to find a notable increase in homicide when states change from mandatory to discretionary use of the death penalty. Specifically, when
examining jurisdictions that have made a change from mandatory to
discretionary capital punishment and comparing them with contiguous
or similar jurisdictions that have not, we should expect the following
propositions to be true:

1.  States that made the change from mandatory to discretionary capital punishment should show higher levels of homicide in the period subsequent to the change than in the period that preceded it.
2.  Change states should show increasing homicide rates after the move to discretionary capital punishment relative to similar or contiguous jurisdictions that made no such change.
3.  Prior to the change, homicide rates in change states should roughly correspond with those in contiguous mandatory states and fall below those in contiguous discretionary states; after the change they should roughly correspond with those in contiguous discretionary states and exceed those in contiguous mandatory states.

When the examination of the mandatory death sentence was begun, as noted above, a complete list of the changes from mandatory to discretionary capital punishment was available only for those occurring since World War II. Information on the move to discretionary capital punishment for all states became available only recently (Garin 1973). With this newly compiled data, we have been able to extend our initial analysis to include four additional states that made the change before World War II. Since the analysis was developed in two distinct phases, we have found it convenient to present the data separately for the periods before and after the Second World War. Notably, this clearly distinguishes changes made during the period of decline in executions under state authority in America from those made during the growth and peak periods of state-imposed executions—a distinction that will, at least tentatively, reveal whether the effect of the mandatory death sentence was contingent upon the historical period in the administration of capital punishment during which it was used.

*After World War II*

Figures 4-10 through 4-14 present homicide rates for six states and the District of Columbia, which have recently changed from a mandatory to a discretionary application of capital punishment for murder. Each graph shows homicide rates for the year the change occurred, for the four years immediately preceding the change and for the four years immediately following it. For each change state the graph also shows one or more contiguous states, and for the District of Columbia it shows a nearby city of comparable size that experienced no such change over the same years.

Figure 4-10 presents North Carolina, the first state to change its statute after World War II. There was clearly no increase in homicide rates after the change to discretionary capital punishment in North Carolina; its rate actually decreased the second year after the change, but this was followed by a return to the previous level in the next year.

**Figure 4-10.** *Annual Homicide Rates under Mandatory and*
*Discretionary Sentencing in North Carolina and*
*South Carolina*

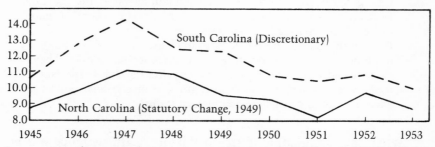

*Sources*: Annual state population estimates 1945 through 1960 from Public Health Ser-
vice, Department of Health, Education and Welfare, *Vital Statistics Rates in the United
States: 1940–1960* (1968). Annual state population estimates 1961 through 1967 from
Bureau of Census, U.S. Department of Commerce, *Statistical Abstract of the United
States* (Annual). Number of homicides for each state 1945 to 1967 from Bureau of Census,
United States Department of Commerce, *Vital Statistics of the United States* (Annual,
1937 to 1945) from 1946 to present published by the Public Health Service, Department
of Health, Education and Welfare.

**Figure 4-11.** *Annual Homicide Rates under Mandatory and*
*Discretionary Sentencing in Connecticut,*
*Massachusetts, New Hampshire, and Rhode Island*

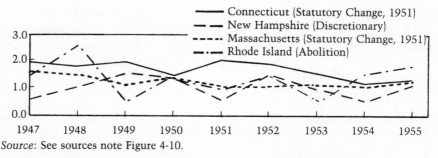

*Source*: See sources note Figure 4-10.

Contiguous South Carolina had consistently higher homicide rates
both before and after the change; indeed its trend in homicide rates
throughout this period was quite similar to that of North Carolina.
There is little if anything in this graph to suggest that the mandatory
death sentence in North Carolina had a greater deterrent effect on
homicide than the discretionary form of sentencing that followed it.

In 1951 two states, Massachusetts and Connecticut (shown in Figure 4-11) changed from mandatory to discretionary death sentences.
Massachusetts experienced remarkable stability of its homicide rate
after the change, and Connecticut actually had a decline in homicide
rate after the change. The two relevant contiguous states, New Hampshire and Rhode Island, showed much more instability, and in Rhode

Island the homicide rate rose relative to the other states a couple years after the change in Connecticut and Massachusetts. Clearly, the statutory changes in Connecticut and Massachusetts did not result in increasing homicide rates, nor even an increase relative to their contiguous states.

A third New England state, Vermont, shown in Figure 4-12, changed to discretionary capital punishment in 1957. The following year the homicide rate increased, only to decrease for the next two years and increase again in the fourth year after the change. Contiguous New Hampshire's annual rates showed a similar instability, although increases and decreases tended to occur in different years. Such instability of homicide rates weakens any suggestion that Vermont's increase in homicide in 1958 is evidence of deterrence, especially in view of the fact that Vermont's rate subsequently dropped to the lowest point on the graph during the next two years.

The legally distinct jurisdiction of Washington, D.C., shown in Figure 4-13, changed from mandatory to discretionary death sentencing in 1962. For purposes of comparison, we have chosen the nearby city of Baltimore. Both cities experienced sharply increasing homicide rates, especially for the critical year of 1962. For Washington, D.C., the sharpest rise came in the second year after the change, while for Baltimore the sharpest increases were in the first and fourth years after the change. In fact, in the four years after 1962, Baltimore's homicide rate increased more than did Washington's. Thus, we find nothing to suggest that the increase in Washington's homicide rate could be a result of the change.

New York, presented in Figure 4-14, was the last state to adopt discretionary capital punishment for first degree murder, doing so in 1963. New York's homicide rate did increase a bit more sharply after the critical year of 1963, yet the pattern of changing homicide rates over the critical years was not much different from that of contiguous Pennsylvania. And indeed, in 1965 New York actually abolished the death penalty entirely, yet only a relatively small increase in homicide rate occurs after 1965 and the homicide rates of contiguous Pennsyl-

**Figure 4-12.** *Annual Homicide Rates under Mandatory and Discretionary Sentencing in Vermont and New Hampshire*

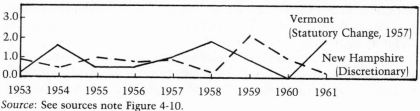

*Source*: See sources note Figure 4-10.

**Figure 4-13.** *Annual Homicide Rates under Mandatory and Discretionary Sentencing in Washington, D.C., and Baltimore, MD.*

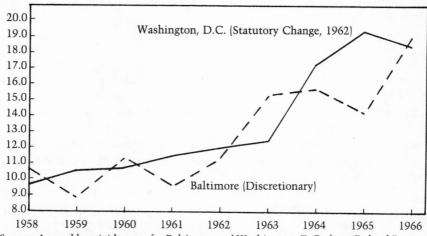

*Source*: Annual homicide rates for Baltimore and Washington, D.C., from Federal Bureau of Investigation, *Uniform Crime Reports* (Annual).

**Figure 4-14.** *Annual Homicide Rates under Mandatory and Discretionary Sentencing in New York, New Jersey, and Pennsylvania*

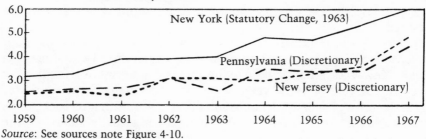

*Source*: See sources note Figure 4-10.

vania and New Jersey also increase. It may be significant that in the postmandatory death penalty period for New York, the homicide rate increases somewhat more rapidly than that of Pennsylvania or New Jersey, for the difference between them is greater in 1967 than in 1963. Yet, examination of the years before 1963 shows that this trend began *before* the statute change. Thus, as evidence for a deterrent effect of mandatory death sentences, this trend is unconvincing.

There is little evidence of a deterrent effect of the mandatory death penalty on homicide rates in the six jurisdictions we have examined. Figure 4-15 shows the average homicide rates for all six jurisdictions

**Figure 4-15.**   *Average Homicide Rates for Six Jurisdictions Examined
in Figures 4-10 through 4-14*

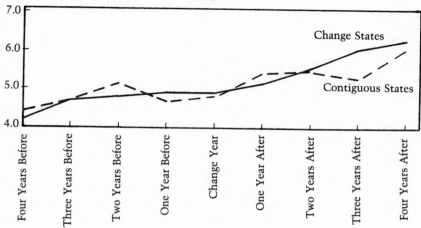

*Note*: The average annual homicide rates for statutory change jurisdictions and also for
their contiguous nonchange jurisdictions were not weighted according to jurisdiction
population. Where a statutory change jurisdiction had more than one contiguous nonchange jurisdiction the homicide rates of the latter jurisdictions were averaged to provide
single annual estimates.

for the year of the change, for four years preceding the change, and for
four years after the change. Both change and contiguous states show
increased average homicide rates after the change from mandatory to
discretionary death penalties. Only in the third year after the change
did they differ greatly, and here, if the two cities of Washington and
Baltimore were removed from the calculations (as cities with very high
homicide rates, they have a strong effect on the summary graph), the
average homicide rates would be the same for change and contiguous
states.

   In summary, the pattern of change in homicide rates of states that
changed their statute from mandatory to discretionary death sentences
is very much like the pattern in their contiguous states. If homicide
rates increased in change states, they increased in contiguous states.
Where homicide rates were unstable, they were so in both change and
contiguous states, and in one case—Connecticut—the homicide rate
actually decreased, while contiguous Rhode Island's homicide rate increased. Finally, as Figure 4-15 shows, when all six jurisdictions are
considered together there was no notable increase in homicide rates
in change states that did not also occur in their contiguous states
(although not always in the same year.) In short, we find no consistent
evidence that the mandatory death penalty was a superior deterrent in
the post-World War II period.

*Before World War II*

The graphs in this subsection present homicide rates for four states that changed from mandatory to discretionary capital punishment prior to the Second World War. Our analysis has been limited by the fact that mortality statistics, including deaths by homicide, were not collected by the Census Bureau before 1900. Since the turn of the century, such statistics have become available for an increasing number of states as they met the death registration standards of the Census Bureau. The last state to meet these standards was Texas in 1933. (For admission dates to the Census Bureau's death registration system, see Bureau of Census, *Vital Statistics of the United States: 1900–1940*, 1943.)

In all, some nine states changed from mandatory to discretionary capital punishment at a time when they were registering homicide data with the Census Bureau. Four of these states—Maryland, Washington, Virginia, and Oregon—were not included in the analysis because in no case were homicide data available for more than two years prior to their statutory changes. And one state—Vermont—was excluded because it made two statutory changes within a span of two years (i.e., to discretionary capital punishment in 1911 and back to the mandatory death penalty in 1913)—too short a time interval to permit a reliable analysis of the effects of either change. For three of the remaining states—New Jersey, Pennsylvania, and New Mexico—homicide rates are available for four years before and after the change and for corresponding periods in contiguous nonchange states. For New Hampshire, rates are available three years before the change and four years after.

New Mexico, shown in Figure 4-16, was the last state to change from mandatory to discretionary capital punishment prior to World War II, doing so in 1939. The relevant years surrounding New Mexico's statutory change—1935 to 1943—were a period of generally declining homicide in the United States, and, as the graph suggests, New Mexico and its contiguous state, Arizona, follow this national trend. Apart from broader secular trends, however, we would expect New Mexico's homicide rate to increase relative to Arizona's rate afer 1939—if New Mexico's change to discretionary capital punishment resulted in any weakening of constraints against homicide. Examination of the graph shows precisely the opposite. After New Mexico's change to discretionary capital punishment its homicide rate actually decreases relative to Arizona's rate.

In 1925 Pennsylvania changed from mandatory to discretionary death sentencing. As shown in Figure 4-17, Pennsylvania's homicide rate actually decreased after its statutory change, but this trend may have been established before 1925. Of the two relevant contiguous states,

**Figure 4-16.** *Annual Homicide Rates under Mandatory and Discretionary Sentencing in New Mexico and Arizona*

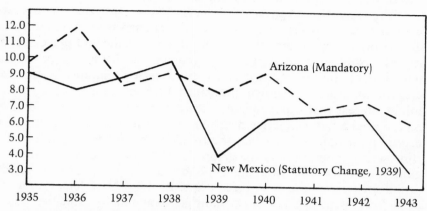

*Sources*: Annual state population estimates from Bureau of the Census, Department of Commerce, *Vital Statistics Rates in the United States: 1900–1940* (1943), and *Vital Statistics Rates in the United States: 1940–1960* (1968). Annual number of homicides for each state, 1900 to 1936, from Bureau of the Census, Department of Commerce, *Mortality Statistics* (Annual prior to 1937). Annual number of state homicides for 1937 to 1943 from Bureau of the Census, United States Department of Commerce, *Vital Statistics of the United States* (Annual, 1937 to 1945).

**Figure 4-17.** *Annual Homicide Rates under Mandatory and Discretionary Sentencing in Pennsylvania, New Jersey, and New York*

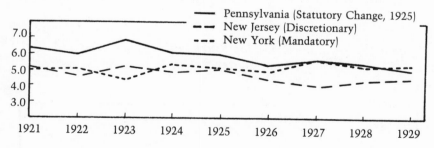

*Source*: See sources note Figure 4-16.

New York had mandatory capital punishment for the period under investigation and New Jersey had discretionary death sentencing. The homicide trends of these two states are contrasting. New Jersey's rate declined but not as much as Pennsylvania's rate, whereas New York's homicide rate showed an absolute as well as relative increase. In other words, the change to discretionary capital punishment in Pennsylvania was accompanied by a *decline* in its homicide rate in absolute terms and relative to both mandatory and discretionary contiguous states.

The same three states—New Jersey, New York, and Pennsylvania—also serve to test the effects of the change from mandatory to discretionary capital punishment at a different time and place. Thus, in 1916 New Jersey moved from mandatory to discretionary capital punishment. In the following year New Jersey's homicide rate increased noticeably, as shown in Figure 4-18. Such an increase by itself might suggest that the mandatory death penalty, at least in this case, represented a more effective deterrent to homicide than discretionary capital punishment. However, the trends in homicide over the entire time series represented in the graph—1912 to 1920—discount this argument. Notice that after the 1917 increase New Jersey's homicide rate decreases for the next three years. By 1920 New Jersey's rate is again lower than either of its two contiguous and then-mandatory death penalty states, having returned to the approximate level exhibited prior to New Jersey's statutory change.

Further comparison of New Jersey with its contiguous states shows that Pennsylvania, which made no statutory change during this period, also experienced a sharp increase in homicide about the same time as (a year prior to) New Jersey. Moreover, Pennsylvania's increase is relatively sustained while New Jersey's is not. In comparison, New Jersey's increase seems like a chance departure from its normal level, whereas Pennsylvania's increase appears to be a more permanent trend.

The final graph, Figure 4-19, compares New Hampshire, which changed to discretionary sentencing in 1903, with two contiguous states, Maine and Vermont. Maine was abolitionist for the entire period under

**Figure 4-18.** *Annual Homicide Rates under Mandatory and Discretionary Sentencing in New Jersey, New York, and Pennsylvania*

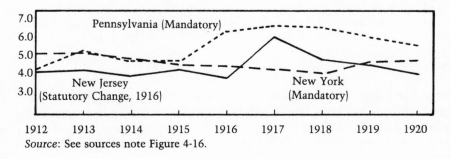

*Source*: See sources note Figure 4-16.

**Figure 4-19.** *Annual Homicide Rates under Mandatory and Discretionary Sentencing in New Hampshire, Maine, and Vermont*

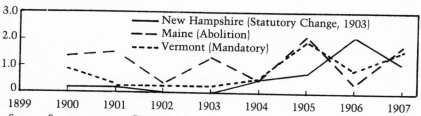

Source: See sources note Figure 4-16.

Note: Homicide data not available from the *Mortality Statistics* of the Census before 1900.

analysis—1900 to 1907—and Vermont was a mandatory death penalty state.

All three states exhibited their highest homicide levels after New Hampshire's statutory change. Notice, moreover, that in the two years immediately following New Hampshire's change, Vermont and Maine are the states that show the increase in homicide. New Hampshire's rate does rise sharply in 1906—three years after its change—but only to drop again below the level of its contiguous states in 1907.

Thus, in this period before World War II, when the use of the death penalty was relatively more common and states had not yet begun to show signs of reluctance to execute, we again find no evidence that the mandatory death penalty had greater deterrent power than discretionary capital punishment. Indeed, a summary of these four cases averaged and shown in the graph in Figure 4-20 shows that change states have on the average had generally lower homicide rates relative to their contiguous states after the change from mandatory to discretionary capital punishment. Thus, for all change states on which adequate homicide data are available both before and after the Second World War, we must unequivocally reject the claim that mandatory death sentencing has any deterrent advantage over the discretionary use of capital punishment.

## Conclusions, Qualifications, and Implications

Simply stated, there is no evidence in the foregoing analysis that the moratorium on executions in the United States contributed to an increasing level of homicide in this country nor that the mandatory application of the death penalty had any greater deterrent effectiveness than its discretionary use. The evidence is remarkably consistent. Vir-

**Figure 4-20.**  *Average Homicide Rates for Four Jurisdictions Examined in Figures 4-16 through 4-19*

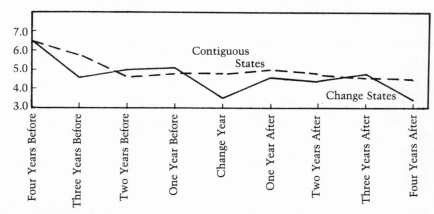

*Note*: The average annual homicide rates for statutory change jurisdictions and also their contiguous nonchange jurisdictions were not weighted according to jurisdiction population. Where more than one contiguous nonchange jurisdiction existed their annual homicide rates were averaged to provide single annual estimates.

tually none of the specific comparisons suggests a deterrent advantage for the use of capital punishment over imprisonment or for mandatory sentencing over discretionary capital punishment. In this respect, our findings are fully consistent with the results of previous research on the deterrent power of the death penalty. Indeed, the words of Thorsten Sellin are appropriate by way of summary:

> Any one who carefully examined the above data is bound to arrive at the conclusion that the death penalty, as we use it, exerts no influence on the extent or fluctuating rates of capital offenses (Sellin 1959, 63).

For the sake of precision, we should add that we are speaking of the death penalty relative to other punishments and one form of the death penalty relative to another, and that our results apply only to homicide—which is, after all, the capital offense for which nine out of ten executions have been performed throughout this century in America.

## On the Judicial Moratorium

Our examination of the moratorium's impact is exhaustive in the sense that it includes all abolition states together with appropriate contiguous death penalty states during the relevant period. Admittedly, the nationwide moratorium on executions is only one aspect—the final phase—in the use of capital punishment. Thus, most of the death penalty states (all except California and Colorado) stopped executing capital offenders before 1967, the majority of them before 1963. (Table 2-1 gives the date of last execution for all death penalty states.) It would be a relatively simple matter to apply this level of analysis to the point at which each state no longer executed capital offenders, thus providing a jurisdictional specific assessment of the cessation of executions.

Apart from the cessation of executions, there is also the effect of the declining use of the death penalty. This may be conceived as a question of the extent to which year-to-year variations in the level of executions cause opposing fluctuations in homicide rates. Two investigations (Ohio Legislative Service Commission 1961; Schuessler 1952) have dealt specifically with homicide rates as a function of prior fluctuations in executions and neither one finds evidence of deterrence. Moreover, the fact that the number of executions in this country has declined steadily during the last thirty years, while homicide rates have remained relatively constant throughout this period (National Commission on the Causes and Prevention of Violence, Mulvihill and Tumin 1969, 54) indicates that the year-to-year decline in executions did not produce a corresponding increase in homicides.

In the face of this evidence against shorter term, jurisdictionally specific deterrent effects of capital punishment, some advocates of the death penalty may be tempted to argue that its deterrent power will be evident only in the long run impact of the decline, cessation, and abolition of capital punishment. Indeed, the recent rise in homicide rates after abandonment and abolition in the United States and Canada might be taken by some as an indication that the death penalty has a potent but indirect deterrent effect—one that is prolonged, pervasive, and generalized in character. Thus, advocates might be tempted to advance the following argument: (1) capital punishment has a *prolonged* or relatively *longlasting* effect, so that the decline in executions will be followed by an increase in capital crimes only some years or decades after the decline has begun; (2) the effect of the death penalty is *pervasive* within a nation: its availability and use in *most* jurisdictions of a country will tend to reinforce the beliefs of citizens in *all* jurisdictions that the behavior in question is truly abhorrent and totally unacceptable; (3) the deterrent effect of the death penalty is *generalized* to all major forms of criminal behavior, including both capital and lesser offenses—it shows that society "means business" in combatting crime across the boards.

In other words, advocates might argue that the long-term decline and eventual abandonment of capital punishment has tended to undermine respect for law and legal authority and to remove an important support for the community's condemnation of criminality, which, in turn, would result in an increase in criminal behavior of all kinds in all jurisdictions once the demise of capital punishment has become a widely recognized fact.

But this argument is suspect even in terms of the evidence we have examined on Canada and the United States. It depends on a very recent upturn in crime rates in both countries that may be only temporary and that could very well be the result of other sociocultural developments. Furthermore, while crime rates (including the incidence of homicide) began to rise precipitously about the same time in both countries, Canada abolished its death penalty five years before the *Furman* decision, and its last execution occurred in 1962, five years prior to the cessation of executions in the United States.

More pointedly, the proper test for the argument that the death penalty may have prolonged, pervasive, and generalized deterrent effects lies in examining the experiences of a number of nations that have abandoned capital punishment for extended periods before and after the transition, not in comparing jurisdictions within nations for relatively brief periods before and after the cessation of executions. When we turn to the experience of other nations, the evidence is much less ambiguous. For instance, Sweden and the Netherlands experienced no precipitous rise or sustained increase in homicide rates after decline, cessation, and/or abolition of capital punishment (Schuessler 1952). The same holds for Belgium, Austria, Switzerland, and Norway (Ancel 1962), and for a host of other nations reviewed in Bowers 1974, Chapter 5 (and discussed in more detail in Canada, Department of Solicitor General 1972, Part I).

In summary, our examination of the national moratorium on executions in the United States, together with the existing evidence on short- and long-term effects of the decline in capital punishment, clearly disputes the claim that the death penalty exercises some constraining effect on homicide rates, above and beyond that of other punishments imposed as alternatives. Unless or until subsequent investigations show quite different results from the consistent evidence thus far accumulated, we must conclude that the declining use of the death penalty, in its various aspects, bears no consistent relationship to the incidence of homicide.

## On the Mandatory Death Penalty

Our investigation of the mandatory death sentence has included all jurisdictions for which homicide rates are available for at least three years before and after the change from mandatory to discretionary capital punishment for murder. Among some ten jurisdictions that made this change both before and after the Second World War and their contiguous nonchange jurisdictions, we have found no indication that the mandatory death penalty was a more effective deterrent of homicide than discretionary capital punishment.

Belief in the mandatory death sentence as a unique deterrent rests on the assumption that it will increase the certainty of execution for capital offenders and that this increased risk of execution will create the impression among prospective offenders that their chances of escaping death as a punishment for such crimes are less. The evidence in Chapter 3 suggests that the mandatory death penalty may indeed increase the risk of execution for capital crimes. In particular, Table 3-10 shows that the number of executions was about 30 percent greater, on the average, under mandatory than under discretionary sentencing in states that imposed executions under both forms of capital punishment.

Yet the risk of execution for capital offenses is really quite low. A precise estimate of the certainty of execution for capitally punishable murder in the United States as a whole is unavailable because the officially published statistics group together homicides that qualify as capital offenses with those that do not. Previous studies have found, however, that capital murders represent from 15 percent in Philadelphia (Wolfgang 1958) to 25 percent in Cleveland (Bensing and Schroeder 1960) of the officially reported homicides. Using the more conservative of these two estimates, Professor Bedau (1967b, 36) has figured that the ratio of executions to capitally punishable homicides in the United States was about 1 to 10 for the period from 1930 to 1960, and about 1 to 16 for the decade of the 1950s.[1]

Thus, an increase of 30 percent, or even 50 percent, in the chances of execution under the mandatory death penalty would mean only an increase from 10 to 13 or 15 percent in the number of capitally punishable offenders who are actually executed. Such an increase is apt to be perceptible only to those who perform the executions and keep the statistics, certainly not to potential offenders as they become involved in the sequence of events leading to a capital crime.

Furthermore, no investigations to date have established or even suggested that variations in the certainty of execution, at least within the range experienced in this country in recent years, have had any effect on homicide rates. Thus, an examination of homicide rates and execution risk for eleven states from 1930 through 1949 found that fluctuations in execution risk were not consistently followed by opposing movements in the level of homicide: "The homicide rate and the execution risk as time series move independently of one another" (Schuessler 1952, 397). And a study of variations in execution and

---

1. These two ratios are transposed in Bedau's (1967b, 36) text, but the data from which they have been derived make their reference clear.

homicide rates for a fifty-year period in Ohio similarly gave no indication that prior fluctuations in the rate of execution affected subsequent levels of homicide (Ohio Legislative Service Commission 1961).

But beyond this, making the death penalty compulsory may reduce
the likelihood that indicted offenders will be convicted. For some time,
observers have reported that juries are less willing to convict when the
death penalty is available or required, and some have offered tentative
documentation of this tendency (Shipley 1910; Bye 1919).

Previous studies of two of the states we have examined above—
Massachusetts and North Carolina—for periods when the death penalty was mandatory revealed quite low conviction rates. The data on
eight counties in Massachusetts for the period from 1925 through 1941
(H. Ehrmann 1952, especially Tables 1 and 2) show that only 8 percent
of those indicted for murder were actually convicted of first degree
murder (which then carried the mandatory death sentence); in fact, in
seven of these eight counties (excluding Middlesex) only 3 percent were
convicted of first degree murder. It is true that the overwhelming majority—84 percent—of the convicted first degree murderers were eventually executed (four of twenty-five had their sentences commuted).
But with a conviction rate of 8 percent, this means that only 7 percent
of those indicted for murder were actually executed under the mandatory death penalty in Massachusetts during this period.

A more detailed analysis of ten counties in North Carolina for the
period from 1930 through 1940 (Garfinkel 1949, especially Tables 2
and 3) shows that 5 percent of those indicted for murder and 10 percent
of those prosecuted specifically on first degree murder charges were
convicted on such charges (for which the death sentence was mandatory). It also appears (Johnson 1957, Tables 1 and 7) that 60 percent at
most of the first degree murderers admitted to death row during this
period had their death sentences carried out. From these figures it
follows that in North Carolina between 1930 and 1940 only about 6
percent of those prosecuted on first degree murder charges and only
about 3 percent of all those indicted for murder were eventually
executed.

We also have no indication that making the death penalty mandatory would eliminate or even reduce racial discrimination in the
administration of capital punishment. Indeed, the evidence in Chapter
3 on states that have imposed the death penalty under both mandatory
and discretionary sentencing shows racial differences in age at execution and in appeals prior to execution for every state under the mandatory death sentence.

Thus, although we have no empirical evidence that the mandatory
death penalty is superior to discretionary sentencing as a deterrent to
murder, we have seen that it has been associated with higher levels of

execution, with comparable levels of racial discrimination, and, very likely, with reduced levels of capital convictions. In view of this evidence, it would appear that the adoption of the mandatory death penalty would mean a greater sacrifice of human life, continued discrimination against blacks, and the inability to convict some guilty offenders—all without deterrent benefit.

## Implications

In a sense, the two issues of this chapter—the moratorium on executions and the mandatory death sentence—focus attention on extremes in the debate over the deterrent effects of capital punishment. The moratorium raises the question of what happens when capital punishment finally *disappears* in practice, and the mandatory death sentence points to the issue of what it would take to make unique deterrent effects *appear*. The fact that neither the moratorium on executions nor the mandatory death sentence had discernible effects on homicide rates holds implications for the kinds of arguments proponents can be expected to advance and for the forms of capital punishment that can be expected to achieve unique deterrent effects.

In the face of the mounting evidence against any deterrent advantage of the death penalty, proponents increasingly find themselves affirming more idiosyncratic explanations for the effects they presume the death penalty has but that research has yet to reveal. In effect, they are forced to fashion arguments that depend on alleged faults in the existing research or are not directly contradicted by the growing empirical evidence against deterrence. With each new set of findings their task becomes more arduous and their arguments less plausible.

The other implication is that for the death penalty to have unique deterrent effects, a form of capital punishment may be required that would be objectionable to even its more ardent proponents—something more arbitrary and excessive than we have yet experienced. And, of course, such use of the death penalty would violate constitutional guarantees of due process and protections against cruel and unusual punishment, not to mention public acceptance. The irony is evident: it is not the absence of the death penalty but its presence, sufficient to be a unique deterrent, that would, in the long run, surely undermine the legal order.

# 5

## CAPITAL PUNISHMENT IN PERSPECTIVE

Death has been justified as an appropriate retribution and a necessary deterrent for the crimes that most offend the public conscience. Yet in practice we find no evidence of its alleged unique deterrent power, and we observe that as retribution it has been contingent on the offender's race and that of his victim. And we have seen that, paradoxically, *the death penalty has been most widely prescribed and imposed where its use has departed most conspicuously from standards of just retribution and effective deterrence.* That is, in the South, where most executions have occurred, its retributive justification is obviously questionable in view of its discriminatory application, and its deterrent power is plainly doubtful in view of the relatively high rates of criminal homicide. Could it be that the death penalty has other functions in society that outweigh those of retribution and deterrence and that govern where and when it will be most widely employed?

The evidence of racial discrimination in the administration of capital punishment suggests that the death penalty may have served as an instrument of *minority group oppression*: to keep blacks in the South in a position of subjugation and subservience. The fact that the death penalty for rape has been imposed primarily on blacks whose victims were white suggests that the death penalty has been used as an instrument of *majority group protection*: to secure the integrity of the white community in the face of threats or perceived challenges from blacks. In the maintenance of a caste system of relations between the races, these two extralegal functions would appear to be quite closely related, but they are distinguishable and may be relatively independent functions of capital punishment in other times and places.

The fact that executions in America rose to a high point during the economic depression of the 1930s suggests that the death penalty may have served as a *repressive response* to conditions of social dislocation and turmoil in that time of economic hardship. It is true that the incidence of homicide increased during this period, but the increase in executions was even more substantial: the *execution rate* peaked in this period (see Table 1-4). Perhaps the more frequent use of the death penalty served to relieve public anxiety about high or rising offense rates. (For a further elaboration of these and related functions, see Bowers 1973.)

Is it not possible that such extralegal functions as majority group protection, minority group oppression, and repressive response are more fundamental to the use of capital punishment in society than are the legal functions of retribution and deterrence—that they dictate where and when the death penalty will be most widely used and that they cause the legal functions of capital punishment to be displaced and compromised? Perhaps an examination of the use of the death penalty at other times and places will help to answer some of these questions and thereby furnish a broader perspective on the functions and effects of the death penalty in society.

## Historical Perspective

The death penalty has an ancient history. The best known of all executions—those of Socrates and Jesus—were performed in the ancient world. The impression, however, that capital punishment was particularly favored or common among ancient or primitive peoples appears to be mistaken. The death penalty fell into disuse during the time of the Roman Republic and, indeed, it was subject to many of the same challenges voiced in modern parliamentary debates (Green 1929; reprinted in Sellin 1967a).[1]

Ironically, the widespread adoption and use of capital punishment in the Western world came with the ascendency of the Christendom in the Middle Ages. The pre-Christian Barbaric Codes contained fewer crimes and milder punishments in general than did the codes of the

---

1. In the later years of the Roman Empire, from about the third through the fifth centuries A.D., the death penalty came into wider use as the Empire expanded to include an increasingly heterogeneous population and as disturbances and disruptions grew among the subject peoples (Sorokin 1937, vol. 2, 611 ff).

twelfth and thirteenth centuries in Western Europe (Sorokin 1937, vol. 2, 584 ff., esp. Table 42). The Middle Ages was, of course, a period of profound change in Western Europe, involving the reconstruction of society under the authority of the Catholic Church. Many of the laws that entered the criminal codes during the Middle Ages provided stricter regulation of family relations and enforced conformity with religious rites and observances. They appear to have encouraged the transfer of allegiances from local, communal, and kinship ties to broader political entities (Cohen 1969) and to have buttressed the dominant position of the Church in medieval society.

Even more ironically, the most gruesome and torturous forms of execution were invented under religious auspices. The rack, the wheel, the iron maiden, burning at the stake, and impaling in the grave are but a few of the diabolical methods devised and employed in the name of religion to cause protracted suffering before death. Such tortures were devised especially for the heretic and were justified as a means of extracting confession and repentance and thus holding out the possibility of salvation. Thus, during a period of religious hegemony in which the church represented the ultimate authority in society and the primary basis for social organization, capital punishment was conspicuously used for religious crimes, especially those tending to challenge or undermine established religious authority.

Witches were the folk counterparts to heretics, and they too were subjected to capital punishment by torturous means including burning, drowning, stoning, staking through the heart, and others. Although claims that as many as 200,000 witches were executed throughout Europe in the fourteenth and fifteenth centuries appear to be exaggerated (Sellin 1950), the recurrent reports of witch burnings during this period undoubtedly reflect the power of religion to sponsor the deaths of those who were suspected of religious deviation.

The religious basis for capital punishment was clearly evident in the "Capital Laws" of Massachusetts circa 1641. The first three capital crimes to be named were offenses against religion (Haskins 1956):

1. If any man after legall conviction, shall have or worship any other God, but the Lord God, he shall be put to death. *Deut.* 13.6, &c. and 17.2 &c. *Exodus* 22.20.
2. If any man or woman be a Witch, that is, hath or consulteth with a familiar spirit, they shall be put to death. *Exod.* 22.18, *Lev.* 20.27, *Deut.* 18.10,11.
3. If any person shall blaspheme the Name of God the Father, Sonne, or Holy Ghost, with direct, expresse, presumptuous, or high-handed blasphemy, or shall curse God in the like manner, he shall be put to death. *Lev.* 24.15,16.

And indeed, biblical authority was cited for each of the remaining twelve capital crimes, which included murder (premeditated, passionate, or guileful), rape (of a minor or married woman, though execution was discretionary in the case of an unmarried female), bestiality, homosexuality, adultery, kidnapping, false witness, and treason.

In view of these statutes it was hardly surprising that theocratic Massachusetts responded to the religious independence of the Quakers with the severely repressive "Quaker Laws" and with capital punishment for banished Quakers who returned to the Bay Colony. And it was essentially the challenge, or at least the perceived threat, to religious authority in Massachusetts of the witchcraft epidemic in Salem that led to the relatively widespread use of capital punishment against alien and deviant elements in the community (Erickson 1966).

With the demise of religious hegemony in Europe and the rise of national monarchies in about the fourteenth century, the number of offenses in the criminal codes again increased, and the prescribed punishments appear to have become even more severe on the average (Sorokin 1937, vol. 2, 584 ff., esp. Table 42). Furthermore, this change from medieval to early modern times showed another substantial change in the structure of the criminal laws, with political crimes displacing religious ones, particularly on the list of capital offenses. Death was still the punishment for those who challenged the basis of authority in society, but the secular state had displaced the church as the authority that might be offended.

The state rivaled the church in devising ungodly and grotesque methods of execution for those who committed crimes against the primary authority. And such punishment was the executioner's duty as late as 1812 when seven men convicted of high treason were sentenced as follows:

> That you and each of you, be taken to the place from whence you came, and from thence be drawn on a hurdle to the place of execution, where you shall be hanged by the neck not till you are dead; that you be severally taken down, while yet alive, and your bowels be taken out and burned before your faces—that your heads be then cut off, and your bodies cut into four quarters, to be at the king's disposal. And God have mercy on your souls (quoted in Scott 1950, 179).

The purpose of such a ghastly execution for political crimes was surely not so much to test the beliefs of the victim as to eliminate him and to dissuade his followers from their pretensions to political power. The risk of escape and renewed political challenge, particularly at a time of political instability, was evidently experienced as a more immediate danger than the possibility of creating a martyr.

Notably, executions appear to have reached their highest level in English history during the period of turmoil and political consolidation that followed Henry VIII's break with the religious domination of the papacy. The number of executions annually is believed to have quadrupled after Henry's break with the Catholic Church; an estimated 560 executions were performed each year in London and Middlesex alone in the last eleven years of Henry's reign and for the six-year reign of Edward VI (Radzinowicz 1948, vol. 1, 142, note 20). Thereafter, the number of executions appears to have declined rather steadily until the last half of the eighteenth century, when executions in London and Middlesex rose to a less auspicious 100 per year for a brief period in the 1780s (Radzinowicz 1948, vol. 1, 147).

Struggles for control of the state at other times and places have also led to the widespread use of capital punishment. In twentieth-century Russia, for example, the unsuccessful Revolution of 1905–1907 brought with it an enormous increase in the use of the death penalty. In the years from 1881 through 1905 there were ordinarily no more than twenty executions per year in Russia. Then, as the revolution got under way, the annual number of executions increased to 547, 1,139, and 1,340 during 1906, 1907, and 1908 respectively. In the next three years, 1909–1911, as the revolutionary activity subsided, the numbers of executions dropped to 717, 129, and 73 (figures reported by Gernet 1915; cited in Sorokin 1937, vol. 2, 601). Concerning the successful Russian Revolution of 1917, Sorokin (1937, vol. 2, 601) has written:

> According to the most conservative estimate, which certainly understates the real number, during the years 1917 to 1922, at least 600,000 (!) persons were executed. The executions during the subsequent years, especially from 1929 to 1935, have also to be counted by the tens of thousands.

Even much more superficial internal political disturbances appear to have been accompanied by increased numbers of executions. Thus, Gernet (1915, 75–76; in Sorokin 1937, vol. 2, 603) quotes an observer of nineteenth-century France who has noted that:

> . . . under any new political regime the number of the death penalty verdicts was greater at the beginning of the new regime, during the first years of its existence, than later on. Thus, the Consulate begins with 605 death verdicts in 1803, while in 1813 the number is only 325, that is, twice less; the Restoration in 1816 starts with 514 death penalties; later on this figure falls to 91. The July Monarchy makes its debut with 108 death penalties in 1831 and ends with 65 in 1847; the Napoleonic Monarchy (Napoleon III) had the greatest number of the death penalties in 1854 (79); in its last year of existence the number was only 11. Finally,

the decrease of death penalties from 1871, when the Republic was established, to the end of the 19th century is evident.

The use of the death penalty to consolidate power and eliminate political adversaries has become institutionalized in the form of "political purges" that often follow both successful and attempted revolutions. The revolutionaries and the *ancien regime* simply change places as victim and executioner depending on the outcome of the attempted revolution. Likewise, the victors in war often execute vanquished leaders after "war crime trials" such as those conducted by the Allies at Nuremberg. Domestic traitors, too, may be executed after "conspiracy trials," as happened in France, Finland, and Austria after the Second World War. The United States also has executed domestic political criminals, including Benedict Arnold, the Lincoln conspirators, Sacco and Vanzetti, and the Rosenbergs, during and after its major wars.

### Eighteenth-century England

With the development of commerce and industry in England, the number of capital offenses expanded from eight major crimes at the end of the fifteenth century (high treason, petty treason, murder, larceny, robbery, burglary, rape, and arson) to some 223 offenses by 1819, according to one estimate (as reported by Radzinowicz 1948, vol. 1, 4). At least a hundred capital offenses were added during the agricultural and industrial revolutions of the eighteenth century alone. By and large, new capital statutes extended the death penalty to offenses against property and commerce, evidently to protect economic interests within English society.

Furthermore, property offenses accounted for the overwhelming majority of capital convictions and executions in eighteenth-century England. Historical data for London at the beginning of the eighteenth century and for London and Middlesex at the beginning of the nineteenth century show that capital convictions and executions for property offenses far outstripped those for crimes involving violence to persons or the threat of bodily harm (Table 5-1).

In the early 1710s most of the capital convictions and executions in London were for larceny, whereas in the early 1800s burglary accounted for most of the capital convictions and forgery for most of the executions in London and Middlesex. A marked increase in convictions and executions for robbery was shown over this period. Notably, at both times murder constituted less than 5 percent of the capital convictions and only about 10 percent of the executions.[2] Thus, throughout

---

2. Similarly, for all of England and Wales in the year 1810—when detailed judicial statistics first became available for all jurisdictions—forgery and burglary accounted for thirty-six of the sixty-seven executions throughout the country, and murder for only nine, or less than 15 percent of all executions (Radzinowicz 1948, vol. 1, 155).

**Table 5-1.** *Convictions and Executions for Various Capital Offenses in London 1710–1714 and in London and Middlesex 1800–1804*

| Offenses | Total Number of Persons | | | |
| --- | --- | --- | --- | --- |
| | London 1710–1714 | | London and Middlesex 1800–1804 | |
| | Capitally Convicted | Executed | Capitally Convicted | Executed |
| Burglary | 10 | 6 | 99 | 11 |
| Horse stealing | 13 | 5 | 33 | 3 |
| Larceny in shops and warehouses | 50 | 10 | 20 | – |
| Murder | 4 | 3 | 6 | 5 |
| Robbery | 4 | 1 | 64 | 11 |
| Forgery | – | – | 26 | 15 |
| Larceny in a dwelling house | 15 | 8 | 89 | 3 |

*Source*: Radzinowicz 1948, vol. 1, 157.

the eighteenth century the application of the death penalty, as well as the statutes providing for its use, seems to have served the interests of private property and commerce.

This unprecedented extension of capital punishment to property offenses occurred at a time of accumulating wealth in the shops and warehouses of England's cities and of growing poverty, idleness, and vagrancy in its streets. Together with the Acts of Enclosure, the revolution in agriculture forced small farmers off their lands to work the farms of others or to leave for the cities. The revolutions in industry forced men, women, and children to leave their home-based crafts and work in factories for long hours and low wages, and to be unemployed when the labor market provided stronger or cheaper hands. Despite the lack of data on those who were executed in eighteenth-century England, there was little doubt in the minds of contemporary observers about who the capital offenders were.

> Most Pick-pockets, House-breakers, Street-robbers and Footpads . . . have once been idle Vagrants . . . You may hang, or transport, or cut off a Number of Felons at this Sitting, but, like Hidra's Heads, there will be more spring up by the next, and ever will do so, as long as idle Vagrants, who continually furnish a fresh Supply, are suffered to go as they do, unmolested (Alcock 1752, 68, 69; quoted in Radzinowicz 1956, vol. 2, 19).

The numbers of capital convictions and executions rose, at least in London and Middlesex, in the latter half of the eighteenth century (Radzinowicz 1948, vol. 1, 147) as the conditions of labor became progressively dehumanizing and the spirit of rebellion took root in the American colonies. In short, the economic growth of the eighteenth century brought with it an impoverished, exploited, and alienated working class that threatened first the property and later the dominant position of the aristocrats and gentry who controlled Parliament throughout this century.

Then, during a period of political reform that included expanding representation for the middle classes in Parliament, emancipation for slaves in the British Empire, and protections for workers in the factories of England, executions for property offenses virtually disappeared. Between 1823 and 1833 many capital statutes were repealed, including those against horse theft, larceny from dwellings, and most forms of forgery.[3] By 1835 there was only one execution for burglary and robbery in all of England and Wales, a decline from twenty-four in 1810 despite an appreciable rise in capital convictions for these two offenses over this period, as shown in Table 5-2.

Convictions for murder remained at 5 percent or less of all capital convictions, as they had throughout the eighteenth century, but executions for murder climbed from their earlier level of about one out of ten to six out of ten in 1835. From this time on, murder accounted for most of the executions in England, and with the penal code revision of 1863 it became the only effective cause of executions (although treason and piracy remained capital offenses) until 1965 when England abolished the death penalty.

In effect, the economic revolution of the eighteenth century brought about a new balance in English society; the middle class gradually grew

**Table 5-2.** *Convictions and Executions for Various Capital Offenses in England and Wales in 1810 and 1835*

| Offenses | England and Wales | | | |
|---|---|---|---|---|
| | 1810 | | 1835 | |
| | Capitally Convicted | Executed | Capitally Convicted | Executed |
| Murder | 15 | 9 | 25 | 21 |
| Attempted murder | 13 | 2 | 60 | 2 |
| Burglary | 88 | 18 | 193 | 1 |
| Robbery | 39 | 6 | 202 | – |
| Other offenses | 346 | 32 | 43 | 10 |

Source: Radzinowicz 1948, vol. 1, 155, and 1968, vol. 4, 310.

3. Forgery alone had accounted for eighteen of the sixty-seven executions in 1810, but by 1832 the repeal of the capital statutes for bank-note forgery was supported by the London Banker's Association on grounds that requiring the death penalty for such forgery was inhibiting convictions (Radzinowicz 1956, vol. 3, 305).

in size and gained economic and political power at the expense of the nobility and landed gentry. The sacredness of property and property rights, as proclaimed by Locke, was displaced by a new-found reverence for human rights and liberties associated with the Enlightenment—providing a mandate for the full political incorporation of all citizens, not just the propertied classes. It was in the spirit of this movement that Beccaria asked by what right the state can take human life as punishment for crime. In this historical context, Englishmen came to view the death penalty as harsh and unworkable for property offenses. Its use in the nineteenth century after 1835 was restricted almost exclusively to murder—itself a crime against human life.

### Nineteenth-century America

In America, too, changing economic and social conditions had a profound impact on the character of capital statutes. By 1785, when Massachusetts had been transformed from a Puritan colony into a center of trade and commerce and the patriotic sentiments associated with the Revolutionary War were still ripe, treason and piracy had entered and moved to the head of the list of capital statutes of the Commonwealth of Massachusetts, and idolatry, witchcraft, and blasphemy were no longer punishable by death (*Law Reporter* 1846, 387).

But the more dramatic change in capital statutes in America—one that rivaled the expansion of capital statutes in England as a response to changing socioeconomic conditions—occurred with the growth of slavery and the development of a large-scale plantation economy in the South. In contrast with the eight or so capital crimes of Massachusetts and Pennsylvania in the postrevolutionary period, North Carolina, for example, had some twenty-six capital crimes in 1837, including the following:

> slave-stealing
> concealing a slave with intent to free him
> inciting slaves to insurrection (second conviction)
> circulating seditious literature among slaves (second conviction).

These four offenses reflect the view of slaves as valuable property not to be tampered with by others. It is noteworthy in this respect that some slave owners received compensation as high as three hundred dollars for slaves who had to be executed (Teeters and Hedblom 1967, 104–105).

Perhaps more portentous than the proliferations of capital statutes to protect the institution of slavery was the differentiation of capital offenses for blacks and whites. Thus, for example, in Virginia in the 1830s there were five capital crimes for whites; for black slaves the offenses punishable by death numbered seventy by one count (Spear 1844, 227–231). In 1848 a blanket statute was passed in the Virginia Assembly requiring the death penalty for blacks for any offense that was punishable by three or more years imprisonment for white free-men. This was later amended to provide for sale and transportation of convicted slaves outside of the United States, thus providing compensation for slave owners in some cases (*Virginia Law Review* 1972, 102).

Still further differentiation by race was provided in rape statutes that specified punishment according to the race of both offender and victim. In 1816, Georgia explicitly required the death penalty for a slave or "freeman of colour" who raped or attempted to rape a white female while at the same time it reduced the minimum sentence from seven to two years and removed "hard labor" for a white convicted of rape. And for a white convicted of raping a slave woman or a free woman of color, the punishment was a fine and/or imprisonment at the discretion of the court (NAACP Legal Defense and Educational Fund, Inc., brief for *Jackson* 1971, Appendix B). Without differentiating offender-victim combinations in the law, Virginia achieved the same effect in 1849 by rendering blacks incompetent by statute to testify against a white criminal defendant (*Virginia Law Review* 1972, 104).

These statutory developments suggest that the death penalty served not only to protect and control the institution of slavery in the South but also to articulate white supremacy in the social order. Grouping "freemen of colour" with slaves in the capital statutes tended to confirm the "caste" nature of the relations between the races. [4] Elaborating these statutes, with respect to rape in particular, underscored restrictions on the kinds of interracial contact that could be tolerated. And providing little if any punishment for whites who raped blacks was a "testimony" in the law to the superior status and privileges of whites in their dealings with blacks.

Although the Black Codes may not have served exclusively to protect the institution of slavery in the South, they undoubtedly had their roots in the character of this institution. Thomas Jefferson saw the devastating effects of slavery on whites as well as on blacks and wondered about its portent for the future of a society committed to human rights and liberties as a basis of government:

---

4. It should be noted that treating black freemen like slaves under the law in the South tended to buttress the institution of slavery by depriving the freeman status of appeal to slaves who might be considering an alternative to their servitude—in effect, it served notice that there was no meaningful alternative to slavery for blacks in the South. Notably, as slavery came under more intense attack from the abolitionists in the 1850s, some southern states considered forcing black freemen to affiliate with slave owners or leave the South (Elkins 1968).

The whole commerce between master and slave is a perpetual exercise of the most boisterous passions, the most unremitting despotism on the one part, and degrading submissions on the other. Our children see this, and learn to imitate it. . . . The man must be a prodigy who can retain his manners and morals undepraved by such circumstances. And with what execration should the statesman be loaded, who, permitting one half the citizens to trample on the rights of the other, transforming those into despots, and these into enemies, destroys the morals of one part, and the "amor patriae" of the other. . . . [Can] the liberties of a nation be thought secure when we have removed their only firm basis, a conviction in the minds of the people that these liberties are the gift of God? That they are not to be violated but with His wrath? Indeed, I tremble for my country when I reflect that God is just; that His justice cannot sleep forever (Washington 1859, 103–104).

Slavery in the American colonies took a particularly dehumanizing form. In Latin America as a contrast, the family and religious lives of slaves were the province of the church, and the right to work independently was guaranteed under the royal paternalism of the Spanish Crown. The forms of slavery that developed in the British colonies of North America were altogether unregulated by church or crown. Indeed, slaves in the American colonies were explicitly deprived by law of civil rights, including the right to own property, thus discouraging manumission. And locally established Protestantism afforded little if any support for stable family relations among the slaves. As British subjects, American slave owners were free to treat slaves exclusively as property whose disposition was wholly determined by conditions in the tobacco and cotton markets. In the spirit of *laissez faire* capitalism, slaves were bought and sold, housed and husbanded like livestock (Elkins 1968).

This form of absolute servitude and dependency gave the black person no basic human qualities in the eyes of the white community. Surely one immediate consequence was the belief that blacks required more severe and dramatic forms of punishment, including the death penalty, as provided in the antebellum Black Codes.[5] But this dehumanization of black people under slavery in the South also had the enduring effect of producing a form of institutionalized racism in America, with consequences that would continue to be intensely felt generations after the abolition of slavery.

With the Emancipation Proclamation of 1864 the southern Black

---

5. Blacks were subjected to particularly torturous executions under the law in some jurisdictions. In fact, burning at the stake was prescribed by law in some states and actually performed as late as 1825 in South Carolina (Teeters and Hedblom 1967, 109).

Codes were abolished. All men were punishable for their crimes according to the codes for white freemen. Yet neither the Proclamation nor the period of Reconstruction that followed seriously altered the long-standing and deeply felt sentiments behind these Black Codes. By enforcing racial equality under the law, however, Reconstruction in the South at least symbolically threatened white dominance in southern society. And predictably, as Reconstruction ended the white majority reasserted its dominance. Jim Crow laws effectively established racial segregation, poll taxes and literacy tests secured the voting franchise for whites alone, and lynching provided a de facto extralegal restoration of the antebellum Black Codes.

Although we lack data on the use of the death penalty in the antebellum South, we do have relatively comprehensive information on lynchings in the late nineteenth century (see Table 2-3). These data show that such extralegal executions—directed primarily against blacks in the South—far outnumbered all legally imposed executions under state and local authority in America during the last two decades of the nineteenth century. Obviously the reaction of the South to what was perceived as a racial challenge brought on by Reconstruction was violent and extensive. As one observer espousing the prevailing view of the black man, explained:

> It was assumed, after the emancipation of the slaves, that a judicial system, adapted to a highly civilized and cultured race, would be equally applicable to a race of inferior civilization. . . . Measured by white man's standard of judgment, the frequent atrocity of the crimes committed by negroes of low character, without apparently any particular provocation, is something scarcely to be understood—the adjectives wanton, bestial, outrageous, brutal, and inhuman, all seem wholly inadequate to express the feeling of utter disgust and abhorence that is aroused . . . In the midst of the increased criminality that has been manifested among the negroes since emancipation, the Southern whites have found the law and its administration utterly unsuited to the function of dealing with negro criminals—hence, the frequent adoption of summary and extra-legal methods of punishment. (Cutler 1907, 622–623)

The characteristics of those who have been executed in America in the twentieth century are a matter of record. Most of the executions in this century have been imposed in the South, and most of those executed have been black (Chapter 2). Particularly in the South, blacks have been executed for lesser offenses, at younger ages, and more often without appeals (Chapter 3). And for rape, the death penalty has been reserved out of all proportion for blacks whose victims were white (Wolfgang 1972; Wolfgang and Riedel 1973, 1975; Bowers 1974, Chapter 4)—the pattern implied by the antebellum Black Codes in the South.

Other studies (referred to in Chapter 3) have revealed racial discrimination in capital cases at indictment, conviction, sentencing, and execution. And although the data have been less adequately developed, there are strong indications of discrimination against the socially deprived and impoverished in the administration of capital punishment (see Chapter 3 for references and a discussion of this issue).

It is doubtful that the death penalty has ever been applied in a strictly uniform manner to offenders from all strata of society. Historically, "Benefit of Clergy" and "Royal Prerogative" have protected higher echelons of society and given the Crown discretion to discriminate in its own interests. And upon occasion common people have rallied to support clemency for distinguished citizens, thus leaving those to be executed more uniformly undistinguished when such appeals have succeeded (see, for example, the case of Dr. Doud, Radzinowicz 1948, vol. 1, 450 ff.).

In this century, American society appears to have tolerated the use of the death penalty only against the racially subjugated and the impoverished—those who are socially unacceptable despite their nominal membership in society. Perhaps the more recent narrowing of offenses for which capital punishment can be imposed (chiefly to crimes of violence against the person) has tended to preselect social outcasts and misfits—those most likely to confront continuing frustration in society and least able to resist violence in the face of it. But when preselection has failed to yield a uniformly wretched group of capital offenders, society has stepped in to confer the death sentence and to carry it out with added selectivity.

### In Summary

The foregoing historical review indicates that a wide variety of crimes have been punished by death and that their description has changed with the changing locus of power and authority in society. In a period of religious hegemony, death was prescribed first and foremost for religious crimes; in a time of expanding economic wealth, it was imposed primarily for offenses against property. Thus, whatever else its function, the death penalty appears to have been used to protect the interests and position of the dominant group in the social order—to punish the offenses defined as gravest by those in power.

At times of crisis in the relations between status groups, particularly when the dominant group in society has been threatened or attacked, the use of the death penalty seems to have flourished. Thus, we have noted that executions reached high points in the reign of Henry VIII, during the Industrial Revolution in England, and in the post-Reconstruction South. In the reign of Henry VIII his separation from the Catholic Church precipitated a crisis of authority; in eighteenth-century England the dominance of landed aristocracy was increasingly threatened as the economic revolution progressed; and in nineteenth-century America white dominance in southern society was first threatened by Abolitionists, then attacked in the Civil War, subsequently abolished de jure under Reconstruction, and ultimately reaffirmed with the aid of the death penalty in both its legal and extralegal forms.

The death penalty may also have been more commonly used when opposition to the established authority had no legitimate or institutionalized status. We know, for example, that it was used more often in England under the divine right monarchies than under the more pluralistic parliamentary system. This might also account for the fact that totalitarian regimes in the modern world have been both conspicuously ready to conduct "political purges" and conspicuously reluctant to give up capital punishment (see Table 5-3).

As much as to protect dominant interests in society, the death penalty appears to have been used to oppress disenfranchised and dispossessed minorities. Although little systematic data are available on those who were executed before the twentieth century, it was the impression of observers in eighteenth-century England that the victims of the executioner typically came from the ranks of vagrants, idlers, and the unemployed. In nineteenth-century America, the pre–Civil-War Black Codes and the post-Reconstruction lynchings leave little doubt as to the foremost targets of execution by legal and illegal means.

The evidence of racial discrimination in capital punishment in twentieth-century America is now hardly contestable. And there is mounting evidence that social class may also have served as a basis for the discriminatory treatment of capital offenders within the criminal justice system. Indeed, the research on social class suggests that discrimination against the socially deprived and impoverished may have been quite pronounced outside the South and that it may, in fact, account for some of the racial disparity in treatment inside the South— two points deserving further research.

The essential feature of poverty and racial subjugation is their dehumanizing effect. These conditions breed contemptuous stereotypes that deprive people of their human qualities in the eyes of others and even in their own eyes if they are sensitive to prevailing social definitions. Injustices against them evoke little sympathy, and their deaths cause little remorse. Indeed, the death penalty can even be— and surely has been—used carelessly and arbitrarily against such powerless victims without generating substantial concern or objection.

In times of social tension and turmoil, particularly when dominant interests seem threatened, the alleged subhuman qualities of minority group members and poor people become more prominent in prevailing stereotypes. Such real or imagined threats on the part of racial minorities within this country have led to "mass executions" whose victims have invariably been blacks or Indians (Teeters and Hedblom 1967, 114 ff.). Racial dehumanization and threatened social upheaval in the presence of the absolute power of a dictatorial regime are the elements that may promote the massive use of executions under civil authority. These were the elements present when Hitler executed more than six million Jews.

## Comparative Perspective

The legacy of the Enlightenment and its expression in the French and American revolutions was a new-found human dignity and newly proclaimed rights for all people. The nineteenth century witnessed the struggle to extend these human rights and liberties to all those within national boundaries, and the twentieth century has seen the ascendency of the common man to a position of influence and participation in the governments of most democratic Western societies. These historical developments have meant a reduction in the size of dispossessed or disenfranchised minorities and in the disparities of power and influence between the upper and lower strata of society. And these changes have been accompanied by a long-term movement away from the use of capital punishment.

Inspired by the Enlightenment, Cesare di Beccaria's attack on the death penalty in 1764 led to criminal code reforms including the abolition of capital punishment in several European countries—Russia, Austria, and Tuscany—in the late eighteenth century. And while these initial reforms did not last, they marked the beginning of a movement that was evident throughout most of the nineteenth and twentieth centuries. In 1848, France abolished the death penalty for all political crimes; in 1863, England effectively restricted the death penalty to murder, though it remained on the books for treason and piracy. Some eleven nations abandoned or abolished capital punishment in the nineteenth century and remained abolitionist thereafter; others, like Italy, abolished it in the nineteenth century but restored it under facism for a period in the twentieth century. Table 5-3 shows when countries abandoned or abolished the death penalty for crimes of violence against the person (including murder, rape, robbery, arson, and kidnapping); the dates indicate when the most recent period of abolition began or when the last execution was imposed.

The movement away from capital punishment gained momentum in the twentieth century, particularly in the years after World War II. This accelerating pace of abolition is highlighted by the fact that virtually half the abolitions listed in Table 5-3 have occurred since 1940.

**Table 5-3.** *Abolition and Abandonment of the Death Penalty among Jurisdictions throughout the World, Excluding the United States*

| Jurisdiction | Date of Abolition or Abandonment | Jurisdiction | Date of Abolition or Abandonment |
|---|---|---|---|
| Lichtenstein | 1798 [b] | Switzerland [c] | 1942 |
| Luxembourg | 1821 [a, b] | India, Travencore | 1944 |
| San Marino | 1848 | Italy [c] | 1944 |
| Belgium | 1863 [b] | Australia, Federal [c] | 1945 |
| Venezuela | 1863 | Brazil [c] | 1946 |
| Mozambique | 1867 | Germany, West | 1949 |
| Portugal | 1867 | Finland [c] | 1949 |
| Costa Rica | 1880 | Nepal [c] | 1950 |
| Netherlands [c] | 1886 [d] | Greenland | 1954 |
| Nicaragua | 1892 [a] | Israel [c] | 1954 |
| Ecuador | 1897 | Australia, New | |
| Norway [c] | 1905 [d] | South Wales [c] | 1955 |
| Uruguay | 1907 | Honduras | 1957 |
| Columbia | 1910 | Netherlands, | |
| Panama | 1915 | Antilles [c] | 1957 |
| Sweden [c] | 1921 | Bolivia | 1961 |
| Argentina | 1922 | New Zealand [c] | 1961 |
| Australia, Queensland [e] | 1922 | Monaco | 1962 |
| Dominican Republic | 1924 | United Kingdom, | |
| Surinam | 1927 [a] | Great Britain [e] | 1965 |
| Denmark [c] | 1930 | United Kingdom, | |
| Mexico | 1931 [f] | Northern Ireland [e] | 1966 |
| Iceland | 1940 | Canada [e] | 1967 |
| | | Austria | 1968 |
| | | Australia, Tasmania [e] | 1968 |
| | | Vatican City State | 1969 |

*Source*: Legal Defense Fund brief for *Aikens*, 1971: Appendix E; drawn from Joyce 1961; Ancel 1962; Patrick 1965; Pena De Morte 1967; Secretary General's Note 1968.

*Note*: All jurisdictions within the United States abandoned the death penalty by 1967; thirteen states abolished it prior to 1972 when the U.S. Supreme Court invalidated existing capital statutes in the remaining thirty-nine U.S. jurisdictions, as indicated in Table 1-1.

[a] Date of de facto abandonment of capital punishment.
[b] Excludes one execution.
[c] Permits the death penalty in time of war or under military law.
[d] Executed Nazi collaborators after World War II.
[e] Retains the death penalty for certain extraordinary civil offenses.
[f] Twenty-nine of thirty-two states within Mexico abolished the death penalty between 1931 and 1970.

The rapid expansion of abolitionist ranks after the Second World War was undoubtedly linked to the experience of atrocities and brutality before and during the war. Justice Marc Ancel of the French Supreme Court has observed:

... by its very excesses totalitarianism provoked a reaction which made itself felt immediately after the Second World War. It was shown in the prosecution of war crimes, even if, here and there, at the time, it was marked by a temporary recrudescence of capital executions. The Universal Declaration of Human Rights of 1948 proclaimed anew to the world the rights of individuals and the eminent dignity of human beings. The abolitionist movement was invigorated and scored successes even— and sometimes especially—in the countries where totalitarianism had imposed a return of the death penalty. Free from facism, Italy returned to the great tradition of Beccaria and of the Zanardelli code. Austria, which had been forcibly incorporated in the Hitlerian system, returned to its earlier condition, which also had repudiated capital punishment. The German federal republic in turn excluded it by a constitutional provision (Ancel 1967; in Sellin 1967a, 8).

In France and England during the 1950s the banner of opposition to capital punishment was raised by intellectuals—notably Albert Camus (1957) and Arthur Koestler (1957)—who were distinguished by their tireless resistance to facism during World War II.

In addition to the growing abolitionist ranks, many countries that retain the death penalty have used it only rarely in recent years. A survey for the period 1958–1962, with responses from 128 countries, identified some 89 countries that provided for capital punishment. Of the 89 death penalty nations, only 60 percent had actually performed an execution during this five-year period, and only 45 percent had performed more than one per year on the average. Thus, about half the death penalty countries made little or no use of capital punishment between 1958 and 1962 (Patrick 1965).

Of the 500 or so executions reported annually during this period, fully half were performed in just four of the eighty-nine countries with capital punishment, and the United States was one of these four despite two decades of decline in executions by that time. (See Table 5-4.)

South Africa, which heads the list, is notorious for its apartheid system of caste relations between the races which is not unlike racial segregation in the southern United States in earlier times, when executions were as common as they have been during the recent period in South Africa.[6]

6. South Africa, like the southern United States, is one of the few jurisdictions to have executed for rape in recent years; and as in the United States, its use of the death penalty against black rapists has been out of all proportion to their numbers among convicted rapists. Thus, it has been reported that between 1947 and 1969, 844 rape convictions of black South Africans resulted in 121 death sentences, while 288 rape convictions of white South Africans resulted in three death sentences (*The Manchester Guardian Weekly*, August 14, 1971, 4; cited in the NAACP Legal Defense Fund brief for Jackson 1971, 20, note 36). Other former British colonies with "race problems"

**Table 5-4.**  *Average Number of Executions Annually for the Period 1958–1962 for the Top 4 of 89 Countries with Capital Punishment*

|  | Annual Average, 1958–1962 | Percentage |
|---|---|---|
| South Africa | 100 | 18.7 |
| Korea | 68 | 12.7 |
| Nigeria | 51 | 9.5 |
| United States | 49 | 9.2 |
| Remaining 49 countries conducting some executions during this period [a] | 267 | 49.9 |
| Additional 36 countries conducting no executions during this period | 0 | 0 |
| Total | 535 | 100.0 |

*Source*: Patrick 1965, Table 1.
*Note*: The data in this table do not precisely correspond with those in Patrick 1965, Table 6; reprinted in Reckless 1969, Table 3; and McCafferty 1972, Table 2.3. Patrick's Table 6 appears to be an inaccurate summary of the information in his Table 1.
[a] The highest annual average number of executions reported by a country in this group is 29.

In addition to South Africa and the United States, Korea and Nigeria are among the four nations responsible for half the executions reported for the period 1958–1962, as shown in Table 5-4. Internal strife and political coerciveness may account, in varying degrees, for the relatively high number of executions in these two countries. It should also be noted that many of the communist bloc nations failed to respond to Patrick's question about the number of executions imposed from 1958 through 1962. However, their conspicuous absence from the list of abolitionist countries in Table 5-3 suggests that the death penalty remains relatively unchallenged in these nations.

These data from the Patrick survey on capital punishment in most nations of the world circa 1960 afford an unusual opportunity for a more systematic examination of factors associated with the availability and use of the death penalty at a time of evident movement away from capital punishment among a growing number of nations. Our historical analysis in the preceding section has identified various conditions under which the application of the death penalty has been relatively common in the past. These include:

---

were among the last to retain the death penalty for rape; Malawi (formerly Nyasaland) retains the death penalty for rape, and Zambia (formerly Northern Rhodesia) gave it up in 1965. China (Taiwan) is the only other country that retains the death penalty for rape (NAACP Legal Defense Fund brief for Jackson 1971, 13, esp. notes 13 and 14). In 1963, there appear to have been some eighteen countries that provided the death penalty for rape (Patrick 1965, Table 1).

*Centralization*   the extent to which political power in society is concentrated or centralized in the hands of a single elite or dominant group

*Coerciveness*   the degree to which the government or ruling regime employs force or violence to restrain or suppress opposition, dissent, and civil liberties

*Instability*   the presence of dislocation, disorder, strife, and violence in political and economic life

*Nonincorporation*   the extent to which local, regional, ethnic, and class identities and interests take precedence over national citizenship rights and commitments, and thus deprive diverse social elements of full membership status in the national community

*Discrimination*   the degree to which racial, linguistic, ethnic, and religious groups are subjected to systematic deprivation of social and economic opportunities.

To the extent that the association between these societal characteristics and the use of the death penalty in the past reflects basic extralegal functions of capital punishment, we expect these factors or conditions to make nations reluctant to abandon or abolish capital punishment, even in the face of recent trends toward abolition. In effect, these factors should, if our historical analysis is correct, predict which nations have continued to retain and use capital punishment in recent years, and which ones have given it up.

To reflect these conditions or characteristics among the nations in the Patrick survey, we have chosen five indicators or measures available in existing data sets, which have been compiled and coded from various sources for cross-national research purposes.[7] These five variables with references to their sources are identified as follows:

*Political Centralization*   as reflected in political party systems in the following ordered categories: (a) no parties or one-party systems, (b) two-party systems, and (c) multiparty systems. The fewer the parties, the greater the political centralization. The data were drawn from Banks and Textor (1963, 97).

*Political Coerciveness*   as measured by a scale of Permissiveness-Coerciveness of the political regime incorporating annual data on the

---

7. Our choice of indicators was necessarily somewhat arbitrary. We were guided, in part, by the desire to minimize the intercorrelations among the independent variables in order to avoid instability and "tilting" as a result of multicollinearity in the regression analyses. The highest correlation among the indicators we have chosen is 0.47 between Political Centralization and Political Coerciveness. We considered several alternative measures of political centralization available in the Banks and Textor (1963) data file, including Horizontal Power Concentration, Constitutional Form, and Representativeness, but found that they had relatively high correlations with Political Coerciveness (exceeding 0.60 in each case).

suppression of suffrage, press censorship, unwillingness to tolerate political opposition, lack of respect for civil rights, and rule by executive
fiat, from 1945 through 1965. The scale was drawn from I. K. Feierabend,
R. L. Feierabend, and B. A. Nesvold (1969).

*Political Instability* as indexed by the number of political assassina-
tions, general strikes, guerilla attacks, major government crises, purges,
riots, revolutions, and antigovernment demonstrations per year from
1956 through 1965. The data were drawn from Banks (1971, xvi, Segment
10, Fields A-H).

*Incomplete Incorporation* as reflected by a measure of interest articulation by nonassociational groups in the following ordered categories: (a)
significant, (b) moderate, (c) limited, and (d) negligible. The more significant the articulation of interest by nonassociational groups, the more
inchoate the level of national political incorporation. This measure is
drawn from Banks and Textor (1963, 92–93), who indicate that "ascrip-
tive" might be preferable to "nonassociational" as a designation for the
types of groups in question. The imagery for this measure is provided by
Almond and Coleman (1960, 33).

*Group Discrimination* as measured by a Group Discrimination Index
designed to specify the "approximate proportion of a population which
is substantially and systematically excluded from valued economic, political, or social positions because of ethnic, religious, linguistic, or regional characteristics" (Gurr 1966, 71). The scoring judgments reflect
discriminatory conditions in the late 1950s or early 1960s, although
"such discrimination is seldom time-dependent, at least in the short
span" (Gurr 1966, 75). The index was drawn from Gurr (1966, Table 5).

Our approach in this section will be to see how each of these
societal characteristics, individually and in conjunction with the other
four, predicts the availability and use of capital punishment among the
nations of the world.[8] Correlation coefficients will tell us the strength
of each characteristic's association with capital punishment, and beta
weights from multiple regression analyses will indicate how much of
the correlation can be attributed to the unique or independent contribution of each variable.[9] To see how these factors affect the avail-

8. Of the 146 nations surveyed by Patrick, 128 provided information on capital punishment, but 16 of these were unclassifiable on all five of the societal characteristics
specified. Therefore, our largest working sample from the Patrick survey will be 112
countries. These are of course most of the world's nations, and they include well
over 90 percent of the world's population. The nations that did not respond or could
not be classified in terms of societal characteristics are not a random or representative subgroup. Statistical significance tests, therefore, do not apply.

9. The correlations, which also serve as the basis for the regression analyses, are calculated using pair-wise deletion of missing values, and the number of nations for
which data are available on each of the independent variables will be indicated in
the upcoming tables.

ability and use of the death penalty among nations like the United States, we shall examine their effects not only for the full sample of nations, but also for "highly developed" and "less developed" subsamples of nations.[10]

How well, then, do these societal characteristics predict the availability of capital punishment circa 1960? Which ones show the strongest effects? Are the effects comparable in highly developed and less developed nations? The answers are to be found in Table 5-5 for the full sample and for each of the development subsamples. The table shows the correlation, beta weights, and regressions of each of the

**Table 5-5.** *Societal Characteristics Predicting the De Jure Availability of the Death Penalty Circa 1960 for Most Nations of the World, and by Level of Economic Development*

| Societal Characteristics | Correlations | Beta Wgts. | Regressions | Number |
|---|---|---|---|---|
| *Total Sample of Nations (N=112)* | | | | |
| Political Centralization | 0.46 | 0.23 | 0.110 | 88 |
| Political Coerciveness | 0.41 | 0.15 | 0.042 | 78 |
| Political Instability | 0.00 | 0.05 | 0.001 | 98 |
| Incomplete Incorporation | 0.55 | 0.40 | 0.179 | 105 |
| Group Discrimination | 0.00 | −0.04 | −0.001 | 105 |
| Multiple Correlation = | | 0.62 | | |
| *Highly Developed Subsample (N=36)* | | | | |
| Political Centralization | 0.52 | 0.30 | 0.172 | 32 |
| Political Coerciveness | 0.52 | 0.26 | 0.066 | 34 |
| Political Instability | 0.14 | 0.12 | 0.001 | 34 |
| Incomplete Incorporation | 0.43 | 0.24 | 0.145 | 34 |
| Group Discrimination | 0.23 | 0.01 | 0.000 | 36 |
| Multiple Correlation = | | 0.64 | | |
| *Less Developed Subsample (N=63)* | | | | |
| Political Centralization | 0.41 | 0.29 | 0.126 | 46 |
| Political Coerciveness | −0.12 | −0.01 | −0.005 | 40 |
| Political Instability | −0.12 | −0.12 | −0.002 | 56 |
| Incomplete Incorporation | 0.54 | 0.47 | 0.261 | 61 |
| Group Discrimination | −0.20 | 0.11 | 0.001 | 65 |
| Multiple Correlation = | | 0.60 | | |

*Note*: Thirteen nations could not be classified by development level, therefore the subsamples are thirteen fewer than in the total sample of nations.

10. To distinguish between development subgroups, we employ a measure of economic development used by Gurr (1969, 489–491) which was scored on the basis of conditions in the late 1950s and early 1960s. In our working sample of 112 nations, this measure of economic development classifies 36 countries as "high" in economic development, 63 as "medium" or "low" in economic development, and leaves 13 unclassified.

independent variables with the presence of capital punishment on the statute books.[11]

In the full working sample, three factors are clearly associated with the presence of the death penalty. Thus, Incomplete Incorporation, Political Centralization, and Political Coerciveness show substantial correlations with the presence of capital punishment (0.55, 0.46, and 0.41, respectively). The beta weights indicate that nonincorporation is the strongest independent predictor of the presence of capital punishment (0.40), followed by centralization (0.23) and coerciveness (0.15).

Among highly developed nations, the same three factors show reasonably strong correlations and beta weights with the presence of the death penalty. In contrast with the full sample, however, political centralization and coerciveness play a relatively more prominent role among the developed nations than does nonincorporation. Among the less developed nations it is nonincorporation that dominates as a predictor of capital punishment; centralization plays a secondary role; and coerciveness has lost its place as a noteworthy predictor.

Thus, Incomplete Incorporation at the national level and the centralization of political power are prominent as predictors of capital punishment in both highly developed and less developed nations. The primary difference is that centralization plays a relatively more important role among developed nations, whereas nonincorporation has a relatively stronger effect among less developed nations. The regression coefficients, which permit direct comparisons between samples, show that the effect of centralization is stronger in the highly developed than in the less developed sample (0.17 compared with 0.13), while nonincorporation is stronger in the less developed as opposed to the highly developed sample (0.26 as opposed to 0.15).

The prominence of centralization as a predictor among highly developed nations undoubtedly reflects the fact that the communist bloc countries have typically retained the death penalty. As we noted earlier, they were conspicuous by their absence from the list of abolitionist nations in Table 5-3. They also score relatively high on the measure of coerciveness, which may, in part, account for the connection between coerciveness and the death penalty that appears to be restricted to the sample of highly developed nations.

The prominent effect of Incomplete Incorporation in the less de-

11. In the working sample of 112 nations, 39 are classified as abolitionist. These include fourteen countries having a limited form of the death penalty according to Patrick's data. Typically, the death penalty could only be imposed in these nations during time of war or for narrowly defined threats to national security (other than treason). The only person to have been executed in these 14 nations between 1958 and 1962 was Adolph Eichmann, for Nazi crimes and genocide under a special statute in Israel.

veloped countries presumably reflects the fact that people without fully institutionalized citizenship rights are subject to more excessive and dehumanizing treatment at the hands of ruling groups.[12] It could also mean that where political interests are organized and articulated around local and regional concerns, conditions are not present for the kind of nationally organized movement that could bring pressure to bear for the abolition of capital punishment.

We can pursue this matter of trends or movements toward abolition somewhat further with the data in the Patrick survey. One of the questions asked nations with the death penalty was whether there had been any trend toward abolition in recent years. Table 5-6 presents correlations, beta weights, and regressions for the total sample and for

**Table 5-6.** *Societal Characteristics Predicting Trends toward Abolition among Nations with the Death Penalty Circa 1960*

| Societal Characteristics | Correlations | Beta Wgts. | Regressions | Number |
|---|---|---|---|---|
| *Total Sample of Nations (N = 78)* | | | | |
| Political Centralization | −0.15 | 0.02 | 0.012 | 60 |
| Political Coerciveness | −0.34 | −0.26 | −0.079 | 50 |
| Political Instability | 0.24 | 0.15 | 0.002 | 68 |
| Incomplete Incorporation | −0.26 | −0.20 | −0.103 | 73 |
| Group Discrimination | −0.05 | −0.02 | 0.000 | 72 |
| Multiple Correlation = | | 0.42 | | |
| *Highly Developed Subsample (N = 20)* | | | | |
| Political Centralization | −0.35 | 0.04 | 0.033 | 18 |
| Political Coerciveness | −0.56 | −0.55 | −0.140 | 19 |
| Political Instability | 0.28 | 0.01 | 0.000 | 19 |
| Incomplete Incorporation | −0.39 | −0.34 | −0.227 | 19 |
| Group Discrimination | −0.19 | 0.08 | 0.002 | 20 |
| Multiple Correlation = | | 0.64 | | |
| *Less Developed Subsample (N = 51)* | | | | |
| Political Centralization | 0.00 | 0.01 | 0.004 | 35 |
| Political Coerciveness | −0.08 | −0.05 | −0.018 | 29 |
| Political Instability | 0.18 | 0.17 | 0.002 | 43 |
| Incomplete Incorporation | 0.11 | 0.10 | 0.056 | 47 |
| Group Discrimination | 0.04 | 0.00 | 0.000 | 50 |
| Multiple Correlation = | | 0.21 | | |

12. Cohen (1969) has shown in a sample of societies drawn from the Human Relations Area File that those at the very beginning or "inchoate" stage of political incorporation were particularly likely to employ the death penalty for adultery, incest, and violations of celibacy. He argues that the availability of the death penalty for these crimes relating to the family and kinship structure have the function of displacing local and ethnic sources of authority with a broader national basis of authority.

development subgroups among those nations with the death penalty circa 1960. (Seven nations could not be classified by development level, therefore the number of cases in the development subsamples is seven fewer than in the total sample of nations.)

Among the death penalty nations in our sample, three factors—coerciveness, nonincorporation and instability—show modest correlations with trends toward abolition. However, the beta weights indicate that the independent effects of these are hardly noteworthy, and the overall predictability as indicated by the multiple correlation (0.42) is clearly less than it was for the availability of the death penalty shown in Table 5-5.

The effects of societal characteristics on trends toward abolition are much stronger in the highly developed nations. For every indicator, the correlation with the move toward abolition is stronger in the highly developed subsample than in the total sample of death penalty nations, and the overall predictability (0.64) is comparable to the levels of prediction of abolition in the preceding table. The beta weights attribute independent effects primarily to coerciveness ($-0.55$) and secondarily to nonincorporation ($-0.34$). Evidently, coercive political regimes are unwilling to countenance moves toward abolition, perhaps because death as punishment is altogether consistent with a coercive approach to the control of internal political turmoil and disorder.

For the less developed nations, the societal characteristics under investigation have little individual or joint effect on trends toward abolition (no correlations or beta weights reach 0.20 and the multiple correlation is only 0.21). Actually, only six of the fifty-one less developed nations with capital punishment reported any trends toward abolition in response to the Patrick survey.

Thus, among less developed nations nonincorporation is strongly related to abolition but not to organized or persistent movements toward abolition. Abolition in these nations appears to have occurred independently of such movements, perhaps more often in conjunction with an abrupt political succession or change of regime. Among highly developed nations, on the other hand, political incorporation is not only associated with abolition (Table 5-5) but also with movements toward abolition (Table 5-6). Perhaps incorporation has proceeded far enough in these developed countries to provide a forum within which nationally organized associational groups can effectively pursue such ends.

In addition to the availability of the death penalty, and moves to alter its availability, we have information from the Patrick survey on the extent of its use, as we have noted with respect to Table 5-4. Specifically, Patrick reported the average annual number of executions imposed between 1958 and 1962 for each country. Because, as noted in Table 5-4, a small number of countries was responsible for many of the executions imposed at this time, we shall employ the log of the number of executions in our analyses to minimize the effects of relatively high levels of executions in a few nations. We have also performed the regression analyses with and without log of population as a predictor. It would, of course, be valuable to have a measure of the number of capital offenses committed in each country. But since no such measure is available, log of population will serve as a rough control on the number of candidates for execution. Finally, for this analysis, we have only the death penalty nations that reported the number of executions imposed over this period. The reduction in sample size is evident in Table 5-7. (Seven nations could not be classified by development level; therefore the number of cases in the development subsamples was seven less than in the total sample of nations.)

The use of the death penalty circa 1960 is predicted primarily by political instability in the full sample of nations reporting executions. When we add (log of) population to the regression equation, the independent effect of instability is reduced (to 0.27) but it remains the dominant predictor of executions among the societal characteristics we have been considering. (Population size is clearly a strong predictor of execution.)

The dominance of political instability is even more pronounced in the sample of less developed nations. (Its correlation with log of execution is 0.54, its beta weight without population in the equation is 0.73, and with population its beta is 0.53). Indeed, instability shows a stronger effect than does (log of) population on the use of the death penalty among the less developed nations.

Instability is also a strong predictor of executions among the highly developed nations, but it no longer dominates the picture. Group discrimination and political centralization show comparable correlations with (log of) executions, and the correlation with nonincorporation is also substantial. Only coerciveness fails to show a sizable correlation with the use of the death penalty in the highly developed sample, and this may be because highly coercive nations were unlikely to provide information on executions.[13]

With a sample of only fourteen highly developed nations, the regression analysis gives relatively unstable coefficients. The three factors with the strongest correlations yield a multiple correlation of 0.99. In this equation all three factors continue to show strong independent effects, and when we add (log of) population to it their effects are

13. All six of the highly developed nations that were available for the analysis of moves toward abolition, but not for the analysis of execution, scored in the highest category on the coerciveness scale.

**Table 5-7.** *Societal Characteristics Predicting (Log of) the Number of Executions Imposed per Year among Nations with the Death Penalty Circa 1960*

| Societal Characteristics | Correlations | Without Log of Population | | With Log of Population | | Number |
|---|---|---|---|---|---|---|
| | | Beta Wgts. | Regressions | Beta Wgts. | Regressions | |
| *Total Sample of Nations (N = 63)* | | | | | | |
| Political Centralization | −0.01 | 0.04 | 0.052 | 0.04 | 0.064 | 49 |
| Political Coerciveness | 0.10 | 0.21 | 0.204 | 0.14 | 0.138 | 36 |
| Political Instability | 0.45 | 0.54 | 0.020 | 0.27 | 0.010 | 53 |
| Incomplete Incorporation | 0.07 | 0.08 | 0.120 | 0.13 | 0.204 | 58 |
| Group Discrimination | 0.14 | 0.04 | 0.002 | 0.15 | 0.006 | 56 |
| Log of Population | 0.56 | | | 0.49 | 0.471 | 63 |
| Multiple Correlation = | | 0.52 | | 0.66 | | |
| *Highly Developed Subsample (N = 14)* | | | | | | |
| Political Centralization | 0.59 | 0.55 | 1.072 | 0.57 | 1.114 | 12 |
| Political Coerciveness | 0.10 | | | | | 13 |
| Political Instability | 0.61 | 0.43 | 0.011 | 0.46 | 0.011 | 13 |
| Incomplete Incorporation | 0.39 | | | | | 13 |
| Group Discrimination | 0.61 | 0.64 | 0.041 | 0.64 | 0.041 | 14 |
| Log of Population | 0.66 | | | −0.04 | −0.052 | 14 |
| Multiple Correlation = | | 0.99 | | 0.99 | | |
| *Less Developed Subsample (N = 42)* | | | | | | |
| Political Centralization | −0.26 | 0.23 | 0.342 | 0.22 | 0.325 | 30 |
| Political Coerciveness | 0.16 | 0.08 | 0.140 | 0.04 | 0.078 | 21 |
| Political Instability | 0.54 | 0.73 | 0.068 | 0.53 | 0.050 | 34 |
| Incomplete Incorporation | 0.06 | 0.21 | 0.445 | 0.17 | 0.371 | 38 |
| Group Discrimination | 0.05 | 0.05 | 0.002 | 0.10 | 0.004 | 40 |
| Log of Population | 0.60 | | | 0.43 | 0.571 | 42 |
| Multiple Correlation = | | 0.60 | | 0.71 | | |

essentially unaltered, although the effect of population is totally absorbed by the other three factors. While the regression results are problematic, they nevertheless indicate that the very high correlations of instability, centralization, and discrimination with (log of) executions are not simply redundant.

Thus, the volume of executions performed between 1958 and 1962 was strongly predicted by the extent of political instability for the period from 1955 through 1965, corresponding rather closely to the period of executions. Evidently, the actual use of capital punishment is responsive to the political tensions, conflicts, turmoil, and strife that prevail at the time. No doubt the death penalty serves in many nations as a reprisal for political crimes. In the highly developed nations centralization and discrimination also played important roles. Presumably the concentration of political power tends to overcome constraints on the use of capital punishment; and the presence of discrimination provides ready scapegoats and victims for executions.

The abolition and abandonment of executions are obviously not identical processes. Whether the death penalty will be available seems to be more contingent on relatively stable structural factors such as the centralization of power in society and the incorporation of diverse social elements into the national polity. Whether and to what extent the death penalty will actually be used where it exists, is apparently more subject to relatively short-term fluctuation in political and social tension. In all societies with the death penalty, political instability appears to prompt its use; among highly developed nations the tensions that characterize systematic discrimination against minority groups appear also to promote executions. Perhaps the force of tradition is insufficient to keep minorities "in their place" in economically modernized and developed countries.[14]

The fact that the number of executions imposed is strongly affected by the level of tension or instability implies, of course, that whether a man is executed for a given crime will depend to an important degree on the timing rather than the seriousness of his offense.

In summary, all five of the societal characteristics we have examined are associated in one way or another with the availability or

14. This difference in the factors predicting the availability and the use of capital punishment may explain the apparent contradiction between the theories of Durkheim and Sorokin with respect to the severity of criminal punishment. Durkheim speaks of the absolutism and unlimitedness of centralized power when accounting for the wide applicability of capital punishment in the late Roman Empire, whereas Sorokin argues that heterogeneity, transition, and instability in society contribute to the application of the death penalty (for a reference to this debate see Sorokin 1937, vol. 2, 611). To the extent that Durkheim's argument refers to the de jure availability of capital punishment and Sorokin's to its de facto application, both would appear to be correct.

use of the death penalty. Political Centralization and Incomplete Incorporation predict the availability of capital punishment with only minor variations between highly and less developed nations. Political Instability predicts the use of capital punishment in both development subsamples. Political Coerciveness displays effects primarily among the highly developed nations; it is the most decisive negative predictor of trends toward abolition, and it appears to have a noteworthy effect on the availability of capital punishment as well. Likewise, group discrimination shows an effect only among highly developed nations, but in this case it is with respect to the actual use of capital punishment. The ability of these few variables to predict the presence and use of the death penalty is reasonably strong by standards of social science research (multiple correlations of 0.60 or higher mean that at least 36 percent of the variance in the dependent variable has been accounted for).

This comparative analysis must be regarded as preliminary and exploratory in character. We have used a narrow and somewhat arbitrary selection of indicators to represent the social conditions presumed to predict the availability and use of capital punishment. The data on these societal characteristics are incomplete in some cases and perhaps biased in others. We have noted, for example, that several highly coercive nations failed to report information on executions (and they may have tended to overlook trends toward abolition). Yet it is evident, despite these shortcomings, that it has further confirmed the implications of our historical analysis in the preceding section. Its results show that the same factors that were related to the presence and application of capital punishment in the past were also associated with the reluctance to abolish capital punishment or to abandon executions in recent years.

The results of the historical and comparative analyses together suggest that the reasons for the existence and use of capital punishment are quite different from those that are generally advanced as the justifications for such punishment. Thus it is not the broadly representative society, but the one in which power is concentrated in the hands of one dominant political group, that retains the death penalty. It is not the egalitarian society in which all men have a full and equal share, but the society in which some men are more equal than others, that preserves capital punishment. It is not the society with orderly processes of political succession and change, but the one that experiences turmoil and strife, that most commonly finds victims for the executioner. And it is not the just society ruled by laws, but the coercive society in which law is an instrument of power, that resists the movement to abolish capital punishment.

As the United States faces the prospect of a return to capital punishment in some modified form, it would be well to consider this evidence of the death penalty's extralegal functions. Most of this book has been devoted to the legal functions of capital punishment, and in the remainder of this chapter we shall review those findings and their implications. Yet the historical and comparative analyses in this chapter reveal that the legal functions of capital punishment are only part of the issue. The death penalty's extralegal functions must also be weighed, perhaps in equal measure, in deciding whether we should turn back to or turn away from the death penalty at this watershed between abolition and restoration.

## Contemporary Perspective

On June 29, 1972, the U.S. Supreme Court found that capital punishment violated the Eighth and Fourteenth Amendments of the U.S. Constitution because, in the opinions of the majority, its use has been rare, arbitrary, and discriminatory. Several justices, though not a majority, also held that the death penalty was cruel and unusual because it was "excessive" punishment—lacking additional value or legitimate purpose over more commonly used alternatives. And some, again not a majority, deemed it unconstitutional because such punishment does not comport with contemporary standards of morality, decency, and human dignity.

In effect, the last legal execution has taken place in America *if* the majority who have found the death penalty rare, arbitrary, and discriminatory in its application will not accept revised capital statutes alleged to preclude these faults, *or if* the minority who held (a) that the death penalty is excessive punishment or (b) that it violates standards of human decency and dignity, will, in the face of new evidence, be joined by other justices to form a majority in opposition to capital punishment on either of these other grounds.

What does the research reported here, most of it developed since the Supreme Court's *Furman* decision, have to say about these important issues? What implications do these data of "recent vintage" hold for the future of capital punishment in America?

### On Discrimination

The fact that the death penalty has been used only rarely—for perhaps one in five convicted first degree murderers at most even during the highpoint in its use in the 1930s—clearly indicates that it has not generally served as retribution even for society's most serious crimes. The fact that it has been used in a discriminatory way against blacks in America further demonstrates that the death penalty has been imposed as retaliation against a selected group of offenders, without regard for retributive justice. Capital punishment used for crimes only or chiefly when they are committed by the members of a racial minority is not retribution; it is minority group oppression. Thus, the legal function of retribution has clearly been compromised in the discriminatory use of the death penalty.

To suppose that such discrimination can be remedied by a change in judicial procedures would seem to mistake the problem. The findings in Chapter 3, together with the results of earlier studies, strongly imply that such discrimination is deeply rooted in American society. The judicial process can function effectively only within the boundaries that society is willing to accept for it. It cannot, therefore, be expected to provide evenhanded justice however the statutes are drawn if society will not tolerate the equal application of the death penalty.

The jury system was originally devised to protect defendants from arbitrary and discriminatory treatment at the hands of the state, but it is peculiarly ill designed to afford such protection from the local community. As a representative cross-section of the community, the jury can be expected to include those who hold the prevailing prejudices against social or racial minorities. To the extent that such prejudices are widely disseminated and deeply felt, the jury will enter the courtroom predisposed against "socially disfavored" defendants. Studies of jury decisions have shown that blacks as compared with whites are described more often as "unattractive" and less often as "sympathetic" defendants in criminal cases of all kinds (Kalven and Zeisel 1966, 210 ff).[15]

Making the death penalty mandatory upon conviction in capital cases, and thus removing jury discretion in sentencing, has been recommended as a way of eliminating discrimination. But research shows that conviction as well as sentencing is affected by the race of the defendant (Johnson 1941). And we have noted that discrimination remained at the points of indictment, charge, conviction (Garfinkel 1949), and execution (Johnson 1957) under the mandatory death sentence in North Carolina. Furthermore, the experience of states that moved from mandatory to discretionary capital punishment, as examined in Chap-

---

15. Parenthetically, poor defendants have also been described as "unattractive" and "unsympathetic" in the trial situation; females, on the other hand, have typically been "sympathetic" defendants (Kalven and Zeisel 1966, 210). There can be little doubt that the small number of females executed for capital crimes in America— 32 of 3,859 since 1930 (Federal Bureau of Prisons 1971, Table 14)—reflects another extreme form of discrimination in capital punishment. In light of the fact that the defendant's sex is a wholly extralegal consideration in the determination of guilt and punishment, this gross disparity in executions between men and women simply underscores the way in which social definitions, irrelevant to the facts of the case, enter the judicial process and affect the outcomes of capital cases.

ter 3, suggests that the mandatory death penalty is no solution to the problem of racial discrimination in capital punishment.

The judicial appeal process is, of course, supposed to correct such injustices. But it has not done so in the past, as we have observed, even during the recent period of increased judicial review when executions in America were in decline. The problem is that it is difficult to demonstrate discrimination in the details of a specific case when it is not the result of direct procedural violations of the rights of the defendant but rather of the prejudiced way jurors view him and weigh the evidence against him. If such discrimination is present, however, it will be evident in an analysis of the outcomes of a large number of similar cases; it will manifest itself in a systematic pattern of differential treatment or outcomes by race or other legally irrelevant social characteristics, as we have seen in Chapter 3.

The unique character of death as a punishment is that it forecloses the defendant's right of review and redress for injustices that might subsequently come to light (Rubin 1969). To permit a return to capital punishment in America, in view of its unequivocal and persistent racial discrimination under varying statutory arrangements, of the jury system's susceptibility to such discrimination, and of the evident difficulty of purging it by means of judicial review, would surely be to endorse a judicial system that finalizes a known injustice.

It might have been appropriate to assume that no such discrimination existed without systematic documentation, and when such documentation first became available it might have been appropriate to assume that such discrimination was limited to the sample within which it was documented. (Appeals courts took this latter position as late as 1970 in *Maxwell* v. *Bishop*; see *Virginia Law Review* 1972, 136 ff.) However, with the mounting evidence of widespread discrimination by race, particularly in the South, and the suggestion of substantial social class discrimination outside the South, such assumptions are untenable. To suppose that the administration of capital punishment could be free of discrimination in the face of the existing evidence would be to deny social reality in favor of legal fiction.

Racial discrimination in the criminal justice system is not, of course, restricted to the administration of capital punishment. As we have noted in Chapter 3, studies have shown that blacks are more likely to have been arrested, detained without bail, convicted, and sentenced to a longer term of imprisonment than whites. Such differential treatment for lesser offenses serves to underscore the fact that prevailing social attitudes will cause the criminal justice process to function in a discriminatory way, despite safeguards such as judicial review. Many who have been sentenced for lesser crimes have suffered discriminatory treatment at the hands of the judicial system and have received no redress. But this is no justification for irretrievably depriving offenders of such redress—as the death penalty does. The justice system that places known discrimination beyond redress will surely encourage it.

## On Deterrence

By virtually all standards, death is regarded as the most severe punishment in society (cf. Barzun 1962). Does it serve any legitimate purpose beyond that provided by lesser criminal sanctions, or is it excessive punishment? As we noted above, the claim that death is necessary as retribution has been invalidated by the rare and discriminatory way in which it has been used in practice. The claim that it is necessary for its deterrent value seems equally doubtful.

To assess the deterrent effects of capital punishment, investigators have conducted studies of various descriptions—examining and comparing nations and jurisdictions within nations for the effects of abolition and other changes in the status of the death penalty, for the effects of fluctuations in and the cessation of executions, and for the impact of the death sentence and execution in specific cases. Not one of these studies has turned up evidence that the death penalty is superior as a deterrent to other punishments. The data presented in Chapter 4 restrict claims for the deterrent power of the death penalty by showing that neither the nationwide moratorium on executions nor the move from mandatory to discretionary capital punishment encouraged or contributed to a rise in criminal homicide.

The failure of the death penalty to display any unique deterrent effect has been attributed to the fact that it was imposed almost exclusively for *irrational* actions and that even for such conduct it was *unlikely* to be imposed. Murder and rape are typically committed in rage, drunkenness, and/or stupefying passion. The offender acts in madness or out of hatred, because of insult or betrayal, without expecting to be caught or not caring if he is. While the objective likelihood of being put to death for his crime is quite low, it is doubtful that the capital offender is aware of his chances of escaping execution. Thus even under the mandatory death penalty, which presumably contributes to the impression that offenders are certain to be executed if caught, potential offenders appear equally oblivious to their fate.

Less commonly considered in the failure of the death penalty as a unique deterrent is the fact that death is not seen as something to be feared under all circumstances in our society. Indeed, risking death is sometimes seen as a way of demonstrating such virtues as courage, bravery, loyalty, and patriotism. Courageous persons will risk death to save a drowning stranger; everyone is expected to risk death in defense of his country. Our society also rewards the willingness to risk death

for adventure, sports, and redressing insult. Daring sportsmen and adventurers are typically admired for their fearless challenges to death,
and honorable men are supposed to be willing to accept death sooner
than insult.

Society encourages this willingness to risk death essentially by
teaching people to be irrational about death; that is, to deny objectively
based fears about death, to regard it as a remote possibility even when
it is close at hand, and to adopt the fatalistic attitude that their own
deaths will utlimately be the result of forces and designs operating
outside themselves and therefore largely unaffected by what they do.
The capital offender may well have learned these lessons better than
most other people.

Of course, some few deliberate and dispassionate potential murderers may have been deterred by the death penalty; the research on
deterrence does not categorically deny this possibility. What it does
imply is that for those who may have been deterred, there was an equal
number for whom the death penalty was a stimulus to murder. As we
have just noted, the need or opportunity to demonstrate one's willingness to risk death may have encouraged some potential murderers
to go ahead with their crimes. The death penalty may also have contributed to homicide, as some have suggested, by affording mentally
disturbed people a way of attracting attention to themselves and even
of bringing death upon themselves when they could not face the prospect of taking their own lives directly (West 1967). And, of course,
there is the very real possibility of a "brutalizing effect"—that the
use of death as punishment by the state deadens people's sense of
respect for human life and thus legitimates the use of death-dealing
violence as a response to insult, offense, and frustration from others
(see Chapter 1).

Recent research has also cast serious doubt on the deterrent efficacy of imprisonment. Studies have long shown that imprisonment
has little salutary effect on the offender. And, more recently, data on
the likelihood and duration of imprisonment for the major felonies
have, upon critical scrutiny, revealed little if any indication that
more certain or long-term imprisonment will deter potential offenders
(Bowers 1973). These findings, together with the evidence on capital
punishment, point generally to the likelihood that variations in legal
punishment are remote to potential offenders. There is no question
that rewards and punishments alter the course of people's behavior,
but to do so they must usually be experienced in a meaningful way in
the individual's immediate social environment. The failure of criminal
sanctions in general and the death penalty in particular to function as
effective deterrents may, indeed, be because they are not transmitted
or articulated in terms of more specific and immediate sanctions in

the potential offender's social context or because they present a challenge that, if accepted, can win him admiration within the small and insulated interpersonal environment he typically occupies (Salem and Bowers 1970, 136).

If society continues to believe in and to use the death penalty as if it were a superior deterrent, when by all objective indications it is not, it will not only be "excessive" punishment but it will also be applied in an unnecessarily arbitrary way. That is, if the death penalty is regarded as an effective deterrent, it is apt to be more commonly imposed in times of social turmoil, particularly when the incidence of serious criminal offenses is relatively high or increasing. Indeed, this is precisely what we noted in Chapter 1 for the relationship between the homicide rate and the rate of executions during the 1930s (see Table 1-4). The data revealed that in the decade of the Great Depression, when homicides rose well above previous levels, the rate of executions—not simply the number, but the number per 100 homicides—rose to a high point shortly after homicides reached their peak. In effect, the death penalty appears to have been used as a "repressive response" to high or rising crime rates (Bowers and Salem 1972).

This means that the death penalty will be imposed for reasons wholly distinct from the facts or considerations relevant to the particular case; its imposition is a function of the extent to which others are committing like crimes. If the exemplary use of the death penalty could be shown to reduce the subsequent incidence of such offenses, then it might be justified in terms of deterrence. When, however, there is no evidence whatsoever that the death penalty has a deterrent effect, its resulting use as a "repressive response" will simply introduce a further element of arbitrariness that cannot be justified in terms of any of the legal functions capital punishment is supposed to serve.

The continued belief in and use of the death penalty as a deterrent will also have the unfortunate effect of diverting attention from more constructive approaches to the prevention and control of serious and violent criminal behavior in society. It might be, for example, that the strict control of handguns in the United States would cut the criminal homicide rate substantially (and the rate of robbery as well)—a step that society might be more willing to take if it were forced to recognize the myth of the death penalty as a superior deterrent.

## On Dehumanization

In addition to retribution and deterrence, another function of the criminal sanction—namely, rehabilitation—has taken a prominent place among the standards for legal punishment in the modern world. The requirements for successful rehabilitation of criminal offenders are not yet adequately understood or implemented. The prison experience for many convicted offenders remains a degrading one, without salutary effect. Yet imprisonment is explicitly conceived by society as a device for reclaiming the offender, and the purpose of rehabilitation, however poorly achieved, has become a broadly accepted function of the criminal sanction in our society.

By contrast, death as a punishment disclaims the offender and the responsibility for his rehabilitation. Instead, the death penalty proclaims the worthlessness of his life and deprives him of the "human condition" itself. In this sense it is fundamentally and ultimately "dehumanizing" as a punishment.

But beyond this, there is little doubt that the execution itself is a degrading and dehumanizing experience both for the condemned offender and for those who attend it. The fact that the torture is not primarily physical makes it no less real; the condemned man's agony is clearly apparent, and in some ways is shared by the few people who watch him as his execution approaches.

The next morning, a Friday, I went into the Holding Cell area about eight-thirty. The guard said Leanderess had slept for only fifteen minutes, around six o'clock. I offered to read from the Bible; he appeared to listen. I read from the Psalms, and parts of two hymns: "Rock of Ages" and "Abide with Me." Leanderess held up his hands, palms out, in a gesture for me to stop. He had not paid any noticeable attention at any time and had continued pacing around his tiny cell.

He still had about an hour to live. I sat down outside his cell door. The guards talked about retirement, and whether the golf course would be too wet the next morning. At nine-fifty, Associate Warden Rigg and the doctors came in. I told Leanderess to say a prayer to himself, if he did not care to have me pray, and to relax into God's care. He did not seem to hear me. When the doctors started to approach his cell, he made a throaty, guttural growling sound. Frantically, at random, he picked up some of the old legal papers on his table and began passing them through the bars to the associate warden, as if they were appeals or writs.

A guard unlocked his cell. He gripped the bars with both hands and began a long, shrieking cry. It was a bone chilling wordless cry. The guards grabbed him, wrested him violently away from the bars. The old shirt and trousers were stripped off. His flailing arms and legs were forced into the new white shirt and fresh blue denims. The guards needed all their strength to hold him while the doctor taped the end of the stethoscope in place.

The deep-throated cry, alternately moaning and shrieking, continued. Leanderess had to be carried to the gas chamber, fighting, writhing all the way. As the witnesses watched in horror, the guards stuffed him into a chair. One guard threw his weight against the struggling little Negro while the other jerked the straps tight. They backed out, slammed the door on him.

Leanderess didn't stop screaming or struggling. Associate Warden Rigg was about to signal for the dropping of the gas pellets when we all saw Riley's small hands break free from the straps. He pulled at the other buckles, was about to free himself.

The Associate Warden withheld his signal. San Quentin had never executed a man ranging wildly around the gas chamber. He ordered the guards to go in again and restrap the frenzied man. One of the guards later said he had to pinch the straps down so tightly the second time that he "was ashamed of himself."

Again the door was closed. Again Leanderess managed to free his small, thin-wristed right hand from the straps. Riggs gave the order to drop the pellets. Working furiously, Leanderess freed his left hand. The chest strap came off next. Still shrieking and moaning, he was working on the waist strap when the gas hit him. He put both hands over his face to hold it away. Then his hands fell, his head arched back. His eyes remained open. His heart beat continued to register for two minutes, but his shrieking stopped and his head slowly drooped (Duffy and Hirshberg 1962, 102–103).

In some people this account will evoke contempt for the victim. In others it will evoke contempt for the system of justice that promotes terror in the name of legal punishment. Some will see this as necessary and even worthwhile for the offender to endure—a way of exorcising his sins and gaining his atonement. Others will see it as a fundamentally degrading and dehumanizing form of punishment that affirms vengeance over retribution and deterrence.

Let us be frank about that penalty which can have no publicity, that intimidation which works only on respectable people, so long as they are respectable, which fascinates those who have ceased to be respectable and debases or deranges those who take part in it. It is a penalty, to be sure, a frightful torture, both physical and moral, but it provides no sure example except a demoralizing one. It punishes, but it forestalls nothing; indeed, it may even arouse the impulse to murder. . . . Let us call it by the name which, for lack of any other nobility, will at least give the nobility of truth, and let us recognize it for what it is essentially: a revenge (Camus 1960, 197).

It will be argued that there is an element of revenge in all punishments, that it is only a corrupted form of capital punishment in which vengeance dominates and displaces the legally prescribed functions, and that statutory reform can restore just retribution and effective deterrence as the principal purposes of such punishment. But note that the foremost solution now being proposed to remedy such corruption— the mandatory death penalty—implicitly blames citizens in their role as jurors for past injustices and calls upon the state in the person of police, prosecutors, judges, and governors to play a greater role in these decisions of life or death. The doubtful and perhaps dangerous assumption is that such officials, unlike the public, can exercise their responsibilities without arbitrariness or discrimination. If citizens cannot make these decisions of life or death justly, should the state take them over? Suppose, as many have argued, that under the mandatory death penalty juries will discriminate in convictions just as they have in sentencing. Under existing discretionary statutes, should citizens then be excluded from such decision-making altogether? Or should the punishment that finalizes such arbitrary and discriminatory decisions be eliminated?

And what about the fact that around the world capital punishment has been associated with the centralization and coercive use of power, the presence of internal instability and strife, the deprivation and poverty of large numbers of people, and the failure to incorporate or represent diverse social elements in the national political structure? In England and America the use of the death penalty has been historically associated with conditions of servitude and exploitation of labor and political and legal disenfranchisement of oppressed or minority groups. Quite recently in the United States and South Africa, the death penalty has been used against ethnic and racial groups in ways that defy justification by any standard of legal punishment. Does all this historical and contemporary experience with capital punishment simply reflect statutory and administrative defects in its application?

Capital punishment is now on trial in America. The time has come to take account of all the evidence—not simply to debate the legal and social purposes it is supposed to serve, but to evaluate the institution in operation and the functions it actually serves in society. Tradition, unfamiliarity, and (for some) the desire for vengeance may have deadened our moral sensibilities about the inhumane character of capital punishment—just as economic considerations deadened the sensibilities of most white southerners to the barbarism of human slavery before the Civil War. Justices Brennan and Marshall have charged that the death penalty is "degrading to the dignity of human beings" and "offensive to contemporary moral values." The fact that the victims of the executioner have been the most inarticulate and dispossessed members of society may have blinded society to the moral reality of such charges, but it does not refute their validity. Little more than a century ago, America became the last nation in the Western world to rid itself of the widespread practice of human slavery. The chance to avoid this distinction in the case of capital punishment is now at hand.

# The Death Penalty on Trial

THE DECADE AFTER *FURMAN*

# TWO

# 6

## CAPITAL PUNISHMENT UNDER REVIEW

Since colonial times some 13,630 executions performed under legal, nonmilitary authority have been documented in this country (Espy 1982). More than half this number, an estimated 7,573, were conducted in the six decades between 1890 and 1950 (see Table 2-3). Historical estimates indicate that executions exceeded 100 a year on the average from the 1890s through the 1920s (see Table 2-3) and we know from official statistics that they exceeded 100 every year during the 1930s and 1940s (see Table 1-4). Then in 1950 the officially recorded number dropped below 100 for the first time; by 1960 the annual average was about 50 executions; and seven years later a de facto nationwide moratorium on executions began, largely owing to legal challenges in the courts. In effect, after six decades with more than 100 executions annually, legally imposed executions disappeared from the American scene in less than two decades.

This cessation of executions in America came at a time when other nations of the world were repudiating the death penalty in increasing numbers; the ranks of abolitionist nations doubled between 1940 and 1970 (see Table 5-3). Indeed, in the mid-1960s, when executions were ending in America, the two nations perhaps closest to the United States in cultural and legal traditions—Great Britain and Canada—both abolished capital punishment. Notably, for the period 1958–1962, less than a decade earlier, the United States had ranked among the four nations responsible for half of the world's executions imposed under legal authority, behind South Africa, Korea, and Nigeria (see Table 5-4).

The demise of executions in the late 1960s was followed by the demise of existing capital statutes in the early 1970s. The U.S. Supreme Court in *Furman* v. *Georgia* (1972) held that the administration of capital punishment under the existing laws violated the constitutional prohibition against cruel and unusual punishment because of the arbitrary way the death penalty was being imposed. This brought legal reforms. The legislatures of most states enacted new capital statutes intended to remedy the arbitrariness experienced under previous laws. Death sentences began again to be sought by prosecutors and imposed by juries, especially in the rural areas of southern states, and most often for killings that occurred in the course of another crime (usually robbery), and for the killing of whites by blacks (as documented in Chapter 7).

In the post-*Furman* era, death sentences soon became more common than they had been before *Furman*, as shown in Table 6-1. In the five years before the *Furman* decision, 93 persons a year on the average were admitted to state and federal prisons under sentence of death. In the year of and the year immediately following the *Furman* decision (when existing capital statutes were invalidated and new laws had not replaced them in many states), death row admissions dropped to 66 and 34 persons, respectively. Then, over the next five years the annual average rose to 187 admissions—almost exactly twice the pre-*Furman* level—and this marked increase held for both black and white offenders.

Practitioners of civil rights and poverty law renewed their attack on the constitutionality of the death penalty. Their legal challenges

**Table 6-1.**  *Persons Received by State Prisons under Sentence of Death by Race, 1967–1978*

| Year | Nonwhites | Whites | Total |
|------|-----------|--------|-------|
| 1978 | 74  | 108 | 182 |
| 1977 | 64  | 68  | 132 |
| 1976 | 88  | 136 | 224 |
| 1975 | 143 | 121 | 264 |
| 1974 | 65  | 67  | 132 |
| 1973 | 23  | 11  | 34  |
| 1972 | 40  | 26  | 66  |
| 1971 | 51  | 45  | 96  |
| 1970 | 52  | 64  | 116 |
| 1969 | 36  | 49  | 85  |
| 1968 | 45  | 51  | 96  |
| 1967 | 38  | 36  | 74  |

*Source*: U.S. Federal Bureau of Prisons, National Prisoner Statistics, *Capital Punishment* (1971); U.S. National Criminal Justice Information and Statistics Service, *Capital Punishment* (1979).

led to state and federal court decisions overturning many death sentences and extending the de facto moratorium on execution. But after ten years without an execution, the moratorium was broken on January 17, 1977, when one of the mounting number of condemned persons—Gary Gilmore—chose death in preference to continued imprisonment. Once Gilmore's request for a new trial had been denied by the Utah Supreme Court and life in prison appeared to be the only alternative to death by firing squad, he dismissed his attorney, refused all further legal assistance, and sought to hasten his execution. Likewise, in 1978 Jesse Bishop chose execution by lethal gas in Nevada over life imprisonment. He too refused to have his case appealed in the federal courts after his death sentence was upheld by the Nevada Supreme Court. These executions were followed in 1979 by the electrocution of John Spinkelink [1] in Florida; in 1981, by the electrocution of Steven Judy in Indiana; and in 1982 by the electrocution of Frank Coppola in Virginia and the lethal injection of Charles Brooks in Texas. Of these six persons put to death since *Furman*, only two—John Spinkelink and Charles Brooks—sought to avoid execution by all legal means. The irony is that for most of those executed since *Furman* the death penalty was not the most dreaded legal alternative, but the preferred punishment, if not an escape from punishment.

These few executions could be just the beginning. At latest count, there were some 1,134 persons under sentence of death in 32 civil jurisdictions[2]. At one a day, it would take almost three years to carry out these executions, and the annual number would far exceed the previous highpoint of 199 executions in 1935. The annual average for the 1980s is well above 200 death sentences a year. Either executions will resume in unprecedented numbers and the United States will become the world's unrivaled leader in this respect, or the institution of capital punishment will be drastically altered or eliminated. This is a precarious moment in the history of capital punishment in America—the death penalty is on trial.

## The Judicial Assault Renewed

The roots of this precarious situation reach back into the 1960s when the NAACP Legal Defense and Educational Fund, Inc. (Legal Defense Fund or LDF), undertook a concerted national assault on the

1. This name was sometimes spelled "Spenkelink" or "Spinkellink" in the media and in court briefs.
2. This is the number of nonmilitary death sentences listed in the December 20, 1982, issue of *Death Row USA* (LDF, bimonthly). Six death sentences imposed under the U. S. Military Code are also listed, but excluded from this total. The total of both military and nonmilitary death sentences was 1,140, not the reported 1,137 (LDF December, 1982: 1).

death penalty (Meltsner 1973a) by appealing death sentences and challenging the constitutionality of capital statutes. This led to the nationwide moratorium on executions and to U.S. Supreme Court decisions limiting the applicability of capital punishment. The breakthrough in Supreme Court rulings came when the Legal Defense Fund attacked the death penalty on Eighth Amendment grounds as cruel and unusual punishment. It presented legal argument and evidence amassed by social scientists to the effect that capital punishment is inconsistent with evolving standards of decency in America and around the world, that it has no deterrent advantage over the commonly used alternative punishments, and that it is imposed in an arbitrary and discriminatory fashion. The LDF consolidated this three-fold attack in terms of contemporary values, utility, and fairness in a group of appeals to the U.S. Supreme Court in 1971, with *Furman* v. *Georgia* as the lead case.

On June 29, 1972, the Supreme Court declared in *Furman* that capital punishment was being administered in violation of the Eighth Amendment prohibition against cruel and unusual punishment. That ruling invalidated the capital statutes of some thirty-five states and spared the lives of more than six hundred persons condemned to death. Each of the nine Justices filed an opinion in the case. The common thread of agreement among the plurality was that the death penalty was being applied in an arbitrary manner under existing statutes. Justices Douglas and Marshall saw the arbitrariness as a systematic bias against those disadvantaged by race and poverty; whereas Stewart, White, and Brennan saw the arbitrariness as "uncommon," "rare," or "freakish," like being struck by lightning or being picked in a lottery. Several members of the plurality blamed this arbitrariness on the failure of the existing laws to guide or to control the exercise of discretion in the imposition of the death sentence. The *Furman* decision did not, however, abolish capital punishment per se; it simply ruled out the uncontrolled, unguided exercise of discretion in its application.

State legislatures responded to *Furman* with new capital punishment laws of two basic types: "mandatory" statutes, making the death penalty automatic upon conviction for specifically defined capital offenses; and "guided discretion" statutes, providing guidelines for sentencing in the form of explicitly enumerated aggravating and mitigating circumstances. For the 30 states that reinstated capital punishment by the fall of 1974, Table 6-2 shows the specific elements of homicide requiring or justifying the death sentence—by statutory definition under mandatory statutes, as aggravating circumstances under guided discretion statutes, and by either method under statutes that combine both components. Of the many elements outlined in the various statutes, only three were present in more than half the jurisdictions with each type of statute: killings committed in the course of another felony

**Table 6-2.** *Elements of Capital Homicide in Post-*Furman *Statutes as of 1974*

| Elements of Capital Homicide | Statutory Method of Indicating Elements of Capital Homicide | | |
|---|---|---|---|
| | Statutory definition only | Both statutory definition and aggravating circumstances | Aggravating circumstances only |
| Offender characteristics | | | |
| Hired, paid killer | 8 | 5 | 9 |
| Serving prison sentence | 7 | 3 | 5 |
| Prior criminal conviction | 5 | 5 | 8 |
| Offense Characteristics | | | |
| During other specified felony | 10 | 5 | 9 |
| Heinous, vile, atrocious method | – | 4 | 4 |
| Knowingly endangering others | – | 3 | 4 |
| Premeditated | 6 | 3 | 2 |
| Use of explosives | 4 | 1 | 3 |
| Hindering government functions | – | 2 | 1 |
| Preventing arrest | 2 | 2 | 3 |
| During sale of narcotics | 1 | 6 | – |
| Victim Characteristics | | | |
| Policeman, prison guard | 10 | 5 | 8 |
| Multiple victims | 4 | 3 | 5 |
| Kidnapped victim | 1 | 2 | 3 |
| Victim a witness to a crime | 1 | – | 2 |
| Victim a government official | – | – | 2 |
| *Number of statutes* | 14 | 6 | 10 |

*Source*: Petitioner's brief in *Fowler* v. *North Carolina* (1974, App. A)

(especially rape or armed robbery); killings of a police officer, prison guard or fireman (usually in the course of his duty); and killing for hire. Aside from these three, there is little consistency or agreement across jurisdictions on what should justify or mandate death as punishment. And what consensus there is appears to reflect a shift in the legal justification for death as punishment from the traditional grounds of deliberation and premeditation embodied in the concept of "first degree" murder or "crime-linked" killings perpetrated during other crimes, by paid criminals, or against crime control agents. Indeed, killings that occurred in the course of another crime, usually resulting from surprise, alarm, or self-protective instincts, were responsible for four out of five death sentences in the three states—Florida, Georgia, and Texas—that accounted for half the persons under sentence of death five years after *Furman* (see Chapter 7).

These new laws and their application set in motion a renewed

judicial assault on the death penalty led by members of the Legal
Defense Fund. Many were veterans of the judicial battles of the sixties;
they included individual defense attorneys, typically public defenders,
working in the trial courts of states with new capital statutes; groups
of attorneys, such as Team Defense of Atlanta, Georgia, and the Southern Poverty Law Center of Montgomery, Alabama, which concentrated
their efforts in state trial and appellate courts; and the Legal Defense
Fund, which assisted trial and appellate lawyers throughout the country and brought appeals to the federal courts.

In 1974 LDF brought North Carolina's mandatory capital statute
to the U.S. Supreme Court in *Fowler* v. *North Carolina*, but the court
reached no decision in the case. A year later, however, the Court heard
appeals from North Carolina, Georgia, Florida, Louisiana, and Texas
attacking both mandatory and discretionary statutes, with *Gregg* v.
*Georgia* as the lead case. The Fund's lawyers renewed the Eighth
Amendment attack in terms of contemporary values, utility and fairness, with additional evidence and arguments focusing on the particulars of these post-*Furman* statutes.

On July 2, 1976, the Supreme Court took a further but not final
step: it abolished the mandatory death penalty but upheld guided discretion statutes. In *Woodson* v. *North Carolina* and *Roberts* v. *Louisiana* the Court concluded that mandatory statutes were unconstitutional
because contemporary standards of justice require "individualized
sentencing" in capital cases and because the mandatory death sentence
for murder had been abandoned by all states prior to *Furman*, evidence
that it is inconsistent with current social values. On the other hand,
in *Gregg* v. *Georgia, Proffitt* v. *Florida*, and *Jurek* v. *Texas*, guided discretion statutes were approved—at least in principle. For the plurality,
Justice Stewart wrote (emphasis added): "On their face these procedures
*seem* to satisfy the concerns of *Furman*. No longer *should* there be 'no
meaningful basis for distinguishing the few cases in which [the death
penalty] is imposed from the many cases in which it is not' " (quoting
from Justice White's *Furman* opinion). The Court thus did not explicitly make a judgment on the guided discretion statutes *as applied*, but
reasoned that they should—theoretically—remedy the ills identified
in *Furman*.

After *Gregg*, the Supreme Court went on to make further decisions
limiting and guiding the use of capital punishment. In *Coker* v. *Georgia*
(1977) it abolished the death penalty for rape of an adult woman on
grounds that it was inconsistent with contemporary standards and
values. For the plurality, Justice White observed that the death penalty
was not available as a punishment for rape in the great majority of
countries with capital punishment, that it was available in only one
of the United States, namely Georgia, and that nine out of ten Georgia

juries refused to impose it on convicted rapists. Then, in *Lockett* v. *Ohio* (1978) the Court struck down Ohio's capital statute because it restricted the consideration of mitigating circumstances. Extending the standard used to invalidate mandatory capital statutes in *Woodson*, it held that the sentencing authority, either judge or jury, must be permitted to hear all evidence of mitigation, in order to provide "individualized sentencing" appropriate to the particular circumstances of the crime and the defendant. Chief Justice Burger made clear that this requirement rests on concepts of human dignity and "respect due the uniqueness of the individual" (438 U.S. 586,605). Later, in *Godfrey* v. *Georgia* (1980), the Court clarified the monitoring function of the appellate review process. It found that the Georgia Supreme Court had failed to ensure that juries throughout the state were interpreting and applying one of the statutory aggravating circumstances in a consistent manner. This ruling did not invalidate the Georgia statute or this particular aggravating circumstance, but it did make clear that the death sentence cannot be imposed unless in comparable factual situations juries throughout the state find the same aggravating circumstances. It held that the appellate review process must ensure such uniformity.

Conspicuous by its absence is a decision the U.S. Supreme Court did *not* make on the death penalty *as applied*. In September 1977, John Spinkelink challenged Florida's guided discretion statute as applied. Before the Federal District Court in Tallahassee, on Spinkelink's behalf, the LDF presented systematic statistical evidence of the racially biased use of the death penalty in Florida since *Furman*. This evidence, supporting what has been characterized as the "white victim argument," showed that the death sentence was imposed almost exclusively when the murder victim was white, hardly ever when the victim was black—and that this pattern held for murders committed in the course of another crime (felony-murder)—the kind of offense that Spinkelink was alleged to have committed. Ignoring the fact that the evidence pertained specifically to felony-type murders, the Florida attorney general responded that murders involving black victims are usually not capital offenses but are simply the "result of family quarrels, lovers' quarrels, liquor quarrels, [and] barroom quarrels."

A month later, Spinkelink's appeal was denied by the Federal District Court and ten months after that it was denied by the Fifth Circuit Court of Appeals. In its opinion, the Fifth Circuit Court restated the Florida attorney general's argument and even quoted his characterization of black victim killings (*Spinkelink* v. *Wainwright*, 578 F.2d 582, 612 n.37)—again disregarding the evidence pertaining specifically to potentially capital felony-murders. Beyond this, the court went on to rule that statistical evidence of differential treatment was insufficient even if correct; a case-by-case demonstration of *intent to dis-*

*criminate* would be necessary. When, two years later in *Jurek* v. *Estelle* (1979), a three-judge panel of the Fifth Circuit ruled that statistical patterns of this kind *could* constitute prima facie evidence of arbitrariness and discrimination, this decision was recalled for reconsideration by the full circuit membership and the opinion was reissued without reference to the evidentiary role of statistical data—thus leaving the Fifth Circuit's *Spinkelink* ruling intact.

The U.S. Supreme Court had a history of reluctance to consider the race issue in capital punishment when the Legal Defense Fund appealed the Fifth Circuit's *Spinkelink* ruling. Fifteen years earlier, it is reported (Meltsner 1973a), Justice Goldberg was persuaded by other members of the Court to drop references about the racially biased application of the death penalty for rape in his opinion in *Rudolph* v. *Alabama* (1963). Several years later, in *Maxwell* v. *Bishop* (1970), the Court agreed to review a rape case in which powerful statistical evidence of racial disparities in the sentencing of convicted rapists had been introduced; but in its statement of acceptance, the Court excluded the question of racial discrimination from consideration. The issue of discrimination figured in the judgments of only two of the concurring five Justices in *Furman* and not at all in the plurality decisions in *Woodson* and *Gregg*. And even the *Coker* decision, which finally abolished the death penalty for rape, totally ignored the strong evidence of racism in the use of the death penalty for this crime. Consistent with this pattern, the Supreme Court refused to hear the evidence of racial disparities in Spinkelink's case. He became the first person to be unwillingly executed after 1967.

## The New Capital Statutes and Their Application

The federal court decisions from *Furman* on set standards and endorsed procedures intended to remove arbitrariness and to ensure evenhandedness in capital punishment. To see the impact of these rulings on the laws and their application in the various states, we first consider the attempts of state legislatures and supreme courts to replace old laws with new ones. Then we look at how the state criminal justice system responded to these new laws.

The legal availability of the death penalty by state in the post-*Furman* era is summarized in Figure 6-1.[3] For each state, the figure

3. The statutes represented in Figure 6-1 all cover capital homicide of one form or another. Statutory provisions for capital homicide in effect in 1974 are compiled by state in the petitioner's brief in Fowler v. North Carolina, 1974, Appendix A. Specific statutory provisions for the death penalty under Georgia, Florida, and Texas post-

shows when capital statutes were enacted (E) or amended (A) by the state legislature and invalidated (I) or revised (R) by the state supreme court. Periods for which the death penalty was legally available in each state are represented by lines beginning with legislative enactments, except when they follow incomplete invalidations or replace already existing capital statutes. They end with judicial invalidations, except when they are partial or incomplete, leaving some capital provisions in force, and are sometimes interrupted by legislative amendments and judicial revisions. Where there appears to be no state supreme court invalidation of the pre-*Furman* statute, the dashed line extends to the first post-*Furman* enactment. An inventory of legislative and judicial actions on capital punishment since *Furman* with specific statutory and case law citations is presented in Appendix B of this volume; information on judicial invalidations of pre-*Furman* capital statutes was drawn from the December 1982 issue of *Death Row USA* updated bimonthly by the Legal Defense Fund.

The decisive effect of the *Furman* decision is clearly evident in Figure 6-1. At the time of *Furman*, 13 of 51 jurisdictions had no effective capital statute. The latest to join this group were California and New Jersey, whose supreme courts had ruled their respective statutes violated their state constitutions shortly before the *Furman* decision. In the remaining 38 capital jurisdictions, state supreme courts explicitly invalidated pre-*Furman* statutes in thirty-two cases and appear to have taken no explicit action in six cases, perhaps because there was no one under sentence of death to initiate appellate action or because the state legislature responded with new capital statutes before such ruling was issued. Most state supreme courts responded with complete invalidation orders before the end of 1972; the high courts of eight states did so in 1973; Massachusetts rendered a complete invalidation in 1975; and the District of Columbia did not respond with an invalidation order until 1980.

*Key to Figure 6-1*

E  =  Legislative *enactment* or *reenactment*, introducing a new capital statute or reworking one as part of a major criminal code reform usually following judicial invalidation.

A  =  Legislative *amendment*, considerably less far-reaching than en-

---

Furman statutes are presented in Chapter 7, footnotes 3 through 7. Other categories of crime covered by capital statutes in each state, such as treason, aggravated kidnapping, rape of a minor, etc., are indicated in the annual reports entitled *Capital Punishment* now published by the U.S. National Criminal Justice Information and Statistics Service. For capital homicide, however, these reports provide no information beyond the statutory language of the respective states, such as "murder," "first degree murder," "aggravated murder," or "Class A felony murder."

actment, usually involving minor additions or alterations of an existing capital statute.

I  =  Judicial *invalidation* by a state supreme court declaring all or most of a capital statute inoperative, usually pursuant to a federal court ruling.

R  =  Judicial *revision* by a state supreme court interpreting a statute so as to keep it in force as law or altering it to the same effect, often by severing unconstitutional provisions.

**Figure 6-1.** *Enactments, Amendments, Revisions, and Invalidations of Capital Statutes Annually by State, 1972–1982*

| | 1972 | 1973 | 1974 | 1975 | 1976 | 1977 | 1978 | 1979 | 1980 | 1981 | 1982 |
|---|---|---|---|---|---|---|---|---|---|---|---|
| **Northeast** | | | | | | | | | | | |
| Maine | | | | | | | | | | | |
| New Hampshire | −I | | E | | | A | | | | | |
| Vermont | | | | | | | | | | | |
| Massachusetts | −I | | I | | | | E | I | | | E— |
| Rhode Island | | E | | | | | | I | | | |
| Connecticut | −I | E | | | | | | | A | | |
| New York | −I | | E | | | I | | | | | |
| New Jersey | | | | | | | | | | | E— |
| Pennsylvania | −I | | E | | | I | E | | | | |
| **North Central** | | | | | | | | | | | |
| Ohio | −I | | E | | | | I | | | E | |
| Indiana | −I | E | | | | I E | | | | | |
| Illinois | −I | | E—I | | | E | | | | | |
| Michigan | | | | | | | | | | | |
| Wisconsin | | | | | | | | | | | |
| Minnesota | | | | | | | | | | | |
| Iowa | | | | | | | | | | | |
| Missouri | | | | E | | I E | | | A | | |
| North Dakota | | | | | | | | | | | |
| South Dakota | | | | | | | | E | | | |
| Nebraska | −I | E | | | | | A | | | | |
| Kansas | | I | | | | | | | | | |
| **South** | | | | | | | | | | | |
| Delaware | −I | | | E | I | E | | | | | |
| Maryland | −I | | | E—I | | | E—A | | | | |
| D. C. | | | | | | | | | I | | |
| Virginia | | | | E | | A | | | | | |
| West Virginia | | | | | | | | | | | |
| No. Carolina | | R—E | | | I | E | | A—A | | | |
| So. Carolina | −I | | E | | I | E—A | | | | | |
| Georgia | | I E | | | | | | | | | |

| | 1972 | 1973 | 1974 | 1975 | 1976 | 1977 | 1978 | 1979 | 1980 | 1981 | 1982 |
|---|---|---|---|---|---|---|---|---|---|---|---|
| Florida | I | E | | | | | | A | | | |
| Kentucky | | | I | | E | E | | | | | |
| Tennessee | I | I | E | | | I | E | | A | | |
| Alabama | | I | | | E | | | | R | E | |
| Mississippi | I | | E | | R | E | | | | | |
| Arkansas | I | E | | | | E | A | | | | |
| Louisiana | I | E | | | I | E | | | | | |
| Oklahoma | | I | E | | I | E | | | A | | |
| Texas | I | E | | | | | | | | | |
| *West* | | | | | | | | | | | |
| Montana | I | E | I | E | | | E | | | | |
| Idaho | | I | E | | | | E | | | | |
| Wyoming | I | E | | | | I | E | | | | |
| Colorado | I | | | E | | | I | E | | | |
| New Mexico | | E | | | I | | | E | A | | |
| Arizona | | I | E | | | | | R | E | | |
| Utah | I | E | | | | A | | | | | |
| Nevada | I | E | | | | A | | | | | |
| Washington | I | | | E | | E | | | | I | E |
| Oregon | | | | | | | | E | | I | |
| California | | | E | I | E | A | | | | | |
| Alaska | | | | | | | | | | | |
| Hawaii | | | | | | | | | | | |
| | 1972 | 1973 | 1974 | 1975 | 1976 | 1977 | 1978 | 1979 | 1980 | 1981 | 1982 |

*Sources*: Legislative and Judicial Actions on Capital Punishment since *Furman* (Appendix B of this book) supplemented with information from *Death Row USA* (LDF, December 1982, 3)
*Note*: The jurisdictions of the U.S. territories did not provide for the death penalty, but federal civil and military codes did so during this period.

In the period between *Furman* and *Gregg*, most states returned to capital punishment: 33 states enacted new capital statutes by 1975; one more—Alabama—did so in 1976, before the *Gregg* decision. One state—Illinois—invalidated its post-*Furman* capital statute in 1975 prior to the *Gregg* decision, and one abolitionist state at the time of *Furman*—California—took up the death penalty before *Gregg*. Two other jurisdictions—District of Columbia and Vermont—having made no legislative or judicial response to *Furman*, continued to have capital statutes technically in effect though constitutionally infirm. Only two states with capital statutes in effect at the time of *Furman*—Massachusetts and Kansas—did not return to the death penalty before *Gregg*. In Massachusetts, however, a statute making the death penalty mandatory for rape resulting in murder remained on the books until 1975 when the Massachusetts Supreme Judicial Court ruled that it violated the state constitution. Thus, at the time of the *Gregg* decision,

36 jurisdictions had capital statutes, compared with 38 at the time with *Furman.*

Between the *Gregg* decision and the end of the decade, 17 states experienced an interruption in the availability of the death penalty; in one case—Ohio—this was the result not of *Gregg* but of *Lockett.* Of these, 15 states enacted new capital statutes before 1980, and two—Ohio and Rhode Island—did not. Another 19 states experienced no such interruption although most of these found it necessary to alter their statutes in light of *Gregg;* 10 states responded with amendments or reenactments; Arizona and Mississippi reacted with major judicial revisions; New York largely invalidated its capital statute leaving the death penalty only for an inmate convicted of murder while serving a life sentence; and Vermont and Washington, D.C., continued under their pre-*Furman* statutes without taking notice of *Furman, Gregg,* or *Lockett* throughout the 1970s. Only four states—Alabama, Connecticut, Georgia, and Texas—give no indication of legislative or judicial reaction, and in the case of Georgia, the *Coker* decision altered the application of that state's statute to exclude rape as a capital offense. Finally, four states without capital statutes at the time of Gregg returned to it before the end of the decade: Massachusetts, Oregon, and South Dakota enacted their first post-*Furman* capital statutes during this period, and Illinois returned to capital punishment for the second time after *Furman* during this period. Thus, at the end of the 1970s the count of capital punishment jurisdictions had risen to 38, precisely where it was at the time of *Furman.*

In the 1980s the supreme courts in three states—Massachusetts, Oregon, and Washington—struck down capital statutes enacted after *Gregg,* and the District of Columbia belatedly invalidated its pre-*Furman* statute. However, the legislatures of Washington and Massachusetts subsequently reenacted capital statutes in the 1980s. In addition, Ohio and New Jersey enacted capital statutes after earlier invalidations. New Jersey returned to the death penalty more than a decade after it was ruled unconstitutional by the state supreme court; Massachusetts reinstated capital statutes after its supreme court twice ruled previous capital statutes unconstitutional during the post-*Furman* period. Again, by the end of 1982, the number of jurisdictions with capital statutes on their books, regardless of their constitutional validity or infirmity, was 38—exactly the number at the time of *Furman.*

It is evident from Figure 6-1 that the decisions of the U.S. Supreme Court on capital punishment since *Furman* have not diminished the availability of the death penalty. These rulings have interrupted its availability by causing jurisdictions to give up statutes that violate the standards or procedures the high court has established. But the overriding response of the states has been to return to the death penalty under the substantive and procedural requirements laid down in the Supreme Court's decision.

We observed in Table 6-1 that death sentences declined immediately after the *Furman* decision abolished existing statutes and then rose to twice the level of previous years as new capital statutes replaced the old ones. And we noted that the pace has quickened even more in the 1980s, with death row reaching a historical highpoint of 1,134 persons by the end of 1982. To see how this unprecedented increase in the use of capital punishment has come about, it is necessary to take a closer look at the application of the death penalty under these new statutes in the various states.

The number of persons under sentence of death at the close of each year and the numbers added to and removed from death row during the year (in italics) are shown for each state from 1973 through 1982 in Table 6-3. Thus, the table shows how the year-to-year totals are affected by additions and removals each year.[4]

For the nation as a whole, the number of persons under sentence of death had mounted by more than 100 a year, and the number of death sentences imposed by more than 200 a year on the average. Removals from death row were greatest in 1976, the year of the *Gregg* decision. Additions were least in 1973 and 1977, the years immediately following the *Furman* and *Gregg* decisions, before newly drafted capital statutes were fully in effect. In the 1980s additions have risen above and removals have fallen below most previous levels; 1982 marks the high point of new admissions to death row.

Throughout the entire period, the southern states were responsible for at least two out of every three death sentences imposed and persons under sentence of death, and in most years more than three out of four. Three southern states—Florida, Georgia, and Texas—have dominated this pattern. They were responsible for almost half of the death sentences among southern states and a third of those in the nation at large throughout this ten-year period. These are, of course, the three states whose post-*Furman* capital statutes were affirmed in the Court's *Gregg,*

---

4. These figures represent the numbers of persons under sentence of death as a result of trial and appellate court actions and not the numbers under such sentences in state and federal prisons as reported in *Capital Punishment* (National Criminal Justice Information and Statistical Service, annually). Because persons sentenced to death in some states, such as Georgia and Texas, remain in local jails for extended periods, often without being moved to state or federal prisons before their death sentences are overturned, the officially published statistics (based on corrections reports) tend to underestimate the number of death sentences handed down in a given year, and to record such sentences in the year after they were actually handed down. For a further discussion of these issues see *Capital Punishment* (NCJISS 1980, 4 n. 3, and Appendix iv. Methodology).

**Table 6-3.** *Persons under Sentence of Death Annually by State, 1973–1982*

| Region | Cumulative Totals, Additions, and Removals | | | | | | | | | |
|---|---|---|---|---|---|---|---|---|---|---|
| | 1973 | 1974 | 1975 | 1976 | 1977 | 1978 | 1979 | 1980 | 1981 [a] | 1982 [a] |
| *Northeast* | | | | | | | | | | |
| Massachusetts | 0 | 0 | 1 / 3,−2 | 0 / 0,−1 | 0 | 0 | 0 | 0 | 0 | 0 |
| Rhode Island | 0 | 0 | 2 / 2,0 | 2 / 0,0 | 4 / 2,0 | 4 / 0,0 | 0 / 0,−4 | 0 | 0 | 0 |
| New York | 0 | 0 | 1 / 1,0 | 2 / 1,0 | 0 / 0,−2 | 0 | 0 | 0 | 0 | 0 |
| Pennsylvania | 0 | 2 / 2,0 | 6 / 4,0 | 11 / 7,−2 | 18 / 10,−3 | 16 [b] / 3,−5 | 2 / 0,−14 | 9 / 9,−2 | 23 / 15,−1 | 45 / 24,−2 |
| ALL NORTHEAST | 0 | 2 / 2,0 | 10 / 10,−2 | 15 / 8,−3 | 22 / 12,−5 | 20 / 3,−5 | 2 / 0,−18 | 9 / 9,−2 | 23 / 15,−1 | 45 / 24,−2 |
| *North Central* | | | | | | | | | | |
| Ohio | 0 | 5 / 5,0 | 33 / 28,0 | 66 / 34,−1 | 84 / 26,−8 | 4 / 18,−98 | 4 / 0,0 | 4 / 0,0 | 0 / 0,−4 | 3 / 3,0 |
| Indiana | 0 | 1 / 1,0 | 6 / 5,0 | 7 / 1,0 | 2 / 1,−6 | 4 / 2,0 | 5 / 1,0 | 6 / 4,−3 | 10 / 5,−1 | 14 / 5,−1 |
| Illinois | 0 | 0 | 0 | 0 | 1 / 1,0 | 5 / 4,0 | 19 / 14,0 | 30 / 16,−5 | 40 / 12,−2 | 51 / 12,−1 |
| Missouri | 0 | 0 | 0 | 0 | 0 | 0 | 3 / 3,0 | 8 / 5,0 | 14 / 6,0 | 20 / 7,−1 |
| Nebraska | 0 | 0 | 2 / 2,0 | 5 / 3,0 | 4 / 0,−1 | 7 / 3,0 | 7 / 1,−1 | 10 / 3,0 | 12 / 2,0 | 12 / 0,0 |
| ALL NORTH CENTRAL | 0 | 6 / 6,0 | 41 / 35,0 | 78 / 38,−1 | 91 / 28,−15 | 20 / 27,−98 | 38 / 19,−1 | 58 / 28,−8 | 76 / 25,−7 | 100 / 27,−3 |

| | (1) | (2) | (3) | (4) | (5) | (6) | (7) | (8) | (9) | (10) |
|---|---|---|---|---|---|---|---|---|---|---|
| Delaware | 0 | 0 | 2<br>2,0 | 0<br>8,−10 | 0 | 1<br>1,0 | 1<br>0,0 | 2<br>2,−1 | 4<br>2,0 | 5<br>1,0 |
| Maryland | 0 | 0 | 2<br>2,0 | 0<br>1,−3 | 0 | 0 | 1<br>1,0 | 1<br>1,−1 | 7<br>7,−1 | 14<br>8,−1 |
| Virginia | 0 | 0 | 2[b]<br>2,0 | 0[b]<br>2,−4 | 1<br>1,0 | 6<br>5,0 | 8<br>3,−1 | 13<br>8,−3 | 17<br>5,−1 | 19<br>4,−2 |
| N. Carolina | 0 | 36[b]<br>36,0 | 72[b]<br>36,0 | −1[b]<br>36,−109 | 0<br>2,−1 | 7<br>7,0 | 7<br>7,−7 | 15<br>9,−1 | 17<br>5,−3 | 29<br>13,−1 |
| S. Carolina | 0 | 8[b]<br>8,0 | 16[b]<br>8,0 | 19[b]<br>18,−15 | 20<br>4,−3 | 16<br>3,−7 | 17<br>5,−4 | 24<br>8,−1 | 21<br>5,−8 | 18<br>2,−5 |
| Georgia | 7<br>8,−1 | 26<br>21,−2 | 42<br>24,−8 | 57<br>19,−4 | 72<br>27,−12 | 79<br>18,−11 | 90<br>21,−10 | 90<br>20,−20 | 109<br>22,−3 | 118<br>15,−6 |
| Florida | 11[c]<br>12,−1 | 35<br>26,−2 | 61<br>31,−5 | 83<br>32,−10 | 99<br>29,−13 | 129<br>37,−7 | 141<br>29,−17 | 160<br>34,−15 | 162<br>17,−15 | 189<br>43,−16 |
| Kentucky | 0 | 0 | 3<br>3,0 | 3<br>0,0 | 0<br>1,−4 | 3<br>3,0 | 3<br>0,0 | 5<br>4,−2 | 10<br>5,0 | 13<br>6,−3 |
| Tennessee | 14[b]<br>14,0 | 28[b]<br>14,0 | 42[b]<br>14,0 | 56[b]<br>14,0 | 17<br>2,−41 | 26<br>9,0 | 24<br>0,−2 | 30<br>7,−1 | 26<br>0,−4 | 35<br>10,−1 |
| Alabama | 0 | 0 | 1<br>1,0 | 4<br>3,0 | 21<br>20,−3 | 39<br>22,−4 | 35<br>13,−17 | 28<br>11,−18 | 55<br>28,−1 | 56<br>14,−13 |
| Mississippi | 0 | 3<br>3,0 | 15<br>13,−1 | 17<br>9,−7 | 12<br>7,−12 | 12<br>2,−2 | 12<br>1,−1 | 14<br>5,−3 | 23<br>9,0 | 36<br>13,0 |
| Arkansas | 0 | 0 | 4<br>4,0 | 4<br>2,−2 | 6<br>4,−2 | 10<br>5,−1 | 11<br>4,−3 | 14<br>3,0 | 23<br>13,−4 | 26<br>4,−1 |
| Louisiana | 1<br>1,0 | 15<br>14,0 | 32<br>17,0 | 1<br>14,−45 | 2<br>2,−1 | 12<br>11,−1 | 13<br>5,−4 | 20<br>11,−4 | 30<br>11,−1 | 36<br>10,−4 |
| Oklahoma | 12[b]<br>12,0 | 24[b]<br>12,0 | 36[b]<br>12,0 | 12[b]<br>12,−36 | 17<br>5,0 | 28<br>11,0 | 37<br>9,0 | 44<br>9,−2 | 37<br>0,−7 | 38<br>7,−6 |
| Texas | 0 | 13<br>13,0 | 35<br>24,−2 | 58<br>23,0 | 70<br>22,−10 | 105<br>44,−9 | 119<br>27,−13 | 129<br>29,−19 | 144<br>37,−22 | 153<br>37,−28 |
| ALL SOUTH | 45[c]<br>47,−2 | 188<br>147,−4 | 365<br>193,−16 | 313<br>193,−245 | 337<br>126,−102 | 473<br>178,−42 | 519<br>125,−79 | 589<br>161,−91 | 685<br>166,−70 | 785<br>187,−87 |

**Table 6-3.** (continued)

| | 1973 | 1974 | 1975 | 1976 | 1977 | 1978 | 1979 | 1980 | 1981[a] | 1982[a] |
|---|---|---|---|---|---|---|---|---|---|---|
| *West* | | | | | | | | | | |
| Montana | 2<br>*2,0* | 0<br>*0,-2* | 4<br>*4,0* | 5<br>*1,0* | 3<br>*0,-2* | 5<br>*3,-1* | 4<br>*0,-1* | 4<br>*0,0* | 3<br>*0,-1* | 3<br>*0,0* |
| Idaho | 0 | 0 | 0 | 2<br>*2,0* | 1<br>*1,-2* | 1<br>*0,0* | 1<br>*1,-1* | 1<br>*0,0* | 0<br>*0,-1* | 7<br>*8,-1* |
| Wyoming | 0 | 0 | 4<br>*4,0* | 5<br>*1,0* | 2<br>*0,-3* | 0<br>*0,-2* | 1<br>*1,0* | 1<br>*0,0* | 1<br>*0,0* | 2<br>*1,0* |
| Colorado | 0 | 0 | 1<br>*1,0* | 4<br>*3,0* | 5<br>*2,-1* | 0<br>*1,-6* | 0 | 0 | 1<br>*1,0* | 2<br>*1,0* |
| New Mexico | 0 | 4<br>*4,0* | 6<br>*6,-4* | 3<br>*5,-8* | 0<br>*0,-3* | 0 | 0 | 1<br>*1,0* | 3<br>*2,0* | 5<br>*2,0* |
| Arizona | 0 | 6<br>*6,0* | 13<br>*8,-1* | 15<br>*6,-4* | 21<br>*8,-2* | 21<br>*14,-14* | 29<br>*17,-9* | 32<br>*11,-8* | 37<br>*8,-3* | 46<br>*14,-5* |
| Utah | 0 | 2<br>*2,0* | 5<br>*3,0* | 6<br>*1,0* | 5<br>*0,-1* | 6<br>*1,0* | 7<br>*1,0* | 4<br>*1,-4* | 3<br>*0,-1* | 3<br>*1,-1* |
| Nevada | 0 | 0 | 1<br>*1,0* | 3<br>*2,0* | 3<br>*1,-1* | 6<br>*4,-1* | 7<br>*3,-2* | 10<br>*3,0* | 12<br>*4,-2* | 16<br>*4,0* |
| Washington | 0 | 0 | 0 | 0 | 2<br>*2,0* | 6<br>*4,0* | 5<br>*1,-2* | 5<br>*0,0* | 0<br>*0,-5* | 2<br>*2,0* |
| Oregon | 0 | 0 | 0 | 0 | 0 | 0 | 1<br>*1,0* | 4<br>*3,0* | 0<br>*0,-4* | 0<br>*0,0* |
| California | 0 | 23[b]<br>*23,0* | 46[b]<br>*23,0* | 3[b]<br>*23,-66* | 3<br>*0,0* | 10<br>*7,0* | 26<br>*20,-4* | 43<br>*24,-7* | 80<br>*41,-4* | 118<br>*39,-1* |
| ALL WEST | 2<br>*2,0* | 35<br>*35,-2* | 80<br>*50,-5* | 46<br>*44,-78* | 45<br>*14,-15* | 55<br>*34,-24* | 81<br>*45,-19* | 105<br>*43,-19* | 140<br>*56,-21* | 204<br>*72,-8* |

| ALL STATES | 47 [c] | 231 | 496 | 452 | 495 | 568 | 640 | 761 | 924 | 1,134 |
|---|---|---|---|---|---|---|---|---|---|---|
| | 49, −2 | 190, −6 | 288, −23 | 283, −327 | 180, −137 | 242, −169 | 189, −117 | 241, −120 | 262, −99 | 310, −100 |

*Source:* Admissions to and Removals from Death Row from 1972 to 1980 by State (Greenberg 1982, Appendix) supplemented with *Death Row USA* (LDF, December 1980–December 1982, quarterly)

*Note:* States that imposed no death sentences during this period have been omitted from the table, as has the U.S. Military jurisdiction, which did impose death sentences during this period.

[a] For these two years cumulative totals come from the December 1981 and December 1982 issues of *Death Row USA* (LDF, bimonthly). Annual additions and removals have been obtained by examining the bimonthly listings of persons under sentence of death from December 1980 through December 1982. Where the 1980 cumulative totals derived from Greenberg (1982, Appendix) and those reported in the December 1980 issue of *Death Row USA* did not agree, we report the information drawn from Greenberg's article, which has been more carefully checked. When this occurred we have altered the 1981 additions and removals counts proportionally.

[b] These are estimates obtained by averaging later cumulative totals over periods for which data are missing or not precisely known. Since no effort was made to apportion changes in terms of removals as well as additions, the estimated figures reported by Greenberg tend to underestimate removals relative to additions.

[c] Includes one death sentence imposed in 1972.

*Proffitt*, and *Jurek* decisions of 1976. In most years, Florida led in the cumulative number of persons under sentence of death, if not in the number of death sentences handed down. Georgia has lagged somewhat behind Florida and Texas in death row population, in part because the *Coker* and *Godfrey* decisions in 1977 and 1980, respectively, explicitly invalidated the death sentences of persons on Georgia's death row.

Other states have figured prominently at certain intervals. Between 1973 and 1975 North Carolina, Tennessee, and Oklahoma had more people under sentence of death than did Florida, Georgia, and Texas. Indeed, in 1974 and 1975 North Carolina's death row led all other states, including Florida. However, the *Woodson* and *Roberts* decisions that accompanied *Gregg* in 1976 virtually emptied the death rows of these three states, and North Carolina, in particular, never resumed its earlier pace. Among the states whose statutes survived *Gregg* and accompanying cases, Ohio ranked second to Florida in the number of persons under sentence of death in 1976 and 1977, before the *Lockett* decision of 1978 depleted its death row. In the 1980s, California has become a major contributor to the number of persons under sentence of death, joining Florida, Georgia, and Texas with more than 100 persons on death row. In fact, California had more new death sentences in the 1981 and 1982 period than did any other state.

By the end of 1982, Florida, Georgia, Texas, and California accounted for five out of ten persons on death row. With Alabama, Arizona, Illinois, and Pennsylvania, these eight were responsible for seven out of ten of the death sentences in effect nationwide.

The death penalty as applied across states and over time in the post-*Furman* era suggests elements of the kind of arbitrariness to which the Court objected in *Furman*. Consider first the large number of jurisdictions in Table 6-3 that have imposed only a few death sentences a year. A majority of these thirty-five states have averaged fewer than five death sentences a year for as long as they have had post-*Furman* capital statutes in effect. In a substantial number of these states this may represent no more than two or three death sentences per 1000 criminal homicides, or 100 convicted (death-eligible) murderers. In these jurisdictions the death penalty as applied has been "uncommon," "rare," or "freakish," in the language of the *Furman* court. Capital punishment appears to be not an integral part of the criminal justice process in these states, but an occasional product of chance—an unpredictable occurrence.

Secondly, consider states that display wide differences or abrupt changes in the pace with which death sentences were handed down. For example, both California and Pennsylvania imposed roughly twice as many death sentences per year in 1981 and 1982 as in previous years, without any evident change in their capital statutes (according to Table

6-1 and Appendix B). Barring radical changes in the incidence or pattern of homicides, these sharp increases suggest that the guided discretion statutes in these states do not meet the Court-enunciated standards of "evenhanded justice" and "proportionality of punishment" over time in factually similar cases, perhaps because they fail to intercept political or social influences that periodically come to bear on the legal process.

Consider next the small handful of states responsible for a disproportionate number of death sentences in the post-*Furman* era. We know that three states—Florida, Georgia, and Texas—account for a third of the death sentences imposed (see Table 6-3) in a period when death sentences had become much more common (as shown in Table 6-1). It seems that the guided discretion statutes specifically upheld in *Gregg*, *Proffitt*, and *Jurek* have actually facilitated the use of capital punishment, especially in these three states. Perhaps explicitly enumerated aggravating circumstances do not serve to guide sentencing discretion as much as they become means of justifying arbitrary or discriminatory sentencing practices in places where social or political influences favor such practices. The capital sentencing patterns of Florida, Georgia, and Texas therefore constitute a critical test of the efficacy of guided discretion statutes in controlling arbitrariness and discrimination (see Chapter 7).

Consider also the fact that half the death sentences imposed throughout the country since *Furman* have been legally faulty. The data in Table 6-3 reveal that virtually as many people have been removed from death row as now occupy it; almost half of those sentenced to death are no longer condemned either because the laws under which they were prosecuted were subsequently invalidated or because the procedures under which they were tried and sentenced did not conform to constitutional requirements—in about equal numbers (LDF, December 1982). An error rate of this magnitude is a unique problem for a system that dispenses death as punishment (Greenberg 1982). It places a severe burden on the already overburdened control mechanism of appellate review and, barring flawlessness in the appellate process, it elevates the risk that errors or arbitrariness will go uncorrected until it is too late. The cases of John Spinkelink and Charles Brooks raise serious questions of this sort (see Chapter 10).

The picture that emerges from these relatively gross data on the yearly imposition of death sentences since 1973 is one of arbitrariness and hence unfairness under post-*Furman* capital statutes, as applied. The remaining chapters of this volume will focus in greater detail on questions of fairness, as gauged by the presence of extralegal influences on the imposition of death sentences under these new statutes, and utility, as reflected in the impact of executions on the subsequent incidence of homicides. We conclude this chapter with a preview of the upcoming evidence and an assessment of its implications for the constitutionality of capital punishment.

## Fairness, Utility, and Contemporary Values

Where do we now stand on the questions of fairness, utility, and contemporary values a decade after these challenges were raised in *Furman* and with the experience and mounting evidence of a ten-year trial period under post-*Furman* legal reforms?

The evidence of racism in the administration of post-*Furman* guided discretion statutes is now stronger and more comprehensive than it was at the time of the Spinkelink appeal. We now have data showing that during the first five years after *Furman* in Florida, Georgia, Texas, and Ohio (which were responsible for two out of three persons under sentence of death by 1977), there were marked patterns of differential treatment by race of both offender and victim (see Chapter 7). Indeed, this evidence has recently played a prominent role in the decision to outlaw the guided discretion statute of Massachusetts. In *District Attorney of Suffolk County* v. *Watson* (1980), the Massachusetts Supreme Judicial Court cited these statistics, noted that such disparities were not confined to southern states, and concluded that the Massachusetts statute, modeled after the Georgia law, was unconstitutional.

Although racial bias is a compelling challenge to the administration of a fair death penalty, it is by no means the only one. The location of the crime is as important as the race of the victim or the offender. It is obviously a departure from evenhanded justice for the same crime to be punished by death in some places and not in others within a state. We now know that the likelihood of a death sentence in some judicial circuits of Florida and Georgia is far greater than in others and that, as in the case of race, the appellate review process fails to redress such disparities (see Chapter 7).

The evidence that capital punishment has no deterrent advantage over imprisonment is now stronger and more consistent than when the Court last considered this issue in *Gregg*. Indeed, a comprehensive review of previous studies and recent analyses of refined statistical data both support the contention that the death penalty has a "brutalizing" rather than a deterrent effect—that executions can be expected to stimulate rather than to inhibit homicides (see Chapter 8). In fact, careful scrutiny and further analysis of Isaac Ehrlich's 1975 research, the sole study identified by the plurality in *Gregg* as supporting the death penalty's deterrent effect, have discredited his deterrent claims and shown these data to be more consistent with brutalizing than with deterrent effects (see Chapter 9).

Sentencing behavior poses a further challenge to the constitutionality of capital punishment under the legal standard of contemporary values. In *Coker* the court outlawed the death penalty for rape in part because in the "vast majority" of cases throughout the state convicted rapists received punishments other than death. We now know that essentially the same is true for convicted first-degree murderers. Thus, of the first 607 sentences imposed on convicted murderers under Georgia's post-*Furman* capital statute—not counting guilty pleas resulting in life sentences—113 were death sentences (Baldus, Wordsworth, and Pulaski 1982a). That is to say, more than 80 percent of the death-eligible murderers in Georgia—the vast majority—were given life sentences. And Georgia is among the states most likely to impose death sentences: in most other states the percentage of death-eligible murderers receiving death sentences will be even less.

These criteria—fairness, utility, and contemporary values—are precedent-established tests of cruel and unusual punishment under the Eighth Amendment. Failure to satisfy any one of the three tests will render the death penalty unconstitutional. The empirical evidence with respect to these criteria is becoming stronger and clearer and thus harder to ignore. Yet the Court need not explicitly incorporate statistical data or social science evidence in such a ruling. And in any case, it must rely on constitutional arguments involving concepts such as "respect for human dignity," the "uniqueness of the individual," "excessive punishment," and the "profound difference" between death and other punishments, used by the Court itself to interpret the core meaning of the Eighth Amendment in the context of its previous death penalty rulings in *Furman, Woodson, Coker,* and *Lockett* (Radin 1978, 1980; Sarat 1979).

Both the social science evidence and the legal reasoning for such a Supreme Court decision are at hand. Indeed, both have been incorporated in the recent *Watson* decision of the Massachusetts high court, which employs evidence of unfairness by race and the concept of human dignity as a constitutional standard to invalidate the state's guided discretion statute modeled after the Georgia law. Perhaps *Watson* will be the prophetic forerunner of a definitive Supreme Court decision. Before *Furman,* the California Supreme Court declared that state's fully discretionary capital statute unconstitutional in *People* v. *Anderson* (1972). Again, before *Woodson,* the Massachusetts Supreme Judicial Court ruled that state's mandatory statute unconstitutional in *Commonwealth* v. *O'Neal* (1975). Although the Supreme Court in *Furman* and *Woodson* did not choose the same Eighth Amendment grounds as did the state courts in *Anderson* and *O'Neal*, it did accomplish the same results—abolishing both fully discretionary and strictly mandatory capital statutes. Now that *Watson* has invalidated the guided discretion statute in Massachusetts, will the U.S. Supreme Court do so nationally?

In some ways, present conditions resemble those of fifty years ago when high levels of criminal violence—not to mention economic instability and political uncertainty—provoked public apprehension, and perhaps a taste for simplistic and vindictive solutions. This was the era when the use of the death penalty reached a high point in American society. But there are several critical differences between then and now. One is that the Supreme Court in *Furman* has established a standard that constitutionally prohibits arbitrariness and discrimination in the imposition of the death sentence. Another is that the role of social science evidence in determining the presence of such arbitrariness and discrimination is acknowledged and becoming accepted by the courts. Thus, in the words of Chief Justice Burger's *Furman* opinion, "The case against capital punishment is not the product of legal dialectic, but rests primarily on factual claims the truth of which cannot be tested by conventional judicial processes" (408 U.S. 237, 405). Finally, there is now more reliable and extensive evidence of arbitrariness and discrimination. And, notably, the current patterns are remarkably like those of the pre-*Furman* era (see Table 7-1), when the use of the death penalty also displayed gross disparities of treatment by race of offender and victim—under statutes declared unconstitutional by *Furman*.

Those who will decide the future of capital punishment in America are facing a critical exercise of discretion. At the same time that there is growing evidence of arbitrariness and discrimination under post-*Furman* capital statutes and increasing recognition that the death penalty has no unique deterrent efficacy, there is also mounting potential for an unprecedented parade of executions. The following chapters, which examine the essential character of capital punishment as revealed in the manner and impact of its application, will, I hope, serve to guide the discretion of those who will decide the future of executions in America.

# 7

## ARBITRARINESS AND DISCRIMINATION UNDER POST-*FURMAN* CAPITAL STATUTES

In the *Furman* v. *Georgia* decision on June 29, 1972 (408 U.S. 232, 1972), the United States Supreme Court held by a five-to-four margin that capital punishment, as administered under then-existing statutes, was unconstitutional. In separate opinions, the concurring majority variously characterized the imposition of the death penalty as "freakishly rare," "irregular," "random," "capricious, "uneven," "wanton," "excessive," "disproportionate," and "discriminatory." The majority were united in the finding that the death penalty was being used in an

Originally published under this title in *Crime and Delinquency*, October 1980, pp. 563–635, with Glenn L. Pierce. This study was made possible by the cooperation and assistance of a great many people and organizations, to whom we are deeply grateful. In developing the present analysis, we have consulted with many people. For their assistance and insights, we wish to thank Millard Farmer and Courtney Mullins, of Team Defense; Morris Dees, John Carroll, and Dennis Balske, of the Southern Poverty Law Center; John Boger and Joel Berger, of the Legal Defense Fund; and trial attorneys Bud Siemon and Craig Barnard. We also thank Gwen Spivey for her work on findings of aggravation in the Florida sentencing process, and we owe special thanks to Carol Palmer, of the Legal Defense Fund, for her constant responsiveness to our numerous and detailed questions. The costs of acquiring and processing the data used in our analysis were covered, in part, by funds from the Southern Poverty Law Center and the Legal Defense Fund.

We gratefully acknowledge the contribution of all the persons listed in Supplement B for providing us with these data. Two individuals do deserve special mention because of their extraordinary effort in this regard. Kay Isaly, of Florida Citizens Against the Death Penalty, and Patsy Morris, of the American Civil Liberties Union in Atlanta, who provided information on persons sentenced to death and on the appellate review status of persons who received the death penalty, spent countless hours collecting data used "arbitrary" manner. The Court ruled that because death is a supremely harsh and an irrevocable form of punishment, "different in kind from lesser criminal sanctions," such arbitrariness in capital punishment was a violation of Eighth Amendment prohibitions against "cruel and unusual" punishment.[1]

The *Furman* decision did not, however, put an end to capital punishment in the United States. To be sure, two of the concurring majority—Justices Brennan and Marshall—found death as a form of punishment constitutionally unacceptable, but the other three—Justices Douglas, Stewart, and White—limited their objections to existing statutes "as applied." Justice Douglas contended that the Court's intervention was warranted because the existing statutes gave "uncontrolled discretion" to sentencers and provided "no standards [to] govern the selection of the penalty." Justice Stewart's opinion also reflected concern with discretion in the sentencing process. In his dissenting opinion, Chief Justice Burger suggested that states could restore capital punishment by drafting new statutes that would narrow and restrict the exercise of discretion in sentencing.

Reacting to the *Furman* decision, state legislatures adopted remedies varying in the restrictions they placed on sentencing discretion.

in this analysis. Kay Isaly also obtained the judicial-processing data from selected counties in Florida, aided by William Sheppard and a group of law students who consulted court records. Ms. Isaly supervised this collection of data and checked the accuracy of the information.

We were also helped by people who supplied data not yet directly employed in our analysis. They include Tim Carr, Director of Statistics, Georgia Department of Offender Rehabilitation; Jerry Smith, Chief of Research, Florida Department of Offender Rehabilitation; Cecilia Whitmore and Laura Dixon, of Team Defense, who collected Georgia parole and probation information; and Susan Carey, who collected pre-Furman death sentence data in Florida.

The task of preparing the data for analysis has required considerable effort on the part of a number of persons we were fortunate to have working with us. Over the past three years, Deborah Good, Elaine Lang, and Keith Dubanevich in turn took primary responsibility for managing, updating, and preparing the various data sets for analysis, and assisted in processing various parts of these data for court testimony. Jacques Parenteau, Elise Bender, and Leslie Moffet supervised and carried out major efforts in data coding and preparation. Barbara Kane provided valuable computer-programming assistance, and Donna-Lee Anderson assisted in preparation of data for this project.

Finally, we wish to thank a number of people for their help in preparing the current study. Carol Cain contributed many hours of invaluable research and editorial assistance. Susan Spaar did much of the computer processing for this paper. Robert Kazarian and Charles Kazarian gave technical and legal advice. Jean Stethem ably typed and retyped countless tables and drafts of the manuscript. Lastly, we wish to thank Sarah Dike, editor of *Crime & Delinquency*, for her painstaking attention to our manuscript.

1. The Court had previously held in McGautha v. California, 402 U.S. 183 (1971), that discretion in capital sentencing that might result in arbitrary or discriminatory imposition of the death penalty was not a violation of the Fourteenth Amendment "due process" clause. The finding of arbitrariness in Furman v. Georgia served, however, to sustain an Eighth Amendment challenge that explicitly incorporated the unique severity and finality of capital punishment.

These post-*Furman* capital statutes took two basic approaches: the "mandatory" death sentence, designed to eliminate sentencing discretion altogether, and "guided discretion" statutes, designed to limit or control the exercise of discretion by means of explicit standards to be followed in the sentencing process. Mandatory statutes were narrowly drawn to avoid ambiguity in classifying crimes as capital offenses, and the death sentence was made mandatory upon conviction for such offenses. Guided discretion statutes provide standards, typically in the form of specific aggravating and mitigating circumstances, that must be taken into account before the death sentence can be handed down. These new guided discretion statutes also provide for separate phases of the trial to determine guilt and punishment and for automatic appellate review of all death sentences.

In *Gregg* v. *Georgia* and companion cases, decided on July 2, 1976 (*Gregg* v. *Georgia*, 96 S. Ct. 2909 (1976); *Roberts* v. *Louisiana*, 96 S. Ct. 3001 (1976); *Woodson* v. *North Carolina*, 96 S. Ct. 2978 (1976); *Proffitt* v. *Florida*, 96 S. Ct. 2960 (1976); *Jurek* v. *Texas* 96 S. Ct. 2950 (1976)), the U.S. Supreme Court rejected the mandatory death penalty as provided for by the legislatures of Louisiana and North Carolina, but upheld guided discretion as formulated in the statutes of Florida, Georgia, and Texas. The Court reasoned that making the death penalty mandatory upon conviction removes sentencing discretion that should be exercised in the interest of "individualized" justice and that the total absence of discretion in sentencing may cause the trial of guilt to be colored by considerations of punishment (that is, jury nullification). By contrast, it reasoned that providing specific sentencing guidelines to be followed in a separate postconviction phase of the trial would free the sentencing decision of arbitrariness and discrimination and, for that matter, free the guilt decision of sentencing considerations.

The Court accepted several different forms of guided discretion that vary in the limits they place on sentencing authorities.[2] Least restrictive are "aggravating only" statutes, which enumerate aggravating circumstances and permit the jury to recommend death if it finds at least one such circumstance present. Intermediate in restrictions are "aggravating versus mitigating" statutes, which list both aggravating and mitigating circumstances and give the jury discretion to recommend death, providing it finds that the aggravating "outweigh" the mitigating circumstances. Most restrictive are "structured discretion" statutes, which make the death sentence strictly contingent upon the jury's findings of fact with respect to aggravation.

2. For an analysis of the distinctions among guided discretion statutes in terms of the limits they place upon sentencing authorities, see *Harvard Law Review* 1974, 1690–1719, esp. 1699ff. The distinctions introduced here draw on this analysis.

Georgia's post-*Furman* capital statute is an example of the "aggravating only" type. The statute lists ten aggravating[3] and no mitigating circumstances. If the jury finds at least one aggravating circumstance it may, but need not, recommend death. The judge must sentence the defendant to death if the jury recommends it, but he must not do so if the jury recommends otherwise.

Florida's capital statute is of the "aggravating versus mitigating" type. The statute lists eight aggravating[4] and seven mitigating[5] circum-

3. "(1) The offense of murder, rape, armed robbery, or kidnapping was committed by a person with a prior record of conviction for a capital felony, or the offense of murder was committed by a person who has a substantial history of serious assaultive criminal convictions.
"(2) The offense of murder, rape, armed robbery, or kidnapping was committed while the offender was engaged in the commission of another capital felony, or aggravated battery, or the offense of murder was committed while the offender was engaged in the commission of burglary or arson in the first degree.
"(3) The offender by his act of murder, armed robbery, or kidnapping knowingly created a great risk of death to more than one person in a public place by means of a weapon or device which would normally be hazardous to the lives of more than one person.
"(4) The offender committed the offense of murder for himself or another, for the purpose of receiving money or any other thing of monetary value.
"(5) The murder of a judicial officer, former judicial officer, district attorney or solicitor or former district attorney or solicitor during or because of the exercise of his official duty.
"(6) The offender caused or directed another to commit murder or committed murder as an agent or employee of another person.
"(7) The offense of murder, rape, armed robbery, or kidnapping was outrageously or wantonly vile, horrible or inhuman in that it involved torture, depravity of mind, or an aggravated battery to the victim.
"(8) The offense of murder was committed against any peace officer, corrections employee or fireman while engaged in the performance of his official duties.
"(9) The offense of murder was committed by a person in, or who has escaped from, the lawful custody of a peace officer or place of lawful confinement.
"(10) The murder was committed for the purpose of avoiding, interfering with, or preventing a lawful arrest or custody in a place of lawful confinement, of himself or another."
Georgia Code Ann., sec. 27-2534.1 (Supp. 1975).
4. "(a) The capital felony was committed by a convict under sentence of imprisonment.
"(b) The defendant was previously convicted of another capital felony or of a felony involving the use or threat of violence to the person.
"(c) The defendant knowingly created a great risk of death to many persons.
"(d) The capital felony was committed while the defendant was engaged or was an accomplice, in the commission of, or an attempt to commit, or flight after committing or attempting to commit, any robbery, rape, arson, burglary, kidnapping, or aircraft piracy or the unlawful throwing, placing, or discharging of a destructive device or bomb.
"(e) The capital felony was committed for the purpose of avoiding or preventing a lawful arrest or effecting an escape from custody.
"(f) The capital felony was committed for pecuniary gain.
"(g) The capital felony was committed to disrupt or hinder the lawful exercise of any governmental function or the enforcement of laws.
"(h) The capital felony was especially heinous, atrocious, or cruel."
Florida Statutes Ann., ch. 921, sec. 921.141.
5. "(a) The defendant has no significant history of prior criminal activity.
"(b) The capital felony was committed while the defendant was under the influence of extreme mental or emotional disturbance.

stances. If an aggravating circumstance is found, death is presumed to be the proper sentence, unless one or more mitigating circumstances are also found and judged to "outweigh the aggravating circumstance(s)." The jury weighs the evidence and advises the court as to the sentence. The judge need not follow the jury's advice: He can impose death even if the jury advises life, and he can impose life even if the jury advises death. He cannot, however, impose death unless the jury finds at least one aggravating circumstance.

Texas's capital statute is an example of the "structured discretion" type. For a murder to qualify as a capital offense, the jury must find the defendant guilty of at least one of five forms of aggravated murder defined in the statute.[6] The jury then considers three further questions of aggravation[7] in the determination of sentence. If it answers all three questions in the affirmative by unanimous vote, the judge must impose the death sentence; otherwise, the judge must not do so. Neither jury nor judge has sentencing discretion once findings are made with respect to these three issues of aggravation.

Each type of guided discretion statute upheld in the *Gregg* decision also provided for automatic appellate review of all death sentences. Most elaborate is Georgia's review process, which was explicitly formulated to determine

1) whether the sentence of death was imposed under the influence of passion, prejudice, or any other arbitrary factor, and 2) whether . . . the

---

"(c) The victim was a participant in the defendant's conduct or consented to the act.
"(d) The defendant was an accomplice in the capital felony committed by another person and his participation was relatively minor.
"(e) The defendant acted under extreme duress or under the substantial domination of another person.
"(f) The capacity of the defendant to appreciate the criminality of his conduct or to conform his conduct to the requirements of law was substantially impaired.
"(g) The age of the defendant at the time of the crime."
Ibid., ch. 921, sec. 921.141.

6. "(1) The person murders a peace officer or fireman who is acting in the lawful discharge of an official duty and who the person knows is a peace officer or fireman;
"(2) the person intentionally commits the murder in the course of committing or attempting to commit kidnapping, burglary, robbery, aggravated rape, or arson;
"(3) the person commits the murder for remuneration or the promise of remuneration;
"(4) the person commits the murder while escaping or attempting to escape from a penal institution; or
"(5) the person, while incarcerated in a penal institution, murders another who is employed in the operation of the penal institution."
Texas Penal Code, art. 1257, sec. 19.03 (a).

7. "(1) Whether the conduct of the defendant that caused the death of the deceased was committed deliberately and with the reasonable expectation that the death of the deceased or another would result;
"(2) whether there is a probability that the defendant would commit criminal acts of violence that would constitute a continuing threat to society; and
"(3) if raised by the evidence, whether the conduct of the defendant in killing the deceased was unreasonable in response to the provocation, if any, by the deceased."
Ibid., art. 37.071 (a).

evidence supports the jury's or judge's finding of a statutory aggravating circumstance . . . and 3) whether the sentence of death is excessive or disproportionate to the penalty imposed in similar cases considering the crime and the defendant.[8]

Justice White, in his *Gregg* opinion, observed that Georgia's statute

gives the Georgia Supreme Court the power and the obligation to perform precisely the task . . . this Court . . . performed in *Furman*; namely, the task of deciding whether *in fact* the death penalty was being administered for any given class of crime in a discriminatory, standardless, or rare fashion (*Gregg* v. *Georgia* 1976, 2948).

Moreover, the Georgia statute makes special provisions for the application of this "similarity standard" in the appellate review of death sentences for excessiveness and disproportionality. To establish a baseline for comparison, it requires the state supreme court to compile the records of "all capital cases" in the state of Georgia in which sentences were imposed after January 1, 1970, and it provides the court with a special assistant and staff for this purpose. For the case under review, it requires the trial judge not only to transmit to the state supreme court a transcript and complete record of the trial, but also to complete a separate, standardized, questionnaire-type report about the defendant, the crime, and the circumstances of the trial. This too is submitted to the state supreme court for use in its review. After the court has made a proportionality review that upholds a death sentence, it is required by statute to cite in an appendix to its opinion all cases it has considered that are "similar" to the one reviewed.

The present study examines whether the new post-*Furman* capital statutes affirmed by the Supreme Court in the *Gregg* decision have, in fact, eliminated the arbitrariness and discrimination that rendered pre-*Furman* capital statutes unconstitutional. We first review the Court's assumptions about how the new capital statutes, "on their face," will remedy the previously existing ills to which the Court objected in the *Furman* decision. We next consider the nature of arbitrariness, the forms it takes, and its sources in the extralegal functions of capital punishment. We then turn to the existing evidence of arbitrariness and discrimination under pre-*Furman* statutes that can serve as a baseline against which the operation of the post-*Furman* statutes may be judged. These steps will set the stage for our report of findings to date from an ongoing research project designed to evaluate the application of post-*Furman* capital statutes in terms of arbitrariness and discrimination.

8. Georgia Code Ann., sec. 27-2537.

## The Court's Assumptions

The Supreme Court affirmed these post-*Furman* statutes on their face. That is, it found that the new statutes provided safeguards which should, in the Court's estimation, correct for the arbitrary and discriminatory application of the death penalty to which the Court had objected in *Furman*. The Court's judgment in the *Gregg* case relies on two central premises: (1) that the forces responsible for arbitrariness and discrimination under pre-*Furman* capital statutes are tractable within the legal system and (2) that the "substantial risk" of arbitrariness and discrimination they tend to produce can be removed under a reformed system of capital punishment. The Court's more specific assumptions about how guided-discretion statutes such as those incorporated into the laws of Florida, Georgia, and Texas will serve to correct these ills are reflected in its responses to the challenges brought by the petitioner in *Gregg* and companion cases.

The petitioner in *Gregg* argued that specific statutory aggravating circumstances are too broad and too vague to serve as an effective guide to discretion. As "too broad," the petitioner cited Georgia's seventh statutory aggravating circumstance, which authorizes imposition of the death penalty if the crime was "outrageously or wantonly vile, horrible or inhuman in that it involved torture, depravity of mind, or an aggravated battery to the victim." All murders, the petitioner argued, can be said to involve depravity of the mind or aggravated battery to the victim. Such language, he contended, permits subjective feelings and prejudices to prevail in the sentencing decision—the kinds of feelings and prejudices that have, under pre-*Furman* statutes, resulted in arbitrariness and discrimination. The Court answered this challenge by saying that the language of the circumstance need not be interpreted in such a broad way, "and there is no reason to assume that the Supreme Court of Georgia will adopt such an open-ended construction" when it reviews the death sentences handed down by trial courts (ibid., 2938).

As "too vague" and, therefore, susceptible to widely differing interpretations by Georgia juries, the petitioner challenged two other statutory aggravating circumstances. These authorize a jury to determine whether a defendant has a "substantial history of serious assaultive criminal convictions," and whether a crime creates a "great risk of death to more than one person." The *Gregg* decision noted that in the meantime the Georgia Supreme Court itself had ruled the "substantial history" circumstance impermissibly vague because it fails to provide the jury with "sufficiently clear and objective standards." Concerning the "great risk" circumstance, the Court observed that "while such a phrase might be susceptible to an overly broad interpretation, the Supreme Court of Georgia has not so construed it" (ibid., 2939). In effect, the Court assumed that through the appellate review process the state supreme court will invalidate aggravating circumstances that are consistently or systematically misinterpreted by juries throughout the state and will correct for the occasional misinterpretation of any aggravating circumstance by an aberrant jury.

Beyond findings of aggravating and mitigating circumstances is the exercise of discretion in weighing the circumstances and recommending a sentence. In Georgia, the jury must decide whether to recommend the death penalty whenever it finds at least one aggravating circumstance. In Florida, the jury must decide whether to recommend death whenever it finds both aggravating and mitigating circumstances, and the trial judge has discretion to accept or to reject the jury's recommendation. According to the petitioner, these remaining decisions leave room for the misguided exercise of discretion in sentencing. The Court answered that *Furman* does not require the state to remove all sentencing discretion, but simply to provide safeguards sufficient to prevent arbitrariness and discrimination in sentencing. Indeed, the individualized treatment of convicted capital offenders is a constitutional requirement (a point developed further by the Court in the *Lockett* decision [*Lockett* v. *Ohio*, 438 U.S. 586 (1978)]). The failure of mandatory death penalty statutes to provide such individualized treatment was at the root of their constitutional infirmity.

The ultimate safeguard against abuses in the exercise of this remaining discretionary power lies, according to the Court, in the automatic appellate review of each death sentence, especially in the review for proportionality. In the opinion of Justice Stewart,

> The provision for appellate review in the Georgia capital-sentencing system serves as a check against the random or arbitrary imposition of the death penalty. In particular, the proportionality review substantially eliminates the possibility that a person will be sentenced to die by an aberrant jury.

As Justice White observed,

> In considering any given death sentence on appeal, the Georgia Supreme Court must do much more than determine whether the penalty was lawfully imposed. It must go on to decide—after reviewing the penalties imposed in similar cases—whether the penalty is excessive or disproportionate considering both the crime and the defendant (*Gregg* v. *Georgia* 1976, 2948).

The petitioner argued, however, that the manner in which the proportionality review is performed is inadequate as a safeguard against arbitrariness and discrimination. The similarity standard requires the

Georgia Supreme Court to determine whether a given death sentence is excessive or disproportionate by comparing it with the sentences imposed in other cases that are "similar both in the characteristics of the crime and of the defendant." But the "similar" cases the Georgia Supreme Court considers are, according to the petitioner, chosen only from previously appealed life and death sentences. This systematically excludes capital convictions resulting in life sentences where no appeal was made. It also leaves out "similar" cases that went to trial on capital charges but did not result in a life or death sentence, and cases that might have been tried as capital felonies but were brought to trial on lesser charges. For these reasons, the petitioner contended, the proportionality review procedure will not remove abuses of discretion in the sentencing process and certainly not reduce such abuses before sentencing.

Speaking for the plurality, Justice Stewart responded that nothing in the Georgia capital statutes prohibits the state supreme court from considering nonappealed capital convictions and sentences in applying the similarity standard. Concerning the exercise of discretion before sentencing, Justice Stewart simply noted that *Furman* dealt with the decision to impose the death sentence on a defendant convicted of a capital offense.

> *Furman* held only that in order to minimize the risk that the death penalty would be imposed on a capriciously selected group of offenders the decision to impose it had to be guided by standards so that the sentencing authority would focus on the particularized circumstances of the crime and the defendant (ibid., 2937).

Justice White, with Chief Justice Burger and Justice Rehnquist concurring, went on to say,

> ... the standards by which prosecutors decide to charge a capital felony will be the same as those by which a jury will decide the questions of guilt and sentence. The defendant will escape the death penalty through prosecutorial charging decisions only because the offense is not sufficiently serious; or because the proof is insufficiently strong. Thus the prosecutor's charging decisions are unlikely to have removed from the sample of cases considered by the Georgia Supreme Court any which are similar. If the cases really were similar in relevant respects, it is unlikely that prosecutors would fail to prosecute them as capital cases; and I am unwilling to assume the contrary (ibid., 2949).

In summary, the Court has made several basic assumptions:

1. That sentencing guidelines within the context of a separate sentencing phase of the trial will effectively focus the attention and

concern of sentencing authorities on selected legally salient characteristics of the crime and the convicted defendant, and thus effectively remove legally irrelevant factors from consideration in the
sentencing decision.

2. That automatic appellate review of all death sentences will serve as
   a check on findings of fact with respect to aggravating and mitigating
   circumstances and, by application of the similarity standard, will detect
   and correct any tendency of sentencing authorities to use the remaining discretionary powers in an arbitrary or discriminatory manner.

3. That the sentencing and review procedures under these statutes will
   counteract any tendency toward the displacement of arbitrariness or
   discrimination to other (earlier) points in the handling of potentially
   capital cases, in part because the sentencing guidelines will also
   influence the exercise of discretion at other decision points.

4. That variations among these statutes in the restrictiveness of sentencing
   guidelines and the particular rules and procedures governing the sentencing decision, providing they do not eliminate individualized
   treatment, will not impair their effectiveness in removing arbitrariness and discrimination from the administration of capital punishment.

Whether, in fact, these reforms will remove arbitrariness and discrimination from the administration of capital punishment is ultimately an empirical question. As Chief Justice Burger put it in his
*Furman* opinion, "The case against capital punishment is not the product of legal dialectic, but rests primarily on factual claims, the truth
of which cannot be tested by conventional judicial processes" (*Furman
v. Georgia* 1972, 405). Indeed, Burger complained that the Court had
insufficient empirical research on the administration of the death penalty at the time of the *Furman* decision and called for "evidence of
more recent vintage" (ibid., 399, note 29, which refers to note 12, in
which the statement is actually made). Lacking such evidence about
the operation of the new post-*Furman* statutes at the time of the *Gregg*
decision, the Court has concluded on the basis of legal analysis that
these reforms will "on their face" remove the potential for the abuses
found under pre-*Furman* statutes. To see whether they have, in fact,
done so, we need to be clear about the nature of arbitrariness, the forms
it takes, and its likely sources.

## The Forms and Sources of Arbitrariness

In the *Gregg* decision, the Court articulated a model of retributive
justice, made most explicit in its discussion of the proportionality
review. Under this model, the severity of the punishment must be

proportional to the seriousness of the crime and independent of legally irrelevant considerations. The death sentence must be strictly a function of legally relevant characteristics of the crime and of the defendant. The statutes themselves provide legally relevant standards for imposing the death penalty in the form of explicit, enumerated aggravating and mitigating circumstances; these establish the retributive appropriateness of death as punishment under the law. The similarity standard applied upon review further requires that sentencing decisions be consistent with legally acceptable criteria evolving in practice throughout the state; it rules out legally acceptable considerations that have typically not figured in the decision to impose the death sentence.

Within this framework arbitrariness can be made quite explicit. Simply stated, it is any departure from the retributive model requiring death as punishment to be strictly a function of statutory guidelines and evolving standards of practice. That is, arbitrariness exists to the extent that legally relevant factors enumerated in statutes and emerging in practice *do not* distinguish between those who are sentenced to death and those who are not.

We can identify forms of arbitrariness in terms of "what else" accounts for the imposition of the death sentence.[9] If the extralegal influences are different in every case or occur randomly without rhyme or reason, the arbitrariness is unsystematic. We may call it "caprice." On the other hand, if the extralegal influences are systematic or consistent, they may be legally irrelevant characteristics of the defendant or of the crime. When they are characteristics of the defendant (for example, race of offender), the form of arbitrariness is what we traditionally call "discrimination" (against the category of defendants whose legally irrelevant characteristics make them more apt to receive the death penalty). When the legally irrelevant factors are characteristics of the crime (for example, size of community in which it occurred) or of the victim (for example, race of victim), the arbitrariness is a form of discrimination, but not in the traditional sense of the term. That is, offenders will be treated differently depending on where and whom they kill rather than who they are. We may call this kind of arbitrariness "disparity" or "partiality" of treatment. Of course, discrimination

---

9. In this connection, Charles Black, Jr., has written, ". . . where the technical materials (precedents, statutes, constitution) do not produce a clear answer—a condition often evidenced by disagreement as to the answer among equally competent and disinterested people—then obviously, since an answer is given, *something else* produces it. This something else may be the judge's sense of policy, justice, fairness. This is undoubtedly the usual case, in overwhelming preponderance. The judge may, in obedience to the style of our law, conceal the operation of these factors from the public or, quite often, from himself, but they must be there, or disagreement on questions of law among equally learned and honest judges could not occur" (Black 1974, 78–79).

and disparity of treatment can have the same source. For example, deeply rooted racism might result in more severe punishment for black than for white killers, and in less severe punishment for the killers of blacks than of whites.

Arbitrariness in its various forms—caprice, discrimination, and disparity—may be linked to the extralegal functions of capital punishment. An examination of the historical and international availability and the use of the death penalty has suggested that three distinct extralegal functions of capital punishment—minority group oppression, majority group protection, and repressive response—play a role in determining who, among capital offenders, will receive the death penalty (Bowers 1974, 165ff).

Minority group oppression refers to the selective or disproportionate use of capital punishment against offenders from groups that are subjugated, impoverished, or dehumanized by the political, economic, or social conditions they face. Majority group protection refers to the disproportionate use of the death penalty against those whose crimes victimize members, interests, or institutions of the powerful or dominant groups in society. Repressive response refers to the selective use of the death penalty against those whose crimes occur at times and places of tension, turmoil, conflict, or crisis, when fear of crime or other forms of social disorder is heightened.

The presumed link between these extralegal functions of capital punishment and the forms of arbitrariness defined above should be clear. Minority group oppression will tend to create arbitrariness in the form of discrimination by offender characteristics. Majority group protection will tend to produce arbitrariness in the form of victim-based disparity of treatment. Repressive response will tend to generate arbitrariness in terms of differential treatment by time and place of offense that reflects conditions apart from the crime. What may seem capricious or freakish—like being struck by lightning (to paraphrase Justice Stewart)—in a particular case may in the aggregate and over a period of time be revealed as part of a systematic pattern of differences in treatment depending on legally irrelevant characteristics of the offender, victim, or crime.

The historical and comparative evidence has raised the following question:

Is it not possible that such extralegal functions as majority group protection, minority group oppression, and repressive response are more fundamental to the use of capital punishment in society than are the legal functions of retribution and deterrence—that they dictate where and when the death penalty will be most widely used and that they cause the legal functions of capital punishment to be displaced and compromised (ibid., 165–66)?

Perhaps, indeed, it is inevitable that capital punishment will be used in an arbitrary and discriminatory manner. Because death is the supreme punishment, it will be reserved for the crimes people find most shocking and abhorrent—those that most provoke anger, inflame emotions, and incite fear and apprehension. In other words, this form of punishment, which, according to the Supreme Court, must be held most strictly to the standards of just retribution because it is "different in kind" from other forms of punishment, may at the same time be the one most subject to the deeply rooted passions and prejudices that will cause its application to depart from the retributive justice model. It can serve to draw distinctions among crime and criminals that are not, and cannot be, reflected in the law, but that do reflect social realities—such as who the victims and offenders are. In effect, the symbolic and definitive character of death as punishment may make its use peculiarly sensitive to social forces beyond the realm of law and justice.

Has the Court correctly evaluated the power of these statutory reforms to control and to correct the arbitrariness and discrimination prevailing under pre-*Furman* capital statutes? As the first step in answering this question, we turn next to the empirical research on the administration of capital punishment in the pre-*Furman* era. This will show in greater detail the nature and extent of the problem and will establish a baseline in terms of which post-*Furman* statutory reforms can be evaluated for their success in altering the prevailing patterns of arbitrariness and discrimination or in overcoming the extralegal functions of capital punishment.

## Pre-*Furman* Patterns of Arbitrariness and Discrimination

Historically, race has figured prominently in the use of the death penalty in America. Before the Civil War, Black Codes in southern and border states made selected crimes punishable by death if committed by blacks. Some statutes even made the death penalty contingent upon race of both offender and victim; for example, an 1816 Georgia statute explicitly required the death penalty for rape or attempted rape if the crime was committed by a black against a white. After the Civil War, discriminatory patterns persisted de facto if not de jure. We know from data on more than five thousand state-imposed executions since 1864 that over the past century blacks, as compared with whites, have been executed for lesser crimes, at younger ages, and more often without appeals, and that each of these differences is independent of the other two (ibid.). And these data, of course, exclude the thousands of illicit executions, largely of blacks, carried out by lynch mobs during this period.

We know a good deal more about the administration of capital punishment in this century—and race again figures prominently. Since 1930, the beginning date for officially recorded statistics on executions nationwide, some 3,865 persons have been put to death under legal authority in the United States. Of these, 2,067 or slightly more than half were blacks.[10] This is roughly five times the proportion of blacks in the population over this period. Yet, this disproportion does not, in itself, constitute evidence of differential treatment of or discrimination against blacks in the application of the death penalty. Historically, blacks have had much higher homicide rates than whites. They have lived in circumstances of poverty and subjugation, which are conducive to criminal violence in general and homicide in particular. Indeed, statistics on homicide since the 1930s show that the homicide rates of blacks have been between four and seven times those of whites (Mulvihill and Tumin 1969). Thus, evidence of discrimination or disparity by race within the criminal justice system depends on information about potentially capital offenses and not on population proportions.

*Three Early Studies*

In the 1940s, three studies appeared that were highly significant for what they revealed about differential treatment by race in the administration of capital punishment. Two of these investigations (Johnson 1941, 93–104; Garfinkel 1949, 369–381) spanned the criminal justice process from indictment to sentence and uncovered racial differences that would have been obscured in ordinary statistics on the disposition of potentially capital cases. The other (Mangum 1940) focused on one particular discretion point, the question of executive clemency, with data on commutations by race of offender from a number of states. Each of these studies merits a brief review.

In 1941, Guy Johnson published information on homicide indictments, convictions, and sentences in selected counties in Georgia, North Carolina, and Virginia for various time intervals within the period from 1930 to 1940. A critical feature of the data Johnson collected was information on race of victim as well as race of offender. His rationale was stated as follows:

10. These figures include all executions from January 1, 1930, through December 31, 1982.

... differentials in the treatment of Negro offenders ... do exist but are obscured by the fact that conventional crime statistics take into account only the race of the offender. If caste values and attitudes mean anything at all, they mean that offenses by or against Negroes will be defined not so much in terms of their intrinsic seriousness as in terms of their importance in the eyes of the dominant group. Obviously the murder of a white person by a Negro and the murder of a Negro by a Negro are not at all the same kind of murder from the standpoint of the upper caste's scale of values, yet in crime statistics they are thrown together. Therefore, instead of two categories of offenders, Negro and white, we really need four offender-victim categories, and they would probably rank in seriousness from high to low as follows: (1) Negro versus white, (2) white versus white, (3) Negro versus Negro, (4) white versus Negro (Johnson 1941, 98).

Johnson's data were incomplete with respect to sentence in Georgia, and there was only one death sentence handed down among the homicide indictments in Virginia. However, for five counties of North Carolina, his data showed that the likelihood of a death sentence given an indictment for criminal homicide varied substantially by offender-victim racial combinations, as he had hypothesized.

In 1949, Harold Garfinkel published a more detailed study of the movement of potentially capital homicides through successive stages of the criminal justice process in North Carolina. Garfinkel (who had provided the data on North Carolina for Johnson's analysis) extended the coverage to ten counties in North Carolina for the period 1930–1940 and focused on three discretion points on the way to a death sentence: (1) the grand jury's decision to indict for first degree murder among all criminal homicide indictments, (2) the prosecutor's decision to go to trial on a first degree murder charge given a first degree indictment, and (3) the trial jury's or judge's decision to convict on first degree murder charges and (thus) impose the death sentence (North Carolina's capital statute made the death sentence mandatory upon conviction for first degree murder).

In Table 7-1 we have combined elements from two of Garfinkel's tables to show the likelihood of moving toward a death sentence at successive stages of the criminal justice process. This was done separately for each offender-victim racial combination, for cases grouped by race of offender, and for cases grouped by race of victim.

The column at the extreme right in Table 7-1 summarizes the movement from beginning to end of the process covered by these data. It shows the likelihood of a death sentence given a criminal homicide indictment for the various offender and victim racial categories. The figures in Part A of the table clearly show differential treatment by race of both offender and victim. When matched for race of victim,

**Table 7-1.** *Indictments, Charges, Convictions, and Death Sentences in Ten Counties of North Carolina for Criminal Homicide, by Race of Offender and Victim, 1930–1940*

| | Numbers at Each Stage | | | | Conditional Probability of Moving between Successive Stages | | | |
| | (1) All Homicide Indictments | (2) First Degree Murder Indictments | (3) First Degree Murder Charges at Trial | (4) Death Sentences for First Degree Convictions | (5) First Degree Murder Indictment Given Homicide Indictment | (6) First Degree Charge Given First Degree Indictment | (7) Death Sentence Given First Degree Charge | (8) Overall Probability of a Death Sentence Given Indictment |
|---|---|---|---|---|---|---|---|---|
| A. Offender-victim racial combinations | | | | | | | | |
| Black kills white | 51 | 48 | 35 | 15 | 0.94 | 0.73 | 0.43 | 0.29 |
| White kills white | 165 | 138 | 73 | 11 | 0.84 | 0.53 | 0.15 | 0.07 |
| Black kills black | 581 | 531 | 307 | 15 | 0.91 | 0.58 | 0.05 | 0.03 |
| White kills black | 24 | 17 | 8 | 0 | 0.71 | 0.47 | 0.00 | 0.00 |
| B. Race of offender | | | | | | | | |
| White | 189 | 155 | 81 | 11 | 0.82 | 0.52 | 0.14 | 0.06 |
| Black | 632 | 579 | 342 | 30 | 0.92 | 0.59 | 0.09 | 0.05 |
| C. Race of victim | | | | | | | | |
| White | 216 | 186 | 108 | 26 | 0.96 | 0.58 | 0.24 | 0.12 |
| Black | 605 | 548 | 315 | 15 | 0.91 | 0.57 | 0.05 | 0.02 |

*Source:* Garfinkel, "Research Note on Inter- and Intra-Racial Homicides," tables 2 and 3.

black killers were more likely than white killers to receive a death sentence; and among offenders of a given race, the killers of whites were more likely than the killers of blacks to receive a death sentence. Moreover, race of victim was a more prominent basis for differential treatment than race of offender. (The differences in likelihood by race of victim are 0.29 versus 0.03 and 0.07 versus 0.00, as compared with 0.29 versus 0.07 and 0.03 versus 0.00 for race of offender.)

When the effects of one variable are underestimated because of the failure to control for another variable, the latter is said to have a "suppressor effect." To see how differences in treatment by race of offender are obscured (as Johnson put it) in statistics that exclude race of victim, examine Part B of Table 7-1. The rightmost column shows virtually no difference in the likelihood of a death sentence given indictment by race of offender. Because the killing of a black person is so unlikely to be punished by death and because black offenders are so likely to have black victims, *without* race of victim as a control the clear and consistent differences by race of offender shown in Part A of the table are altogether obscured, even slightly reversed, as shown in Part B of the table. Even the differences by race of victim tend to be somewhat masked when presented *without* controls for race of offender, as shown in Part C of the table.[11] Thus, with respect to treatment differences within the criminal justice process, race of victim and race of offender tend to have suppressor effects on one another.

Note that in Table 7-1 the racial differences from indictment to sentence (in column 8) are the cumulative result of differential treatment by race of both offender and victim at each stage of the process (columns 5, 6, and 7 in the table). At indictment and charge, differences by race of offender are more pronounced than those by race of victim (columns 5 and 6);[12] at conviction and sentencing, differences by race of victim exceed those by race of offender (column 7). Furthermore, at each successive stage of the process, race tends to be a stronger factor: The difference in likelihoods between black-offender–white-victim and white-offender–black-victim categories increases in both absolute and relative terms at each subsequent stage of the process. In effect, at least in North Carolina in the 1930s, there were pervasive racial differences

11. In absolute terms, the 0.10 difference in Part C of the table is less than an average of 0.165 for the relevant differences in Part A of the table (0.26 for black offenders and 0.07 for white offenders). In relative terms, the six-to-one ratio in Part C of the table is less than the roughly ten-to-one ratio when the offender was black. A ratio cannot be computed for white offenders because no white had been sentenced to death for killing a black.

12. Note that the consistent race of victim differences with respect to first degree murder charges in Part A of the table (0.15 and 0.06 for an average of 0.105) are obscured when tabulated by race of victim disregarding race of offender (a difference of 0.01) in Part C of the table.

across stages in the processing of potentially capital cases, with variations in priority and magnitude of offender and victim race at particular stages of the process.

The third significant study in this period (which actually predates the other two) dealt solely with the stage in the process between sentencing and execution. In 1940, Charles Mangum reported that execution clemency disproportionately favored white over black offenders condemned to death. With data (supplied to him by Johnson) on commutations of death sentences in the 1920s and 1930s for nine southern and border states—Florida, Kentucky, Missouri, North Carolina, Oklahoma, South Carolina, Tennessee, Texas, and Virginia—Mangum showed that in every state commutations were more likely for whites than for blacks on death row. Thus, in contrast with Garfinkel's study showing differential treatment by race across stages of the criminal justice process in a single state, Mangum showed differential treatment by race across states at a single stage of the process.

Notably, the suppressor effect of victim's race revealed in Johnson's and Garfinkel's studies suggests that Mangum's data may actually have underestimated differences in the use of executive clemency by race of offender. Indeed, a year after the publication of Mangum's work, Johnson actually demonstrated a suppressor effect of victim's race at the postsentencing stage of the process as well. Working with a restricted sample of cases in North Carolina from the period 1933–1939 for which race of victim could be obtained, he tabulated the data separately for offenders only and for offender-victim combinations (Johnson 1941, table 2). "When the data are tabulated merely by race of offender," Johnson wrote, "they show that 71.6 percent of the Negroes and 69.0 percent of the whites get executed. When they are tabulated by offender-victim groupings the picture is different" (ibid., 100). Johnson reported that 80.5 percent of the blacks who killed whites were executed, compared with only 68.3 percent of the whites who killed whites. And the difference attributable to race of victim among black offenders was even greater.

These early studies established several things: (1) that there were very substantial differences by race of both offender and victim in the administration of capital punishment in selected southern and border states, (2) that the pattern was repeated with minor variations at successive stages of the criminal justice process, and (3) that the magnitude of racial differences was obscured by the lack of information on race of both offender and victim in the analysis. These studies do not directly control for the possibility that the crimes of blacks and crimes against whites were more serious or aggravated in nature and thus more likely to qualify for the death penalty. The magnitude of racial differences especially at later stages of the process does, however, cast doubt on the possibility that legally relevant factors are responsible for these differences. After all, the defendants who reach each successive stage of the process are, presumably, more nearly alike in personal culpability and the character of their crimes.

## Further Evidence of Systematic Arbitrariness

In the years that followed, research on the criminal justice processing of potentially capital cases spread to states in other regions of the country, and investigators focused in more detail on discrete stages of the criminal justice process, explicitly introducing interpretive variables into their analyses in an effort to account for observed racial differences in terms of legally relevant factors. The earliest and most numerous of the studies dealt with the postsentencing stage of the process; the most extensive and detailed dealt with the sentencing stage; the fewest and most recent have examined the presentencing stage of the process. We review them in this order.

The greatest number of these studies have focused on the postsentencing stage of the process, perhaps because data on death row inmates, commutations, and executions are relatively complete and accessible from prison records. Following Mangum's lead, investigators have documented racial differences in the likelihood of execution among death row inmates in Maryland (Maryland Legislative Council 1962), New Jersey (Bedau 1964, 1–64), Ohio (Ohio Legislative Service Commission 1961), Pennsylvania (Wolfgang, Kelly, and Nolde 1962, 301–311), and, for longer periods than Mangum examined, in Texas (Koeninger 1969, 132–141), and North Carolina (Johnson 1957, 165–169). These studies extend the coverage of Mangum's research to nonsouthern states with sufficient numbers of blacks sentenced to death for reliable comparisons. Two of these studies are notable for their extensions beyond Mangum's research and refinements of the work he initiated.

The first to appear was carried out by Elmer H. Johnson in 1957 with data on commutations and executions in North Carolina for the period 1909–1956 (ibid.). He showed substantial differences in execution rates for specific types of offenses, by race of offender within broad offense categories such as murder, rape, and burglary, and by race of victim for the crime of rape. His analysis also traced changes over time in execution rates by race of offender and by reasons for commutation as given in official commutation statements. His analysis did not, however, attempt to account for racial differences in execution rates in terms of interpretive variables nor did it attempt to evaluate the independent effects of offender's and victim's race.

The first study that attempted to interpret racial differences in execution rates among condemned murderers in terms of legally relevant variables was conducted with data on death row inmates in Pennsylvania for the period 1914–1958. In 1962, Marvin Wolfgang, Arlene Kelly, and Hans Nolde examined the possibility that higher execution rates for blacks occurred because black condemned murderers were more likely than their white counterparts to have committed felony-type murders, for which commutations were less apt to be granted (Wolfgang, Kelly, and Nolde 1962). They found that blacks were, indeed, more likely to have committed felony-type murders, *but* that they were less likely to receive commutations than whites for both felony and nonfelony murders. The investigators also found that the greater incidence of court-appointed as opposed to private defense attorneys among condemned blacks did not account for their higher execution rates. This research carried the analysis of racial differences further than other studies of the postsentencing disposition of condemned offenders. But it too failed to take race of victim into account, as Johnson had done (Johnson 1957), and may therefore have underestimated the extent of execution rate differences by race of offender.

The sentencing phase of the process in capital cases has received the most detailed attention. In 1964, Edwin Wolf examined the sentencing of 159 convicted capital offenders in New Jersey over the period 1937–1961 (Wolf 1964, 56–64). He found that blacks convicted of capital crimes were more likely than whites to be sentenced to death—47.5 percent of the blacks compared with 30.4 percent of the whites received death sentences. He then introduced type of murder (felony versus nonfelony), murder weapon (gun versus other), and offender's age as possible interpreting variables. The difference in treatment by race of offender remained evident under each of these controls.

In a concluding footnote citing Johnson's work, Wolf indicated that race of victim was available for about half the cases, and presented a tabulation of these data showing that 72.0 percent of the blacks who killed whites were sentenced to death as compared with 31.6 percent of the whites who killed whites. Although he made no effort to examine the effect of interpretive factors on offender-victim differences in the likelihood of a death sentence, it is clear from the magnitude of the disparity that none of the control variables available to him could account for it.

The most extensive and ambitious effort to examine the racial factor in capital sentencing was undertaken in the summer of 1965 by Wolfgang and his associates. They gathered extensive data on some three thousand convicted rapists in selected counties of eleven southern and border states for the period 1945–1965. In various reports of their findings, these investigators have shown that the death sentence was more likely for blacks than for whites, and especially so for blacks whose victims were white (Wolfgang 1972, in Bowers 1974, 109–120;

Wolfgang and Riedel 1973, 119–133; Wolfgang and Riedel 1975, 658–668). Furthermore, they have shown that the legally relevant aggravating circumstance of an acompanying felony plays no part in the interpretation of the stark racial differences. For both felony and non-felony rapes, 39 percent of blacks with white victims were sentenced to death; for the other three offender-victim racial categories combined, 3 percent were sentenced to death for felony rape and 2 percent for nonfelony rape.

The first reports of findings from this study presented felony circumstance as the only interpretive variable, although the investigators have indicated that more thorough analyses confirming marked racial differences were carried out separately for Alabama, Arkansas, Florida, Georgia, Louisiana, South Carolina, and Tennessee. In the latest report of their work, however, Marvin Wolfgang and Marc Riedel included an analysis of the Georgia data with a number of control variables introduced not one at a time but simultaneously (Wolfgang and Riedel 1975). Using discriminant function analysis, the investigators estimated the independent effects of fourteen variables. Only two—black-offender–white-victim and felony circumstance—had independent effects that were statistically beyond the 0.01 probability level.

In 1969 a study of the sentencing of 238 persons convicted in California of first degree murder between 1958 and 1966 shifted the focus from race to social class as a basis for differential treatment (Judson, Pandell, Owens, McIntosh, and Matschullat 1969, 1297–1497). This study used extensive information on the offender, victim, crime, and trial, coded from court and prison records. Controlling for some eighteen other variables by means of partial correlation analyses, the investigators found that by occupation, blue-collar defendants were more likely and white-collar defendants less likely to be sentenced to death. A broader measure of social class incorporating unemployment, job instability, and education (available in the data set) as well as occupation might show an even stronger sentencing difference. Notably, race of offender and victim was not significantly related to the likelihood of a death sentence in this western state after other correlated variables were taken into account. Could it be that where race is not so prominent a basis of stratification in society, other more prominent bases will be substituted for it?

And, finally, what do studies of the presentencing stages in the handling of potentially capital cases show? The tendency for social class to be a basis for differential treatment before sentencing is reflected in research on convictions in murder cases by Victoria Swigert and Ronald Farrell (Swigert and Farrell 1976; and Swigert and Farrell 1977, 16–32). With data on 444 persons arrested for criminal homicide in an urban jurisdiction in an unnamed northeastern state for the period

1955–1973, these investigators studied factors affecting severity of conviction (as a five-point ordinal scale from first degree murder conviction and eligibility for capital punishment to acquittal).

They first reported that lower-status occupation of the defendant was a significant determinant of conviction severity, independent of other legally relevant factors controlled by multiple regression techniques (Swigert and Farrell 1977). They later showed that killings that crossed class lines, particularly those with offenders from lower and victims from upper occupational categories, were more likely to result in conviction on murder charges subject to more severe punishment (Farrell and Swigert 1978, 565–576). In effect, they demonstrated that social class of both offender and victim was a significant determinant of conviction level—just as previous studies of the racial factor had indicated that both offender's and victim's race figured in the handling of cases across stages of the process. Again, in this study of a non-southern jurisdiction, race of offender and victim was not found to be significantly associated with conviction outcome.

Concerning prosecutorial discretion, in 1979 Steven Boris examined the decision to prosecute or dismiss charges against 383 arrested murder suspects in an unnamed large northern industrial city for the year 1972 (Boris 1979, 139–158). The study incorporated data on race and occupation of both offender and victim, as well as other legally relevant control variables. Using multiple regression techniques, Boris found that the decision to prosecute was associated with the status of the offender (disadvantaged) and the status of the victim (advantaged) in terms of both race and occupation, with occupation a stronger determinant than race. By focusing on occupation as an indicator of social class of offender and victim, this research and the work of Swigert and Farrell have suggested a more general tendency for the crossing of social boundaries in murder to be singled out as a reason for especially severe treatment of offenders.

Still another element of arbitrariness besides race and class differentials has been documented in studies comparing courts or court districts in a given state, namely, differential treatment according to where, within a jurisdiction, the crime occurred. In 1952, Herbert Ehrmann reported data on convictions for murder in eight counties of Massachusetts for the period 1925–1941 (Ehrmann 1952, 73–84). These data revealed that, overall, 8 percent of those indicted for murder were actually convicted of first degree murder (which then carried a mandatory death sentence). Furthermore, his data showed disparities in conviction rates by county; in particular, Middlesex County had a much higher conviction rate than the others. Indeed, Middlesex had five times the first degree conviction rate of all other counties and four times the rate of Suffolk County, its nearest neighbor geographically, the closest in size, and the most similar in demographic characteristics.

Some seventeen years later, most of these same counties were examined in a study of murder indictments and plea bargaining for the period 1955–1964, after Massachusetts had abandoned the mandatory death sentence for first degree murder (but not for felony murder/rape). In 1969, Frank Carney and Ann Fuller reported vast differences in the proportion of first degree among all murder indictments across six counties (ranging from a high of 87.5 to a low of 26.17 percent) and a substantial spread in the proportion of guilty pleas (to lesser charges in nine out of ten cases) among first degree murder indictments (from 81.3 to 40.0 percent) (Carney and Fuller 1969, 292–304). The authors concluded that it was not so much court congestion or overcharging at indictment as it was pressure to prosecute in courts with infrequent murder trials that accounted for the disparities in plea bargaining by court.

Notably, during this period Middlesex County had proportionately fewer first degree murder indictments than Suffolk County (32.8 v. 47.0 percent), but was not significantly different in the proportion of guilty pleas in first degree murder cases (65.0 and 69.0 percent, respectively). Thus, unless Middlesex had a radically higher conviction rate than Suffolk among those not pleading to a lesser charge, the differences in first degree conviction rates reported by Ehrmann for 1925–1941 were not maintained in this later period, 1955–1964.

Differential treatment over time in potentially capital cases in a given jurisdiction was largely ignored until Thorsten Sellin's most recent work (1980). With information on indictments, prosecutions, and/or convictions drawn from historical records in selected states for various periods (Alabama, 1908–1926 [interrupted]; California, 1952–1966; Massachusetts, 1931–1970; Ohio, 1886–1904; Pennsylvania, 1971–1975), Sellin documented wide fluctuations and consistent trends in prosecution and conviction rates. Although the information is admittedly limited in reliability and comparability from year to year, these data suggest that the processing of potentially capital offenses is responsive to changing social, economic, or political considerations apart from the nature of the crime committed. Certainly, the dramatic decline in execution rates on a state-by-state basis from the mid-1930s through the mid-1960s illustrates such external influences, independent of the offender, the victim, or the crime.

Two relatively recent studies of Pennsylvania and Massachusetts murder statutes have documented arbitrariness in prosecutorial decisions to bring capital charges and to accept guilty pleas to lesser charges. With a sample of all homicide indictments in Philadelphia for the year

1970, Franklin Zimring, Sheila O'Malley, and Joel Eigen in 1976 examined the operation of the state's mandatory minimum life sentence for first degree murder (Zimring, O'Malley, and Eigen 1976, 227–252). They showed that successive stages of the process tended to single out black offenders for the mandatory life sentence—and, more particularly, black offenders whose victims were white for the death sentence.

With data on murders of females by males in Middlesex and Suffolk counties of Massachusetts for the period 1946–1970, Hugo Bedau in 1976 examined the operation of that state's mandatory death sentence for felony murder/rape (Bedau 1976, 493–520). For the 128 indictments examined, not one death sentence was imposed over this period; one death sentence was later handed down in a black offender/white victim felony murder/rape case. The Massachusetts study showed that a felony murder/rape defendant ran twice the risk of a first degree murder conviction in Middlesex compared with Suffolk County, again documenting differential treatment by court jurisdiction under the same law.

### Evidence of Unsystematic Arbitrariness

Beyond the systematic biases in terms of race, class, time, and place, there is also evidence of unsystematic arbitrariness, or "caprice," in the imposition of the death sentence. Thus, in their 1966 study of the American jury, Harry Kalven and Hans Zeisel identified thirty-five capital convictions in which either judge or jury favored the death penalty (Kalven and Zeisel 1966). Notably, in only fourteen, or 40 percent of these cases, did the trial judge report agreement between himself and the jury about whether the death sentence should be imposed. In the disputed 60 percent of these cases, judges compared with juries favored the death penalty two to one. The reasons for disagreement in the disputed cases, as reported by the responding trial judges, cover a broad range of factors. Indeed, some sixteen different factors were cited among the twenty-one cases of disagreement. In view of the evidence we have reviewed thus far, it should not be surprising to learn that one of these factors, as related in the words of the judge who tried the case, was "a Negro killing a Negro, that is, the jury did not attach enough importance to the value of a human life due to race" (ibid., 442).

This level of disagreement—in a majority of the cases, with one party accepting the death penalty, the other rejecting it—and the fact that there were nearly as many reasons for as cases of disagreement certainly point to the idiosyncratic or freakish nature of the decision to impose death as punishment in the absence of clear and workable standards that would yield consensus among sentencing authorities (see Black 1974, especially the passage cited earlier in note 9, and 1982).

Yet, what seems to be caprice in a single case or a small sample may turn out to be a systematic bias in a larger sample of cases. To be sure, the devaluation of human life in a black killing of another black may come up only once in a sample of twenty-one cases of judge-jury disagreement over the death penalty. It will come up only as often as it is a source of disagreement and is recognized as such. Indeed, the more powerful and pervasive its influence, the less likely it is to be a source of disagreement. Perhaps this racial factor plays an unrecognized part in many of the seventy-six capital cases studied by Kalven and Zeisel in which both judge and jury agreed that a term of imprisonment rather than the death sentence was appropriate (Kalven and Zeisel 1966).

Nor does the absence of aggregate differences in other extralegal factors in treatment by race guarantee that they are not a source of arbitrariness. As a hypothetical example, suppose that in a given jurisdiction some judges hold discriminatory attitudes that make them punitive toward blacks, while other hold compensatory attitudes that make them lenient toward blacks. Such racial attitudes might, then, make the death penalty more or less likely for a black as compared with a white defendant depending on which judge handles the case. If, however, there were about equal numbers of judges with discriminatory and compensatory attitudes, there would be little aggregate difference in the treatment of black and white defendants in this jurisdiction. The differential treatment attributable to racial attitudes on a case-by-case basis in this hypothetical example would be obscured at the aggregate level by the offsetting effects of the divergent racial attitudes.

To our knowledge, no studies have documented such divergent and possibly offsetting sources of arbitrariness among judges—or juries or prosecutors, for that matter—in the handling of potentially capital cases. However, such an offsetting pattern within a given jurisdiction has been quite effectively documented for lesser offenses—among the same judges who would handle capital cases (Gibson 1978, 455–478). The obvious implication is that such a pattern could also be present in the handling of capital cases and hence introduce an additional component of arbitrariness above and beyond any systematic differences in treatment that are evident at the aggregate level.

## Hypotheses and Research Questions

The evidence from historical and cross-national research and from the studies of the administration of capital punishment in the United States during the pre-*Furman* era suggests several hypotheses about the operation of post-*Furman* capital statutes, particularly about the presence of arbitrariness and discrimination under those statutes. In this section, we present four general hypotheses, each with more specific subhypotheses. We conclude this section with a statement of the research questions to which this initial report of our research will be addressed.

The historical and cross-national evidence that capital punishment has consistently served extralegal functions suggests that arbitrariness and discrimination are inherent in the use of death as punishment and not contingent upon the nature or form of capital statutes. The evidence from studies of capital punishment during the pre-*Furman* era in the United States showing that differences by race and social class of offender and victim were consistent and cumulative over successive stages of the criminal justice process and could not be attributed to legally relevant crime or offender characteristics further suggests that the extralegal functions of capital punishment are deeply rooted in our society; they are not likely to be eliminated by the reform of capital statutes. To be sure, such reforms might produce some measure of "process displacement," or transfer of discrimination, from the sentencing phase to other stages of the criminal justice process. But, to the extent that the arbitrary and discriminatory imposition of the death penalty is tied to deep-seated patterns of racism and classism in our society, any reduction of arbitrariness or discrimination in the sentencing process may be offset by a compensatory increase in differential treatment before sentencing. Thus, under post-*Furman* capital statutes, the extent of arbitrariness and discrimination, if not their distribution over stages of the criminal justice process, might be expected to remain essentially unchanged. These considerations are incorporated in the following set of hypotheses:

1. The death sentence will be imposed in an arbitrary and discriminatory manner under post-*Furman* capital statutes.
    1.1 It will be imposed disproportionately by race and/or social class of offender (minority group oppression).
    1.2 It will be imposed disproportionately by race and/or social class of victim (dominant group protection).
    1.3 It will be imposed disproportionately by offender/victim combinations in terms of race and/or social class (social boundary maintenance).
    1.4 It will be imposed disproportionately by time and/or place within a given capital jurisdiction (repressive response).

2. The disproportionate imposition of the death sentence under post-*Furman* capital statutes will not be attributable to legally relevant aggravating or mitigating circumstances.
    2.1 It will be independent of legally relevant crime characteristics (e.g., contemporaneous felony, murder weapon, number slain).

2.2 It will be independent of legally relevant offender characteristics (e.g., motive, alcohol involvement, prior criminal record).

2.3 It will be independent of legally relevant victim characteristics (e.g., relation to offender, vulnerability, provocation).

3. The post-*Furman* procedural reforms, providing separate sentencing hearings, sentencing guidelines, and automatic appellate review, will not eliminate a substantial risk of arbitrariness and discrimination from the criminal justice process.

3.1 Disparities will not be removed from the sentencing phase of the process (despite the purpose of the sentencing guidelines).

3.2 Disparities will not be removed from earlier stages of the process (despite the inferred consequence of these reforms on the exercise of discretion by prosecutors and police).

3.3 Disparities that enter at the sentencing phase or earlier stages of the criminal justice process will not be corrected in the post-sentencing stage of the process (despite the purpose of automatic appellate review).

4. The restrictiveness of post-*Furman* capital statutes in how they guide or limit sentencing discretion will not eliminate a substantial risk of arbitrariness and discrimination.

4.1 Differential treatment will not be removed under "aggravating only" statutes (e.g., Georgia).

4.2 Differential treatment will not be removed under "aggravating versus mitigating" statutes (e.g., Florida).

4.3 Differential treatment will not be removed under "structured discretion" statutes (e.g., Texas).

In our ongoing program of research on the administration of capital punishment under post-*Furman* statutes, we have adopted an "incremental evaluation strategy" which entails the progressive acquisition of data and examination of the hypotheses stated above (Bowers and Pierce 1979a). In the analysis that follows, we examine arbitrariness and discrimination over the criminal justice process from the point of the crime itself to the point at which the death sentence is handed down. In particular, we consider disparities in the likelihood of a death sentence by race of both offender and victim and by location of crime and prosecution within the state. We also consider whether the observed discrepancies can be attributed to the legally relevant aggravating circumstances of accompanying felonies that could be differentially distributed by time or place of offense or by race of offender or victim.

More specifically, the present analysis will address the following research questions, which put into operation the broader hypotheses stated above:

1. Are patterns of differential treatment by race of offender and victim main-

tained under post-*Furman* capital statutes, and are such patterns independent of the aggravating circumstance of an accompanying felony?

2.  Is differential treatment by location of judicial circuit within a state
    present under post-*Furman* capital statutes, and is it independent of
    the aggravating circumstances of an accompanying felony?
3.  Is differential treatment by race and by location present at the presen-
    tencing and sentencing stages of the criminal justice process in the
    handling of potentially capital cases?
4.  Does the postsentencing review process correct for disparities of treat-
    ment that enter in the sentencing and presentencing stages of the process?
5.  Do the form and restrictiveness of post-*Furman* capital statutes affect
    the extent of differential treatment in presentencing and sentencing
    stages of the process, or the extent to which the postsentencing
    review process will correct for it?

What follows is the first interpretive report of the findings. Portions of these data have been circulated in tabular form to lawyers and
social scientists (Bowers and Pierce 1978; Bowers and Pierce 1979b;
Bowers and Pierce 1979c), presented in testimony before the Senate
Judiciary Committee (Bedau 1978), entered as evidence in capital cases,[13]
used as documentation in claims filed with the Inter-American Commission on Human Rights (International Human Rights Law Group
1980), and cited by the Massachusetts Supreme Court in support of its
recent decision finding the state's latest capital statute unconstitutional (*District Attorney for the Suffolk District* v. *James Watson et
al.*, 381 Mass. 648, 1980).

Most of the tables presented in this chapter were initially developed in conjunction with litigation in capital cases at the trial or appellate levels. Although our further analyses of these data will go well
beyond these early reports, in our judgment the analyses developed
thus far are sufficiently important with respect to their findings about
the administration of capital punishment under post-*Furman* statutes
to be brought to the attention of those whose decisions can affect the
present status and use of the death penalty in the United States.

## Data for the Analysis

In the fall of 1977, the Center for Applied Social Research at Northeastern University began collecting data on capital punishment under
post-*Furman* statutes, following a national conference on capital pun-

---

13.  Sierra v. Texas (September 1976), Raymer v. Colorado (April 1977), Street v. Georgia
     (November 1977), Thomas v. Alabama (February 1978), Taylor v. Georgia (April
     1978), Valle v. Florida (May 1978), Harris v. Alabama (June 1978), Johnson v. Florida
     (November 1978), Lamb v. Georgia (December 1978), McCampbell v. Florida (Feb-
     ruary 1979), Wilson v. Georgia (February 1979), Jackson et al. v. Georgia (August
     1977), Spinkelink v. Florida (October 1977), Evans v. Alabama (June 1979), and House
     and McCorquodale v. Georgia (June 1979).

ishment attended by lawyers and social scientists.[14] This meeting underscored the need for a centralized effort (1) to gather the kinds of systematic information that might yield *prima facie* evidence of arbitrariness and discrimination under post-*Furman* statutes, and (2) to build a data archives that would contain the refined and detailed kinds of information needed to develop an integrated and exacting picture of the administration of capital punishment following the *Furman* decision.

In gathering data, we have relied on the cooperation of federal, state, and local agencies of government, the help of trial attorneys, and the paid and volunteered assistance of a number of other individuals. We have obtained systematic data on (1) criminal homicides in all states since the 1972 *Furman* decision, (2) death sentences handed down and appellate review in selected states since *Furman*, and (3) the criminal justice processing of potentially capital cases from charge through sentencing in one state under the post-*Furman* capital statute.

## Criminal Homicide Data

In 1976 the FBI began to include in the Supplementary Homicide Reports (see Supplement B at the end of this chapter for full citation) information on arrested and/or suspected offenders. Before 1976, these reports contained information on the offense (for example, felony circumstances, murder weapon, offender-victim relationship, time and location of the crime, number of offenders and victims) and on the victim (for example, age, sex, race). In 1976, the reports were modified to include such information on the arrested or suspected offender as age, sex, race, alcohol involvement, and motive for or purpose of the crime (Federal Bureau of Investigation 1976). Thus, since 1976 both offender and victim characteristics have been available for most killings that could be prosecuted as capital offenses.

The Supplementary Homicide Reports are filled out voluntarily by local police departments and are transmitted to a state crime-reporting agency, which compiles state-level crime statistics and forwards the data to the Uniform Crime Reporting section of the FBI. We have obtained from the FBI the data on all states for the period 1973–1976, and, from the state-level crime-reporting agencies of Florida, Georgia, Texas, and Ohio, the data for the year 1977.[15]

---

14. 1977 Death Penalty Conference, Howard University, Washington, D.C. The meeting was jointly sponsored by the NAACP Legal Defense Fund and the Center for Studies in Criminology and Criminal Justice, University of Pennsylvania.
15. We subsequently obtained the Supplementary Homicide Reports data on all states for 1977 and 1978 from the FBI, but not in time for the information to be incorporated into this report of findings.

In Florida, the Supplementary Homicide Reports are filed by all local jurisdictions for full statewide coverage; in Georgia, Texas, and Ohio, they are reported by most but not all local agencies. To correct for the incomplete geographic coverage in the latter states, and to estimate offender characteristics for the pre-1976 period in all four states, we have also obtained the complete willful homicide data from the Vital Statistics programs of these states for the period 1973–1977.[16] With these data, we have developed victim-based adjustments for undercoverage of Supplementary Homicide Reports offender data (see Supplement A at the end of this chapter).

## Death Sentence and Appellate Review Data

In the fall of 1977, we began to compile detailed information on all persons sentenced to death in the states whose capital statutes were specifically upheld in the *Gregg* and companion decisions—Florida, Georgia, and Texas. These three states were responsible for approximately half of all death sentences handed down under post-*Furman* capital statutes in effect at that time. In the spring of 1978, we also began to compile such data for Ohio, which brought the representation of post-*Furman* death sentences to approximately 70 percent.[17] We have periodically updated our data files and now have death sentence information through August 1980 for Florida and Georgia and through May 1978 for Texas. For Ohio, we were able to obtain information on persons under the sentence of death as of the *Lockett* decision of the U.S. Supreme Court, which overturned Ohio's capital statute on July 3, 1978 (*Lockett* v. *Ohio* 1978).[18] With respect to appellate review status, we now have complete information for Florida and Georgia through August 1980.

The data collection effort has involved trial attorneys and others who have helped in compiling and validating the information in the respective states; with their assistance, we have acquired extensive information on offense, defendant, victim, and processing of the case from indictment through appellate review. In particular, the instruments used to compile these data have provided comparable information on felony circumstances of the crime; race of offender and victim; the statutory, aggravating, and mitigating circumstances found

16. These data are published by the Public Health Service, Department of Health and Human Services.
17. These estimates are based on a state-by-state count of death sentences compiled by the National Criminal Justice Information and Statistics Service, *Capital Punishment* (Washington, D.C.: Dept. of Justice, November 1978). This is part of the National Prisoner Statistics series.
18. Unlike that on Florida, Georgia, and Texas, our information on Ohio does not include data on persons sentenced to death; it is restricted to those persons who were under sentence of death at the time of the Lockett decision.

by sentencing authorities; and the current status of the case in the appellate review process.

## Judicial-processing Data

In collaboration with Professor Hans Zeisel of the University of Chicago Law School and Dr. Linda Foley of North Florida University, we began, in the fall of 1977, to collect data designed to follow the criminal justice processing of potentially capital cases in Florida from charge through sentencing. In the first stage of this project, information was gathered on all first degree murder indictments from 1973 through 1976 in twenty-one Florida counties, accounting for approximately 75 percent of Florida's death sentences over that period. Six months later, a second stage of data collection was undertaken to obtain a broader initial sampling of homicide cases, including all homicide charges at arraignment. These data were gathered for the period 1976–1977 in a sample of twenty Florida counties, including some but not all of the counties sampled in the first phase of the data collection.

In both phases, data were collected by law students instructed in the use of a standard form designed to gather information on the disposition of the case at successive stages and to obtain characteristics of the crime, the victim, and the accused defendant. All decisions concerning the coding of verbatim material were reviewed by a consulting attorney.

## Scope of the Analysis

The upcoming analysis deals with the first five years following the *Furman* decision. For Florida, Georgia, Texas, and Ohio, we examine criminal homicides committed between the effective dates (if occurring on the first of the month; if not, tabulations begin with the first of the following month) of their respective statutes (that is, Florida: December 8, 1972; Georgia: March 28, 1973; Texas: January 1, 1974; Ohio: November 1, 1974) and the end of 1977, and the death sentences imposed under the post-*Furman* statutes for homicides occurring before 1978.[19] The analysis of judicial processing in Florida is restricted to offenses

19. The number of death sentences for the states in this analysis (Table 7-2) will generally exceed the number imposed by 1977 (see Table 6-3, *additions*) because the present figures include death sentences imposed after 1977 for offenses committed in that year or earlier. Georgia is an exception because death sentences for rape prior to the Coker decision are included among those reported in Table 6-3. For Ohio, the Lockett decision brought post-1977 death sentences to an end, at least temporarily, in July 1978, and data were available only on death sentences in effect at the time of Lockett. But owing to the relatively small number of pre-1978 removals and the relatively large number of pre-Lockett death sentences in 1978 imposed for offenses committed in 1977 and earlier, the number of Ohio death sentences in this analysis does exceed the number reported through 1977 in Table 6-3.

that occurred before 1978 and reached the trial court dockets before the collection of data. Thus, December 31, 1977, is our cutoff date in the sense that offenses occurring after 1977, regardless of sentencing date, are excluded from this analysis.

The analysis proceeds in five sections: (1) arbitrariness by race; (2) arbitrariness by place; (3) arbitrariness by stages of the process; (4) arbitrariness and the review process; and (5) arbitrariness and the form of the law. In our analysis of racial differences all four states are examined, although we do not carry the Ohio data as far as we do the data for Florida, Georgia, and Texas. In our analysis of regional differences, we examine Florida and Georgia, excluding Texas because of ambiguities with respect to judicial circuits as a basis for grouping jurisdictions. Our analysis of judicial processing is based on information that was available only from Florida. Our analysis of appellate review incorporates data available only on Florida and Georgia. The final section of the empirical analysis, on the form of the law, draws a comparison between Florida and Georgia based on data available only from these two states.

## Analysis

The stage is now set for the analysis. The questions are clear. Have the new post-*Furman* capital statutes removed the substantial risk of arbitrariness and discrimination present under pre-*Furman* statutes? Have they eliminated differential treatment by race of offender and victim, by time and place within a jurisdiction, at presentencing and sentencing stages of the process? Has appellate review corrected differential treatment that might have entered earlier in the process? And are the different forms that post-*Furman* capital statutes take equally effective in purging the process of differential treatment?

### Arbitrariness by Race

By far the most substantial and consistent extralegal basis of differential treatment under pre-*Furman* statutes was race. All but a few studies found gross racial differences in the likelihood of a death sentence; race of both offender and victim was associated with differential treatment, and race of victim was a more prominent basis of differential treatment than race of offender. If the post-*Furman* statutes have remedied the previous ills, we should find no substantial or consistent differences by race in the likelihood of a death sentence for criminal homicide under the new statutes.

The likelihood of a death sentence by offender-victim racial categories in Florida, Georgia, Texas, and Ohio is shown in Table 7-2. It

**Table 7-2.** *Probability of Receiving the Death Sentence in Florida, Georgia, Texas, and Ohio for Criminal Homicide, by Race of Offender and Victim (from Effective Dates of Respective Post-*Furman* Capital Statutes through 1977)*

| Offender-Victim Racial Combinations | (1) Estimated Number of Offenders [a] | (2) Persons Sentenced to Death | (3) Overall Probability of Death Sentence |
|---|---|---|---|
| **Florida** | | | |
| Black kills white | 240 | 53 | 0.221 |
| White kills white | 1768 | 82 | 0.046 |
| Black kills black | 1922 | 12 | 0.006 |
| White kills black | 80 | 0 | 0.000 |
| **Georgia** | | | |
| Black kills white | 258 | 42 | 0.163 |
| White kills white | 1006 | 43 | 0.043 |
| Black kills black | 2458 | 12 | 0.005 |
| White kills black | 71 | 2 | 0.028 |
| **Texas** | | | |
| Black kills white | 344 | 30 | 0.087 |
| White kills white | 3616 | 56 | 0.015 |
| Black kills black | 2597 | 2 | 0.001 |
| White kills black | 143 | 1 | 0.007 |
| **Ohio** | | | |
| Black kills white | 173 | 44 | 0.254 |
| White kills white | 803 | 37 | 0.046 |
| Black kills black | 1170 | 20 | 0.017 |
| White kills black | 47 | 0 | 0.000 |

*Sources* (keyed to Supplement B): Florida—A1, A2, C1; Georgia—A1, A3, A6, C2; Texas—A1, A5, A8, C4; Ohio—A1, A4, A7, C3.

[a] Based on information submitted by the police in the Supplementary Homicide Reports. The number of offenders is estimated as described in Supplement A, with the following adjustment factors: Florida, 2.861; Georgia, 4.453; Texas, 2.473; Ohio, 1.871.

presents the estimated number of criminal offenders,[20] the number of persons sentenced to death, and the probability or likelihood of a death sentence given a homicide for each offender-victim racial combination in each state from the effective date of the post-*Furman* statute through 1977. The likelihood of a death sentence given a criminal homicide spans the criminal justice process from the initial investigation of the crime by the police through the sentencing of a convicted offender. That is, unlike studies that begin with a sample of indictments, these

20. The method of estimating the number of criminal homicides by offender-victim category is described in Supplement A, and the specific adjustment factors employed for each state are given in note *a* below Table 7-2.

data will reflect the effects of differential law enforcement as well as differential court processing of criminal homicide cases. They incorporate the effects of discretion at arrest, charging, indictment, conviction, and sentencing in the handling of potentially capital crimes.

And what do these data show? Stark differences by race of both offender and victim in all four states are apparent in Table 7-2. The racial pattern is consistent across states and similar to the experience under pre-*Furman* statutes. Thus, black killers and the killers of whites are substantially more likely than others to receive a death sentence in all four states. And, as in the pre-*Furman* era, race of victim tends to overshadow race of offender as a basis for differential treatment (in fact, differences by race of offender would be altogether obscured if the data were tabulated without race of victim).[21] In Florida, the difference by race of victim is great. Among black offenders, those who kill whites are nearly forty times more likely to be sentenced to death than those who kill blacks. The difference by race of offender, although not as great, is also marked. Among the killers of whites, blacks are five times more likely than whites to be sentenced to death. To appreciate the magnitude of these differences, consider the following implications of these data: If all offenders in Florida were sentenced to death at the same rate as blacks who killed whites, there would be a total of 887 persons sentenced to death; 53 blacks who killed whites, 391 whites who killed whites, 425 blacks who killed blacks, and 18 whites who killed blacks—instead of the 147 death sentences actually imposed by the end of 1977.

In Georgia, the chances of a death sentence are slightly less in magnitude but remarkably similar in pattern to those in Florida. Overall, the likelihood of a death sentence is 30 percent lower in Georgia than in Florida (0.026 for Georgia; 0.037 for Florida), but much of this difference is due to the greater proportion of black-black killings in Georgia. For the respective offender-victim racial categories, the differences are less: 24 percent lower for black-offender–white-victim killings, 9 percent lower for white-white killings, and 17 percent lower for black-black killings. Only the category of white offenders-black victims is noticeably different, as a result of two death sentences in Georgia and none in Florida. Hence, the difference in statutory form in these two states—"aggravating only" in Georgia and "aggravating versus mitigating" in Florida—appears to have only a slight and not an altogether consistent effect on the chances of a death sentence and virtually no effect in controlling or correcting racial disparities.

21. When race of victim is ignored, white offenders are more likely to receive a death sentence in three of these four states: Florida (white = 0.044, black = 0.030), Georgia (white = 0.040, black = 0.020), Texas (white = 0.015, black = 0.011). Without considering race of victim, black offenders exceed whites in the chances of a death sentence only in Ohio (white = 0.044, black = 0.048).

In Texas, the chances that a murder will result in a death sentence are considerably less; indeed, the likelihood is only about one-third the chances in Florida and one-half the chances in Georgia.[22] But the pattern of racial differences is still very much the same. In fact, despite the reduced chances of a death sentence in Texas, the racial differences, in relative terms, are generally greater.[23] Among black offenders, those with white victims are eighty-seven times more likely than those with black victims to receive the death penalty; and among the killers of whites, black offenders are six times more likely than white offenders to be sentenced to death. Perhaps the lower likelihood of a death sentence in Texas than in Florida and Georgia is a result of the more restrictive procedures of the "structured discretion" statute in Texas or of the more limited kinds of offenses that qualify for the death sentence in Texas. But it is clear that the Texas statute, despite its restrictiveness, has not eliminated differential treatment by race of offender and victim. On the contrary, race of offender and race of victim are responsible for more variation in the chances of a death sentence in Texas than in Florida or Georgia.

In Ohio, the pattern is the same; black killers and the killers of whites are more likely to receive the death sentence. Here the chances of a death sentence are greater overall than in the other three states. The relative differences by race of offender and victim are generally somewhat less than in Florida, Georgia, and Texas. Perhaps the greater likelihood of a death sentence in Ohio reflects the "quasi-mandatory" character of the Ohio statute (see *Harvard Law Review* 1974, p. 1709, note 133, for discussion of the definition of *quasi-mandatory*), which was overturned in the *Lockett* decision for its failure to provide individualized treatment for convicted capital offenders.[24] Since Ohio's statute

22. The latest statewide listing of death sentences available from the Texas Judicial Council was current as of May 1978, so it may not include some death sentences that were eventually imposed for murders committed in 1977 or earlier. Given a pace of about twelve death sentences per year in Texas, with an average elapsed time between offense and sentence of six to eight months, we estimate that roughly six to eight death sentences might have been missed. Our figures for Texas, therefore, may underrepresent death sentences by six to eight cases, not more than 10 percent of the total.

23. Furthermore, the Texas figures probably underestimate the extent to which blacks and whites, or members of minority groups versus the majority group, are treated differently. We know from the Texas Judicial Council reports that persons with Spanish surnames were overrepresented among those sentenced to death; eleven death sentences of such persons were imposed. But, because it was not possible to distinguish Hispanics from whites in the Supplementary Homicide Reports data, we could not tabulate the figures for blacks and whites excluding Hispanics or differentiate between blacks and Hispanics on the one hand and whites on the other.

24. Under the Ohio statute, the jury considered only aggravating circumstances. If the jury found an aggravating circumstance, death was automatically the recommended punishment. The judge was then required to take evidence on mitigating circumstances. If the judge found no mitigating circumstances, the death sentence was imposed; otherwise, it was not.

has been invalidated by the Supreme Court, we have given the Ohio data less priority in our analysis and will not examine the operation of this statute further here.

In these four states, which accounted for approximately 70 percent of the nation's death sentences in the first five years after *Furman*, race of both offender and victim had a tremendous impact on the chances that a death sentence would be handed down. To understand to some extent the size of the effect of these racial differences, consider the following: The probability that a difference of this magnitude in the four states combined could have occurred by chance is so remote that it cannot be computed with available statistical programs. As computed, the probability is greater than 1 in 1 million for a chi square of 769.5 with 3 degrees of freedom. And this is a conservative estimate, since the overall pattern is not a composite of widely different patterns from state to state, but rather is a reflection of the same essential pattern in states with differing mechanisms and procedures for guiding discretion.

The presence of differential treatment by race is unmistakable. But does it reflect the direct influence of race on the decisions made in the criminal justice process or could it be the result of legally relevant differences in the kinds of crimes committed by and against blacks and whites? A recent statement of this latter possibility can be found in the Fifth Circuit Court of Appeals opinion in *Spinkelink* v. *Wainwright* (578 F.2d 582 [CA5, 1978]). As recounted by the court, the Florida Attorney General argued

> that murders involving black victims have, in the past, generally been qualitatively different from murders involving white victims; as a general rule, . . . murders involving black victims have not presented facts and circumstances appropriate for the imposition of the death penalty (ibid., 617).

In a footnote, the court went on to quote Attorney General Chevin's enumeration of these alleged differences: "Murders involving black victims have in the past fallen into the categories of family quarrels, lovers' quarrels, liquor quarrels, [and] barroom quarrels" (ibid., 617, note 37).

In response to this argument, it would obviously be desirable to examine the chances of a death sentence by race of offender and victim separately for two categories of murder: those which by definition qualify for the death penalty and those which may or may not so qualify. In this connection, the statutes of Florida and Georgia make a felony circumstance—the fact that a homicide is committed in the course of another felony (for example, rape, robbery)—an aggravating factor that qualifies the homicide for the death penalty.[25] The Texas statute explicitly defines felony killing as one of the five categories of

25. See notes 3 and 4.

homicide that may lead to a death sentence.[26] In effect, the distinction between felony and nonfelony homicides corresponds to the difference between crimes that definitely qualify for capital punishment and those that may or may not so qualify.

In the Supplementary Homicide Reports, the police indicate for each homicide whether it was committed in the course of another felony. The data we have obtained on death sentences imposed in the several states show for each crime whether it was accompanied by one or more felony circumstances. Notably, these data reveal that fewer than one out of five of the homicides in Florida, Georgia, and Texas were felony-type murders, but that more than four out of five of the death sentences in each of these states were imposed for felony-type murders. If, as the Florida attorney general contended, blacks are typically the victims of nonfelony-type murders, which do not present the "facts and circumstances appropriate for the imposition of the death penalty," the pattern of racial differences observed in Table 7-2, at least with respect to race of victim, might possibly be attributable to this legally relevant difference in the types of homicide committed against blacks and whites.

The likelihood of a death sentence by offender-victim racial category is presented separately in Table 7-3 for felony and nonfelony-type murders in Florida, Georgia, and Texas. The importance of a felony circumstance as a determinant of the death sentence is immediately evident. For nearly every offender-victim racial category in each state, the death sentence is more likely for felony than for nonfelony murder—five to ten times more likely on the average within offender-victim racial categories.

But the table makes it equally clear that type of murder does not account for the racial differences in treatment observed earlier in Table 7-2. For felony homicides and for nonfelony homicides alike, the differences by race of both offender and victim shown in Table 7-2 are again evident. To be sure, as the Florida attorney general argued in the *Spinkelink* case, black homicide victims are less likely than their white counterparts to be killed under the potentially capital felony circumstances (evident from the base figures in the first and fourth columns of Table 7-3). But it is not true, as he alleged, that this difference in the kinds of murder perpetrated against blacks as compared with whites explains or accounts for the racial differences in treatment shown in Table 7-2.[27]

---

26. See note 6.
27. Ironically, the evidence of gross differences in the likelihood of a death sentence by race of victim presented in the Spinkelink appeal was restricted to cases of murder committed under felony circumstances (essentially the data for Florida in the first three columns of Table 7-3). With respect to these data, the argument that blacks were typically or disproportionately the victims of killings provoked by quarrels was essentially irrelevant. The data explicitly excluded the overwhelming majority of killings attributed to quarrels or similar passion-filled conflicts. The failure to appreciate this point would appear to have been a fatal mistake even at the appellate level.

**Table 7-3.** *Probability of Receiving the Death Sentence in Florida, Georgia, and Texas for Felony and Nonfelony Murder, by Race of Offender and Victim (from Effective Dates of Respective Post-Furman Capital Statutes through 1977)*

| Offender-Victim Racial Combinations | Felony-type Murder | | | Nonfelony-type Murder | | |
|---|---|---|---|---|---|---|
| | (1) Estimated Number of Offenders [a] | (2) Persons Sentenced to Death | (3) Probability of Death Sentence | (4) Estimated Number of Offenders [a] | (5) Persons Sentenced to Death | (6) Overall Probability of Death Sentence |
| Florida | | | | | | |
| Black kills white | 143 | 46 | 0.323 | 97 | 7 | 0.072 |
| White kills white | 303 | 65 | 0.215 | 1465 | 17 | 0.012 |
| Black kills black | 160 | 7 | 0.044 | 1762 | 5 | 0.003 |
| White kills black | 11 | 0 | 0.000 | 69 | 0 | 0.000 |
| Georgia | | | | | | |
| Black kills white | 134 | 39 | 0.291 | 124 | 3 | 0.024 |
| White kills white | 183 | 37 | 0.202 | 823 | 6 | 0.007 |
| Black kills black | 205 | 8 | 0.039 | 2253 | 4 | 0.002 |
| White kills black | 13 | 2 | 0.154 | 58 | 0 | 0.000 |
| Texas | | | | | | |
| Black kills white | 173 | 28 | 0.162 | 171 | 2 | 0.012 |
| White kills white | 378 | 48 | 0.127 | 3238 | 8 | 0.002 |
| Black kills black | 121 | 2 | 0.017 | 2476 | 0 | 0.000 |
| White kills black | 30 | 1 | 0.033 | 113 | 0 | 0.000 |

*Sources* (keyed to Supplement B): Florida—A1, A2, C1; Georgia—A1, A3, A6, C2; Texas—A1, A5, A8, C4.

[a] See Table 7-2.

A closer examination of Table 7-3 reveals a slight but consistent pattern of racial differences in treatment by type of killing. For felony homicides, race of victim becomes more clearly the dominant factor. In each of the three states, by far the most substantial differences in the chance of a death sentence occur between those offenders who kill whites and those who kill blacks. In the case of nonfelony homicides, the overall pattern of differential treatment by race of offender and victim persists, but the greatest difference in both absolute and relative terms tends to be between the killings by blacks of white victims and all other racial combinations.

It appears, then, that among the kinds of killings least likely to be punished by death (that is, nonfelony killings), the death sentence is used primarily in reponse to the most socially condemned form of boundary crossing—a crime against a majority group member by a minority group member. Among those offenders more commonly (but not usually or typically) punished by death (that is, those committing a felony homicide), there is some suggestion that cases of boundary crossing in the opposite direction—with majority group offenders and minority group victims—are selected occasionally against the prevailing race of offender and victim influences for more severe treatment.[28] But this latter pattern is a minor variation on a major theme. The primary point is this: Among felony killings, for which the death penalty is more apt to be used, race of victim is the chief basis of differential treatment.

Table 7-3 also helps to clarify the effects of differences among the capital statutes of Florida, Georgia, and Texas. We noted in connection with Table 7-2 that the overall likelihood of a death sentence was somewhat greater in Florida than in Georgia but that the differences were less for specific offender-victim racial categories. With the control for felony circumstances in Table 7-3, the differences between corresponding categories are still further reduced for killings under felony circumstances. Thus, compared with Florida, the likelihood of a death sentence in Georgia is 10 percent lower for black-offender–white-victim felony killings, 6 percent lower for white-white felony killings, and 11 percent lower for black-black felony killings. (The corresponding figures for all homicides in Table 7-2 are 24, 9, and 17 percent, respectively.) Among nonfelony killings, for which the death sentence is relatively unlikely, there are greater differences in some of the categories between the two states in relative terms. But by and large, the statutes of these two states yield similar levels and patterns in the use of the death penalty.

---

28. In each state the fewest homicides are reported for the white-offender–black-victim category. Hence, the likelihood estimates for this category are least stable, and comparisons between this category and the others are least reliable.

Moreover, Table 7-3 addresses a question raised earlier about the manner in which the Texas "structured discretion" statute affects the likelihood of a death sentence. It is clear from Table 7-3 that the death sentence is less likely in Texas than in Florida or Georgia for felony as well as nonfelony killings. Obviously, the low likelihood of a death sentence in Texas is not simply the result of the statutory restrictions on the kinds of killings that qualify for the death penalty. It is evident that, for the kinds that qualify in all three states—namely, felony murders—Texas has relatively fewer death sentences. Apparently, the procedural questions of aggravation the Texas jury must answer have the effect of limiting the imposition of the death sentence in that state. These inferences are, of course, only as strong as the assumption that the killers are no more culpable and their crimes no more heinous in one state than another, or that the prosecutors, judges, and juries in the three states do not differ in their predilection for capital punishment.

The data in this section point to more than arbitrariness and discrimination in isolation. They reflect a twofold departure from evenhanded justice that is consistent with a single underlying racist tenet: that white lives are worth more than black lives. From this tenet it follows that death as punishment is more appropriate for the killers of whites than for the killers of blacks and more appropriate for black than for white killers. Either discrimination by race of offender or disparities of treatment by race of victim of the magnitudes we have seen here are a direct challenge to the constitutionality of the post-*Furman* capital statutes. Together, these elements of arbitrariness and discrimination may represent a two-edged sword of racism in capital punishment that is beyond statutory control.

## Arbitrariness by Place

We observed in the preceding section considerable differences among states in the likelihood of a death sentence: Texas was well below and Ohio was somewhat above Florida and Georgia for corresponding offender-victim racial categories. These differences by place could plausibly be attributed to legally relevant variations—to the statutes' differences in the restrictiveness of their standards and guidelines for imposing the death penalty. Within a state, however, the law is the same from one court jurisdiction or county to another. If justice is evenhanded throughout the state, the same crime should not be two or three times more likely to result in a death sentence in one part of a state than in another.

In the *Gregg* decision, the U.S. Supreme Court cited the Georgia review process for its commitment to equalize the imposition of the death sentence throughout the state. Specifically, the Court quoted the words of the Georgia Supreme Court in *Moore* v. *State*, "We view it to be our duty under the similarity standard to assure that no death sentence is affirmed unless in similar cases throughout the state the death penalty has been imposed generally" (*Gregg* v. *Georgia* 1976, 2940). In so doing, the highest court gave explicit endorsement to the premise that the death penalty must be administered in a manner consistent with the legally relevant characteristics of the crime and of the defendant and independent of where and when the crime occurred or was tried within a state.

There are as many possibilities for differential treatment by place as there are places where police, prosecutors, juries, and judges exercise discretion in the processing of potentially capital cases. This means that a statistical analysis that groups specific locations, counties, or court jurisdictions into broader geographic or regional categories runs the risk of obscuring substantial disparities in treatment by place. That is, in the course of an examination of differences that are relatively broadly based—covering major portions or regions of a state—stark and consistent differences in treatment by court, judge, prosecutor, and so on, within one of these broader areas, may tend to offset one another and thus be masked in the aggregate statistics. For this reason, the findings that follow will be a conservative or partial reflection of the true variations by location within the respective states.

In this section, we examine the likelihood of a death sentence by judicial circuits grouped regionally within Florida and Georgia. We exclude Texas from this analysis because it does not have judicial circuits for the handling of criminal cases.[29] To develop such regional groupings of judicial circuits, we first combined the homicide and death sentence data for the counties in a circuit and tabulated death sentence rates for each circuit within a state. We next combined judicial circuits into regional groupings which follow north-south and east-west co-ordinates or natural boundaries (for example, panhandle), tend to be homogeneous with respect to death sentence rates, and do not yield conspicuously small numbers of reported homicides (that is, not fewer than 200 or less than 5 percent of the total for the state). We then calculated death sentence rates for the principal population centers (circuits with 1970 populations exceeding 500,000) within the respective regional groupings. Those population centers with less than half or more than twice the death sentence rate for their region are presented separately in the tables that follow.

The chances of a death sentence in the various regional groupings

---

29. Texas has 281 district courts in 254 counties. Some of these courts serve only a portion of a single county, some serve portions of several counties, and some specialize in noncriminal cases. However, all criminal appeals go directly to the state supreme court; there are no judicial circuits for the handling of criminal cases.

of judicial circuits in Florida and Georgia are shown in Table 7-4.[30] A glance at the table reveals that there is considerable variation by region and by population centers within these two states. In Florida, the death sentence is nearly two and one-half times more likely in the panhandle than in the southern portion of the state; the northern and central regions fall about midway between these two extremes. In Georgia, the regional variations are even greater. The death sentence in the central region of Georgia is over six times more likely than it is in the northern region. It is between seven and eight times as likely in the central region as in Fulton County (where Atlanta is located). The

**Table 7-4.** *Probability of Receiving the Death Sentence in Florida and Georgia for Criminal Homicide, by Judicial Circuits/Counties Grouped Regionally (from Effective Dates of Respective Post-Furman Capital Statutes through 1977)*

| Regional Grouping of Judicial Circuits/Counties | (1) Number of Homicides | (2) Number of Death Sentences | (3) Overall Probability of Death Sentence |
|---|---|---|---|
| Florida [a] | | | |
| Panhandle | 415 | 20 | 0.048 |
| North | 976 | 34 | 0.035 |
| Central | 1526 | 54 | 0.035 |
| South | 1927 | 39 | 0.020 |
| Georgia [b] | | | |
| North | 289 | 2 | 0.007 |
| Central | 1011 | 45 | 0.045 |
| Fulton County (Atlanta) | 1133 | 7 | 0.006 |
| Southwest | 985 | 23 | 0.023 |
| Southeast | 837 | 22 | 0.026 |

*Sources* (keyed to Supplement B): Florida—A-1, A-2, C-1; Georgia—A6, C2.
[a] Regional groupings of circuits are as follows: panhandle (1, 2, 3,14), north (4, 5, 6, 7, 8), central (6, 9, 10,12,13,18,19), south (11,15,16,17).
[b] Regional groupings of circuits are as follows: north (Lookout Mountain, Conasauga, Blue Ridge, Mountain, Northeastern, Rome, Cherokee), central (Tallapoosa, Cobb, Coweta, Griffin, Clayton, Stone Mountain, Gwinnett, Alcovy, Piedmont, Western, Ocmulgec, Northern, Toombs, Flint), Fulton County (Atlanta), southwest (Chattahoochee, Macon, Houston, Southwestern, Pataula, Cordege, Tifton, Dougherty, South Georgia, Southern, Alapaha), southeast (Augusta, Middle, Dublin, Ogeechee, Oconce, Atlantic, Eastern, Waycross, Brunswick).

30. The homicide figures in this section of the analysis are adjusted only for geographic undercoverage owing to the failure of some agencies within a state to file Supplementary Homicide Reports. The adjustment for temporal undercoverage is unnecessary since no offender characteristics (unavailable before 1976) will be examined here. For Florida, where all local police agencies have reported Supplementary Homicide Reports data at least since 1973, no adjustment factor has been applied.

southeastern and southwestern regions are again roughly midway between the extremes. The probability that such differences occurred by chance, given evenhanded disposition of the death penalty and comparable offenses committed across the states, is extremely rare, well beyond accepted standards of chance variation (that is, the regional differences in Florida would occur 2 times in 1,000 and the Georgia differences would occur no more often than 1 in 1 million times for a chi square of 76.3 with 4 degrees of freedom).

One might quarrel with the assumption that there are no regional differences in the kinds of killings that occur. That is, regional disparities in the chances of a death sentence could reflect regional variations in the kinds of homicides committed. For example, regions with higher death sentence rates might have relatively more felony murders. But there is reason to believe that the opposite is true. Felony-type murder is more characteristic of urban areas, and these are the locations in Florida and Georgia—southern Florida and Fulton County, Georgia—that had the lowest death sentence rates in Table 7-4.

In fact, regional differences in the likelihood of a death sentence are even greater when we take type of killing into account. Table 7-5 shows the chances of a death sentence for felony and nonfelony homicides within each of the regional groupings of judicial circuits in Florida and Georgia. For felony-type murder in Florida, the death sentence in the panhandle is four to five times more likely than in the southern and northern regions of the state, and more than twice the probability in central Florida; the level in central Florida is twice that in the northern and southern regions. In fact, felony homicides are less likely to be punished by death in those places—the southern and northern regions—where they are a greater fraction of all homicides committed (as reflected in the base figures of Table 7-5).

Among nonfelony homicides in Florida the death sentence is three times more likely in the northern region than in any of the others. Indeed, the northern region of Florida shows a pattern quite different from the rest of the state. This region is among the least likely to impose the death sentence for felony-type murder but is by far the most likely to do so for nonfelony murder. The contrast between the pattern in this region and that in the panhandle draws attention to widely discrepant practices in the imposition of the death sentence under the same law in geographically contiguous court jurisdictions.

There are a number of similarities in Georgia. Among felony-type murders, the regional differences are again greater than those in Table 7-4. Courts in the central, southwestern, and southeastern regions are three to four times more likely to impose the death sentence for felony murder than those in northern Georgia, and about eight times more likely to do so than those in Fulton County. Again, those areas with

**Table 7-5.** *Probability of Receiving the Death Sentence in Florida and Georgia for Felony and Nonfelony Homicide, by Judicial Circuits/Counties Grouped Regionally (from Effective Dates of Respective Post-Furman Capital Statutes through 1977)*

| Regional Grouping of Judicial Circuits/ Counties | Felony-type Murder | | | Nonfelony-type Murder | | |
|---|---|---|---|---|---|---|
| | (1) Number of Homicides | (2) Number of Death Sentences | (3) Overall Probability of Death Sentence | (4) Number of Homicides | (5) Number of Death Sentences | (6) Overall Probability of Death Sentence |
| Florida | | | | | | |
| Panhandle | 31 | 18 | 0.581 | 384 | 2 | 0.005 |
| North | 140 | 19 | 0.136 | 836 | 15 | 0.018 |
| Central | 172 | 47 | 0.273 | 1354 | 7 | 0.005 |
| South | 270 | 34 | 0.126 | 1657 | 5 | 0.003 |
| Georgia[a] | | | | | | |
| North | 36 | 2 | 0.056 | 253 | 0 | 0.000 |
| Central | 162 | 37 | 0.228 | 849 | 8 | 0.009 |
| Fulton Co. (Atlanta) | 154 | 4 | 0.026 | 979 | 3 | 0.003 |
| Southwest | 103 | 23 | 0.223 | 882 | 0 | 0.000 |
| Southeast | 116 | 20 | 0.172 | 721 | 2 | 0.003 |

*Sources* (keyed to Supplement B): Florida—A-1, A-2, C-1; Georgia—A1, A3, A6, C2.
[a] The numbers of homicides for Georgia are estimates. They are estimated as described in Supplement A, with the following adjustment factors for Georgia regional groupings: north, 1.818; central, 1.879; Fulton County, 1.166; southwest, 1.820; southeast, 2.152.

the highest proportion of felony versus nonfelony homicides—northern Georgia and Fulton County—are less likely than the other regions to impose the death sentence for felony homicides.

In Georgia, too, one of the regions—central Georgia—is much more likely than any of the others to use the death sentence for nonfelony homicides. Indeed, the central region of Georgia is more likely than any of the others to hand down the death sentence for both felony and nonfelony homicides. Gross disparities of treatment by jurisdiction in Georgia for similar kinds of killings are aptly illustrated by the comparison of Fulton County with central Georgia, which virtually surrounds the county. The death sentence is three times more likely for nonfelony homicides and almost ten times more likely for felony homicides in central Georgia than in Fulton County.

So far, we have documented gross differences in the likelihood of

chances of a death sentence by race and by location within a state
(Tables 7-2 and 7-4) and shown that these differences are independent
of the kinds of killings for which the death penalty may be imposed
(Tables 7-3 and 7-5). We now carry the analysis one step further by
asking to what extent the observed differences by race and by region
are independent of one another.

In Table 7-6, we examine the joint effects of region and race of
victim on the likelihood of a death sentence for felony-type murder in
Florida. We do not attempt to examine the offender's as well as the
victim's race for two reasons. First, race of victim is a more pronounced
basis for differential treatment among felony homicides than is race
of offender, as shown in Table 7-3. And second, the race of victim data
do not need to be adjusted for temporal undercoverage, as would the
race of offender figures. We present only felony-type murders in Table
7-6 because death sentences for nonfelony homicides are few in
number and seldom imposed when the victim is a black person.

Table 7-6 demonstrates quite unmistakably that both race and
place contribute independently to the likelihood of a death sentence
in Florida. Within each region, the felony killers of whites are decidedly
more likely to be sentenced to death than are those of blacks. The
differences range from about three to one in southern Florida to much
greater levels in the other regions. Moreover, the regional differences
remain apparent and follow the pattern shown for felony murders without respect to race demonstrated in Table 7-5. So few persons who
killed blacks under felony circumstances were sentenced to death that
the pattern is erratic by region; only seven death sentences were imposed for felony killings of blacks.

Here we see extraordinary variation in the likelihood of a death
sentence for killings committed under felony circumstances. Not only
are there large differences in terms of the region in which the offense
occurred, but there are also large differences by race of victim. Together,
these two extralegal sources of variation in the likelihood of a death
sentence produce extreme disparities. Consider, for instance, the difference in the probability that a death sentence will be given the felony killer of a white in the panhandle and the probability that a felony
killer of a black in the northern region will be sentenced to death: For
killings under similar circumstances the death sentence is roughly
thirty times more likely for the killer of a white in the panhandle than
for the killer of a black in the northern region.

These differences by judicial circuit in the likelihood of a death
sentence are, at this point, a conservative uninterpreted estimate. We
know that the death sentence is more likely where felony murders are
less frequent, and that such murders are relatively infrequent in rural
as opposed to urban areas. Why this should be so is unclear at this

**Table 7-6.** *Probability of Receiving the Death Sentence in Florida for Felony-type Murder, by Race of Victim and Judicial Circuits Grouped Regionally (from Effective Date of Post-Furman Statute through 1977)*

| Regional Grouping of Judicial Circuits | White Victim | | | Black Victim | | |
|---|---|---|---|---|---|---|
| | (1) Number of Homicides | (2) Number of Death Sentences | (3) Overall Probability of Death Sentence | (4) Number of Homicides | (5) Number of Death Sentences | (6) Overall Probability of Death Sentence |
| Panhandle | 24 | 18 | 0.750 | 7 | 0 | 0.000 |
| North | 101 | 18 | 0.178 | 38 | 1 | 0.026 |
| Central | 138 | 45 | 0.326 | 34 | 2 | 0.059 |
| South | 192 | 30 | 0.156 | 76 | 4 | 0.053 |

*Sources* (keyed to Supplement B): A1, A2, C1.
*Note:* The total number of homicides that appears in this table is lower than the total for Florida as shown in Table 7-5 because of the exclusion of homicide victims of races other than black or white.

point, but it seems likely that regional differences in death sentence rates for killings under similar circumstances are even greater than the tables in this section show. Thus, killers in rural areas are probably less likely than those in urban areas to have a prior record of convictions—a legally relevant aggravating circumstance that should make the death sentence more likely. And, as we noted at the beginning of this section, the aggregate regional data we have presented here will tend to "average out" and thus obscure some of the disparity by place within a state. But without our knowing why they occur or how much greater the variations actually are, the regional disparities presented above represent a striking departure from the standard of similar punishment for similar crimes throughout a state, which the Supreme Court affirmed in the *Gregg* decision.

### Arbitrariness by Stages of the Process

We now know that there have been gross variations in the handling of cases from offense through sentence by both race and location within the state, that these two extralegal factors have contributed independently to these variations in treatment, and that their effects are not attributable to the legally relevant difference between felony and nonfelony homicides. What we do not yet know is where in the criminal justice process the effects of race and place intrude and whether they are corrected by appellate review. In this section we examine discrete stages in the handling of potentially capital cases to find out whether the effects of such extralegal factors are concentrated at a particular point in the process or diffused and pervasive throughout the process.[31] In the following section we will examine the appellate review process to see whether the differential treatment in presentencing and/or sentencing stages is corrected in the postsentencing stage of the process.

In the *Gregg* decision the Supreme Court held that mandatory capital statutes were unconstitutional and noted that they run the risk of having arbitrariness and discrimination displaced to earlier stages of the process—especially through "jury nullification" (the failure of a jury to convict an offender of a crime for which the death sentence is mandatory because, even though the jury may be convinced of the defendant's guilt, it is unwilling for other reasons to see the death sentence imposed). The Court reasoned that guided discretion statutes, on the other hand, would preserve individualized treatment in sentencing, eliminate arbitrariness and discrimination in sentencing (*Gregg v. Georgia* 1976, 2940), and, indeed, purge these ills from the exercise of discretion at earlier stages of the process (ibid., 2948).

---

31. Although we are examining stages before conviction, for ease of reference we continue to use the term *offender* throughout.

In view of our findings thus far, the Court's assumption about the ability of guided discretion statutes to remove arbitrariness and discrimination from the overall processing of potentially capital cases appears to be mistaken. Whether the narrower assumption that such sentencing guidelines will eliminate these ills at the sentencing stage of the process remains uncertain at this point. This is particularly relevant since automatic appellate review of all death sentences is apt to become less effective as a tool for correcting such ills the further removed they are from the sentencing step of the process.

For this analysis we turn to the data on the processing of potentially capital cases in selected counties of Florida. Information was obtained on charges, indictments, convictions, and sentences in selected Florida counties (see Supplement B at the end of this chapter). These data can be used to examine discrete stages or decision points in the process: the decision to bring a first degree versus a lesser charge among all cases charged with criminal homicide; the decision to convict on a first degree murder charge versus acquit or convict on a lesser charge among all cases charged with first degree murder; and the decision to impose the death sentence versus a lesser sentence among all persons convicted of first degree murder.

Table 7-7 shows the likelihood of moving from one stage to the next in the judicial process for the various offender-victim racial categories. The pattern is clear and consistent. At each stage of the process, race of both offender and victim affects a defendant's chances of moving to the next stage. Race of victim differences are larger than race of offender differences at each stage, as they were from offense to death sentence in Florida, as shown earlier in Table 7-2. As might be expected, the overall chances of a death sentence are greater in Table 7-7 than in Table 7-2; more of those charged with criminal homicide at arraignment (Table 7-7) than of those suspected and possibly arrested for criminal homicide (Table 7-2) will end up with a death sentence. Table 7-7 may look familiar, because it follows the same form as Table 7-1, which was drawn from Harold Garfinkel's work of more than thirty years ago. What is remarkable about Table 7-7, however, is how closely it resembles not the form but the content of Table 7-1. Although the stages of the process shown in the tables do not correspond exactly, the same kinds of racial differences are evident at successive stages of the process in both periods. We may conclude from these similar patterns, over stages defined somewhat differently in the two states, that the overall chances of a death sentence for offender-victim racial categories in Florida in the 1970s were remarkably similar to those in North Carolina in the 1930s (compare the rightmost columns in the two tables). However these differences are distributed stage by stage, the end products are virtually the same. Three decades after the early

**Table 7-7.**   *Charges, Indictments, Convictions, and Death Sentences in Selected Counties in Florida for Criminal Homicide, by Race of Offender and Victim (from Effective Date of Post-Furman Statute through 1977)*

| Offender-Victim Racial Combinations | Numbers at Each Stage | | | | Conditional Probability of Moving between Successive Stages | | | |
|---|---|---|---|---|---|---|---|---|
| | (1) All Homicide Charges at Arraignment | (2) First Degree Murder Indictments | (3) First Degree Murder Convictions | (4) Death Sentences | (5) First Degree Indictment Given Charge | (6) First Degree Conviction Given First Degree Indictment | (7) Death Sentence Given First Degree Conviction | (8) Overall Probability of Death Sentence Given Charge |
| Black kills white | 67 | 193 | 83 | 39 | 0.925 | 0.430 | 0.470 | 0.187 |
| White kills white | 305 | 457 | 169 | 49 | 0.666 | 0.370 | 0.290 | 0.071 |
| Black kills black | 314 | 288 | 56 | 11 | 0.366 | 0.194 | 0.196 | 0.014 |
| White kills black | 21 | 20 | 3 | 0 | 0.429 | 0.150 | 0.000 | 0.000 |

*Sources* (keyed to Supplement B): B1 and B2.

*Note:* The figures in column 1 and the probabilities in column 5 are based on the subset of cases collected in the Zeisel study (source B2) of all homicide charges for offenses that occurred in 1976 or 1977.

*Note:* The probability of a death sentence given charges (column 8) is calculated as the joint probability of columns 5, 6, and 7.

study, under a capital statute designed to eliminate differential treatment by race and other extralegal factors, such differences are every bit as clear and consistent as they were under a former statute now ruled unconstitutional.

With the data now available, we can carry this analysis a step beyond Garfinkel's work by focusing on felony and nonfelony murder cases. We have seen in Table 7-3 that felony circumstances, as reported by the police, do not account for racial differences in the likelihood of a death sentence in Florida, contrary to arguments advanced by that state's attorney general. We are now in a position to see at what stage or stages of the criminal justice process such differential treatment of felony and nonfelony murder cases occurs, with these data from court case records.

It should be noted that the proportion of felony murders in the court data is substantially greater than that in the police data for Florida: 26 percent of the judicial-processing cases are classified as felony homicides, as compared with 11 percent of those reported by police in the Supplementary Homicide Reports. This undoubtedly reflects prosecutorial discretion in the decision not to bring some police-reported nonfelony homicides to the grand jury for a homicide indictment, and/or to classify some police-reported nonfelony killings as felony killings.[32]

The processing of felony- and nonfelony-type murder cases by race of offender and victim is shown in Table 7-8. For felony-related murders, racial differences are again present at each stage of the process (as in Table 7-7), and race of victim again predominates as the basis for differential treatment (as in Tables 7-3 and 7-7). For the nonfelony murder cases, the pattern is different; for the most part, differential treatment occurs before sentencing. Differences by race of victim are evident at the conviction stage, and differences by race of both offender and victim are evident at the indictment stage. Thus, from charge through sentence (column 8 of Table 7-8), the overall race of offender difference is due almost exclusively to the indictment stage, the overall difference by race of victim is due to the indictment and conviction stages, and very little of the overall difference is due to the sentencing stage of the process.

Two anomalies in Table 7-8 suggest further elements of differential treatment by race. The first is that the likelihoods of a death sentence

---

32. The case of John Spinkelink appears to fall into this category. A Supplementary Homicide Report was filed fitting the description of his crime in terms of time, place, and victim characteristics, with no felony circumstances indicated. Spinkelink was later charged with killing his criminal traveling companion for money—a felony (robbery) murder.

**Table 7-8.** Charges, Indictments, Convictions, and Death Sentences in Selected Counties in Florida for Felony and Nonfelony Homicide, by Race of Offender and Victim (from Effective Date of Post-Furman Statute through 1977)

| Offender-Victim Racial Combinations | Numbers at Each Stage | | | | Conditional Probability of Moving between Successive Stages | | | |
|---|---|---|---|---|---|---|---|---|
| | (1) All Homicide Charges at Arraignment [a] | (2) First Degree Murder Indictments | (3) First Degree Murder Convictions | (4) Death Sentences | (5) First Degree Indictment Given Charge [a] | (6) First Degree Conviction Given First Degree Indictment | (7) Death Sentence Given First Degree Conviction | (8) Overall Probability of Death Sentence Given Charge [b] |
| Felony | | | | | | | | |
| Black kills white | 49 | 162 | 74 | 38 | 1.000 | 0.456 | 0.514 | 0.234 |
| White kills white | 100 | 208 | 101 | 42 | 0.970 | 0.486 | 0.416 | 0.196 |
| Black kills black | 35 | 66 | 22 | 7 | 0.800 | 0.333 | 0.318 | 0.085 |
| White kills black | 1 | 10 | 2 | 0 | — | 0.200 | 0.000 | — |
| Nonfelony | | | | | | | | |
| Black kills white | 18 | 31 | 9 | 1 | 0.722 | 0.290 | 0.111 | 0.023 |
| White kills white | 205 | 249 | 68 | 7 | 0.522 | 0.273 | 0.103 | 0.015 |
| Black kills black | 279 | 222 | 34 | 4 | 0.312 | 0.153 | 0.118 | 0.006 |
| White kills black | 20 | 10 | 1 | 0 | 0.450 | 0.100 | 0.000 | 0.000 |

*Sources* [keyed to Supplement B]: B1 and B2.
a See Table 7-7.
b See Table 7-7.

for black-offender–white-victim and for white-white felony killings in Table 7-8 are less than the corresponding likelihoods in Table 7-3. This would seem unlikely. The felony-related cases in Table 7-8 have been charged with some level of criminal homicide in the courts, while those in Table 7-3 have only been reported as felony-type homicides by the police. We might reasonably expect more of those who reach the charging stage to receive a death sentence than of those who are reported and perhaps booked on a homicide charge by the police. Of course, this discrepancy could reflect a bias in the counties selected for the collection of court data.

Secondly, more black felony killers of whites were indicted for first degree murder (Table 7-8) than were identified by the police for such murders (Table 7-3). This is even more incongruous; the larger number comes from a selected sample of counties while the smaller one represents the state as a whole.

The key to these two anomalies may be selective "upcharging." Perhaps many black-offender–white-victim killings filed by the police as nonfelony homicides are subsequently charged as felony murders by the prosecutors. And, to a lesser extent, white-white killings reported by the police as nonfelony homicides may also be subjected to the same kind of reclassification. It is hard to imagine how the discrepancies between Tables 7-3 and 7-8 can be reconciled except by such selective upgrading of aggravating felony circumstances by prosecutors. (And to the extent that other Florida prosecutors share the view expressed by the state's attorney general in the *Spinkelink* case, such upgrading of circumstances in white victim as opposed to black victim killings would be consistent with their perceptions and predispositions, if not prejudices.)

Indeed, there is a clear suggestion in these data that blacks who kill whites are being *over*charged. In column 6 of Table 7-8, we see that among cases with alleged felony circumstances, blacks who killed whites are slightly less likely to be convicted than are whites who killed whites, contrary to prevailing race of offender differences. This at least suggests that in black-offender–white-victim cases prosecutors may have alleged felony circumstances to enhance their plea-bargaining position or as a demonstration of concern for the kind of crimes the community finds most shocking on racial grounds, without sufficient evidence for a conviction.

We can pursue this matter of discretion with respect to felony circumstances a few steps further. For cases in the judicial-processing sample we have attempted to identify the corresponding Supplementary Homicide Reports. It was possible to identify Supplementary Homicide Reports for roughly 30 percent of the sample indictments without ambiguity, and thus to learn what circumstances the police reported in these cases. This is not, of course, a random subsample; it over-represents those police districts with relatively few homicides and relatively careful reporting norms—two factors that have tended to enable the matching of police reports with court case data. Also, when victim's age was unavailable in the judicial-processing data, it was generally not possible to match, with confidence, Supplementary Homicide Reports data with murder indictment data. Table 7-9 shows for each offender-victim racial combination the likelihood of a felony circumstance in the court case records for police-reported felony, suspected felony, and nonfelony circumstances.

The differential treatment of these cases in terms of felony circumstances by race of offender and victim is unmistakable. When the cases reach the prosecutor's office, selective transformation occurs. Among blacks who kill whites, a majority of the cases in which police report no felony circumstance become felony-related cases in the court records. This occurs in every case the police report as a suspected felony. Among white-white killings this upgrading occurs for suspected felony cases, but it is less pronounced in the case of police-reported nonfelony killings. Among black-black killings there is little tendency for the courts to classify the circumstances of the cases as more severe than the police reports; indeed, there is a tendency for the courts to downgrade the court case records to reflect nonfelony circumstances when the police have reported a felony circumstance present. Either the police are peculiarly blind to the presence of a felony circumstance in the case of black killings of white victims and overly sensitive to the hint of such a circumstance in black-black killings, or prosecutors

**Table 7-9.**  *Probability, by Race of Offender and Victim, of a Felony Circumstance in Court Case Records, Given Police-reported Circumstances, among Persons Indicted for First Degree Murder in Selected Counties in Florida (from Effective Date of Post-*Furman* Statute through 1977)*

| Offender-Victim Racial Combinations | Police Reports Indicate: | | |
|---|---|---|---|
| | Felony Circumstance | Suspected Felony Circumstance | No Felony Circumstance |
| Black kills white | 0.891 (46) | 1.000 ( 7) | 0.688 (16) |
| White kills white | 0.867 (45) | 0.786 (14) | 0.239 (109) |
| Black kills black | 0.667 (12) | 0.167 (6) | 0.133 (83) |
| White kills black | — (12) | — (2) | — (4) |

*Sources* (keyed to Supplement B): A1, A2, B1, B2.

are selectively transforming circumstances in police reports, not simply for advantage in any and all cases, but quite specifically in cases with white victims, especially if the offender is black.

What about the decision to bring an accompanying felony charge? Is this charging decision also affected by race apart from circumstances in the court case records? The Florida judicial-processing data contain information on charges in addition to the first degree murder indictment filed by prosecutors. Table 7-10 shows the probability, by race of offender and victim, of such an accompanying charge for cases with and without felony circumstances in the court records. Here we see a tendency for the prosecutor to file an accompanying felony charge disproportionately against black offenders if there is a felony circumstance in the court case record, and disproportionately against offenders whose crimes cross racial boundaries if there is no felony circumstance in the court record. Again, with or without such a felony circumstance in the court record, blacks who kill whites are most likely to be charged with an accompanying felony. This tendency to charge an accompanying felony differentially by race of offender and, to a lesser degree, by race of victim among court felony cases, and for racial boundary crossings among court nonfelony cases, further compounds the pattern of differential treatment by race within the criminal justice process.

And what about felony as an aggravating circumstance in the sentencing stage of the process? Is there a tendency for sentencing authorities to find a felony aggravating circumstance depending on race of the convicted offender or his victim apart from whether an accompanying felony was also charged? The Florida judicial-processing data also indicate whether an aggravating felony circumstance was found

**Table 7-10.** *Probability, by Race of Offender and Victim, of an Accompanying Felony Charge, Given Court-recorded Circumstances, among Persons Indicted for First Degree Murder in Selected Counties in Florida (from Effective Date of Post-*Furman *Statute through 1977)*

| Offender-Victim Racial Combinations | Court Records Indicate: | |
| --- | --- | --- |
| | Felony Circumstance | No Felony Circumstance |
| Black kills white | 0.479 (167) | 0.194 (31) |
| White kills white | 0.385 (218) | 0.105 (256) |
| Black kills black | 0.418 (67) | 0.097 (226) |
| White kills black | 0.100 (10) | 0.182 (11) |

*Sources* (keyed to Supplement B): B1 and B2.
*Note:* The total number of first degree indictments that appears in this table is greater than the number that appears in Tables 7-7, 7-8, and 7-9. In this case, there are no cases excluded because of missing information on offenders convicted.

in the sentencing phase of the trial among those convicted of first degree murder. Table 7-11 shows the probability, by race of offender and victim, of a felony finding of aggravation by sentencing authorities among those convicted of first degree murder with and without an accompanying felony charge. Notice, first, that the findings of sentencing authorities are relatively independent of the prosecutor's charge of an aggravating felony. An aggravating felony circumstance is found in 15 percent of the cases where prosecutors made no charge of an accompanying felony, and in only 35 percent of the cases where such an accompanying felony charge was filed. Note, further, that the prosecutor's charge, which is of course based on police investigation of felony circumstances and evidence developed by the prosecutor's office, has less effect on sentencing authorities than does race of victim. Thus, the presence of an accompanying felony charge roughly doubles the chances of an aggravating felony finding on the part of sentencing authorities, whereas the effect of race of victim among blacks convicted of first degree murder far exceeds the impact of an accompanying felony charge. Indeed, among blacks charged with an accompanying felony, virtually half were found to have an aggravating felony circumstance by sentencing authorities if their victims were white, while not one was found to have such an accompanying circumstance if the victim was black.

The determination of an aggravating felony circumstance at sentencing would seem to be, on the face of it, a relatively objective matter. But this appearance is deceptive. It is the final decision in a process

**Table 7-11.**  *Probability, by Race of Offender and Victim, of an Aggravated Felony Finding by Sentencing Authorities, Given Accompanying Charge, among Persons Convicted of First Degree Murder in Selected Counties in Florida (from Effective Date of Post-*Furman* Statute through 1977)*

| Offender-Victim Racial Combinations | Trial Charges Include: | |
|---|---|---|
| | Accompanying Felony Charge | No Accompanying Felony Charge |
| Black kills white | 0.488  (43) | 0.275   (40) |
| White kills white | 0.352  (54) | 0.158  (114) |
| Black kills black | 0.000  (17) | 0.077   (39) |
| White kills black | —   (3) | —   (0) |

*Sources* (keyed to Supplement B): B1, B2, D1.
*Note:*  The probabilities have been adjusted for missing information on aggravating felony circumstances found by the sentencing authorities for forty-eight persons sentenced to death. These cases have been assigned to aggravating felony and nonfelony circumstance categories in the same proportions as they occur for those death sentence cases on which we have aggravating felony circumstance data.

with much slippage from one decision point to the next, and a process in which race of offender and victim count as much as or more than police investigations, court case records, and charges at trial. Narrowing the pool of offenders who may have an aggravating felony circumstance assigned and determining which ones in the pool will have such an aggravating circumstance found are a race-linked series of decisions. In effect, the dice are loaded against black offenders and the killers of whites in the allegation, charge, and finding of a felony circumstance. With each additional throw of the dice, or successive decision about felony-related circumstances, they are more likely to be losers ultimately.

These decisions within stages of the criminal justice process reveal a consistent pattern of differential treatment that favors white over black offenders and the killers of blacks over those who kill whites. Just as the movement from stage to stage through the process reflects a cumulative pattern of differential treatment, the effects of felony-related decisions on the part of prosecutors and sentencing authorities within stages of the process show a progressive tendency to move offenders closer to a death sentence, depending on their race and that of their victims. Indeed, the examination of these decision points helps to illuminate the way in which racially biased movement between the stages of the process comes about.

By way of summary at this point, suffice it to say that race is truly a pervasive influence on the criminal justice processing of potentially capital cases, one that is evident at every stage of the process we have been able to distinguish. It is an influence revealed not only in the movement from one stage to the next, but also in the decisions about circumstances, accompanying charges, and sentencing findings within the respective stages of the process. And it is an influence that persists despite separate sentencing hearings, explicitly articulated sentencing guidelines, and automatic appellate review of all death sentences.

In the remainder of this section, we turn to variations in the processing of potentially capital cases by judicial circuits grouped regionally. Table 7-12 presents the stages of the process for all persons indicted for criminal homicide, and Table 7-13 shows the process separately for felony and nonfelony homicides, according to the court records. In these two tables, counties are grouped into three categories: north/panhandle, which combines sampled counties from the northern and panhandle circuits as defined earlier in Table 7-4, and central and southern regions, which include the sampled counties identified in Table 7-4.

In Table 7-12, we see the same overall ordering of regional differences from charge through sentence as we did from offense through sentence (combining the panhandle and northern regions) in Table 7-4.

**Table 7-12.** *Probability of Receiving the Death Sentence in Selected Counties in Florida for Criminal Homicide, by Judicial Circuits Grouped Regionally (from Effective Date of Post-Furman Statute through 1977)*

| Regional Grouping of Judicial Circuits | Numbers at Each Stage | | | | Conditional Probability of Moving between Successive Stages | | | |
|---|---|---|---|---|---|---|---|---|
| | (1) All Homicide Charges at Arraignment[a] | (2) First Degree Murder Indictments | (3) First Degree Murder Convictions | (4) Death Sentences | (5) First Degree Indictment Given Charge[a] | (6) First Degree Conviction Given First Degree Indictment | (7) Death Sentence Given First Degree Conviction | (8) Overall Probability of Death Sentence Given Charge[b] |
| North/Panhandle | 221 | 257 | 84 | 34 | 0.489 | 0.327 | 0.405 | 0.065 |
| Central | 241 | 267 | 99 | 28 | 0.574 | 0.371 | 0.283 | 0.060 |
| South | 295 | 498 | 133 | 37 | 0.573 | 0.267 | 0.278 | 0.043 |

*Sources* (keyed to Supplement B): B1 and B2.

*Note:* The numbers of arraignments, indictments, and convictions appearing in this table are greater than those appearing in Tables 7-7, 7-8, 7-9, and 7-10. Here there are no cases excluded because of missing information on race of victim and/or race of offender.

[a] See Table 7-7.
[b] See Table 7-7.

But this result appears to be the product of a hodgepodge of different practices in the various regions. Relatively speaking, the southern region is likely to indict but not to convict or to impose the death sentence; the central region is likely to indict and to convict but not likely to impose the death sentence; and the northern/panhandle region is unlikely to indict, likely as not to convict, and likely to sentence to death. These differences appear not to follow any consistent pattern. It might be argued that they reflect random variations in the treatment of potentially capital cases, and hence are an indication of caprice or unsystematic arbitrariness.

What are bizarre variations in Table 7-12 become more systematic in Table 7-13 when we examine the process separately for felony and nonfelony killings. In the first place, the overall differences are greater by region. Among felony killings the overall differences from charge through sentence are decidedly higher in the northern/panhandle and central regions than in southern Florida; among nonfelony homicides the northern/panhandle region is well above the other two in overall likelihood of a death sentence. For both kinds of offenses, the differences are most pronounced in the sentencing stage of the process. The death sentence is relatively unlikely to be handed down for felony murders in the southern region and relatively likely to be imposed for nonfelony murders in the northern/panhandle region. These variations are consistent with the differences we saw in Table 7-5. What we can see here is that they are concentrated in the sentencing process more than anywhere else in the handling of potentially capital cases.

Admittedly, these data are subject to challenge. They come from a selected sample of counties not chosen to be representative of the state as a whole, and they were collected by persons associated with and employed by an advocacy group opposing the death penalty in Florida. Yet, they are the only data known to us on the processing of potentially capital cases post-*Furman*, and they were collected in consultation with and under the guidance of professional social scientists. Moreover, the patterns in these data replicate those in the statewide data on homicides and death sentences we have examined in the earlier sections of the analysis.

Unmistakably, the pattern of racial differences revealed in these data closely follows the pattern shown more than thirty years ago in Garfinkel's research on North Carolina (reproduced in Table 7-1). Although the stages of the process do not correspond exactly, the patterns are quite similar. Certainly, the magnitude and pervasive character of the effects in both periods—the 1930s in North Carolina and the 1970s in Florida—convey a grim message that the previous ills, now supposed to be purged from the process, are present in very much the same form and extent as before. These remarkably similar patterns both before

**Table 7-13.**  Probability of Receiving the Death Sentence in Selected Counties in Florida for Felony and Nonfelony Homicide, by Judicial Circuits Grouped Regionally (from Effective Date of Post-Furman Statute through 1977)

| Regional Grouping of Judicial Circuits | Numbers at Each Stage [a] | | | | Conditional Probability of Moving between Successive Stages | | | |
|---|---|---|---|---|---|---|---|---|
| | (1) All Homicide Charges at Arraignment [b] | (2) First Degree Murder Indictments | (3) First Degree Murder Convictions | (4) Death Sentences | (5) First Degree Indictment Given Charge [b] | (6) First Degree Conviction Given First Degree Indictment | (7) Death Sentence Given First Degree Conviction | (8) Overall Probability of Death Sentence Given Charge [c] |
| Felony | | | | | | | | |
| North/Panhandle | 51 | 118 | 56 | 28 | 0.902 | 0.475 | 0.500 | 0.214 |
| Central | 52 | 106 | 52 | 26 | 0.884 | 0.491 | 0.500 | 0.217 |
| South | 94 | 247 | 93 | 33 | 0.979 | 0.377 | 0.355 | 0.131 |
| Nonfelony | | | | | | | | |
| North/Panhandle | 170 | 139 | 28 | 6 | 0.365 | 0.201 | 0.214 | 0.016 |
| Central | 189 | 161 | 47 | 2 | 0.487 | 0.292 | 0.043 | 0.006 |
| South | 201 | 251 | 40 | 4 | 0.383 | 0.159 | 0.100 | 0.006 |

*Sources* (keyed to Supplement B): B1 and B2.

[a] See Table 7-12.
[b] See Table 7-7.
[c] See Table 7-7.

and after *Furman* suggest that the sources of differential treatment are so deeply rooted that they will bend the law to their uses, and that differential treatment is not the result of flaws in the judicial process that permit underlying tendencies toward arbitrariness and discrimination to be manifested occasionally or at an isolated weak point in the process.

## Arbitrariness and Appellate Review

The judicial-processing data show, at least for the counties studied, that differential treatment by race and by region is present at various stages of the process; hence, the overall level of arbitrariness is the product of a cumulative process. To remove differential treatment in sentencing, the U.S. Supreme Court has required automatic appellate review of all death sentences as a necessary instrument for monitoring the sentencing process and for correcting arbitrariness and discrimination that might enter the process leading to a death sentence. It has, in particular, applauded the Georgia statute that requires that state's supreme court to consider the influence of passion and prejudice on the processing of cases. Furthermore, the Georgia statute charges appellate review with responsibility for applying the similarity standard to ensure that the death sentence not be excessive or disproportionate to sentences imposed in similar cases throughout the state. In effect, the appellate review process is supposed to eliminate arbitrariness and discrimination from the processing of potentially capital cases; at the very least, it is supposed to purge the sentencing stage of the process of arbitrariness and discrimination.

To examine this issue we have tabulated the outcome of appellate review of death sentences imposed in Florida and Georgia from the effective dates of their statutes through 1977. Most death sentences from that period have now been reviewed, so our information on review status is virtually complete. In the tables that follow we examine the probability, among all reviewed death sentences in Florida and Georgia, of an affirmation, given information on race and place.

To obtain the information on appellate review status, the Florida and Georgia *Supreme Court Reports* were consulted in the summer of 1980.[33] For Florida, ninety-one reviewed cases were identified; for Georgia, ninety such cases were found. Table 7-14 shows the number of

33. The Florida Supreme Court is taking much longer in its review of death sentences than the Georgia Supreme Court. Thus, by mid-1980, Florida Supreme Court opinions could be found for only 63 percent of the death sentences handed down before 1978, whereas published reviews were available for 91 percent of the pre-1978 death sentences in Georgia. This substantial delay in the appellate review of death sentences in Florida appears to reflect an extraordinary backlog of cases before the

**Table 7-14**   *Probability that the Death Sentence for Criminal Homicide in Florida and Georgia Will Be Affirmed upon Appellate Review, by Race of Offender and Victim (for Offenses Committed after Effective Dates of Respective Post-*Furman* Capital Statutes through 1977)*

| Offender-Victim Racial Combinations | (1) Number of Death Sentences Reviewed | (2) Number of Death Sentences Affirmed | (3) Probability of Affirmed Death Sentence |
|---|---|---|---|
| Florida | | | |
| Black kills white | 36 | 18 | 0.500 |
| White kills white | 50 | 25 | 0.500 |
| Black kills black | 5 | 3 | 0.600 |
| White kills black | 0 | – | – |
| Georgia | | | |
| Black kills white | 40 | 29 | 0.725 |
| White kills white | 37 | 26 | 0.703 |
| Black kills black | 11 | 9 | 0.818 |
| White kills black | 2 | 2 | 1.000 |

*Sources* (keyed to supplement B): Florida—C1; Georgia—C2.

death sentences reviewed, the number affirmed, and the probability of an affirmation given review, by race of offender and victim in Florida and Georgia.

Looking first at Florida, the figures in Table 7-14 show that the Florida Supreme Court has affirmed exactly half the death sentences imposed for killings by blacks of white victims and for white-white killings, which jointly represent virtually 95 percent of all death sentences reviewed up to this point in Florida. Thus, with respect to these two categories the review process does nothing to redress the imbalance of treatment by race of offender. Only with respect to black-black killings is the likelihood of affirmation greater; in view of the very small number of cases here, this action has no discernible effect on the overall offender-victim racial disparities of treatment in Florida. Thus, after appellate review, the offender-victim racial categories stand in virtually the same relationship to one another as they did before the review (column three of Table 7-12).

With respect to Georgia, the story is nearly the same. Here 88

Florida Supreme Court (some fifteen hundred cases awaiting review by March of 1980). This has led to a state constitutional amendment in Florida, limiting the appellate responsibilities of the Florida Supreme Court but not altering its responsibility for reviewing death sentences (*Florida Times Union* [Jacksonville, Fla.], Mar. 12, 1980).

percent of the reviewed cases are white-victim killings, and the difference in the likelihood of an affirmation by race of offender is very
small—with slightly more death sentences of blacks affirmed than
death sentences of white offenders. A death sentence imposed for the
killing of a black person is somewhat more likely to be affirmed—a
circumstance tending, although not to any substantial degree, to reduce
disparities of treatment by race of victim. Thus, appellate review in
Georgia has the effect of adding slightly to the imbalance by race of
offender and subtracting slightly from the imbalance by race of victim.
Again, the overall impact on racial differentials is hardly perceptible.

It is noteworthy that the Florida Supreme Court affirmed only
about five out of each ten death sentences reviewed, as opposed to at
least seven out of ten affirmed by the Georgia Supreme Court; but this
apparently more critical approach to trial court sentencing in Florida
has no greater effect in alleviating the imbalance of treatment by race
of offender and victim.

We observed earlier (Table 7-3) that among felony-type murders
differential treatment by race is reduced somewhat and that race of
victim predominates as the basis for differential treatment. And, we
observed further (Table 7-8) that a substantial portion of the difference
by race of victim in felony murder cases in Florida occurs at the sentencing stage of the process. Since more than 80 percent of the death
sentences in both Florida and Georgia were handed down for felony
murder, they cannot differ greatly from the pattern shown in Table
7-14. But we may at least examine whether the review process shows
any tendency to correct for the conspicuous differences by race of
victim among felony murder cases, which are particularly pronounced
at the sentencing stage of the process, at least in Florida.

Table 7-15 shows the extent to which appellate review of death
sentences imposed for felony-type murders reduces the imbalance of
treatment by race of offender and victim. In Florida, there is no clear
difference, by offender-victim racial categories, in the likelihood that
a death sentence for felony-type murder will be affirmed or reversed.
In Georgia, as well, the likelihood of an affirmation differs only slightly
for the various offender-victim racial categories. What differences there
are in Georgia actually tend to accentuate rather than diminish the
disparities in treatment by race of both offender and victim. In effect,
Tables 7-14 and 7-15 make it clear that there is no tendency for the
appellate review process to correct the racial differences in treatment,
whether at the sentencing or the presentencing stages of the process.

What about the power of the review process to correct regional
disparities in treatment? We observed earlier (Table 7-4) that there are
gross variations in the chances of a death sentence by regional groupings of judicial circuits in both Florida and Georgia, and that, at least

**Table 7-15.**   *Probability that the Death Sentence for Felony-type Homicide in Florida and Georgia Will Be Affirmed upon Appellate Review, by Race of Offender and Victim (for Offenses Committed after Effective Dates of Respective Post-*Furman* Capital Statutes through 1977)*

| Offender-Victim Racial Combinations | (1) Number of Death Sentences Reviewed | (2) Number of Death Sentences Affirmed | (3) Probability of Affirmed Death Sentence |
|---|---|---|---|
| Florida | | | |
| Black kills white | 32 | 15 | 0.469 |
| White kills white | 39 | 19 | 0.487 |
| Black kills black | 3 | 2 | 0.667 |
| White kills black | 0 | 0 | 0.000 |
| Georgia | | | |
| Black kills white | 37 | 29 | 0.784 |
| White kills white | 31 | 23 | 0.742 |
| Black kills black | 7 | 5 | 0.714 |
| White kills black | 2 | 2 | 1.000 |

*Sources* (keyed to Supplement B): Florida—C1; Georgia—C2.

for Florida (Table 7-12), the regional variations among a selected subset of the counties are the result of differences among particular regions occurring at particular stages of the process. In effect, the case of regional disparities presents a possible test of the "reach" of appellate review in detecting and correcting differential treatment at earlier stages of the process, depending on which differences (if not all) are eliminated.

The probability, by regional groupings of judicial circuits in Florida and Georgia, of having a death sentence affirmed is shown in Table 7-16. For the differences in treatment by region to be removed, the probability of an affirmation would have to be relatively high in regions with relatively low death sentence rates, such as the southern region in Florida and Fulton County in Georgia. In fact, the reverse is true. The affirmation levels are the lowest for these two areas in the respective states. Thus, at least for the places where the death sentence is least likely to be imposed, appellate review adds to the disparities separating these regions from the rest of the respective states, considered as a whole.

Indeed, the appellate review process in Florida definitely tends to reinforce and accentuate the overall regional differences. If we combine the panhandle and northern regions of Florida in Table 7-16 to form a northern region similar to the one in Table 7-9, the probability of an

**Table 7-16.** *Probability that the Death Sentence for Criminal Homicide in Florida and Georgia Will Be Affirmed upon Appellate Review, by Judicial Circuits/Counties Grouped Regionally (for Offenses Committed after Effective Dates of Respective Post-Furman Capital Statutes through 1977)*

| Regional Grouping of Judicial Circuits/ Counties | (1) Number of Death Sentences Reviewed | (2) Number of Death Sentences Affirmed | (3) Probability of Affirmed Death Sentence |
|---|---|---|---|
| Florida |  |  |  |
| Panhandle | 15 | 7 | 0.467 |
| North | 19 | 12 | 0.632 |
| Central | 32 | 16 | 0.500 |
| South | 25 | 11 | 0.440 |
| Georgia |  |  |  |
| North | 2 | 2 | 1.000 |
| Central | 41 | 28 | 0.683 |
| Fulton County (Atlanta) | 6 | 4 | 0.667 |
| Southwest | 23 | 19 | 0.826 |
| Southeast | 18 | 13 | 0.722 |

*Sources* (keyed to Supplement B): Florida—C1; Georgia—C2.

affirmation for this combined region is 0.559. The resulting empirical generalization for Florida is evident: The more likely a region is to impose the death sentence, the more likely it is to have the sentence affirmed upon review. Appellate review in Georgia does not show as clear a tendency to add to the differential treatment by region already present in the sentencing stage of the process, apart from the tendency for Fulton County to drop further below the average of the rest of the state.

We have seen (Table 7-5) that the regional differences among felony-type murders are even greater than for all criminal homicides. That is, regional differences in the handling of felony murders are somewhat masked in tables showing all homicides without separation of those committed under felony circumstances.

Is there any indication that the appellate review process will detect and correct the more exaggerated regional differences in the handling of felony murders? Table 7-17 shows the probability that a death sentence for felony murder will be affirmed in Florida and Georgia. Here again, the review process adds to an already wide range of regional disparities. Southern Florida and Fulton County, Georgia, are again the two places with the lowest death sentence rates and the lowest affirmation rates.

The appellate review process is evidently blind to these social and

**Table 7-17.** *Probability that the Death Sentence for Felony-type Homicide in Florida and Georgia Will Be Affirmed upon Appellate Review, by Judicial Circuits/Counties Grouped Regionally (for Offenses Committed after Effective Dates of Respective Post-*Furman *Capital Statutes through 1977)*

| Regional Grouping of Judicial Circuits/ Counties | (1) Number of Death Sentences Reviewed | (2) Number of Death Sentences Affirmed | (3) Probability of Affirmed Death Sentence |
|---|---|---|---|
| Florida | | | |
| Panhandle | 14 | 7 | 0.500 |
| North | 11 | 5 | 0.455 |
| Central | 26 | 14 | 0.538 |
| South | 23 | 10 | 0.435 |
| Georgia | | | |
| North | 2 | 2 | 1.000 |
| Central | 33 | 25 | 0.758 |
| Fulton County (Atlanta) | 3 | 2 | 0.667 |
| Southwest | 23 | 19 | 0.826 |
| Southeast | 16 | 11 | 0.688 |

*Sources* (keyed to Supplement B): Florida—C1; Georgia—C2.

regional treatment differentials, despite the Supreme Court's insistence that the death penalty be imposed in an evenhanded manner, free of extralegal influences. Requiring review of all death sentences provides the appearance of "quality control": The affirmed cases are stamped "reviewed and approved." To be sure, at least half the death sentences handed down in Florida are reversed upon review, suggesting that the Florida Supreme Court is taking its responsibility seriously and finding much to be concerned about in the application of the death penalty. Perhaps the kind of proportionality review required by the *Gregg* decision exceeds the traditional functions and practices of appellate review in criminal cases. Indeed, these flaws in the system of capital punishment may not often nor necessarily be evident in the details of a specific case; they may only be exposed in the aggregate, over a number of cases. The evidence in this section surely indicates that the appellate courts have failed to meet their responsibility to remove strong and systematic extralegal influences on the imposition of the death penalty.

## Arbitrariness and the Form of the Law

We have seen that the form of the law, as reflected in Ohio's quasi-mandatory statute and Texas's structured discretion statute, may affect the overall likelihood that a death sentence will be imposed, but without eliminating disparities of treatment by race of offender and victim. Furthermore, these racial disparities appear to be pervasive throughout the judicial process, as they were in the pre-*Furman* era, and they remain uncorrected by appellate review. Could it be that the laws themselves are the servants of extralegal purposes that "dictate where and when the death penalty will be most widely used . . . and cause the legal functions of capital punishment to be displaced and compromised?" (Bowers 1974, 166, in Chapter 5 of this volume). Indeed, could it be that the form of the law, especially the nature of the sentencing guidelines, will be irrelevent except insofar as it establishes the legal framework through which extralegal purposes can be converted into legal actions?

If the death penalty's extralegal functions are the essential reason for its use, then we might expect to find that the laws under which it is imposed will be bent to accomplish these extralegal purposes. To illustrate the point, we offer the following hypothetical example. Suppose two states, A and B, have capital statutes with the very same list of aggravating circumstances. The statutes differ, however, in that A's statute requires one aggravating circumstance and B's requires two such circumstances to be found for a death sentence to be imposed. Suppose, further, that the courts of states A and B are trying identical cases that vary among themselves in both legal and extralegal respects. Now, if the death sentence were strictly a function of legally relevant aggravating circumstances, we should expect to find more death sentences in state A, which requires fewer aggravating circumstances. If, on the other hand, the death sentence were a function of extralegal factors, such as race of offender and victim, we might expect to find the same number of death sentences in each state, but more aggravating circumstances cited by sentencing authorities in state B with the stricter requirement. Indeed, we might expect the aggravating circumstances found in state B to be disproportionately the less factual and more subjective of those circumstances enumerated in the statute.

Florida and Georgia have capital statutes that list very similar aggravating circumstances. Georgia's statute lists ten such circumstances (see note 3) and Florida's lists eight (see note 4). In Georgia, a jury needs a finding of one and only one aggravating circumstance to recommend the death sentence. The trial judge is bound by the jury's recommendation. In Florida, on the other hand, aggravating must "outweigh" mitigating circumstances for the jury to recommend death as punishment, and the judge need not follow the jury's recommendation. It follows that sentencing authorities in Florida intent upon having the death penalty imposed can buttress this intention with each additional aggravating circumstance they find, whereas a Georgia jury can accomplish this purpose without risk by finding a single aggravating circumstance. If the death penalty is grounded in the extralegal functions it serves, we would expect Florida courts to find more aggravating circumstances than do courts in Georgia.

To examine this possibility, we have tabulated the aggravating circumstances found in Georgia and Florida for all cases on which reliable information could be obtained.[34] In Table 7-18 we list in abbreviated form the seven aggravating circumstances for which both Florida and Georgia have close counterparts in wording and substance; and for each circumstance we show the percentage of cases in which the circumstance was found. At the bottom of the table we show the average number of aggravating circumstances found per case in each state.

To begin with, on the average there are twice as many aggravating

**Table 7-18.**   *Aggravating Circumstances Found among Death Sentences in Florida and Georgia (from Effective Dates of Respective Post-***Furman*** Capital Statutes)*

| Aggravating Circumstances | Florida: Percentage of Total | Georgia: Percentage of Total |
|---|---|---|
| Accompanying felony | 71 | 87 |
| Vile, heinous, torturous, cruel | 89 | 46 |
| Pecuniary gain/Contracted murder | 43 | 15 |
| Prior felony conviction | 35 | 6 |
| Avoiding arrest/Escaping conviction/In confinement | 30 | 3 |
| Risk to others | 28 | 1 |
| Murdering officials/Disrupting government | 20 | 4 |
| *Average number of circumstances found per case* | *3.16* | *1.63* |
| *Total number of cases* | *92* | *99* |

*Sources* (keyed to Supplement B): D1 and D2.

34. In Georgia, the jury findings are reported by the trial judge in a questionnaire filed with the Georgia Supreme Court together with the transcript and other case materials as required by statute. The data on the jury findings with respect to aggravating circumstances were drawn from the published opinions of the Georgia Supreme Court, which routinely indicates the jury's findings of aggravation. In Florida, the jury makes a recommendation of life or death without submitting a written statement of findings of aggravation. The trial judge files a written sentencing memorandum with the Florida Supreme Court, which must report the aggravating and mitigating circumstances present in the case and justify the finding that the aggravating outweigh the mitigating circumstances. For Florida judges, memoranda available in sixty-three cases were consulted as the primary data source. Florida Supreme Court opinions, which provided statements of aggravating and mitigating circumstances quoting or paraphrasing the trial judge's memorandum, were also used as a data source.

circumstances reported for Florida as compared with Georgia cases receiving the death sentence—consistent with the argument that extralegal functions predominate. The findings of aggravation in the two states are most alike with respect to the supposedly objective felony circumstance. In both states the large majority of death sentences are handed down with felony circumstances found by the sentencing authorities. In contrast, the findings of aggravation most discrepant between the two states are those including the relatively ambiguous terms, that is, the judgment that the crime was vile, heinous, torturous, cruel. In fact, there is a forty-three-point percentage spread between the two states in this circumstance. Less than half Georgia's cases are judged vile and heinous, compared with nine out of ten in Florida. For the remaining five aggravating circumstances, Florida exceeds Georgia in the proportion of cases found to have each of these circumstances. By every indication here apart from the felony circumstance, it would appear that Florida's death sentences are handed down for much more aggravated murders than are Georgia's.

Are Florida's capital murders twice as heinous as Georgia's? In Table 7-19 we list seven objective indicators of aggravation, which can be expected to reflect the vile or heinous character of a killing. They include use of a gun as the murder weapon, which may reflect intent or premeditation; multiple offenders and multiple victims, both of which suggest an imbalance or excess in the circumstances leading to the killing; and youthful, elderly, and female victims, suggesting a relatively vulnerable victim whom the offender has attacked or exploited.

**Table 7-19.**  *Aggravating Factors Reported among Death Sentences in Florida and Georgia (from Effective Dates of Respective Post-Furman Capital Statutes)*

| Aggravating Factors | Florida: Percentage of Total | Georgia: Percentage of Total |
|---|---|---|
| Gun as murder weapon | 56 [a] | 65 [c] |
| Multiple offenders | 50 | 64 |
| Female victim | 36 | 36 |
| Multiple victims | 14 | 20 |
| Victim 60 years or older | 11 [b] | 23 |
| Victim 16 years or younger | 8 [b] | 10 |
| Felony-related | 82 | 87 |
| *Total number of cases* | 92 | 99 |

*Sources* (keyed to Supplement B): C1 and C2 (for the subsample of cases in B1 and B2).
[a] Based on the 86 cases for which there is information on the murder weapon.
[b] Based on the 69 cases for which there is information on age of victim.
[c] Based on the 92 cases for which there is information on the murder weapon.

By most of these objective indicators, however, Georgia's capital murders would appear to be more heinous than Florida's. They are more often committed with a gun, by multiple offenders, and against female and elderly victims. Perhaps more important, the differences between the two states in any of the aggravating factors are not large, meaning that the crimes in these two states for which death sentences are imposed appear to be very much alike in objective indicators of aggravation.

These results are consistent with the proposition that the laws are bent to accomplish the extralegal functions of capital punishment. The crimes for which the death sentence is imposed in both states appear quite similar in objectively measured aggravating factors (Table 7-19); they are also quite similar in extralegal characteristics of offender and victim (Table 7-2). If the requirement that aggravating circumstances must outweigh mitigating circumstances in Florida were actually guiding sentencing discretion, then we might expect the sentencing rate to be lower in Florida than in Georgia; but we know this is not the case. The likelihood of a death sentence is actually somewhat higher in Florida—0.037 compared with 0.026 in Georgia.

These data suggest that sentencing authorities in Florida are finding aggravating circumstances in cases in which Georgia sentencing authorities would not find aggravating factors. That the relatively ambiguous and subjective aggravating circumstance—namely, that the crime is vile and heinous—is the factor that most distinguishes the sentencing practices of Florida and Georgia provides support for this interpretation. In fact, this analysis suggests that the sentencing guidelines become the instruments of arbitrariness and discrimination, not their cure.


# Conclusion

In the first five years after the *Furman* decision, racial differences in the administration of capital statutes have been extreme in magnitude, similar across states and under different statutory forms, pervasive over successive stages of the judicial process, and uncorrected by appellate review. Moreover, these differentials have been fully consistent with the pattern of racial disparity occurring under capital statutes invalidated by the *Furman* decision. That is, differential treatment by race of offender and victim has been shown to persist in the post-*Furman* period to a degree comparable in magnitude and pattern to the pre-*Furman* period. It is not that the new statutes have failed to eliminate all or most of these racial differences; it is, rather, that they have failed to alter in any substantial way the cumulative pattern of differential treatment by race that was present under the now unconstitutional pre-*Furman* capital statutes.[35]

We have also seen substantial differentials in treatment by judicial circuits within states under different kinds of capital statutes, evident at discrete stages of the criminal justice process and unaltered by appellate review. And, we have established that the observed differences by judicial circuits within a state are quite independent of race of offender and victim, and hence an entirely separate source of differential treatment under post-*Furman* capital statutes.

Is it possible that the patterns of differential treatment we have documented here do not actually reflect arbitrariness and discrimination in the administration of capital punishment? The answer turns on whether these apparent departures from evenhanded justice can be explained in terms of legally relevant factors or are the result of legally irrelevant influences.

A critical limitation on the available legally relevant explanations for such treatment differentials is that they must come from a strictly defined set of legally relevant factors which are enumerated as aggravating and mitigating circumstances in the statutes that provide for

---

35. Gary Kleck (1981) has disputed earlier evidence of racial discrimination in capital punishment for homicide in light of methodological weaknesses in previous studies and national aggregate statistics showing slightly higher execution rates (1930–1967) and death sentencing rates (1967–1978) for white than for black offenders, *without race of victim* as a control. The fact is that Kleck's race of offender differences correspond quite closely to the post-Furman data for all homicides, shown in Table 7-2, and for felony homicides, shown in Table 7-3, *if race of victim is excluded as a variable in the tables*. And, in fact, his data correspond to the results published by Garfinkel (1949) for the pre-Furman period, again *disregarding race of victim* (as we explicitly showed in Table 7-1 by excluding race of victim in Part B of the table to demonstrate its suppressor effect on the relationship between offender's race and death sentencing rate). As we noted there, "because the killing of a black person is so unlikely to be punished by death and because black offenders are so likely to have black victims, *without* race of victim as a control the clear and consistent differences by race of offender [more severe treatment of black than of white offenders] shown in Part A of the table are altogether obscured, even slightly reversed, as shown in Part B of the table."

Ironically, Kleck failed to recognize that the data he presented on homicide victim death sentences and executions by race actually underscore the importance of race of victim as a control. Specifically, they reveal that in a given year the number of white victims, as compared with the number of black victims, was not only a better predictor of the total number of persons sentenced to death and executed in the following year, but also a better predictor of the number of blacks (as opposed to whites) sentenced to death and executed a year later (Bowers 1983b). This is because the relatively small number of blacks who kill whites contributes more to black death sentences and executions than the relatively large number of blacks who kill blacks. This is confirmed for Florida, Georgia, Texas, and Ohio during the post-Furman era, as was shown in Table 7-2. For North Carolina in the pre-Furman era, as shown in Table 7-1, white victim and black victim killings contributed equally to the number of black death sentences, although the latter outnumbered the former nearly ten to one.

the death penalty. In other words, a plausible explanation of these racial and geographic disparities of treatment would have to be found among these statutory provisions.

A further limitation is set by the empirical fact that only a subset of these legally possible explanations is found sufficiently often to account for racial and regional differences in the likelihood of a death sentence. That is, aside from the heinous-and-vile and felony-related aggravating circumstances, the others are not found often enough to constitute a sufficient explanation, statistically, for the observed racial and regional differences in treatment.

We have noted the argument that the kinds of killings in which whites are victims and blacks are offenders differ from other homicides in legally relevant ways—that is, the allegation that killings of whites are more often committed under felony circumstances and killings by blacks are more often heinous and vile. The evidence presented here has taken felony circumstance, specifically, into account as it is determined by police who investigate the crime and by prosecutors who prepare cases for trial. The data show that whether police or prosecutors' classifications are used, there are clear differences in treatment by both victim's and offender's race among felony-type murders and among killings classified as nonfelony homicides. In other words, felony circumstances do not account for the racial differences.

Furthermore, we have seen that there is a tendency to apply the felony category differentially by race of offender and victim within certain stages of the criminal justice process. That is, decisions about whether to introduce felony-related circumstances in the court case records, whether to charge an accompanying felony at trial, and whether to find an aggravating felony circumstance at sentencing are each independently affected by race of offender and victim.[36]

Such a tendency also seems likely with respect to the other statutory aggravating circumstances. In particular, we observed wide differences in the use of the vile-and-heinous circumstance between Florida and Georgia for crimes similar in objective indicators of victim vul-

---

36. Perhaps the shift in the primary legal basis for the imposition of capital punishment away from the determination that a homicide was intentional, deliberate, and premeditated to the finding that a killing was committed in the course of another felony will preserve, in the present legal framework, the tendency to inflict capital punishment on those for whom it has traditionally been reserved. However, this shift raises a question about the constitutionality of the existing system of capital punishment. Thus, Justice White has commented, in Lockett v. Ohio, "I agree with the contention of the petitioner, ignored by the plurality, that it violates the Eighth Amendment to impose the penalty of death without a finding that the defendant possessed a purpose to cause the death of the victim" (at 2983). "The infliction of death upon those who had no intent to bring about the death of the victim is not only grossly out of proportion to the seriousness of the crime but also fails to significantly contribute to acceptable, or indeed any perceptible goals of punishment" (at 2984).

nerability, multiple offenders or victims, and intent or preparation for killing. Hence, the argument that these racial differences in treatment can be attributed to legally relevant aggravating circumstances—that they are heinous and vile or felony-related murders—is unsupported in these data.

This is not to say that killings of whites and killings by blacks will not seem more vile and heinous to most people. Where there is animosity, prejudice, and stereotyping along racial lines—resulting, perhaps, from long-standing patterns of discrimination and deeply rooted racial attitudes and fears—people will be more shocked and outraged by crimes that victimize members of the dominant racial group, by crimes that are perpetrated by members of the subjugated or subordinated racial group, and especially by killings in which a minority group offender crosses racial boundaries to murder a majority group victim.[37]

Moreover, the people who have these attitudes and fears are also the ones who serve as jurors and who elect prosecutors and judges to execute their laws. In effect, the stereotype and similarity of racial difference in treatment under different laws in different states and over different stages of the criminal justice process, and particularly at points of discretion for prosecutors and sentencing authorities within steps

37. Walter Berns has advanced anger, outrage, and the need for vengeance as the rationale for capital punishment (see Berns 1979), but what he ignores is that these are often sources of injustice. They serve, for example, as the lynch mob's justification. This argument confuses the desire for vengeance with the principle of retribution. Vengeance is a human sentiment; retribution is a standard of justice. Vengeance rooted in anger ignores the distinction between legal and extralegal considerations in the act of vindictive punishment; retribution requires only that the punishment be proportional to the legally relevant characteristics of the crime and the offender— not that the punishment replicate the crime. Punishment that imitates the crime is not imposed for rape, assault, or arson—and surely, such punishment would be regarded as cruel and unusual for its obviously vengeful nature. The imposition of death as punishment for murder has the same primitive, vengeful nature. To be sure, motives of anger and the desire for revenge are implicit in the willingness to punish, and more so the more serious and shocking the crime. The irony is that the crimes for which capital punishment is advocated most strenuously are those in which extralegal influences are most powerful. When the punishment is death, the sensitivity of the motives of anger and revenge to extralegal influences makes arbitrariness and discrimination irrevocable.

The argument that society needs the death penalty for its deterrent or educative function is ignorant of the empirical facts. If anything, the effect of executions, according to the overwhelming bulk of credible empirical evidence, has been to increase rather than to decrease the incidence of homicides (see Bowers and Pierce 1975a; and Chapter 9 of this book, especially the review of previous research). If capital punishment teaches anything, it appears to be the lesson of lethal vengeance. Once the extralegal influences of capital punishment become clear, as they are in these data, it is not difficult to see how and why the death penalty has a brutalizing effect on society. Simply stated, the death penalty encourages the exercise of lethal vengeance in the name of justice, rather than just retribution under law.

of the process, are consistent with this explanation in terms of extralegal influences.

With respect to region or judicial circuit within a state, we know of no remaining plausible explanations, in terms of legally relevant aggravating and mitigating circumstances, for the differences in treatment. Indeed, what we know about variations in types of crimes by geographic areas would suggest that murders of a more aggravated sort occur disproportionately in urban as opposed to rural areas. Urban areas are more likely than small towns and rural areas to have killings that occur in the course of another felony, to have murders involving multiple victims and multiple offenders, and to have murders committed by offenders with prior criminal records. Thus, taking legally relevant factors into consideration, especially those which, at least on statistical grounds, could possibly account for the regional differences, suggests that regional differences in treatment are actually greater than they appear. The fact that legally relevant factors tend to enhance rather than to eliminate the observed differences simply strengthens the argument that extralegal influences are responsible for the regional differences.

Previous studies of jurisdictional differences in the handling or treatment of potentially capital cases have suggested explanations based on extralegal considerations, such as the pressures of court congestion and plea-bargaining practices. In the courts of urban communities with heavy criminal caseloads and established plea-bargaining practices, a long murder trial and subsequent sentencing hearing may seem less attractive to prosecutors than they would in smaller counties with less congested courts. Under such circumstances, a guilty plea to a lesser charge, which the prospect of a death sentence could help to obtain, may be a more welcome substitute. And where there are many such cases, the prosecutor's reputation and reelection prospects are less likely to be affected by his decision to seek the death penalty in a given case.

In addition, defense attorneys in urban areas may be better prepared to handle capital cases in court and to make the kinds of motions and appeals that would effectively challenge death sentence upon review. This could explain the greater likelihood of having a death sentence overturned upon review in the urban areas of Florida and Georgia.

Beyond this, the same crimes may be viewed as more heinous and vile in one place than in another. If relations in the community between majority and minority groups or between social classes are precarious, or the lines are strictly drawn, a killing that crosses class or racial boundaries may be viewed as especially shocking, heinous, and threatening. Furthermore, in a smaller community, elected prosecutors and judges may answer more directly to community sentiments. Zealous prosecutors can make a reputation and perhaps even a career of seeking the death penalty whenever the opportunity presents itself. The point is that extralegal social conditions of these kinds introduce substantial elements of arbitrariness which are reflected in regional differences that cannot be attributed to the legally relevant factors which are supposed to guide the sentencing decision.

More can be and is being done to show how the differentials by race, judicial circuit, and other sources come about. But we have come far enough to see that the system of capital punishment under post-*Furman* statutes has done little, if anything, to remedy the ills of the pre-*Furman* era. The burden of proof should now be shouldered by those who argue that the death penalty can be imposed without arbitrariness and discrimination. Those charged with judicial and executive responsibility for the present system of capital punishment should now take the initiatives needed for bringing the present system of injustice to a halt.

## Supplement A:
## Adjustment Procedures for Temporal and Cross-Sectional Undercoverage of Homicide Offender Data

In 1976 the Supplementary Homicide Reports compiled by local police agencies and filed with the Uniform Crime Reporting Section of the FBI were revised to include information on offenders as well as victims of criminal homicide in those cases where offenders or suspected offenders were arrested or known to the police. Since 1976, offender characteristics have been reported for roughly 85 percent of all homicide incidents or victims. These Supplementary Homicide Reports are filed on a voluntary basis and not all agencies comply, thus producing cross-sectional undercoverage of homicides.

Since reports may not be filed by all local jurisdictions within a given state (cross-sectional undercoverage) and since the information on offenders was not reported before 1976 in any state (temporal undercoverage), this data source will undercount the number of homicide offenders since the effective date of post-*Furman* capital statutes. To obtain adequate estimates of the numbers of homicide offenders arrested by or known to the police during the effective periods of post-*Furman* capital statutes in the states under analysis, we must adjust for temporal and cross-sectional undercoverage.

Our adjustment for undercoverage of homicide offenders is based on full coverage homicide victim statistics. The Vital Statistics Program of the National Center for Health Statistics provides a virtually complete accounting of the victims of willful homicide in all states. Willful homicides as classified or defined by the Vital Statistics Program correspond quite closely to the *Uniform Crime Reports* definition or classification of criminal homicides. (Where coverage is complete for both data sources, the reported number of homicide victims is very nearly the same, 95 percent, on the average.)

Our victim-based adjustment factor is the number of homicide victims in a state for the period to be studied divided by the number of homicide victims in that state for the period over which offender characteristics are available; the number of victims for the period of analysis is drawn from the Vital Statistics records or reports and the number of victims during the period for which offender data are available comes from the Supplementary Homicide Reports. The adjustment employed corrects for both temporal and cross-sectional undercoverage when the effective date of the post-*Furman* statute was earlier than 1976 and not all police agencies in the state consistently filed Supplementary Homicide Reports. Where a state has a post-1976 capital statute (as in Alabama), the adjustment is strictly for cross-sectional undercoverage; and where all police agencies in a state file Supplementary Homicide Reports (as in Florida), the adjustment is strictly for temporal undercoverage. In the latter case, homicide victim figures from the Supplementary Homicide Reports provide full coverage of homicide victims and are used in place of Vital Statistics figures to correct for temporal undercoverage.

It should be noted that this adjustment procedure assumes comparable arrest or suspect rates and offender/victim ratios for the time periods and geographic areas where offender data are not available.

A modification of these adjustment procedures was used in estimating the number of felony homicides for each of the Georgia regional groupings in Table 7-5. Since these estimates are based on homicide victim statistics and do not incorporate offender information, it is not necessary to adjust for temporal undercoverage. In Georgia, however, it is still necessary to adjust for geographic undercoverage, because of the failure of some police agencies to report crime to the UCR Program. For each of Georgia's regional groupings, an undercoverage adjustment factor was computed by dividing the number of complete coverage Vital Statistics homicides by the reported number of Supplementary Homicide Reports homicides within each of the respective regions.

# Supplement B:
# Data Sources

Homicide data from crime-reporting agencies:

(A1)  All states, 1973–1976: computerized Supplementary Homicide Reports, supplied by Paul Zolbe, Chief, Uniform Crime Reporting Program, Federal Bureau of Investigation, United States Department of Justice, Washington, D.C.

(A2)  Florida, 1977: computerized Supplementary Homicide Reports, supplied by Alan Knudson, Bureau Chief, Uniform Crime Reports, Department of Law Enforcement, P.O. Box 1489, Tallahassee, Fla. 32302.

(A3)  Georgia, 1977: xeroxed copies of individual Supplementary Homicide Report forms supplied by Jan Trace, Criminal Activity Reporting Unit, Georgia Bureau of Investigation, Georgia Crime Information Center, P.O. Box 1456, Atlanta, Ga. 30301.

(A4)   Ohio, 1977: computerized Supplementary Homicide Reports, sup-
       plied by Herman Slonecher, Data Systems Division Chief, Ohio
       Bureau of Criminal Investigation, P.O. Box 365, Columbus, Ohio,
       43140.
(A5)   Texas, 1977: computerized Supplementary Homicide Reports, sup-
       plied by Cal Killingsworth, Manager, Uniform Crime Reporting
       Bureau, Texas Department of Public Safety, P.O. Box 4143, Austin,
       Tex. 78765.

Homicide data from vital statistics agencies:

(A6)   April 1973–December 1977: computerized Vital Statistics records
       supplied by Anne Allen and Sarah Odom, statisticians, Office of
       Health Services Research and Statistics, Division of Physical Health,
       47 Trinity Ave. S.W., Atlanta, Ga. 30334.
(A7)   Ohio, 1975–1977: Vital Statistics figures supplied by Karl Wise,
       Chief, Division of Vital Statistics, Rm. 620, Ohio Departments
       Building, 65 South Front St., Columbus, Ohio 43215.
(A8)   Texas, 1974–1977: Vital Statistics tabulations supplied by Tom Pollard,
       Statistician, Bureau of Vital Statistics, Texas Department of Health,
       1100 West 49th St., Austin, Tex. 78756.

Judicial-processing data from court records:

(B1)   First degree murder indictment followed through sentencing for twenty
       Florida counties for 1973–1976: forms supplied by Kay Isaly, Citizens
       Against the Death Penalty, 215 Washington St., Jacksonville, Fla.
       32202.
(B2)   All homicide arraignments followed through sentencing for twenty
       Florida counties, 1976–1977: forms supplied by Kay Isaly, Citizens
       Against the Death Penalty, 215 Washington St., Jacksonville, Fla.
       32202.

Death sentence data and appellate review status:

(C1)   Florida: data sheets on persons sentenced to death and appellate
       review status supplied by Kay Isaly, Citizens Against the Death
       Penalty, 215 Washington St., Jacksonville, Fla. 32202.
(C2)   Georgia: data sheets on persons sentenced to death and appellate
       review status supplied by Patsy Morris, American Civil Liberties
       Union, 88 Walter St. N.W., Atlanta, Ga. 30303.
(C3)   Ohio: data sheets on persons under the sentence of death supplied
       by William Gilbert and Steve Van Dine, research coordinators, Adult
       Parole Authority, 1050 Freeway Dr., North Columbus, Ohio 43229.
(C4)   Texas: reports by the Texas Judicial Council and information on
       persons sentenced to death supplied by Eric Troseth, Office of Court
       Administration of the Texas Judicial System, 1414 Colorado St.,
       Suite 600, P.O. Box 12066, Capital Station, Austin, Tex. 78711.

Aggravating circumstance information:

(D1)   Florida: information obtained from (1) trial court sentencing memoranda and (2) Florida State Supreme Court opinions as reprinted in *Florida Law Weekly*. In some cases in which information from these sources was not directly available, a study of aggravating and mitigating circumstances by Gwen Spivey, completed under the Howe Fellowship from Harvard Law School, was used. Ms. Spivey's study drew on the above data sources.

(D2)   Georgia: information supplied by Patsy Morris, American Civil Liberties Union, 88 Walter St. N.W., Atlanta, Ga. 30303.

# 8

## DETERRENCE OR BRUTALIZATION: WHAT IS THE EFFECT OF EXECUTIONS?

A critical feature of the continuing debate over capital punishment has been the impact of executions on society. Advocates of the death penalty say that it protects society by dramatically demonstrating to would-be murderers that such crime does not pay. Opponents argue that capital punishment brutalizes society because executions show that lethal violence is an appropriate response to those who offend.

Historically, these arguments came into bold relief in the debate over public executions in America in the 1830s and 1840s. Advocates argued that removing executions from public view would deprive them of their unique power as a deterrent. Opponents said that public executions stimulate the kinds of violence for which they are imposed. These opposing arguments also figured in the controversy over press coverage of executions in the 1890s and later. Indeed, they surfaced again recently in response to a proposal to televise executions in Texas. Some, including once-presidential-hopeful John Connally, see this as the best way to "harness the deterrent power" of the death penalty. Others are afraid that televising executions would incite imitative execution-

Originally published under this title in *Crime and Delinquency*, October 1980, pp. 453–484, with Glenn L. Pierce. An earlier version of this paper was presented at the meetings of the Southern Economic Association, New Orleans, November 1977. The authors wish to thank Shari Wittenberg, Elaine Lang, and Robert Kazarian for their help at various stages of the project. The work for this paper was supported in part by the National Science Foundation, Grant Number 7804603.

like behavior in society. They cite Gary Gilmore's execution as a case in point, saying it was followed by a rash of bizarre acts of violence by mentally unstable persons apparently seeking public attention. What are the assumptions and implications of these two opposing positions?

## Deterrence

The deterrence argument assumes a rationalistic perspective in which human behavior is seen as a function of individually perceived costs and benefits of alternative choices or actions. The individually perceived costs and benefits are further assumed to reflect directly, if imperfectly, objectively ascertainable variations in these costs and benefits to the individual. Thus, in the case of murder, not unlike other less violent and more instrumental crimes, deterrence theory assumes that potential offenders exercise rational judgment in deciding whether to kill and that they are predictably sensitive to the actual range of variation in certainty and severity of legal punishment for murder at the time of the decision to act. This rationalistic view is familiar in economics, and has served as the basis for a theory of legal punishment, at least since Jeremy Bentham.

From what we know about murder, however, there is reason to doubt these assumptions. Most murders are acts of passion between angry or frustrated people who know one another (Wolfgang 1958). Indeed, many murders are the result of assaults occurring under the influence of alcohol (ibid.), and many of the murderers are persons who have previously and repeatedly assaulted the victim (Kelling et al. 1974). Encounters that result in murder typically involve "face saving" (Luckenbill 1977) or the maintenance of favorable "situational identities" (Felsen and Steadman 1979) in the presence of threats, insults, and demands for compliance. In a recent study, having intoxicated and unarmed victims is what best distinguished imprisoned killers from those incarcerated for aggravated assault (ibid.). We know further that extreme brutality or cruelty toward the victim and killing in the act of another crime are the circumstances most likely to bring down a death sentence.[1] In effect, most murderers, and particularly those who reach death row, do not fit the model of the calculating killer.

1. After the United States Supreme Court's 1972 Furman v. Georgia decision invalidating existing capital statutes, Florida and Georgia were the first states to enact new death penalty statutes that listed aggravating circumstances, at least one of which must be found by the jury before a death sentence can be imposed. The only two aggravating circumstances found as many as half of the cases receiving the death sentence in either state are those identifying murders as occurring in the course of another felony and those identifying murders as particularly heinous or as committed in a vile or wanton manner (see Table 7-18).

Moreover, it is doubtful that the calculating potential offender, even if he wanted to do so, could make a rational decision that takes risk of execution into account. Police statistics reported to the Federal Bureau of Investigation and execution records from the National Bureau of Prisons indicate that only a small fraction of criminal homicides have resulted in executions—no more than 2 percent per year since 1930 (see Table 1-4). It has been virtually impossible for the public to know the proportion of first degree or capital murders for which executions were carried out in a given jurisdiction over a given period of time. Even experts (Bailey 1975, 669–688) have found it difficult to estimate the number of capital murders.[2] About the only way potential offenders can develop some vague impression that committing murder has become more or less risky is from the number and pacing of executions as reported in the press.

Beyond these misgivings about the rational model of the murder decision, there is further reason to doubt that potential offenders actually get the deterrence message executions are presumed to convey. An execution can be viewed from various vantage points. If one could put himself in the shoes of the offender who gets executed, he might see that the same could be in store for him were he to follow in that offender's footsteps. That is, the person who identifies with an executed offender may get the deterrence message. But the psychology of identification tells us that people identify personally with those they admire or envy. What we know about those murderers who are eventually executed makes it seem quite unlikely that any sane or rational person will identify with them. They are characteristically uneducated, impoverished social misfits whose crimes appear to be the stupid or senseless manifestations of anger or fear, not well planned, or well executed acts of deliberation and purpose. Will calculating potential murderers identify with them, or will they not, instead, contrast themselves with these wretches? Might they not infer that the death penalty is reserved as punishment only for people unlike themselves?

## Brutalization

The argument that executions have a brutalizing effect draws on different assumptions about the message that executions convey. The first serious critic of capital punishment in modern times, Cesare di

2. Notably, first degree murder of the deliberate, calculated, and premeditated kind, which executions supposedly have the unique power to deter, is no longer sufficient grounds for the imposition of the death penalty. Under post-Furman capital statutes, for an offender to qualify for the death sentence the murder must be found to have occurred under aggravating circumstances that suggest an irrational or spontaneous response to fear or anger on the part of the offender. It would appear, therefore, that the deterrence argument has become a relatively empty justification for execution.

Beccaria, in 1764 attacked the death penalty for the "savage example" it presents to men:

> ... laws designed to temper human conduct should not embrace a savage example which is all the more baneful when the legally sanctioned death is inflicted deliberately and ceremoniously. To me it is an absurdity that the law which expresses the common will and detests and punishes homicide should itself commit one (cited in Sellin 1967, 43).

A similar argument was advanced in 1846 by Robert Rantoul, Jr., who was among the first to present statistical evidence on the brutalizing effect of execution: "... after every instance in which the law violates the sanctity of human life, that life is held less sacred by the community among whom the outrage is perpetrated" (Hamilton 1854, 494).

The lesson of the execution, then, may be to devalue life by the example of human sacrifice. Executions demonstrate that it is correct and appropriate to kill those who have gravely offended us. The fact that such killings are to be performed only by duly appointed officials on duly convicted offenders is a detail that may get obscured by the message that such offenders deserve to die. If the typical murderer is someone who feels that he has been betrayed, dishonored, or disgraced by another person—and we suggest that such feelings are far more characteristic of those who commit murder than is a rational evaluation of cost and benefits—then it is not hard to imagine that the example executions provide may inspire a potential murderer to kill the person who has greatly offended him. In effect, the message of the execution may be lethal vengeance, not deterrence.

Implicit in the brutalization argument is an alternative identification process, different from the one implied by deterrence theory. The potential murderer will not identify personally with the criminal who is executed, but will instead identify someone who has greatly offended him—someone he hates, fears, or both—with the executed criminal. We might call this the psychology of "villain identification." By associating the person who has wronged him with the victim of an execution, he sees that death is what his despised offender deserves. Indeed, he himself may identify with the state as executioner and thus justify and reinforce his desire for lethal vengeance.

Granted, it is uncommon to think of potential murderers as self-righteous avengers who identify with the executioner; but the more common view that they will think of themselves as criminals and identify with those who are executed may be wishful thinking. We have already observed that those who get executed are a wretched lot with whom few would identify—the kinds with whom one might identify his worst enemies. Perhaps the reason people are inclined to believe that potential murderers will recognize their criminal tendencies and be deterred by the executions of other murderers is that this distinguishes "them" from the rest of "us" and provides a justification for executions that masks the desire for lethal vengeance. Also, by imagining that potential murderers will get the deterrence message, the "law-abiding" have the satisfaction of believing that they are taking effective steps to combat society's most heinous and feared crimes.[3]

Executions might stimulate homicides in other ways. For some people the psychology of suggestion or imitation may be activated by an execution. In this connection, research on the aftermath of the John F. Kennedy assassination and two highly publicized mass murders has shown that they were succeeded by significantly increased rates of violent crime in the months immediately following (Berkowitz and McCauley 1971, 238–260). The investigators offer the following three-point interpretation of imitative violence:

> One, aggressive ideas and images arise. Most of these thoughts are probably quite similar to the observed event, but generalization processes also lead to other kinds of violent ideas and images as well. Two, if inhibitions against aggression are not evoked by the witnessed violence or by the observers' anticipation of negative consequences of aggressive behavior, and if the observers are ready to act violently, the event can also evoke open aggression. And again, these aggressive responses need not resemble the instigating violence too closely. Three, these aggressive reactions probably subside fairly quickly but may reappear if the observers encounter other environmental stimuli associated with aggression—and especially stimuli associated with the depicted violence (ibid.).

Furthermore, there is evidence that such a process of suggestion or stimulation may also include an element of identification with the victim. Thus, research on highly publicized suicides has shown that they are followed in the succeeding month by a significantly higher than expected number of suicides in the population (Phillips 1974, 340–354). It is estimated, for example, that Marilyn Monroe's suicide provoked some 363 suicides in the United States and Britain (ibid.).

As an escape from life, execution may be preferable to suicide to some troubled individuals. Although most people find it hard to imagine, there are many cases of persons who have killed others for self-destructive motives.[4] In these cases, the individuals typically have a

3. The absence of any consistent or reliable empirical evidence that the death penalty has a unique deterrent effect is amply documented in recent reviews of this body of literature (see Zeisel in Kurland, ed., 1977, 317–343; McGahey 1980, 485–502; and Lempert 1980).
4. For discussion and elaboration of this point, see Sellin 1959, 65–69; West 1975, 689–700; Solomon 1975, 701–711; and Diamond 1975, 712–722.

deep-seated antipathy toward themselves and others, a need to express and act on their feelings, and a guilt-inspired desire to be punished for their feelings and actions. For those burdened with self-hatred, death by execution is punishment as well as escape. With the crime that leads to execution, the offender also strikes back at society or particular individuals. The execution itself may provide an opportunity to be seen and heard, to express resentment, alienation, and defiance. Thus, even for the troubled few who may find it possible to identify with the executed criminal, or at least with his situation, the message of an execution may be imitation rather than deterrence.

In the era of public executions, such imitative behavior was noted in the press and commented on by prominent social critics. The *Times* of London on January 25, 1864, contained the following observation:

> It has often been remarked that in this country a public execution is generally followed closely by instances of death by hanging, either suicidal or accidental, in consequence of the powerful effect which the execution of a noted criminal produces upon a morbid and unmatured mind (quoted in Feuer 1959, 485–486).

Writing in the New York *Daily Tribune* of February 18, 1853, no less a social critic than Karl Marx elaborated specifically on this observation. Citing data on executions, suicides, and murders for forty-three days in 1849, he commented as follows: "This table . . . shows not only suicides but also murders of the most atrocious kind following closely upon the execution of criminals" (ibid., 487).

Even after executions had been largely removed from public view, it was argued that they still had a brutalizing impact in stimulating imitation of the crimes of the condemned through their coverage in the press: "This morbid press publicity has a most demoralizing effect upon the community and many weak-minded persons of inadequate self-control are thus enabled to dwell on the details of horrible crimes with the real danger of repeating them" (Calvert 1927, 111–112). The suggestion is that publicizing an execution, let alone allowing people to witness one, may cause some people—perhaps those on the fringe of sanity—to become fascinated or obsessed with the condemned person's crime, even to the point of imitating it.

Nor is the suggestive or imitative impact of an execution necessarily limited to the condemned person's crime. Thus, some have suggested that the execution itself may be imitated:

> . . . lynchings are the sequel of the imposition of the death penalty by the state, which, setting the example of sending criminals to the gallows, leads mobs to adopt similar methods of punishment when aroused. This

is not unlike the argument . . . that the public executions of old, instead of deterring criminals from crime, led them into it by brutalizing their feelings and cheapening the value of human life (Bye 1919, 70–71).

Notably, the fact that lynching was itself a capital offense in most states where it prevailed did not deter thousands of otherwise "law-abiding" citizens; there have been roughly thirty-five hundred documented lynchings since 1890 (see Table 2-3).

Indeed, death-risking behavior is sometimes a way of affirming one's commitments and winning favor in society. It is a sign of courage and bravery in wartime, a source of recognition and admiration among sportsmen and adventurers, an affirmation of honor in the face of insults, and a demonstration of allegiance with others who share a common cause or fear. The very existence of the death penalty may provide some fanatical or troubled people with an unparalleled opportunity to "prove a point" or draw attention to themselves. Of the last four to be executed, Gilmore sought death and publicity, Jesse Bishop and Steven Judy accepted death and did not refuse publicity, and only John Spinkelink preferred not to die.

## Existing Evidence

Most studies have examined variations in the availability or use of executions over extended periods of time with officially recorded statistics on murder or homicide for evidence of whether death as punishment prevented or provoked the kinds of crimes for which it was imposed. A few studies have focused on the more immediate impact of executions by examining homicides in the days, weeks, and months surrounding executions. In our review of this empirical literature, it will be convenient to distinguish between studies of the longer term effects of executions conducted with data on homicides for years or longer periods of time and studies of their more immediate impact done with data on homicides nearer to the time of execution.

### Long-term Effects

Well over a century ago, when capital punishment was under attack and public executions in the United States were coming to an end, the impact of executions on homicides was being studied with statistics from various countries covering extended periods of time. Perhaps America's most prominent compiler and interpreter of these data was Massachusetts legislator and man of letters, Robert Rantoul, Jr.[5] In

5. We are grateful to Russ Immarigeon of the National Council on Crime and Delinquency for bringing Rantoul's work to our attention.

1846, he addressed a series of six letters containing detailed tabulations and interpretations of these data to the legislature and governor of Massachusetts. Rantoul's analyses of these data were broadly comparative across jurisdictions and time periods:

> In England, France, Prussia, Belgium, and Saxony, as well as many other nations that might be mentioned, where the proportion of executions to convictions is much smaller than in Massachusetts, and much smaller than fifty years ago in the same countries, murders have rapidly diminished in those countries in which executions are scarcely known; slightly in France where the change of policy was not so great; while in England, down to about 1835, murders and attempts to murder increased, since which, under a milder administration of the law, there has been a change for the better (Hamilton, ed., 1854, 504).

Rantoul was also sensitive to short-term fluctuations in executions as they might affect the incidence of homicides. Thus, for the period 1796–1833 in Belgium, he observed:

> Not only does this result follow from the table taken as a whole, but each period in which a change in the degree of severity occurs, teaches the same lesson.
> The three years in which more than fifty executions occurred in each year, were followed respectively by the three years of most numerous murders (ibid., 498).

Rantoul's analysis is remarkable even by modern standards for its scope, logic, and attention to detail. If he did not convincingly rule out the possibility that declining homicide rates or other associated factors might have relaxed the public's desire for executions—as an alternative to the brutalizing hypothesis—he did at least address the issue of causal priority with selected data on the temporal sequence of movements in executions and homicides. Certainly, the deterrence argument finds no support in these data; they are, instead, consistent with the argument that executions, at least public executions, have a brutalizing effect on society.[6]

In a second reform era when capital punishment was again under attack and public executions had virtually disappeared, the focus of research shifted from the actual use to the legal availability of executions. The development of Census Bureau registration of mortality statistics around the turn of the century provided a new, more reliable

6. The possibility of "jury nullification," or the tendency for murder conviction to be less likely where death may be the punishment, suggests that the apparent brutalizing effect of executions might even be stronger than these data indicate, since the official statistics available to Rantoul typically counted murders in terms of the numbers of persons convicted of or imprisoned for murder.

measure of homicide—one more strictly comparable across states and over time. In 1919, using these data, Raymond Bye compared abolitionist states with neighboring death penalty states, and periods of abolition with periods of retention in states that had abolished or reinstated the death penalty (Bye 1919). This work marked the beginning of a series of such investigations based initially on the willful homicide data of the Census Bureau and later on the criminal homicide statistics of the FBI.[7] Best known in this tradition of research is the work of Thorsten Sellin.[8]

Each of these investigations concluded that the study provided no consistent or reliable evidence that the de jure availability of executions had a deterrent effect on homicides. Yet, as a group, these investigations suggest a different conclusion: The balance of evidence is consistent with a brutalizing effect of executions. Thus, every study comparing abolitionist and neighboring retentionist states has shown that the former tend to have lower homicide rates than the latter.[9] Studies of the killing of policemen, prison guards, and prison inmates have found that the rates tend to be lower in abolitionist than in death penalty states.[10] And, in studies comparing abolition and retention periods in a given state with contiguous states to control for trends,

---

7. See, for example, Sutherland 1925, 522–529; Vold 1932, 1952; Schuessler 1952, 54–62; Sellin 1961, 3–11; and Sellin and Reckless 1969, 43–56.
8. Partially reprinted in Sellin 1967a and Bedau, ed., 1967b; prominently reviewed in Baldus and Cole 1975, 170–186; and Zeisel 1976.
9. Of seven abolitionist states examined over the period 1906–1915, six were below the mean homicide rate for retentionist states in their census registration area (Bye 1919, 42–43). Of eight abolitionist states examined in 1932, the 1928–1929 homicide rates of seven were below the mean for retentionist states in their more narrowly drawn (by that time) census registration areas (Vold 1932, 6, table 1). Of five abolitionist states studied for the period 1931–1946, four had lower homicide rates than retentionist states selected according to contiguity (Schuessler 1952, 58, table 2). Of three abolitionist states studied over the period 1933–1951, all three had lower homicide rates than either of two contiguous death penalty states (Vold 1952, 4, table 3). Of eight abolitionist states studied over the period 1920–1955, six had lower homicide rates than the mean for their contiguous death penalty states during their periods of abolition (Sellin 1959, 25–33, tables 6–8). Of nine abolitionist states compared with paired retentionist states for the year 1967, lower homicide rates were found in five of the abolitionist states, in three of the retentionist states, and there was one tie (Reckless 1969, 52ff., tables 9 and 10). Reckless also found lower rates of aggravated assault and other violent crimes in abolitionist than in matched retentionist states in most comparisons (ibid.).
10. In Sellin (1955, 718–728), the cities in abolitionist states have slightly lower rates in police homicides than those in death penalty states, and this difference holds within three of five categories of city size and within two regional groupings of states in the East and Midwest. In Donald Campion (1955, 729–735), the rates standardized by police force size were lower in abolitionist than in death penalty states in New England, east north central, and west north central regions (although the results are ambiguous in the east north central region since the data for Ohio cannot be grouped for overlapping periods). Sellin's (1967, 154–160) study of the killing of prison guards and prison inmates does not contain sufficient information to make standardized comparisons of rates within regional groupings of contiguous states, but the qualitative results certainly give no indication of a deterrent effect.

the differences tend to be more consistent with the brutalization than with the deterrence argument.[11]

At the critical juncture in the history of capital punishment in the United States, after executions had ceased and the Supreme Court had declared previous capital statutes unconstitutional, a new brand of research on the effects of executions appeared using annual execution and homicide data—as Rantoul had done well over a century earlier. Instead of comparing matched abolition and retention jurisdictions as Sellin and others had done, this econometric modeling approach attempted to adjust statistically, by multiple regression techniques, for differences across states or over time that could be expected to produce differences in homicide rates that otherwise might mistakenly be attributed to the imposition of executions.

In 1975, Isaac Ehrlich published the first econometric study of execution risk and homicide rates, based on data for the nation as a whole over the period 1933–1969 (Ehrlich 1975, 397–417). This study purported to show—contrary to all previous investigations—that each

11. In Bye's (1919) study of the period 1906–1915, Kansas, Minnesota, and Washington abolished the death penalty, but before-after homicide rates for the change state and no-change comparison states were available only in the case of Minnesota, where homicide rates increased less (mean homicide rate after the change as a percentage of the mean homicide rate before the change) after abolition than in Wisconsin, Michigan, Indiana, or Ohio for comparable before-after periods. In Sellin's (1959) study of the period 1920–1955, South Dakota and Kansas reinstated the death penalty; homicide rates decreased less in South Dakota than in its contiguous states of North Dakota and Nebraska, but homicide rates decreased more in Kansas than in its contiguous states of Colorado and Missouri. In Reckless's (1969) study of the period 1963–1967, Oregon, Iowa, West Virginia, and New York abolished capital punishment. Although Reckless did not show the corresponding homicide rates for nonchange states contiguous to these four, they are readily available from the *Uniform Crime Reports* for the respective years. They show that homicide rates in Oregon increased less than in Washington, Idaho, California, or Nevada; homicide rates in West Virginia increased less than in Virginia, Maryland, Pennsylvania, Ohio, or Kentucky; homicide rates in Iowa increased less than in Minnesota, Wisconsin, Illinois, or Nebraska but more than in Missouri or South Dakota; and homicide rates in New York increased less than in Connecticut, Massachusetts, or Ohio but more than in Pennsylvania or New Jersey. Thus, of the seven cases in which a state abolished or reinstated the death penalty and homicide rates were available before and after the change for the change state and for contiguous or comparison nonchange states, in four cases the brutalization argument is supported in all comparisons with nonchange states, in two cases the results are mixed, with some comparison states supporting brutalization and others supporting deterrence, and in one case the result is consistent with the deterrence argument in both comparisons with nonchange states. The two cases with mixed results favor the brutalization argument if the homicide rates for the contiguous states are averaged. In the one case that is fully consistent with the deterrence argument, one of the two comparisons with contiguous nonchange states is very close (Kansas versus Missouri). To the extent that abolition is apt to follow a period of abnormally low homicide rates and reinstatement is likely to follow a period of exceptionally high homicide rates, these patterns provide even stronger support for the brutalization argument, especially the results for the relatively brief period examined by Reckless.

execution saved seven or eight innocent lives by deterring murders that would otherwise occur (ibid., 414). This work is noteworthy not for the validity of its claims, which have now been discredited by a number of reanalyses of these data,[12] but for its impact in promoting the cause of capital punishment[13] and for the series of further studies it provoked. These latter studies have, on balance, yielded more empirical support for the brutalizing than for the deterrent effect of executions.[14]

What did careful reanalyses of these data show? First, execution risk tended to be positively associated with homicide rates from the mid-1930s through the early 1960s, using Ehrlich's data and analytic approach.[15] Second, the relationship also tended to be positive in the 1960s when this period was examined independently of the earlier years.[16] Third, the relationship tended to be even more positive, approaching statistical significance, when less flawed homicide data were used in the analyses.[17]

In this connection, the National Academy of Sciences's critique of Ehrlich's work on capital punishment noted that errors in the measurement of homicides would tend to introduce a negative bias[18] or "illusion of deterrence" into Ehrlich's findings:

12. The flaws in Ehrlich's data and analysis have been amply reviewed elsewhere. See Bowers and Pierce unpub., 1975a; Bowers and Pierce, 1975b; Passell and Taylor, in Bedau and Pierce, eds., 1976; Zeisel, Klein, Forst, and Filatov, in Blumstein, Cohen, and Nagin, eds., 1978; and McGahey 1980. See also Chapter 9.
13. Ehrlich's research figured prominently in the Supreme Court's decision in Gregg v. Georgia, as justification for the majority opinion that social science evidence concerning the deterrent effect of capital punishment was "inconclusive." Only Justice Marshall's dissenting opinion reflected an appreciation of the flaws in Ehrlich's work and the judgment that it could not legitimately be regarded as inconsistent with the overwhelming body of previous evidence indicating that the death penalty has no deterrent effect.
14. The terms *counterdeterrent effect* and *stimulation effect* have been used by other investigators to describe a positive association between execution risk and homicide rates which we have referred to here as a "brutalizing effect of executions."
15. Strictly following Ehrlich's analytic procedures with data virtually identical to his, the estimates for all six of his alternate measures of execution risk are positive for the period 1935–1963 (Bowers and Pierce 1975b, 198, table IV; also Chapter 9 of this volume).
16. In a crude analysis of year-to-year changes in executions and homicides in states that performed executions after 1962, there was, overall, a positive association between changes in executions and changes in homicide rates (ibid., 203–204, esp. table VII; also Table 9-9 of this volume); and a more sophisticated analysis of changes in execution risk and homicide rates over the period 1960–1970 found positive "counterdeterrent" effects of execution risk on homicide rates (Forst 1977, 743–767).
17. The substitution of census-based homicide figures that are more nationally representative than the FBI-based homicide estimates, especially for the early years of Ehrlich's time series, yields more positive estimates of the effects of execution risk on homicide rates (Bowers and Pierce 1975a, 32ff., esp. table 11; also Chapter 9 of this volume).
18. The problem arises when the same measured variable (in this case the number of homicides occurring annually) appears in the numerator of one variable (the hom-

If the homicide rate were in fact totally insensitive to changes in the execution rate, measurement errors even as small as those caused by Ehrlich's having used a homicide series rounded to the nearest 10 murders would have biased his estimate of this key relationship toward a negative unit elasticity. That Ehrlich has estimated elasticities for $P_{e/c}$ [probability of execution given conviction] considerably nearer to zero than to $-1$ could be regarded as evidence that the true elasticity is positive, indicating a counterdeterrent effect of capital punishment (Klein, Forst, and Filatov 1978, 347).

Studies have gone on to show with Ehrlich's data and with other time series and cross-sectional data sets that positive execution effects occur with the addition of explanatory variables omitted from Ehrlich's analysis. Thus, positive execution effects have emerged in time series analyses with measures of hand gun ownership (Kleck 1979, 882–910) and noncapital violent crime rates (Klein et al. 1978) and in cross-sectional analyses with variables reflecting certainty and severity of imprisonment for criminal homicide (Passell 1975, 61; Forst 1977; Bailey 1977, 239–260)—despite the negative bias that error in measuring homicides may introduce.[19] In the only analysis we know of that is not subject to the negative bias introduced by the common term problem (execution risk is a conditional measure computed by dividing the number of persons executed in 1960 by the number of murderers imprisoned in that year), William Bailey (1980, 1308–1333) found statistically significant positive effects of execution risk on homicide rates consistent with a brutalizing effect of executions.

## Short-term Impact

At the high point of executions in America in the mid-1930s, research began to deal with the more immediate impact of executions—in the spirit of Marx's commentary on forty-three days of executions and homicides in London in 1849 (cited above) but more systematic in its approach. In 1935 Robert Dann examined five executions in Philadelphia (occurring in 1927, 1929, 1930, 1931, and 1932) which had in common the fact that no other execution had been imposed within sixty days (Dann 1935, 1). Dann then tallied the homicides occurring

---

icide rate) and in the denominator of another (the arrest or execution rate). Either random or systematic errors in measuring homicides will tend to produce an artifactual negative correlation between the two rates (Klein et al. 1978).

19. In a series of studies also subject to the negative bias introduced by the common term problem, Bailey nevertheless found more positive than negative estimates of the effect of execution risk on homicide rates with annual time series data for each of five states. Positive outnumbered negative estimates in California, Oregon, and North Carolina, while the converse was true for Ohio and Utah. See the following works by Bailey: 1979a, 1979b, 1978a, 1979c, 1978b.

in sixty-day periods before and after each of these executions and reported a total of 91 homicides before and 113 homicides after these five executions—an average increase of 4.4 homicides in the sixty days after each execution. As it happens, Dann's results are not independent of seasonal fluctuations in homicides. A crude adjustment for seasonal variations in homicides in Philadelphia indicates that a total of 105 homicides might have been expected in the postexecution period.[20] Thus, a more reliable estimate of the impact of these five executions would be eight additional homicides—an average of 1.6 more homicides in the sixty days following each execution.

Dann's work inspired a parallel study of the impact of death sentences on homicides in Philadelphia. In 1958, Leonard Savitz examined the eight weeks before and after death sentences were handed down in four well-publicized cases (Savitz 1958, 338). He tallied "definite capital" and "possible capital" murders, which represented about one-quarter of all homicides, in order to focus his analysis on the particular kinds of homicides the death penalty is supposed to deter. Savitz's analysis showed a total of forty-three capital murders in the eight-week period before and forty-one in the eight-week period after these four death sentences. Like Dann, Savitz overlooked the impact on his analysis of seasonal variations in homicides. When the Savitz data are adjusted for monthly variations in homicides in Philadelphia, they yield an expected number of thirty-six capital murders in the eight-week periods after these four death sentences,[21] indicating that there were five more murders than would be expected—an average of 1.25 more murders per death sentence—in the eight weeks after these death sentences were handed down. There was also a shift toward more "definitely capital" and fewer "possibly capital" murders in the periods after death sentences were imposed, which is clearly inconsistent with the deterrence argument.

Dann's work also stimulated a study of the more immediate impact of executions in California. In 1956, William Graves tabulated homicides from the records of San Francisco, Los Angeles, and Alameda counties over the period 1946–1955 for each day of the week in which an execution was imposed and for each day of execution-free weeks

20. Using Wolfgang's (1958, table 8) data on homicides in Philadelphia by month for the period 1948–1952, we have calculated an expected before-after ratio of homicides for each execution date in Dann's study. To obtain the expected before-after ratio for a given execution, each of the 120 days in the before-after period is weighted by the proportion of homicides occurring in the month in which it falls (according to Wolfgang's table 8). Multiplying the observed number of homicides in the sixty days before each execution by its estimated before-after ratio and summing over the five executions yields an expected number of 105 postexecution homicides.
21. The procedure was the same as that described in note 20.

immediately before and after the week of an execution (excluding execution-free weeks between two execution weeks). Executions in California were routinely carried out on Fridays during this period. There were seventy-four weeks with Friday executions in these ten years. Graves found that on Thursdays and Fridays during execution weeks (the day before and the day of execution) homicides were slightly higher, and on Saturdays and Sundays of execution weeks (the first and second days after execution) homicides were slightly lower than in the corresponding days of the execution-free weeks immediately before and after. Graves observed that the slight depression in homicides in the two days immediately after an execution "is almost exactly canceled out by its earlier 'brutalizing' effect." (Graves 1956, 137) He noted that the difference in patterns between execution and execution-free weeks would occur by chance with a probability of less than 0.05. By way of interpretation, he asked the following question: "May it be that minds already burdened with conscious or subconscious homicidal intent are stimulated by the example of the state's taking of life to act sooner?" (ibid.).

What Graves failed to notice is that homicides were higher in the weeks after than in the weeks before executions (ibid.). If he had used the execution-free weeks preceding executions as a baseline, instead of combining the weeks before and the weeks after in his analysis, he would have seen that there were, on the average, 0.05 more homicides in the execution week and 0.20 more homicides in the week immediately following an execution week. This suggests that one out of four executions stimulates a homicide within ten days in the three California counties studied. If this brutalizing effect lasted for forty days, there would be one homicide for every execution.

Quite recently, another study of this sort appeared that quite specifically addressed itself to the brutalizing effect of executions. In 1979, David King examined the monthly incidence of homicides in South Carolina for the effect of newspaper publicity about executions. Over the period of 1951–1962 he identified twenty months in which stories on executions appeared in the state's daily paper with the largest circulation.[22] He compared the number of homicides in the month of an execution story and in the month after an execution story with the number that would be expected as an average of the homicides occurring in these months the year before and the year after (with an adjustment if there was an execution story in one of these comparison months). King found 0.6 fewer homicides in the month of a story

22. This is barely discernible in Grave's chart I but is clear in his table I, rows 1 and 2 (King 1978, 683–687). It is noteworthy that there were twenty-four different months in which executions occurred over this period (see Appendix A). Hence, the vast majority of executions that occurred were covered in this newspaper.

and 1.8 more homicides in the month after a story, for a net increase of 1.2 homicides in the months in which and immediately after an execution story appeared. He reported that the delayed brutalizing effect in the month after an execution story was statistically significant in his relatively small sample of twenty cases at the 0.10 probability level.

In summary, studies of the long-term effect and short-term impact of executions give ample indication that executions may have—contrary to prevailing belief—not a deterrent but a brutalizing effect on society by promoting rather than preventing homicides. The earliest research in the period of public executions was fully and strongly consistent with such a brutalizing effect. Later studies comparing periods of abolition and retention between and within jurisdictions consistently show lower homicide rates at times and places of abolition, suggesting that the availability, and by implication the use, of the death penalty stimulates homicide. And, recent studies using econometric modeling and regression estimation techniques have begun to reveal more positive than negative estimates of the effects of execution risk on homicide rates—notwithstanding analytic problems that have tended to bias results in favor of deterrence.

Among the smaller number of studies that have examined homicides in the days, weeks, and months following executions, the evidence of a slight brutalizing effect is again consistent. In three California counties, there was a slight but discernible increase in homicides (0.25 per execution) within ten days of an execution. In the relatively large city of Philadelphia, there was a slightly larger increase in homicides after executions (1.6 per execution) and after death sentences (1.2 per death sentence) within roughly two months after these events. And statewide in South Carolina there was a comparable increase in homicides after execution stories (1.2 per execution story) within roughly two months of publication, the increase concentrated in the month after an execution story appeared.

Given the size of the brutalizing effect as reflected in the short-term impact studies, it is not surprising that most investigators working with aggregate annual homicide data failed to detect brutalizing effects. For perspective on this point, take the study of execution stories in South Carolina as an example. South Carolina had an estimated 24 additional homicides over the period 1951–1962 as a result of executions (20 execution stories × 1.2 homicides per story). This is an average of 2 more homicides per year—less than 1 percent of the annual average of 222 homicides, and less than 10 percent of the average year-to-year fluctuation of 20.4 homicides over this period. The stronger effect of other factors on homicide rates and the fact that such variables are imperfectly controlled by contiguous matching procedures and not

286 | Legal Homicide

all included or accurately measured in regression adjustments would further obscure such a brutalizing effect. The impact of an execution story is less apt to be lost in the monthly average of 18.5 homicides or the average monthly fluctuation of 5.3 homicides. And other factors affecting homicide rates, but inadequately controlled by matching procedures or regression adjustments, are likely to change less from month to month than from year to year.

For research to evaluate an effect of this sort, then, there will be premiums in the data used for analysis on (1) *temporal refinement*, enabling one to isolate effects that may be relatively immediate and short lived for the duration of their impact, and at the same time to restrict the period over which potentially confounding effects of other influences may operate, and (2) *larger sample size*, so that relatively slight effects that are nevertheless consistent and recurrent can be detected with statistical reliability and estimated with accuracy and precision. The study described below was designed with these considerations in mind.

## Data and Analysis

With the publication of the Teeters-Zibulka inventory of *Executions under State Authority: 1864–1967*,[23] systematic information became available on some 5,706 executions imposed over the past century. For most states this represented a complete listing of executions since they were moved from local jurisdictions to the central authority of the state. The inventory included information on type of offense, county of prosecution, race and age of offender, appeals before execution, and, for present purposes, date of execution.

With the development of the Vital Statistics program of the United States Bureau of the Census, systematic information became available by states on the numbers of deaths from various causes, including "willful homicide." A willful homicide is defined in the International Classification of the Causes of Death as ". . . a death resulting from an injury purposely inflicted by another person" (Public Health Service 1967, 9). Notably, the definition of willful homicide has remained relatively unchanged (with one critical but tractable exception[24]) throughout successive revisions of the classification scheme:

Since 1900 the causes of death have been classified according to seven different versions of the International Classification of Diseases. Each

23. Corrected and updated as Appendix A of this volume.
24. Described in note 25.

revision has produced some breaks in the comparability in the causes-of-death statistics. However, homicide is among the causes for which the classifications are essentially comparable for all revisions (ibid.).

Of all states, New York has imposed the most executions under state authority, some 695 since 1890 when it became the first state to use the electric chair. New York has also had more homicides than any other state for most of this period. Moreover, New York has had an active Vital Statistics program at the state level since 1907. The numbers of homicides recorded monthly for New York state since 1907 are available from the Department of Health. The comparatively high incidence of homicides and executions in New York and the relatively long period of time over which data are available on a monthly basis make New York the state best suited to the purposes of our analysis.

The analysis to be presented here is a simple one. It asks how the number of homicides in a given month is affected by the occurrence of executions throughout the preceding year. The data are homicides and executions occurring monthly.[25] The monthly homicide figures run from their starting point in January 1907 through August 1964, a year after the last execution in New York state. The monthly execution data for this analysis cover the period from January 1906 through the date of New York's last execution, in August 1963. For purposes of statistical analysis, this is a time series of fifty-seven years and eight months, or some 692 monthly observations.

Our concern is with the impact of executions on homicides. We estimate by multiple regression techniques how homicides in a given month, $HO_t$, are affected by executions occurring in each of the twelve preceding months, $EX_{t-i}$ (where $i = 1, 2, \ldots, 12$). Thus, we have chosen to examine the effects of executions on the incidence of homicides for up to a year. The fundamental form of the regression model is

$$HO_t = EX_{t-i}.$$

We know that there are seasonal variations in homicides. Homicides are generally more numerous in the summer months. December, however, is an exception; apparently the holiday season creates conditions conducive to homicide.

It also happens that in New York state, executions have been

25. In 1949, with the sixth revision of reclassification of the International Classification of Diseases, Injuries, and Causes of Death, death by legal execution was included in the category of willful homicides. We have, therefore, corrected the number of homicides in each month from 1949 through 1964 by subtracting from it the number of executions in that month.

consistently more numerous in some months than in others. January has been the leading month for executions, with an average of 2.0 over the period of the study. July and August rank second and third, with averages of 1.5 and 1.2, respectively. October and November are conspicuously low execution months, with averages of 0.1 and 0.2—perhaps authorities are reluctant to schedule executions as Christmas approaches.

The point is that both homicides and executions vary systematically on a seasonal or monthly basis. In order to obtain unbiased estimates of the effects of executions on homicides, we must therefore control for their seasonal covariation. This we do by introducing the months of the year (minus 1 as a reference category) as dummy variables, $MO_i$s (where $i$ = January, February, ..., December), into the regression model. Thus, the regression equation becomes

$$HO_t = EX_{t-i} + MO_i.$$

Furthermore, we know that both homicides and executions display disparate long-term trends. In parallel fashion, they both rise to a peak in the mid-1930s. After that, homicides drop off to a plateau in the 1940s and 1950s, and then begin a precipitous rise as our time series comes to an end. By contrast, executions show a consistent downward trend after the mid-1930s.

These movements over time in homicides and executions require that we attempt to control for exogenous factors producing relatively long-term trends in these data. This we do by introducing successively higher-order polynomials of chronological time in months, $TM^i$ (where $i$ = 1, 2, ..., 10). In this way we can control more or less efficiently for the long-term covariation in these two variables. Thus, our regression equation becomes

$$HO_t = EX_{t-i} + MO_i + TM^i.$$

In the sections that follow we first show the estimated effects of the presence of executions in one month on homicides in subsequent months with controls for seasonality and time trend. We then introduce further controls for temporal fluctuations in the data and adjustments for autocorrelated errors of prediction.[26]

26. A dummy variable for the month September 1920 was also included in the estimation equations. Inspection of the homicide distribution revealed that the number of homicides recorded for September 1920 (81) was far above the monthly figures for this period. The *New York Times* of September 17, 1920, reported that 30 people were killed and 300 people injured in a bomb blast on Wall Street attributed to a "red plot." The death toll undoubtedly rose further by the end of the month, and we presume that the cause of death in those cases was recorded in the mortality statistics as willful homicide.

# Findings

The figures reported in the upcoming tables are the unstandardized regression coefficients or "$b$" 's that reflect the estimated change in number of homicides produced by the occurrence of executions in earlier months. Each row reports the effect of executions a designated number of months earlier (viz., 1, 2, . . . , 12). Each column presents effects as estimated in equations with a time trend polynomial of designated order (viz., 1, 2, . . . , 10). (It should be noted that we employed a default option that eliminates statistically redundant predictors at or below a 0.001 tolerance level. This option caused some powers of the time trend to be deleted in the higher-order polynomials.) The estimated effects are calculated in all instances with month dummy variables, $MO_i$s, as controls for seasonality and for variations in the length of the months, although their effects are not shown. For each estimated equation the table shows the adjusted $R^2$ as a measure of goodness of fit and the Durbin-Watson statistic as an indication of correlated errors of prediction.

*Estimated Effects of Executions Controlling for Seasonality and Time Trend*

The most substantial, the most consistent, and the only statistically significant coefficients in Table 8-1 represent a brutalizing effect of executions on homicides the following month. In the first row of the table, the estimated effects range from 1.00 in the equation without control for chronological time to 1.92 in the equation with the seventh-order time trend polynomial. Moreover, in all equations with polynomial time trends of fourth order and higher, these estimated effects, ranging from 1.70 to 1.92, are statistically significant at the 0.05 level. These figures say that, on the average, the presence of one or more executions in a given month adds two homicides to the number committed in the next month.

A similar but weaker effect appears for the presence of executions two months earlier. Equations estimated with time trend controls (excluding *no TM*) show effects ranging from 1.01 to 1.41. This suggests that, on the average, executions imposed in a given month add one homicide to the number committed two months later. We say "suggest" here because the observed pattern in the data is not sufficiently strong under any of the time trend controls in this sample of 692 observations to be statistically significant at the 0.05 probability level.

The estimated effects of executions three to six months earlier are weaker than those in months $t-1$ and $t-2$ and alternate between positive and negative values. Thus, on the balance, the coefficients are negative at $t-3$, positive at $t-4$, negative at $t-5$, and again positive

**Table 8-1.** *Estimated Effects of Execution on Homicides, Controlling for Seasonality with Increasing Time Trend Polynomials (January 1907 through August 1964)*

| Executions Lagged 1–12 Months | Estimated with Successively Higher-order Time Trend Polynomials (time in months) | | | | | | | | | | |
|---|---|---|---|---|---|---|---|---|---|---|---|
| | No TM | TM[1] | TM[2] | TM[3] | TM[4] | TM[5] | TM[6] | TM[7] | TM[8] | TM[9] | TM[10] |
| EX $_{t-1}$ | 1.00 | 1.68 | 1.47 | 1.73 | 1.85* | 1.90* | 1.70* | 1.92** | 1.81** | 1.76** | 1.75** |
| EX $_{t-2}$ | 0.55 | 1.22 | 1.01 | 1.18 | 1.30 | 1.39 | 1.18 | 1.41 | 1.27 | 1.22 | 1.22 |
| EX $_{t-3}$ | -1.62 | -0.98 | -1.18 | -1.01 | -0.93 | -0.84 | -1.03 | -0.83 | -0.94 | -1.00 | -1.01 |
| EX $_{t-4}$ | 0.32 | 0.93 | 0.74 | 0.86 | 0.97 | 1.06 | 0.87 | 1.08 | 0.95 | 0.91 | 0.90 |
| EX $_{t-5}$ | -0.86 | -0.29 | -0.48 | -0.47 | -0.32 | -0.20 | -0.39 | -0.18 | -0.34 | -0.37 | -0.37 |
| EX $_{t-6}$ | -0.06 | 0.46 | 0.27 | 0.19 | 0.37 | 0.52 | 0.33 | 0.54 | 0.33 | 0.31 | 0.33 |
| EX $_{t-7}$ | -0.20 | 0.27 | 0.07 | -0.18 | 0.05 | 0.27 | 0.06 | 0.29 | 0.25 | 0.01 | 0.04 |
| EX $_{t-8}$ | -0.75 | 0.32 | 0.12 | -0.22 | 0.00 | 0.24 | 0.04 | 0.26 | -0.02 | -0.04 | -0.01 |
| EX $_{t-9}$ | -0.33 | 0.13 | -0.07 | -0.50 | -0.23 | 0.03 | -0.17 | 0.62 | 0.24 | -0.26 | -0.23 |
| EX $_{t-10}$ | -0.41 | 0.06 | -0.16 | -0.63 | -0.31 | -0.02 | -0.24 | 0.00 | -0.30 | -0.31 | -0.27 |
| EX $_{t-11}$ | -0.39 | 0.09 | -0.14 | -0.61 | -0.23 | 0.05 | -0.18 | 0.08 | -0.21 | -0.21 | -0.17 |
| EX $_{t-12}$ | -0.14 | 0.31 | 0.05 | -0.52 | -0.09 | 0.23 | -0.01 | 0.26 | -0.06 | -0.05 | -0.01 |
| Adj. R² | 0.03 | 0.04 | 0.05 | 0.35 | 0.45 | 0.48 | 0.48 | 0.48 | 0.55 | 0.54 | 0.53 |
| D/W statistic | 0.62 | 0.62 | 0.62 | 0.91 | 1.09 | 1.14 | 1.15 | 1.15 | 1.34 | 1.32 | 1.28 |

*p <.05, t test.
**p <.01, t test.

at $t-6$. The estimated effects of executions seven or more months earlier are still weaker, on the average, and tend to run slightly positive or negative depending on the order of the time trend control.

By statistical standards, the equation with eighth-order time trend controls fits the data best. It shows a higher adjusted $R^2$ and a more favorable D/W statistic than any of the other equations. To be sure, the strongest positive coefficients for $EX_{t-1}$ and $EX_{t-2}$ appear in equations with fourth-, fifth-, and seventh-order time trend polynomials. Indeed, the coefficients in the equation with fifth-order controls are all higher (more positive or less negative) than their counterparts in the best-fitting equation. Yet the best-fitting eighth-order time trend equation provides statistically significant evidence of a brutalizing effect in the month following an execution and suggests that this effect may extend into the next month as well.

Can we do better in estimating the effects of executions on homicides? The adjusted $R^2$ tells us that roughly 30 percent of the variance in homicides is accounted for by our best equation. If we can improve the fit in terms of the adjusted $R^2$, our parameter estimates will be more reliable. The D/W statistic tells us that the errors of prediction from this equation are serially correlated. A better-fitting equation may remove this correlated error; if not, we can adjust for such autocorrelation and thus inverse the efficacy of our estimates. Our approach will be first to try to improve the fit of the equation and then to deal with the problem of autocorrelation.

## Further Controls for Temporal Variation

The time trend polynomials will trace the broad contours of the movement in homicides, but they will not follow relatively abrupt and temporary departures from these steadier trends, departures that may, for example, be the product of discrete historical events. To the extent that such shifts in the level of homicides are not traced by the time trend controls, they will add to the errors of prediction and to the correlation among these errors. Furthermore, to the extent that executions are affected by such a historical event, perhaps increased or diminished in number, biases will be introduced into our estimates of execution effects. It is important, therefore, that our temporal controls incorporate the effects of such events.

War is one of the most disruptive events societies experience. Those who go to war are disproportionately from the groups in society that contribute most to the homicide rate. It is reported, for example, that New York City shrank by three-quarters of a million persons, mostly young males, during World War II (von Hentig 1947). Studies have shown that domestic homicide rates tend to drop off during wartime (ibid.) and that they tend to climb precipitously immediately after war (Archer and

Gartner 1976, 937–963). Though not fully understood, these systematic temporal fluctuations are certainly affected by the movement of more homicide-prone individuals out of civilian society during wartime and by the impact of war on those who return from combat to face problems of adjusting to civilian life. War may also foster an acceptance of lethal violence in the broader society—as some say executions do.

This raises the possibility that our analysis of the impact of executions on homicides is missing an important component that would improve the fit of our regression equations, and thus increase the reliability of our results. On the assumption that major wars and their aftermaths tend to produce significant departures from secular trends in domestic homicides, we have extended the analysis to include variables representing the period of United States involvement in World War II and a two-year postwar adjustment period. Specifically, we have introduced each year from 1941 through 1947 as a dummy variable, $YR_i$ (where $i$ = 1941, 1942, . . . , 1947), into the equations estimated in Table 8-1, thus extending our analytical model to

$$HO_t = EX_{t-1} + MO_i + YR_i + TM^i.$$

The values reflecting each year's departure from the secular time trend as estimated in our best-fitting equation with the eighth-order time trend polynomial are as follows:

| Year | Departure |
|------|-----------|
| 1941 | − 5.48 |
| 1942 | − 4.50 |
| 1943 | − 6.47 |
| 1944 | − 6.48 |
| 1945 | + 3.95 |
| 1946 | + 10.63 |
| 1947 | + 8.63 |

The war years obviously dropped well below the trend line; from 1941 to 1944 there were on the average six fewer homicides per month than would otherwise be expected. In the year the war ended and the troops returned home in massive numbers, homicides increased substantially, to a monthly average four homicides above the trend line. In the two years after the war, homicides rose further, to ten per month above the trend line. Perhaps those who went to war came back more violent, maybe they returned to a more violent society, or possibly problems of reintegration and adjustment were the cause. In any case, the war evidently had a brutalizing effect on postwar society.

Notably, we also examined the values during the two years after World War I, introducing dummy variables for the years 1917 through 1920. None of these variables was statistically significant or displayed effects comparable in magnitude to the World War II dummies. We have therefore omitted them from our analysis.

The evidence of brutalization is even stronger in Table 8-2 than it was in Table 8-1. First, estimated parameters for executions at $t-1$ and $t-2$ are now larger (more positive) in nine of the eleven corresponding equations. The only exceptions are the equations with no time trend variable and the one with a second-order time trend polynomial. Second, more of the $EX_{t-1}$ parameters are statistically significant at the 0.05 level, and several have now reached the 0.01 level of significance. Thus, the coefficient for $EX_{t-1}$ is now significant at the 0.05 level for all equations with $TM^3$ or higher and at the 0.01 level for those with $TM^8$ or higher-order time trend polynomials. Third, the full range of parameter estimates are now more consistently positive. There are now fewer negative coefficients in every one of the eleven equations; they have dropped in number from thirty-eight to eight among equations of fourth-order polynomial or higher. The only consistently negative coefficient across equations appears for executions at $t-3$, and it is far from statistically significant. And fourth, all of the equations in Table 8-2 have higher adjusted $R^2$ values and more favorable D/W statistics than do their counterparts in Table 8-1.

Again, as in Table 8-1, the best-fitting equation is the one estimated with the eighth-order time trend polynomial. Compared with its counterpart in Table 8-1, in this equation the brutalizing effect of executions at $t-1$ has increased slightly (from 1.81 to 1.95) and become statistically more significant (from the 0.05 to the 0.01 probability level). The suggested brutalizing effect of executions at $t-2$ also shows a slight increase (from 1.27 to 1.40), with an estimated probability level of exactly 0.05.[27] In fact, with controls for World War II, every coefficient in this equation has increased (become more positive or less negative); six have changed from negative to positive values, leaving only one negative estimate for executions at $t-3$. The increase in adjusted $R^2$ (from 0.55 to 0.59) is highly significant, and the D/W statistic has improved (from 1.34 to 1.43), although it remains problematic.

The problem of autocorrelation arises when variables omitted from the explanatory regression model shift their values over time. When this occurs, the residuals associated with observation from different points in time are likely to be correlated. In the present analysis, autocorrelation might arise from short-term business cycles not accounted for by either our polynomial controls for secular trends or our monthly dummy variable controls for seasonal variations which may systematically affect the residuals.

Although autocorrelation of the residuals will not lead to biased

---

27. It is conventional to speak of an effect as statistically significant with a probability of less than a given level; hence, we have not supplied an asterisk in this case.

**Table 8-2.** *Estimated Effects of Execution on Homicides, Controlling for Seasonality and World War II, with Increasing Time Trend Polynomials (January 1907 through August 1964)*

| Executions Lagged 1–12 Months | Estimated with Successively Higher-order Time Trend Polynomials (time in months) | | | | | | | | | | |
|---|---|---|---|---|---|---|---|---|---|---|---|
| | No TM | TM 1 | TM 2 | TM 3 | TM 4 | TM 5 | TM 6 | TM 7 | TM 8 | TM 9 | TM 10 |
| EX $_{t-1}$ | 0.77 | 1.87 | 1.41 | 1.79* | 1.94* | 2.01* | 1.82* | 1.99* | 1.95* | 1.91** | 1.90** |
| EX $_{t-2}$ | 0.33 | 1.41 | 0.95 | 1.23 | 1.38 | 1.47 | 1.28 | 1.45 | 1.40* | 1.36 | 1.35 |
| EX $_{t-3}$ | -1.65 | -0.60 | -1.03 | -0.80 | -0.66 | -0.57 | -0.75 | -0.59 | -0.60 | -0.65 | -0.66 |
| EX $_{t-4}$ | 0.12 | 1.12 | 0.71 | 0.91 | 1.03 | 1.11 | 0.92 | 1.09 | 1.00 | 0.95 | 0.95 |
| EX $_{t-5}$ | -0.77 | 0.15 | -0.25 | -0.18 | 0.53 | 0.15 | -0.24 | 0.13 | 0.35 | 0.99 | 0.64 |
| EX $_{t-6}$ | 0.09 | 0.99 | 0.56 | 0.57 | 0.88 | 0.99 | 0.82 | 0.98 | 0.83 | 0.81 | 0.81 |
| EX $_{t-7}$ | -0.01 | 0.78 | 0.34 | 0.17 | 0.53 | 0.68 | 0.50 | 0.67 | 0.47 | 0.46 | 0.47 |
| EX $_{t-8}$ | -0.23 | 0.50 | 0.08 | -0.10 | 0.19 | 0.36 | 0.18 | 0.35 | 0.12 | 0.11 | 0.11 |
| EX $_{t-9}$ | -0.20 | 0.56 | 0.10 | -0.17 | 0.23 | 0.42 | 0.23 | 0.41 | 0.18 | 0.17 | 0.18 |
| EX $_{t-10}$ | -0.35 | 0.39 | -0.11 | -0.36 | 0.95 | 0.30 | 0.11 | 0.30 | 0.11 | 0.12 | 0.12 |
| EX $_{t-11}$ | -0.33 | 0.44 | -0.08 | -0.36 | 0.15 | 0.35 | 0.13 | 0.34 | 0.12 | 0.13 | 0.14 |
| EX $_{t-12}$ | 0.10 | 0.84 | 0.30 | -0.15 | 0.42 | 0.63 | 0.40 | 0.62 | 0.36 | 0.37 | 0.37 |
| Adj. $R^2$ | 0.13 | 0.17 | 0.20 | 0.40 | 0.53 | 0.54 | 0.54 | 0.54 | 0.59 | 0.59 | 0.59 |
| D/W statistic | 0.65 | 0.69 | 0.72 | 0.95 | 1.23 | 1.25 | 1.26 | 1.26 | 1.43 | 1.41 | 1.40 |

*$p$ <.05, $t$ test.
**$p$ <.01, $t$ test.

parameter estimates, it can lead to inefficient statistical inferences. Because the error variance formulas are no longer valid in the presence of autocorrelation and consequently we are unable to establish reliable confidence intervals with which to test hypotheses (Kelegian and Oates 1974), we have therefore obtained estimates of the autocorrelation parameters from the equation with the eighth-order polynomials. Using these estimates we have removed the systematically correlated portion of the residuals, thereby providing more accurate estimates of statistical significance.

Indeed, the problem that remains to be dealt with is reflected in the Durban-Watson statistics. Although in every case they are improved over their values in Table 8-1, they are still substantially below the 2.00 standard that reflects no first-order autocorrelation. Even the value of 1.43 for our best-fitting equation in Table 8-2 indicates the presence of an autocorrelative process that may cause us to evaluate improperly the statistical significance of our results.

### Adjustments for Autocorrelation Errors of Prediction

The problem of autocorrelated errors of prediction arises when explanatory variables omitted from the regression equation shift their values over time. In the present analysis such autocorrelation might arise from business or employment cycles that are not accounted for by either our polynomial controls for secular trends or our monthly dummy variable controls for seasonal variations.

The result is that errors of prediction associated with observations from successive points in time are likely to be correlated. Although such autocorrelation will not necessarily bias parameter estimates, it will weaken our statistical inferences. Error variance formulas are no longer valid in the presence of autocorrelation and consequently we are unable to establish reliable confidence intervals with which to test hypotheses (ibid., Malinvaud 1970).

To adjust for the effect of autocorrelation, we have obtained estimates of autocorrelation parameters and applied them to yield revised estimates of the effects of executions on homicides and more reliable estimates of statistical significance.[28] We have obtained these adjustments for autocorrelation for up to a year's duration (from first- to twelfth-order adjustments). Table 8-3 shows the best-fitting equation in Table 8-2—namely the one with eighth-order time trend polynomials—reestimated with successively higher-order autocorrelative adjustments. The top half of the table shows the reestimated execution effect parameters with designated significance levels; the bottom half of the table shows the estimated autocorrelative adjustments also with significance level estimates.

---

28. The autocorrelation parameters were estimated using the AUTOREG procedure of SAS (Statistical Analysis System).

**Table 8-3.**  Estimated Effects of Execution on Homicides, Controlling for Seasonality, World War II, and Eighth-order Time Trend Polynomials with Successively Higher-order Adjustments for Autocorrelated Errors

| Executions Lagged 1–12 Months | Estimated with Successively Higher-order Adjustments for Autocorrelated Errors | | | | | | | | | | | | |
|---|---|---|---|---|---|---|---|---|---|---|---|---|---|
| | No Adj. | 1st | 2d | 3d | 4th | 5th | 6th | 7th | 8th | 9th | 10th | 11th | 12th |
| $EX_{t-1}$ | 1.95** | 1.79** | 1.66** | 1.71** | 1.67** | 1.69** | 1.70** | 1.79** | 1.79** | 1.78** | 1.77** | 1.74** | 1.75** |
| $EX_{t-2}$ | 1.40* | 1.35 | 1.22 | 1.16 | 1.23 | 1.22 | 1.24 | 1.27* | 1.33* | 1.33* | 1.33* | 1.31* | 1.33* |
| $EX_{t-3}$ | -0.60 | -0.63 | -0.72 | -0.78 | -0.86 | -0.81 | -0.80 | -0.75 | -0.73 | -0.69 | -0.69 | -0.70 | -0.69 |
| $EX_{t-4}$ | 1.00 | 0.97 | 0.89 | 0.84 | 0.79 | 0.77 | 0.79 | 0.82 | 0.86 | 0.87 | 0.91 | 0.90 | 0.90 |
| $EX_{t-5}$ | 0.35 | 0.01 | 0.03 | 0.08 | 0.12 | 0.14 | 0.14 | -0.08 | -0.06 | -0.04 | 0.03 | 0.02 | -0.03 |
| $EX_{t-6}$ | 0.83 | 0.82 | 0.79 | 0.75 | 0.68 | 0.68 | 0.67 | 0.67 | 0.69 | 0.70 | 0.74 | 0.73 | 0.72 |
| $EX_{t-7}$ | 0.47 | 0.49 | 0.49 | 0.45 | 0.42 | 0.42 | 0.42 | 0.39 | 0.39 | 0.43 | 0.43 | 0.45 | 0.45 |
| $EX_{t-8}$ | 0.12 | 0.12 | 0.12 | 0.11 | 0.09 | 0.10 | 0.09 | 0.11 | 0.11 | 0.09 | 0.11 | 0.12 | 0.11 |
| $EX_{t-9}$ | 0.18 | 0.19 | 0.19 | 0.17 | 0.17 | 0.14 | 0.14 | 0.18 | 0.17 | 0.15 | 0.14 | 0.18 | 0.17 |
| $EX_{t-10}$ | 0.11 | 0.11 | 0.10 | 0.11 | 0.08 | 0.07 | 0.08 | 0.06 | 0.06 | 0.06 | 0.05 | 0.05 | 0.03 |
| $EX_{t-11}$ | 0.12 | 0.11 | 0.10 | 0.09 | 0.11 | 0.13 | 0.11 | 0.11 | 0.11 | 0.11 | 0.12 | 0.13 | 0.13 |
| $EX_{t-12}$ | 0.36 | 0.41 | 0.37 | 0.38 | 0.45 | 0.42 | 0.42 | 0.42 | 0.43 | 0.43 | 0.46 | 0.48 | 0.50 |
| $R^2$ | 0.59 | 0.49 | 0.43 | 0.40 | 0.37 | 0.36 | 0.35 | 0.34 | 0.33 | 0.33 | 0.32 | 0.31 | 0.31 |

Estimated Autoregressive Parameters

| Parameters | 1st | 2d | 3d | 4th | 5th | 6th | 7th | 8th | 9th | 10th | 11th | 12th |
|---|---|---|---|---|---|---|---|---|---|---|---|---|
| $\rho^1$ | -0.28** | -0.23** | -0.21** | -0.20** | -0.19** | -0.19** | -0.19** | -0.18** | -0.18** | -0.18** | -0.18** | -0.18** |
| $\rho^2$ | | -0.17** | -0.14** | -0.12** | -0.12** | -0.11** | -0.11** | -0.11** | -0.11** | -0.11** | -0.11** | -0.11** |
| $\rho^3$ | | | -0.10** | -0.07** | -0.06 | -0.06 | -0.05 | -0.05 | -0.05 | -0.05 | -0.05 | -0.05 |
| $\rho^4$ | | | | -0.12** | -0.11** | -0.11** | -0.10** | -0.10** | -0.10** | -0.10** | -0.09** | -0.09** |
| $\rho^5$ | | | | | -0.06 | -0.05 | -0.04 | -0.04 | -0.04 | -0.04 | -0.04 | -0.04 |
| $\rho^6$ | | | | | | -0.03 | -0.01 | -0.01 | -0.01 | -0.00 | -0.00 | -0.00 |
| $\rho^7$ | | | | | | | -0.06 | -0.05 | -0.05 | -0.05 | -0.04 | -0.05 |
| $\rho^8$ | | | | | | | | -0.04 | -0.03 | -0.03 | -0.03 | -0.03 |
| $\rho^9$ | | | | | | | | | -0.03 | -0.02 | -0.02 | -0.02 |
| $\rho^{10}$ | | | | | | | | | | -0.02 | -0.02 | -0.02 |
| $\rho^{11}$ | | | | | | | | | | | -0.03 | -0.03 |
| $\rho^{12}$ | | | | | | | | | | | | -0.01 |

*$p < .05$, $t$ test.
**$p < .01$, $t$ test.

Table 8-3 shows that the adjustments for autocorrelated error have confirmed and extended the evidence of a brutalizing effect. By way of confirmation, for executions at $t-1$ the brutalizing effect remains statistically significant at the 0.01 level across all adjustments. The estimated effect is slightly less, on the average, than it was in the $TM^8$ equation of Table 8-2, but it still represents roughly two additional homicides in the month immediately after an execution was carried out.

By way of extension, note the indications of statistical significance for executions at $t-2$. What we previously referred to as a "suggested" brutalizing effect for lack of statistical significance is now supported by estimates significant at the 0.05 probability level under six of the twelve adjustments in Table 8-3. Again, the estimated coefficients for executions at $t-2$ are, on the average, slightly less than they were in the $TM^8$ equation of Table 8-2, but they continue to represent roughly one more homicide two months after an execution. It is obviously the increased efficiency of the estimates and not the changed values of the coefficients that produces statistical significance under half of these adjustments.

It might be argued that the fourth-order autocorrelative adjustment is the most appropriate; all four of the adjustment parameters are statistically significant. Higher-order adjustments do not register additional significant adjustment coefficients at the 0.05 level (although they do render the third-order coefficient insignificant at the 0.05 level). On the other hand, the adjustment coefficients in the bottom half of the table and the parameter estimates in the top half appear to stabilize with the seventh- and higher-order adjustments. The fourth-order adjustment is clearly required; the seventh-order adjustment may be an improvement. The safest conclusion, in either case, is that the one additional homicide occurring two months after an execution according to this analysis is an estimated effect of borderline statistical significance.[29]

## Conclusions

There is room to quarrel about whether these data show a brutalizing effect of two or three homicides, on the average, occurring after a month in which an execution is carried out. It is certainly consistent with the notion of a brutalizing effect of two homicides in the first month immediately after an execution to have some "temporal spillover" into the second month after an execution. Indeed, if, on the aver-

---

29. Throughout, we have employed the conservative two-tailed test of statistical significance, which assumes no effect of executions as the null hypothesis. In view of the existing evidence reviewed above, however, the one-tailed test of no brutalizing effect as the null hypothesis could be justified, in which case the effects of executions at $t-1$ and $t-2$ would both be statistically significant.

age, executions tend to fall in the middle of a month, then the fact of two homicides in the following month suggests a six-week brutalizing effect. For executions imposed at the end of a month, this would naturally extend the duration of effect into the second month after the execution. The point is that such a distributive effect—two homicides one month later and one homicide two months later—is thoroughly consistent with a commonly observed pattern of dissipating effects over time.

The fact that we see a consistently negative (though statistically nonsignificant) coefficient for the effect of executions at $t-3$ at least suggests that some of those who were stimulated to kill by the occurrence of an execution would have done so anyway, but did so *sooner* because of the execution. That is, just as these data suggest a third additional homicide in the second month after an execution, they also suggest (though less strongly) that one of the three might have occurred a month or so later anyway. In any case, the data definitely show an addition of at least two to the incidence of homicides, not simply a change in the timing of homicides.

Furthermore, the largely positive (but nonsignificant) coefficients for $EX_{t-4}$ through $EX_{t-12}$ may reflect a longer-term brutalizing effect of executions over a period from four to twelve months after an execution. Although these coefficients are slight and somewhat erratic, together they sum up to a positive value of roughly 3.00, or three additional homicides. That is to say, the presence of executions at a given point in time adds very little to the monthly number of homicides after three months have elapsed, but the data at least suggest that such an execution adds roughly three more to the number of homicides in the next nine months of the year after the execution.

It should be noted that in this analysis we have probably underestimated the brutalizing effect of executions. We have ignored those instances in which a brutalizing effect may have occurred in the same month as an execution. The analysis of this issue is complicated, however, by the possibility of a "repressive response" effect (Bowers and Salem 1972, 427–441). That is, whether or not an execution occurs may, in some measure, be affected by the incidence of homicides in that month (and/or the preceding one). Thus, for example, the decision to grant a stay of execution may be more difficult to make in the presence of an exceptionally high level of homicides in the days and weeks immediately preceding the scheduled execution date.[30] Hence,

30. In this connection, Savitz's data (1958b) show an increased level of capital murders in the four weeks immediately after death sentences as compared with the preceding four weeks (twenty-six v. seventeen) and Dann's data (1935) show an increased level of homicides in the thirty days immediately after executions as compared with the preceding thirty days (fifty-four v. thirty-seven). In some measure, these death sentences and executions may have been a repressive response to relatively high or rising offense levels.

a greater than expected number of homicides in a month with an execution might reflect the impact of homicides on the occurrence of executions instead of executions on the occurence of homicides. This matter, to be addressed in subsequent research, requires the use of a more complicated analytic model than we have dealt with here.

Of course, in states with smaller populations and/or fewer executions the brutalizing effect will yield fewer homicides (unless it extends beyond jurisdictional boundaries). Parenthetically, this may, in part, account for the failure of previous studies based on state-level aggregate annual homicide data to detect brutalizing effects. Notably, the studies that have suggested a brutalizing effect of executions have worked with data on homicides occurring days (Graves 1956), weeks (Dann 1935), and months (King 1978) before and after executions. Indeed, the only other study to examine monthly homicide data found borderline statistical support for a brutalizing effect in the month after the occurrence of an execution story in South Carolina (ibid.). In fact, the magnitude of the brutalization effect relative to the incidence of homicides was roughly similar in South Carolina and New York; South Carolina had about half the homicides in an average month (20.4 versus 40.4) and about half the brutalizing effect (1 as opposed to 2 additional homicides), despite the fact that its population was approximately one-sixth that of New York for the respective periods of analysis.

This suggests that the brutalization occurs among the pool of potential killers (as this may be reflected in the actual number of homicides) and not the population at large. This tends to confirm the notion that the brutalizing effect is specific to the person who has reached a state of "readiness to kill," in which the potential killer has a justification, a plan, a weapon, and above all a specific intended victim in mind.[31] It is precisely for such people with a victim in mind that an

31. In an analysis of psychiatric case records of persons who have committed homicide, Shervert Frazier has explicitly identified a state of readiness to kill. "A second phase—not always present—is the buildup state or state of readiness—often of hours' to weeks' duration and in rare instances of 1 or 2 years' duration. This state of readiness, by no means uniform, was universal in this series of preplanned and prearranged murders—both for murderers of single individuals as well as of multiple individuals. The buildup state consists of biological, cyclic, intrapsychic, and social factors" (p. 306). In this state of readiness, the killer frequently identifies one or more victims by name or status group: "Delusional ideas of the need to murder a named individual or individuals with characteristic detailed planning and processing of the act was present in eight murderers, five of whom were multiple—a physician with a list of persons, an exconvict with a list of guards, an adolescent with a family list, a parent with a family list, a young adult with a family list, and a neighbor with a list of members of another family. Three murderers of one individual had named a spouse, a famous person, and an employee. In each instance reasons were stated and the buildup was accompanied by a planned progression of organized behavior, detailed and carefully executed goal-oriented purposive behavior despite delusional reasons and active delusional thinking sustained from three days to over one year in duration" (p. 307) (Frazier 1974, ch. 16).

execution may convey the message of lethal vengeance. They need only place the intended victim in the shoes of the executed criminal, the process we have called "villain identification." Of course, some guilt-laden, self-destructive persons in a state of readiness to kill might be prompted by the execution to imitate the crime for which it was imposed.

The implications of this research, given the present status of capital punishment in the United States, are ominous. At this writing (summer 1980) there are some 642 persons under sentence of death. If the execution of each one produced two or three homicides, the cost in innocent lives would be outstanding. Moreover, the audience for executions in this era may not be jurisdictionally specific—it may be nationwide, suggesting that the increase in homicides experienced by New York state represents only a fraction of what might be expected for the nation as a whole.

To be sure, many questions remain about the nature and magnitude of such a brutalizing effect. Strictly speaking, our findings pertain only to the impact of months with one or more executions, not to the effect of each execution in a given month. As noted above, the impact on homicides of executions in the same month has yet to be examined, as does the role of the publicity executions receive. And there are questions about the social and psychological dynamics of brutalization. Is a message of lethal vengeance an essential ingredient? Must the brutalized person associate the executed offender with persons he has come to fear or hate? Do some people, in fact, identify with the executed offender and seek to imitate his crime through some obsessive desire to gain attention, as a way of expressing abject alienation, or to act out a sublimated death wish? Is there also a deterrent effect that is simply outweighed by the brutalizing effect?

Although these questions deserve answers, they do not alter the conclusion that executions as they have been imposed historically in New York state have contributed to homicides in the month immediately following. It might be argued that this is not a necessary result, that changes in the conduct of executions could offset or neutralize the brutalizing effect we have observed. Indeed, to anticipate the argument that the fewest innocent lives would be sacrificed if all pending executions were imposed in a massive, one-month bloodbath, we hasten to add that execution months in New York state had, on the average, two and seldom more than six electrocutions. Hence, these data cannot be generalized to support the argument that concentrating a great many executions into a brief time period would minimize the sacrifice of innocent lives.

The point is that the way we have carried out executions historically in the United States appears to have contributed slightly but significantly to the increase in homicides. Any argument that packaging, pacing, or publicizing executions differently would do otherwise finds no support in these data. In view of these findings, the burden of proof that a brutalizing effect can be avoided lies with those who advance this argument. Without evidence on how the observed brutalizing effect could be converted into the desired deterrent effect, these findings represent a direct challenge to the constitutionality of the death penalty for its impact on those who have not been convicted of any crime.

# 9

## BRUTALIZATION, NOT DETERRENCE: A CLOSER LOOK AT EHRLICH'S RESEARCH

Not long after the U.S. Supreme Court's *Furman* decision had invalidated existing capital statutes in 1972, reports began to circulate that Professor Isaac Ehrlich (1973) had developed hard empirical support for the deterrent advantage of execution over alternative punishments. Ehrlich was said to have applied sophisticated statistical techniques to overcome significant investigatory flaws in the earlier studies showing no deterrent advantage of the death penalty. Writing in *The Public Interest*, for example, Gordon Tullock (1974, 108) said of Ehrlich's work, "By using a much more sophisticated method, [Ehrlich] has demonstrated a very sizable deterrence payoff to the death penalty for murder." Of the earlier studies, he wrote, "Computers were not then readily available, the modern statistical techniques based on

This is a revised version of a more extensive and detailed critique of Ehrlich's work (Bowers and Pierce 1975a), which includes as appendices the full regression results for equations used to estimate coefficients presented here. Portions of that earlier study have also been published elsewhere (Bowers and Pierce 1975b).

We wish to thank Andrea Carr, Elizabeth Chambers, Robert Kazarian, Phyllis Lakin, and Shari Wittenberg for their help in this research. We also wish to thank the staff of the Northeastern University Computation Center for providing frequent and extended access to the computer in connection with this work. The research was supported in part by Grant No. RR07143 from the U.S. Department of Health, Education and Welfare, and this revision was carried out with the assistance of Grant No. SOC 78-04603 from the National Science Foundation.

the computer had not yet been fully developed, and, last but by no means least, the scholars who undertook the work were not very good statisticians."

Even before Ehrlich's research was published or openly circulated to the scientific community, it became prominent in the continuing litigation over the constitutionality of capital punishment. Thus, Ehrlich's unpublished work was submitted by the U.S. solicitor general as a lodging with the Court in *Fowler* v. *North Carolina* (1975) and cited in his *amicus* brief (Bork et al. 1974) as providing "important empirical support for the *a priori* logical belief that use of the death penalty deters the number of murders" (ibid. 36). The solicitor general argued that:

> All of the studies that have shown no measurable deterrent effects of the death penalty have shared certain investigatory flaws (ibid.).
>
> For example, these studies have relied not upon the actual *use* of the death penalty but upon its statutory authorization as the independent variable against which the murder rate was compared (ibid.).[1]
>
> And, perhaps, most importantly, all of these studies failed to hold constant factors other than the death penalty that might influence the rate of murder (ibid. 37).[2]
>
> Unless [such] factors . . . are held constant—as the most recent study [Ehrlich 1973] alone has done—no valid conclusions can be drawn (ibid. 38).

1. On the contrary, there are several time series analyses of variations in the use of capital punishment: Schuessler (1952) has studied the correlation between homicide rates and execution rates for eleven states over a seventeen-year period; the Ohio Legislative Service Commission (1961) has performed a similar analysis of homicide rates and execution risk for a fifty-year period in Ohio; Bailey (1975) has conducted a correlational analysis of execution and homicide rates covering 1910 to 1967 for most states that performed executions during that time. In addition, there are a number of quasi-experimental studies of the actual use of the death penalty: Dann (1935) has examined homicide rates in the weeks before and after well-publicized executions; Savitz (1958) has examined homicide rates in the weeks before and after the death sentence was handed down in court; Graves (1956) has examined the incidence of homicide in the days before and after executions were performed; Bowers (1974, Chapter 6, included here as Chapter 4) has examined homicide rates in the years before and after the cessation of executions in the United States for contiguous death penalty and abolitionist states.
2. Actually, many previous investigations incorporate strong quasi-experimental design features that control for both known and unknown determinants of criminal homicide. These include the comparison of homicide rates (1) between contiguous jurisdictions differing in the availability or use of the death penalty, and (2) within a given jurisdiction before and after a change in the availability or use of capital punishment. For a further discussion of the methodological strengths of this previous research, see Baldus and Cole (1975).

As early reports of Ehrlich's "findings" appeared (for example, Tullock 1974), social scientists interested in this area were able with difficulty to obtain prepublication versions of his analysis.[3] Ehrlich's work was then subjected to close scrutiny. Investigators found fault with his methodological approach and his criticisms of previous studies (Baldus and Cole 1975; Friedman 1975), and they identified flaws in his empirical data and his statistical analysis (Bowers and Pierce 1975a, 1975b; Passell and Taylor 1975, 1976).

The Supreme Court reached no decision in the *Fowler* case; the NAACP Legal Defense and Educational Fund, Inc. (LDF) renewed its attack on capital punishment with appeals to the High Court in the fall of 1975 from Georgia, Florida, Texas, North Carolina, and Louisiana; *Gregg* v. *Georgia* was the lead case. This time the Solicitor General tempered his claims somewhat, saying that the social science evidence on deterrence was "inconclusive." He contended that Ehrlich's work had broken the previously consistent pattern of no-deterrence findings and raised serious questions about the validity of earlier studies (Bork et al. 1975, esp. App. B). In turn, LDF attorneys argued that Ehrlich's "deterrence findings" were erroneous for the reasons indicated in the various critiques of his work and that correctly conducted analyses of such data showed no evidence of deterrence—thus adding to the conclusiveness of previous research, which shows that the availability and use of the death penalty are not associated with reduced homicide rates.

The first court ruling to consider Ehrlich's research came not from the U.S. Supreme Court, but from the Supreme Judicial Court of Massachusetts. After the Supreme Court announced no decision in *Fowler*, the Massachusetts high court began deliberating the constitutionality of that state's remaining provision for the death penalty (in *Commonwealth* v. *O'Neal* (1975)). This court's December 1975 decision, which struck down the state's mandatory death penalty for rape resulting in murder, included an extensive review of the deterrence research that concluded:

> Despite the most exhaustive research by noted experts in the field, there is simply no convincing evidence that the death penalty is a deterrent superior to lesser punishments. In fact, the most convincing studies point in the opposite direction (ibid. 252).

3. The lodging of Ehrlich's unpublished work with the U.S. Supreme Court in the Fowler case made his research publicly available; however, his supply of prepublication copies was exhausted when we inquired in August 1974 and he "found it necessary to discontinue distribution prior to publication in June 1975" (correspondence cited in Bowers and Pierce 1975a, note 8).

Specifically with respect to Ehrlich's research the Massachusetts court commented:

> While the overwhelming majority of serious studies in this area have concluded that capital punishment has no special deterrent effect, one recent study . . . indicated a contrary result . . . . However, serious flaws have been revealed both in Ehrlich's approach and in his results. We are not persuaded that this study adds much, if anything, to our analysis (ibid. 257).

Six months later, in its July 1976 *Gregg* decision upholding "guided discretion" but not "mandatory" capital statutes, the U.S. Supreme Court adopted a different view of the deterrence evidence. The nation's highest court cited the debate between Ehrlich and his critics as indicating that the deterrence evidence was "inconclusive." In the words of Justice Stewart for the plurality,

> Statistical attempts to evaluate the worth of the death penalty as a deterrent to crimes by potential offenders have occasioned a great deal of debate. The results simply have been *inconclusive"* (ibid. 184–185, emphasis added).

By contrast, in his dissenting opinion, which contains a more extensive review of Erhrlich's work, Justice Marshall found that the evidence "remains convincing" that capital punishment has no superior deterrent effect, sufficiently so to justify the conclusion that the death penalty is "excessive punishment" and therefore unconstitutional. In Marshall's words,

> The Ehrlich study, in short, is of little, if any, assistance in assessing the deterrent impact of the death penalty. . . . The evidence I reviewed in *Furman* remains convincing, in my view, that "capital punishment is not necessary as a deterrent to crime in our society" (ibid. 346).

The impact of Ehrlich's research is obvious. It came at a time when it seemed that the institution of capital punishment was being dismantled. The *Furman* decision had struck down existing capital statutes in 1972 and executions had been halted five years earlier. For advocates of capital punishment, the Ehrlich study's conclusions and timing were fortuitous. It appeared to provide scientific support for the critical argument that the death penalty is a necessary protection against society's most serious crimes. It did so at a time of desperation among proponents of capital punishment and in a way that seemed to obviate the consistent no-deterrence findings of previous studies. Right or wrong, this study was seized upon by advocates of the death penalty as the long overdue empirical support for one of their principal claims.

But who is right? Is it Ehrlich or his critics; the solicitor general or the Legal Defense Fund; the U.S. Supreme Court or the Supreme Judicial Court of Massachusetts; Justice Stewart for the plurality or Justice Marshall in dissent? Or are all of them wrong about the effect of executions? We examine here the possibility that Ehrlich's data and analysis, upon close scrutiny, may actually show the opposite of what he concluded: specifically, that executions stimulate the behavior they are supposed to deter—that they have a "brutalizing" rather than a deterrent effect.

In the sections that follow, we briefly summarize Ehrlich's analytic approach, review the data he used to estimate the effects of execution risk on homicide rates, reproduce his estimates to verify that we have independently replicated his data set, evaluate the sensitivity of his results to specific assumptions and restrictions he placed on the analysis, and demonstrate how flaws in his analysis have generated an illusion of deterrent effects. We then carry our earlier critique of Ehrlich's work a step further by introducing a census-based measure of homicide in place of FBI statistics and a measure of execution *level* as an alternative to execution *risk* for its effect on homicide rates.

## Overview of Ehrlich's Approach

Ehrlich adopts an "economic" theory of murder. He sees the act of murder, or the decision to commit murder, as a function of perceived costs and benefits on the part of the potential murderer. These perceived costs and benefits, he argues, reflect the balance of illegitimate against legitimate opportunities for economic gain in society. The socially imposed costs of such an illegitimate act are the certainty and severity of legal punishments for murder. Among these "deterrence variables," the probability that convicted murderers will be executed is a key element, according to Ehrlich's theory.

This theory is assessed using annual aggregate data on the United States for the period 1933 through 1969. Legitimate and illegitimate opportunities for economic gain are represented by measures of labor force participation $(L)$, unemployment $(U)$, permanent income $(Y_p)$, and proportion of the population aged fourteen to twenty-four $(A)$. These variables are regarded as antecedent (exogenous) causes of the murder rate in society. They are also treated—in conjunction with measures of nonwhite population $(NW)$, total civilian population $(N)$, government expenditures $(XGOV)$, and police expenditures $(XPOL_{-1})$—as determinants of the certainty and severity of legal punishments for murder.

Certainty and severity of punishment for murder are measured by the observed probability of arrest for criminal homicide $(P°a)$, of conviction among those arrested $(P°c/a)$, and of execution among those convicted $(P°e/c)$. These arrest, conviction, and execution rates are regarded as intervening (endogenous) variables that directly affect the murder rate and are, themselves, affected by the murder rate, by one another, and by the antecedent variables described in the preceding paragraph. In particular, these deterrence variables are presumed to be inversely related to one another because, according to Ehrlich's theory, society will tend to compensate for a reduction in one of these dimensions of deterrence with increased levels of the others.[4]

The murder rate, to be explained by the foregoing factors, includes offenses classified by the police as "murder" and "non-negligent manslaughter" but not "manslaughter by negligence." To adjust for a presumed increase over time in the proportion of capital to noncapital homicides and for a likely decrease over time in the overall homicide rate due to improved health care, Ehrlich also includes chronological time $(T)$ among the factors predicting the criminal homicide rate. The symbolic notations and operational definitions of all the variables described above are presented in the supplement to this chapter.

To estimate the extent to which the use of capital punishment may have affected the murder rate, Ehrlich employs a two-stage multiple regression procedure with the Cochrane-Orcutt correction for serially correlated disturbances.[5] On the assumption that the function

4. Ehrlich relies heavily on this proposition to challenge the methodological adequacy of previous investigations. He argues that short-term compensatory movement among the deterrence variables will tend to obscure the effect of a change in the availability or use of capital punishment. Since previous contiguous state comparisons and before-after studies have not tried to isolate or to control for quickly compensating changes in arrest or conviction rates, they are unlikely, according to this logic, to pick up the direct effect on the homicide rate of a change in execution risk.

This argument fails, however, to recognize that the net impact of a change in execution risk (whether it comes about through abolition or some other mechanism) must include not only the pure (direct) effect of the change on the murder rate, but also the mediated (indirect) effects that are the result of any compensatory changes in arrest and/or conviction rate. Indeed, if reduced execution risk leads to increased arrest and conviction rates, and if the latter two have a more pronounced deterrent effect than the former, the net result would be a lower, not a higher, level of murder. Notably, Ehrlich's analysis of the tradeoff between executions and murders—the claim that each additional execution saved seven or eight lives—altogether ignores the presumed impact of a change in execution risk on arrest and conviction rates and through them on the murder rate (see Passell and Taylor 1976).

5. In the first stage of this regression procedure, Ehrlich obtains adjusted values for the endogenous arrest and conviction measures by regressing their observed values on the $X_1$ and $X_2$ variables as identified in Table 9-3, plus lagged values of the $y_1$, $Y_1$ and $X_1$ variables (also including contemporaneous $P°e/c$ and excluding lagged $T$). In the second stage, he estimates the elasticity of the homicide rate with respect to eight independent variables—the conditional probability of execution $(P°e/c)$, the first stage adjusted values of arrest and conviction rates $(P°a$ and $P°c/a)$ and the five exogenous

explaining the murder rate is multiplicative (of the Cobb Douglas variety) Ehrlich uses the logarithmic, rather than the natural, values of the variables throughout his analysis.

For each of the causal variables specified by his theory, this analytic procedure yields a partial regression coefficient (or elasticity) representing the strength of its direct effect on the murder rate, and a $t$ value indicating the statistical significance of its effect. Ehrlich's analysis focuses chiefly on the partial regression coefficients and significance values associated with the conditional probability of execution.

## Problems in Ehrlich's Data

Ehrlich's conclusions are only as sound as the data on which they are based. For measures of the variables at the core of his theoretical approach, he relies chiefly on the Uniform Crime Reporting Section (UCRS) of the FBI (Ehrlich 1975, 406). The behavior he seeks to explain (the dependent variable) is the annual criminal homicide rate of the United States for the period 1933–1969 as reported by the UCRS. His deterrence variables are the rates of arrest, conviction, and execution for homicide over the same period, which also come entirely or in part from the UCRS. How sound are these data for the time period covered by Ehrlich's analysis?

### The Dependent Variable: $(Q/N)°$

The annual homicide rate for the United States $(Q/N)$ is represented by the annual number of murders and non-negligent manslaughters $(Q)$ estimated by the FBI's Uniform Crime Reporting Section, divided by the annual civilian population $(N)$ estimates from the U.S. Bureau of the Census.

The FBI's national homicide statistics, especially in the early years of the UCRS, are problematic. A staff report of the National Commission on the Causes and Prevention of Violence has described this problem:

> [M]any reporting agencies, especially in the nonurban areas, were slow in joining the UCR network; there were only 400 agencies reporting to

---

variables (identified as the $X_1$ variables in Table 9-3). The Cochrane-Orcutt iterative method corrects for serial correlation by subtracting a constant fraction of once lagged values from contemporaneous values of the variables. Accordingly, the parameter estimates reported in Ehrlich's tabulations are based on the "modified first differences" of the variables entering the second stage of the regression procedure. (See Fair 1970 for further details on this procedure.)

the UCR in the 1930's, while today there are about 8,500. Thus trends of both violent and nonviolent crimes during the early years of the UCR are highly questionable as representative of national figures (Mulvihill et al. 1969, 17).

Furthermore, the President's Commission on Law Enforcement and the Administration of Justice has warned that "figures prior to 1958, and particularly those prior to 1940, must be viewed as neither fully comparable with nor nearly so reliable as later figures" (1967, 20).[6]

Unlike the voluntary reporting system of the FBI, Bureau of the Census reports of willful homicide are mandated by law in each state. The annual collection of mortality statistics including willful homicide started in 1900, thirty years before the beginning of the FBI reporting system. By 1933, all states had met the 90 percent coverage requirement for admission to the national Vital Statistics program (Public Health Service 1954, 29). Thus, the Census homicide statistics for the nation have been relatively complete since the early 1930s.[7]

Furthermore, the classification of "willful homicide" has remained essentially constant over time. The National Center for Health Statistics reports:

> Since 1900, the causes of death have been classified according to seven different revisions of the International Classification of Diseases. Each revision has produced some breaks in the comparability of cause-of-death statistics. However, homicide is among the causes for which the classifications are essentially comparable for all revisions (1967, 9).[8]

For these reasons, perhaps, the Census homicide figures have gained a reputation for reliability and have been used more widely than the FBI figures in previous studies of the deterrent effects of capital punishment (for example, Sellin 1959; Schuessler 1952).

6. Ehrlich (1975a, 406) indicates that he used "readjusted" estimates of the homicide rate supplied by the FBI. The FBI has periodically adjusted their estimates of offenses for earlier years on the basis of recent data from jurisdictions that entered the reporting program after 1958. But the adjustment of national homicide figures for several decades on the basis of the current homicide levels of agencies recently added to the sample is of dubious value.
7. According to a U.S. Public Health Service (1954) report, tests of the completeness of birth registrations made in 1940 and 1950 indicated that these statistics were, respectively, 92.5 and 97.9 percent complete. Although precise studies of the completeness of death registrations are not available for this period, the compilers of the Vital Statistics believe that they are even more complete than birth registrations.
8. One exception is that death by legal execution is included under willful homicide through 1949 but not thereafter. In calculating annual homicide rates with Census data, we have therefore subtracted executions as reported by the National Prisoner Statistics program from the total number of willful homicides recorded for each year before 1950.

**Table 9-1.** *Correlations between Homicide Rates Based on FBI and Census Data by Decade*

| Effective Period | Annual Homicide Rates | Year-to-Year Changes in Homicide Rates |
|---|---|---|
| 1960–1969 | 0.98 | 0.79 |
| 1950–1959 | 0.95 | 0.76 |
| 1940–1949 | 0.81 | 0.86 |
| 1933–1939 | 0.24 | −0.69 |

*Source*: see supplement to this chapter, numbers 1 and 13.

If both FBI and Census data were accurate they would, of course, agree. But Table 9-1 shows that the level of agreement between these two data sources drops off for successively earlier time periods. Thus, the correlation of 0.24 between FBI and Census annual homicide rates for the 1930s means that there is little consistency (only 6 percent common variance) during that period. Moreover, the negative correlation between year-to-year changes in the two data sets for the 1930s reflects opposing year-to-year changes. Notably, the FBI homicide estimates are 15 percent below the Census figures for the 1930s, but only about 3 percent lower for the period after 1940. By all indications, these discrepancies are the result of inadequacies in the early years of the UCRS.

*The Deterrence Variables: $P°a$, $P°c/a$, and $P°e/c$*

Ehrlich's deterrence variables are the probabilities of arrest among those committing criminal homicide ($P°a$), of conviction among those arrested for criminal homicide ($P°c/a$), and of execution among those convicted of criminal homicide ($P°e/c$). The first two of these rates are drawn directly from the annual *Uniform Crime Reports (UCR)*. Since conviction rates for homicides were first reported in 1936, Ehrlich estimated the values for the missing years 1933–1935 (with an auxiliary equation provided in Ehrlich 1975b).

The arrest and conviction data from the UCRS are even more problematic than the FBI's criminal homicide figures. The agencies reporting these statistics have remained a relatively small, self-selected subsample for most of the period during which these data have been compiled.[9] The number of agencies reporting arrest and conviction data by years is shown in Figure 9-1, and the average size in terms of population coverage of reporting agencies over time appears in Figure 9-2.

---

9. It is noteworthy in this connection that as of 1978 the FBI dropped conviction data from the Uniform Crime Reporting System. Among the explanations given by the director of the UCRS is that the data were too unrepresentative to be relied upon for national estimates.

**Figure 9-1.** *Number of Agencies Reporting Arrest and Conviction Statistics by Year*

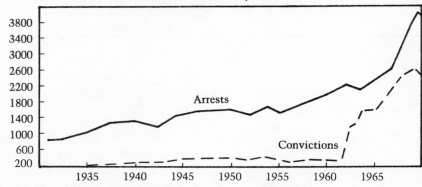

*Source*: see supplement to this chapter, numbers 2 and 3.

**Figure 9-2.** *Population Coverage per Agency Reporting Arrest and Conviction Statistics by Year*

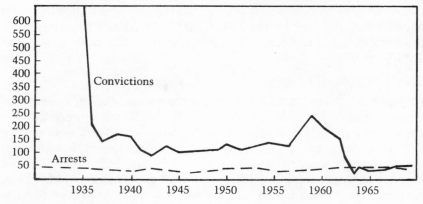

*Source*: see supplement to this chapter, numbers 2 and 3.

As Figure 9-1 shows, until the 1960s conviction figures were available from fewer than three hundred (or less than 5 percent) of all agencies, and arrest data were reported by fewer than two thousand (or about one-quarter) of the agencies. Notably, in 1936, the first year of conviction data, the national estimate used by Ehrlich was based on only thirteen jurisdictions; in 1937 the base number was only fifty-seven.

Moreover, as Figure 9-2 shows, agencies reporting conviction statistics changed abruptly and substantially in population coverage over this period. Thus, conviction rates were reported by a few very large agencies in the first several years and by several hundred relatively large agencies for most of the period. The population coverage of agencies reporting arrest rates was relatively constant over this period, but substantially different from the coverage of those reporting conviction rates for most of this period.

Furthermore, there is evidence that conviction rates are relatively low in the nation's largest jurisdictions. For example, tabulations for 1974 show that only 32 percent of those charged with criminal homicide in jurisdictions with populations of 200,000 or more were convicted, compared with 50 percent in smaller jurisdictions. Hence, the conviction data drawn from disproportionately large agencies, especially in 1936 and 1937, can be expected to underestimate the national conviction rates. In fact, the conviction levels for 1936 and 1937 published in the *UCR* are far below those for other years—respectively −5.94 and −4.54 standard deviations below the mean for the rest of the time series, 1938–1969.

The problem is further compounded by the fact that the 1936 and 1937 conviction rates greatly influence Ehrlich's estimates for the years 1933–1935 when no conviction data were collected. Thus, using an auxiliary equation that estimates earlier conviction rates on the basis of later data, Ehrlich obtained conviction estimates for 1933 through 1935 that are also four to five standard deviations below the mean for 1938–1969. To show the effect of these two values on the earlier estimates, we have applied Ehrlich's auxiliary equation to the data for the 1938–1969 period to obtain alternative estimates for 1933–1937 conviction rates. The alternative estimates, presented together with Ehrlich's values in Table 9-2, make it clear that the conviction figures for the first five years of Ehrlich's time series are far below those for the rest of the series, and that this is due in large measure to the influence of the unrepresentative 1936–1937 conviction values.

Finally, the key deterrence variable in Ehrlich's research—execution risk—incorporates the inadequacies in the FBI's homicide, arrest, and conviction data. Execution risk, as defined by Ehrlich, is the number of executions for murder divided by the number of criminal hom-

**Table 9-2.**  *Comparison of Ehrlich's Conviction Rate Estimates with Those of an Alternative Estimate*

| Year | Ehrlich's Rates | | Alternative Estimates | |
|------|---------------------|-------------------------------------------------|---------------------|-------------------------------------------------|
|      | Annual Estimates | Standard Deviations from the 1938–1969 Mean | Annual Estimates | Standard Deviations from the 1938–1969 Mean |
| 1937 | 30.3 | −4.54 | 43.7 | −0.40 |
| 1936 | 25.8 | −5.94 | 44.1 | −0.29 |
| 1935 | 28.3 | −5.18 | 44.1 | −0.26 |
| 1934 | 26.9 | −5.59 | 42.8 | −0.69 |
| 1933 | 30.2 | −4.58 | 43.3 | −0.53 |

icide convictions (specified somewhat differently with respect to time in six alternative indices). The annual number of executions as reported by the National Prisoner Statistics program is presumably accurate. The annual number of homicide convictions, however, is obtained for a given year by multiplying the number of homicides by the arrest rate by the conviction rate, all as reported by the FBI. Thus, measurement problems in the dependent variable and in the other two deterrence variables are combined in the denominator of execution risk.

There is a further problem. Since reported homicides are the numerator of the homicide rate and a component in the denominator of execution risk (see the supplement to this chapter, nos. 1 and 4), errors in the FBI's homicide figures will tend to produce an artifactual negative relationship between the dependent variable and the key deterrence variable. Thus, if too few homicides are reported, the homicide rate will be underestimated and execution risk will be overestimated. In effect, the mismeasurement of homicides will create an illusion of deterrence in Ehrlich's research because of the way in which the homicide rate and execution risk are defined.[10]

## Problems in Ehrlich's Analysis

Our purpose here is to evaluate Ehrlich's analytic results, apart from the inadequacies of his data. Ehrlich declined to make his data available to us,[11] so we independently reproduced his data set and replicated his results by applying his analytic techniques and assumptions to our data set. We examine below the extent to which his results are the idiosyncratic product of the analytic restrictions he imposed.

### Reproducing Ehrlich's Data

After Ehrlich denied our request for access to his data we attempted to constuct a data set comparable to the one he used. For each variable in his analysis, Table 9-3 shows the mean and standard deviation (in logarithmic values) as reported by Ehrlich (1975a, table 2) and as calculated from the data set we developed. (We indicate the precise data

10. An empirical estimate of the extent of this bias in Ehrlich's analysis has been obtained with simulation techniques by Klein, Forst, and Filatov (1978).

11. In response to a November 1974 request to make his data available to us for further analysis, Ehrlich refused, saying that his "work on issues relating to capital punishment [was] still in progress." Shortly after the publication of his research in June 1975, he did circulate a memorandum on *Sources of Data* (1975b) to researchers who had requested copies of his data set. He first made the data set he employed available for reanalysis in 1978 at the request of the National Academy of Sciences Task Force on Deterrence and Incapacitation (see Klein et al. 1978).

**Table 9-3.**   *Variables Used in the Regression Analysis: Annual Observations 1933–1969 (Means and Standard Deviations in Natural Logarithms)*

|  |  | Variable | Data Set | Mean | Standard Deviation |
|---|---|---|---|---|---|
|  | $(Q/N)°$ = | Crime rate: offenses known per 1,000 civilian population | Ours<br>Ehrlich's | −2.853<br>−2.857 | 0.156<br>0.156 |
|  | $P°a$ = | Probability of arrest: clearance rates | Ours<br>Ehrlich's | 4.497<br>4.497 | 0.038<br>0.038 |
| $Y_1$ | $P°c/a$ = | Conditional probability of conviction: fraction of those charged who were convicted of murder | Ours<br>Ehrlich's | 3.742<br>3.741 | 0.172<br>0.175 |
|  | $P°e/c$ = | Conditional probability of execution. $PXQ_1$ = the number of executions for murder in year $t + 1$ as a percentage of the total number of convictions in year $t$. | Ours<br>Ehrlich's | 0.172<br>0.176 | 1.748<br>1.749 |
|  | $L$ = | Labor force participation rate of the civilian population | Ours<br>Ehrlich's | −0.544<br>−0.546 | 0.029<br>0.030 |
|  | $U$ = | Unemployment rate of the civilian labor force | Ours<br>Ehrlich's | 1.743<br>1.743 | 0.728<br>0.728 |
| $X_1$ | $A$ = | Fraction of residential population in the age group 14–24 | Ours<br>Ehrlich's | −1.759<br>−1.740 | 0.122<br>0.118 |
|  | $Y_p$ = | Friedman's estimate of permanent income per capita | Ours<br>Ehrlich's | 6.889<br>6.868 | 0.337<br>0.338 |
|  | $T$ = | Chronological time (years) | Ours<br>Ehrlich's | 2.685<br>2.685 | 0.867<br>0.867 |
|  | $NW$ = | Percentage of nonwhite residential population | Ours<br>Ehrlich's | −2.216<br>−2.212 | 0.061<br>0.063 |
|  | $N$ = | Civilian population in 1,000s | Ours<br>Ehrlich's | 11.944<br>11.944 | 0.161<br>0.161 |
| $X_2$ | $XGOV$ = | Per capita (real) expenditures by all governments in million dollars | Ours<br>Ehrlich's | −7.753<br>−7.661 | 0.256<br>0.501 |
|  | $XPOL-_1$ = | Per capita (real) expenditures on police in dollars lagged one year | Ours<br>Ehrlich's | 2.200<br>2.114 | 0.146<br>0.306 |

*Sources*: see supplement to this chapter and Ehrlich 1975a. In his memorandum on data sources, Ehrlich (1975b) indicated that the mean of $P°a$ is 4.497, not 4.997 as shown in Ehrlich 1975a, tables.

sources from which each of our variables was drawn in the supplement to this chapter.)

For most of the variables, our measures correspond quite closely to Ehrlich's. With two exceptions, means differ only in the third significant digit and standard deviations only in the second. Such differences may reflect the effects of rounding error or the choice of different published sources for essentially the same data. Ehrlich's (1975b) memorandum on data sources has enabled us to account for differences between the two data sets.

The two variables that show greater discrepancies—$XGOV$ and $XPOL_{-1}$—differ primarily in standard deviations. In both cases, we believe that our measures more faithfully reflect Ehrlich's definitions of the variables. Although Ehrlich described $XGOV$ as per capita expenditures of local, state, and federal governments, his memorandum (1975b) on data sources indicates that he actually used government purchases of goods and services. His memorandum further indicates that he failed to exclude defense purchases. Since defense expenditures and purchases represent resources not available for law enforcement activity, this tends to jeopardize the intended role of $XGOV$ as an instrumental variable. Our measure is based on government expenditures and excludes defense expenditures. We could not replicate $XPOL_{-1}$ exactly because Ehrlich used an unspecified auxiliary regression equation to estimate unavailable police expenditure data for odd numbered years prior to 1952. His memorandum also indicates that he used a price deflator for government purchases rather than for government expenditures.

We constructed two other variables—$A$ and $NW$—differently than Ehrlich did. While $A$ is described as the proportion of the residential population aged fourteen to twenty-four, Ehrlich's memorandum reveals that he used fourteen to twenty-four-year-olds in both the residential population and the armed forces overseas as a proportion of the total residential population. Clearly, persons in this age group overseas cannot contribute to the domestic homicide rate. The slightly greater standard deviation of our measure, based exclusively on residential population figures, undoubtedly reflects movements of this age group in and out of the country during the war years. Although $NW$ is described as the proportion of nonwhites in the residential population, Ehrlich's memorandum indicates that he took nonwhites in the total population as a proportion of the residential population. Moreover, he used annual estimates of the nonwhite population from the *Current Population Reports* for the 1960s instead of readjusted estimates based on the 1970 census. Again, our measure, based exclusively on residential population figures and readjusted annual estimates, is a more accurate representation of the variable as originally defined.

*Reproducing Ehrlich's Results*

If our data set is comparable to Ehrlich's, as it appears to be, we should be able to replicate the results of his regression analysis. Table 9-4 contains estimated deterrent effects for six alternative measures of execution risk as reported by Ehrlich and as calculated by applying his statistical techniques to our data.

The six measures of execution risk given in Table 9-4 are alternative ways of representing the conditional probability of execution given conviction for murder. In most of these measures, except $PXQ_2$, Ehrlich provides for a delay between conviction and execution; that is, he divides the number of executions in one year by the estimated number of convictions at an earlier time. In two cases $(TXQ_1$ and $PDL_1)$ he estimates execution risk at a given point in time in terms of the numbers of convictions over a period of three or four years. (For further details concerning the calculation of $TXQ_1$, $PDL_1$, and $PXQ_1$, see Ehrlich 1973, 30, 31; 1975, 407, 408).

The estimated effects are represented by partial regression coefficients, elasticities[12] in this case; the statistical significance of these effects is indicated by the ratio of these coefficients to their standard errors, or approximately the $t$ values of the coefficients.[13] (More complete tabulations of these regression results appear in Bowers and Pierce 1975a, App. B equations 1.1, 2.1, 3.1, 4.1, 5.1, and 6.1.)

Our results are similar to Ehrlich's in a number of ways. We both obtain negative regression coefficients for all six measures of execution risk, with $PXQ_2$ showing the strongest effect. In four cases, his negative coefficients are more than twice their standard errors; three of our coefficients meet this standard and they are included among his four.

Curiously, two of Ehrlich's regression equations (nos. 3 and 4 in his table 4) appear to be misspecified in terms of effective period.[14] It

12. When the execution and homicide variables are in logarithmic form, the partial regression coefficients indicate the elasticity of the homicide rate with respect to execution risk—that is, the percentage change in the homicide rate that can be expected from a 1 percent change in execution risk. Thus, an elasticity of $-0.068$ (associated with $PXQ_2$) means that a 1 percent increase in this measure of execution risk can be expected to yield a decrease of 0.068 percent in the homicide rate.

13. A $t$ value of 2.0 is generally taken as an indication of statistical significance because if the true value of the regression coefficient were actually zero, an estimated regression coefficient with a $t$ value greater than 2.0 would only occur approximately 5 times out of 100. A $t$ value greater than 2.0 is required for this level of statistical significance when the number of data observations exceeds the number of explanatory variables by five or less.

14. Given Ehrlich's data and analytic procedures, 1935 is the earliest possible beginning date for regression analysis using any of the measures of execution risk. The first stage regression estimates of arrest and conviction rates cannot be obtained prior to 1934 since values of many variables lagged one year are required by the reduced form equation. The modified first differences obtained in the second stage of the regression analysis by the Cochrane-Orcutt procedure cannot be obtained prior to 1935 since all exogenous and endogenous variables must be lagged one year.

With $PXQ1_{-1}$ as the measure of execution risk, however, the earliest possible

**Table 9-4.** *Estimated Effects of Execution Risk on the Criminal Homicide Rate*

| Six Alternative Measures of Execution Risk | | Data Set | Effective Period | Partial Regression Coefficients | $t$ Values |
|---|---|---|---|---|---|
| $PXQ_1$ | $= (E_{t+1}/C_t)$ The number of executions in the year after the presumed effect on the homicide rate divided by the number of convictions one year earlier. | Ours | 1935–1969 | $-0.018$ | $-0.69$ |
| | | Ehrlich's | 1935–1969 | $-0.039$ | $-1.59$ |
| $PXQ_2$ | $= (E_t/C_t)$ The number of executions in the year of the presumed effect on the homicide rate divided by the number of convictions in the same year. | Ours | 1935–1969 | $-0.068$ | $-3.15$ |
| | | Ehrlich's | 1935–1969 | $-0.068$ | $-3.69$ |
| $PXQ_{1-1}$ | $= (E_t/C_{t-1})$ The number of executions in the year of the presumed effect on the homicide rate divided by the number of convictions one year earlier. | Ours | 1936–1969 | $-0.023$ | $-1.12$ |
| | | Ehrlich's | 1935–1969 | $-0.065$ | $-3.29$ |
| $TXQ_1$ | $=$ A linear distributed lag regression of $PXQ_1$ on three of its prior values. | Ours | 1938–1969 | $-0.059$ | $-2.76$ |
| | | Ehrlich's | 1937–1939 | $-0.049$ | $-2.26$ |
| $PDL_1$ | $=$ A second degree polynomial lag function of $PXQ_1$ on four of its prior values. | Ours | 1939–1969 | $-0.065$ | $-3.45$ |
| | | Ehrlich's | 1939–1969 | $-0.062$ | $-3.82$ |
| $P\hat{X}Q_1$ | $=$ The systematic part of $PXQ_1$ estimated via a reduced form regression equation. | Ours | 1935–1969 | $-0.004$ | $-0.113$ |
| | | Ehrlich's | 1935–1969 | $-0.059$ | $-1.73$ |

might, therefore, be more accurate to say that Ehrlich obtained negative coefficients twice their standard errors in two of four valid equations. In our data, the same two of these four equations show effects that are twice their standard errors. Specifically, in Ehrlich's results and ours, $PXQ_2$ and $PDL_1$ meet this standard, whereas $PXQ_1$ and $P\hat{X}Q_1$ do not.

In addition, the relative strengths of the effects of arrest $(P°a)$, conviction $(P°c/a)$, and execution $(P°e/c)$ in our regression results are the same as Ehrlich (1975a, 411) reports.

The regression results regarding the effects of $P°a$, $P°c/a$, and $P°e/c$ constitute perhaps the strongest findings of the empirical investigation. Not only do the signs of the elasticities associated with these variables conform to the general theoretical expectations, but their ranking, too, is consistent with the predictions. [15]

---

starting date is 1936. The reduced form first-stage equation requires that a lagged value of $PXQ1_{-1}$ is that for 1934, not for 1933, since the denominator of this measure incorporates values of homicides, arrests, and convictions lagged one year. This means that estimated arrest and conviction rates cannot be obtained before 1935 and that modified first differences cannot be estimated for periods beginning before 1936. Since Ehrlich gives 1935 as the beginning of the effective period, he may have used an erroneous (probably zero) value for $PXQ1_{-1}$ in the first-stage estimation procedure.

With $TXQ_1$ as the measure of execution risk, the earliest beginning point for the effective period should be 1938. Since values of $TXQ_1$ depend on data from three prior years, the first values cannot be obtained before 1936; the first stage estimation of arrest and conviction rates with lagged $TXQ_1$ cannot be made for years earlier than 1937, and hence modified first differences cannot be calculated for effective periods starting earlier than 1938. If, as Ehrlich indicates, 1937 is actually used as the beginning date of the effective period, lagged $TXQ_1$ in the first-stage equation will be an arbitrary (probably nonzero) value based on data from only two prior years (and a zero value for the third year).

$PXQ1_{-1}$ and $TXQ_1$ are used more extensively than any of the other execution measures in Ehrlich's regression analyses, and in virtually all cases the effective period of analysis begins one year too soon. The following equations in both his papers would appear to be misspecified and, therefore, improperly estimated, in terms of the effective period of analysis: equations 3 and 4 in table 4 of Ehrlich (1973, 53), table 3 of Ehrlich (1975a, 410), equations 2 through 5 in table 5 of Ehrlich (1973, 54), equations 1 through 6 in table 6 of Ehrlich (1973, 55), table 4 of Ehrlich (1975a, 410), and equations 3 and 4 in table 7 of Ehrlich (1973, 57).

We believe these equations are not simply mislabeled but are, in fact, improperly specified with respect to the effective period of analysis. With the data generated from information in Ehrlich's memorandum, we have estimated each of the above equations for its maximum proper effective period and for the apparently incorrect one indicated in Ehrlich's tabulations. In every case, we found that the results reported by Ehrlich correspond more closely with the estimates we have obtained for the incorrectly defined effective period. However, the resulting errors of estimation are small in magnitude since they enter the second-stage regression results through one of eighteen variables in the first-stage estimation of arrest and conviction rates.

15. Hoenack and Weiler (1980) attribute this ordering of effects to misspecification of Ehrlich's murder supply equation, which, they show, empirically violates the imposed identification restrictions. They propose an alternative structural equation model for the criminal justice processing of capital cases that satisfies their identification assumptions, acccounts for Ehrlich's ordering of effects in terms of other components of the model, and yields significant negative (deterrent) effects for arrest rate but nonsignificant positive effects for conviction and execution rates.

Thus, by replicating the rank order of effects among arrest, conviction, and execution rates, we have reproduced what Ehrlich regards as an especially important aspect of his regression results. Our full regression results are also comparable to Ehrlich's (as shown in Bowers and Pierce 1975a, App. B). Because we have clearly reproduced Ehrlich's results, our data can now be used to examine the adequacy of his analytic approach.[16]

## Temporal Specification

If the results of a time series regression analysis are a faithful representation of underlying causal processes, the estimated coefficients should be independent of the specific time period chosen for the analysis. Thus, if the coefficients associated with execution risk change substantially when they are estimated for alternative time intervals, the values reported in Table 9-4 are not a reliable basis for inferring that executions have a deterrent effect on murder.

Ehrlich addressed this issue by conducting the regression analysis for selected subperiods. He performed regressions with a few years removed from the beginning of the time series and others with a few years dropped from the end of the series. These alterations in the effective period of analysis did not appreciably change the elasticities associated with execution risk. Ehrlich did, however, concede in his unpublished paper that the deterrent effects of arrest, conviction, and execution rates become "weaker" when as many as seven years are dropped from the recent end of the time series.

> Indeed, regression results pertaining to the effect of these variables in the subperiod 1935–1962 or 1937–1962 are found to be generally weak . . . (Ehrlich 1973, note 10).

We find that all empirical support for the deterrent effect of executions disappears when as few as five years are removed from the recent end of Ehrlich's time series. Table 9-5 shows the estimated effects of execution risk on the criminal homicide rate for ten periods with successively earlier ending dates. For the period ending in 1964, there are no statistically significant negative elasticities associated with the various measures of execution risk. For the period ending in 1963, the estimated elasticities have become positive in every case. Indeed,

16. Ehrlich (1975c, 210) and Bork et al. (1974, App. B, 11a) have represented these results as independent confirmation of the deterrent effect of executions. At this point, we wish to make it clear that they are, instead, a demonstration that we reproduced a data set comparable to Ehrlich's and applied his analytic techniques in a similar manner—a demonstration required because Ehrlich would not supply us with copies of the data set he used.

**Table 9-5.** *Estimated Effects of Execution Risk on the Criminal Homicide Rate for Effective Periods with Successively Earlier Ending Dates*

| Ending Date of Effective Period | Six Alternative Measures of Execution Risk | | | | | |
|---|---|---|---|---|---|---|
| | $PXQ_1$ | $PXQ_2$ | $PXQ_{1-1}$ | $TXQ_1$ | $PDL_1$ | $P\hat{X}Q_1$ |
| 1969 | −0.018 | −0.068 | −0.023 | −0.059 | −0.065 | −0.004 |
| | (−0.69) | (−3.15) | (−1.12) | (−2.70) | (−3.45) | (−0.11) |
| 1968 | −0.026 | −0.069 | −0.030 | −0.059 | −0.069 | −0.049 |
| | (−0.99) | (−3.50) | (−1.41) | (−2.76) | (−4.09) | (−1.36) |
| 1967 | −0.031 | −0.064 | −0.061 | −0.064 | −0.068 | 0.060 |
| | (−1.38) | (−3.65) | (−3.18) | (−3.64) | (−4.55) | (−1.98) |
| 1966 | −0.020 | −0.055 | −0.053 | −0.050 | −0.056 | −0.043 |
| | (−1.00) | (−3.79) | (−3.31) | (−2.88) | (−3.40) | (−1.59) |
| 1965 | −0.016 | −0.041 | 0.034 | −0.025 | −0.037 | −0.031 |
| | (−0.99) | (−1.51) | (−1.20) | (−0.98) | (−1.53) | (−1.41) |
| 1964 | 0.028 | −0.021 | −0.017 | −0.009 | −0.013 | 0.013 |
| | (0.91) | (−0.70) | (−0.58) | (−0.34) | (−0.40) | (0.37) |
| 1963 | 0.057 | 0.003 | 0.003 | 0.065 | 0.048 | 0.037 |
| | (1.77) | (0.08) | (0.08) | (1.63) | (1.00) | (1.02) |
| 1962 | 0.052 | −0.030 | −0.021 | 0.060 | 0.021 | 0.040 |
| | (1.14) | (−0.60) | (−0.54) | (1.30) | (0.35) | (0.83) |
| 1961 | −0.015 | 0.041 | 0.011 | 0.086 | 0.050 | −0.019 |
| | (−0.28) | (0.67) | (0.29) | (2.10) | (1.02) | (−0.33) |
| 1960 | 0.013 | 0.029 | 0.009 | 0.070 | 0.067 | 0.013 |
| | (0.24) | (0.52) | (0.25) | (1.72) | (1.36) | (0.22) |

*Note*: Variables are expressed as natural logarithms and $t$ values are given in parentheses.

of the twenty-four coefficients reflecting the effects of execution risk for periods ending in 1963 and earlier, twenty are positive.

Not only does the evidence for deterrence disappear, but Ehrlich's anticipated ordering of the effects of arrest, conviction, and execution rates also vanishes. When we examine the results for periods ending in 1964 or earlier, we find only three instances out of thirty possible comparisons that conform to his rank order predictions of the relative strengths of the deterrence variables.

Furthermore, we find that the regression results are more statistically reliable and consistent for the periods with earlier ending dates. The standard errors of the regressions are less, the $F$ statistics are consistently higher, and the Durbin-Watson statistics are generally more acceptable for the periods with earlier ending dates. (See equations 1.1–6.4 in App. B of Bowers and Pierce 1975.) Corresponding coefficients for the other variables in the regression equations are generally in closer agreement in the shorter than in the longer periods. Hence, for the periods in which the model gives evidence of being more adequately specified, the regression analysis consistently shows a slightly *positive*, though not statistically significant, effect of execution risk on the homicide rate.

## Functional Form

A theoretical formulation, such as Ehrlich's economic model of murder, seldom dictates the mathematical function that describes the true relationships among the variables. When the functional form is open to question or when the analyst wishes to establish the generality of his findings, he will typically examine regression results obtained under different assumptions about the form of the model.

Ehrlich assumes that the factors that determine the murder rate have a multiplicative effect. He therefore uses logarithmic values of the variables to transform this multiplicative model into a form suitable for linear regression analysis (see Johnston 1972; Wonacott and Wonacott 1970). He reports (Ehrlich 1975, 412-413), however, that his regression results are not dependent on the specific assumptions he has made about the form of the relationships among the variables— that there is evidence of a deterrent effect even when he performs the regression analysis with the natural values of his variables (which corresponds to an additive rather than a multiplicative relationship among the variables).

> The regression results are found to be robust with respect to the functional form of the regression equation. Running the regressions . . . by introducing the natural values of all the relevant variables instead of their natural logarithms does not change the qualitative results reported therein (Ehrlich 1973, 36–37).

Using the natural values of these variables, we have re-estimated the coefficients shown in Table 9-5 to obtain the results in Table 9-6.[17] There are, among the sixty estimates in Table 9-6, more positive than negative coefficients associated with the various measures of execution risk. Only two, both of them positive, are statistically signif-

---

17. When execution risk and homicide rates are expressed in natural values rather than in logarithms, the regression coefficients indicate the change in the homicide rate to be expected from one unit change in execution risk. For example, a coefficient of $-0.000621$ (for $PXQ$ in the period 1935–1969) means that a reduction in the number of executions from ten to nine (per 100 convictions for murder) can be expected to increase the homicide rate from 5.00000 to 5.00061 (per 100,000 population), or to add twelve homicides for a population of 200 million.

**Table 9-6.** *Estimated Effects of Execution Risk on the Criminal Homicide Rate for Effective Periods with Successively Earlier Ending Dates*

| Ending Date of Effective Period | Six Alternative Measures of Execution Risk | | | | | |
|---|---|---|---|---|---|---|
| | $PXQ_1$ | $PXQ_2$ | $PXQ_{1-1}$ | $TXQ_1$ | $PDL_1$ | $P\hat{X}Q_1$ |
| 1969 | 0.00008 | −0.00061 | 0.00132 | 0.00135 | 0.00085 | 0.00054 |
| | (0.05) | (−0.73) | (1.02) | (0.64) | (0.43) | (0.33) |
| 1968 | 0.00038 | −0.00068 | 0.00126 | 0.00134 | 0.00085 | 0.00053 |
| | (0.25) | (−0.79) | (0.96) | (0.61) | (0.41) | (0.34) |
| 1967 | 0.00021 | −0.00051 | 0.00629 | 0.00106 | 0.00039 | 0.00016 |
| | (0.16) | (−0.63) | (0.56) | (0.47) | (0.18) | (0.11) |
| 1966 | −0.00023 | −0.00040 | −0.00013 | −0.00110 | −0.00046 | −0.00046 |
| | (−0.20) | (−0.52) | (−0.17) | (0.54) | (0.22) | (−0.38) |
| 1965 | −0.00027 | −0.00027 | −0.00038 | 0.00124 | 0.00087 | −0.00053 |
| | (−0.29) | (−0.40) | (−0.60) | (0.81) | (0.52) | (−0.55) |
| 1964 | 0.00009 | −0.00024 | −0.00034 | 0.00104 | 0.00123 | −0.00004 |
| | (0.11) | (−0.37) | (−0.57) | (0.78) | (0.78) | (−0.04) |
| 1963 | 0.00026 | −0.00019 | −0.00023 | 0.00123 | 0.00189 | 0.00022 |
| | (0.29) | (−0.28) | (−0.37) | (0.87) | (1.10) | (0.24) |
| 1962 | −0.00030 | −0.00023 | −0.00032 | 0.00058 | 0.00120 | −0.00035 |
| | (−0.38) | (−0.35) | (−0.56) | (0.53) | (0.80) | (−0.44) |
| 1961 | −0.00032 | 0.00027 | −0.00003 | 0.00147 | 0.00216 | −0.00044 |
| | (−0.50) | (0.45) | (−0.05) | (1.35) | (2.00) | (−0.68) |
| 1960 | −0.0004 | 0.00041 | 0.00005 | 0.00139 | 0.00235 | −0.00013 |
| | (−0.06) | (0.69) | (0.09) | (1.30) | (2.17) | (−0.20) |

*Note*: Variables are expressed in natural values whose coefficients are rounded to five decimal places, and $t$ values are shown in parentheses.

icant. Again, there is more evidence of a *positive* than of a negative effect.

The direction and size of the estimated coefficients do not appear to be systematically affected by the choice of time period. In other words, the years at the recent end of the time series, which suggest a deterrent effect when logarithmic values are used, yield no such suggestion with the natural values of the variables.

## Further Diagnosis of the Problems

In our review of the data used by Ehrlich we found serious problems of unreliability in the FBI-based measures of the dependent and deterrence variables, especially in the early years of his time series. In our review of his analytic approach we found serious problems with the temporal and functional specifications of his model, especially in the later years of his time series. Here we take a closer look at the two ends of his time series to see in more detail how they affected his analysis and why they have created the appearance of deterrence.

## The Recent Years

What is it about the middle and late 1960s that causes the measures of execution risk to show negative effects on the homicide rate when they are in logarithmic, but not in natural, form? This was a time when the national homicide rate was rising and executions literally came to an end. Hence execution risk—the number of executions among those convicted of murder—took on extremely low values. The logarithmic transformation emphasizes variations at the lower range of a variable. For example, a decline of 1 percentage point at lower levels of execution risk (from 2 to 1 executions per 100 convictions) will be equal to a drop of 30 percentage points at higher levels (from 60 to 30 executions per 100 convictions) when they are transformed into logarithms.

To show the effect of the logarithmic transformation on recent values of execution risk, we present in Table 9-7 the corresponding logarithmic and natural values of one of these measures $(PXQ_2)$ for the years 1950 through 1969. For purposes of comparison, these values are also expressed in terms of standard deviations (S.D.) from their respective means for the 1933–1969 period. In natural values the decline from 1960 to 1969 is about one-half standard deviation $(-0.521$ S.D.), whereas the decline in logarithms over this period is almost two-and-a-half standard deviations $(-2.487$ S.D.).[18] The point of greatest re-

**Table 9-7.** *Logarithmic and Natural Values of Execution Risk* $(PXQ_2)$ *for Each Year 1960–1969*

| Year | Logarithms | | Natural Values | |
|------|----------------|-----------------------------------------|----------------|-----------------------------------------|
|      | Absolute Value | Standard Deviations from the Mean | Absolute Value | Standard Deviations from the Mean |
| 1969 | −3.823 | −2.524 | 0.022 | −1.123 |
| 1968 | −3.873 | −2.554 | 0.021 | −1.124 |
| 1967 | −3.134 | −2.103 | 0.044 | −1.114 |
| 1966 | −3.774 | −2.494 | 0.023 | −1.123 |
| 1965 | −1.742 | −1.252 | 0.175 | −1.059 |
| 1964 | −1.456 | −1.077 | 0.233 | −1.034 |
| 1963 | −0.642 | −0.580 | 0.526 | −0.911 |
| 1962 | 0.174 | −0.081 | 1.191 | −0.630 |
| 1961 | −0.042 | −0.214 | 0.959 | −0.728 |
| 1960 | 0.229 | −0.048 | 1.257 | −0.602 |

18. There were no executions in 1968 and 1969. In order to extend the effective period of analysis through 1969, Ehrlich had to generate nonzero execution values for the years after 1967 since the logarithm of zero has not differed. He did this by supplying one (mythical) execution for 1968 and 1969 in the calculation of the other measures (see Ehrlich 1973, table 3, note b; 1975, table 2, note b).

duction in logarithmic values (−1.240 S.D.) comes between 1965 and 1966 when the number of executions nationally dropped from seven to one. In logarithms, this change is virtually twenty times the corresponding change in natural values (0.064 S.D.), five times the largest difference between consecutive years (1962–1963) in natural values (−0.281 S.D.) and more than twice the difference in natural values over the entire period from 1960 to 1968 (−0.521 S.D.).[19]

To show how the recent years affect the relationship between execution risk and homicide rates when these variables are in natural or in logarithmic form, we present the correlations between these two variables for periods with successively later ending dates in Table 9-8. Adding recent years to the time series in natural form has the modest effect of reducing the correlation by 0.176 (from 0.729 to 0.553). But when the annual values are in logarithmic form, the addition of these years dramatically reduces the correlation by 0.712 (from 0.835 to 0123). Indeed, in logarithmic values adding the one year 1966 to the period ending in 1965 reduces the correlation more than does adding all nine years after 1960 in natural values. The sensitivity of least squares regression to extreme values has given extraordinary weight to the very low level of execution risk during the period of relatively high homicides in the middle and late 1960s when these values are in logarithmic form.

What reality is there behind these statistics? Was there any con-

**Table 9-8.**  *Correlations of Execution Risk (PXQ$_2$) with Homicide Rates in Logarithmic and Natural Values for Effective Periods with Successively Earlier Ending Dates*

| EffectivePeriods | Logarithms | Natural Values |
|---|---|---|
| 1933–1969 | 0.123 | 0.553 |
| 1933–1968 | 0.270 | 0.644 |
| 1933–1967 | 0.442 | 0.720 |
| 1933–1966 | 0.563 | 0.758 |
| 1933–1965 | 0.748 | 0.773 |
| 1933–1964 | 0.806 | 0.772 |
| 1933–1963 | 0.858 | 0.763 |
| 1933–1962 | 0.857 | 0.750 |
| 1933–1961 | 0.846 | 0.741 |
| 1933–1960 | 0.836 | 0.729 |

19. In fact, the log transformation has so changed the form of the execution variable that the correlation between its logarithmic and natural versions for the period 1933–1969 is only 0.744, as compared with correlations of not less than 0.943 between logarithmic and natural versions of the other variables in the analysis for the same period. Notably, between execution rates in logarithmic and natural form for the period 1933–1960, the correlation is 0.954.

nection between the rising homicide rates and the declining risk of execution in the 1960s? Did homicide rates rise more in those states with declining executions and less (or actually fall) in those states with increasing executions—as deterrence theory would predict?

For the period 1962 to 1968, Table 9-9 shows year-to-year changes in homicide rates (relative to the national trend) among states that increased and those that decreased the number of executions imposed for murder between successive years. The changes are expressed in homicides per 100,000 persons and are obtained by subtracting annual changes in the national homicide rate from the corresponding changes in the states that decreased and increased executions. The table also reports the number of states that increased or decreased executions between successive years and the proportion of the nation's population they represent.

For the six annual changes between 1962 and 1968, states that reduced executions had homicide rates increase more than the national figure in two of the intervals but less than the national figure in four. For the five intervals in which at least some states increased executions, their homicide rates fell more than the national average in one case, were very nearly the same in one case, and actually rose more than the national average in the three other cases. That is to say, compared to the year-to-year changes in the national homicide rate, states that increased executions more often had increased homicide rates and those that reduced executions more often had reduced homicide rates. Thus, even in the middle and late 1960s changes in homicide rates were more often associated *positively* than negatively with changes in the risk of execution.[20]

Table 9-9 also shows that the use of capital punishment during this period was progressively restricted to a small minority of states with effective jurisdiction over a very small proportion of the nation's population. Even if the homicide rate in these states were responsive to changes in execution risk, such effects would hardly be perceptible in the national homicide figures. Moreover, by calculating execution risk for the nation as a whole in this period, Ehrlich overestimated the actual "pool of executables" and, consequently, further exaggerated the low levels of execution risk (especially in logarithms) for this period. Thus, apart from problems of temporal specification and functional form, it would have been more appropriate for Ehrlich to have ended the effective period of analysis earlier—perhaps after 1963, when only a minority of states representing a minority of the nation's population continued to impose executions.

20. Using more sophisticated statistical techniques, Forst (1977) also found a positive "counterdeterrent" effect of execution risk on homicide rates over the period 1960–1970.

**Table 9-9.**   Annual Changes in Criminal Homicide Rates among States that Have Increased and Decreased Executions Relative to Annual Homicide Rate Changes in the Nation as a Whole, 1962–1968

| Annual Change | States Decreasing Executions | | | States Increasing Executions | | |
|---|---|---|---|---|---|---|
| | Number of States | Proportion of Population | Homicide Rate Change Relative to Nation | Number of States | Proportion of Population | Homicide Rate Change Relative to Nation |
| 1962–1963 | 14 | 0.44 | −0.10 | 6 | 0.17 | −0.03 |
| 1963–1964 | 8 | 0.33 | 0.19 | 3 | 0.06 | −0.33 |
| 1964–1965 | 3 | 0.13 | −0.41 | 4 | 0.05 | 0.88 |
| 1965–1966 | 4 | 0.05 | −0.93 | 1 | 0.01 | 0.50 |
| 1966–1967 | 1 | 0.01 | 0.62 | 2 | 0.11 | 0.09 |
| 1967–1968 | 2 | 0.11 | −0.23 | — | — | — |

*Note*: States imposing executions for murder during this period are identified in Appendix A; criminal homicides annually by state were obtained from FBI *Uniform Crime Reports* for the United States (Table 3, 1962–1964; Table 4, 1965–1968); annual population estimates by state taken from U.S. Bureau of the Census (1971). Changes in homicide rates for groups of states that increased and decreased executions are essentially the average of the annual changes in the states in the group weighted by their respective population sizes. The data for these states are directly comparable with the national figures in the *Uniform Crime Reports*.

*The Early Years*

We have seen in the early years of the Uniform Crime Reporting Section that there was relatively little correspondence between FBI and Census annual homicide statistics (see Table 9-1); that arrest and conviction statistics were reported by relatively few agencies (see Figure 9-1); that the agencies reporting arrest and conviction statistics differed widely in population coverage (see Figure 9-2); and that the reported (and estimated) conviction rates, in particular, were far below those reported throughout the rest of the time series (see Table 9-2). By reproducing his regression analysis for effective periods with later beginning dates, Ehrlich may have hoped to test for the effects of measurement problems in the early years of the time series. But in so doing he has also given greater weight in the analysis to the later years, which are responsible for his "evidence" of a deterrent effect. To determine the effects of data inadequacies in the early years, we must first drop the idiosyncratic recent years, and then successively remove years from the beginning of the time series. Accordingly, we have performed regressions for periods with 1963 as the ending date and with successively later beginning dates from 1935 through 1940. The estimated coefficients for logarithmic and natural values of two measures of execution risk—$PXQ_{1-1}$ and $P\hat{X}Q_1$ are shown in Table 9-10.[21]

For each measure of execution risk in both logarithmic and natural form, the estimated effects tend to become more positive as years are

**Table 9-10.**   *Estimated Effects of Execution Risk on FBI-based Criminal Homicide Rate for Effective Periods Ending in 1963 with Successively Later Beginning Dates (t Value in Parentheses)*

| Beginning Date of Effective Period | Logarithms | | Natural Values | |
|---|---|---|---|---|
| | $PXQ_{1-1}$ | $P\hat{X}Q_1$ | $PXQ_{1-1}$ | $P\hat{X}Q_1$ |
| 1935 | — | 0.037 (1.02) | — | 0.000219 (0.24) |
| 1936 | 0.003 (0.08) | 0.034 (0.95) | −0.000225 (−0.37) | 0.000082 (0.08) |
| 1937 | 0.007 (0.19) | 0.038 (1.02) | −0.000079 (−0.12) | −0.000004 (−0.00) |
| 1938 | 0.038 (0.91) | 0.033 (0.95) | 0.001147 (1.10) | 0.000833 (0.64) |
| 1939 | 0.062 (1.39) | 0.061 (1.73) | 0.001858 (1.35) | 0.001772 (1.20) |
| 1940 | 0.095 (1.95) | 0.056 (1.56) | 0.004581 (3.03) | 0.001848 (1.19) |

21. In the interests of space and ease of exposition, we present only these two measures of execution risk in subsequent tabulations. Of all the measures, $PXQ1_{-1}$ is the one most commonly used by Ehrlich and $PXQ_1$ is perhaps least biased by measurement error since the (one year lagged) homicide rate is only one of eighteen variables that figure in its estimation.

dropped from the beginning of the series. In fact, the estimated effects are positive in all twelve cases with beginning dates of 1938, 1939, and 1940. Evidently, the problematic early years of the UCRS also contributed to the "appearance" of deterrent effects in Ehrlich's analysis.

We observed above that census-based homicide statistics are apt to be more reliable than the FBI figures, especially in the early years of the *UCR* when the national homicide estimates provided by these two sources are relatively uncorrelated (see Table 9-1). To explore the impact of *UCR* data inadequacies one step further, we have reproduced the analysis in Table 9-10 with census homicide data. Table 9-11 shows the Census-based estimates that correspond to the FBI-based estimates in Table 9-10.

The estimates based on census homicide data tend to confirm a negative bias in Ehrlich's results due to the early *UCR* data. As in Table 9-10, the estimated coefficients are predominantly positive; indeed, a few more of them (four as opposed to one) have reached $t$ values above 2.00. By contrast with Table 9-10, the variations in effective beginning date have relatively little impact on the estimated coefficients in Table 9-11; for each measure in logarithmic and natural form the estimates are relatively independent of beginning date. The main differences in estimated effects in Table 9-11 come between the alternative measures of execution risk and between their logarithmic and natural forms, apart from effective period of analysis.

It is commonly assumed that data inadequacies will have the conservative effect of making a hypothesis less likely to be confirmed. But for the deterrence hypothesis used here the opposite is true. With homicides represented in the numerator of the homicide rate and in the

**Table 9-11.** *Estimated Effects of Execution Risk and Execution Level on Census-based Willful Homicide Rate for Effective Periods Ending in 1963 with Successively Later Beginning Dates for Variables in Logarithmic and Natural Forms (t Value in Parentheses)*

| Beginning Date of Effective Period | Logarithms | | Natural Values | |
|---|---|---|---|---|
| | $PXQ_{1-1}$ | $P\hat{X}Q_1$ | $PXQ_{1-1}$ | $P\hat{X}Q_1$ |
| 1935 | — | −0.023 (−0.55) | — | 0.001222 (1.01) |
| 1936 | 0.052 (1.41) | −0.023 (−0.62) | 0.001681 (2.42) | 0.001085 (0.72) |
| 1937 | 0.053 (1.41) | −0.023 (−0.56) | 0.001545 (2.22) | 0.001324 (0.86) |
| 1938 | 0.057 (1.41) | −0.012 (−0.31) | 0.001586 (1.97) | 0.000826 (0.55) |
| 1939 | 0.065 (1.34) | −0.015 (−0.41) | 0.003865 (2.66) | 0.000501 (0.26) |
| 1940 | 0.051 (1.00) | −0.004 (−0.11) | 0.004773 (2.81) | 0.000866 (0.43) |

denominator of the execution rate, errors in the measurement of homicide will tend to produce an artifactual negative relationship between
these two variables (see note 9). Accordingly, the effects associated
with the measures of execution risk become more negative (less positive) with the addition of faulty homicide figures from the early years
of the UCR, but not with the addition of less faulty census homicide
data for these years. Thus, measurement problems in the early years
of the UCRS have tended not to obscure a true deterrent effect but to
generate an illusion of deterrence.

## Brutalizing vs. Deterrent Effects

From the standpoint of deterrence theory, the predominantly positive coefficients, especially the statistically significant ones, in Table
9-10 and 9-11 are anomalous. Indeed, they suggest that the risk of
execution actually stimulates homicide, or that the imposition of executions has a "brutalizing" effect on society. This is not a new idea.
It was advanced by Cesare di Beccaria, the first modern opponent of
capital punishment, more than two centuries ago, and by Robert Rantoul, Jr., who spearheaded the movement to ban public executions in
Massachusetts more than a century ago. But solid empirical support
for this idea is new. We refer here to the development of statistically
significant evidence of such a brutalizing effect over the period 1907–
1964 in New York state and to the recognition that the balance of
empirical evidence from the full range of previous studies weighs more
heavily on the side of a brutalizing than of a deterrent effect of the
death penalty (see Chapter 8).

If executions stimulate rather than inhibit homicide, the critical
causal variable may be the number of executions imposed—not the
risk of execution given conviction for criminal homicide. Indeed, the
positive coefficients for execution risk in Tables 9-10 and 9-11 may
mean that this variable is serving as a surrogate for execution level, or
the annual incidence of executions. If so, direct measures of the incidence of executions should show stronger positive effects than do these
measures of execution risk, and the positive effects should be stronger
with the more reliable homicide figures from the Census Bureau than
with the relatively faulty criminal homicide data from the FBI.

We employ two measures of execution level: $NXQ$ is simply the
number of executions imposed in the year of the presumed effect on
the homicide rate, and $N\hat{X}Q$ is the systematic part of $NXQ$ estimated
by means of the reduced form regression equation used to estimate
$P\hat{X}Q_1$ by Ehrlich (1973, table 4; 1975a, table 3). This second measure
is intended to adjust for the bias that might occur if the number of

executions in a given year is affected to some degree by the homicide rate in that year.

In Tables 9-12 and 9-13 we have substantiated these measures of execution level for Ehrlich's measures of execution risk in Tables 9-10 and 9-11, respectively. They show the estimated effects of $NXQ$ and $N\hat{X}Q$ on FBI homicides (Table 9-12) and census homicides (Table 9-13) in both logarithmic and natural form for effective periods ending in 1963 and beginning at successive points between 1935 and 1940. (Detailed regression results appear in equations 17.1 to 20.3, App. B of Bowers and Pierce 1975a.)

**Table 9-12.** *Estimated Effects of Execution Level on FBI-based Criminal Homicide Rate for Effective Periods Ending in 1963 with Successively Later Beginning Dates for Variables in Logarithmic and Natural Forms* (t *Value in Parentheses)*

| Beginning Date of Effective Period | Logarithms | | Natural Values | |
|---|---|---|---|---|
| | $NXQ_1$ | $N\hat{X}Q_1$ | $NXQ_1$ | $N\hat{X}Q_1$ |
| 1935 | 0.024 (0.63) | 0.114 (1.83) | 0.000021 (0.79) | 0.000055 (1.64) |
| 1936 | 0.019 (0.51) | 0.195 (2.22) | 0.000018 (0.66) | 0.000048 (1.43) |
| 1937 | 0.026 (0.67) | 0.235 (2.29) | 0.000043 (1.28) | 0.000077 (1.89) |
| 1938 | 0.041 (1.04) | 0.198 (2.26) | 0.000065 (1.84) | 0.000082 (2.05) |
| 1939 | 0.059 (1.39) | 0.144 (2.15) | 0.000059 (1.72) | 0.000059 (1.57) |
| 1940 | 0.074 (1.65) | 0.111 (2.00) | 0.000085 (2.37) | 0.000079 (2.09) |

**Table 9-13** *Estimated Effects of Execution Level on Census-based Willful Homicide Rate for Effective Periods Ending in 1963 with Successively Later Beginning Dates for Variables in Logarithmic and Natural Forms* (t *Value in Parentheses)*

| Beginning Date of Effective Period | Logarithms | | Natural Values | |
|---|---|---|---|---|
| | $NXQ_1$ | $N\hat{X}Q_1$ | $NXQ_1$ | $N\hat{X}Q_1$ |
| 1935 | 0.045 (1.10) | 0.053 (0.88) | 0.000079 (2.54) | 0.000107 (2.63) |
| 1936 | 0.075 (1.68) | 0.151 (1.94) | 0.000110 (4.17) | 0.000105 (3.43) |
| 1937 | 0.078 (1.67) | 0.177 (2.11) | 0.000113 (3.78) | 0.000108 (3.11) |
| 1938 | 0.082 (1.65) | 0.181 (2.06) | 0.000113 (3.51) | 0.000108 (2.96) |
| 1939 | 0.076 (1.51) | 0.153 (1.70) | 0.000113 (3.33) | 0.000111 (2.94) |
| 1940 | 0.061 (1.17) | 0.057 (0.79) | 0.000115 (3.08) | 0.000114 (2.77) |

The results in Table 9-12 are impressive. All twenty-four coefficients are positive; eight show $t$ values above 2.00. Note also that the positive coefficients and $t$ values do not drop off for the periods with earlier beginning dates as much as they did in Table 9-10. This may reflect the fact that these measures of execution level, unlike Ehrlich's measures of execution risk, do not incorporate UCRS arrest, conviction, and homicide figures, which are especially flawed in the early years of the reporting system. These results are clearly and uniformly consistent with the hypothesis that executions have a brutalizing effect on society.

The results in Table 9-13 are even more impressive. The census-based homicide measures yield stronger evidence of brutalization effects than do the *UCR*-based measures shown in Table 9-12. Again in Table 9-13, every one of the estimated coefficients is positive. In this case all but two of the $t$ values are greater than 1.00 and a majority (fourteen out of twenty-four) exceed a $t$ value of 2.00. Note further that the effects are strongest for the two measures of execution level in natural values. All twelve of them have $t$ values above 2.00; in fact, the lowest is 2.54. Moreover, the estimated effects are remarkably stable over variations in effective period and between $NXQ$ and $N\hat{X}Q$.

From this table, especially, it would appear that executions have a brutalizing effect. The fact that evidence of this effect is most pronounced among the natural versions of $NXQ_1$ and $N\hat{X}Q_1$ suggests that executions are equally likely to contribute to the homicide rate, apart from how many have been imposed in a given period. It is executions weighted equally, and not inversely, to the frequency of their occurrence that better predicts the homicide rate, according to these data. This is clearly consistent with the notion that each execution may evoke or trigger lethal violence in distressed or disturbed individuals.[22]

## Conclusion

Ehrlich's analysis has generated an illusion of deterrence in the relationship between execution risk and homicide rates. His so-called deterrent effects are a statistical artifact produced by the conjunction in his analysis of two disparate periods in the history of capital punishment, neither of which displays evidence of deterrence when examined separately. We have seen (in Tables 9-5 and 9-6) that Ehrlich's

22. The sociopsychological mechanisms through which such brutalizing effects may occur have been elaborated above (chapter 8) and similar contagion-of-violence effects have been documented in recent studies showing that well-publicized suicides and murders have been followed by periods of increased suicide and criminal violence, respectively (Phillips 1974; Berkowitz and McCauley 1971).

"deterrence findings" emerge *only* if the period of analysis is extended beyond 1965 to include years when executions had dwindled to one or two or had actually ceased, and *only* if logarithmic values of the variables are used, giving disproportionate weight to these recent years in the regression analysis.

It is true that homicide rates increased in the middle and late 1960s, but not as a result of declining executions in America. This was a period of generally rising crime rates and, in fact, other crimes of violence not punishable by death increased at a faster pace than did criminal homicides. Moreover, we have seen (in Table 9-9) that, compared with yearly changes in the national homicide rate from 1962 on, states with reduced executions tended to have reduced homicide rates and those with increased executions tended to have increased homicide rates.

The fact is that for the years when the death penalty was actively enforced in most states, Ehrlich's analytic framework reveals "brutalizing" rather than "deterrent" effects; executions appear to have provoked rather than to have prevented homicides. In particular, Ehrlich's analytic approach applied to the period 1935–1963 shows: (1) that execution risk tends to make a positive contribution to the homicide rate as measured by the FBI (Table 9-10) and by the Census Bureau (Table 9-11); (2) that the number of executions imposed (a better index of possible brutalizing effects) makes a stronger and more consistent positive contribution to the FBI homicide rate (Table 9-12); and (3) that the evident brutalizing effects become even stronger and more statistically significant with the more reliable census measure of willful homicide (Table 9-13).

We hasten to add that these results cannot be regarded as strong evidence of a brutalizing effect. Ehrlich's theoretical framework is hardly adequate as an explanatory model for the occurrence of criminal homicide, and it utilizes relatively few observations at a high level of aggregation. Yet these data do show mostly positive effects of execution risk and mostly significant positive effects of execution level for the period when the analytic model and the empirical data are less obviously flawed. This outcome clearly contradicts Ehrlich's claim that the death penalty has a deterrent effect and places his work among those recent empirical studies that point to a brutalizing effect of executions. If, at the time of its circulation, Ehrlich's research was sufficient to render the accumulated evidence "inconclusive" with respect to deterrence, this futher analysis of the data should be sufficent to rescind that judgment, if not to replace it with a judgment that the death penalty "brutalizes" society and is therefore "excessive" in violation of the Eighth Amendment prohibition against cruel and unusual punishment.

## Supplement: Variable Definitions and Data Sources

1. $(Q/N)°$   *Criminal Homicide Rate* = Number of criminal homicides per year/annual civilian population.
(a) $Q$ = Annual number of murders and nonnegligent manslaughters from 1933 to 1939. Revised figures, 1971, provided by the FBI. And as an alternative: $Q$ = annual number of willful homicides (minus the annual number of executions after 1948, when the two mortality categories were combined). Sources: for 1933–1936, U.S. Bureau of the Census (1933–1936); for 1937–1969, U.S. Bureau of the Census (1937–1945) and U.S. Public Health Service (1946–1969), all from annual reports.
(b) $N$ = Civilian population of the United States in 1,000s from 1933 to 1969 (U.S. Bureau of the Census 1973).

2. $P°a$   *Clearance Rate for Criminal Homicide* = Fraction of murders and nonnegligent manslaughters cleared by arrest (Federal Bureau of Investigation 1933–1969).

3. $P°c/a$   *Conviction Rate for Criminal Homicide* = Fraction of individuals found guilty as charged for murder and nonnegligent manslaughter (Federal Bureau of Investigation 1936–1939). After 1962 separate estimates are reported in the FBI's *Uniform Crime Reports* annual bulletin. Estimates from the time series which is continuous over the 1936 to 1969 period were chosen. These estimates were generally based on larger population bases. The value for 1961 is the average of the 1960 and 1962 estimates. Values for 1933 to 1935 were obtained from Ehrlich (1973).

4. $P°e/c$   *Execution Risk for Criminal Homicide ($PXQ_1$, $PXQ_2$, $PXQ_{1-1}$, $TXQ_1$, $PDL_1$, $P\hat{X}Q_1$)*. The measures of execution risk are all variations of the form $E/C$, where $C = Q \cdot P°a \cdot P°c/a$.
(a) $E$ = The number of executions for murder (U.S. Bureau of Prisons 1971).
(b) $C$ = Number of convictions for murder.
(c) $Q$ = The annual number of criminal homicides as defined in item 1(a).
(d) $P°a$, $P°c/a$ are as defined in items 2 and 3.

5. $L$   *Labor Force Participation Rates*. For 1940–1969, $L = CL/(TN - TL + CL)$. For 1933–1939, $L = CL/(N - P13)$.
(a) $CL$, $TL$ = The civilian and total labor force in 1,000s from 1933 to 1969 (U.S. Bureau of Labor Statistics 1971).
(b) $TN$ = Total noninstitutional population from 1940 to 1969 (U.S. Bureau of Labor Statistics 1971).
(c) $N$ = Annual civilian population as defined in item 1(b).
(d) $P13$ = Annual population thirteen years old and under from 1933 to 1939 (U.S. Bureau of the Census 1965b).

6. $U$   *Unemployment Rate of the Civilian Labor Force, 1933 to 1969*. (U.S. Bureau of Labor Statistics 1971).

7. A   *Fraction of the Resident Population Fourteen to Twenty-Four Years of Age. A = (P1424)/(RP).*

(a) *P1424* = Number of persons fourteen to twenty-four years of age in the resident population. Sources: for 1933–1939, U.S. Bureau of the Census (1965b); for 1940–1949, U.S. Bureau of the Census (1954); for 1950–1959, U.S. Bureau of the Census (1965a); for 1960–1969, U.S. Bureau of the Census (1974).

(b) *RP* = Residential population in 1,000s. References same as given in 7(a) for each of the respective time periods.

8. $Y_p$   *Friedman's Estimate of Real Permanent Income per Capita.* The following equation was used to compute $Y_p$:

$$Y_t = (.330)\ Y_{t-1} + (.226)\ Y_{t-2} + (.154)\ Y_{t-3} + (.106)\ Y_{t-4} + (.072)\ Y_{t-5} + (.049)\ Y_{t-6} + (.033)\ Y_{t-7} + (.023)\ Y_{t-8}$$

(a) The weights in the above equation were obtained from Karni, Table 33 (1971).

(b) $Y_{t-1}$ through $Y_{t-8}$ are logarithmic estimates of per capita real national income for the years 1925 to 1969. The national income figures were provided by Karni (1971). Population figures for per capita estimates for 1925–1929 were obtained from U.S. Bureau of the Census (1973); for 1930–1968, from U.S. Department of Commerce (1969).

(c) The per capita income was measured in terms of 1919 dollars using a price deflator obtained from Karni (1971).

9. NW   *Percentage of Nonwhite Residential Population.* References same as given in item 7(a) for each of the respective time periods.

10. N   *Civilian Population in 1,000s.* Reference same as given in item 1(b).

11. XGOV  *Per Capita Real Expenditures on All Governments in Millions of Dollars. XGOV = (FE + SLE − D)/RP\*PD\*10.*

(a) *FE, SLE* = Federal and state/local expenditure on all governments. Sources: for 1933–1938, U.S. Department of Commerce (1960); for 1939–1965, U.S. Department of Commerce (1966); for 1966–1969, U.S. Department of Commerce (1970).

(b) *D* = National defense expenditures. Sources: for 1933–1938, U.S. Department of Commerce (1960); for 1939–1952, purchases of goods and services, U.S. Department of Commerce (1966); for 1953–1969, purchases of goods and services, U.S. Department of Commerce (1970).

(c) *RP* = Residential population as defined in item 7(b).

(d) *PD* = Implicit price deflator for all governments. Sources: for 1932–1965, U.S. Department of Commerce (1966); for 1966–1969, U.S. Department of Commerce (1970).

12. $XPOL_{-1}$ *Per Capita Real Expenditures on Police Lagged One Year in Dollars. XPOL = POLE\*100,000/RP\*PD.*

(a) *POLE* = Total police expenditure. Sources: for 1932–1966, U.S. Bureau of the Census (1969); for 1967–1969, U.S. Bureau of the Census (1971).

(b) *RP* = Residential population as defined in item 7(b).

(c) *PD* = Price deflator as defined in item 11(d).

# 10

## THE EXERCISE OF CAPITAL DISCRETION

The *Furman* decision was not a clear statement reflecting a single perspective on the ills of capital punishment. Rather, it was nine separate statements reflecting the particular views and concerns of each justice. Of the five concurring justices, Brennan and Marshall found that the death penalty was cruel and unusual punishment per se, arbitrariness aside; Marshall also found that it was used in a discriminatory way against blacks and other minorities. Justices Douglas, Stewart, and White, on the other hand, found the death penalty unconstitutional because of the arbitrariness of its administration under then existing statutes. Douglas identified discrimination against minorities, blacks, and disadvantaged persons as an aspect of the arbitrariness. But Stewart and White described the arbitrariness in different terms—as "freakish," "random," and "rare"—like being "struck by lightning" or being "chosen in a lottery." These two pivotal members of the *Furman* plurality thus adopted formulations of the arbitrariness as unsystematic in nature: dissociated from specific extralegal sources, such as race or class, that might exercise a systematic effect. The problem, according to their diagnosis, was like that faced by a traveler following an unclear or imprecise map; he must rely on intuition and guesswork and is thus apt to make mistakes. The solution for the traveler is, obviously, a better map.

By a similar logic, the Court blamed this arbitrariness on shortcomings in the pre-*Furman* capital statutes. These laws provided unclear or insufficient guidance to those who must decide whether to impose a sentence of death. The unguided, standardless exercise of discretion in capital sentencing is subject to errors of judgment in much the same way as is the traveler with an inadequate map. The solution was the formulation of capital statutes with clear standards that would guide juries in sentencing (that is, explicit aggravating and mitigating circumstances), with procedures that would remove these decisions from extraneous influences (that is, separate guilt and sentencing hearings), and with provisions that would subject these decisions to oversight (that is, automatic appellate review). This was the remedy approved four years after *Furman* in the *Gregg* decision, which upheld the capital statutes of Florida, Georgia, and Texas with the concurrence of Justices White and Stewart of the *Furman* plurality.

There is, however, another view of the arbitrariness found unacceptable in *Furman*. The fact that some persons are sentenced to death and others are not for essentially the same crime is not, according to this interpretation, simply the result of confusion owing to insufficient guidance, insulation, and oversight in the exercise of discretion. Rather, it exists because those who exercise such discretion are consistent *and* because their behavior reflects systematic, though perhaps unrecognized, extralegal influences such as race, class, and origin.

Behind this alternative diagnosis is a perspective on capital punishment that has been developed in the preceding chapters of this volume, especially Chapter 5. It holds that death as punishment is unique in its power to express community sentiments of condemnation, and will, therefore, be imposed on those criminals who most offend the community conscience, not strictly because they are the most legally culpable, but because they violate social mores and boundaries. Thus offenses will be viewed as more or less shocking and abhorrent depending on who the victims and offenders are in social, not just legal, terms. Persons disfavored or disadvantaged by class, race, or origin will be disproportionately singled out for capital punishment, especially when their victims are members of the dominant group in the community. And the death penalty's expressive functions will be sought especially when cultural mores and boundaries are threatened by social change, when social change is associated with rising crime rates, and when those crime rates are attributed to socially disfavored or disadvantaged persons. Whether it is legally justified, community sentiments will call for capital punishment under such conditions.

As a representative cross-section of the community, the jury embodies community sentiments. Jurors are not like travelers in an unfamiliar territory. They have their own internalized maps of the social landscape. Jurors will have difficulty replacing their socially conditioned views of victims and offenders with strictly legal considerations, especially for the crimes they find most shocking and abhorrent. Thus, interpretations of statutory aggravating and mitigating circumstances in the sentencing decision are apt to be colored by extralegal considerations. Nor will extralegal influences be restricted to the sentencing process; indeed, according to this view, they will be deeply imbedded at other discretion points in the processing of potentially capital cases.

Prosecutors, who are typically elected, must be sensitive to community sentiments and reactions to crime, which they will encounter in the media, among associates, and from police, families of victims, and prominent community spokesmen. In addition to the courtroom presentation of a case, such sentiments and reactions may influence a host of less public actions that greatly affect the likelihood of a death sentence: whether to bring a capital charge, whether to accept a guilty plea in return for a reduced charge or sentence, whether to offer a reduced charge or sentence to one defendant in return for testimony against another, whether to develop evidence of statutory aggravating circumstances, and whether to seek a death sentence given conviction. To maintain community support and to win reelection, prosecutors are likely to seek the death penalty when the community wants it, apart from strictly legal considerations.

Defense attorneys in capital cases are also affected by community sentiments. A disproportionate number of them are court-appointed rather than privately retained attorneys, who work with severely limited resources for conducting investigations, hiring expert witnesses, and generally preparing an effective capital defense. Intense community hostility toward defendants can add to the difficulty of investigating the case, identifying rebuttal witnesses, and developing evidence of mitigation. Community sentiment may also develop into mistrust or animosity toward the lawyer who aggressively attempts to build a strong trial record, to expose police, prosecutorial, or judicial errors, and to challenge the constitutionality of capital punishment itself. For court-appointed attorneys, in particular, this sort of defense can provoke impatience and resentment from the bench, and thus jeopardize future court appointments. In other words, the system assigns the defense of most capital cases, where the defendant's life is at stake and extralegal influences are strongly felt, to the least experienced, resourceful, and independent members of the bar.

Nor are judges—federal, state, or local—immune from extralegal influences. Like prosecutors, defense attorneys, and jurors, they are the products of the cultures and the communities from which they come. In many places, state and local judges, like prosecutors, are elected and thus accountable to the public. Appellate court judges are, of course, usually removed from the specific influences at work in the local community where a crime occurs, but they are not removed from the broader historical, political, and social context that has supported the arbitrary and discriminatory imposition of capital punishment. Indeed, most appellate court judges are only a step or two removed from the trial court where they themselves may have imposed the death penalty.

To summarize the argument: If the death penalty exists for the extralegal functions it serves, and if the arbitrariness found unacceptable in *Furman* is a systematic reflection of this fact, as our theory maintains, then this arbitrariness should be evident in the decisions of participants at the various stages throughout the processing of potentially capital cases. Statutory reforms designed to regulate the exercise of discretion at one stage of the process, such as those approved in *Gregg*, are predicated on a diagnosis that fails to recognize the pervasive and systematic character of the problem. To the extent that such reforms are effective at one point in the process, they may simply produce a shift or displacement of arbitrariness to other points in the process.

In the following sections of this chapter, we turn our attention to the decisions and actions of those involved at four stages in the handling of potentially capital cases: the exercise of prosecutorial discretion in bringing charges and going to trial; the allocation and effectiveness of defense services; the decisions to seek and to impose the death sentence upon convicted offenders; and the proportionality review of death sentences by state appeals courts. We conclude this chapter with a closer look at the exercise of discretion in the federal appeals process.

## Prosecutorial Discretion in Charging and Trying Cases

A beneficial effect of post-*Furman* guided discretion statutes, according to Justice White in *Gregg* (1976, 2937), is that prosecutors will be guided in their exercise of discretion by the same statutory aggravating and mitigating standards "as those by which a jury will decide questions of guilt and sentence." Our earlier analysis in Chapter 7, however, suggested that in the hands of prosecutors the statutory guidelines approved in *Gregg* may be serving as instruments of, rather than curbs on, arbitrariness and discrimination early in the handling of potentially capital cases. Using data on the grand jury indictments of persons charged with criminal homicide in Florida, we observed that indictment disparities by race and location within the state contribute substantially to the overall level of arbitrariness and discrimination in the process leading to a death sentence (Tables 7-7, 7-8, 7-12, and 7-13). These data suggested, further, that racial considerations lead prosecutors to "upgrade" some cases by alleging an aggravating felony circumstance or charging the defendant with an accompanying felony, and to "downgrade" others by ignoring evidence in police reports or withholding an accompanying charge, depending on the race of the offender and the victim (Tables 7-9 and 7-10).[1]

Using the same Florida court processing data, we can now carry the analysis of prosecutorial discretion a step further by examining factors that may affect the prosecutor's ability to obtain a first degree murder indictment. Using the 1976–1977 sample of persons charged with criminal homicide in twenty Florida counties (as described in Chapter 7 and its Supplement B), we have conducted a multiple regression analysis (see Table 10-1) to determine how the indictment decision was affected by extralegal factors such as race, region, and attorney type, and a broader group of legally relevant factors than we have previously taken into account.[2]

The aggravating circumstances include: the presence of an accompanying felony; more than one alleged offender; more than one murder victim; the fact that the murder victim was old, young, or female (suggesting victim vulnerability); and the use of a gun as the murder weapon (suggesting intent to kill). (These are the same aggravating factors used in Table 7-19.) The mitigating factors include evidence from the court record that: the defendant was an accomplice or accessory to the crime, but not the triggerman or actual killer; the crime was the result of, or precipitated by, an argument, dispute, or quarrel; and the offender was less than eighteen years of age.

Among the factors that should *not* systematically affect the handling of the defendant's case, we have included three variables designating the racial character of the crime: black-kills-white, white-kills-white, and white-kills-black (black-kills-black is omitted); two variables identifying the location of the crime within the state: the northern region (equivalent to the judicial circuits classified as North/Panhandle in Table 7-4) and the central region (equivalent to the same judicial circuits classified as Central in Table 7-4)—the circuits of the southern

---

1. This study of the upgrading and downgrading of cases in terms of an aggravating felony circumstance is now being extended (Radelet and Pierce 1983). With additional information on homicide victims from the Florida Bureau of Vital Statistics, Michael Radelet has succeeded in matching many more police reports and court records. The pattern observed in Table 7-9 continues to hold and is more statistically reliable in this larger sample of cases. These data show, moreover, that in upgraded cases (those having a felony circumstance added in the court case records when the police reports indicated no such circumstances), prosecutors were less likely to offer or accept a plea bargain—further suggesting their determination to seek a death sentence. Similar patterns are now under investigation in South Carolina by Joseph Jacoby and Raymond Paternoster (1982). See also Paternoster (1983).
2. These were restricted to variables in the Florida court processing data with information unavailable on no more than 15 percent of the cases.

region are omitted; and two variables indicating type of attorney: private attorneys appointed to the case and paid for their services by the court, and attorneys employed as public defenders by the state to provide services to indigent clients (privately retained counsel is the omitted category).

The interpretation of the regression coefficient is straightforward. All variables in the analysis have been entered in binary forms,[3] hence the regression coefficient for a given variable corresponds to the percentage difference in first degree murder indictments between the category of that variable in the table and the omitted or reference category (controlling statistically for all other variables in the analysis). For instance, a coefficient of .25 for felony-related killing corresponds to a 25-point difference in the percentage receiving first degree murder indictments between cases with and cases without an accompanying felony, controlling for the other variables entered into the regression analysis. In cases where several mutually exclusive binary variables have been constructed, as with race, region, and attorney type, the reference category is restricted to those cases excluded from all the component variables. That is, they share the common reference category of the cases they jointly exclude. Consequently, for example, the coefficients for the three racial combinations in Table 10-1 (0.19, 0.15, and -0.08) represent the percentage difference in first degree murder indictments between the respective categories and the black-kills-black category (the jointly excluded cases). In the 1976–1977 sample, data are available on all seventeen of these variables for 508, or 66 percent, of the 771 cases.[4] The regression results appear in Table 10-1.

The analysis shows that four legally aggravating factors play a substantial role in determining a first degree murder indictment; a felony-related killing has the greatest effect, followed by multiple offenders, multiple victims, and female victims. Three of the four variables show effects significant beyond the .01 probability level. Contrary to expectation, one other factor advanced as a mitigating circumstance, namely, the offender's youthfulness, appears also to contribute to a first degree murder indictment, though not significantly so. The remaining legally relevant factors show slight effects, not exceeding coefficients of .10.

Critically, the variables designating racial combinations show sub-

3. The characteristic or category of the variable identified in the table is scored "1" and all other cases are given a value of "0".
4. Michael Radelet has supplemented the information available at the time of our earlier analysis in Table 7-7 (column 1) and Table 7-12 (column 1) with additional data on race of victim and date and location of offense from the Florida vital statistics records. The 1976–1977 sample of criminal homicide arraignments used here excludes four cases used by Radelet (1981).

**Table 10-1.** *Estimated Effects of Legal and Extralegal Factors on First Degree Murder Indictment Among Persons Charged with Criminal Homicide in Florida, 1976–1977*

| Variables | Regression Coefficients |
|---|---|
| A. *Legally Relevant Factors* | |
| Felony-related killing | 0.25 ** |
| More than one offender | 0.20 ** |
| More than one victim | 0.18 |
| Female victim | 0.18 ** |
| Victim 60 years or older [a] | 0.04 |
| Victim 16 years or younger [a] | −0.07 |
| Gun used as murder weapon | −0.06 |
| Defendant accessory | −0.04 |
| Defendant 18 years or younger | 0.12 |
| Quarrel precipitated killing | −0.04 |
| B. *Race* [b] | |
| Black kills white | 0.19 * |
| White kills white | 0.15 ** |
| White kills black | −0.08 |
| C. *Region* [c] | |
| North | −0.02 |
| Central | 0.10 * |
| D. *Type of Attorney* [d] | |
| Court-appointed | 0.17 ** |
| Public defender | 0.03 |
| Adjusted R² | 0.27 |
| Number of Cases | 508 |

[a]Victims aged 17–59 is the reference category.
[b]Black kills black is the reference category.
[c]Southern region of Florida is the reference category (as defined in Table 7-4).
[d]Privately retained attorneys is the reference category.

*p < .05, *t* test
**p < .01, *t* test

stantial and significant effects. That a black has killed a white is virtually as strong a predictor of a first degree indictment as any of the legally relevant factors except felony circumstance.[5] When the offender and victim are both white, the effect is not quite as strong but even more significant statistically. Together, of course, these two racial variables represent a white-victim effect on first degree indictment that

5. Because there are *relatively* few black-kills-white cases among all criminal homicide arraignments in these Florida counties, the statistical significance of this effect ( a .03 probability) is less than that of some other variables showing comparable regression coefficients.

is statistically significant well beyond the effect of either alone. A further examination of the data shows white-victim cases tend to be more aggravated, but the remaining strongly significant race-of-victim effect seen in Table 10-1 means that race figures prominently in the first degree indictment decision above and beyond legally relevant considerations.

The location of the crime within the state is also significant. The analysis shows a significantly higher level of first degree murder indictments in the central region of Florida (the southern region is the reference category), when other legally relevant factors have been controlled. Moreover, the disparity is even greater and more highly significant if we compare this region with the rest of Florida (the combined southern and northern regions are the reference category). In other words, the chances of a first degree murder indictment for otherwise comparable cases were significantly greater in the central region than elsewhere in Florida.

Finally, the analysis shows that defendants with court-appointed attorneys were far more likely to receive a first degree murder indictment (compared to those with privately retained attorneys as the reference category). The data further indicate that court-appointed attorneys typically handle more difficult cases in terms of legally aggravating and mitigating considerations than do public defenders or privately retained counsel. But the highly significant regression coefficient for court-appointed attorneys in the presence of these legally aggravating and mitigating factors strongly suggests that these attorneys are less effective in averting a first degree murder indictment than are other types of attorneys.

Thus, the statistical evidence now shows more emphatically than did the evidence presented in Chapter 7 that race and location are powerful and independent influences on the likelihood of a first degree murder indictment; it is important to remember that the prosecutor exercises almost total discretion over the decision to indict for first degree murder at this early stage in the process that leads to a death sentence. The effects of race and place remain strong not only in the presence of felony circumstance, but also with control for other legally relevant considerations.

How does this statistical evidence square with the experiences of those who handle capital cases? The decisions of prosecutors to bring a capital charge and to take such a charge to trial have recently been examined by Mary Brennan (1982), who interviewed judges, prosecutors, and defense attorneys for the Florida Justice Institute. The sample was drawn from the same counties as the Florida court processing data presented earlier in Tables 7-7 through 7-13 and 10-1; many of the respondents had participated in the cases that constitute the data base for the analyses presented earlier.

The respondents reported a wide range of extralegal influences on prosecutors' decisions to charge and try capital cases. The answers of a state circuit court judge illustrate the point. To the question, "What influences the decision to indict for first degree murder?" he answered:

> A high publicity case is more likely to be filed first degree murder. [Also] pressure from the police—the police will convince themselves they've got a better case than they do, and the Assistant State Attorney assigned to charge the case may not be strong enough to stand up to a particular police investigator.

And in response to the question, "What influences the decision to take the case to trial on a first degree murder charge?" he answered:

> Facts of the case plus how well the attorneys know each other and how closely they worked together. You pay more attention to a good attorney than one you know is a lightweight, when he communicates with you about the case. . . .
>
> [Also] pressure from the top, the supervisor of the Assistant State Attorney assigned to try the case. Even if the Assistant State Attorney assigned to try the case knows he can't win it, he may go to trial anyway because a directed verdict by the judge [a ruling that first degree murder is not proved as a matter of law so the jury is not allowed to convict for first degree murder regardless of the original charge] looks better publicity-wise on the elected State Attorney's record than the office dropping [dismissing or reducing] the case.

Pressure from the police, the division of responsibility in the prosecutor's office, the prosecutor's relationship with the defense attorney, and the political advantage of seeking a death sentence even when the facts of the case do not warrant it are only a few of the extralegal considerations described by respondents. A more comprehensive picture emerges from the answers of all respondents. The two questions about filing a capital charge and taking such a charge to trial yielded some 188 codable responses from sixteen judges, sixteen prosecutors, and thirty-eight defense attorneys.[6] These responses have been grouped into fifteen categories under four general headings in Table 10-2.

---

6. Responses to these two questions were forwarded to us for tabulation and do not appear in the Florida Justice Institute's report (Brennan 1982), which deals chiefly with defense services.

**Table 10-2.** *Factors Affecting the Decision to Bring a Capital Charge and to Take Such a Charge to Trial, According to Florida Judges, Prosecutors, and Defense Attorneys*

|  | No. of Responses | Percentage of Responses |
|---|---|---|
| A. *Legal Factors or Considerations* | 75 | 39.9 |
| A1. Facts of the case, fact pattern, facts (e.g.: do facts fit the definition of first degree murder?) | 20 | 10.6 |
| A2. Aggravating or mitigating considerations (presence, number, relative weight) | 16 | 8.5 |
| A3. Particular aggravating circumstance (prior record, accompanying felony, premeditation, heinous or execution-type killing) | 16 | 8.5 |
| A4. Overall strength of case, probability of conviction | 13 | 6.9 |
| A5. Evidence, quality of evidence/witness credibility, reliability | 10 | 5.3 |
| B. *Personal Orientations or Values of Prosecutors* | 30 | 15.9 |
| B1. Aggressiveness, competitiveness, ambition (e.g.: personal pride, win-loss record, notch-in-the-gun syndrome, desire to be reelected) | 16 | 8.5 |
| B2. Orientation toward punishment (deterrence, retribution, appropriateness) | 8 | 4.2 |
| B3. Attitude toward particular defendant or victim (prominence, character, class, race) | 6 | 3.2 |
| C. *Situational Pressures or Constraints in Handling Cases* | 44 | 23.5 |
| C1. Plea-bargaining strategy, opposing counsel (e.g.: indict high to force plea, plead second degree for accomplice testimony, experience of defense counsel) | 19 | 10.1 |
| C2. Time, caseload, office policies, judge's reputation | 11 | 5.9 |
| C3. Influence of victim's family (e.g.: victim's family wants death, can't reduce charge) | 8 | 4.3 |
| C4. Pressure from police (e.g.: police press for first degree charge) | 6 | 3.2 |
| D. *Social Influences or Pressures from the Community* | 39 | 20.7 |
| D1. Media coverage, publicity, notoriety (including effects on political climate, plea bargaining, reelection) | 17 | 9.0 |
| D2. Public opinion, reaction (community conscience, confidence, outrage, anger) | 17 | 9.0 |
| D3. Political/racial climate (politics, political realities, race, racism) | 5 | 2.7 |

Respondents mentioned more extralegal considerations, including personal orientation of the prosecutor, situational pressures and constraints in handling a case, and social influences and pressures from the community, than factors falling within the general category labeled "legal factors or considerations." The personal characteristics of prosecutors most frequently mentioned were aggressiveness, competitiveness, and ambition (B1). The only legal consideration that is cited more often than these personal attributes is "facts of the case" (A1). Among situational pressures and constraints, most common were those referring to plea bargaining (C1). This category includes statements such as "indict high to force a plea," and "plead to second degree murder for accomplice testimony." Two themes were prominently mentioned under "social influences or pressures from the community": media coverage, publicity, and notoriety (D1), and public opinion and reactions (D2). Only two other specific categories, facts of the case (A1) and plea bargaining (C1), were more frequently mentioned.

Thus, the influence of extralegal considerations on the decision to bring a capital charge and to take it to trial is broadly recognized by those who prosecute, defend, and judge such cases. One could quarrel with the placement of certain categories of response in the general groupings in Table 10-2. For instance, pressures from the victim's family (C3) or from the police (C4) might be regarded as social rather than situational factors; the use of a single aggravating factor to the exclusion of others (A3) might be considered a personal predisposition of the prosecutor rather than a strictly legal consideration. But these objections do not alter the fundamental picture of a decision-making process responding to social influences from the community, situational pressures in handling cases, and personal orientations of prosecutors, as well as legal considerations.

It should not, therefore, be surprising to learn that the first man executed against his will in the post-*Furman* era may have been a victim of prosecutorial arbitrariness. According to former United States Attorney General Ramsey Clark, who entered John Spinkelink's last appeal, prejudices, political ambitions, local idiosyncracies, and community attitudes all figured in the prosecutor's decision to seek the death penalty. In his words (Clark, 1979, 402):

> This should not have been a capital case. . . . Here there was a claim of self-defense, that the defendant had been homosexually raped and his money taken from him, that he had entered the motel room to recover his money and go his own way. The other man [murder victim] was older, bigger, stronger, had spent decades in prison and was in violation of parole at the time. . . . The death penalty is not normally asked for or given in such cases.
>
> But Leon County, Florida, is special. More than half of the people on death rows in the nation [as of 1979] are in three Southern states— Florida, Texas and Georgia. This unequal distribution only begins to suggest the severely limited number of jurisdictions prosecuting capital

cases. Most of the more than 300 men in these three states were convicted in a handful of counties in each state. The prejudices of the prosecutors, political ambitions, local idiosyncracies, and community attitudes in these counties were the determinants. Had these events occurred in nearly any of America's 3,000 other counties—or even in Leon County at another time—it is very unlikely the prosecutor would have asked for death.

## Allocation and Effectiveness of Defense Services

People will readily say that a good lawyer can frequently affect the outcome of a case. The unavoidable implication is that those who can afford to retain a good lawyer will have a distinct advantage in the legal process. Does it work the other way as well? Are impoverished defendants who must rely on public defenders or court-appointed attorneys at a distinct disadvantage in the legal process? Type of attorney is not a legally relevant factor that should influence the outcome of any case, certainly including the sentence imposed in a capital case.

We have seen in Table 10-1 that defendants with court-appointed attorneys are more likely to be indicted for first degree murder than those with public defenders or privately retained counsel, and that this is not simply because the most difficult cases devolve on court-appointed attorneys. Indeed, in equally death-prone cases, court-appointed attorneys seem to be less effective than other types of attorney in maneuvering to avert a first degree murder indictment. For whatever reasons, they appear to provide less effective defense services at this early stage in the process. Is this disadvantage to their clients cumulative? Does the defendant with a court-appointed attorney lose ground at each successive stage of the process?

To learn more about how attorney type affects the defendant's chances of receiving a death sentence, we take another step in our analysis of the Florida court processing data.[7] Here we examine the separate and joint effects of attorney type, race, region, and legally relevant factors on the likelihood of a first degree murder conviction from the sample of those indicted for first degree murder from 1973 through 1977. The independent variables and the analytic procedures are the same as those used in Table 10-1. The difference is that we are now considering only those defendants from the Florida sample indicted for first degree murder. The data on all variables are available for 613 or 59 percent of the 1045 cases in the 1973–1977 combined

7. Linda Foley and Richard Powell (1982) have reported differences in the likelihood of death sentence by attorney type, but without controlling for other factors associated with the imposition of a death sentence.

sample. (These data correspond to those reported in column 2 of Tables 7-7, 7-8, 7-12, and 7-13.) The results of the regression analysis appear in Table 10-3.

Again, as with first degree murder indictment, felony circumstance, number of offenders, and female victim are statistically significant predictors, and number of victims is comparable in magnitude but not significant among the legally aggravating factors. There are, however, two distinct differences between Tables 10-1 and 10-3 in the presumably mitigating factors. First, the youthfulness of the defendant has become a significant mitigating factor in the process leading to conviction, as compared to its apparently aggravating role at indict-

**Table 10-3.** *Estimated Effects of Legal and Extralegal Factors on First Degree Murder Conviction among Persons Indicted for First Degree Murder in Florida, 1973–1977*

| Variables | Regression Coefficients |
|---|---|
| **A.  *Legally Relevant Factors*** | |
| Felony-related killing | 0.15** |
| More than one offender | 0.10* |
| More than one victim | 0.11 |
| Female victim | 0.13** |
| Victim 60 years or older[a] | −0.06 |
| Victim 16 years or younger[a] | 0.09 |
| Gun used as murder weapon | −0.03 |
| Defendant accessory | −0.29** |
| Defendant 18 years or younger | −0.16** |
| Quarrel precipitated killing | 0.02 |
| **B.  *Race*[b]** | |
| Black kills white | 0.29** |
| White kills white | 0.18** |
| White kills black | −0.07 |
| **C.  *Region*[c]** | |
| North | 0.07 |
| Central | 0.13** |
| **D.  *Type of Attorney*[d]** | |
| Court-appointed | 0.06 |
| Public defender | 0.00 |
| Adjusted $R^2$ | 0.14 |
| Number of Cases | 613 |

[a]Victims aged 17–59 is the reference category.
[b]Black kills black is the reference category.
[c]Southern region of Florida is the reference category (as defined in Table 7-4).
[d]Privately retained attorneys is the reference category.

*$p < .05$, $t$ test
**$p < .01$, $t$ test

ment. Secondly, the fact that a defendant was an accessory rather than the triggerman significantly reduces his chances of a first degree murder conviction. The corresponding reduction in the coefficient for multiple offenders from Table 10-1 to Table 10-3 suggests that prosecutors will typically indict all offenders for first degree murder in multiple-offender cases in order to bargain for testimony that will convict the alleged triggerman. Again, the age of the victim, quarrel as a precipitating factor, and a gun as the murder weapon show little effect in the presence of the other predictors.

Again, race and region are statistically powerful determinants independent of legally relevant considerations. Black-kills-white has as strong an effect as any other variable in the analysis. In fact, the effect on a black offender of having killed a white rather than a black person (the reference category) is equivalent to the effect on any offender of committing the murder rather than being an accessory to the crime. White-kills-white is the third strongest predictor of a first degree murder conviction; race of defendant given a white victim has a nearly significant effect (p = .067) on the likelihood of a first degree murder conviction, controlling for legally relevant factors.[8] The racial bias is stronger in the conviction process for first degree murder than it is at indictment (see Table 10-1).

Region has a statistically significant impact as well in the conviction stage of the process, and again it is the central region of Florida where first degree murder convictions are most likely compared with otherwise comparable cases in the rest of the state. The northern region also shows a greater likelihood of first degree murder conviction than the southern region (as the reference category), but the difference does not reach statistical significance. Thus, there are substantial regional disparities in the likelihood that a person indicted for first degree murder will actually be convicted on that charge, and this pattern is compounded when we consider the indictment and conviction stages together.

Attorney type appears to have less effect on conviction than it did on indictment, and less effect on conviction than race, region, or legally relevant factors do. In otherwise comparable cases, court-appointed attorneys are less likely to avert a first degree murder conviction than either public defenders or privately retained counsel, a finding consistent with the pattern at indictment, though the effect shown in Table 10-3 is not statistically significant.

That attorney type appears to have less effect on conviction is

8. To estimate this effect we have omitted the white-kills-white category and included black-kills-black in the regression equation. Black-kills-white shows a regression coefficient of .11 (equal to the difference between .29 and .18 in Table 10-1), with a probability of p = .067.

contrary to our expectation. One reason the difference at conviction is not greater may be that privately retained counsel and public defenders are more effective than court-appointed attorneys in negotiating an agreement that the prosecutor not ask for the death penalty in return for a guilty plea to first degree murder from the defendant. The data to be presented in Table 10-4 bear further on this possibility.

Most members of the bar interviewed in the Florida Justice Institute study (Brennan 1982, 16-18) believe that type of attorney will affect the outcome of capital cases. The study concentrated chiefly on the provision of defense services, rather than the exercise of prosecutorial discretion in capital cases. The interviews with judges, prosecutors, and defense attorneys dealt with the selection and appointment of defense counsel in such cases, the remuneration available to them, their motives and justifications for taking such cases, the training and experience they bring to these cases, and the conditions of independence or interference under which they work. Their responses help to explain the relatively poor performance of court-appointed attorneys revealed in Tables 10-1, 10-3, and 10-4.

In response to questions about the impact of limited resources, especially the $3,500 cap on the payment for defense services in capital cases, respondents made the following observations:

> The court won't give you anywhere near the kind of money you need to try a capital case—the defendant is supposed to be on the same footing [as one who can afford an attorney] and in no way is he—you can't prepare any case for $2-3,000 and that's about what you're going to get.

> You're doing a disservice to your other clients if you take the appointment and get $3,500 and your paying clients suffer. . . . the cap deters competent attorneys and leaves the judges a smaller pool of good attorneys to appoint from . . . [and] doesn't provide much incentive to do the job competently.

> Dollar-wise [appointed attorneys] peak out before going to trial, meaning the trial is his gift to the defendant—it's free—that's his practice he's cutting into. His bills continue to pile up, his clients call and ask "Where is he?" The cap makes hungry, inexperienced guys take cases, but attorneys who can command fees can't afford to.

How do court-appointed attorneys approach their cases? What do they think about them?

> . . . where a judge appoints an attorney [that attorney's] natural reaction is not to give the judge too hard a time.

> If the defendant has to have an attorney appointed for him, he is lower class and nobody cares if you lose the case.

... an appointed attorney is more likely to plead a defendant guilty—
even to first degree murder. They're happy, they got their fee and if they
don't negotiate the judge gets pissed.

It's insane to ruin your practice with a case like that *unless* to curry
favor with the judge.

Some members of the bar say that the way appointments are made
tends to load the dice against some categories of defendants. According
to one judge, "I don't go down the list and automatically appoint the
next name but try to use discretion and appoint a qualified attorney,
but not the 'best.' " Another said that a judge in the city where he
practices is believed to be "matching up incompetent attorneys with
heinous defendants."

Respondents also reported a lack of independence, if not interference from the bench. One attorney commented,

"There's a problem where the judge holds the purse strings; judges make
it clear to the appointed attorney (that his) fee will be diminished and/
or he won't be appointed again, according to what he does outside of
what they expect of him (i.e., to plead guilty, not make motions, etc.)"

Another attorney voiced similar sentiments: "Regularly appointed attorneys feel if they don't plead guilty or don't give the judge an easy
time, they won't get any more appointments." Those who take such
appointments are generously characterized by their colleagues as "new
inexperienced attorneys" or more disparagingly as attorneys who "appear to be competent in the sense that they are not disbarred."

Brennan's analysis of these data presents a detailed picture of a
system that assigns the most death-prone defendants to the least experienced attorneys, who lack the resources, incentives, and indeed
the independence to provide the kind of defense their clients especially
require. Moreover, even if the perceptions of these respondents are not
accurate in all instances, they nevertheless constitute a "social reality"
that is bound to have a demoralizing influence on the way court-appointed
attorneys approach their work. Thus, the statistical data on court processing of homicide cases in Florida and these interview data from the
Florida Justice Institute's study tell the same story in different but
complementary ways.

John Spinkelink's case again serves as documentation. His last
appeal was made on Sixth Amendment grounds of ineffectiveness of
counsel. According to Ramsey Clark (1979, 400),

John Spenkelink's trial attorneys were court-appointed. They lacked sufficient resources to prepare and conduct the defense. One publicly stated

that the case was beyond his competence. One was absent during part of the jury selection to be with his wife in childbirth. He had not sought a delay in the proceeding or permission of the court to be absent.

Spenkelink's lawyers also failed to challenge the composition of the grand and petit juries. Both were later found to underrepresent blacks, women and young people—groups considered by most experienced attorneys to be favorable to the defense in capital cases. The lawyers failed to ask that Spenkelink be tried separately from his co-defendant who was acquitted. Severance was authorized under Florida law and would seem strategically important. Counsel failed to challenge excessive security measures in the courtroom, which are generally thought to be prejudicial to a defendant. . . . They had (wrongly) informed the jury in their closing argument that the judge could not impose a more severe sentence than the jury recommended. This may have encouraged the jury to ask for a maximum sentence, leaving the judge the full range of punishment alternatives. Counsel failed to obtain a transcript of questions asked prospective jurors, which was necessary in determining if they were constitutionally selected. The Florida Supreme Court ruled that all objections had been waived. With their client facing death, counsel did not request oral argument on appeal in the Supreme Court of Florida.

## The Exercise of Discretion in the Sentencing Process

Sentencing decisions were the chief locus of arbitrariness in capital punishment according to the Supreme Court's diagnosis. As a solution, the *Gregg* Court approved sentencing reforms that were supposed to insulate and to guide the exercise of sentencing discretion and were believed also to eliminate arbitrariness that might otherwise enter at earlier stages of the process. But, as we have seen, the Court was wrong about the presumed derivative benefits of these sentencing reforms; arbitrariness by race and location is strongly in evidence at indictment and conviction. What about the primary target of post-*Furman* statutory reforms? Has this solution succeeded in purging arbitrariness at least from the sentencing process?

There is mounting evidence of continuing arbitrariness despite statutory sentencing guidelines and separate sentencing hearings. In Chapter 7, we saw racial disparities in the sentencing of convicted first degree murderers in Florida (Table 7-7); these disparities were not attributable to differential involvement in felony-type killings by race, but were actually concentrated among those found guilty of a felony-type murder (Table 7-8). We also saw wide geographical disparities in the sentencing of convicted first degree murderers in Florida (Table 7-12), which were not due to regional differences in the felony-related character of the killings (Table 7-13).

As we did for the indictment and conviction decisions, we now carry our analysis of the sentencing decision a step further with the Florida court processing data. We have performed a multiple regression analysis using the same legal and extralegal factors examined in Tables 10-1 and 10-3. The analysis is based on 191 cases with complete information, or 63 percent of 305 first degree murder convictions in the 1973–1977 combined sample. The results of this analysis appear in Table 10-4.

Among the legally aggravating factors, felony-related killing and, to a lesser (and nonsignificant) extent, multiple offenders and multiple victims appear to contribute to the imposition of a death sentence. In

**Table 10-4.** *Estimated Effects of Legal and Extralegal Factors on Death Sentences among Persons Convicted of First Degree Murder in Florida, 1973–1977*

| Variables | Regression Coefficients |
|---|---|
| A. *Legally Relevant Factors* | |
| Felony related killing | 0.23** |
| More than one offender | 0.11 |
| More than one victim | 0.10 |
| Female victim | 0.00 |
| Victim 60 years or older[a] | 0.03 |
| Victim 16 years or younger[a] | 0.20 |
| Gun used as murder weapon | 0.02 |
| Defendant accessory | −0.12 |
| Defendant 18 years or younger | −0.14 |
| Quarrel precipitated killing | −0.06 |
| B. *Race*[b] | |
| Black kills white | 0.13 |
| White kills white | 0.13 |
| White kills black | −0.17 |
| C. *Region*[c] | |
| North | 0.22** |
| Central | 0.09 |
| D. *Type of Attorney*[d] | |
| Court appointed | 0.22** |
| Public defender | 0.16* |
| Adjusted R² | 0.18 |
| Number of Cases | 191 |

[a]Victims aged 17–59 is the reference category.
[b]Black kills black is the reference category.
[c]Southern region of Florida is the reference category (as defined in Table 7-4).
[d]Privately retained attorneys is the reference category.

*p < .05, t test
**p < .01, t test

contrast to the indictment and the conviction stages, however, female victim shows no effect and youthful victim shows a sizable though nonsignificant effect on sentencing. All three mitigating factors apparently impede the imposition of a death sentence. Because this sample of first degree murder conviction is much smaller than the samples used in Tables 10-1 and 10-3, estimated effects of a given size are less likely to achieve statistical significance. Thus, of six legally relevant variables with coefficients of .10 or more, only felony-related killing has an effect that is statistically significant.

Among the variables reflecting offender-victim racial combinations, there is evidence of a white-victim effect at the sentencing stage. Both black-kills-white and white-kills-white cases are more likely to receive a death sentence than the black-kills-black reference category, and far more likely than the (relatively few) white-kills-black cases. When the white-victim cases are combined and examined with black-victim cases as the reference category, the effect of having a white victim (b = .13) approaches statistical significance (p = .11).[9] Thus, racial considerations appear to affect each successive stage of the process and to have a consistent cumulative effect over the entire process, apart from a number of legally aggravating and mitigating factors.

Regional disparities in sentencing are even greater than they were at other stages of the process. Courts in the northern region are far more likely to impose a death sentence on convicted first degree murderers than are those elsewhere in the state. The difference between the northern and the southern regions (as the reference category) is highly significant and virtually as great as any other effect in the table. The likelihood of a death sentence is also greater in the central than in the southern region, though not significantly so, given the size of the sample. Since the central region is also more likely to indict and convict on capital charges, the cumulative effect of the process in the central region may nevertheless rival the death sentence proneness of the northern region at the sentencing stage. At each stage of the process, the southern region is clearly less likely than the rest of the state to move otherwise comparable cases along the path toward a death sentence. These disparities are statistically significant at each stage of the process and their cumulative effect over the entire process is far beyond chance statistical variation.

Finally, type of attorney continues to be among the strongest extra-

9. It should be noted at this point that the use of the felony circumstance variable drawn from the court case records may spuriously reduce our estimates of racial effects because of the apparent "upgrading" of white-victim cases to include allegations of a felony circumstance in the court case records where none appeared in the police reports (Table 7-9). The true effect of victim's race may therefore be even stronger than is shown in Tables 10-1, 10-3, and 10-4.

legal factors contributing to a death sentence among convicted first degree murderers. Having a court-appointed attorney is on par with having committed a felony-related murder as a predictor that a convicted defendant will be sentenced to death. Having a public defender is also significantly associated with receiving a death sentence. The disadvantage of having a court-appointed attorney in the sentencing process may, in part, reflect his or her ineffectiveness at an earlier stage in trading a guilty plea to first degree murder charges for the prosecutor's promise not to seek the death penalty. This would mean that more of the court-appointed attorney's cases that resulted in a first degree murder conviction were subjected to a penalty trial. In any case, over the entire process from indictment through sentencing, having a court-appointed attorney is almost as great a disadvantage as having killed a white rather than a black person.

Our findings in Florida were replicated recently by a study conducted in Georgia. There, still stronger evidence of racial and regional disparities in sentencing were compiled in the preliminary report of David Baldus, George Woodworth, and Charles Pulaski (1982a). They collected extensive data on more than 600 cases in which the defendants were found guilty by a jury or pleaded guilty to first degree murder charges between 1973 and 1978. They obtained data on over 250 potentially aggravating or mitigating factors for each case from official records of the Georgia Supreme Court, the Georgia Department of Offender Rehabilitation, the Georgia Department of Probations and Paroles, and Georgia's Bureau of Vital Statistics; data were also obtained from questionnaires sent to defense counsel and prosecutors. With these data Baldus and his associates have examined race-of-victim disparities in sentencing for cases that are: (1) eligible for a death sentence on each of Georgia's ten statutory aggravating circumstances; (2) matched in terms of the number of statutory aggravating circumstances present; (3) equated on an index constructed to reflect both aggravating and mitigating factors most predictive of sentencing outcomes; (4) similar in terms of specific aggravating and mitigating factors identified as most important in regression analyses; and (5) alike in "salient features" as determined on an *ad hoc* basis from a close reading of the cases. In each of these analyses, they have found substantial and consistent sentencing differences by race of victim in otherwise comparable cases. They find, moreover, that these disparities are due more to prosecutorial decisions to seek the death sentence by holding a penalty trial than to jury decisions to impose the death sentence given a penalty trial.

The role of prosecutorial discretion in the sentencing process is presented in Table 10-5. For white-victim and black-victim murderers convicted by a jury, it shows the likelihood of a sentencing trial at

**Table 10-5.**   *Likelihood of a Penalty Trial by Race of Victim at Various Levels of Aggravation/Mitigation among Convicted First Degree Murderers in Georgia, 1973–1978*

| Level of aggravation/mitigation | White-victim cases | Black-victim cases |
|---|---|---|
| 1 (low) | 0.05(41) | 0.00(70) |
| 2 | 0.08(52) | 0.07(54) |
| 3 | 0.15(60) | 0.06(53) |
| 4 | 0.30(50) | 0.22(23) |
| 5 | 0.71(41) | 0.35(26) |
| 6 | 0.88(50) | 0.64(11) |
| 7 | 0.91(34) | 0.87(7) |
| 8 (high) | 1.00(32) | 1.00(3) |

*Source*: Baldus et al. 1982a, part II, n. 98

corresponding levels on an index constructed to reflect both aggravating and mitigating factors that best predict a penalty trial (the third and most conservative of their analytic approaches presented).[10] According to Table 10-5, Georgia prosecutors decide to hold penalty trials disproportionately in white-victim cases as opposed to black-victim cases at most levels of aggravation/mitigation. There are consistent and sometimes striking disparities of treatment by race of victim, notwithstanding the conservative bias of this regression-based aggravation/mitigation index. As a consequence, sentencing juries see mostly white-victim cases at relatively high levels of aggravation. Race-of-victim comparisons of jury decisions to impose death sentences are thus limited by the small number of black-victim cases at a given aggravation/mitigation level. The differences that do appear, however, tend to compound further the disparities at intermediate levels of aggravation/mitigation.

Baldus and his associates also examined specific sentencing disparities for convicted first degree murderers in the same five regional groupings of judicial circuits in Georgia that we examined in Tables 7-4 and 7-5. Their analysis reveals extreme sentencing disparities by region, especially as aggravation level increases, as shown in Table 10-6. Thus, among the most aggravated cases, no more than 40 percent of the convicted murderers receive a death sentence in the northern region and Fulton County, compared to at least two-thirds of their counterparts in the other three regions. The investigators show, moreover, that these extreme disparities persist when the comparisons are

10. This regression-based index of aggravating and mitigating factors was constructed specifically to provide a conservative test of hypothesized racial disparities by excluding race of victim as a regressor. Thus, some of the effects of victim's race are incorporated into the index by the presence of factors correlated with it, such as victim's social class.

**Table 10-6.**  *Likelihood of a Death Sentence by Region at Various*
*Levels of Aggravation/Mitigation among Convicted*
*First Degree Murderers in Georgia, 1973–1978*

| Levels of aggravation/ mitigation | North | North Central | Fulton County | South- east | South- west |
|---|---|---|---|---|---|
| 1 (low) | 0.00(1) | 0.00(5) | — | — | — |
| 2 | 0.00(11) | 0.00(12) | 0.00(7) | 0.00(14) | 0.00(14) |
| 3 | 0.00(14) | 0.00(34) | 0.00(24) | 0.00(45) | 0.00(25) |
| 4 | 0.00(9) | 0.00(21) | 0.00(20) | 0.07(14) | 0.00(26) |
| 5 | 0.00(9) | 0.14(28) | 0.06(17) | 0.00(11) | 0.17(12) |
| 6 | 0.00(2) | 0.05(21) | 0.10(10) | 0.14(7) | 0.11(9) |
| 7 | 0.00(6) | 0.61(18) | 0.17(6) | 0.07(14) | 0.10(10) |
| 8 (high) | 0.40(10) | 0.75(51) | 0.38(16) | 0.77(26) | 0.68(28) |

Source: Baldus et al. 1982a, 109, Table 25

restricted to white-victim cases (Baldus et al. 1982a, 110, Table 26).
These regional disparities are underscored by the fact that just 26, or
15 percent, of Georgia's 159 counties were responsible for 85 percent
of the death sentences imposed between 1973 and 1978 in that state
(Baldus et al. 1982a, 106, note 107).

In continuing research, Baldus and his associates have gathered
additional data on the processing of Georgia homicide cases from indictment through sentencing and extended the period of coverage through
1979. Although the analyses of these data are still preliminary, Baldus
summarized the cumulative findings of this research in an affidavit of
June 22, 1982, prepared for the petitioner in *Smith* v. *Balkcom*:

> Differential treatment of white and black victim cases appears to prevail
> at each stage of the capital charging and sentencing process beyond initial
> indictment—specifically in plea bargaining decisions, jury guilt deci-
> sions, the prosecutor's decision to proceed to a penalty trial, and the
> jury's decision at sentencing.

With the evidence of race- and region-linked sentencing differences
in Florida (Tables 7-7, 7-8, 7-12, 7-13, and 10-4) and with stronger, more
rigorously controlled evidence of this sort now becoming available on
Georgia (Tables 10-5 and 10-6), it is obvious that despite statutory
sentencing guidelines and separate sentencing hearings, the sentencing
stage of the process is still subject to the extralegal influence of race
and place. Thus, of the three reforms approved in *Gregg*—statutory
sentencing guidelines, separate sentencing hearings, and automatic appellate review—the last of these must bear a heavy burden if the post-
*Furman* capital statutes are to meet the *Furman* standard.

## State Appellate Review

The Supreme Court declared in *Gregg* that automatic appellate review of all death sentences "serves as a check against the random or arbitrary imposition of the death penalty." In this connection, Justice White (*Gregg* v. *Georgia* 1976, 2948) commented that Georgia's statutory provision for "proportionality review" requires the Georgia Supreme Court to "do much more than determine whether the penalty was lawfully imposed." He noted that "it must go on to decide—after reviewing the penalties imposed in 'similar' cases—whether the penalty is 'excessive or disproportionate' considering both the crime and the defendant."

But state appellate courts may be ill-prepared and disinclined to perform the oversight and monitoring functions assigned to them under the new capital statutes. They do not generally compare the sentence in one case with those in others, nor do they directly collect and evaluate evidence; instead, they usually review arguments based on evidence that has been admitted in other courts. Evidence that the appellate review process is not living up to the High Court's expectations is mounting. We observed in Tables 7-14 through 7-17 that racial and locational disparities in the imposition of death sentences are not being reduced by the actions of the state supreme courts of Florida and Georgia.

David Baldus, Charles Pulaski, and George Woodworth (1982b) have recently studied Georgia's appellate review process in more detail. For its proportionality review, the Georgia Supreme Court is required by statute to identify cases "similar" in characteristics of the crime and the defendant to the one under review, and then to compare the sentence under review with those imposed in these similar cases. The pool from which the Court may select "similar" cases should, according to the Georgia statute, include capital cases in which sentences were imposed after January 1, 1970. The statute also requires that the cases selected as similar be cited in an appendix to each of the Court's publicized opinions upholding a death sentence.

Baldus and his associates examined the Court's selection of similar cases for the proportionality reviews of sixty-eight affirmed post-*Furman* death sentences for murder. Using the detailed data they collected on some 750 capital cases (approximately 150 pre-*Furman* and 600 post-*Furman*) during the period 1970–1978, they compared the cases cited as similar by the Court with cases identified as (1) comparable in terms of aggravation/mitigation index scores; (2) matched on the basis of specific facts or main determinants analysis; and (3) alike with respect to the salient features of the case.[11] They found that the cases cited as

11. These correspond to procedures 3 through 5 as enumerated under the preceding heading and they are described in detail in Baldus et al. 1982b.

similar by the Georgia Supreme Court are more highly aggravated and more likely to have received a death sentence than those identified as similar by any of the three empirically based and objectively specified methods they have employed.

We too are currently conducting an analysis of the Georgia review process using a somewhat different approach (Bowers, McDevitt, and Diana 1983). Instead of identifying similar cases by some objective standard and then comparing them with those the Court cited as similar, our approach has been to identify the factors that distinguish the cases the Court chose as similar from the eligible cases the Court did not select. That is, we have attempted to discover the criteria the Georgia Supreme Court actually applies, knowingly or otherwise, in the selection of similar cases.[12]

We are using the Georgia Supreme Court's own data, collected specifically for purposes of proportionality review as directed by Georgia's capital statute, on all capital cases resulting in life or death sentences that were appealed to the Georgia Supreme Court after January 1970. The data came from a six-page questionnaire completed by trial judges in cases where a death sentence was imposed under the post-*Furman* statute, and by a clerk of the Court for all cases where the sentence was life and pre-*Furman* cases where the sentence was death. The questionnaires provide data on the crime, the defendant, the trial process, and the outcome or disposition of the case, including jury findings and sentence imposed. The data for some 297 murder cases between 1970 and 1977 (including the first thirty-six post-*Furman* death sentences for murder reviewed for proportionality) were obtained under a motion for discovery filed by Atlanta attorney Millard Farmer. (The Georgia Supreme Court has since refused to release the data on subsequently reviewed cases.)

These data show that the Georgia Supreme Court chose cases that are not more consistently similar to the ones under review than the other cases in the pool. By statute, the characteristics of the crime and the defendant should determine which cases are similar and the court should compare the sentence imposed in the case under review with the case found to be similar. Instead, the court seems to have reversed the procedure. What most distinguishes the cases chosen by the court

12. This approach avoids the difficulty of making *a priori* assumptions about the standards of comparability the Georgia Supreme Court should have used in specific cases. A federal district court raised this objection (in evidentiary hearings for House and McCorquodale [1979]) to our earlier analysis of these data in which we generated groups of similar cases in terms of the number of persons killed, the presence of accompanying felony circumstances, a prior record of criminal violence, and the use of a firearm as the murder weapon.

from those eligible[13] but not chosen is the fact that the original sentence was death and had been upheld by the Georgia Supreme Court. In effect, the court defines as similar those cases in which the death sentence has been handed down and upheld, whether the characteristics of the crime or the defendant are similar to the one under review.

Our complex statistical analysis led us to the simple but revealing picture of the proportionality review process given in Table 10-7. It shows, for each of the first thirty-six affirmed death sentences for murder, how many of the cases cited as "similar" were life cases after 1970, how many were death cases under the pre-*Furman* statute, and how many were death cases under the present post-*Furman* statute effective April 1973.

In all, the Georgia Supreme Court cited only eighteen life cases (the total of the second column of figures), or less than 10 percent, of the more than 200 life sentences appealed to the Court between 1970 and 1977. Moreover, seventeen of these were pre-April 1973 life cases cited in the first six reviews, and not cited again after the thirteenth case (A. Smith). The Court cited only one life case under the new statute (as similar to Dix). In only one case (Moore) were more life than death sentences cited as similar.[14]

The Court cited twenty-two pre-*Furman* death cases, almost two-thirds of them in the very first review. Over half of these were cited in ten of the first fourteen reviews, and no additional pre-*Furman* death cases were cited after the ninth review (Jarrell). Then, as post-*Furman* death sentences were reviewed and affirmed, virtually all were cited by the Court in subsequent reviews. Indeed, the Court had cited all but one (Street) of the first thirty-two affirmed death cases by the thirty-sixth review (rightmost column). Moreover, of the first four post-*Furman* death sentences upheld by the Court, three were cited at least twenty-seven times subsequently; another seven were cited in ten or more subsequent reviews. And there was a tendency for the Court simply to draw "similar" cases from the group cited in the immediately preceding review (see the notes to Table 10-7).

Thus, from the substantial pool of almost 300 cases available for proportionality review by 1977, the Georgia Supreme Court repeatedly

13. For a given proportionality review, the eligible pool is defined as all life and death cases after 1970 that have been appealed to and reviewed by the Georgia Supreme Court on or before the review date of the case in question.
14. Moore's case is truly extraordinary in that the trial judge imposed death—without jury recommendations—after the defendant pleaded guilty and despite the mitigating facts that the defendant had cooperated with the police, had no prior criminal record, was youthful, had been intoxicated, and was first shot at by the victim. Federal District Judge Edenfield later reversed the Georgia Supreme Court's proportionality review in a decision quoted later in this chapter.

**Table 10-7.** *Cases Cited as Similar by the Georgia Supreme Court in the First 36 Proportionality Reviews of the Death Sentence for Murder*

| Defendants | Number of cases cited as similar | Life sentences between 1970 and 1977 | | Death sentences prior to June 1972 | | Death sentences since April 1973 | | Number of citations in later reviews |
|---|---|---|---|---|---|---|---|---|
| | | First cited | Pre- viously cited | First cited | Pre- viously cited | First cited | Pre- viously cited | |
| House | 18 | 4 | – | 14 | – | – | – | 30 |
| Gregg | 18 | – | 3a | 1 | 13a | 1 | – | 27 |
| Ross | 6 | – | 1a | 1 | 4a | – | – | 3 |
| Floyd | 18 | – | 3b | – | 13 | 1 | 1 | 27 |
| McCorquodale | 20 | 4 | 3 | – | 11 | – | 2a | 6 |
| Moore | 23 | 9 | 4 | 4 | 5 | – | 1a | 13 |
| Mitchell | 16 | – | 1a | 1 | 10 | 2 | 2 | 9 |
| Chenault | 15 | – | – | – | 12 | – | 3a | 12 |
| Jarrell | 19 | – | 1 | 1 | 12 | 1 | 4b | 11 |
| Berryhill | 7 | – | – | – | 7 | – | – | 10 |
| Tamplin | 16 | – | – | – | 11 | 1 | 4 | 2 |
| R. Smith | 19 | – | 3 | – | 13 | – | 3a | 12 |
| A. Smith | 19 | – | 3a | – | 13a | – | 3a | 12 |
| Mason | 16 | – | – | – | 12a | 1 | 3a | 11 |
| Dobbs | 15 | – | – | – | 7 | 3 | 5 | 5 |
| Goodwin | 12 | – | – | – | 5a | – | 7a | 4 |
| Pulliam | 15 | – | – | – | 7b | – | 8b | 8 |
| Spencer | 5 | – | – | – | 4 | – | 1a | 1 |
| Davis | 15 | – | – | – | 5 | 3 | 7 | 4 |
| Birt | 14 | – | – | – | 8 | 2 | 4a | 6 |
| Gibson | 15 | – | – | – | 5 | – | 10 | 2 |
| Coleman | 19 | – | – | – | 12 | 1 | 6 | 6 |
| Isaacs | 19 | – | – | – | 12a | – | 7a | 6 |
| Street | 15 | – | – | – | 5 | – | 10 | 0 |
| Dungee | 19 | – | – | – | 12 | – | 7 | 6 |
| Banks | 19 | – | – | – | 12a | – | 7a | 7 |
| Stephens | 19 | – | – | – | 12a | – | 7a | 4 |
| Harris | 16 | – | – | – | – | 10b | 6c | 3 |
| Hill | 26 | – | – | – | 4 | 2 | 20b,c | 1 |
| C. Young | 26 | – | – | – | 4a | – | 22a,c | 2 |
| Dix | 17 | 1d | – | – | – | 5 | 11c | 2 |
| Pryor | 22 | – | – | – | – | 2 | 20 | 1 |
| Douthit | 19 | – | – | – | 6 | 1 | 12 | 0 |
| J. Young | 24 | – | – | – | 12 | – | 12 | 0 |
| Gaddis | 24 | – | – | – | 12a | – | 12a | 0 |
| Blake | 5 | – | – | – | – | 1 | 4 | 0 |
| TOTALS | | 18 | | 22 | | 37 | | |

aIncludes only cases of this type cited in the preceding review.
bIncludes all cases of this type cited in the preceding review.
cIncludes three post-*Furman* death cases reversed by the Georgia Supreme Court on procedural grounds.
dImposed under the post-*Furman* capital statute.

relied upon a small and highly selective subsample. It cited predominantly death cases, then exclusively death cases, and increasingly death cases it had affirmed in previous proportionality reviews: fewer than one in ten of the available life cases and virtually nine out of ten previously affirmed post-*Furman* death cases.[15]

This is not proportionality review as mandated by the Georgia capital statute and approved by the U.S. Supreme Court in *Gregg*, but a process of legally rationalizing trial court decisions to impose death as punishment, regardless of proportionality or excessiveness relative to the sentences in similar cases. Thus, arbitrariness is evident in the decisions and actions of state appellate court judges, as well as those of prosecutors, defense attorneys, and juries; automatic appellate review, like sentencing guidelines and separate penalty hearings, has also failed to serve its intended purpose.

## Federal Appellate Review

The burden of detecting and correcting arbitrariness and discrimination in capital sentencing and at earlier stages of the process has fallen of necessity on the federal appellate courts. Challenges to the death penalty as applied came first to the federal district courts in southern states where death sentences were most commonly imposed. These courts, in turn, looked to the Fifth Circuit Court of Appeals (whose decisions then governed the actions of trial and appellate courts in Florida, Georgia, and Texas, as well as most other southern states) for standards in judging death penalty appeals. Those standards were established in the case of John Spinkelink.

---

15. Of course, these same data could be used by the Georgia Supreme Court to see whether there are systematic statewide disparities of treatment among cases similar in legally relevant ways. For example, the data show substantial differences in likelihood of a death sentence by race of offender and victim and by geographical location within the state among cases comparable both in felony circumstance and prior criminal record, the principal legally aggravating factors alleged to account for racial differences (cf. Kleck 1981). Further, these data reveal that 72 percent of the convicted offenders who were transients in the community where the crime occurred—as compared with 25 percent of those who were residents—received a death sentence; although the number of transient offenders is relatively small for statistical comparisons, this difference is not attributable to differences in the felony circumstances of the crime or the prior record of the defendants. With these continually accumulating data on hand, and these leads to pursue, the Georgia Supreme Court might be expected to investigate disparities of treatment associated with place, race, residence, etc., and make available the accumulating data for what they may reveal about the constitutionality of the death penalty as applied and reviewed for proportionality.

In September 1977 the Legal Defense Fund, representing John Spinkelink, presented evidence of racial bias—specifically, the disproportionate use of the death sentence in white-victim cases—in the administration of Florida's capital statute. At that time there were 114 men on death row, of whom 94 percent had killed only whites, two percent had killed both whites and blacks, and four percent had killed only blacks—in a state where most homicide victims are blacks. Eighty-five of 114 had committed murder in the course of another felony, typically robbery. Of these, eighty-three were white-victim cases, one was a mixed-race case, and one was a black-victim case. Compared to their incidence in the population, white-victim felony-related killings (a felony was alleged in Spinkelink's case) were thirty-one times more likely to be punished by death than were black-victim felony-related killings. These statistics were presented by expert witnesses for Spinkelink at an evidentiary hearing in federal district court at Tallahassee with the following statement:

> The statistics provide *prima facie* evidence of bias, strong enough to suggest that the burden of proving that no such bias exists should shift to the prosecutor. He should be required to show that the statistical discrepancy is the result of some factor other than bias (quoted in Zeisel 1981, 461).

The district court denied Spinkelink's petition, and this ruling was appealed to the Court of Appeals for the Fifth Circuit. A three-judge panel of the Fifth Circuit then ruled that these statistical data were irrelevant, and that the defendant must show "racially discriminatory intent or purpose" in terms of specific actions taken against him in his case in order to demonstrate a violation of constitutional protection. The court held that the Florida statute itself was immune from constitutional challenges of arbitrariness and that such a statistical analysis was, therefore, unwarranted and beyond the court's review obligations. It relied on language in *Proffitt* v. *Florida* (1976) for the proposition that the Florida statute was not subject to challenge as applied except in those cases where the petitioner can show specific acts of intentional discrimination against him because of his or his victim's race.[16]

---

16. The Fifth Circuit Court's response to the statistical evidence of racial bias in Spinkelink v. Wainwright closely resembles the Eighth Circuit Court's reaction to similar evidence in Maxwell v. Bishop ten years earlier. Despite vast racial disparities in the likelihood of a death sentence, both courts held that the statistical evidence was inadequate because some legally relevant but omitted factors could conceivably

In effect, the *Spinkelink* decision erected a judicial shield against challenges of arbitrariness and discrimination in the states of the Fifth Circuit, where the death penalty is now and has been most widely used. By closing the door on statistical evidence and restricting the scope of federal appellate review, the Fifth Circuit Court's ruling in *Spinkelink* effectively impeded constitutional challenges. In other words, *Spinkelink* provided the protection behind which the new statutes approved in *Gregg* might operate relatively free of monitoring by the federal courts for the kinds of constitutional violations that invalidated the former statutes.[17]

In June 1979, shortly after Spinkelink's execution in Florida, the Legal Defense Fund challenged Georgia's capital statute presented in the federal district court in Atlanta at combined evidentiary hearings in the cases of *House* and *McCorquodale*. Here the data revealed both disparities by race like those presented in *Spinkelink* and disparities by region within the state. As in Florida, the data documented disproportionate imposition of the death sentence, especially for white-victim killings (see Table 7-2), and the pattern was present for both felony and nonfelony homicides (see Table 7-3). The data further revealed

---

account for the racial disparities, and irrelevant because the data were not specific to the handling of the case under review. (On the latter point, in Maxwell the data on rape cases from nineteen representative counties in Arkansas did not include the county in which Maxwell was tried.)

Ironically, eight years after the Maxwell Court had ruled that this evidence was inadequate and irrelevant, the solicitor general of the United States conceded, in his *amicus* brief supporting capital punishment for Gregg and companion cases, that the statistical evidence presented in Maxwell clearly justified conclusions of racial discrimination: "We do not question the conclusion that during the twenty years in question, in southern states, there was discrimination in rape cases." Hans Zeisel (1981, 458) has characterized this as an emerging pattern of

. . . government officials admitting after it no longer matters legally, that discrimination has affected capital sentencing and executions, but professing that such discrimination is all a matter of the past and that current data are too scanty to support conclusions of continuing racial discrimination.

17. The Fifth Circuit Court's commitment to this Spinkelink shield was underscored a year later. In August 1979, a panel of the Fifth Circuit held in Jurek v. Estelle (1979, note 26) that statistical patterns of racial disparities could suffice as *prima facie* evidence of "intent to discriminate," citing the legal principle that actors are responsible for the natural and forseeable consequences of their actions. Within weeks, Jurek v. Estelle had been withdrawn for rehearing before the full membership of the Circuit. In three months' time a replacement version of Jurek v. Estelle appeared with no reference to the role of statistical evidence in demonstrating intent to discriminate, thus leaving intact the judicial shield established by Spinkelink v. Wainwright.

disparities of treatment for judicial circuits grouped regionally (see Table 7-4); for felony- or nonfelony-type killings (see Table 7-5); and for white-victim or black-victim felony-type murders (a table for Georgia was presented that corresponded to Table 7-6 for Florida).

To challenge this evidence, the state engaged as an expert Timothy S. Carr, the Director of Research for the Georgia Department of Corrections, but did not call him to the witness stand. In a letter to the presiding federal magistrate, Mr. Carr offered his professional evaluation, saying that the magnitude of the racial disparities "is as great as anything I have ever seen in my seven years of processing and interpreting criminal justice data in Georgia," and that he "did not believe that a difference of this magnitude would 'wash out' statistically even if all the [legally relevant] factors . . . were to work *in concert* to nullify it" (cited in *Smith* v. *Balkcom*, petition for cert. No. 81, 1981. 25).[18]

The federal magistrate's order in *House* and *McCorquodale* disallowed further consideration of this statistical evidence of racial and regional disparities, explicitly indicating that such evidence did not meet the standard established in *Spinkelink*. This evidence eventually reached the Fifth Circuit Court in the case of *Smith* v. *Balkcom* (*Smith I*, 1981), at which point the Circuit Court rejected it, also invoking *Spinkelink*.

Then came the first scoring of the *Spinkelink* shield. The Fifth Circuit withdrew its *Smith* opinion for rehearing and issued a modification of its opinion in *Smith* v. *Balkcom* (*Smith II*, 1982), which explicitly recognized that statistical evidence could serve as proof of "intent to discriminate" under a Fourteenth Amendment "equal protection" challenge. The court, however, rejected the particular statistical evidence presented in *Smith I*, saying that it "falls short . . . of establishing an equal protection violation" (1982, 859, esp. note 33).[19] This turnaround came just as the Fifth Circuit was split into the Fifth

---

18. Carr, who was called as the petitioner's witness, made it clear that although he personally favored the death penalty, he was convinced by these data that it was being imposed in a racially biased manner:

> I favor the death penalty . . . in specific cases. I favor it in these two cases here. . . . I talked at some length with my wife about this. She told me, "What would you do if some of these men possibly as a consequence of my testimony were actually released from prison and were to commit another crime of the magnitude that they did before?" and asked me if I would ever be able to forgive myself. That gave me pause. . . . But by the morning the strength of the numbers had come back to me. I can see that it's not being fairly applied (Smith v. Balkcom, petition for cert. No. 81, 1981, 25 note 22).

and Eleventh Circuits. However, because the case was argued before the bifurcation, the modified *Smith* decision was binding on the courts of both the Fifth and the Eleventh Federal Circuits.

The new Eleventh Circuit Court recently took a further step in *Proffitt* v. *Wainwright* (1982). Citing the U.S. Supreme Court's decision in *Godfrey* v. *Georgia* (1980) as precedent, the Eleventh Circuit held that both sentencing and review decisions of state trial and appellate courts were open to Eighth Amendment challenges to the application of statutory and non-statutory sentencing criteria. In the words of *Proffitt* v. *Wainwright* (1982, 2731, note 52):

> In view of *Godfrey*, we can only conclude that the language in the *Spinkelink* opinion precluding federal courts from reviewing state courts' application of capital sentencing criteria is no longer sound precedent.

In effect, the protection afforded post-*Furman* capital statutes by *Spinkelink*—which itself arbitrarily impeded constitutional challenges to their application—was weakened by *Smith II* in the geographically restricted jurisdiction of the Fifth Circuit, and by *Smith II* and *Proffitt* in the jurisdiction of the newly formed Eleventh Circuit Court of Appeals. The actions taken in *Smith II* and *Proffitt* mean that federal appeals courts will now have a freer hand in monitoring the application of existing capital statutes, and that statistically based challenges to the death penalty as applied will soon be brought to the U.S. Supreme Court on appeal. That is to say, the High Court will soon again be faced with the question it sidestepped when it declined to hear *Spinkelink* v. *Wainwright*—this time with considerably stronger evidence of arbitrariness and discrimination.

## Final Appeals

By the end of 1982, two men—John Spinkelink and Charlie Brooks, Jr.—had been executed against their will under post-*Furman* capital statutes. Their cases illustrate how the federal appellate courts have acted on specific cases apart from the legal standards they have formulated to govern the handling of such cases in lower courts. They are examples of the extent to which the federal courts are or are not immune from the arbitrariness that infects earlier stages of the process,

---

19. This represented a return to the position purged from the first Jurek v. Estelle decision—a slight but definite weakening of the Spinkelink shield (see note 17).

and the degree to which death as a form of punishment invites or provokes arbitrariness even at the highest levels of appellate review. Moreover, Spinkelink and Brooks passed the last safeguard against arbitrariness when the U.S. Supreme Court denied their final appeals; any arbitrariness or other constitutional breaches in the handling of their cases have become permanent and irreparable. And these cases foreshadow what lies ahead if the High Court chooses not to bring legal homicides to an end.

John Spinkelink was the first to be executed against his will in the post-*Furman* era. We have reviewed the circumstances of his crime, and the handling of his case by prosecutors and defense attorneys as recounted by former United States Attorney General Ramsey Clark. However, Clark's account deals primarily with the details of Spinkelink's final appeal.

Two days after Clark and his associates obtained a stay of execution from federal Judge Elbert Tuttle of Atlanta on the grounds that Spinkelink had been denied his Sixth Amendment right to effective trial counsel, Clark received a call at 7:30 P.M. from the clerk of the Fifth Circuit Court in New Orleans who said he was setting up a conference call between the Florida Attorney General, lawyers for Spinkelink, and three judges of the Court of Appeals—Judges James P. Coleman, Peter T. Fay (who later turned out to be unavailable) and Alvin B. Rubin. These three were to rule on a request from the State of Florida that Judge Tuttle's stay of execution be set aside. According to Clark's account (1979, 403):

> The telephone conference was a nightmare. We were told at the beginning not to record what was said. The court did not have our papers. We had not seen the State's papers. . . . There was loose, unstudied, uninformed discussion about whether Judge Tuttle had jurisdiction, whether he entered a final order, whether the Court of Appeals had the power to review his order. . . . We asked for time to file affidavits and a response to the State's motion. The merits of our petition for a writ of habeas corpus had been barely even discussed . . . the call was over shortly after 8 P.M.

Ten minutes before midnight, the clerk of the Court of Appeals called Clark from New Orleans with a page-and-a-half order to read. According to Clark, it cited four cases that had nothing to do with any issue before the Court of Appeals, and had not been mentioned before. It concluded, "We are convinced, for reasons which will hereafter be stated in a formal opinion, that the aforesaid stay should be vacated." The order added, "The motions of Spenkelink for time in which to file supporting affidavits, etc., is denied. . . . This order vacating the stay execution granted by Judge Tuttle shall become fully and formally effective at the hour of 9:30 o'clock Eastern daylight savings time, Friday, May 25, 1979. . . . Judge Rubin reserves the right to dissent for reasons to be assigned."

According to Clark, the panel acted without jurisdiction (1979, 404):

> Judge Coleman based jurisdiction on an appellate rule even though no appeal had been taken, so the case was not even properly before his court. He ignored the habeas corpus statute, which denies the Court of Appeals jurisdiction over original petitions for habeas corpus. He considered a stay order a "final order" in violation of a statute that required a certificate of probable cause—a stay order that was clearly made in order to preserve jurisdiction.

With the following litany of unanswered questions, Ramsey Clark raised the spectre of unconstitutional arbitrariness in response to Spinkelink's final appeal (1979, 404):

> Why did Coleman proceed after years of careful, painstaking litigation to compel exhausted lawyers and the court to discuss a life-and-death case late at night over the phone, without exchanging papers, without giving time for review or study, without allowing time for supporting affidavits? Why did he not wait until Judge Fay could hear the argument? Why did he cite four irrelevant cases never mentioned in the papers or the discussion in an order written at home and dictated over the phone to a clerk?
>
> How could he decide the matter without having facts to judge whether there had been effective assistance of counsel? Since Judge Fay did not hear argument and should not have voted, and because Judge Rubin ultimately dissented, how could he decide to vacate Judge Tuttle's order? And why had he not given his reasons? Judges deciding death cases ought to give reasons.

Prompted by Clark's long list of questions, Robert Kastenmeier, the chairman of the congressional Subcommittee on Courts, Civil Liberties, and the Administration of Justice, requested an inquiry that was undertaken by Judge John R. Brown of the Fifth Circuit. Judge Brown defended the panel's failure to issue a formal opinion on the grounds that it could not have "operational effect" now that Spinkelink was dead. He did not, however, discuss the question of the panel's jurisdiction over Judge Tuttle's stay, which, according to Michael Meltsner (1980), "can only lead one to conclude that upon reflection the panel realized that it had none." Concerning the rush to execution, Meltsner observed:

It is my understanding that the warrant of execution signed by the governor of Florida expired at noon on the 25th of May. . . . Judge Brown
offers no explanation of why the panel did not at the very least extend
the stay for several days in order to permit counsel a reasonable amount
of time to prepare considered papers for the Supreme Court of the United
States. The only reason that appears for the failure of the panel to grant
such time was the desire to have Mr. Spenkelink executed before the
death warrant then in force expired.

 

Charlie Brooks, Jr., was the first black man, and only the second
person, to be executed against his will in over fifteen years in the United
States. Brooks and, in a separate trial, his co-defendant, Woodie Loudres,
were both sentenced to death for a murder in which only a single shot
had been fired. No eyewitness or forensic evidence decisively pointed
to Brooks rather than Loudres as the killer. On appeal Loudres was
granted a new trial. At his second trial, the prosecutor offered him a
forty-year sentence—which made him eligible for parole after one-third
of his term—in exchange for a guilty plea to the charge that Loudres
"caus[ed] the death of [the victim] by shooting him with a firearm"
(*Texas* v. *Loudres* 1980) and Loudres accepted the offer. This left one
man in prison with the prospect of parole and his co-defendant under
sentence of death awaiting execution. The chief prosecutor in both the
Brooks and the Loudres trials declared in an affidavit supporting Brooks's
appeal to the Supreme Court that

> the evidence against Brooks and the evidence against Loudres was sub-
> stantially identical. . . . No fact surrounding the offense suggests that one
> defendant was more culpable than the other (brief in support of appli-
> cation for a stay of execution to the U.S. Supreme Court, *Brooks* v. *Estelle*
> 1982).

In his appeal, Brooks raised issues about jury selection as well as
disproportionality of punishment. He challenged the prosecutor's re-
moval of a prospective juror in part on the grounds that she could not
impose a death sentence without proof that the defendant had himself
committed murder. Although Texas state law permitted the juror to
be excused, the U.S. Supreme Court subsequently held that it was
unconstitutional to impose a death sentence without proof that a defendant participated in or intended the victim's death (*Enmund* v. *Florida* 1982). The juror in Brooks's case appeared to have been excused
because she took a viewpoint later held to be constitutionally required.

Although Brooks raised serious constitutional questions about his
jury selection and the manifestly disproportionate punishments meted
out to the two men, he was denied a full hearing before the Fifth Circuit

Court. He was instead given "expedited" treatment—rushed through the appeals court in a matter of days without a stay of execution and without full briefing or argument. In denying Brooks these procedural rights, the three-judge panel announced that, henceforth, their court would grant stays of execution only to those capital inmates who could make a preliminary demonstration of a likelihood of success on appeal (*Brooks* v. *Estelle* 1982, 586). Before Brooks, every capital inmate in the past decade who sought review by the federal appellate courts had been granted an opportunity to file a federal appeal, submit a brief, and argue his case, through counsel, to three appellate judges. In an earlier case, a federal judge described this review process as "so long and so well established that [it] . . . must be counted among the basic protections with which our system has surrounded all persons convicted of crime" (*Shaw* v. *Martin* 1980, 487, 491). Brooks's last-minute complaint to the U.S. Supreme Court about the appeals court's precipitous change in procedures fell on deaf ears, and he was executed without ever receiving a full federal appeal.

Ironically, on the morning of December 7, 1982, the day Brooks was put to death, the Fifth Circuit Court of Appeals, the same court that had hastened Brooks's execution, held in another capital case that without an express jury finding that a defendant himself, and not a codefendant, had been the triggerman, a death sentence could not be carried out (*Clark* v. *Louisiana State Penitentiary* 1983, 699). The "expedited" treatment of Brooks's case denied him the obvious constitutional claim afforded by this ruling.

Ironically, again, less than two months later, when Thomas Barefoot, the second capital defendant to be denied a stay of execution under these new "expedited" procedures, reached the Supreme Court, the Court stayed his execution in order to decide whether the procedures under which Brooks was executed complied with federal law (*Barefoot* v. *Estelle* 1983). To decide in favor of Barefoot, however, would be to indict the Fifth Circuit Court for the legally unacceptable homicide of Brooks.

These two cases display unmistakable indications of arbitrariness in their federal appeals beyond whatever arbitrariness may have entered earlier in the process. And they show that arbitrariness can take on different forms.

In Brooks's case the arbitrariness had a capricious character that left him "struck by lightning" in precisely the fashion condemned by Justice Stewart in *Furman*. It was the "luck of the draw" that denied him the three judges who ruled in *Clark* that death could not be imposed without a finding that the defendant himself was actually the triggerman, and provided him instead with three judges who prescribed the "expedited" treatment that deprived him of the opportunity for a full appeal on the constitutional grounds that his jury was selected unlawfully and that his punishment was disproportionate.

In Spinkelink's case the arbitrariness seemed to depend less on the luck of the draw than on the determination of the Florida attorney general. He vowed that Spinkelink would be executed as planned despite the stay. The day after it was issued he tried to have the U.S. Supreme Court set it aside, and when that failed he tried the Fifth Circuit where, it appears, at least one judge was sympathetic and willing to take the extraordinary steps that would permit Florida to execute Spinkelink before his death warrant expired and that would deny Spinkelink's attorneys the time to mount an effective appeal to the U.S. Supreme Court. It is the Court, of course, and not the Florida attorney general, that bears the responsibility for the arbitrariness. "As a lawyer," Clark (1979, 404) observed, "I have no doubt that Judge James P. Coleman violated John Spinkelink's right to due process of law. There can be only one explanation. Coleman wanted the man executed quickly, regardless of the law." Here the three-judge panel went a step further than the Brooks panel: they actually overturned a stay of execution without seriously considering the grounds on which it had been granted and without even having proper legal jurisdiction.

The final appeals of Spinkelink and Brooks reveal arbitrariness at the highest levels of legal authority. Federal judges are not exempt from or immune to personal, social, or situational influences; they are subject to the same pressures and temptations as everyone else who handles capital cases. As judges most have spent many years deciding what is appropriate and desirable punishment. They will surely have strong personal feelings about the desirability and appropriateness of the ultimate punishment of death. It is a seductive illusion to believe that the highest courts can intercept arbitrariness wherever it occurs in the handling of capital cases. Indeed, the assumption that the federal appellate process can serve as a fail-safe mechanism against arbitrariness and discrimination now sustains the institution of capital punishment in America. But the truth revealed here is that the federal courts themselves are an independent source or conduit of such arbitrariness.

## Conclusion

The evidence of arbitrariness and discrimination presented here is qualitatively more than a statistical demonstration that certain states' sentencing practices have failed to meet the *Furman* standard. Beyond this, we have seen that the arbitrariness is manifold in its links to race, location within state, and other personal, situational, and social influences; that it is pervasive in its presence at various decision-making points in the handling of capital cases; that it is intractable under different kinds of statutes in different states; and that it is replicated in different kinds of studies using different kinds of data. These findings represent an extension of our perspective on arbitrariness in capital punishment in the sense that they explicate some of the ways in which extralegal influences operate even in the presence of post-*Furman* statutory reforms—how prosecutors, defense attorneys, and judges, as well as jurors, become the agents of both systematic and unsystematic arbitrariness.

The evidence further confirms our view (developed especially in Chapter 5 and applied to the post-*Furman* era in Chapter 7) that arbitrariness is inherent in the use of capital punishment. Where death is available as punishment, according to this theory, it will be used in ways that reflect dominant community sentiments and override standards of evenhanded justice whatever form the capital statutes take. To be sure, statutory reforms may affect how and where arbitrariness occurs in the handling of cases, but changes are apt to be more apparent than real. Thus, the vast differences in the use of the death penalty by location within states observed since *Furman* appear to have been a pattern consistent with the pre-*Furman* era (Baldus et al. 1982a 105ff). And differential treatment by race of victim, so apparent in the post-*Furman* era, has also long been in existence (see Table 7-1). A great many other extralegal factors, such as wealth, property ownership, resident/transient status in the community, and unpopular political or religious beliefs, may also affect the handling of cases; but these have not been examined owing to a lack of systematic data. The consistent cumulative effect of attorney type adds a further element of arbitrariness and may reflect the influence of factors yet to be examined.

Above all, the evidence presented here should dispel the notion that the problem of arbitrariness is confined to sentencing. It is clearly present in the sentencing process—disparities by race and place persist under strong statistical controls for legally relevant considerations— but such arbitrariness also appears at every other stage of the process we have been able to examine. Greater guidance in sentencing and stricter separation between the guilt and punishment decisions have failed not only as a solution to the arbitrary sentencing of convicted offenders, but also, contrary to Justice White's hopes, as a statutory guide to the exercise of prosecutorial discretion. The data show that neither prosecutorial decisions of guilt made before or after the trial nor the judgment of guilt itself is free of recurrent biases. And over successive stages of the process these biases—especially the racial bias— are cumulative in nature.

So far, the federal courts, especially the Fifth Circuit Court of

Appeals, have taken the narrow view that arbitrariness must be demonstrated strictly and specifically in sentencing and that statistical evidence is irrelevant, as in *Spinkelink*, or insufficient (not strictly focused on sentencing or controlled for conceivably confounding factors), as in *Smith*. But the *Furman* justices objected to the freakish, rare, arbitrary use of the death penalty that left one defendant but not another condemned to death with no meaningful distinction between their cases—whether this was the product of sentencing or decisions elsewhere in the process. That statutory sentencing guidelines would seem on their face to remedy the problem, according to the *Gregg* court, does not mean that the court found arbitrariness constitutionally acceptable if it occurred elsewhere. Why else would Justice White address himself to the presumed derivative benefits of sentencing guidelines on the exercise of prosecutorial discretion? Is it not cynical to suppose that the Supreme Court is concerned only with the biases of jurors, that it has granted to the regular participants in the criminal justice process the privilege of caprice and systematic bias at the expense of the capital defendant whose cost may be his life? The language of Chief Justice Burger in *Furman* was "evenhanded justice," not "evenhanded sentencing."

Statistical evidence of arbitrariness and discrimination is becoming more broadly recognized and appreciated among members of the judiciary. Even under the *Spinkelink* standard of the former Fifth Circuit, Georgia federal district judge Avant Edenfield in an appendix to his opinion in *Moore* v. *Balkcom* (1981), indicted Georgia's post-*Furman* guided discretion statutes as applied. Citing the evidence on Georgia (presented in Chapter 7), he observed:

> There is simply no basis whatever for believing that sentencing procedures have changed significantly in Georgia since the current statute was enacted. . . . In sum, it appears to this Court that the procedures mandated by *Furman* do not now and in fact never will achieve the standard set out in that opinion and in succeeding cases. . . . Far from guiding juries to rational choices, the statute merely catalogues a laundry list of considerations which would be obvious to any jury considering an appropriate case, but provide little, if any, real basis for their determination (p. 824).

Although these words do not have the standing of law, written as they were in an appendix to the formal opinion, they do nevertheless represent an outspoken condemnation of the post-*Furman* system of capital punishment.

Beyond the reaches of the Fifth Circuit, statistical evidence was explicitly incorporated into the Massachusetts Supreme Judicial Court's decision in *District Attorney of Suffolk County* v. *Watson* (1980) as a basis for abolishing capital punishment under that state's constitutional protection against cruel or unusual punishment. The death penalty was declared unconstitutional in Massachusetts, in part because of the arbitrary and discriminatory manner of its application under post-*Furman* statutes in other states (as revealed in preliminary tabulations of the data presented here in Chapter 7). In the words of the Massachusetts court:

> Examination of death sentences imposed in Florida, Georgia, and Texas under post-*Furman* statutes upheld by the Supreme Court in 1976 indicates that very little has changed as to arbitrariness and discrimination (p. 2251).

This court also recognized the pervasive and inevitable character of such arbitrariness and discrimination:

> Power to decide rests not only in juries but in police officers, prosecutors, defense counsel, and trial judges. In the totality of the process, most life or death decisions will be made by these officials, unguided and uncurbed by statutory standards. In any given case, decisions may rest upon such considerations as the level of public outcry (p. 2250).

This judgment of the Massachusetts court, written of course without knowledge of the newly accumulated evidence presented here, is nevertheless an apt summary of this chapter. Our examination of the actors and stages in the processing of potentially capital cases supports the diagnosis of this arbitrariness as a systematic, pervasive, and inexorable problem. We see it in the actions of prosecutors, defense attorneys, jurors, and judges; in charging, trying, and defending cases; in seeking, imposing, and reviewing death sentences; and in the presence of sentencing guidelines, bifurcated sentence hearings, and automatic appellate review. The results are plain: the system of capital punishment is riddled with arbitrariness from beginning to end.

# 11

## THE FINAL DISCRETION

A decade ago, the United States Supreme Court delivered a stunning appraisal of capital punishment in America. It ruled in the *Furman* decision of 1972 that the death penalty was being imposed in violation of the Eighth Amendment prohibition against cruel and unusual punishment but, as we have seen, it left open the possibility that the death penalty could be imposed without violating the constitution. Since then the Supreme Court has presided over changes in the institution of capital punishment designed to remedy these constitutional ills, and hence preserve the death penalty itself. The chief instruments of change have been the Eighth Amendment standards of fairness, utility, and contemporary values.

In *Furman* the High Court ended capital punishment, at least temporarily, by declaring that, because of the arbitrary way death sentences were being handed down, it failed the fairness test. The members of the plurality did not agree on the precise character or source of this arbitrariness, but they did agree that its presence represented a departure from the constitutional standard of "evenhanded justice." On Eighth Amendment tests of utility as a deterrent and compatibility with contemporary values, the death penalty was found acceptable by most of the justices.

After most state legislatures had responded with new capital statutes designed to remove such arbitrariness, the Court again applied the standards of the Eighth Amendment. In *Gregg* and companion cases, the Court shifted ground on fairness and contemporary values.

On the one hand, it invoked the contemporary values test to outlaw the mandatory death penalty. In *Woodson* and *Roberts*, the Court held that the almost complete transition from mandatory to discretionary capital statutes in the United States prior to *Furman* (see Table 1-2) and the tendency of juries under mandatory statutes not to convict when they were unwilling to see the death penalty imposed (jury nullification) indicated that contemporary standards of respect for the person require "individualized treatment in sentencing" when the punishment is death.

On the other hand, the Court restricted its application of the fairness test to the new capital statutes "on their face," not "as applied." In *Gregg*, *Proffitt*, and *Jurek*, it found that guided discretion statutes should, on their face, remove the arbitrariness to which it had objected in *Furman*; it did not consider whether, in practice, they had—and thus did not subject the remedies adopted by the various states to an empirical test of fairness. As it had in *Furman*, the Court rejected the challenge that the death penalty had no deterrent advantage, this time citing Ehrlich's research (1975) and indicating that the evidence against the death penalty's unique deterrent power was "inconclusive."

After *Gregg*, the Supreme Court further extended its application of the contemporary values test and further restricted its use of the fairness test. In *Coker* it ruled that the death penalty for rape violated contemporary values. The unwillingness of most legislatures to provide the death penalty for rape and the reluctance of most juries to impose death as punishment for rape in the post-*Furman* era, in the words of the Court, "do not wholly determine . . . [but] strongly confirm our own judgment which is that death is indeed a disproportionate penalty for the crime of raping an adult woman." In *Lockett* the High Court declared that statutes limiting the consideration of mitigating circumstances violated the contemporary standard of "individualized treatment," as articulated in *Woodson*. But when the death penalty was again challenged as unfair in its application under post-*Furman* guided discretion statutes, the High Court, in its discretion, chose not to consider the arguments and evidence in the case of *Spinkelink* v. *Wainwright*.

The Supreme Court has final discretion over the availability and use of capital punishment in America and a continuing obligation to act in the presence of laws and practices that violate the constitution. At the time of *Furman*, Chief Justice Burger wrote of the need for "data of more recent vintage" and observed that the future of the death penalty "rests primarily on factual claims." The facts are mounting. Concerning fairness, the evidence is now stronger than it was when Spinkelink appealed, or for that matter, when Federal Judge Edenfield issued his opinion in *Moore* or the Massachusetts Supreme Judicial

Court rendered its opinion in *Watson*. Evidence on the question of utility is also stronger and more consistent now than it was when the Court last considered this issue in *Gregg*. And this accumulating evidence sheds new light on the question of contemporary values.

In this concluding chapter, we review the evidence as it now stands in the context of the three Eighth Amendment standards of fairness, utility, and contemporary values. This will serve to summarize our findings and to bring them to bear on the chief constitutional challenges to capital punishment. We also take a closer look at the punishment itself to consider what it means to those in whose names it is carried out.

*Fairness: The death penalty under post-*Furman *capital statutes continues to be imposed in an arbitrary manner; the arbitrariness is not localized at one stage but pervades the entire process; and the arbitrariness is both systematically linked to race and unsystematic in nature.*

There is unmistakable evidence that the imposition of the death sentence under the various post-*Furman* guided discretion statutes has departed substantially from the Eighth Amendment standard of "evenhanded justice." In Chapter 7 we saw gross disparities of treatment by race and by geographical location within states during the first five years under post-*Furman* statutes in states responsible for more than half the death sentences imposed in that period. Furthermore, both types of disparities were shown to be independent of the principal aggravating circumstance among cases resulting in a death sentence, namely, the presence of an accompanying felony. For four states, these disparities by race and place were established for the overall processing of cases from offense through sentencing, and for Florida, where data were available on the successive stages of indictment, conviction, and sentencing, these disparities of treatment appeared at each discrete stage of the process. The data also revealed that in Florida and Georgia the appellate review process failed to remove or even to reduce the disparities that had entered earlier in the process.

The evidence of pervasive race-linked arbitrariness is stronger now than it was at the time Judge Edenfield or the Massachusetts Supreme Judicial Court rendered their opinions. In Chapter 10 we saw that racial disparities at indictment, conviction, and sentencing in Florida were independent of legally relevant aggravating and mitigating factors (in addition to felony circumstance), and that the race-of-victim bias was cumulative in progressive stages of capital cases. The decisions of prosecutors, in particular, display evidence of racial bias in allegations of an accompanying felony circumstance (Table 7-9), in charging an accompanying felony (Table 7-10), in obtaining a first degree murder indictment (Table 10-1), and in seeking a death sentence given a first degree murder conviction (Table 10-4).

At the appellate level, courts have ignored or actively shielded racial bias. We now know that the Georgia Supreme Court disregards race as well as legally relevant characteristics of the crime and of the defendant in conducting its proportionality review. In identifying "similar" cases, the Court has endorsed prevailing patterns of race-linked arbitrariness instead of testing for proportionality of punishment. In addition, there is now evidence that the Florida Supreme Court has actually contributed to disparities of treatment by race (Radelet and Vandiver 1983). In turn, federal court decisions have further perpetrated this arbitrariness and discrimination in capital punishment by greatly restricting the kinds of evidence that might be offered to demonstrate the influence of race.

There is also much stronger evidence of arbitrariness apart from race. Where within a state a crime occurs is another element of arbitrariness; it has a substantial independent effect on the handling of cases in both Florida and Georgia. Unlike race, location's effects are not strictly cumulative over stages of the criminal justice process. The region in Florida where death sentences were most likely was not the one where capital indictments and convictions were most common; to the contrary, capital indictments, convictions, and sentences were least likely in the southern region of Florida. For each stage of the process where data were available in both states, regional disparities of treatment were statistically independent of a wide range of aggravating and mitigating considerations, as well as race. Clearly, the death sentence is not being imposed in similar cases throughout the state.

Race and location aside, judges, prosecutors, and defense attorneys cite a wide variety of additional extralegal considerations including personal, situational, and community factors that they say influence the prosecutor's critical decision to charge a capital offense and to take such a capital charge to trial. The availability of effective defense services in capital cases is influenced by a number of extralegal factors that work against the defendant who has a court-appointed attorney, regardless of race. In the sentencing process, the death penalty is being sought and imposed at levels of aggravation where similar cases do not typically receive a death sentence; this holds for both black-victim and white-victim cases. In effect, these death sentences are freakish, random, and rare—the standard applied in *Furman*—by comparison with cases similar in legally aggravating and mitigating characteristics.

The evidence of arbitrariness in appellate review does not point so much to differential treatment by race (cf. Radelet and Vandiver 1982) as it does to the failure to detect treatment disparities of any kind—racial bias being the most prominent of these—at earlier stages in the handling of capital cases. The Georgia Supreme Court, for whatever reasons, simply fails to comply with the statutory standard for reviewing proportionality of punishment by comparing the case under review with similar cases.

These latter elements of arbitrariness are independent of race. Together they infect the processing of potentially capital cases with unsystematic arbitrariness from beginning to end.[1] This arbitrariness may appear unsystematic because the processes involved are essentially random or because we do not adequately understand them. But either way, this arbitrariness will be reflected in departures from the rational standards of evenhanded justice required by *Furman* and thought to be established by *Gregg*. The Eighth Amendment fairness test requires only that arbitrariness be demonstrated, not that its nature be understood, for the death penalty to be held unconstitutional.

*Utility: Executions have no unique deterrent advantage over alternative punishments; the evidence shows that executions promote rather than prevent the homicides of innocent people; the brutalizing effect is a consistent finding of various studies of the short-run impact of executions.*

There is strong support for the Eighth Amendment challenge that the death penalty is an "excessive" punishment in the sense, elaborated by Justice Brennan in *Furman*, that it has "no penological advantage" over less severe punishments. In Chapters 4, 8, and 9, we addressed the claims for capital punishment as a unique deterrent. The most credible evidence now available indicates the contrary, namely, that executions cause more, not fewer, homicides—that the death penalty brutalizes rather than deters.

Scores of studies spanning more than a century have reported that capital punishment has no deterrent advantage over alternative punishments. They typically examined how changes in the availability and use of capital punishment affected homicide rates within and between states. (Our analysis in Chapter 4 of the effect of the cessation of executions in the 1960s on homicide rates is an example of this kind of research.) Then in 1975, Isaac Ehrlich published a study using econometric techniques that claimed to show that execution has a deterrent effect. And, despite the evidence to the contrary of all previous studies and the methodological critiques of Ehrlich's work then available (Bowers and Pierce 1975b; Passell and Taylor 1976), the Supreme Court in *Gregg* concluded that the evidence against the deterrent effect of capital punishment was "inconclusive."

---

1. This perspective on the death penalty under post-Furman statutes is best articulated in Black (1982, 1974).

The balance of evidence has now shifted even more decisively in favor of the proposition that capital punishment does not deter but brutalizes. The strongest evidence of this brutalizing effect comes from our analysis (in Chapter 8) of the monthly incidence of executions and homicides over a period of fifty-seven years in New York state. This investigation shows that there were two *more* homicides than otherwise expected, on the average, in the month immediately after an execution, controlling for the influence of secular trends, seasonal variations, and the occurrence of warfare on the incidence of homicide. This effect is statistically significant well beyond chance variation.

Among the limited number of other studies of homicides in the days, weeks, and months following executions, several have explicitly suggested the possibility of a brutalizing effect (Dann 1935; Graves 1956; King 1978) and still others are consistent with such an effect (Savitz 1958b; Phillips 1981, as shown below). Furthermore, a review of the evidence from studies of the availability and use of capital punishment between and within states reveals that the variations in homicide rates are more often consistent with brutalizing than with deterrent effects. And still further, our critical reexamination of Ehrlich's work (in Chapter 9) shows that when the more reliably reported vital statistics data on willful homicides are substituted for the FBI's criminal homicide statistics, Ehrlich's reported deterrent effects are converted into statistically significant brutalizing effects.

We can now cite still further evidence of brutalizing effects. In a recent study (Phillips 1981) of the incidence of homicides in the weeks before, during, and after twenty-two highly publicized executions in England, the author claimed to have shown, in what he described as the "first compelling statistical evidence" of deterrence, that there was a statistically significant reduction in homicides in the week of and in the week immediately after these executions. We have now established (Bowers 1983a) that this conclusion was based on errors in the data presented by Phillips. The corrected weekly homicide figures are shown in Table 11-1. When the correct figures are substituted for the incorrect ones, the pattern changes from deterrence to brutalization. The data show an average of two more homicides in the six weeks after than in the six weeks before an execution (forty-one more homicides after than before these twenty-two executions). Significantly, the corrected data show that the executions that received greater newspaper publicity (measured in column inches of type) were the ones that had a greater brutalizing effect.

Perhaps a predisposition or desire to believe in the deterrent advantages of the death penalty led commentators and even investigators to herald studies purporting to demonstrate deterrence as "more sophisticated" than previous research (Tullock 1974) and as the "first

**Table 11-1.** *Number of Homicides in the Weeks Before, During, and After 22 Highly Publicized Executions in England, 1853–1921*

| Weeks before, during, and after | Number of homicides |
| --- | --- |
| Sixth week before | 25 |
| Fifth week before | 13 |
| Fourth week before | 28 |
| Third week before | 30 |
| Second week before | 30 |
| First week before | 24 |
| Week of execution | 25 |
| First week after | 21 |
| Second week after | 34 |
| Third week after | 38 |
| Fourth week after | 37 |
| Fifth week after | 31 |
| Sixth week after | 30 |

*Note*: Elizabeth Hanoway of Amnesty International in London collected these homicide statistics from the British Museum and verified the figures where they differed from those published by Phillips (1981).

statistically reliable evidence" of a unique deterrent effect (Phillips 1981). Indeed, such a predisposition may explain why the U.S. Supreme Court relied on Ehrlich's work alone for its judgment that the evidence was "inconclusive" in *Gregg*. The fact that both these studies, as well as others, are now shown to be more consistent with brutalizing than with deterrent effects adds significantly to the strength of the evidence that the death penalty fails the Eighth Amendment test of utility.

*Contemporary Values: Capital punishment offends contemporary values because it sacrifices innocent human lives as well as the lives of convicted offenders, because it systematically deprives black citizens as well as black convicted offenders of equal justice, and because these ills are beyond the reach of legal reform.*

This is a broader test that goes beyond fairness and utility to consider the acceptability or appropriateness of punishment in light of society's fundamental values. It asks whether the punishment is consistent with underlying social values and morality. For this test, the Court has invoked criteria such as "evolving standards of human decency," "respect for the individual," and "excessiveness" or "disproportionality" of punishment. And it has looked to public opinion, legislative action, and jury behavior for indications, though not determinative evidence, of whether these standards were being met.

If the death penalty does not deter then it should fail the utility test; the fact that it provokes lethal violence in society offends contemporary values. The absence of a deterrent effect has one implication; the presence of a brutalizing effect has another. With consistent evidence that the death penalty is not safeguarding but sacrificing innocent human life, it is no longer our responsibility to move cautiously so as not to do away with executions that might yet be discovered to have a deterrent effect, but to move expeditiously to halt executions because the best available evidence shows that they actually promote homicide. The brutalizing effect may be slight in numbers—very few additional homicides in a very large population—but it is profoundly cruel and unusual for the supreme sacrifice it requires of innocent persons, if not for the life it takes from the convicted murderer. Studies of the kind that might verify or further specify such brutalizing effects are limited by a lack of temporally refined data on the relationship between executions and homicides—unless those now on death row become part of a grotesque experiment on the brutalizing effect of executions. In such a case, the available research indicates that as many as two thousand additional human lives would be sacrificed if the more than one thousand persons now on death row were executed.

If the death penalty is arbitrarily imposed it should fail the test of fairness; the fact that it is imposed in a systematic racially biased manner offends contemporary values. It is a violation of fairness when one person is sentenced to death and another is not for crimes that cannot meaningfully be distinguished in legally relevant terms. It is a violation of a broader and more fundamental social value when a class of persons distinguished by race is consistently subjected to discrimination in the administration of capital punishment. This applies to a class of convicted criminal offenders *and* to a class of innocent victims of capital crimes, both identified by race. When the law disregards or disfavors black victims, it deprives black citizens of equal rights.

Evolving standards of human decency no longer tolerate discrimination that deprives any social group, especially by race, in terms of access to voting rights, public accommodations, education, and housing—nor does the law, thanks to the Supreme Court's leadership in recognizing and articulating contemporary values in landmark decisions on these issues. Surely the same contemporary values will not tolerate systematic disparities of treatment by race of convicted offender or by race of innocent victims. Moreover, the Supreme Court itself has ruled in *Furman* that the constitution demands a higher standard of justice when the crime is murder and the punishment may be death. Surely that includes greater intolerance for racial disparities.

Furthermore, these two violations of contemporary values—brutalization and discrimination—are beyond redemption by legal reform. Laws would have to rid capital punishment of the extralegal functions that are responsible for its very existence. The new capital statutes accepted by the Supreme Court in *Gregg* have not removed systematic and pervasive racial bias. They may have reduced unsystematic arbitrariness somewhat (Baldus et al. 1982a), but the intransigence of systematic arbitrariness to legal reform is suggested by evidence that the post-*Furman* reforms have been answered not by a reduction of racial bias but by shifts in the character and locus of such bias: there may have been some displacement of bias from race of offender to race of victim and within the sentencing process from jury to prosecutorial discretion (Baldus et al. 1982a). Yet race-linked differences in treatment remain evident throughout the process—in the charging and trying decisions of prosecutors, in the allocation of effective defense services, and even in the sentencing process, which was specifically targeted by these reforms. And even if arbitrariness and discrimination could be reversed, no law could halt the brutalizing effect of executions, short of having them conducted secretly, a step that would surely be unconstitutional.

There is a parallel between the Supreme Court's present experience with capital punishment and its earlier experience with segregation in the public schools. About the turn of the century the Court held in *Plessy* v. *Ferguson* (1897) that racially segregated public schools could be "separate but equal." The next sixty years of segregated schooling led the Court to the alternative diagnosis in *Brown* v. *Board of Education* (1954): segregated schooling was inherently discriminatory and therefore unconstitutional. In similar fashion, the Court's initial diagnosis was that the death penalty could be administered free of any constitutional violation under guided discretion statutes. The experience of the past ten years, as it becomes better documented, indicates, however, that an alternative diagnosis is now in order, a diagnosis of the kind formulated by the Massachusetts Supreme Judicial Court in *Watson*, which concludes, on the basis of this post-*Furman* experience, that the death penalty is inherently and inexorably discriminatory in its application. The Massachusetts Court ruled that the death penalty violates the constitutional protection provided in that state's Declaration of Human Rights against "cruel or unusual punishment."

## The Meaning of Death as Punishment

Why do we still have it? Its heritage is suspect. It has flourished in America with the institution of slavery, with racial strife during Reconstruction, and with economic adversity at the time of the Great Depression, especially in the regions where these conditions were most keenly felt. Its use has been aberrant, racially biased, and far exceeding that in most other nations. And, according to the evidence we have examined here, the system remains replete with arbitrariness and is liable for the loss of innocent human lives.

Despite this, a majority of Americans say they favor the death penalty for convicted murderers—60 percent in 1973 and 67 percent in 1967, according to the Harris polls (Bedau 1982, 85, Table 3-2-1). Public attitudes toward capital punishment have fluctuated: a majority favored it in the 1950s, opposed it in the 1960s, and again favored it in the 1970s. Not surprisingly, the polls have consistently found that most blacks oppose the death penalty. And those who are better informed about capital punishment are more likely to oppose it (Sarat and Vidmar 1976; Ellsworth and Ross 1983)—a finding consistent with Justice Marshall's opinion in *Furman* that "the great mass of citizens would conclude [if they knew the facts] that the death penalty is immoral" (p. 363).

Moreover, the expressions of support for capital punishment given in public opinion surveys are evidently at odds with how people would actually behave as jury members. In a recent article, Ellsworth and Ross (1983) report that when people were given actual case descriptions and asked whether the death penalty was appropriate, they were reluctant to recommend it.

> [T]he strength of people's support for the death penalty in the abstract is considerably qualified when they are asked to imagine themselves on a capital jury. . . . In not one of the three descriptions of cases where the defendant actually received the death penalty did more than 15 percent of the respondents recommend death, even though a majority said that they were in favor of the death penalty in general (pp. 138–139).

If they are reluctant to use the death penalty, why do so many people say they favor it? They say they do so above all because they believe it will have a deterrent effect (Sarat and Vidmar 1976; Ellsworth and Ross 1983). However, this belief in deterrence may not be the only reason for their support. Most (62 percent) of those who favor the death penalty do so even though they believe that it will be imposed in a discriminatory manner (Ellsworth and Ross 1983); most (66 percent) of those who favor it and believe in its deterrent effect say they would support the death penalty even if it could be proved to their satisfaction that it did not have a deterrent effect (Ellsworth and Ross 1983).[2]

2. This does not imply that a majority of the population would support the death penalty if they were convinced that it was not an effective deterrent. Only a minority of the respondents to Harris polls in 1973 (35 percent) and 1977 (46 percent) said they would favor the death penalty in answer to the question: "Suppose that it could be proven to your satisfaction that the death penalty was NOT more effective than life imprisonment in keeping people from committing crimes such as murder; would you be in favor of the death penalty or opposed to it?" (Bedau 1982, 91, Table 3-2-7).

These responses suggest that some death penalty advocates may be so desperate for the protection they hope it will bring that they are willing to support it even though they concede that it will be imposed discriminatorily. Others may support it for reasons that are socially less acceptable than deterrence, such as a desire for vengeance, especially for certain kinds of offenses and against certain kinds of offenders. "[I]t may be that the belief in deterrence is seen as more 'scientific' or more socially desirable than other reasons; people mention it first because its importance is obvious, not because its importance is real (Ellsworth and Ross 1983, 149)."

On the basis of their research, Ellsworth and Ross have concluded that general statements of support for capital punishment—and opposition as well—reflect "symbolic attitudes," that is, attitudes untested by experience, as a juror's would be in a capital case. Consequently, they remain abstract and ideological, part of a person's political or social orientation that does not depend on any particular knowledge about capital punishment.[3] In other words, these attitudes are empty ideological statements that do not guide people's actions in concrete situations.

In sentencing a convicted offender, however, the jurors' attitudes can no longer remain symbolic. The prosecutor's task is, of course, to overcome the resistance the jurors may feel to sentencing the defendant to death. By examining how a prosecutor constructed his argument before the sentencing jury in one such case, we may learn something more about what makes people choose death as punishment when they must actually decide on the sentence.

The role of deterrence as an underlying rationale is aptly illustrated in the prosecutor's closing arguments before the sentencing jury in the case of William Brooks, a black man sentenced to death for killing a white woman in Columbus, Georgia, in 1977 (petitioner's brief in *Brooks* v. *Francis* 1981 [filed sub nom. in *Brooks* v. *Zant*]):

I can tell you this; the last person in Georgia was electrocuted in 1964, and since that date, crime has increased year by year, time after time,

---

3. A majority of the proponents for capital punishment in the study by Ellsworth and Ross (1983) were either unsure or mistaken about the truth of the following statements:

Over the years, states which have had the death penalty have shown a lower murder rate than neighboring states which did not have the death penalty [False].
Studies have not found that abolishing the death penalty has any significant effect on the murder rate in a state [True].
After the Supreme Court struck down the death penalty in 1972 the murder rate in the United States showed a sharp upturn [False].
Studies have shown that the rate of murder usually drops in weeks following a publicized execution [False].

every time the statistics come out, we have an increase in crime rate. We didn't have that when we had capital punishment. We didn't have this kind of murder, these kinds of crimes you've heard about here this week, when we had capital punishment, if they were they were very seldom, we heard about them somewhere else, but not around here.

Let me say this to you, during my lifetime this country has been in three wars, each war we've taken our young men down to the age of seventeen, we've trained them, we've put guns in their hands, we've taught them how to kill the enemy and we've sent them overseas, and they have killed other human beings who were enemies of our country, and when they did a good job of killing them, we decorated them and gave them citations, praised them for it. . . .

Well, I say to you that we're in a war again in this country, except it's not a foreign nation, it's against the criminal element in this country, that's who we're at war with, and they're winning the war, is what's so bad, and if you don't believe they're winning, just look about you. You don't dare get out on the streets at night and walk around, you don't dare leave your house unlocked.

And, if we can send a 17-year-old young man overseas to kill an enemy soldier, is it asking too much to ask you to go back and vote for the death penalty in this case against William Brooks and I submit to you that he's an enemy, and he's a member of the criminal elements, and he's our enemy, and he's an enemy of the law-abiding citizens and the people who want to live peacefully in this country, and who want to be secure in their persons and their homes.

This argument began with an impassioned appeal for deterrence and ended with a patriotic call to arms against an enemy within. The alleged deterrent power of capital punishment was transformed into a promise of protection for society in a war against the "criminal element" (left ill-defined, evidently to include criminals of all sorts). The prosecutor spoke of William Brooks not as a man guilty of murder but as a representative of the criminal element that threatens to destroy our way of life. The issue was not Brooks, but the class of people he represented. Thus, the deterrence ideology, as it was embellished with the appeal to patriotism, invited the jurors to act on their fantasies and prejudices in deciding Brooks's fate. In this way the socially acceptable deterrence ideology made room for other less acceptable motives for capital punishment.

But there is still more in the prosecutor's closing arguments than inflammatory rhetoric about patriotism and deterrence. He also focused the jury's attention on the victim and her family:

. . . Let's talk a minute about the person who is not here, about Carol Jeannine Galloway. What kind of person was she? We know that she was a pretty young lady, a beautiful young lady. We know that she was about twenty-three years old, she was not married, that she still lived with her mother and father, and we know that she was a person of high morals. We know that she was a considerate person. She went out picking up the garbage can to save her mother or father from having to do that. We know that she was a thoughtful person, she was going to treat her friend to breakfast before her friend left town.

. . . think about the Galloway family. And think about Carol Jeannine Galloway, who is not here in the Courtroom today, and who will never be here again.

. . . What has the Galloway family gone through, what have they gone through? Next week when it's Thanksgiving, and they are sitting around the table, Carol Jeannine won't be there, and never will be there again.

. . . who knows who it will be next time, whose daughter will it be next time? It was Mrs. Galloway's daughter this time, Bobby Murray's girlfriend; whose girlfriend or daughter will it be next time? (29)

Here the prosecutor tried to make the crime more immediate and personal for the jurors by having them identify with the victim and empathize with her family and friends. He described her as someone they would like to know, and asked them to share the anguish of her family and friends and to experience her death as they did. He knew that the anger and indignation jurors naturally feel about a crime such as this would be stronger if they felt close to the victim or to her family. He then suggested that one of them could be next; this frightening prospect was more credible to the jurors if they identified with the victim. By evoking their feelings of identification, the prosecutor evidently persuaded the jurors to set aside whatever aversion or reluctance they may have had to calling for Brooks' death. Needless to say, his closing argument to the jury misrepresented what is known about deterrence and obscured the legal issues of aggravation and mitigation.

Beyond the particulars of the Brooks case, the prosecutor's focus on the victim may provide further insight into why the death penalty is used disproportionately in white-victim cases. Because it is natural to identify with those who share one's personal qualities and social identities, most jurors in most communities are more likely to identify with white rather than with black murder victims. As Gross and Mauro (1983, 73) have observed:

There is, undoubtedly, wide variation among jurors both in the degree and in the type of horror that will tip the balance toward death. Particular gruesome facts will be more horrifying to some than to others. But one influential process cuts across this uneven range: we are more readily horrified by a death if we empathize or identify with the victim, or see the victim as similar to a relative or friend, than if the victim appears to us as a stranger. In a society which is still segregated socially if not legally, and in which the great majority of jurors are white, jurors will rarely identify with black victims or see them as family or friends. This reaction is not an expression of racial hostility, it is simply a reflection of an emotional fact of inter-racial relations in our society.

Feelings of identification with the murder victim are not, of course, confined to the courtroom or to the small group of community members who become jurors in a particular case. Indeed, such feelings are likely to affect the publicity a murder attracts, the outrage the community feels, and each of the successive decisions that move a defendant along the path toward capital punishment.

Identification with the victims of murder, then, may be what transforms symbolic attitudes of support for the death penalty into votes for the death sentence in a particular case. The realities of murder naturally and inevitably make people feel angry, vengeful and fearful; and the feelings become stronger when people feel closer to the murder victim. Anger may be a healthy sign that people care about justice and about the well-being of their fellow citizens (see Berns 1979a), but it provides no guarantee that punishment will be justly imposed. Indeed, it is precisely because we respond emotionally to the personal tragedy of murder that our use of the death penalty in specific cases will be affected by our feelings about the victim. Individuals who identify with specific murder victims will undoubtedly feel that they are responding genuinely to the issues of justice in a given case. But jurors' judgments in the aggregate, because they reflect their personal preferences, have meant that those who kill whites are sentenced to death more often than those who kill blacks. The point is that people's motives for punishment and the legally acceptable standards for its imposition are not the same. The law allows the seriousness of the crime and the culpability of the criminal, not feelings for the victim, to figure in the determination of punishment. But personal feeling for the murder victim will inevitably, if unconsciously, introduce arbitrary extralegal influences into the process that leads to death as punishment.

Identification with the victim of a murder may affect those who become murderers as well as those who judge murderers. We would like to believe that potential murderers identify with actual murderers—who have been condemned and executed—and are thus deterred. Indeed, this is the justification most people give for capital punishment. But the evidence of brutalizing effects in the month following an execution suggests, on the contrary, that a potential murderer who feels he has been outraged, betrayed, or dishonored by someone else learns from the example of an execution that persons who grievously offend others deserve to die for their crimes. In other words, he may actually identify with victims of murder, and, by murdering, exact lethal vengeance. Thus, personal identification with the victims of murder may be a common underpinning for legal and illegal homicides. Indeed, this factor may be responsible, in part, for the failure of the death penalty on both Eighth Amendment tests of fairness and of utility—for the presence of arbitrariness and the absence of deterrence.

The public opinions polls and the prosecutor's arguments in the Brooks case strongly suggest that America's fear of criminal violence is the mainstay of capital punishment. And indeed the fear is justified. The murder rate in America is among the highest anywhere in the modern industrial world, and within the United States it is highest in the south. The irony is that our adherence to the death penalty is not a cure for but a symptom of the violence and fear in our society; it is used most often in the places where such violence is most intense or extreme.

Survey research suggests that the public desperately wants to prevent murder, supposes that making would-be murderers believe they might be punished by death will help, and knows that this cannot be accomplished without having capital statutes on the law books. The enactment of revised capital statutes after *Furman* was surely a testimony to the public's desire for the protection they hope the threat of the death penalty will provide.

The discrepancy between the advocacy for capital punishment and its rare application is a sign that the death penalty is no longer compatible with contemporary values. Death sentences are "freakishly rare," to use the *Furman* court's language, in most states and even in most counties of those states where they are not as rare. Indeed, the character of the prosecutor's appeal for William Brooks's death suggests that the jurors would not have chosen death as punishment strictly on the basis of legally aggravating and mitigating considerations.

Our society has always been ambivalent about the final stage of the process: imposing legal homicide. We have removed executions from public view, sought more "humane" methods of execution, and devised ways to obscure the identity of the executioner. More recently, our ambivalence has given way to aversion and abstinence. About a half-century ago, the number of executions began to decline and some fifteen years ago came to a halt. In the six years since that moratorium ended, we have so far averaged one execution a year, and most of these have been state-assisted suicides.

America has been trying to preserve the threat of capital punishment without conducting executions; we want the death penalty without legal homicides. But laws that provide for capital punishment are being applied whether or not we want legal homicides. There are now more than a thousand persons condemned to death in the United States, and their numbers are mounting week by week. Their executions are being blocked by legal appeals that will ultimately be carried to the United States Supreme Court. As the final arbiter, the Supreme Court is regularly confronted with evidence and arguments against the constitutionality of the death penalty. Because of the consistency and strength of the evidence, the court must ultimately decide against capital punishment. The question is, before that happens, will we begin a grim parade of legal homicides in unrivaled numbers that will distinguish us in the invidious manner that our tenacious adherence to legal slavery did a century ago? How long will it be before we join virtually all other nations that share our social and cultural traditions and abolish the death penalty?

Capital punishment in the United States is guilty on three counts. It is unfair, ineffective, and offensive to contemporary values. Its legitimacy has been sustained in the public mind by an erroneous belief in its deterrent effect. Its legality is now being sustained by the U.S. Supreme Court under the false assumption that it has been purged of unfairness by statutory reforms. The public desires and believes in deterrence, and the Court requires evenhanded justice; but neither exists. Instead its application is discriminatory and its effect is brutalizing; and this offends the social as well as the legal values of our society. Its failure on any one of these counts makes it cruel and unusual punishment. Its failure on all three counts must hasten the verdict that it is unconstitutional.

# APPENDICES

# APPENDIX A

## EXECUTIONS UNDER STATE
## AUTHORITY: AN INVENTORY

This appendix contains a listing of state-imposed executions since 1864 and those imposed in Washington, D.C., since 1853. The listing was originally compiled by Negley K. Teeters and Charles J. Zibulka for the period January 20, 1864, through August 10, 1967, and first published in its entirety in the 1974 edition of *Executions in America.* * For this second edition of that book, M. Watt Espy, Jr., has provided numerous additions and corrections to the original Teeters-Zibulka inventory. With the information supplied us by Mr. Espy through December 1981, we have made some 2,900 corrections in the more than 5,700 executions listed by Teeters and Zibulka, and added some 40 executions occurring between 1864 and 1967 but omitted from the original Teeters-Zibulka inventory. In addition, we have updated the historical record through December 1982 with information on the six executions imposed since 1967.

## Teeters and Zibulka's Description
## of the Original Inventory

This is a compilation of the names, counties, and dates of execution of every individual executed at a state penal institution from

*A portion of this inventory (*Alabama* through *Kentucky*, alphabetically) has appeared in *Hearings Before the Subcommittee on Criminal Laws and Procedures of the U.S. Senate Committee on the Judiciary, 90th Congress, 2nd Session, on S 1760*, March 21, 22, and July 2, 1968 (1970, 209–236).

the first executions in the Vermont State Prison in 1864. Executions in the District of Columbia have been included, together with the electrocutions at the Cook County Jail, Chicago, Illinois, and the county jail hangings in Kentucky for rape. In the latter two instances, county authorities exercised concurrent jurisdiction with state authorities.

This compilation is presented and distributed in the hopes that it will lead to further studies of capital punishment on the state level. With this list, which compiles executions from every state having capital punishment, it will be possible to use newspapers and the published opinions of appellate courts as sources of information on these individuals, especially regarding their crimes.

Information on appeals has been derived from the Indices to the *Decennial Digests* published by West Publishing Company. *These are not completely accurate*, as the Indices alone were hurriedly consulted for legal citations. Many defendants with common surnames have had their appeals confused with other defendants of the same name not executed, or some appeals have been docketed under the name of a crime partner who was not executed. A listing of appeals for executions since 1956 is very incomplete, as a ten-year table of cases has not been compiled for that period. Many appeals so reported are either summarily affirmed or argued upon legal points only, and no information on the crime is included in the opinion.

Our heartfelt thanks to the wardens and departments of correction of the various states who have taken the trouble to furnish us with the information which is, in part, reported in this compilation.

## Espy's Explanation of the Updating Procedure

I have undertaken to research and confirm every execution imposed under both state and local authority in the history of the United States. The master list I have compiled as of September 1982 includes 13,630 executions. As one aspect of this project, I obtained from wardens and departments of correction lists of all persons executed under state authority, as Teeters and Zibulka had done. I noticed that, because many were poorly mimeographed and printed, some of the vital information, including names and dates, was almost illegible. Since my intention was, and still is, to verify all executions in every jurisdiction, including those imposed under state authority, as I researched each individual case I was able not only to fill in gaps left by the states, but also to correct the errors contained in their listings.

The information providing the basis for these changes has been found in contemporary local newspaper coverage of the crimes, trials, and executions, in actual court records of the trials and the various appeals, and through contacts with local historians, historical societies, museums, and county clerks. Not all cases have yet been thoroughly researched, and corrections and additions have been made only in those cases where further research has been carried out.

Where a question of spelling has been involved and the case was taken to a higher tribunal, I have used the spelling given in the appeals decisions as found in the various regional reports. Where the case was not appealed, I have relied on local court records and the contemporary newspaper coverage for spelling verification. Changes in dates have been verified by newspaper coverage of the execution as well as by further correspondence with prison officials and departments of corrections. In most instances where an incorrect date was listed in the original inventory, a typing error was the cause or the date originally set by the court was given even though the actual execution was, in fact, delayed by judicial or executive action.

I have found that, in many instances, the ages quoted in the lists provided by the states were the ages of the individuals at the time of their conviction or admission to the prison system and not at the time of the execution. I have endeavored to correct these to show the actual age at the time of execution. Many of the errors with respect to age and race were typographical and I have also endeavored to correct these.

In a number of states, there were local hangings at the county level after the state began executing persons at the penitentiaries. In these instances, I have included the pertinent information on those persons whose executions I have confirmed in order that the listings might be as complete as possible from the inception of executions on the state level.

## Key to Symbols and Abbreviations Used in the Inventory

*Race*:

W = White
B = Black
C = Chinese
P = Puerto Rican
M = Mexican
J = Japanese
F = Filipino
E = Eskimo
I = Indian
O = Other

*Age*: Age at date of execution

*Date*: month/day/year

| | |
|---|---|
| *Offense*: | A = Assault |
| | A, L = Assault by a person under a life sentence |
| | Awira = Assault with intent to rape |
| | B = Burglary |
| | CK = Carnal knowledge |
| | E = Espionage |
| | K = Kidnapping |
| | M = Murder |
| | M, Acc = Accessory to murder |
| | M, Ar = Arson-Murder |
| | M, Att = Attempted murder |
| | M, B = Murder-Burglary |
| | M, Con = Murder-Conspiracy |
| | M, Ra = Rape-Murder |
| | Ra = Rape |
| | Ra, Att = Attempted rape |
| | Ra, B = Rape-Burglary |
| | Ra, Ro = Rape-Robbery |
| | Ro = Robbery |
| | Ro, Arm = Armed robbery |
| | Ro, Fr = Robbery-Firearms |
| | Ro, Hwy = Highway robbery |

*Appeals*: 
S = appeal to the highest state appellate court
F = appeal to a federal court (including application for the writ of habeas corpus to the United States District Court and/or appeal to the United States Circuit Court of Appeals)
U = appeal to the United States Supreme Court (including petitions for writs of certiorari, most of which are denied)
N.T. = new trial awarded by order of one of the above courts

*County*: County of prosecution. Spelled out in full except: N.Y. = New York; L.A. = Los Angeles; S.F. = San Francisco; Fed = execution was imposed under federal authority within the state

*Missing data*: A dash (—) is used to indicate where data are unavailable.

*Footnotes*: Footnotes to particular cases within the inventory are indicated with arabic numerals and located at the end of the list of executions for each state in which they occur.

## ALABAMA

*Period of Executions*: 1927–1965
*Total Number*: 153
*Method*: Electrocution
*Other Data*: Automatic appeal began in 1943. This applies to 53 cases.

| Name | Race | Age | Date of Execution | Offense | Appeal [1] | County |
|------|------|-----|-------------------|---------|-----------|--------|
| DeVaughn, Horace | B | 35 | 4/ 8/1927 | M | | Jefferson |
| Murphy, W. Virgil | W | 37 | 4/23/1927 | M | | Houston |
| Batchelor, Clyde Reese | W | 26 | 7/15/1927 | M | S | Elmore |
| Hall, Sam | B | — | 9/ 9/1927 | M | S | Autauga |
| Coleman, Jeff | B | — | 12/16/1927 | M | | Jefferson |
| Eatman, Bob | B | — | 12/30/1927 | M | | Hale |
| Washington, Charlie | B | — | 3/ 9/1928 | M | S | Jefferson |
| Burchfield, John | W | 25 | 3/ 9/1928 | M | S | Chambers |
| Brooks, Isiah | B | — | 4/ 6/1928 | M | | Crenshaw |
| Shelton, Robert | B | — | 6/15/1928 | M | S | Mobile |
| Peoples, Rodel | B | — | 7/20/1928 | M | | Jefferson |
| Jiles, Dock | B | — | 3/15/1929 | M | S | Lee |
| Carter, Will | B | 26 | 7/26/1929 | M | S | Jefferson |
| Harris, Charlie | B | 38 | 8/23/1929 | M | | Barbour |
| Jarvis, Jack | W | 28 | 4/11/1930 | M | S | Mobile |
| Miles, Roy Lee | B | 29 | 6/20/1930 | M | S | Bullock |
| Harris, Edgar | B | — | 6/20/1930 | M | S | Marengo |
| Brown, Jack | B | — | 6/20/1930 | M | S | Marengo |
| Gilmore, Silena (Female) | B | — | 1/24/1930 | M | | Jefferson |
| Malone, Cleveland | B | — | 2/27/1931 | Ra | | Talladega |
| Daniels, Mose | B | 19 | 3/27/1931 | Ra | S | Montgomery |
| Bates, Spencer | B | 27 | 5/29/1931 | M | S | Sumter |
| Stokes, William | B | — | 6/10/1931 | M | | St. Clair |
| Ashe, Richard | B | 24 | 1/15/1932 | M | | Hale |
| Williams, Charley | B | — | 1/15/1932 | Ra | S | Mobile |
| Irvin, Percey | B | — | 3/11/1932 | Ro | | Lowndes |
| Mims, Isaac | B | — | 3/11/1932 | M | S | Lowndes |
| Jones, Charlie | B | — | 2/ 3/1933 | M | S | Jefferson |
| Johnson, Willie James | B | — | 2/ 3/1933 | M | S | Jefferson |
| Meadows, George | B | 27 | 10/27/1933 | Ro | | Montgomery |
| Waller, Ernest | B | 21 | 2/ 9/1934 | M | | Dallas |
| Thompson, John | B | 38 | 2/ 9/1934 | M | S | Mobile |
| White, Hardie | B | 32 | 2/ 9/1934 | M | S | Mobile |
| Foster, Bennie | B | 21 | 2/ 9/1934 | M | S | Dallas |
| Roper, Soloman | B | 24 | 2/ 9/1934 | M | S | Dallas |
| Thomas, Ed | B | — | 3/ 1/1935 | M | | Hale |
| Ruff, Blake | B | — | 3/22/1935 | M | S | Clay |
| Preston, Johnny | B | 36 | 2/ 2/1936 | M | S | Lee |
| Dudley, Robert | B | 27 | 3/20/1936 | M | S | Jefferson |
| Roper, Eddie | B | 30 | 3/20/1936 | M | S | Jefferson |
| Peterson, Henry | B | 29 | 3/27/1936 | M | S | Montgomery |
| Bynum, Willie E. | B | 26 | 4/17/1936 | M | S | Montgomery |
| Cosey, Waddie | B | 30 | 5/15/1936 | M | S | Morgan |
| Stewart, Jimmie | B | 33 | 5/15/1936 | M | S | Montgomery |

| Name | Race | Age | Date of Execution | Offense | Appeal | County |
|------|------|-----|-------------------|---------|--------|--------|
| Gast, Joseph Wheeler | W | 37 | 6/ 5/1936 | M | | Tuscaloosa |
| Vincent, Wesley | W | 20 | 6/12/1936 | M | S,U | Jefferson |
| Waters, Gabel | B | 19 | 6/12/1936 | M | | Sumter |
| Harrell, Tyrle | B | 44 | 6/12/1936 | M | S | Elmore |
| Arrant, Elmer N. | B | 34 | 6/19/1936 | M | S | Lowndes |
| Miller, Walter | B | 38 | 6/19/1936 | M | | Madison |
| Perkins, Tom | B | 29 | 7/ 3/1936 | M | | Monroe |
| Smiley, A.B. | B | 30 | 7/10/1936 | M | | Elmore |
| Patterson, Oscar | B | 24 | 7/31/1936 | Ra | | Coosa |
| Summerville, Ed Lee | B | 35 | 8/ 7/1936 | M | | Pickens |
| Skelton, Edgar Prude | W | 36 | 1/29/1937 | M | S | Tuscaloosa |
| Franklin, James Victor | W | 31 | 2/26/1937 | M | S | Tuscaloosa |
| Collins, Roosevelt | B | 31 | 6/11/1937 | Ra | S | Calhoun |
| Oliver, Arthur | W | 46 | 9/10/1937 | M | S | Elmore |
| Millhouse, Frank | B | 18 | 1/28/1938 | M | S | Mobile |
| Vaughn, R.P. | B | 20 | 1/28/1938 | M | S | Mobile |
| Davidson, Mack | B | 28 | 7/22/1938 | Ro | | Baldwin |
| Young, Gary | B | 41 | 7/22/1938 | M | | Mobile |
| Whitfield, Willie James | B | 17 | 8/19/1938 | M | | Montgomery |
| Cobb, Curtis | B | 22 | 8/19/1938 | Ra | S | Jefferson |
| Brown, Jimmie | B | 25 | 11/25/1938 | Ra | S | Jefferson |
| Vaughan, Connie | W | 27 | 11/25/1938 | Ra | S | Jefferson |
| Smith, Adolph | B | 23 | 12/30/1938 | Ro | | Geneva |
| Ware, Fred | B | 24 | 2/17/1939 | Ra | S | Randolph |
| Kennedy, Joe Lee | B | 33 | 3/17/1939 | M | S | Jefferson |
| Wimbush, Edward | B | 22 | 3/17/1939 | M | S | Jefferson |
| Williams, Tom | B | 28 | 4/14/1939 | M | | Elmore |
| Tubbs, Grady | B | 21 | 6/ 9/1939 | M | S | Hale |
| Frazier, Joseph | B | 22 | 6/ 9/1939 | M | S | Marengo |
| White, Charles | B | 51 | 6/ 9/1939 | Ra | S | Pike |
| Anderson, Ray | B | 26 | 6/ 9/1939 | Ra | S | Jefferson |
| Sanders, Robert | B | 37 | 7/ 7/1939 | M | | Montgomery |
| Jackson, Mack[2] | B | 23 | 8/18/1939 | Ra | S | Jefferson |
| Tucker, Calvin | B | 24 | 2/16/1940 | M | | Mobile |
| Avery, Lonnie | B | 32 | 3/15/1940 | M | S,U | Bibb |
| Bell, Herman | B | 23 | 3/29/1940 | Ra | S | Mobile |
| Williams, David | B | 22 | 3/29/1940 | M | S | Jefferson |
| Jackson, Mack[2] | B | 28 | 3/29/1940 | M | S | Jefferson |
| Ragland, Judge | B | 34 | 5/ 3/1940 | M | S | Lee |
| McGuire, David | B | 25 | 5/24/1940 | M | S | Jefferson |
| Williams, Willie C. | W | 31 | 6/14/1940 | M | S | Jefferson |
| Brandon, Willie James | B | 23 | 8/ 9/1940 | Ra | | Coffee |
| Jackson, Julius | B | 29 | 7/11/1941 | M | | Talladega |
| Clark, William | B | 18 | 1/17/1941 | Ra | S,U | Limestone |
| Bass, Frank | B | 22 | 8/ 8/1941 | B | S | Morgan |
| Jones, Robert | B | 24 | 8/ 8/1941 | M | S | Greene |
| Dyer, Albert | W | 34 | 1/ 9/1942 | M | S | Jefferson |
| Powell, Dock | B | 27 | 1/23/1942 | M | | Clay |
| Gibson, Esker W. | W | 32 | 3/13/1942 | M | S | Mobile |
| Herring, Bud Phelps | B | 69 | 3/13/1942 | M | | Coffee |
| Hayes, Ed, Jr. | B | 34 | 5/ 1/1942 | M | | Marengo |
| Hardy, Clarence | B | 42 | 5/ 1/1942 | M | | Jefferson |

| Name | Race | Age | Date of Execution | Offense | Appeal | County |
|------|------|-----|-------------------|---------|--------|--------|
| Patterson, William M. | B | 25 | 6/26/1942 | M | S | Jefferson |
| Snead, William N. | B | 34 | 6/26/1942 | Ra | S | Jefferson |
| Mealer, Paul | W | 39 | 7/10/1942 | M | S | Tuscaloosa |
| Bossie, Haywood | B | 24 | 2/19/1943 | M | | Marengo |
| Johnson, Frank | B | 24 | 6/ 4/1943 | Ra | S,U | Jefferson |
| Goldsmith, Leroy | B | 38 | 8/ 6/1943 | M | S | Montgomery |
| Daniels, Henry Jr. | B | 19 | 8/13/1943 | Ra | S,U | Mobile |
| Robinson, Curtis | B | 20 | 8/13/1943 | Ra | S,U | Mobile |
| Mitchell, Lewis | B | 38 | 3/24/1944 | M | S | Montgomery |
| Vernon, Joe | B | 38 | 11/ 3/1944 | M | S,U,NT | Jefferson |
| Reddy, Daniel T. | W | 20 | 3/16/1945 | Ra | S | Jefferson |
| Hockenberry, Joseph H. | W | 23 | 3/16/1945 | Ra | S | Jefferson |
| Patton, Ed Lucky | B | 45 | 7/20/1945 | M | S | Hale |
| Hall, Peter Paul | B | 23 | 1/18/1946 | M,Ra | S | Barbour |
| Johnson, Ernest | B | 17 | 1/25/1946 | M | S | Hale |
| Brown, Richard | B | 18 | 2/ 1/1946 | M | S | Hale |
| Burns, Elbert J. | W | 65 | 3/15/1946 | M | S | Jefferson |
| Pilley, Robert S. | W | 26 | 4/19/1946 | M | S | Jefferson |
| Wingard, Lester | B | — | 5/24/1946 | M | S | Montgomery |
| Hicks, Fred | B | 33 | 5/24/1946 | M | S | Hale |
| Mincey, Joe | B | 30 | 6/14/1946 | M | S | Pike |
| Alston, William Edgar | W | 41 | 8/16/1946 | M | S | Walker |
| Smith, John B. | B | 24 | 12/13/1946 | Ra | S | Tuscaloosa |
| Brooks, Booker T. | B | 31 | 3/14/1947 | M | S | Chambers |
| Garrett, Israel | B | 45 | 5/23/1947 | M | S | Hale |
| Grant, Noel J. | W | 40 | 3/19/1948 | M | S | Baldwin |
| Munson, John Henry, Jr. | B | 28 | 3/19/1948 | M | S | Jefferson |
| Cobb, Philip | B | 23 | 3/11/1949 | M | S | Montgomery |
| Haygood, Perry Lee | B | 26 | 3/18/1949 | M | S | Jefferson |
| Snead, Buster | B | 41 | 3/25/1949 | M | S | Bibb |
| Green, Nehemiah | B | 26 | 8/12/1949 | M | S | Jefferson |
| Winters, J.C. | B | 20 | 8/12/1949 | M | S | Elmore |
| Smith, Charlie | B | — | 5/16/1950 | M | S | Mobile |
| Odom, Homer Garland | W | 23 | 7/21/1950 | M | S | Jefferson |
| Sims, Claude B. | B | 20 | 7/21/1950 | M | S | Jefferson |
| Keith, Joe | B | 29 | 7/21/1950 | M | S | Limestone |
| Drake, Cooper | B | 31 | 5/ 2/1952 | M,Att | S | Shelby |
| Smith, Andrew Lee | B | 31 | 5/ 2/1952 | M | S | Jefferson |
| Forrest, Levert | B | 27 | 5/ 9/1952 | M | S | Mobile |
| Miles, Desmond | W | 34 | 10/10/1952 | M | S | Covington |
| Myhand, Reuben | B | 20 | 8/28/1953 | Ra | S | Geneva |
| Dennison, Earle (Female) | W | 54 | 9/ 4/1953 | M | S | Elmore |
| Hardie, Will | B | 54 | 1/22/1954 | M | S | Tuscaloosa |
| Jones, Albert Lee | B | 23 | 4/23/1954 | M | S | Russell |
| Grimes, Arthur Lee | B | 23 | 4/23/1954 | M | S | Russell |
| Jackson, Jessie Frank | B | 23 | 6/ 4/1954 | Ra | S | Montgomery |
| Jackson, Melvin | B | 18 | 9/28/1956 | Ra | S | Russell |
| Johnson, Clarence | B | 56 | 3/22/1957 | M | S | Wilcox |
| Martin, Rhonda Bell (Female) | W | 48 | 10/11/1957 | M | S | Montgomery |
| Reeves, Jeremiah | B | 23 | 3/28/1958 | Ra | U,NT | Montgomery |
| Walker, Ernest Cornell | B | 25 | 12/ 4/1959 | Ra | S | Jefferson |
| Dockery, Edwin Ray | W | 25 | 12/11/1959 | M | S | Morgan |

| Name | Race | Age | Date of Execution | Offense | Appeal | County |
|------|------|-----|-------------------|---------|--------|--------|
| Boggs, Columbus | B | 26 | 4/29/1960 | M | S | Dallas |
| Johnson, Joe Henry | B | 19 | 11/24/1961 | M | S | Limestone |
| Gosa, Wilmon | B | 43 | 8/31/1962 | M | S | Tuscaloosa |
| Coburn, James | W | 38 | 9/ 4/1964 | Ro | S | Dallas |
| Bowen, William Frank, Jr. | W | 33 | 1/15/1965 | M | S | Madison |

[1]Automatic appeal started in 1943.
[2]The records of the state correctional authority show that Jackson (8/18/1939) and Jackson (3/29/1940) are different persons though executed within a year of each other.

## ARIZONA

*Period of Executions*: 1910–1963
*Total Number*: 64
*Method*: Hanging 1910–1916, 1918–1932; lethal gas 1933–1963
*Period of Abolition*: 1916–1918
*Other Data*: Arizona was a territory until 1915.

| Name | Race | Age | Date of Execution | Offense | Appeal | County |
|------|------|-----|-------------------|---------|--------|--------|
| Lopez, Jose | W | — | 1/ 5/1910 | M | | Pinal |
| Sanchez, Cesario | W | — | 12/ 2/1910 | M | | Coconino |
| Barela, Rafael | W | — | 12/ 2/1910 | M | | Coconino |
| Franco, Domingo | W | — | 7/ 7/1911 | M | | Santa Cruz |
| Galles, Alejandra | W | — | 7/28/1911 | M | | Yavapai |
| Villalobo, Ramon | W | — | 12/10/1915 | M | S | Pinal |
| Rodriquez, Francisco | W | — | 5/19/1916 | M | S | Maricopa |
| Chavez, N.B. | W | — | 6/ 9/1916 | M | S | Yavapai |
| Peralta, Miguel | W | — | 7/ 7/1916 | M | S | Yavapai |
| Torrez, Sinplicio | W | — | 4/16/1920 | M | S | Coconino |
| Dominguez, Pedro | W | — | 1/14/1921 | M | S | Greenlee |
| Martin, Michan | W | 24 | 9/ 9/1921 | M | S | Yavapai |
| Lauterio, Ricardo | W | — | 1/13/1922 | M | S | Maricopa |
| Roman, Tomas | W | — | 1/13/1922 | M | S | Maricopa |
| West, Theodore | W | — | 9/29/1922 | M | S | Mohave |
| Hadley, Paul V. | W | — | 4/13/1923 | M | S | Pima |
| Martinez, Manuel | W | — | 8/10/1923 | M | | Santa Cruz |
| Ward, William B. | B | — | 6/20/1924 | M | | Pinal |
| Flowers, Sam | B | — | 1/ 9/1925 | M | S | Maricopa |
| Lawrence, William | W | 27 | 1/ 8/1926 | M | S,U | Maricopa |
| Blackburn, Charles J. | W | 40 | 5/20/1927 | M | S | Graham |
| Sam, B.W.L. | C | — | 6/22/1928 | M | S | Mohave |
| Chin, Shew | C | — | 6/22/1928 | M | S | Mohave |
| Har, Jew | C | — | 6/22/1928 | M | S | Mohave |
| Long, Gee King | C | — | 6/22/1928 | M | S | Mohave |
| Dugan, Eva (Female) | W | 49 | 2/21/1930 | Ro | S | Pima |
| Macias, Refugio | W | — | 3/ 7/1930 | M | S | Greenlee |
| Young, Herman | W | 26 | 8/21/1931 | M | S | Pima |
| Hernandez, Manuel | W | 18 | 7/ 6/1934 | M | S | Pinal |
| Hernandez, Fred | W | 19 | 7/ 6/1934 | M | S | Pinal |
| Shaughnessy, George | W | 18 | 7/13/1934 | M | S | Santa Cruz |

| Name | Race | Age | Date of Execution | Offense | Appeal | County |
|------|------|-----|-------------------|---------|--------|--------|
| Douglas, Louis Sprague | W | 46 | 8/31/1934 | M | | Yuma |
| Sullivan, Jack | W | 23 | 5/15/1936 | M | S | Cochise |
| Rascon, Frank | W | 26 | 7/10/1936 | M | S | Maricopa |
| Gardner, Earl[1] | I | 31 | 7/13/1936 | M | S | Federal |
| Cochrane, Roland H. | W | 28 | 10/ 2/1936 | M | S | Maricopa |
| Duarte, Frank | W | — | 1/ 8/1937 | M | S | Pinal |
| Patten, Ernest | B | 37 | 8/13/1937 | M | S | Apache |
| Anderson, Burt | W | 54 | 8/13/1937 | M | S | Yavapai |
| Knight, David Benjamin | W | — | 9/ 3/1937 | M | S | Maricopa |
| Odom, Elvin Jack | W | — | 1/14/1938 | M | | Maricopa |
| Bailey, James | W | — | 4/28/1939 | M | | Pinal |
| Conner, Frank | B | — | 9/22/1939 | M | S | Santa Cruz |
| Burgunder, Robert | W | — | 8/ 9/1940 | M | | Maricopa |
| Levice, J.C. | B | — | 1/ 8/1943 | M | S | Cochise |
| Sanders, Charles | B | — | 1/ 8/1943 | M | S | Cochise |
| Cole, Grady B. | B | — | 1/ 8/1943 | M | S | Cochise |
| Rawling, James C. | W | — | 2/19/1943 | M | | Greenlee |
| Macias, Elisandro | W | — | 4/27/1943 | M | S | Pima |
| Ransom, John Earnest | B | — | 1/ 5/1945 | M | S | Maricopa |
| Smith, Lee Albert | W | — | 4/ 6/1945 | M | S | Cochise |
| Holley, U.L. | B | — | 4/13/1945 | M | | Gila |
| Serna, Angel | W | — | 7/29/1950 | M | S,U | Pinal |
| Lantz, Harold Thomas | W | — | 7/18/1951 | M | S | Cochise |
| Folk, Carl J. | W | 55 | 3/ 4/1955 | M | S | Navajo |
| Bartholomew, Lester Edward | W | — | 8/31/1955 | M | | Maricopa |
| Coey, Leonard | W | — | 5/22/1957 | M | S | Maricopa |
| Thomas, Arthur | B | — | 11/17/1958 | M | S,U | Cochise |
| Jorden, Richard Lewis | W | — | 11/22/1958 | M | S,U | Pima |
| Craft, Lonnie | W | — | 3/ 7/1959 | M | S | Maricopa |
| Fenton, Robert D. | W | — | 3/11/1960 | M | S,U | Pima |
| Robinson, Honor | B | — | 10/31/1961 | M | S | Maricopa |
| McGee, Patrick M. | W | 52 | 3/ 8/1963 | M | S,U | Coconino |
| Silva, Manuel E. | W | — | 3/14/1963 | M | S,U | Pinal |

[1]Execution by hanging under Federal authority in the Gila County Jail at Globe.


## ARKANSAS

*Period of Executions*: 1913–1964
*Total Number*: 172
*Method*: Electrocution
*Other Data*: After Arkansas began electrocuting its condemned felons at the state penitentiary, three men (identified by footnote 1) were hanged under local authority in the counties of their convictions at the county seat designated.

| Name | Race | Age | Date of Execution | Offense | Appeal | County |
|------|------|-----|-------------------|---------|--------|--------|
| Simms, Lee | B | — | 9/ 5/1913 | Ra | S | Prairie |
| Davis, Owen[1] | — | — | 9/11/1913 | M | | Fayettville |
| King, Ed | B | — | 12/12/1913 | M | S | Ashley |

| Name | Race | Age | Date of Execution | Offense | Appeal | County |
|------|------|-----|-------------------|---------|--------|--------|
| King, Will[1] | B | — | 3/14/1914 | M | | |
| Felton, Fred | B | — | 3/28/1914 | Ra | | Lincoln |
| Tillman, Arthur[1] | W | 23 | 7/15/1914 | M | S | Paris |
| Neely, Will | B | — | 12/ 8/1914 | M | | Union |
| Hodges, Arthur | W | 21 | 12/18/1914 | M | S | Clark |
| Hall, John | B | — | 4/ 2/1915 | M | S | Craighead |
| Owens, Walter | B | — | 4/ 2/1915 | M | S | Craighead |
| Simms, Clay | B | — | 3/19/1915 | M | | Desha |
| Derrick, Sam | W | — | 7/28/1915 | M | S | Monroe |
| Hawkins, John | B | — | 3/ 3/1917 | M | | Little River |
| Smith, Henry | B | — | 3/31/1917 | M | S | Crittenden |
| Diggs, Tom | B | 39 | 6/22/1917 | M | S | Conway |
| Johnson, Aaron | B | — | 6/22/1917 | M | S | Desha |
| Daffron, Solomon | B | — | 7/26/1918 | M | | Polk |
| Caughron, Ben | W | — | 8/23/1918 | M | | Polk |
| Tobay, Vick | I | 24 | 8/14/1920 | M | | Washington |
| Cooper, Charlie | B | — | 11/19/1920 | M | S | Ouachita |
| Reynolds, Revertia | B | — | 4/29/1921 | M | | Lincoln |
| Clarke, Virgil | B | — | 6/17/1921 | M | | Chicot |
| Ratcliffe. Amos | W | 24 | 10/14/1921 | M | | Carroll |
| Price, John | B | — | 12/30/1921 | M | | Phillips |
| Wells, James | B | 18 | 3/10/1922 | M | S | Drew |
| Sease, Herbert | W | 40 | 7/27/1923 | M | S | Baxter |
| Richardson, Duncan | W | 29 | 2/ 2/1923 | M | S | Ashley |
| Richardson, Ben | W | 19 | 2/ 2/1923 | M | S | Ashley |
| Bullen, E.G. | W | 50 | 2/ 2/1923 | M | S | Ashley |
| Debord, Will | W | — | 2/ 2/1923 | M | | Stone |
| Owens, John | W | — | 8/24/1923 | M | S | Little River |
| Sullivan, Joe | W | 34 | 4/18/1924 | M | | Pulaski |
| Ruck, Spurgeon | B | — | 6/27/1924 | M | | Crawford |
| Bettis, Will | B | — | 6/27/1924 | M | S | Crawford |
| Buster, Jack | B | — | 6/26/1925 | M | | Jefferson |
| Kelley, J.C. | W | 30 | 11/13/1925 | M | | Pulaski |
| Flowers, Perk | B | — | 6/26/1925 | M | S | Columbia |
| Harris, Aaron | B | — | 1/ 8/1926 | M | S | Ashley |
| Clark, Tyrus | W | — | 1/ 8/1926 | M | S | Benton |
| Edmons, Roy | B | — | 2/ 5/1926 | M | | Union |
| Walker, Lee | B | — | 2/ 5/1926 | M | | Union |
| Johnson, Cephus | B | — | 2/12/1926 | M | S | Ouachita |
| Canady, John | B | — | 2/12/1926 | M | S | Ouachita |
| Mason, Clint | B | — | 2/12/1926 | M | S | Ouachita |
| Jones, Ishman | B | — | 2/12/1926 | M | S | Ouachita |
| Martin, Willie | B | 36 | 6/ 9/1926 | M | | Pulaski |
| Jones, Albert | B | — | 6/ 9/1926 | M | | Mississippi |
| Dixon, Lonnie | B | 18 | 6/24/1927 | M | | Pulaski |
| Martin, Booker | B | — | 9/ 2/1927 | M | | Monroe |
| Cathey, Horace | B | — | 9/ 2/1927 | M | | Monroe |
| Eutsey, Willie | B | — | 3/30/1928 | M | | Ouachita |
| McKenzie, Will | B | — | 3/30/1928 | M | | Ouachita |
| Brown, Sinner | B | — | 7/10/1928 | M | S | Hempstead |
| Robinson, Pete | B | — | 9/10/1928 | M | S | Union |
| Evers, Ben | B | — | 1/24/1930 | M | S | Arkansas |

| Name | Race | Age | Date of Execution | Offense | Appeal | County |
|------|------|-----|-------------------|---------|--------|--------|
| Brown, Mack | B | 27 | 3/21/1930 | M | | Little River |
| Green, John | B | 28 | 3/21/1930 | M | | Little River |
| Alford, Ambrosia | B | — | 6/20/1930 | M | | Ouachita |
| Nolan, Bud | B | — | 7/25/1930 | M | S | Little River |
| Howell, W.H. | W | 62 | 8/15/1930 | M | S | Crawford |
| Washington, George | B | 30 | 11/14/1930 | M | S | Pulaski |
| Turnage, James | B | 29 | 11/14/1930 | M | S | Pulaski |
| Davis, Willie | B | — | 11/14/1930 | M | S | Pulaski |
| Long, Eddie | B | — | 11/14/1930 | M | S | Pulaski |
| Lawson, James | B | — | 7/31/1931 | M | | Bradley |
| McBryde, Louie | B | — | 7/ 8/1932 | M | S | Clark |
| Daniels, Freeling | B | — | 11/25/1932 | Ra | S | Miller |
| Hill, James | B | 19 | 6/30/1933 | Ra | S | Phillips |
| Williams, Woodie | B | 39 | 7/14/1933 | M | S | Pulaski |
| Banks, J.C. | B | 24 | 12/ 8/1933 | M | S | Pulaski |
| McDaniels, Len | B | — | 12/ 8/1933 | M | S | Lonoke |
| Butler, Ben | B | — | 2/ 9/1934 | M | | Craighead |
| Jackson, Luther | B | 25 | 5/11/1934 | M | | Pulaski |
| Mitchell, Purcell | B | 21 | 11/ 2/1934 | M | | Union |
| Rose, Robert | W | — | 2/23/1935 | M | | Independence |
| Barnes, Frank | W | — | 3/ 1/1935 | M | S | Mississippi |
| Shank, Mark | W | 43 | 3/ 8/1935 | M | S | Saline |
| Freeman, Tom | B | 28 | 8/23/1935 | M | | Chicot |
| Nelson, Paul | W | 23 | 9/28/1935 | M | S | Jackson |
| Barnes, Bill | W | — | 9/28/1935 | M | S | Mississippi |
| Dobbs, Frank | W | 40 | 11/11/1935 | M | S | Saline |
| Hawkins, Ben | B | — | 12/13/1935 | M | S | Mississippi |
| Nelson, Mack | B | — | 12/13/1935 | M | S | Mississippi |
| House, Roy | W | 22 | 10/23/1936 | M | S | Garland |
| Turner, Dennis | W | 47 | 11/ 6/1936 | M | S | Calhoun |
| Smith, Willie | B | — | 12/11/1936 | M | S | Drew |
| White, Beverly | B | — | 12/11/1936 | M | S | Drew |
| McCormick, F. | B | — | 12/11/1936 | M | S | Drew |
| Mattock, Clinton | B | — | 4/23/1937 | M | | Calhoun |
| Austin, James | B | 22 | 5/14/1937 | M | S | Garland |
| Hutto, Tom M. | W | — | 9/ 3/1937 | M | | Union |
| Edwards, Sandy | B | — | 9/24/1937 | M | | Hempstead |
| Amos, Jessie | B | — | 10/15/1937 | Ra | S | Lonoke |
| Pigue, Duncan | B | — | 2/ 4/1938 | M | | Lonoke |
| Ware, Leroy | B | — | 2/25/1938 | M | | Ashley |
| Noble, Willie | B | — | 3/11/1938 | M | S | Miller |
| Sims, Joe | W | — | 3/18/1938 | M | S | Saline |
| Brocklehurst, Lester | W | 23 | 3/18/1938 | M | | Lonoke |
| Thomas, Theo | B | 28 | 6/24/1938 | Ra | S | Crittenden |
| Carter, Frank | B | 26 | 6/24/1938 | Ra | S | Crittenden |
| Anderson, Joe | W | — | 3/10/1939 | M | S | Garland |
| Dickerson, Fred | W | — | 5/19/1939 | M | S | Garland |
| Arnell, Fred | B | 18 | 5/19/1939 | Ra | | Miller |
| Williams, Milton | B | 27 | 8/18/1939 | M | | Pulaski |
| Carruthers, James | B | — | 6/30/1939 | Ra | | Mississippi |
| Clayton, Bubble | B | — | 6/30/1939 | Ra | | Mississippi |
| Williams, Sylvester | B | — | 6/30/1939 | M | S | Jefferson |

| Name | Race | Age | Date of Execution | Offense | Appeal | County |
|------|------|-----|-------------------|---------|--------|--------|
| Charles, James | B | 24 | 1/19/1940 | M | S | Pulaski |
| Manning, Otis | B | — | 4/12/1940 | M | | Union |
| Gulley, Jack | B | — | 11/15/1940 | M | S | Nevada |
| Dillard, James | B | — | 12/13/1940 | M | | Desha |
| Mooney, John | B | — | 1/24/1941 | M | | Woodruff |
| Peyton, A.C. | B | — | 5/15/1941 | M | | Crittenden |
| Lewis, Percy | B | — | 6/ 6/1941 | M | S | Phillips |
| Riney, John Henry | B | — | 6/20/1941 | Ra | | Desha |
| Washington, John | B | — | 10/11/1941 | M | | White |
| Herron, Jimmie | B | — | 1/23/1942 | M | | Little River |
| Adams, Ben | W | — | 6/ 5/1942 | M | S | Woodruff |
| Jones, A.T. | B | — | 7/31/1942 | M | S | Phillips |
| Luchyardo, A.D. | B | — | 11/20/1942 | M | | Lonoke |
| Allison, Stoney | B | — | 11/20/1942 | Ra | S | Desha |
| Thomas, Adolph | B | — | 3/19/1943 | M | | Columbia |
| Thompson, Henry | B | — | 8/ 6/1943 | M | S | Cleveland |
| Mack, Seke | B | — | 6/ 2/1944 | M | | Mississippi |
| Hudson, Walker | B | — | 7/ 7/1944 | M | S | Clark |
| Tacker, Jim | W | — | 7/14/1944 | M | | Crittenden |
| Clingham, Levi | B | — | 12/ 1/1944 | M | S | Crittenden |
| Brown, Tony | B | 39 | 3/30/1945 | M | S | Mississippi |
| Yaates, James | B | — | 5/25/1945 | M | | Arkansas |
| Hall, James Wayburn | W | 24 | 1/ 4/1946 | M | | Pulaski |
| Riley, Willie | B | — | 4/12/1946 | M | | Chicot |
| Chitwood, Elton | W | — | 11/22/1946 | M | S | Polk |
| Thomas, Andrew | B | 24 | 11/22/1946 | M | S | Jefferson |
| Holmes, Clifton | B | 26 | 1/10/1947 | Ra | S | Jefferson |
| Hodges, Albert | B | — | 1/17/1947 | Ra | S | Pulaski |
| Henley, Jeff | B | — | 1/24/1947 | M | S | Lee |
| Bates, Vollie Bill | W | — | 5/16/1947 | M | S | Polk |
| Johnson, Gubie Lee | B | 24 | 8/ 8/1947 | M | S | Pulaski |
| Dukes, Lawrence W. | B | 40 | 8/ 8/1947 | M | | St. Francis |
| Hyde, James H. | W | — | 2/13/1948 | M | S | Carroll |
| Pugh, Edward | B | 20 | 7/ 2/1948 | Ra | S | Pulaski |
| Palmer, Edward | B | — | 6/17/1949 | Ra | S,U | Pulaski |
| Rorie, Harvie | W | — | 7/22/1949 | M | S | Jefferson |
| Pierce, Walter | B | — | 12/ 9/1949 | M | | Chicot |
| Hildreth, Wesley | B | 26 | 12/23/1949 | Ra | | Phillips |
| Black, Thomas | W | 28 | 3/10/1950 | M | S,U | Pulaski |
| Needham, Hollis | W | 26 | 3/17/1950 | Ra | S | Mississippi |
| Smith, Robert L. | W | 40 | 4/24/1950 | M | S | Pulaski |
| Ezell, Matthew | B | 38 | 2/23/1951 | M | S | Mississippi |
| Ferguson, George | B | 35 | 2/23/1951 | M | | Pulaski |
| Smith, Aubrey | B | — | 7/27/1951 | M | S | Phillips |
| Dorsey, Peter | B | — | 11/23/1951 | M | S,U | Phillips |
| Grays, Arthur | B | — | 11/23/1951 | M | S | Mississippi |
| Maxwell, Herman | B | 22 | 6/ 6/1952 | Ra | S,U | Hempstead |
| Wright, Wilson | B | — | 8/ 1/1952 | M | | Dallas |
| Jenkins, Bill | B | — | 5/ 7/1954 | M | S | Garland |
| Scarber, Leo | B | — | 9/21/1956 | Ra | S | Nevada |
| Smith, Lawrence | B | — | 7/24/1959 | M | S | Chicot |

| Name | Race | Age | Date of Execution | Offense | Appeal | County |
|------|------|-----|-------------------|---------|--------|--------|
| Lee, Leo | B | 53 | 9/25/1959 | M | S | Pulaski |
| Walker, Thomas | B | 52 | 10/ 2/1959 | M | S | Crittenden |
| Young, William | B | 39 | 10/ 2/1959 | M | S | Mississippi |
| Hayes, Arthur | B | — | 10/23/1959 | M | S | Mississippi |
| House, J.T. | B | — | 10/23/1959 | M | S | Phillips |
| Moore, James | B | 22 | 5/13/1960 | M | S,F,U | Miller |
| Boone, Roger | B | 27 | 5/13/1960 | M | S,F,U | Miller |
| Boyd, James | B | 21 | 5/20/1960 | M | S,F,U | Miller |
| Byrd, Willie | B | 22 | 5/20/1960 | M | S,F,U | Miller |
| Leggett, Emett | W | 19 | 9/16/1960 | M | S,F,U | Pulaski |
| Nail, William | W | — | 9/16/1960 | M | S | Jefferson |
| Moore, Lawrence | B | — | 10/28/1960 | M | S | Crittenden |
| Bracy, John | B | 27 | 10/28/1960 | M | S | Chicot |
| Fields, Charles F. | W | — | 1/24/1964 | Ra | S,U | Jefferson |

¹Davis (9/11/1913), Tillman (7/15/1914), and King (3/14/1914) were hanged under local authority in the counties of their convictions after Arkansas began electrocuting its condemned felons at the state penitentiary.

## CALIFORNIA

*Period of Executions*: 1893–1967
*Total Number*: 502
*Method*: Hanging until 1933, then lethal gas
*Other Data*: Executions were performed at two prisons, Folsom and San Quentin. Effective August 27, 1937, the gas chamber, located at San Quentin Prison, was adopted as the means of execution. Prisoners on death row at the time of the adoption of the gas chamber were to be executed according to their original sentences. Appeals were automatic beginning in April 1936. The San Quentin data were provided by courtesy of Associate Warden James W. L. Park, San Quentin Prison. After the state of California began executing its condemned felons at the state penitentiaries, one man (identified in footnote 1) was hanged under local authority in the county of his conviction at the county seat designated.

| Name | Race | Age | Date of Execution | Offense | Appeal | County |
|------|------|-----|-------------------|---------|--------|--------|
| FOLSOM | | | | | | |
| Hane, Chin | C | 35 | 12/13/1895 | M | S | Sacramento |
| Kovalev, Ivan | W | 29 | 2/21/1896 | M | | Sacramento |
| Craig, John | W | 42 | 6/12/1896 | M | S | L.A. |
| Kamaunu, Paulo | O | 29 | 6/19/1896 | M | S | El Dorado |
| Howard, John E. | W | 37 | 7/17/1896 | M | S | Tulare |
| Roberts, George W. | W | 46 | 9/ 4/1896 | M | | El Dorado |
| Lopez, Benito | M | 70 | 5/21/1897 | M | | Calaveras |
| Berry, James | B | 38 | 8/13/1897 | M | | Stanislaus |
| Raymond, C.H. | W | 49 | 4/ 8/1898 | M | | San Mateo |

| Name | Race | Age | Date of Execution | Offense | Appeal | County |
|------|------|-----|-------------------|---------|--------|--------|
| Barthelman, John T. | W | 31 | 5/12/1898 | M | S | L.A. |
| Belew, Franklin | W | 40 | 6/16/1898 | M | | Solano |
| Winters, Harry | W | 48 | 12/ 8/1899 | M | S | San Mateo |
| Puttman, George | W | 25 | 11/19/1900 | M | S | Sacramento |
| Haines, Frank M. | W | 40 | 9/26/1902 | M | | Marin |
| Glover, William | W | 28 | 2/ 6/1904 | M | S | Placer |
| Hidaka, Kokichi | J | 27 | 6/10/1904 | M | | Sacramento |
| Lawrence, Charles | I | 26 | 10/ 7/1904 | M | S | Sacramento |
| Yow, Sing | C | 30 | 1/ 6/1905 | M | S | Sacramento |
| Murphy, Joseph | W | 26 | 7/14/1905 | M | S | Sacramento |
| Eldridge, Harry | W | 43 | 12/ 1/1905 | M | S | Sacramento |
| Easton, George | W | 25 | 4/ 6/1906 | M | S | Solano |
| Gray, W.M. | B | 32 | 4/13/1906 | M | S | Sacramento |
| Weber, Adolph J. | W | 21 | 9/27/1906 | M | S | Placer |
| Cipolla, Antonio | W | 26 | 4/30/1909 | M | S | Sacramento |
| Benjamin, Wilbur | I | 22 | 10/28/1910 | M | S | Yolo |
| Leahy, Michael | W | 33 | 2/ 8/1911 | M | | Placer |
| Delhantie, Edward | B | 26 | 12/ 6/1912 | M | S | Marin |
| Oppenheimer, Jacob | W | 35 | 7/11/1913 | A | S,U | Marin |
| Raber, Samuel | W | 27 | 3/15/1915 | M | S | Sacramento |
| Creeks, Frank | W | 32 | 8/27/1915 | M | S | Sacramento |
| Fountain, David | W | 48 | 9/10/1915 | M | S | Sacramento |
| Harris, Burr L. | B | 28 | 10/ 8/1915 | M | S | L.A. |
| Loomis, Earl M. | W | 19 | 11/ 5/1915 | M | S | Sacramento |
| Bargas, Rito | M | 28 | 1/21/1916 | M | | Kern |
| Ung, Sing | O | 23 | 2/18/1916 | M | S | San Joaquin |
| Witt, Glenn | W | 23 | 3/13/1916 | M | S | L.A. |
| Kromphold, Kosta | W | 23 | 9/ 1/1916 | M | S | Yuba |
| Schoon, Joseph | W | 27 | 7/12/1918 | M | S | San Joaquin |
| Negrete, Jesse | M | 61 | 11/29/1918 | M | S | Sacramento |
| Shortridge, William | B | 34 | 5/ 2/1919 | M | S | Yuba |
| Tyren, James | W | 59 | 5/23/1919 | M | S | Sacramento |
| Clifton, David | B | 35 | 10/21/1921 | M | S | Sacramento |
| Bisquerre, Felipe | F | 20 | 1/26/1923 | M | | Plumas |
| Donnely, George | W | 53 | 2/23/1923 | M | S | Sacramento |
| Kels, Alex A. | W | 39 | 1/ 4/1924 | M | | San Joaquin |
| Sliskovitch, Mike | W | 30 | 8/22/1924 | M | S | Sacramento |
| Matthew, Robert | B | 24 | 12/12/1924 | M | S | L.A. |
| Simnel, Joe | B | 23 | 12/19/1924 | M | S | L.A. |
| Geregac, John | W | 22 | 1/16/1925 | M | S | L.A. |
| Montijo, Ed | W | 19 | 7/10/1925 | M | S | L.A. |
| Connelly, John | W | 38 | 7/24/1925 | M | S | Yuba |
| Ballinger, Alfred | W | 41 | 10/ 9/1925 | M | S | Yuba |
| Sloper, Felix | W | 29 | 6/25/1926 | M | S | S.F. |
| Peevia, Charles | B | 53 | 8/27/1926 | M | | Kern |
| Arnold, Ray | W | 28 | 1/28/1927 | M | S | Placer |
| Sayer, Edward K. | W | 24 | 2/ 4/1927 | M | S | Placer |
| Shannon, Willard C. | W | 27 | 5/ 4/1928 | M | | Amador |
| Kuryla, George | W | 41 | 1/25/1929 | M | | Amador |
| Randolph, Harrison H. | W | 24 | 2/ 8/1929 | M | | Kern |
| Rowland, Paul | W | 36 | 9/27/1929 | M | S | Sacramento |
| Brown, Anthony | W | 31 | 1/ 3/1930 | M | S,U | Sacramento |

| Name | Race | Age | Date of Execution | Offense | Appeal | County |
|---|---|---|---|---|---|---|
| Stokes, Roy E. | W | 24 | 1/ 3/1930 | M | S,U | Sacramento |
| Burke, Walter E. | W | 33 | 1/10/1930 | M | S,U | Sacramento |
| Gregg, James H. | W | 34 | 1/10/1930 | M | S,U | Sacramento |
| Gleason, James | W | 30 | 1/17/1930 | M | S,U | Sacramento |
| Boss, Alfred | W | 31 | 12/ 5/1930 | M | S | Sacramento |
| Davis, George | W | 30 | 12/ 5/1930 | M | S | Sacramento |
| Mott, Fred | W | 36 | 7/17/1931 | M | S | S.F. |
| McCabe, Wilbur | W | 40 | 7/24/1931 | M | S | L.A. |
| Hudson, William | W | 25 | 10/ 2/1931 | M | | L.A. |
| O'Neil, Robert | W | 21 | 10/ 2/1931 | M | | L.A. |
| Burkhart, William H. | W | 29 | 1/29/1932 | M | S | L.A. |
| Walker, Thomas H. | W | 49 | 8/19/1932 | M | | Kern |
| Johnson, C.W. | W | 28 | 1/19/1933 | M | | S.F. |
| Farrington, Peter | W | 33 | 3/24/1933 | M | S,U | S.F. |
| Fleming, John C. | W | 42 | 11/17/1933 | M | | San Bernardino |
| Villon, Dick | – | 29 | 12/ 1/1933 | M | | Santa Clara |
| Harris, Daniel | B | 37 | 7/ 6/1934 | M | S | Contra Costa |
| Nobles, Pat | B | 43 | 11/23/1934 | M | S | L.A. |
| Lami, Mike | W | 39 | 1/11/1935 | M | S | Sacramento |
| Bieber, Harold P. | W | 41 | 2/ 1/1935 | M | | Tulare |
| McQuate, Tellie | W | 44 | 5/24/1935 | M | S | San Diego |
| Bermijo, Anastacio | F | 38 | 5/31/1935 | M | S | Sacramento |
| Lutz, Aldrich W. | W | 19 | 6/21/1935 | M | | Siskiyou |
| Garcia, Harry | M | 33 | 7/10/1935 | M | S | Sacramento |
| Hall, George | W | 26 | 3/27/1936 | M | S,U | Siskiyou |
| Kimball, Earl B. | W | 21 | 5/22/1936 | M | S | Placer |
| Stone, Elton M. | W | 30 | 6/12/1936 | M | S | Fresno |
| James, Charles | B | 32 | 8/14/1936 | M | S | Sacramento |
| Berryman, John B. | W | 42 | 8/14/1936 | M | S | Sacramento |
| Dale, Lloyd A. | B | 36 | 10/16/1936 | M | S | San Joaquin |
| McGuire, Charles | W | 30 | 12/ 3/1937 | M | S | Sacramento |

SAN QUENTIN

| Name | Race | Age | Date of Execution | Offense | Appeal | County |
|---|---|---|---|---|---|---|
| Gabriel, Jose | I | 60 | 3/ 3/1893 | M | | San Diego |
| Vincent, Frederick Oscar[1] | W | — | 10/27/1893 | M | | Fresno |
| Sing, Lu | C | 26 | 2/ 2/1894 | M | | S.F. |
| Sullivan, P.J. | – | 41 | 4/21/1894 | M | | S.F. |
| Azoff, Anthony | – | 32 | 6/ 7/1895 | M | S | Santa Cruz |
| Collins, Patrick J. | – | 36 | 6/ 7/1895 | M | S | S.F. |
| Garcia, Emilio | – | 37 | 6/ 7/1895 | M | S | San Bernardino |
| Fredericks, William M. | – | 22 | 7/26/1895 | M | S | S.F. |
| Smith, Fremont | – | 47 | 8/ 9/1895 | M | S | Colusa |
| Hansen, Hans | W | — | 10/18/1895 | M | U | Fed |
| St. Clair, Thomas | W | — | 10/18/1895 | M | U | Fed |
| Young, William | W | 23 | 10/25/1895 | M | S | Monterey |
| Miller, N.S. | – | 50 | 12/ 6/1896 | M | S | Yuba |
| Sing, Chung | C | 40 | 2/17/1897 | M | | Mono |
| Kloss, Frank C. | – | 27 | 4/23/1897 | M | S | S.F. |
| Allender, Harvey | W | 36 | 12/10/1897 | M | S | Santa Clara |
| Durrant, William H.T. | W | 24 | 1/ 7/1898 | M | S,F,U | S.F. |
| Jung, Wee | C | 42 | 3/11/1898 | M | | S.F. |

| Name | Race | Age | Date of Execution | Offense | Appeal | County |
|------|------|-----|-------------------|---------|--------|--------|
| Hill, Benjamin L. | W | 36 | 4/ 6/1898 | M | S | Alameda |
| Ebanks, Joseph J. | B | 33 | 5/27/1898 | M | S | San Diego |
| Miller, John | W | 41 | 10/14/1898 | M | S | S.F. |
| Clark, George W. | W | 37 | 10/21/1898 | M | S | Napa |
| Chavez, Manuel | – | 28 | 4/15/1899 | M | S | San Diego |
| Owens, George C. | W | 48 | 4/21/1899 | M | S | Stanislaus |
| See, Go | C | 47 | 1/ 5/1900 | M | | Tulare |
| Eslabe, Joaquin | I | 29 | 4/23/1900 | M | S | Alameda |
| Flannelly, Thomas W. | – | 31 | 6/29/1900 | M | S | Santa Clara |
| Sullivan, William | – | 40 | 11/16/1900 | M | S | Tuolumne |
| Methever, E.V. | W | 57 | 5/10/1901 | M | S | L.A. |
| Daily, Isaac | W | 45 | 2/21/1902 | M | S | Kings |
| Wheelock, James | – | 43 | 6/13/1902 | M | S | Butte |
| Keong, Chung | C | 45 | 8/ 1/1902 | M | | S.F. |
| Cota, Jose | – | 20 | 2/13/1903 | M | | San Benito |
| Gonzales, Juan | – | 36 | 2/13/1903 | M | | San Benito |
| Fischer, F.C. | W | 31 | 7/14/1903 | M | | Riverside |
| Martinez, Julius | – | 22 | 12/11/1903 | M | | Calaveras |
| Ross, Bert | – | 27 | 12/18/1903 | M | S | San Luis Obispo |
| Wardrip, Charles | W | 21 | 2/26/1904 | M | S | Sacramento |
| Ochoa, Francisco | M | 38 | 6/10/1904 | M | S | Kern |
| Suesser, George | – | 23 | 7/15/1904 | M | S | Santa Clara |
| Ong, Chew Lan | C | 32 | 7/22/1904 | M | S | S.F. |
| Milton, Henry | – | 55 | 1/ 6/1905 | M | S | S.F. |
| Lock, Lee | C | 26 | 5/19/1905 | M | S | Santa Clara |
| Howard, Wilson R. | – | 27 | 6/ 9/1905 | M | | Santa Clara |
| Anthony, Miguel R. | – | 20 | 9/29/1905 | M | S | San Bernardino |
| Woods, Frank | W | 29 | 10/ 6/1905 | M | S | S.F. |
| Snaidecki, Joe | – | 43 | 10/27/1905 | M | | L.A. |
| Warner, William | W | 18 | 12/ 8/1905 | M | S | Santa Barbara |
| Trebilox, W.J. | – | 40 | 8/ 9/1906 | M | S | Nevada |
| Brown, Henry | – | 18 | 9/ 7/1906 | M | S | Del Norte |
| Soeder, Leon | W | 38 | 3/29/1907 | M | S | S.F. |
| Willard, Frank | I | 43 | 6/14/1907 | M | S | Mendocino |
| Grill, A.J. | – | 30 | 11/ 7/1907 | M | S | Sonoma |
| Buck, Morris | – | 28 | 12/13/1907 | M | S | L.A. |
| Dabner, Louis | W | 18 | 7/31/1908 | M | S | S.F. |
| Seimsen, John | W | 28 | 7/31/1908 | M | S | S.F. |
| Albitre, Delfino | – | 27 | 8/28/1908 | M | S | L.A. |
| Borsei, C. | – | 27 | 9/11/1908 | M | | L.A. |
| Fallon, Thomas P. | – | 40 | 1/ 8/1909 | M | S | S.F. |
| Baldesar, Charley | – | 36 | 1/29/1909 | M | | San Joaquin |
| Wirth, Ernest | – | 49 | 6/17/1910 | M | | L.A. |
| Magana, Juan | M | 24 | 6/16/1911 | M | | Tulare |
| Treschenko, Dimitry | – | 52 | 8/ 4/1911 | M | S | S.F. |
| Wilkins, Mark A. | – | 62 | 1/13/1912 | M | S | Alameda |
| Szafcsur, Alex | – | 43 | 11/22/1912 | M | S | S.F. |
| Williams, Ed | I | 28 | 11/29/1912 | M | | Butte |
| Louis, Willie | C | 44 | 12/ 6/1912 | M | | San Luis Obispo |
| Rogers, John S. | – | 29 | 12/27/1912 | M | | S.F. |
| Prantikos, Poolis | W | 28 | 3/14/1913 | M | S | S.F. |
| Bauweraerts, Frank | W | 37 | 7/11/1913 | M | S | Riverside |

| Name | Race | Age | Date of Execution | Offense | Appeal | County |
|------|------|-----|-------------------|---------|--------|--------|
| Green, Thomas | W | 23 | 4/ 3/1914 | M | | Riverside |
| Allen, Jerry | W | 39 | 4/10/1914 | M | S | Colusa |
| Chin, Lee Nam | C | 30 | 4/17/1914 | M | S | San Joaquin |
| Bostic, John | W | 24 | 3/15/1915 | M | S | L.A. |
| Larson, Louis A. | W | 46 | 1/22/1915 | M | S | L.A. |
| Bundy, Louis | W | 19 | 11/ 5/1915 | M | S | L.A. |
| Coutcure, Lawrence | W | 46 | 1/ 7/1916 | M | S | San Luis Obispo |
| Oxnam, Charles E.T. | W | 18 | 3/ 3/1916 | M | S | L.A. |
| Fortine, Louis | W | 31 | 7/21/1916 | M | | Ventura |
| Wilt, Joseph Vance | W | 37 | 2/ 9/1917 | M | S | Glenn |
| Hadley, Lon | – | 22 | 10/ 5/1917 | M | S | L.A. |
| Miller, Fred | B | 33 | 8/ 9/1918 | M | S | Ventura |
| Quiroz, Damasco | M | 31 | 2/28/1919 | M | | Tulare |
| Collins, Clarence | – | 20 | 6/20/1919 | M | S | Tuolumne |
| Rogers, Joe | – | 26 | 6/20/1919 | M | S | Tuolumne |
| Furuya, M. | J | 37 | 7/11/1919 | M | | San Joaquin |
| Morisawa, R. | – | 43 | 7/18/1919 | M | S | Sonoma |
| Rico, Pedro | – | 36 | 9/19/1919 | M | S | San Bernardino |
| Bellon, Tom | – | 42 | 10/17/1919 | M | S | Merced |
| Newell, Lafayette | W | 36 | 1/ 2/1920 | M | | El Dorado |
| Niino, T. | J | 40 | 8/27/1920 | M | S | Kings |
| Gibson, Moses | B | 36 | 9/24/1920 | M | | Orange |
| Collins, Arthur | – | 22 | 10/29/1920 | M | | L.A. |
| Foo, Ong Mon | C | 22 | 12/ 3/1920 | M | S | S.F. |
| Singh, Maher | O | 30 | 12/17/1920 | M | | Contra Costa |
| Clark, James C. | – | 43 | 2/ 4/1921 | M | S | Yolo |
| Nakis, Ernest | – | 34 | 2/18/1921 | M | S | Fresno |
| Williams, George | – | 53 | 6/ 3/1921 | M | S | S.F. |
| Guillen, Louis | – | 19 | 2/24/1922 | M | | Riverside |
| Valcalda, John | – | 40 | 5/26/1922 | M | S | Amador |
| Sisneres, Marcis | – | 50 | 9/22/1922 | M | | Orange |
| Manriquez, Miguel | – | 27 | 10/ 6/1922 | M | S | Imperial |
| Fat, Lew | – | 28 | 11/24/1922 | M | S | S.F. |
| Chavez, Gregorio | – | 50 | 3/ 2/1923 | M | | Imperial |
| Mohammed, Ullah | – | 32 | 4/13/1923 | M | S | Sonoma |
| Marui, T. | – | 45 | 5/ 4/1923 | M | S | Monterey |
| Campbell, Lawrence C. | – | 18 | 6/22/1923 | M | | Imperial |
| Parisi, Mauro | – | 28 | 6/29/1923 | M | S | Fresno |
| Sam, Jung | – | 35 | 8/ 3/1923 | M | S | Monterey |
| Pompa, Aurelio | – | 23 | 3/ 7/1924 | M | S | L.A. |
| Hendriz, J.V. | – | 53 | 4/11/1924 | M | S | San Diego |
| Thompson, Willard | – | 40 | 4/21/1924 | M | S | L.A. |
| Bringhurst, William | – | 38 | 4/21/1924 | M | S | L.A. |
| Casarez, Mariano | – | 69 | 5/ 9/1924 | M | | Imperial |
| Champion, A.F. | – | 29 | 8/15/1924 | M | S | L.A. |
| Yeager, Walter | W | 42 | 1/ 9/1925 | M | S | Madera |
| Sears, John | – | 21 | 1/16/1925 | M | S | L.A. |
| Ferdinand, Jack | – | 30 | 1/16/1925 | M | S | L.A. |
| Casade, Francisco | – | 42 | 2/13/1925 | M | S | L.A. |
| Reid, Clarence | – | 21 | 4/24/1925 | M | S | L.A. |
| Erno, Ronald C. | – | 26 | 5/ 8/1925 | M | S | Siskiyou |
| Bailey, Tom | W | 22 | 7/10/1925 | M | S | L.A. |

| Name | Race | Age | Date of Execution | Offense | Appeal | County |
|------|------|-----|-------------------|---------|--------|--------|
| Perry, Lewis | W | 19 | 7/10/1925 | M | S | L.A. |
| Craig, Charles | W | 23 | 7/31/1925 | M | S | Tehama |
| Garbutt, Harry | – | 39 | 2/13/1926 | M | S | L.A. |
| Wolfgang, Isaac | – | 57 | 9/10/1926 | M | S,U | L.A. |
| Adams, Willie | – | 23 | 10/ 8/1926 | M | S | L.A. |
| Rincon, Alfonse | – | 24 | 10/ 8/1926 | M | S | L.A. |
| Watts, Joseph H. | – | 32 | 10/15/1926 | M | S | San Bernardino |
| Trinidad, Mauricio | M | 33 | 10/15/1926 | M | S | San Bernardino |
| Slater, William J. | – | 24 | 1/ 7/1927 | M | S | San Bernardino |
| Adams, Sydney | W | 40 | 1/21/1927 | M | S | L.A. |
| Clark, Earl J. | – | 37 | 9/23/1927 | M | | L.A. |
| Vukich, Milan | W | 37 | 10/ 7/1927 | M | S | Placer |
| Sieber, Charles | – | 38 | 10/21/1927 | M | S | L.A. |
| Kelly, Clarence | W | 23 | 5/11/1928 | M | S | S.F. |
| Dowell, Mark | – | 24 | 8/17/1928 | M | S,U | S.F. |
| Hickman, William E. | W | 20 | 10/19/1928 | M | S,U | L.A. |
| Malone, John, J. | – | 30 | 12/ 7/1928 | M | S | L.A. |
| Lapierre, Edgar | W | 31 | 2/15/1929 | M | S | Alameda |
| Coen, Perry | W | 27 | 3/22/1929 | M | S | Kings |
| Thomas, Samuel | B | 30 | 3/22/1929 | M | S | Alameda |
| Fook, Leong | C | 54 | 4/ 5/1929 | M | S | Tulare |
| Beitzel, Russell S. | W | 28 | 8/ 2/1929 | M | S | L.A. |
| Price, Jack H. | – | 42 | 8/30/1929 | M | S | L.A. |
| Costello, George | W | 27 | 12/13/1929 | M | S | Alameda |
| Negra, Antone | W | 50 | 12/13/1929 | M | S | Merced |
| Croce, Mario | W | 40 | 12/20/1929 | M | S | Mendocino |
| Lazarus, Louis | W | 37 | 1/ 3/1930 | M | S | Alameda |
| Chandler, James | – | 48 | 2/10/1930 | M | S | L.A. |
| Reilly, Alphonse Dan | – | 22 | 3/14/1930 | M | S | L.A. |
| Boltares, Armando | M | 24 | 5/16/1930 | M | | L.A. |
| Lehew, Thomas | W | 33 | 8/ 1/1930 | M | S | Mendocino |
| Gomez, John | M | 22 | 8/15/1930 | M | S | Alameda |
| Northcott, Gordon S. | W | 22 | 10/ 2/1930 | M | S | Riverside |
| Ryley, George | W | 21 | 12/ 5/1930 | M | | Alameda |
| Simpson, Charles H. | W | 18 | 7/17/1931 | M | | S.F. |
| La Verne, Edward | W | 25 | 7/24/1931 | M | S | Alameda |
| Brown, Benjamin F. | W | 27 | 7/31/1931 | M | | L.A. |
| Magsaysay, Pedro | F | 40 | 11/13/1931 | M | S | Fresno |
| King, Clarence | W | 26 | 12/ 4/1931 | M | S | Humboldt |
| Lacang, Treso | F | 24 | 4/15/1932 | M | S | Fresno |
| Franco, Frank | W | 53 | 5/13/1932 | M | S | Santa Clara |
| Farolan, Victor | – | 46 | 6/10/1932 | M | S | Santa Clara |
| Monroe, Billy | – | 30 | 10/28/1932 | M | | Lassen |
| Hatamoto, Koji | J | 35 | 5/19/1933 | M | | L.A. |
| Paciga, Frank J. | W | 29 | 6/30/1933 | M | | L.A. |
| Fuller, Albert | W | 44 | 7/14/1933 | M | S | Madera |
| Regan, Joseph F. | W | 26 | 8/18/1933 | M | S | L.A. |
| Smith, George | W | 23 | 9/22/1933 | M | S | Alameda |
| Egan, Dallas | W | 40 | 10/20/1933 | M | S | L.A. |
| Forbes, Claude | I | 25 | 12/ 8/1933 | M | S | Alameda |
| Shick, Quang | C | 41 | 2/ 9/1934 | M | | Colusa |
| Williams, George | B | 26 | 6/29/1934 | M | | San Bernardino |

| Name | Race | Age | Date of Execution | Offense | Appeal | County |
|------|------|-----|-------------------|---------|--------|--------|
| Mix, John | B | 22 | 7/ 6/1934 | M | | San Bernardino |
| Rippey, Walker | B | 24 | 7/13/1934 | M | | San Bernardino |
| Aragon, Jose | M | 25 | 7/13/1934 | M | | Riverside |
| Alosi, Peter | W | 42 | 10/ 5/1934 | M | | Lassen |
| Murphy, Leo Dwight | W | 41 | 12/ 7/1934 | M | S | L.A. |
| Sison, Eulogia B. | F | 28 | 1/25/1935 | M | S | Yuba |
| Rogan, James S. | W | 35 | 2/ 8/1935 | M | S | L.A. |
| Anderson, Edward | – | 25 | 2/15/1935 | M | S | S.F. |
| Griffin, Rush | B | 19 | 4/ 5/1935 | M | | L.A. |
| Lang, Edward L. | – | 26 | 6/ 7/1935 | M | S | L.A. |
| Ramos, Augustin | – | 32 | 8/16/1935 | M | S | Monterey |
| McNabb, Ethan | W | 37 | 9/ 6/1935 | A,L | S,U | Marin |
| Bagley, William | W | 43 | 9/ 6/1935 | A,L | S,U | Marin |
| Hawkins, John | – | 25 | 10/24/1935 | M | S | L.A. |
| Latona, Ellis J. | – | 41 | 12/ 6/1935 | M | S | L.A. |
| West, Arthur D. | W | 33 | 12/13/1935 | M | S | S.F. |
| De Moss, Clarence[2] | – | 42 | 4/ 3/1936 | M | S | Merced |
| Dugger, Thomas E. | W | 30 | 5/ 1/1936 | K | S | L.A. |
| Kristy, Joe | W | 27 | 5/22/1936 | K | U | Marin |
| McKay, Alexander | W | 29 | 5/22/1936 | K | U | Marin |
| Boulton, J.C. | W | 48 | 6/ 5/1936 | M | S | Butte |
| Gosden, Louis | W | 33 | 6/19/1936 | M | S | Alameda |
| Ottey, Irwin B. | W | 33 | 7/10/1936 | M | S | Monterey |
| Cabrera, Tony | M | 22 | 7/24/1936 | M | S | San Bernardino |
| Sam, Bill | – | 33 | 9/11/1936 | M | S | San Joaquin |
| Kellogg, John | B | 21 | 9/18/1936 | M | S | Fresno |
| Walter, Albert, Jr. | W | 28 | 12/ 4/1936 | M | S | S.F. |
| Joven, Joe | – | 32 | 1/ 8/1937 | M | S | Santa Clara |
| Shaver, Louis R. | W | 51 | 1/15/1937 | M | S | Alameda |
| Valenzuela, Natividad | – | 24 | 1/22/1937 | M | S | Orange |
| Pacren, Petronillo | – | 40 | 3/31/1937 | M | S | San Joaquin |
| Hart, Fred | W | 44 | 4/16/1937 | M | S | Riverside |
| Woods, John | – | 49 | 5/28/1937 | M | S | Alameda |
| McNeill, John D. | W | 52 | 7/ 9/1937 | M | S | Riverside |
| Wilhelm, Frank | – | 24 | 1/ 7/1938 | M | S | L.A. |
| Righthouse, Roy Leon | W | 27 | 2/18/1938 | M | S | Fresno |
| Goodwin, Lee Grant | – | 28 | 2/18/1938 | M | S | L.A. |
| Aguirre, Afrncisco | M | 30 | 9/ 2/1938 | M | S | Riverside |
| Dyer, Albert | W | 33 | 9/16/1938 | M | S | L.A. |
| Wells, Harrison | – | 47 | 10/14/1938 | M | S | Plumas |
| Kessell, Albert | – | 29 | 12/ 2/1938 | M | S | Sacramento |
| Cannon, Robert Lee | – | 24 | 12/ 2/1938 | M | S | Sacramento |
| Barnes, Fred | – | 40 | 12/ 9/1938 | M | S | Sacramento |
| Eudy, Wesley E. | – | 34 | 12/ 9/1938 | M | S | Sacramento |
| Davis, Ed | – | 37 | 12/16/1938 | M | S | Sacramento |
| David, Claude | W | 25 | 7/21/1939 | M | S | Modol |
| Smith, William G. | W | 25 | 9/ 8/1939 | M | S | Sacramento |
| McLachlan, Charles | – | 57 | 9/15/1939 | M | S | L.A. |
| Green, William | B | 39 | 10/20/1939 | M | S | Fresno |
| Williams, James Charles | W | 33 | 2/16/1940 | M | S | Riverside |
| Anderson, Neil | W | 23 | 3/15/1940 | M | S | Fresno |
| Spinelli, Vergilio | W | 60 | 5/17/1940 | M | S | L.A. |

| Name | Race | Age | Date of Execution | Offense | Appeal | County |
|------|------|-----|-------------------|---------|--------|--------|
| Perry, Robert C. | W | 71 | 7/19/1940 | M | S | San Diego |
| Parman, Everett Gilbert | W | 30 | 8/16/1940 | M | S | Placer |
| Greig, Rodney | W | 22 | 8/23/1940 | M | S | Alameda |
| Cook, DeWitt Clinton | W | 21 | 1/31/1941 | M | S | L.A. |
| Smith, Thomas B. | W | 60 | 4/18/1941 | M | S | Stanislaus |
| Kay, Wong Don | C | 57 | 7/11/1941 | M | S | Placer |
| Hawk, Eldon Richard | W | 27 | 8/29/1941 | M | S | Yolo |
| Lininger, John | W | 41 | 8/29/1941 | M | S | Tehama |
| Johansen, William | W | 36 | 9/ 5/1941 | M | S | S.F. |
| Reed, John | – | – | 9/26/1941 | M | S | San Bernardino |
| Spinelli, Eithel Leta (Female) | W | 51 | 11/21/1941 | M | S | Sacramento |
| Simone, Mike | W | 32 | 11/28/1941 | M | S | Sacramento |
| Hawkins, Gordon | W | 21 | 11/28/1941 | M | S | Sacramento |
| Clark, Dewey | – | 30 | 4/10/1942 | M | S | San Joaquin |
| Jones, Henry E. | – | 50 | 4/10/1942 | M | S | San Joaquin |
| Lisemba, Major Raymond | W | 47 | 5/ 1/1942 | M | U | L.A. |
| Briggs, Maurice Louis | W | 26 | 8/ 7/1942 | M | S | L.A. |
| Crimm, Steve | B | 28 | 8/21/1942 | M | S | Sacramento |
| Arnold, Delmar | – | 24 | 11/13/1942 | M | S | S.F. |
| Hoyt, Barzen | – | – | 11/13/1942 | M | S | S.F. |
| Frazier, Arthur | – | 22 | 11/20/1942 | M | S | S.F. |
| Wells, Albert | W | 32 | 12/ 4/1942 | M | S | San Bernardino |
| Gireth, Leslie B. | W | 38 | 1/22/1943 | M | S | Alameda |
| Cramer, Warren | – | 25 | 5/14/1943 | M | S | S.F. |
| Coleman, John L. | W | 43 | 8/13/1943 | M | S | San Diego |
| Bautista, Marcellino | F | 32 | 1/21/1944 | M | S | Tulare |
| Hill, Farrington Graham | W | 33 | 1/28/1944 | M | S | L.A. |
| Brown, Glenard | W | 19 | 2/15/1944 | M | S | Placer |
| Kolez, Daniel | – | 50 | 5/12/1944 | M | S | Lassen |
| Shaw, William | B | 35 | 6/16/1944 | M | S | San Bernardino |
| Alcalde, Florencio | W | 30 | 8/18/1944 | M | S | Santa Clara |
| Baa, Charles Ivan | B | 22 | 11/ 3/1944 | M | S | San Diego |
| Gonzales, Theodore | M | 21 | 1/ 5/1945 | M | S | L.A. |
| Anderson, Rollie Lee | W | 29 | 1/ 5/1945 | M | S | Lassen |
| Nagle, Djory | W | 32 | 3/ 2/1945 | M | S | Alameda |
| Keeling, Ernest | W | 26 | 3/ 2/1945 | M | S | Monterey |
| Glenn, Hurschel | W | 23 | 3/ 2/1945 | M | S | Monterey |
| Kelso, Silas J. | W | 25 | 5/25/1945 | M | S | L.A. |
| Bolden, Emery | B | 26 | 6/22/1945 | M | S,U | Monterey |
| Harper, McElwee | B | 35 | 6/22/1945 | M | S,U | Monterey |
| Diaz, Manuel Nino | M | 22 | 8/14/1944 | M | S | San Joaquin |
| Brigance, Thomas E. | W | 30 | 9/14/1945 | M | S,U | Alameda |
| Whitson, Benjamin H. | W | 27 | 9/14/1945 | M | S,U | Alameda |
| Jackson, Louie Lee | B | 53 | 10/ 5/1945 | M | S | S.F. |
| Simeone, Albert | W | 33 | 11/30/1945 | M | S | L.A. |
| Ming, Robert Lee | W | 26 | 4/12/1946 | M | S | Kern |
| Williams, Sam | B | 38 | 4/26/1946 | A,L | S | Marin |
| Wilson, Otto Stephen | W | 35 | 9/20/1946 | M | S | L.A. |
| Bernard, Charlie | B | 41 | 9/27/1946 | M | S | L.A. |
| de la Roi, Wilson | W | 28 | 10/25/1946 | A,L | S | Sacramento |
| Crain, William | W | 39 | 11/29/1946 | M | S | L.A. |
| Honeycutt, John T. | W | 33 | 2/ 7/1947 | M | S | L.A. |

| Name | Race | Age | Date of Execution | Offense | Appeal | County |
|------|------|-----|-------------------|---------|--------|--------|
| Hilton, Thomas | W | 29 | 2/26/1947 | M | S | Santa Barbara |
| Simmons, Alger | B | 30 | 3/21/1947 | M | S | L.A. |
| Peete, Louise L. (Female) | W | 58 | 4/11/1947 | M | S,U | L.A. |
| Dunn, Ernest | W | 38 | 6/ 6/1947 | M | S | Sacramento |
| Caetano, Joe | W | 30 | 8/29/1947 | M | S | Humboldt |
| Barnes, Francis Paul | W | 21 | 11/14/1947 | M | S | L.A. |
| Sanchez, Jose R. | M | 28 | 1/26/1948 | M | S | Imperial |
| McMonigle, Thomas H. | W | 33 | 2/20/1948 | M | S | Santa Cruz |
| Peterson, John J. | W | 42 | 4/ 9/1948 | M | S,F,U | L.A. |
| Isby, George | B | 27 | 4/16/1948 | M | S | Alameda |
| Winton, Paul C. | I | 31 | 5/28/1948 | M | S | Mendocino |
| Trujillo, Jose | M | 30 | 10/ 1/1948 | M | S,U | S.F. |
| Eggers, Arthur R. | W | 54 | 10/15/1948 | M | S,U | L.A. |
| Thompson, Miran Edgar | W | 31 | 12/ 3/1948 | M | S,F,U | Fed |
| Shockley, Sam Richard | W | 38 | 12/ 3/1948 | M | S,F,U | Fed |
| Ochoa, Carlos Romero | M | 29 | 12/10/1948 | M | S,F,U | Fed |
| Mehaffey, Robert F. | W | 38 | 12/31/1948 | M | S,U | San Bernardino |
| Shorts, Robert R. | B | 21 | 1/ 7/1949 | M | S,U | Alameda |
| Tuthill, Marvin James | W | 45 | 1/28/1949 | M | S | Riverside |
| Bowie, Maxwell J. | B | 23 | 2/18/1949 | M | S,U | Alameda |
| Williams, Henry A. | B | 24 | 2/18/1949 | M | S,U | Alameda |
| Campbell, Clayburne | B | 33 | 4/ 1/1949 | M | S | L.A. |
| Harrison, Joel | B | 23 | 4/ 1/1949 | M | S | L.A. |
| Zatke, Daniel Jerome | W | 23 | 7/ 1/1949 | M | S | L.A. |
| Sanford, William H. | W | 21 | 7/15/1949 | M | S | S.F. |
| Adamson, Admiral Dewey | B | 49 | 12/ 9/1949 | M | S,F,U | L.A. |
| Murphy, Jesse A. | W | 25 | 12/16/1949 | M | S | Fresno |
| Nixon, Albert E. | W | 34 | 12/16/1949 | M | S | Fresno |
| Corrales, Victoriano | M | 47 | 2/24/1950 | M | S | Sacramento |
| LeTourneau, Armand | W | 40 | 3/31/1950 | M | S | S.F. |
| Huizenga, Edward Albert | W | 59 | 6/ 2/1950 | M | S | Sacramento |
| Hooper, Henry | B | 45 | 8/ 4/1950 | M | S | Stanislaus |
| Avery, Herman | B | 50 | 10/ 6/1950 | M | S | San Diego |
| Gulbrandsen, Henry | W | 36 | 10/ 6/1950 | M | S | Sonoma |
| Gutierrez, Paul | M | 26 | 12/ 1/1950 | M | S | Fresno |
| Jackson, Monroe Arthur | W | 34 | 3/ 2/1951 | M | S | Tulare |
| Sexton, Harold | W | 23 | 3/16/1951 | M | S | Alameda |
| Odle, John Calvin | W | 59 | 8/17/1951 | M | S | Orange |
| Osborn, Claude L. | B | 36 | 9/14/1951 | M | S | Fresno |
| Cullen, Ray | W | 65 | 11/ 2/1951 | M | S | Riverside |
| Chavez, Felix | M | 26 | 11/30/1951 | M | S | Colusa |
| Phyle, William Jerome | W | 37 | 2/29/1952 | M | S,U | San Diego |
| Miller, Doil | B | 31 | 3/ 7/1952 | M | S | Alameda |
| Coefield, William Thomas | B | 23 | 3/21/1952 | M | S | Alameda |
| Sampsell, Lloyd Edison | W | 52 | 4/25/1952 | M | S,U | San Diego |
| Buckowski, Stanley | W | 26 | 5/ 9/1952 | M | S,U | L.A. |
| Martinez, Aurelio | M | 38 | 6/20/1952 | M | S | Tulare |
| Stroble, Fred | W | 70 | 8/25/1952 | M | S,U | L.A. |
| Gilliam, Bernard | W | 38 | 10/31/1952 | M | S | Fresno |
| Cook, William E. | W | 23 | 12/12/1952 | M | S | Imperial |
| Dessauer, Robert Gene | W | 30 | 2/ 2/1953 | M | S,U | L.A. |
| Riley, Leanderess | B | 32 | 2/20/1953 | M | S,U | Sacramento |

| Name | Race | Age | Date of Execution | Offense | Appeal | County |
|------|------|-----|-------------------|---------|--------|--------|
| Reed, Diamond | B | 34 | 4/17/1953 | M | S | Alameda |
| Barclay, Lovell | B | 37 | 5/15/1953 | M | S | Contra Costa |
| Amaya, Dario | W | 21 | 5/22/1953 | M | S | Alameda |
| Gomez, Lloyd | I | 29 | 10/16/1953 | M | S | Sacramento |
| Harrison, Johnnie | B | 51 | 10/23/1953 | M | S | Riverside |
| Lawrence, John Chauncey | W | 38 | 10/30/1953 | M | S | Riverside |
| Thomas, Evan Charles | W | 30 | 1/29/1954 | M | S | L.A. |
| McCracken, Henry Ford | W | 36 | 2/19/1954 | M | S,U | Orange |
| Daugherty, Joseph Arthur | W | 54 | 3/ 5/1954 | M | S,U | Sonoma |
| Ortega, Florentino | M | 25 | 3/ 5/1954 | M | S | L.A. |
| Decaillet, Henry | W | 52 | 4/ 2/1954 | M | S | Yolo |
| McGarry, Charles Leo | W | 66 | 7/ 2/1954 | M | S | L.A. |
| Wolfe, James Franklin | W | 42 | 7/30/1954 | M | S | Sacramento |
| Johansen, Joseph | W | 26 | 7/30/1954 | M | S | Sacramento |
| Dusseldorf, Alfred | B | 33 | 9/10/1954 | M | S,F,U | Alameda |
| Byrd, Walter Thomas | W | — | 2/ 4/1955 | M | S | Ventura |
| Jensen, Richard John | W | 28 | 2/11/1955 | K | S,U | L.A. |
| Caldwell, Johnson William | W | 33 | 5/ 6/1955 | M | S | Riverside |
| Baldwin, Leonard | W | — | 5/13/1955 | M | S,U | San Bernardino |
| Zilbauer, Anthony | W | 53 | 5/18/1955 | M | S | L.A. |
| Graham, Barbara (Female) | W | — | 6/ 3/1955 | M | S,U | L.A. |
| Santo, John A. | W | — | 6/ 3/1955 | M | S,U | L.A. |
| Perkins, Emmet | W | — | 6/ 3/1955 | M | S,U | L.A. |
| Berry, Harold E. | W | 28 | 9/20/1955 | M | S | Monterey |
| Pierce, Robert O. | B | 27 | 4/ 6/1956 | M | S | Alameda |
| Jordan, Smith E. | B | 27 | 4/ 6/1956 | M | S | Alameda |
| Cavanaugh, Michael T. | W | 29 | 4/13/1956 | M | S,U | San Diego |
| Morlock, Eugene A. | I | — | 6/15/1956 | M | S | San Diego |
| Thomas, Henry | B | 28 | 7/13/1956 | M | S,F,U | Siskiyou |
| Smith, Louis Franklin | W | 38 | 2/ 8/1957 | A,L | S,U | Sacramento |
| Allen, John | W | 48 | 2/ 8/1957 | A,L | S,U | Sacramento |
| Abbott, Burton W. | W | 27 | 3/15/1957 | M | S | Alameda |
| Johnston, Thomas Lynn | W | 25 | 6/28/1957 | M | S | Sacramento |
| Cheary, John E. | W | — | 7/19/1957 | M | S | Stanislaus |
| Hardenbrook, David J. | W | — | 8/16/1957 | M | S | Imperial |
| Dement, Foster S. | W | — | 10/ 2/1957 | M | S | L.A. |
| Simpson, Henry C. | W | — | 10/ 4/1957 | M | S,U | Stanislaus |
| Bashor, Donald Keith | W | 27 | 10/11/1957 | M | S | L.A. |
| Reese, James | B | — | 2/14/1958 | M | S | S.F. |
| Rogers, James Alonzo | W | 22 | 4/15/1958 | M | S,F,U | Marin |
| Burwell, Eugene T. | B | 24 | 4/15/1958 | M | S,F,U | Marin |
| Tipton, John Calvin | W | 20 | 9/26/1958 | M | | Orange |
| Caritativo, Bart Luis | F | 52 | 10/24/1958 | M | S,U | Marin |
| Rupp, William Francis, Jr. | W | 18 | 11/ 7/1958 | M | S,F,U | Ventura |
| Feldkamp, James Lewis | W | — | 2/27/1959 | M | S,U | L.A. |
| Riser, Richard G. | W | — | 5/22/1959 | M | S | Stanislaus |
| Duncan, Vender Lee | B | — | 5/29/1959 | M | S,U | S.F. |
| Ward, Cecil Herman | W | 27 | 6/26/1959 | M | S | Kern |
| Nash, Stephen A. | W | 35 | 8/21/1959 | M | S | L.A. |
| Glatman, Harvey Murray | W | 31 | 9/18/1959 | M | S | San Diego |
| Hamilton, Philip Henry | B | — | 1/ 8/1960 | M | S | S.F. |
| Jones, Jimmie Lee | B | — | 1/ 8/1960 | M | S | S.F. |

| Name | Race | Age | Date of Execution | Offense | Appeal | County |
|------|------|-----|-------------------|---------|--------|--------|
| Wade, Lawrence Leroy | B | — | 4/22/1960 | M | S | Alameda |
| Chessman, Caryl Whittier | W | — | 5/ 2/1960 | K | S | L.A. |
| Hooten, James Eugene | W | — | 5/13/1960 | M | S | L.A. |
| Cooper, Richard Thomas | B | — | 7/ 8/1960 | M | S | S.F. |
| Harmon, Robert S. | W | 27 | 8/ 9/1960 | A,L | S | Monterey |
| Scott, George Albert | W | 36 | 9/ 7/1960 | M | S | L.A. |
| Cartier, Raymond L. | W | — | 12/28/1960 | M | S,U | San Diego |
| Robillard, Alexander, XIV | W | 19 | 4/26/1961 | M | S | San Mateo |
| Rittger, Ronald | W | — | 6/29/1961 | M | S,U | Monterey |
| Linden, Marion James | W | — | 7/12/1961 | M | S,F,U | L.A. |
| Combes, David Allen | W | 32 | 10/18/1961 | M | S | Ventura |
| Kendrick, James | W | — | 11/ 3/1961 | M | S | San Bernardino |
| Lindsey, Richard Arlen | W | 30 | 11/21/1961 | M | S | Kern |
| Monk, Billy Wesley | W | 26 | 11/21/1961 | K | S,U | L.A. |
| Gonzalez, Jose Angel | M | 28 | 11/29/1961 | M | S | Riverside |
| Wright, Rudolph | B | — | 1/11/1962 | A,L | S,U | Monterey |
| Carter, Elbert Lyndon | B | 24 | 1/17/1962 | M | S,U | San Joaquin |
| Lane, Henry Roy, Jr. | W | — | 3/ 7/1962 | M | S | San Mateo |
| Hughes, Robert Green | B | 27 | 4/18/1962 | M | S | L.A. |
| Busch, Henry Adolph | W | 30 | 6/ 6/1962 | M | S | L.A. |
| Duncan, Elizabeth Ann (Fe-male) | W | — | 8/ 8/1962 | M | S,F,U | Ventura |
| Baldonado, Augustine | M | — | 8/ 8/1962 | M | S,F,U | Ventura |
| Moya, Luis Estrada | M | — | 8/ 8/1962 | M | S,F,U | Ventura |
| Garner, Lawrence C. | W | 27 | 9/ 4/1962 | M | S,U | San Bernardino |
| Darling, Melvin T. | W | 28 | 10/ 1/1962 | M | S | S.F. |
| Ditson, Allen | W | 42 | 11/21/1962 | M | S,U | L.A. |
| Bentley, James Abner | W | 26 | 1/23/1963 | M | S | Fresno |
| Mitchell, Aaron | B | 37 | 4/12/1967 | M | S,U | Sacramento |

[1]Vincent (10/27/1893) was hanged under local authority in the county of his conviction after California began executing its condemned felons at the state penitentiaries.
[2]Hanged for crimes committed prior to legislation changing method of execution to lethal gas.

## COLORADO

*Period of Executions*: 1890–1967
*Total Number*: 77
*Method*: Hanging 1890–1933; lethal gas 1934–1967
*Period of Abolition*: 1897–1901

| Name | Race | Age | Date of Execution | Offense | Appeal | County |
|------|------|-----|-------------------|---------|--------|--------|
| Criego, Noverto | — | — | 11/ 8/1890 | M | | Las Animas |
| Joyce, James T. | — | — | 1/17/1891 | M | | Arapahoe |
| Davis, William C. | B | — | 9/22/1891 | M | S | Pueblo |
| Smith, Charles | — | — | 12/14/1891 | M | | Huerfano |
| Lawton, Thomas | W | 24 | 5/ 6/1892 | M | | El Paso |
| Jordan, Thomas | — | — | 5/11/1895 | M | S | Arapahoe |
| Augusta, Peter | — | — | 5/11/1895 | M | S | Arapahoe |

| Name | Race | Age | Date of Execution | Offense | Appeal | County |
|------|------|-----|-------------------|---------|--------|--------|
| Taylor, Abe | – | – | 12/13/1895 | M | S | Conejos |
| Ratcliff, Benjamin | W | – | 2/ 7/1896 | M | S | Chaffee |
| Holt, William | – | – | 6/26/1896 | M | S | Las Animas |
| Noble, Albert | – | – | 6/26/1896 | M | S | Las Animas |
| Romero, Deonicio | – | – | 6/26/1896 | M | S | Las Animas |
| Galbraith, Azel | – | – | 3/ 6/1905 | M | | Gilpin |
| Arnold, Fred | – | – | 6/16/1905 | M | S | Denver |
| Andrews, Newton | – | – | 6/16/1905 | M | S | Denver |
| Johnson, Joseph | W | – | 9/13/1905 | M | | Las Animas |
| McGarvey, John | W | 25 | 1/12/1907 | M | | Mesa |
| Alia, Giuseppe | W | – | 7/15/1908 | M | | Denver |
| Lynn, James | B | 50 | 10/ 8/1908 | M | | Pueblo |
| Wechter, Lewis | W | – | 8/31/1912 | M | S | Denver |
| Hillen, Harry E. | – | – | 6/24/1915 | M | S | Denver |
| Quinn, George | – | – | 1/28/1916 | M | S | Denver |
| Cook, Oscar | – | – | 2/26/1916 | M | S | Denver |
| Bosko, George | W | 29 | 12/10/1920 | M | S | Pueblo |
| Borich, Daniel | – | – | 8/18/1922 | M | | Routt |
| McGonigal, Joe | W | – | 4/26/1924 | M | S | Las Animas |
| Shank, R.I. | – | 56 | 9/18/1926 | M | S | Denver |
| Casias, Antonio | – | – | 11/12/1926 | M | | Rio Grande |
| Noakes, Jasper R. | W | – | 3/30/1928 | M | S | Grand |
| Osborn, Arthur | W | – | 3/30/1928 | M | S | Grand |
| Ives, Edward | W | 44 | 1/10/1930 | M | S | Denver |
| Weiss, Harold I. | W | – | 5/28/1930 | M | S | Denver |
| Fleagle, Ralph E. | W | – | 7/10/1930 | M | S | Prowers |
| Abshier, George J. | W | – | 7/18/1930 | M | S | Prowers |
| Royston, Howard L. | W | – | 7/18/1930 | M | S | Prowers |
| Herrera, Amelio | – | – | 8/20/1930 | M | S | Denver |
| Moya, William | W | 30 | 12/12/1930 | M | S | Denver |
| Halliday, Andrew | – | – | 1/30/1931 | M | S | Kiowa |
| Walker, John | – | – | 1/30/1931 | M | S | Kiowa |
| Ray, Claude | – | – | 1/30/1931 | M | S | Kiowa |
| Foster, James V. | W | 49 | 12/11/1931 | M | | Weld |
| Farmer, E.J. | – | – | 3/18/1932 | M | S | Moffat |
| Meastas, Joe | W | – | 5/27/1932 | M | | Costilla |
| Moss, Nelwelt | B | 20 | 3/10/1933 | M | S | Gunnison |
| Jones, Walter | W | 23 | 12/ 1/1933 | M | S | Mesa |
| Kelly, William C. | W | 30 | 6/22/1934 | M | | Delta |
| Pacheco, John | M | 24 | 5/31/1935 | M | S | Weld |
| Pacheco, Louis | M | 37 | 5/31/1935 | M | S | Weld |
| Belongia, Leonard | W | 24 | 6/21/1935 | M | | Weld |
| McDaniel, Otis | W | 30 | 2/14/1936 | M | | San Miguel |
| Aguilar, Frank | M | 34 | 8/13/1937 | M | | Pueblo |
| Arridy, Joe | M | 21 | 1/ 6/1939 | M | S | Pueblo |
| Agnes, Angelo | – | – | 9/29/1939 | M | S | Denver |
| Catalina, Pete | – | – | 9/29/1939 | M | S | Chaffee |
| Leopold, Harry | W | 29 | 12/ 8/1939 | M | S | Denver |
| Coates, Joe | – | – | 1/10/1941 | M | S | Denver |
| Stephans, James | – | – | 6/20/1941 | M | S | Montezuma |
| Sukle, Martin | W | 38 | 5/22/1942 | M | S | El Paso |
| Fearn, Donald H. | W | 23 | 10/23/1942 | M | | Pueblo |

| Name | Race | Age | Date of Execution | Offense | Appeal | County |
|------|------|-----|-------------------|---------|--------|--------|
| Sullivan, John | W | 43 | 9/20/1943 | M | S | El Paso |
| Honda, George | – | – | 10/ 8/1943 | M | S | Denver |
| Potts, Howard C. | W | 41 | 6/22/1945 | M | S | Denver |
| Silliman, Charles F. | W | 35 | 11/ 9/1945 | M | S | Arapahoe |
| Martz, Frank H. | W | — | 11/23/1945 | M | S | Arapahoe |
| Brown, John H. | – | – | 5/23/1947 | M | S | Denver |
| Gillette, Harold | W | 31 | 6/20/1947 | M | | Larimer |
| Battalino, Robert S. | – | – | 1/ 7/1949 | M | | Jefferson |
| Schneider, Paul F. | W | 24 | 12/16/1949 | M | S,U | Washington |
| Berger, John J., Jr. | – | – | 10/26/1951 | M | S,U | Denver |
| Martinez, Besalirez | – | 42 | 9/ 7/1956 | M | S | Eagle |
| Graham, John Gilbert | W | 23 | 1/11/1957 | M | S | Denver |
| Leick, LeeRoy A. | W | 30 | 1/22/1960 | M | S,F,U | Denver |
| Early, David F. | W | 28 | 8/11/1961 | M | S,U | Arapahoe |
| Wooley, Harold D. | W | 36 | 3/ 9/1962 | M | S | Jefferson |
| Hammill, Walter D. | W | 31 | 5/25/1962 | M | S | Denver |
| Bizup, John, Jr. | W | 26 | 8/14/1964 | M | S,F,U | Pueblo |
| Monge, Luis Jose | P | 48 | 6/ 2/1967 | M | | Denver |

## CONNECTICUT

*Period of Executions*: 1894–1960
*Total Number*: 73
*Method*: Hanging 1894–1936; electrocution 1937–1960

| Name | Race | Age | Date of Execution | Offense | Appeal | County |
|------|------|-----|-------------------|---------|--------|--------|
| Cronin, John | W | 38 | 12/18/1894 | M | S | Hartford |
| Hertlein, Kapar | W | 40 | 12/13/1896 | M | | Hartford |
| Kippie, Thomas | W | 42 | 7/14/1897 | M | | New Haven |
| Fuda, Gussippi | W | 31 | 12/ 3/1897 | M | | Fairfield |
| Imposino, Nicodemo | W | 24 | 12/17/1897 | M | | Fairfield |
| Bainay, Charles | W | 34 | 4/14/1898 | M | | Fairfield |
| Willis, Benjamin | W | 21 | 12/30/1898 | M | S | Fairfield |
| Brockhaus, Frederick | W | 21 | 9/ 6/1899 | M | S | Fairfield |
| Cross, Charles | W | 18 | 7/20/1900 | M | S | Fairfield |
| Misik, Paul | W | 34 | 2/11/1904 | M | | Hartford |
| Watson, Joseph | B | 18 | 11/17/1904 | M | | Hartford |
| Marx, Gershom | W | 73 | 5/18/1905 | M | S | New London |
| Sherouk, Ephria | W | 24 | 1/ 9/1906 | M | S | Tolland |
| Bailey, Henry | W | 40 | 4/16/1907 | M | S | Middlesex |
| Herman, Alexander | W | 26 | 5/10/1907 | M | | Fairfield |
| Washelesky, John | W | 32 | 7/ 1/1908 | M | S | New Haven |
| Rossi, Lorenzo | W | 31 | 7/24/1908 | M | | Hartford |
| Zett, John | W | 48 | 12/21/1908 | M | | Tolland |
| Campagnolo, Giuseppe | W | 28 | 2/24/1909 | M | | New Haven |
| Carfaro, Raeffaele | W | 19 | 2/24/1909 | M | | New Haven |
| Zawedzianczek, Johb | W | 28 | 2/ 9/1910 | M | | Hartford |
| Tanganelli, Andrea | W | 26 | 3/29/1912 | M | | New Haven |
| Redding, George | W | 21 | 11/ 1/1912 | M | | Hartford |

| Name | Race | Age | Date of Execution | Offense | Appeal | County |
|------|------|-----|-------------------|---------|--------|--------|
| Saxon, Louis | W | 29 | 7/27/1913 | M | S | Hartford |
| Plew, James | W | 48 | 3/14/1914 | M | | New Haven |
| Rikteraites, Matyius | W | 29 | 5/ 8/1914 | M | | New Haven–Waterbury |
| Buonomo, Joseph | W | 24 | 6/30/1914 | M | S | Fairfield |
| Bergeron, Joseph | W | 40 | 8/11/1914 | M | S | New Haven |
| Montvid, Bernoid | W | 23 | 8/ 6/1915 | M | | Hartford |
| Grela, Frank | W | 41 | 8/13/1915 | M | | Hartford |
| Williams, Isaac | W | 30 | 3/ 3/1916 | M | S | Litchfield |
| Rowe, Harry | W | 22 | 3/ 3/1916 | M | S | Litchfield |
| Zuppa, Pasquale | W | 28 | 3/10/1916 | M | | New Haven |
| Vetere, Francesco | W | 24 | 10/ 5/1917 | M | S | New Haven |
| Castelli, Joseph | W | 25 | 10/ 5/1917 | M | S | New Haven |
| Don Vanso, Giovanni | W | 21 | 11/16/1917 | M | | Hartford |
| Buglione, Stephen | W | 20 | 11/16/1917 | M | | Hartford |
| Wise, William J. | W | 23 | 12/14/1917 | M | | Hartford |
| Lanzillo, Carmine | W | 24 | 6/17/1918 | M | | New Haven |
| Pisaniello, Carmine | W | 21 | 6/17/1918 | M | | New Haven |
| Dusso, Francesco | W | 25 | 6/17/1918 | M | | New Haven |
| Perretta, Erasmo | W | 28 | 6/27/1919 | M | S | Hartford |
| Perretta, Joseph | W | 33 | 6/27/1919 | M | S | Hartford |
| Nechesnook, Nikifor | W | 28 | 12/ 3/1919 | M | | New Haven–Waterbury |
| Cerrone, Daniel | W | 31 | 7/ 5/1920 | M | | New Haven |
| Wade, Elwood B. | W | 24 | 5/20/1921 | M | S | Fairfield |
| Kauarauskas, John | W | 36 | 5/27/1921 | M | | New Haven |
| Schutte, Emil | W | 55 | 10/24/1922 | M | S | Middlesex |
| Chapman, Gerald | W | 35 | 4/ 6/1926 | M | S,F,U | Hartford |
| Lung, Chin | C | 33 | 11/ 8/1927 | M | S | Hartford |
| Wing, Soo Hoo | C | 19 | 11/ 8/1927 | M | S | Hartford |
| Feltovic, John | W | 19 | 12/10/1929 | M | S | Fairfield |
| DiBattista, Frank | W | 26 | 2/21/1930 | M | S | Hartford |
| Lorenzo, Henry | W | 26 | 8/12/1930 | M | | Hartford |
| Simborski, John | W | 30 | 4/ 7/1936 | M | S | New Haven |
| McElroy, James J. | W | 45 | 2/10/1937 | M | | New Haven |
| Palka, Frank J. | W | 25 | 4/12/1938 | M | S,U | Fairfield |
| Cots, Vincent | W | 32 | 4/29/1940 | M | S | Middlesex |
| Weaver, Ira Allen | W | 36 | 4/29/1940 | M | S | Middlesex |
| Gurski, Peter | W | 26 | 2/23/1943 | M | | Litchfield |
| Funderburk, Wilson H. | B | 28 | 4/20/1943 | M | | Hartford |
| DeCaro, Carlo James | W | 19 | 5/ 3/1944 | M | | Hartford |
| Rossi, Nicholas J. | W | 31 | 6/18/1945 | M | S | Hartford |
| McCarthy, James J. | W | 21 | 10/ 1/1946 | M | S | Hartford |
| Tommaselli, Arthur | W | 25 | 10/ 1/1946 | M | S | Hartford |
| Lewis, Raymond | W | 19 | 10/ 1/1946 | M | S | Hartford |
| Bradley, Robert | B | 37 | 4/12/1948 | M | S,U | New Haven |
| Lorain, William | W | 40 | 7/11/1955 | M | S | Hartford |
| Donahue, John B. | W | 33 | 7/18/1955 | M | S,U | Fairfield |
| Maim, Robert Nelson | W | 31 | 7/18/1955 | M | S | Hartford |
| Davies, George James | W | 41 | 10/20/1959 | M | S,U | New Haven–Waterbury |
| Wojculewicz, Frank[1] | W | 42 | 10/27/1959 | M | S,F,U | Hartford |

| Name | Race | Age | Date of Execution | Offense | Appeal | County |
|------|------|-----|-------------------|---------|--------|--------|
| Taborsky, Joseph L.[2] | W | 36 | 5/17/1960 | M | S,U | Hartford |

[1]Wojculewicz (10/27/1959) was permanently crippled by gunshots during the commission of his crime and was carried into the execution chamber on a stretcher. The electric chair was specially altered to receive him.

[2]Taborsky (5/17/1960) had been freed from death row in 1955 on charges of an earlier murder. He subsequently confessed that he was guilty of that one.

## DISTRICT OF COLUMBIA

*Period of Executions*: 1853–1957
*Total Number*: 113
*Method*: Hanging 1853–1925; electrocution 1928–1957
*Other Data*: Appeals were taken to the Supreme Court of the District of Columbia. Since 1920, the decisions of this Court were printed in the Federal Reporter.

| Name | Race | Age | Date of Execution | Offense | Appeal | County |
|------|------|-----|-------------------|---------|--------|--------|
| Woodward, Daniel | W | — | 9/ 2/1853 | M | | (not applicable) |
| Powers, James W. | W | 19 | 6/ /1858 | M | | |
| Hendricks, Jeremiah[1] | W | — | 4/1/1864 | M | | |
| Pollard, Emmanuel | W | — | 7/ 8/1864 | M | | |
| Gordon, P | W | — | 7/ 8/1864 | M | | |
| Tuell, Cornelious | W | — | 7/ 8/1864 | M | | |
| Grady, James | W | — | 3/24/1871 | M | | |
| Jenkins, George W. | B | — | 10/31/1872 | M | | |
| Wood, Barney | W | — | 12/ 6/1872 | M | | |
| Johnson, Charles | B | — | 12/10/1872 | M | | |
| Wright, Thomas | B | — | 6/ 6/1873 | M | | |
| Young, Henry | B | — | 11/28/1873 | M | | |
| Stone, James M.W. | B | 35 | 4/ 2/1880 | M | | |
| Queenan, Edward | B | — | 11/19/1880 | M | | |
| Bedford, Joseph | B | — | 11/19/1880 | M | | |
| Guiteau, Charles Julius | W | 38 | 6/30/1882 | M | | |
| Shaw, Charles | B | — | 1/19/1883 | M | | |
| Langster, John | B | — | 5/15/1885 | M | | |
| Sommerfield, Louis | W | 54 | 4/30/1886 | M | | |
| Lee, Richard | B | — | 4/30/1886 | M | | |
| Nardello, Antonio | W | 22 | 5/28/1886 | M | | |
| Green, Albert | B | — | 4/ 5/1889 | M | | |
| Colbert, Nelson | B | — | 5/17/1889 | M | | |
| Hawkins, Benjamin | B | 29 | 5/29/1890 | M | | |
| Schneider, Howard J. | W | — | 3/17/1893 | M | | |
| Crumpton, Thomas | B | — | 4/27/1894 | M | | |
| Travers, James L. | B | — | 7/19/1895 | M | | |
| Beam, Joseph A. | W | — | 7/26/1895 | M | | |
| Harris, John | B | — | 2/14/1896 | M | | |
| Ford, Irvin | B | — | 6/26/1896 | M | | |
| Strathers, William | B | 25 | 5/ 5/1899 | M | U | |
| Winston, Charles | B | 24 | 5/ 5/1899 | M | U | |

| Name | Race | Age | Date of Execution | Offense | Appeal | County |
|------|------|-----|-------------------|---------|--------|--------|
| Smith, Edward | B | 47 | 5/12/1899 | M | U | |
| Horton, George W. | W | 50 | 12/ 8/1899 | M | | |
| Snell, Benjamin H. | W | 42 | 6/29/1900 | M | | |
| Vale, Nelson | B | 59 | 7/ 6/1900 | M | | |
| Funk, Frank W. | W | 25 | 11/ 9/1900 | M | | |
| Chapman, Elijah | B | 33 | 5/23/1902 | M | | |
| St. Clair, John T. | B | 26 | 1/30/1903 | M | | |
| Hill, Benjamin G. | W | 52 | 7/24/1903 | M | | |
| Burley, John W. | B | 43 | 8/26/1904 | Ra | | |
| Shaffer, Augustus L. | W | 39 | 2/10/1905 | M | | |
| Hamilton, William W. | B | 27 | 2/ 2/1906 | M | | |
| Grant, Edward | B | 21 | 11/16/1906 | M | | |
| Burge, William | B | 23 | 4/23/1907 | M | | |
| Paoleucchi, Joseph | W | 31 | 3/23/1908 | M | | |
| Brown, Albert | B | 23 | 6/29/1908 | M | | |
| Gregory, Richard | B | 37 | 6/29/1908 | M | | |
| Rauen, Samuel W. | W | 25 | 2/14/1913 | M | | |
| Green, Nathaniel | B | 23 | 6/ 9/1913 | Ra | | |
| Allen, James F. | B | 36 | 9/12/1917 | M | | |
| Jackson, James | B | 27 | 3/ 2/1920 | M | F | |
| Bowman, Frank | B | 39 | 10/22/1920 | M | F | |
| Campbell, William H. | B | 22 | 3/11/1921 | M | | |
| McHenry, John | W | 19 | 3/17/1922 | M | F | |
| Shands, Ernest A. | B | 29 | 3/ 9/1923 | M | | |
| Price, Charles | B | 32 | 5/ 3/1923 | M | F | |
| Banton, George S. | B | 20 | 4/20/1923 | M | | |
| Epps, George S. | B | 31 | 5/24/1923 | M | | |
| Gordon, Rufus | B | 37 | 6/23/1923 | M | F | |
| Thomas, Ralph | B | 40 | 1/15/1925 | M | F | |
| Copeland, Herbert L. | B | 50 | 1/22/1925 | M | F | |
| Jackson, Philip | B | 30 | 5/29/1928 | Ra | F | |
| Eagles, Nicholas L. | W | 34 | 6/22/1928 | M | F | |
| Mareno, Sam | W | 21 | 6/22/1928 | M | | |
| Proctor, John R. | W | 20 | 6/22/1928 | M | | |
| Hawkins, Andrew J. | B | 31 | 6/ 5/1930 | M | F | |
| Bell, Cardoza | B | 24 | 3/ 6/1931 | M | F | |
| Aldridge, Alfred S. | B | 21 | 5/ 6/1932 | M | U,F,NT | |
| Logan, John | B | 24 | 6/29/1932 | M | F,U | |
| Borum, John | B | 26 | 6/29/1932 | M | F,U | |
| Morris, Charles | B | 33 | 12/ 2/1932 | M | F | |
| Robinson, William C. | B | 20 | 10/27/1933 | M | F,U | |
| Lowry, James H. | B | — | 11/ 1/1933 | M | | |
| Washington, Charles E. | B | 23 | 11/24/1933 | M | | |
| Montague, Benjamin | B | 29 | 12/ 1/1933 | M | | |
| Murry, Irving | B | 26 | 1/12/1934 | M | F | |
| Jackson, Joseph J. | B | 20 | 1/12/1934 | M | F | |
| Holmes, Ralph E. | B | 25 | 1/12/1934 | M | F | |
| Bolden, Ernest H. | B | 25 | 4/27/1934 | M | F | |
| Pitmond, George H. | B | 34 | 6/ 1/1934 | M | F | |
| Goodman, Joe | B | 38 | 6/ 1/1934 | M | F | |
| Preston, Albert | B | 38 | 3/20/1936 | M | F | |
| Cummings, John R. | B | 27 | 4/23/1937 | M | F | |

| Name | Race | Age | Date of Execution | Offense | Appeal | County |
|------|------|-----|-------------------|---------|--------|--------|
| Marcus, Willett | B | 21 | 4/23/1937 | M | F | |
| Robinson, Norman W. | B | 29 | 3/18/1938 | M | F | |
| Kinard, Will | B | 39 | 2/ 3/1939 | M | F | |
| Haupt, Herbert Hans[2] | W | 22 | 8/ 8/1942 | M | | |
| Heink, Heinrich Harm[2] | W | 34 | 8/ 8/1942 | M | | |
| Kerling, Edward John[2] | W | 33 | 8/ 8/1942 | M | | |
| Neubauer, Herman Otto[2] | W | 32 | 8/ 8/1942 | M | | |
| Quirin, Richard[2] | W | 34 | 8/ 8/1942 | M | | |
| Thiel, Werner[2] | B | 35 | 8/ 8/1942 | M | | |
| Robinson, William I. | B | 36 | 10/ 9/1942 | Ra | F | |
| Mumford, William T. | B | 22 | 12/18/1942 | M | F,U | |
| Catoe, Jarvis T.R. | B | 36 | 1/15/1943 | M,Ra | F | |
| Neely, Monroe D. | B | 37 | 12/14/1945 | M | F,U | |
| McFarland, Earl | W | 23 | 7/19/1946 | M | F,U | |
| Copeland, William | B | 38 | 12/20/1946 | M | F,U | |
| Fisher, Julius | B | 34 | 12/20/1946 | M | F,U | |
| Medley, Joseph | W | 45 | 12/20/1946 | M | F,U | |
| Hawkins, Alfred L. | B | 24 | 10/31/1947 | M | F,U | |
| Patton, Jesse | B | 23 | 12/10/1948 | M | | |
| Wheeler, Reginald J. | B | 28 | 12/10/1948 | M | | |
| Harris, Shirley | B | 25 | 1/14/1949 | M | F,U | |
| Hall, John H. | B | 35 | 2/25/1949 | CK | F | |
| Holmes, Theodore M. | B | — | 3/15/1949 | Ra | F | |
| Garner, George A. | B | 26 | 7/29/1949 | M | | |
| Garner, Lawrence | B | 26 | 7/29/1949 | M | F,U | |
| Pritchard, Fred S. | W | 41 | 2/15/1952 | M | | |
| Tyler, William A. | B | 20 | 7/25/1952 | M | F,U | |
| Allen, Albert | B | 25 | 3/20/1953 | M | F,U | |
| Carter, Robert E. | B | 28 | 4/26/1957 | M | F,U | |

[1]Mr. Espy reports that his listing of executions received from the District does not show Hendricks (4/1/1864).
[2]These men were Nazi spies and saboteurs, convicted by a military commission. A writ of habeas corpus was denied by the U.S. Supreme Court.

## FLORIDA

*Period of Executions*: 1924–1979
*Total Number*: 198 (includes 1 post-*Furman* execution)
*Method*: Electrocution

| Name | Race | Age | Date of Execution | Offense | Appeal | County |
|------|------|-----|-------------------|---------|--------|--------|
| Johnson, Frank | B | — | 10/ 7/1924 | M | S | Duval |
| Coachman, J.C. | B | — | 5/ 6/1925 | Ra | | Manatee |
| Champion, Will | B | — | 1/28/1926 | M | | Duval |
| Dunwood, Roy | B | — | 5/12/1926 | M | | Duval |
| Simmons, John | B | — | 5/18/1926 | M | | Duval |
| Scrimm, Harry | W | — | 5/25/1926 | Ra | | Dade |
| Taylor, Philip | B | — | 10/28/1926 | M | | Dade |
| Green, Willie | B | — | 11/23/1926 | M | S | Dade |

| Name | Race | Age | Date of Execution | Offense | Appeal | County |
|------|------|-----|-------------------|---------|--------|--------|
| Williams, Arthur | B | — | 12/11/1926 | M | S | Dade |
| Salter, Lloyd Odell | B | — | 3/ 1/1927 | M | | Duval |
| Stone, Raymond | B | — | 3/ 8/1927 | M | | Duval |
| Chesser, Rufus | W | 18 | 3/23/1927 | M | S | Clay |
| London, Earl | B | — | 4/ 7/1927 | M | | Polk |
| Ferguson, Fortune | B | 16 | 4/27/1927 | Ra | S | Alachua |
| Levins, Benjamin F. | W | — | 11/22/1927 | M | | Hillsborough |
| Thomas, Louis | W | — | 11/29/1927 | M | S | Pinellas |
| Costello, Thomas | W | 31 | 12/13/1927 | M | S | Hillsborough |
| Henderson, William B. | W | — | 12/21/1927 | M | S | Hillsborough |
| Pittman, Robert C. | B | 26 | 6/13/1928 | M | S | Seminole |
| Vaughn, Will | B | — | 8/28/1928 | M | | Duval |
| Johnson, Melvin | B | 26 | 9/ 4/1928 | Ra | | Dade |
| Crumpler, Paul | B | 29 | 9/18/1928 | Ra | | Hillsborough |
| Turner, James | B | 27 | 9/25/1928 | M | | Calhoun |
| Davis, George | B | — | 10/ 9/1928 | M | S | Putnam |
| Harvey, Herbert | B | 21 | 10/23/1928 | M | | Baker |
| Kirkland, Roosevelt | B | — | 10/30/1928 | M | S | Baker |
| Funderbirk, Boss | B | — | 3/19/1930 | M | | Franklin |
| Bell, Clayton | B | — | 1/27/1931 | M | | Volusia |
| Southworth, T. | W | 27 | 2/12/1931 | M | S | Palm Beach |
| Burton, Nathan | W | 24 | 2/24/1931 | M | | Alachua |
| McQuagge, Robert | W | — | 5/27/1931 | M | | Jackson |
| Graham, John | B | — | 6/18/1931 | Ra | | Marion |
| Johnson, Henry | B | — | 6/24/1931 | M | S | Lake |
| Collins, Jim | B | — | 11/12/1931 | Ra | | Dade |
| Jacobs, Lee | B | 22 | 3/26/1932 | Ra | S | Marion |
| Zangara, Guiseppe[1] | W | 33 | 3/20/1933 | M | | Dade |
| Jeffcoat, Elvin E. | W | 40 | 3/24/1933 | M | S | Pinellas |
| Palmer, Victor | W | 26 | 7/10/1933 | M | S | Hillsborough |
| Leavine, Louis | W | 33 | 7/10/1933 | M | S | Hillsborough |
| Heidt, Norman | W | 26 | 7/10/1933 | M | S | Hillsborough |
| Williams, Walter | B | 31 | 10/ 8/1934 | Ra | | Dade |
| Jefferson, Thomas | B | 23 | 1/22/1935 | M | S | Duval |
| Anderson, Fred | B | 24 | 1/22/1935 | M | S | Duval |
| Robinson, George | B | 46 | 2/25/1935 | Ra | S | Seminole |
| Smith, Herman | W | 36 | 4/ 5/1935 | M | S | Orange |
| Jarvis, Martin | W | 36 | 4/11/1935 | M | S | Sarasota |
| Hasty, Monroe | B | 17 | 9/16/1935 | M | S | Volusia |
| Green, Lonnie | B | 28 | 1/ 7/1936 | M | | Bradford |
| Bradley, Ed | W | 57 | 6/29/1936 | M | | Santa Rosa |
| Dixon, George | B | 27 | 8/24/1936 | M | | Seminole |
| Casey, Clarence D. | W | 23 | 10/19/1936 | M | S | Dade |
| Milligan, James | W | 24 | 10/19/1936 | M | | Dade |
| Padgett, L.D. | W | 28 | 10/19/1936 | M | S | Santa Rosa |
| Clark, Lee | B | 30 | 10/19/1936 | M | S | Escambia |
| Scroggins, George W. | B | 41 | 10/26/1936 | M | S | Dade |
| Johnson, Rufus | B | 20 | 10/26/1936 | M | | Seminole |
| Williams, Richard | B | 32 | 12/14/1936 | M | S | Pinellas |
| Walker, James W. | B | 30 | 12/14/1936 | M | S | Pinellas |
| Walker, Willie | B | 33 | 4/23/1937 | Ra | | Nassau |
| Fields, Simee Lee | B | 21 | 5/10/1937 | M | S | Hillsborough |

| Name | Race | Age | Date of Execution | Offense | Appeal | County |
|------|------|-----|-------------------|---------|--------|--------|
| Powell, Marcus C. | W | 50 | 7/12/1937 | M | S | Duval |
| McDonald, Preston | B | 28 | 7/19/1937 | M | S | Duval |
| Williams, Walter | B | 38 | 7/19/1937 | M | S | Duval |
| Hinds, Robert | B | 17 | 7/23/1937 | Ra | | Leon |
| Williams, Orson | B | 28 | 6/20/1938 | M | S | Hillsborough |
| Randolph, Willie | B | 34 | 7/ 5/1938 | M | | Duval |
| Bunge, Paul | W | 53 | 2/20/1939 | M | | Hillsborough |
| McCall, Franklin Pierce | W | 21 | 2/24/1939 | K | S | Dade |
| Smith, Johnny | B | 30 | 5/12/1939 | M | S | Indian River |
| McGraw, Hervey | W | 20 | 9/ 4/1939 | M | | Santa Rosa |
| Parker, Clarence | B | 29 | 6/ 5/1940 | M | S | Gilchrist |
| Goddard, Herbert | W | 29 | 7/29/1940 | M | S | Palm Beach |
| Williams, Ivory Lee | B | 18 | 11/11/1940 | M | S | Alachua |
| Smith, Richard | B | 48 | 4/15/1941 | M | S | Brevard |
| Ormond, Dan J. | W | 52 | 10/ 6/1941 | M | | Jackson |
| Crews, Wilburn | W | 36 | 10/ 6/1941 | M | S | Duval |
| Henderson, Charlie | B | 34 | 10/ 6/1941 | M | S | Orange |
| McLaren, Frizell | B | 34 | 10/ 6/1941 | M | S | Dade |
| Ranson, Mack | B | 38 | 10/27/1941 | M | | Duval |
| Mardorff, Paul H. | W | 50 | 10/27/1941 | M | S | Dade |
| Walker, Nathaniel | B | 17 | 12/29/1941 | M | S | Duval |
| Powell, Edward | B | 16 | 12/29/1941 | M | S | Duval |
| Clay, Willie B. | B | 16 | 12/29/1941 | M | S | Duval |
| Newsome, George | B | 29 | 3/ 2/1942 | M | S | Leon |
| Roberson, Worth | W | 22 | 3/23/1942 | M | | Gilchrist |
| Gaingetti, Angie Michael | W | 50 | 3/23/1942 | M | | Volusia |
| Crawford, Jicy | B | 28 | 3/23/1942 | M | S | Duval |
| Roberson, Walter | B | 42 | 3/23/1942 | M | | Dixie |
| Stanton, John A. | W | 44 | 5/18/1942 | M | S | Dade |
| Hysler, Clyde | W | 23 | 6/15/1942 | M | S,U | Duval |
| Baker, James | B | 32 | 6/15/1942 | M | S | Duval |
| Hudgins, Byrdl | W | 23 | 7/20/1942 | M | | Dade |
| Williams, Willie M. | B | 37 | 7/20/1942 | M | S | Taylor |
| Robinson, Ernest James | B | 20 | 8/17/1942 | M | S | Duval |
| Saylor, Forrest | B | 35 | 1/18/1943 | M | | Pinellas |
| Christy, Vincent J. | W | 38 | 3/ 1/1943 | M | | Dade |
| Parker, Cornelius E. | B | 24 | 10/ 4/1943 | M | | Hillsborough |
| Leundon, Buffie | B | 44 | 10/25/1943 | M | | Alachua |
| Young, James A. | B | 32 | 10/25/1943 | Ra | | Hillsborough |
| James, G.W. | B | 54 | 10/29/1943 | M | S,U | Polk |
| Acree, Perry | W | 43 | 11/22/1943 | M | S | Levy |
| Flowers, Edgar | B | 21 | 6/26/1944 | Ra | S,U | Hillsborough |
| Thompson, Edward | W | 25 | 8/19/1944 | M | S | Duval |
| Thompson, Earl | W | 33 | 8/19/1944 | M | S | Duval |
| Williams, James C. | B | 25 | 10/ 9/1944 | Ra | S | Alachua |
| Lane, Freddie Lee | B | 18 | 10/ 9/1944 | Ra | S | Alachua |
| Davis, James | B | 16 | 10/ 9/1944 | Ra | S | Alachua |
| Mix, Tom | B | 37 | 12/28/1944 | M | S | Citrus |
| Sparks, Henry | B | 33 | 1/15/1945 | Ra | | Palm Beach |
| Green, Albert | B | 28 | 2/12/1945 | M | S | Lake |
| Anderson, William H. | B | 23 | 7/25/1945 | Ra | | Broward |
| Warren, Ernest | B | 29 | 10/29/1945 | Ra | | Dade |

| Name | Race | Age | Date of Execution | Offense | Appeal | County |
|------|------|-----|-------------------|---------|--------|--------|
| Dixon, Pleas | B | 31 | 10/29/1945 | M | S | Holmes |
| Reed, James | B | 28 | 1/14/1946 | Ra | | Dade |
| Halloway, Charlie | B | 30 | 1/14/1946 | M | | Pinellas |
| Sullivan, George L. | W | 37 | 1/14/1946 | M | S | Marion |
| Lewis, Eddie | B | 52 | 4/22/1946 | M | | Broward |
| Webb, Jacob Sugg | B | 26 | 9/30/1946 | Ra | | Broward |
| Patterson, Wilbur Paul | W | 24 | 3/17/1947 | M | S,U | Volusia |
| Green, Lewis | B | 19 | 4/21/1947 | Ra | | Dade |
| Henderson, Leroy | B | 36 | 6/16/1947 | M | | Palm Beach |
| Maxwell, James Andrew | B | 31 | 8/ 4/1947 | Ra | S | Broward |
| Ferguson, Joe | B | 42 | 8/ 4/1947 | Ra | S | Broward |
| Melson, Tom | B | 32 | 8/ 4/1947 | Ra | S | Duval |
| Harper, Reuben | B | 30 | 1/ 5/1948 | Ra | | Columbia |
| Wiles, Alexander H. | W | 41 | 1/14/1948 | M | S,U | Duval |
| Washington, Alonzo, Jr. | B | 25 | 3/23/1948 | M | S,U | Duval |
| Harper, Ernest Eugene | B | 30 | 9/ 6/1948 | M | S | Polk |
| Enmond, Alphonso | B | 35 | 9/ 6/1948 | Ra | S | Dade |
| Watson, David J. | B | 23 | 9/15/1948 | M | F,U | Fed |
| Talley, Lonnie Lee | B | 25 | 10/ 5/1948 | Ra | S | Duval |
| Stewart, Lacy | B | 17 | 10/25/1948 | M | S | St. Lucie |
| Combs, Felix | B | 23 | 1/24/1949 | Ra | | Pinellas |
| Quince, Aaron | B | 22 | 2/ 7/1949 | M | S | Volusia |
| Berry, Arthur Edward | W | 23 | 4/ 4/1949 | M | S,U | Pasco |
| Griffis, Flem | W | 30 | 8/ 8/1949 | M | S | Nassau |
| Tiliman, Henry V. | W | 51 | 6/ 5/1950 | M | S | Duval |
| McDonald, Walter | B | 21 | 1/ 8/1951 | M | S | Bradford |
| Robinson, L.D. | B | 46 | 1/ 8/1951 | M | S | Bradford |
| Wolfork, George, Jr. | B | 28 | 1/ 8/1951 | M | S | Bradford |
| Gifford, R. Charlie | W | 72 | 2/21/1951 | M | | Pinellas |
| Hilton, Jessie | B | 33 | 6/ 4/1951 | M | | Volusia |
| Washington, John, Jr. | B | 25 | 6/ 4/1951 | M | | Volusia |
| Felton, James Edward | B | 25 | 8/ 6/1951 | M | S | Lake |
| London, Willie | B | 42 | 8/ 6/1951 | M | S | Lake |
| McCann, Coy | B | 48 | 4/ 7/1952 | M | S | Manatee |
| James, Saul | B | 28 | 4/21/1952 | Ra | | Hillsborough |
| Leiby, Merlin James | W | 25 | 6/30/1952 | M | S | Collier |
| Story, George W. | W | 52 | 9/ 8/1952 | M | S | Duval |
| Brown, Jimmie Lee | B | 30 | 7/ 6/1953 | M | S | Duval |
| Brooks, Ed | B | 61 | 9/ 7/1953 | M | S | Franklin |
| Brock, Tanner | W | 57 | 9/28/1954 | M | | Columbia |
| Johnson, Orion, Nath. | B | 19 | 9/28/1954 | M | S,U | Alachua |
| North, A. Ellwood | W | 37 | 10/ 4/1954 | M | S | Polk |
| Henderson, James | B | 47 | 10/ 4/1954 | M | S | Leon |
| Bailey, George | B | 36 | 10/ 4/1954 | M | | Leon |
| Williams, Leroy | B | 37 | 11/ 8/1954 | M | S | Palm Beach |
| Beard, Abraham | B | 18 | 11/ 8/1954 | Ra | | Leon |
| McVeigh, John H. | W | 34 | 4/18/1955 | M | S,U | Duval |
| Gillard, Louis | B | 54 | 8/29/1955 | M | | Hillsborough |
| Dyer, Chester F. | W | 20 | 10/31/1955 | M | | Sarasota |
| Hornbeck, Samuel J. | W | 38 | 12/12/1955 | M | S | Duval |
| Anderson, George | B | 32 | 2/20/1956 | M | S | Dade |
| Ambrister, Percy | B | 25 | 2/20/1956 | M | | Dade |

| Name | Race | Age | Date of Execution | Offense | Appeal | County |
|------|------|-----|-------------------|---------|--------|--------|
| Barwicks, Herman | B | 28 | 2/20/1956 | M | S | Polk |
| Copeland, Charlie, Jr. | B | 24 | 4/28/1956 | Ra | S | Duval |
| LaVoie, Edgar J. | W | 55 | 8/20/1956 | M | | Putnam |
| Colson, Robert Lee | B | 25 | 10/ 1/1956 | Ra | S | Alachua |
| Dunmore, Moses Lee | B | 21 | 10/ 1/1956 | Ra | S | Alachua |
| Ezzell, Joseph L. | W | 42 | 1/21/1957 | M | S | Duval |
| Raulerson, William O. | W | 49 | 7/15/1957 | M | | Columbia |
| Rhone, Roosevelt | B | 33 | 9/30/1957 | M | S | Marion |
| Nelson, Bozzie | B | 45 | 5/26/1958 | M | S | Palm Beach |
| Everett, George L. | W | 23 | 6/14/1958 | M | S | Bay |
| Long, Harry Frank | W | 35 | 9/29/1958 | M | S | Duval |
| Horne, Willie | B | 25 | 1/12/1959 | Ra | S | Duval |
| Thomas, Jimmie Lee | B | 35 | 1/19/1959 | Ra | S | Duval |
| Withers, Dallas E. | W | 38 | 2/ 2/1959 | M | S | Bay |
| Connor, Harley A. | W | 59 | 6/ 1/1959 | M | S | Gilchrist |
| Frazier, John | B | 44 | 6/ 1/1959 | M | S | Union |
| Peterson, Frank | B | 33 | 6/ 1/1959 | M | S | Holmes |
| Odom, Sam Wiley | B | 20 | 8/28/1959 | Ra | S | Lake |
| Daniels, E.C. | B | 49 | 8/28/1959 | M | S | Columbia |
| Paul, John Edward | B | 24 | 11/13/1959 | Ra | S | Pinellas |
| City, Willie George | B | 22 | 11/13/1959 | Ra | S | Pinellas |
| Williams, Ralph | B | 25 | 2/ 1/1960 | Ra | S | Pinellas |
| Brooks, James E. | B | 29 | 6/20/1960 | M | S | Palm Beach |
| Mackiewicz, Norman J. | W | 32 | 8/ 7/1961 | M | S | Dade |
| Davis, Robert Wesley | W | 26 | 8/ 7/1961 | Ra | S | Leon |
| Jefferson, Robert Lee | B | 22 | 5/12/1962 | M | S | Bay |
| Hill, Johnnie | B | 28 | 5/12/1962 | M | S | Escambia |
| Johnson, Samuel | B | 42 | 9/ 6/1962 | M | S | Putnam |
| Leach, William E. | W | 22 | 9/24/1962 | M | S | Union |
| Smith, Joe | W | 21 | 9/24/1962 | M | S | St. Johns |
| Lee, Charles H. | W | 35 | 7/18/1963 | M | S | Levy |
| Dawson, Sie | B | 40 | 5/12/1964 | M | S | Gadsden |
| Blake, Emmett C. | W | 31 | 5/12/1964 | M | S | Bay |
| Spinkellink, John A. | W | 30 | 5/25/1979 | M | S | Leon |

[1]On February 15, 1933, Zangara shot at Franklin Delano Roosevelt, the President-elect, and Anton Cermak, Mayor of Chicago, in a crowded Miami park. His shots missed Roosevelt but killed Cermak.

## GEORGIA

*Period of Executions*: 1924–1964
*Total Number*: 422
*Method*: Electrocution
*Other Data*: After the state of Georgia began electrocuting its condemned felons at the state penitentiary, five men (identified by footnote 1) were hanged under local authority in the counties of their convictions at the county seats designated.

| Name | Race | Age | Date of Execution | Offense | Appeal | County |
|------|------|-----|-------------------|---------|--------|--------|
| Henson, Howard | B | — | 9/13/1924 | M | | DeKalb |
| Walters, Warren[1] | W | 56 | 9/19/1924 | M | S | Hazelhurst |

| Name | Race | Age | Date of Execution | Offense | Appeal | County |
|---|---|---|---|---|---|---|
| Williams, Alex | B | — | 5/15/1925 | M | | Jones |
| Curry, Lee[1] | – | — | 5/21/1925 | M | S | Lyons |
| Jackson, Frank | B | — | 9/26/1925 | M | S | Rabun |
| Bloodworth, Gervis[1] | W | 20 | 1/29/1926 | M | S | Columbus |
| Jones, Willie[1] | W | 19 | 1/29/1926 | M | S | Columbus |
| Walton, Charlie | B | 39 | 3/11/1926 | M | | Fulton |
| Coggeshall, Ted | W | 21 | 3/25/1926 | M | S | Putnam |
| McClelland, Floyd | B | 20 | 3/25/1926 | M | S | Putnam |
| Wooten, Mack[1] | B | 52 | 5/18/1926 | M | | Atlanta |
| Stewart, Amos | B | — | 6/18/1926 | M | | Worth |
| Glover, Ed | B | — | 9/ 9/1926 | M | | Bibb |
| Johnson, Tom | B | 48 | 9/24/1926 | M | S | Jefferson |
| Williams, Pringle | B | 17 | 10/ 8/1926 | Ra | S | Emanuel |
| Johnson, James | B | — | 11/13/1926 | M | | Fulton |
| Gore, Mell | W | 22 | 6/ 3/1927 | M | S | Fulton |
| Fennell, Herbert | B | 30 | 6/ 3/1927 | M | S | Liberty |
| Mars, Oscar | W | 46 | 6/ 6/1927 | M | S | Ben Hill |
| Rounsaville, John | B | 20 | 7/12/1927 | M | S | Chatooga |
| Stewart, Cellus | B | 35 | 7/15/1927 | M | | Early |
| Chambles, Lee | B | 40 | 10/14/1927 | M | | Bartow |
| Galloway, Wilbur | B | 28 | 10/14/1927 | M | | Dodge |
| Parker, Mose | B | 49 | 10/14/1927 | M | | Pike |
| Pryor, Roy | B | 24 | 10/26/1927 | Ra | | Monroe |
| Clark, George | B | 26 | 11/11/1927 | Ra | | Jasper |
| Sanders, John | B | 41 | 11/18/1927 | Ra | | Fulton |
| Fuller, Garfield | B | 44 | 1/13/1928 | M | | Pike |
| Quinn, Albert | B | 25 | 1/20/1928 | M | S | Terrell |
| Coates, Robert | B | 36 | 2/21/1928 | M | S | Jefferson |
| Ellis, Henry | B | 25 | 4/18/1928 | M | S | Fulton |
| Price, Edgar | B | 24 | 5/ 4/1928 | M | S | Grady |
| Grant, James E. | B | 27 | 5/18/1928 | M | | Fulton |
| Hicks, Charlie | B | 21 | 6/ 8/1928 | M | S | Fulton |
| Jones, Robert | B | 22 | 6/28/1928 | M | S | Bibb |
| Hammond, Harold | W | 36 | 7/ 6/1928 | M | S | Fulton |
| McLeod, Medie | B | 29 | 7/ 6/1928 | M | S | Decatur |
| Gower, Sam | W | 42 | 7/13/1928 | M | S | Gwinnett |
| Taylor, Preddie | B | 33 | 7/13/1928 | M | | Fulton |
| Thompson, Clifford | W | 28 | 8/ 3/1929 | M | S | Murray |
| Moss, Jim | B | 27 | 8/ 3/1928 | M | S | Murray |
| Shepherd, R.H. | W | 57 | 12/19/1928 | M | S | Fulton |
| Redding, Marshall | B | 40 | 1/18/1929 | M | S | Coweta |
| George, Willie C. | B | 23 | 1/18/1929 | M | S | Fulton |
| Capers, Ed | B | 19 | 1/18/1929 | M | S | Fulton |
| Gilham, Willie | B | 21 | 1/18/1929 | M | S | Fulton |
| Grinstead, Griff | W | 56 | 2/22/1929 | M | S | Montgomery |
| Clark, John | B | 44 | 3/20/1929 | M | | McIntosh |
| Crumady, James | B | 25 | 5/17/1929 | M | | Colquitt |
| Dozier, Jeff | B | 60 | 7/22/1929 | M | S | Floyd |
| Morrow, Malcolm | W | 31 | 9/11/1929 | M | S | Glynn |
| Simpson, Homer C. | W | 40 | 9/11/1929 | M | S | Glynn |
| Bryant, Willie | B | 23 | 10/ 4/1929 | Ra | | Ware |
| Merritt, Alvin T. | W | 25 | 10/ 4/1929 | Ra | S | Fulton |

| Name | Race | Age | Date of Execution | Offense | Appeal | County |
|------|------|-----|-------------------|---------|--------|--------|
| Ellen, John | B | 41 | 1/27/1930 | M | S | Floyd |
| Barker, James | B | 23 | 2/14/1930 | M | S | Bibb |
| Kelly, Edmond | B | 28 | 2/21/1930 | M | S | Grady |
| Screven, Renty | B | 50 | 3/21/1930 | M | S | Chatham |
| Jolley, Angeline | B | 23 | 6/20/1930 | M | S | Bibb |
| VanDuzer, Emory | B | 24 | 6/27/1930 | M | | Fulton |
| Smith, Wash | W | 21 | 11/22/1930 | M | S | Ben Hill |
| Jenkins, Edgar | B | 22 | 1/16/1931 | Ra | | Early |
| Biggers, William | B | 36 | 1/27/1931 | M | S | Fulton |
| West, Henry | B | 21 | 3/13/1931 | M | | Floyd |
| Newsome, L.B. | B | 21 | 3/27/1931 | M | | Peach |
| Cox, Willie Lee | B | 27 | 4/17/1931 | M | S | Fulton |
| Glaze, Gilbert | B | 30 | 4/17/1931 | M | S | Fulton |
| Berry, Marvin | B | 40 | 4/29/1931 | M | | Early |
| Griffin, Fred | B | 18 | 5/18/1931 | M | | Campbell |
| Green, Willie | B | 27 | 5/22/1931 | M | S | Richmond |
| Adams, Burley | W | 34 | 5/22/1931 | M | S | Columbia |
| Dudley, Eugene | B | 21 | 7/17/1931 | M | S | Walton |
| Higgins, Willie | B | 28 | 9/11/1931 | M | S | Fulton |
| Stevens, Clark | B | 24 | 10/16/1931 | M | | Morgan |
| Chisholm, Robert L. | B | 20 | 10/16/1931 | Ra | | Peach |
| Searcy, William | B | 32 | 10/30/1931 | M | | Talbot |
| Hendrix, O.C. | B | 34 | 10/31/1931 | M | S | Fulton |
| Gaskins, English | W | 50 | 12/21/1931 | M | S | Candler |
| March, Eddie | B | 16 | 2/ 9/1932 | M | | Dougherty |
| Johnson, Major | W | 44 | 2/ 9/1932 | M | S | Dougherty |
| Parker, J.H. | W | 38 | 4/ 8/1931 | M | S | Ware |
| Rounds, Willie | B | 27 | 6/10/1932 | M | S | Houston |
| Jones, Willie | B | 24 | 8/ 8/1932 | M | S | Richmond |
| Jackson, Albert | B | 22 | 10/ 7/1932 | M | S | Peach |
| Baker, Paschall | B | 32 | 10/28/1932 | Ra | | Webster |
| Green, Charlie, Jr. | B | 32 | 10/28/1932 | Ra | | Webster |
| Hulsey, Fred (Son) | W | 31 | 11/ 4/1932 | M | S | Polk |
| Hulsey, William (Father) | W | 55 | 11/ 4/1932 | M | S | Polk |
| Humphreys, John L. | B | 21 | 11/ 5/1932 | M | S | Stewart |
| Jackson, J.C. | B | 23 | 11/16/1932 | M | S | Early |
| Welch, Lawrence | B | 46 | 4/ 4/1933 | M | S | Early |
| Todd, Johnny | B | — | 5/19/1933 | M | | Greene |
| Randall, Pat | B | — | 5/20/1933 | M | S | Randolph |
| Davis, Raider | B | — | 6/14/1933 | M | S | Fulton |
| Morris, Richard | B | 18 | 8/11/1933 | M | S | Fulton |
| Sims, Richard | B | 18 | 8/11/1933 | M | S | Fulton |
| White, Mose | B | 18 | 8/11/1933 | M | S | Fulton |
| McCullough, Thomas A. | W | 58 | 8/25/1933 | M | | Fayette |
| Key, Eugene | B | 25 | 8/25/1933 | M | S | Houston |
| Jackson, Rochelle | B | 27 | 9/ 8/1933 | M | S | Worth |
| Simpson, Harry | B | 34 | 10/20/1933 | M | | Clinch |
| Brooks, Grady | B | 19 | 10/27/1933 | M | | Pickens |
| Zuber, George | B | 29 | 10/27/1933 | M | | Pickens |
| Barbee, James F. | W | 47 | 12/29/1933 | M | S | Pulaski |
| Osborne, Will | B | 18 | 1/12/1934 | Ra | | Fulton |
| Short, Homer Lee | B | 24 | 3/ 2/1934 | M | | Marion |

| Name | Race | Age | Date of Execution | Offense | Appeal | County |
|------|------|-----|-------------------|---------|--------|--------|
| Downer, John | B | 28 | 3/16/1934 | Ra | S | Elbert |
| Walker, Sandy | B | 48 | 3/16/1934 | M | | Worth |
| Lively, Mitcy W. | W | 47 | 4/20/1934 | M | S | Fulton |
| James, Mack | B | 29 | 5/11/1934 | M,Ra | S | Banks |
| Patrick, Hosea | B | 30 | 5/15/1934 | M | S | Fulton |
| Hicks, Claude | B | 27 | 5/15/1934 | M | S | Fulton |
| South, Floyd | B | 22 | 6/15/1934 | M | S | Fulton |
| Castleberry, Reese | B | 24 | 6/15/1934 | M | S | Pickens |
| Duncan, Clifford | B | 26 | 9/14/1934 | Ra | S | Candler |
| Johnson, Frank | B | 42 | 10/ 4/1934 | M | S | Johnson |
| Street, Mose | B | 29 | 11/15/1934 | M | S | Chatham |
| Dodson, Charlie | B | 17 | 1/21/1935 | M | S | Schley |
| Hammett, J.T. | W | 47 | 2/11/1935 | M | S | Troup |
| Barfield, Archie | B | 22 | 2/15/1935 | M | S | Gwinnett |
| Wright, John Henry | B | 28 | 3/ 1/1935 | M | S | McDuffie |
| Reese, Rack | B | 55 | 3/ 1/1935 | M | | McDuffie |
| Tucker, Joe | B | — | 3/ 5/1935 | M | S | Meriwether |
| Brown D.W. | B | — | 3/ 7/1935 | M | S | Webster |
| Bell, Arthur | B | — | 3/ 7/1935 | M | S | Webster |
| Hargroves, Robert | W | 26 | 3/15/1935 | M | S | Effingham |
| Pierce, Victor | W | 35 | 3/29/1935 | M | S | Clayton |
| Rivers, Albert | B | 41 | 4/ 5/1935 | Ra | S | Screven |
| Ashley, Isaiah | B | 18 | 4/ 5/1935 | M | S | Appling |
| Harden, Henry | B | 24 | 5/10/1935 | M | S | Washington |
| Stone, Charlie | B | 30 | 5/10/1935 | Ra | S | Fulton |
| Beasley, Charlie | B | 50 | 6/14/1935 | M | | Troup |
| Mullinax, Robert | W | 34 | 6/14/1935 | M | S | Floyd |
| Hicks, Cleveland | B | 30 | 7/12/1935 | M | | Mitchell |
| Reese, J.B. | B | 19 | 7/19/1935 | Ra | S | Jackson |
| Gaines, Simmie | B | 35 | 10/10/1935 | M | | Oglethorpe |
| McRae, George | W | 24 | 10/18/1935 | M | S | Cherokee |
| Mattox, Jack | B | 26 | 11/22/1935 | M | S | Oglethorpe |
| Honea, Marvin | W | 29 | 12/20/1935 | M | S | Fulton |
| White, John Will | B | 24 | 12/20/1935 | M | S | Cobb |
| Bowen, Eddie B. | B | 18 | 3/ 6/1936 | M | S | Douglas |
| Simmons, John Henry | B | 50 | 3/20/1936 | M | | Camden |
| Nelson, Thomas | B | 38 | 3/20/1936 | M | S | Camden |
| Lowman, Julius | B | 32 | 3/25/1936 | M | S | Chatham |
| McLemore, Hamp | B | 21 | 4/10/1936 | Ra | | Muscogee |
| Thomas, John Henry | B | 21 | 8/ 6/1936 | M | S | Clarke |
| Daniel, John | B | 24 | 8/21/1936 | M | | Hall |
| Charles, Demps | B | 28 | 8/21/1936 | M | S | Hall |
| Coombs, Arthur | B | 30 | 11/12/1936 | Ra | | Henry |
| Boyer, Winton | B | — | 12/ 4/1936 | M | S | Hancock |
| Sloan, John Henry | B | 25 | 12/31/1936 | M | S | Colquitt |
| Burden, Arthur | B | 28 | 2/24/1937 | M | S | Bibb |
| Burke, James | B | 24 | 4/19/1937 | M | S | Richmond |
| Goodman, J.P. | B | 21 | 5/14/1937 | M | S | DeKalb |
| Lacy, Will | B | 41 | 5/21/1937 | M | | Cook |
| Melton, Eli | W | 34 | 5/21/1937 | Ra | S | Muscogee |
| Brown, Leonard | B | 18 | 5/24/1937 | M | S | Richmond |
| Trammell, Mose | B | 36 | 5/28/1937 | M | S | Troup |

| Name | Race | Age | Date of Execution | Offense | Appeal | County |
|------|------|-----|-------------------|---------|--------|--------|
| Hopkins, Willie | B | — | 6/14/1937 | Ra | | Burke |
| Rose, Edgar | W | 27 | 6/18/1937 | M | S | Dougherty |
| Worthy, James | B | 24 | 6/18/1937 | M | S | Fulton |
| Young, Charlie | B | 35 | 6/25/1937 | M | | Burke |
| Jackson, Mitchell | B | 26 | 7/ 9/1937 | M | | Fulton |
| Douberly, Willie E. | W | 25 | 7/30/1937 | M | S | Chatham |
| Ward, Lawrence | W | — | 8/13/1937 | M | S | Jeff Davis |
| Pinson, Clinton | B | 40 | 9/29/1937 | M | S | Fulton |
| Daniels, Willie Frank | B | 25 | 12/27/1937 | M | | Clarke |
| Haywood, Archie | B | 37 | 5/ 6/1938 | M | | Worth |
| Thomas, George | B | 21 | 5/13/1938 | M | | Fulton |
| Rozier, Leavy L. | W | 38 | 6/17/1938 | Ra | S | Ware |
| Benton, Ralph | B | 40 | 10/28/1938 | M | S | Fulton |
| Menton, Walter | B | 31 | 10/18/1938 | M | S | Charlton |
| McBride, Isaac | B | 31 | 11/ 4/1938 | M | S | Clinch |
| Etheridge, Buck | B | 20 | 11/10/1938 | M | S | Henry |
| Knight, Frank | B | 26 | 11/25/1938 | Ra | S | Bryan |
| Gilbert, George | B | 28 | 11/30/1938 | Ra | | Troup |
| Rucker, Charlie | B | 18 | 12/ 9/1938 | M | | Butts |
| Russell, Willie D. | B | 31 | 12/ 9/1938 | M | | Cobb |
| Carter, Raymond | B | 24 | 12/ 9/1938 | M | | Butts |
| Perry, Arthur | B | 25 | 12/ 9/1938 | M | S | Muscogee |
| Mack, Arthur | B | 26 | 12/ 9/1938 | M | S | Muscogee |
| Williams, John Henry | B | 21 | 12/ 9/1938 | M | S | Butts |
| Wright, Wilson | B | 20 | 1/25/1939 | M | S | Chatham |
| Harvey, Floyd Nelson | W | 36 | 6/23/1939 | M | | Ware |
| Vaughn, J.D. | B | 25 | 7/ 7/1939 | Ra | | Walton |
| Barker, Arthur E. | W | 35 | 7/26/1939 | M | S | Gwinnett |
| Hunter, Marion | B | 25 | 8/ 4/1939 | M | S | Chatham |
| Sheffield, Clarence | B | 36 | 9/29/1939 | M | S | Ware |
| Bruno, Sheppard | B | 45 | 11/17/1939 | M | S | Dougherty |
| Bivins, James | B | 19 | 11/21/1939 | M | | Schley |
| Fisher, James | B | 27 | 2/ 9/1940 | M | | Newton |
| Mathis, Joe | B | 27 | 2/ 9/1940 | M | | Newton |
| Mims, William L. | B | 38 | 3/22/1940 | M | S | Bibb |
| Brown, Robert | B | 26 | 5/17/1940 | M | S | Jefferson |
| Barkley, Curtis | B | 34 | 8/16/1940 | Ra | S | Fulton |
| Fields, Oscar | B | 24 | 8/16/1940 | Ra | S | Fulton |
| Josey, Charlie | B | 20 | 8/23/1940 | M | S | Pike |
| Brown, Eddie | B | 30 | 8/23/1940 | Ro | S | Lowndes |
| Anderson, Fred | B | 19 | 10/ 4/1940 | M | S | Laurens |
| Hicks, Henry William | B | 18 | 10/18/1940 | Ra | S | Thomas |
| Sutton, John William | B | 22 | 11/ 8/1940 | M | | Whitfield |
| Lawrence, Buddie | B | 28 | 12/13/1940 | M | | Bacon |
| Brannon, Robert Lee | B | 39 | 12/13/1940 | M | S | Floyd |
| Waddell, Jennings | B | 34 | 12/27/1940 | M | | Toombs |
| Watson, Johnnie | B | 33 | 1/ 3/1941 | M | S | Coweta |
| Hayes, Eddie Bennie | B | 19 | 1/ 3/1941 | M | | Coweta |
| Bland, William Henry | B | 23 | 5/12/1941 | Ra | | Henry |
| Anderson, Charlie | B | 18 | 5/23/1941 | M | S | Fulton |
| Jenkins, Willie | B | 23 | 5/23/1941 | M | S | Fulton |
| Alford, Albert | B | 32 | 10/10/1941 | Ra | S | Hart |

| Name | Race | Age | Date of Execution | Offense | Appeal | County |
|------|------|-----|-------------------|---------|--------|--------|
| Shivers, James | B | 38 | 1/30/1942 | Ra | | Fayette |
| Strickland, Charlie | B | 25 | 1/31/1942 | M | | Terrell |
| Morton, Edward Leroy | B | 28 | 2/ 6/1942 | M | S | Jefferson |
| Miller, John | B | 35 | 3/ 6/1942 | Ra | | DeKalb |
| Cone, Howard P. | W | 24 | 3/11/1942 | M | S | Thomas |
| Williams, Norman | W | 28 | 5/15/1942 | M | S | Elbert |
| Moore, Dock | B | 25 | 7/ 2/1942 | M | S | Fulton |
| Mosley, S.T. | B | 23 | 7/10/1942 | M | | Taylor |
| Martin, Charles E. | W | 24 | 10/16/1942 | M | S | DeKalb |
| Shaw, Buster | B | 20 | 10/16/1942 | M | | Brantley |
| Lewis, W.Z. | B | 26 | 11/26/1942 | M | S | Thomas |
| Dowdell, Raymond | B | 24 | 1/15/1943 | M | S | Muscogee |
| Smith, Richard | B | 24 | 2/ 4/1943 | M | S | Fulton |
| Coates, Charles | W | 29 | 3/12/1943 | M | S | Catoosa |
| Wilcoxon, Lewis | B | 20 | 3/26/1943 | Ra | | Cobb |
| Palmer, Joel Luther | W | 30 | 5/28/1943 | M | S | Tift |
| Franklin, Bernice | B | 17 | 5/28/1943 | Ra | | Wayne |
| Sims, Mose | B | 23 | 6/10/1943 | Ra | S | Fulton |
| Reed, Edmond | B | 26 | 7/19/1943 | M | S | Bibb |
| Johnson, Adel | B | 21 | 8/10/1943 | Ra | S | Fulton |
| Pittman, Eugene | B | 28 | 8/20/1943 | M | S | Polk |
| Russell, John Thomas | B | 43 | 8/20/1943 | M | S | Fulton |
| Sexton, Charlie | B | 16 | 8/20/1943 | M | S | Paulding |
| Hancock, Marlin | W | 43 | 8/20/1943 | M | S | Paulding |
| Hodo, Serina | B | 23 | 9/24/1943 | M | | Meriwether |
| Mathis, Tommie Lee | B | 23 | 10/22/1943 | M | S | Spalding |
| Williams, Robert | B | 20 | 10/23/1943 | M | S | Laurens |
| Allison, S.A. | B | 17 | 12/11/1943 | M | | Meriwether |
| Johnson, H.T. | B | 22 | 12/31/1943 | M | S | Henry |
| Hubbard, Willie | B | 28 | 1/ 5/1944 | Ra | S | Bibb |
| Irwin, Isaac | W | 32 | 1/ 7/1944 | M | S | Bibb |
| Hicks, Willie | B | 18 | 2/ 3/1944 | Ra | S | Fulton |
| Lee, Marvin Lewis | B | 22 | 3/ 7/1944 | Ra | S | Fulton |
| Hooten, Rock | B | 24 | 3/17/1944 | M | | Taylor |
| Rozier, Herbert | B | 72 | 4/ 7/1944 | M | S | Laurens |
| Walker, Robert | B | 26 | 4/28/1944 | Ra | S | Bibb |
| Reed, Oscar | B | 26 | 4/28/1944 | M | S | Bibb |
| Ellison, Grady | B | 36 | 5/25/1944 | M | S | Burke |
| Stroup, William B. | W | 41 | 7/28/1944 | Ra | S | Fulton |
| Glass, Henry | B | 21 | 1/19/1945 | M | S | Fulton |
| Tye, Jimmie Lee | B | 22 | 1/19/1945 | M | S | Fulton |
| Jackson, Willie | B | 28 | 3/ 2/1945 | Ra | S | Fulton |
| Fowler, Walter | W | 22 | 3/ 2/1945 | M | S | Forsyth |
| Baker, Lena (Female) | B | 44 | 3/ 5/1945 | M | S | Randolph |
| Johnson, L.C. | B | 19 | 3/ 9/1945 | M | | Newton |
| Smith, E.V. | W | 39 | 3/ 9/1945 | M | S | Pike |
| Gilbert, Ulysses | B | 24 | 4/27/1945 | M | S | Houston |
| Lamar, Nathaniel | B | 21 | 5/11/1945 | M | S | Bibb |
| Watkins, David | B | 18 | 5/11/1945 | M | S | Cobb |
| Green, Edward, Lee | B | 23 | 6/ 1/1945 | Ra | | Houston |
| Green, Jack Roy | B | 40 | 6/29/1945 | Ra | | Sumter |
| Smithwick, Albert | W | 26 | 7/28/1945 | M | S | Chatham |

| Name | Race | Age | Date of Execution | Offense | Appeal | County |
|------|------|-----|-------------------|---------|--------|--------|
| Gunnells, Robert R. | W | 40 | 8/24/1945 | M | S | Baldwin |
| Hayes, Henry | B | 27 | 8/24/1945 | Ro | S | Fulton |
| Johnson, Charlie | B | 27 | 9/21/1945 | Ra | | Early |
| Collins, Noah | B | 29 | 11/ 9/1945 | M | S | Chatham |
| Craiton, Jesse | B | 23 | 11/ 9/1945 | M | S | Fulton |
| Taylor, Nathaniel | B | 37 | 11/30/1945 | M | S | Laurens |
| Daniels, Eddie | B | 34 | 2/ 8/1946 | M | S | Grady |
| Bonner, Isaac | B | 19 | 3/29/1946 | M | | Bibb |
| Lewis, Leon | B | 26 | 3/29/1946 | Ra | S | Fulton |
| Jones, Willie | B | 28 | 4/19/1946 | M | S | Ware |
| Bryant, Early | B | 30 | 5/31/1946 | Ra | S | Fulton |
| Burke, Anderson | B | 28 | 7/ 5/1946 | Ra | S | Oglethorpe |
| Nappier, Aaron | B | 41 | 7/19/1946 | M | S | Laurens |
| McKethan, James R. | W | 22 | 8/ 2/1946 | M | S | Chatham |
| Yearwood, Walter H. | W | 23 | 10/22/1946 | M | S | Clarke |
| Murray, Alton | W | 29 | 11/ 8/1946 | M | S | Candler |
| Allen, Lee James | B | 16 | 11/15/1946 | Ra | S | Fulton |
| Burns, Johnnie | B | 22 | 11/22/1946 | M | S | Lee |
| Stevenson, Willie | B | 17 | 11/22/1946 | M | | Lee |
| Williams, James Rufus | B | 19 | 11/29/1946 | M | | Irvin |
| Parker, Albert | B | 29 | 12/13/1946 | M | | Cook |
| Hill, J.C. | B | 19 | 12/20/1946 | M | S | Ware |
| Brown, Arthur, Jr. | B | 23 | 2/ 8/1947 | M | S | Chatham |
| Dorsey, Morris | B | 23 | 2/ 8/1947 | M | S | Chatham |
| Knapp, Homer R. | W | 38 | 4/18/1947 | M | | Chatham |
| Porter, Lauren | B | 38 | 4/25/1947 | M | | Oglethorpe |
| Barnes, Willis | W | 29 | 4/25/1947 | M | S | Ben Hill |
| Daniel, Quiller | B | 30 | 5/ 2/1947 | M | S | Franklin |
| Brown, James | B | 24 | 6/17/1947 | M | | Screven |
| Reddick, Herbert L. | B | 17 | 6/30/1947 | M | S | Bibb |
| Scott, Ebenezer | B | 27 | 8/ 1/1947 | M | S | Chatham |
| Stanford, Robert L. | B | 25 | 8/ 1/1947 | M | S | Richmond |
| Loughbridge, Terrell | W | 29 | 8/ 9/1947 | M | S | Jefferson |
| Moore, Roosevelt | B | 26 | 8/15/1947 | M | S | Stewart |
| Owen, Jim | B | 43 | 10/ 6/1947 | M | S | Warren |
| Ford, Oscar L. | B | 21 | 10/10/1947 | M | S | Dougherty |
| Bryant, Sweetie | B | 29 | 10/10/1947 | M | | Mitchell |
| Morakes, Nick | W | 53 | 11/18/1947 | M | S | Morgan |
| Scrutchens, Leroy | B | 37 | 1/ 2/1948 | M | | Sumter |
| Porter, Joe | B | 27 | 1/ 2/1948 | M | | Sumter |
| Brown, Eddie, Jr. | B | 23 | 2/13/1948 | M | S | Carroll |
| Torbert, J.W. | B | 37 | 2/16/1948 | M | S | Randolph |
| Mangum, James | B | 18 | 3/ 5/1948 | Ra | S | Fulton |
| Campbell, L.P. | B | 26 | 3/26/1948 | M | S | Floyd |
| Nunn, Red Lamar | B | 43 | 8/13/1948 | M | S | Jefferson |
| Whitt, Sam | B | 22 | 8/16/1948 | M | S | Fulton |
| Davis, William C. | B | 55 | 10/15/1948 | M | S | Carroll |
| Beetles, J.B. | B | 32 | 10/15/1948 | M | S | Carroll |
| Eller, Jewell | W | 21 | 11/ 5/1948 | M | | Towns |
| Garrett, Charlie | W | 26 | 11/ 5/1948 | M | S | Towns |
| Brown, L.C. | B | 25 | 11/26/1948 | M | | Greene |
| Carroll, Jessie C. | W | 44 | 4/ 8/1949 | M | S | Muscogee |

| Name | Race | Age | Date of Execution | Offense | Appeal | County |
|------|------|-----|-------------------|---------|--------|--------|
| Moore, Junior | B | 25 | 4/20/1949 | M | S | Bibb |
| Persons, Morgan | B | 39 | 5/20/1949 | M | | Worth |
| Williams, A.C. | B | 33 | 6/ 1/1949 | M | S | Fulton |
| Dorsey, Andrew | B | 23 | 8/19/1949 | Ra | S | Fulton |
| Jones, John A., Jr. | B | 17 | 9/12/1949 | M | S | Sumter |
| Jones, Wilbur G. | B | 18 | 9/12/1949 | M | S | Sumter |
| Brown, Lindsey | B | 26 | 12/16/1949 | M | S | Burke |
| Houser, Eddie, Jr. | B | 22 | 1/27/1950 | M | | Peach |
| Wyatt, Jesse | B | 39 | 4/21/1950 | M | S | DeKalb |
| Carrigan, John P. | W | 29 | 4/28/1950 | M | S | Fulton |
| Bryan, Robert F. | B | 19 | 5/28/1950 | M | S,U | Chatham |
| Cade, Charlie L. | B | 20 | 8/18/1950 | M | S | Richmond |
| Mays, Lincoln | B | 24 | 8/18/1950 | M | | Richmond |
| Wynn, Curtis, Jr. | B | 20 | 8/18/1950 | M | S | Richmond |
| McKay, George | B | 30 | 9/29/1950 | M | | Fulton |
| Gardner, Jimmie Lee | B | 27 | 10/28/1950 | Ro | | Clay |
| Wallace, John | W | 54 | 11/ 3/1950 | M | S | Coweta |
| Richardson, Jimmie | B | 47 | 11/ 3/1950 | M | S | Crisp |
| Lynch, Thomas | W | 31 | 11/21/1950 | M | S | Chatham |
| Kersey, George | W | 27 | 11/21/1950 | M | S | Chatham |
| Harris, Willie B. | B | 47 | 3/ 2/1951 | M | S | Worth |
| Williams, Jimmie C. | B | 28 | 5/25/1951 | Ra | S | Clinch |
| Solesbee, George W. | W | 26 | 7/27/1951 | M | S,F,U | Clinch |
| McLendon, E.B., Jr. | W | 37 | 10/ 5/1951 | M | S | Richmond |
| Ballard, Willie Ford | B | 19 | 11/ 2/1951 | Ra | S | Gwinnett |
| Parks, Jim | B | 45 | 12/14/1951 | M | S | Pike |
| McBurnett, Vester | W | 43 | 12/17/1951 | M | S | Floyd |
| Brock, Henry | W | 39 | 2/21/1952 | M | S | Floyd |
| Almond, Homer | B | 48 | 3/ 1/1952 | M | S | DeKalb |
| Williams, Clifton | B | 30 | 3/14/1952 | M | S | Richmond |
| Reese, Pat | W | 33 | 4/ 4/1952 | M | | White |
| Griffin, Eli | B | 42 | 4/17/1952 | M | S | Putnam |
| Darden, Arthur | B | 22 | 4/25/1952 | M | S | Grady |
| Wise, Napoleon | B | 20 | 6/ 6/1952 | M | S | Emanuel |
| Thornton, John Henry | B | 24 | 7/11/1952 | M | S | Fulton |
| Blackstone, James, Jr. | B | 30 | 7/25/1952 | M | S | Coffee |
| Johnson, Horace | B | 29 | 10/ 7/1952 | M | S | Jones |
| Savage, Henry | B | 35 | 11/21/1952 | M | S | Chatham |
| Pinckney, Abraham | B | 67 | 2/27/1953 | M | | Berrien |
| Starr, Jesse | B | 26 | 4/16/1953 | Ra | S | Floyd |
| Patrick, Amos | B | 34 | 5/ 8/1953 | M | S | Clarke |
| Strickland, Robert | W | 20 | 8/24/1953 | M | S | Chatham |
| Bowens, Samuel | B | 23 | 8/28/1953 | M | S | Screven |
| Burgess, Willie | B | 56 | 11/14/1953 | M | S | Chatham |
| Calhoun, Robert E. | B | 31 | 12/18/1953 | M | S | Coweta |
| Harris, Isaiah | B | 33 | 12/23/1953 | Ra | | Ware |
| Wright, Paul | B | 19 | 1/22/1954 | M | S | Walton |
| Scott, Doyal | W | 30 | 2/ 5/1954 | M | S | Glynn |
| Heard, Lindsey | B | 20 | 5/25/1954 | Ra | S | Cherokee |
| Jones, Ozzie | B | 32 | 6/11/1954 | Ra | S | Chatham |
| Miller, Herman Lee | B | 18 | 6/15/1954 | Ra | | Baldwin |
| Jackson, Willie | B | 17 | 6/15/1954 | Ra | | Baldwin |

| Name | Race | Age | Date of Execution | Offense | Appeal | County |
|------|------|-----|-------------------|---------|--------|--------|
| Seymore, Sylvester | B | 35 | 8/ 6/1954 | M | S | Richmond |
| Booker, Howard L. | B | 35 | 9/17/1954 | Ro | S | Fulton |
| Simon, Eliott | B | 55 | 11/ 5/1954 | M | | Colquitt |
| Jones, Joe Lee | B | 17 | 11/19/1954 | M | S | Upson |
| King, Charles L. | B | 19 | 11/19/1954 | M | S | Upson |
| Davis, Calvin E. | B | 19 | 11/12/1954 | M | S | Schley |
| Morgan, James W. | W | 18 | 1/ 7/1955 | M | S | Richmond |
| Jackson, Howard | B | 44 | 4/15/1955 | M | S | Coweta |
| Williams, Tom | B | 53 | 4/15/1955 | M | S | Colquitt |
| Fuller, Sylvester | B | 25 | 6/17/1955 | Ro | | Calhoun |
| Philpot, Walter | B | 39 | 1/27/1956 | M | S | Muscogee |
| Williams, Aubrey | B | 29 | 3/30/1956 | M | S,U | Fulton |
| Cochran, Willie Grady | W | 37 | 4/13/1956 | M | S | Calhoun |
| Turner, James | B | 27 | 6/ 8/1956 | M | | Bartow |
| Mosley, Frederick | B | 25 | 6/29/1956 | Ra | | Fulton |
| Cooper, Paul | B | 48 | 9/21/1956 | M | | Worth |
| Reese, Amos | B | 31 | 1/ 4/1957 | Ra | | Cobb |
| Corbin, John F. | W | 32 | 2/ 8/1957 | M | | Fulton |
| Fields, Jennings E. | W | 32 | 3/ 5/1957 | M | | DeKalb |
| Newberry, John | W | 47 | 3/ 8/1957 | M | | Miller |
| Domingo, Leon I. | B | 23 | 3/15/1957 | M | S | Muscogee |
| Styles, Isaac | B | 34 | 3/15/1957 | M | | Burke |
| Coleman, Don Mitchell | B | 18 | 3/19/1957 | M | | Fulton |
| Toler, James | B | 39 | 3/19/1957 | M | | Fulton |
| Elder, Robert Lee | B | 37 | 3/19/1957 | M | | Fulton |
| Hill, Harold | W | 25 | 3/25/1957 | M | | Richmond |
| Justice, Grady | B | 29 | 7/26/1957 | Ra | | Fulton |
| Mullins, Fred G. | B | 41 | 9/ 6/1957 | M | | Harris |
| DuPree, Lem | B | 59 | 9/16/1957 | M | | Laurens |
| White, John Henry | B | 26 | 10/ 4/1957 | Ra | | Berrien |
| Krull, George | W | 34 | 10/21/1957 | Ra | F,U | Fed |
| Krull, Mike | W | 32 | 10/21/1957 | Ra | F,U | Fed |
| Smith, Edward S. | B | 23 | 1/17/1958 | Ra | | Richmond |
| Golden, William | B | 23 | 4/18/1958 | M | | Chatham |
| Curry, Albert | B | 26 | 9/19/1958 | M | | Harris |
| Dobbs, Leroy | B | 36 | 11/ 7/1958 | M | S | Cobb |
| Adams, Otha A. | W | 54 | 11/14/1958 | M | | Colquitt |
| Woods, Henry R. | B | 20 | 12/19/1958 | M | | Fulton |
| Murray, J.C. | B | 54 | 2/ 6/1959 | M | | Bryan |
| Hill, Frank Junior | B | 36 | 6/ 5/1959 | M | | Dougherty |
| Charlton, William | B | 23 | 8/ 7/1959 | M | | Chatham |
| Wilson, Eddie | B | 37 | 12/18/1959 | M | | Atkinson |
| Bunkley, Homer | B | 26 | 1/15/1960 | M | | Talbot |
| Albert, Ernest | W | 34 | 3/ 4/1960 | M | | Columbia |
| Wilson, Frank | B | 54 | 6/10/1960 | M | | Warren |
| Davis, Herring | B | 40 | 6/24/1960 | M | | Meriwether |
| Johnson, Nathaniel | B | 25 | 7/ 1/1960 | M | | Richmond |
| Wimis, Oscar J. | B | 44 | 11/21/1960 | M | S | Fulton |
| Mullins, Roy Lee | W | 24 | 1/20/1961 | M | | Fannin |
| Johnson, Thurmond | B | 26 | 3/24/1961 | M | | Richmond |
| Watt, George | B | 21 | 8/1/1961 | Ra | S | Muscogee |
| Smith, Sammie Lee | B | 27 | 11/14/1962 | M | | Houston |

| Name | Race | Age | Date of Execution | Offense | Appeal | County |
|------|------|-----|-------------------|---------|--------|--------|
| Jones, Orelander | B | 19 | 10/ 4/1963 | M | | Jasper |
| Chandler, Ollie | B | 21 | 10/18/1963 | M | | Lowndes |
| Pugh, J.W. | W | 35 | 1/14/1964 | M | | DeKalb |
| Dye, Bernard | W | 34 | 10/16/1964 | M | | McDuffie |

¹Walters (9/19/1924), Curry (5/21/1925), Bloodworth (1/29/1926), Jones (1/29/1926), and Wooten (5/18/1926) were hanged under local authority in the counties of their convictions after Georgia began electrocuting its condemned felons at the state penitentiary.


## IDAHO

*Period of Executions*: 1901–1957
*Total Number*: 9
*Method*: Hanging

| Name | Race | Age | Date of Execution | Offense | Appeal | County |
|------|------|-----|-------------------|---------|--------|--------|
| Rice, Edward | W | — | 11/30/1901 | M | S | Shoshone |
| Connors, James | W | — | 12/16/1904 | M | | Bingham |
| Bond, William H. | W | 35 | 8/10/1906 | M | S | Ada |
| Seward, Fred M. | W | — | 5/ 7/1909 | M | | Latah |
| Arnold, Noah | B | — | 12/19/1924 | M | S | Bonner |
| Jurko, John | W | — | 7/ 9/1926 | M | S | Twin Falls |
| Powell, Troy D. | W | 20 | 4/13/1951 | M | S | Ada |
| Walrath, Ernest Lee | W | 19 | 4/13/1951 | M | S | Ada |
| Snowden, Raymond Allen | W | 35 | 10/18/1957 | M | S | Ada |


## ILLINOIS

*Period of Executions*: 1928–1962
*Total Number*: 98
*Method*: Electrocution
*Other Data*: Executions were performed at three prisons: Joliet, Menard, and Cook. Prisoners from the counties (except Cook) north of Springfield were executed at Joliet. Those from countries south of Springfield were executed at Menard. On July 6, 1927, legislation was enacted making electrocution the means of executing the death sentence. Counties with more than one million inhabitants were to have their own electric chairs. Cook County exercises concurrent jurisdiction with the state penitentiaries in this matter and is included. The data were provided by courtesy of Virgil W. Peterson, Director of the Chicago Crime Commission.

| Name | Race | Age | Date of Execution | Offense | Appeal | County |
|------|------|-----|-------------------|---------|--------|--------|
| JOLIET | | | | | | |
| Clark, Claude | B | 48 | 12/15/1928 | M | | Lake |
| Brown, John | B | 32 | 12/15/1928 | M | | Lake |
| Bressette, Dominick | I | 33 | 12/15/1928 | M | | Lake |

| Name | Race | Age | Date of Execution | Offense | Appeal | County |
|------|------|-----|-------------------|---------|--------|--------|
| Preston, John | W | 30 | 10/ 9/1931 | M | S | DuPage |
| Blink, Fred | W | 43 | 4/23/1935 | M | | Whiteside |
| Thielan, Arthur | W | 42 | 5/10/1935 | M | | LaSalle |
| Gerner, Fred | W | 27 | 5/10/1935 | M | | LaSalle |
| Hauff, John | W | 32 | 5/10/1935 | M | | LaSalle |
| Thompson, Gerald | W | 25 | 10/15/1935 | M | | Peoria |
| Jelliga, John | W | 39 | 10/21/1938 | M | | Will |
| Wood, Elvyn | W | 23 | 4/14/1939 | M | | Grundy |
| Jordan, Leo | W | — | 5/13/1942 | M | | Whiteside |
| Weber, Herman Frederick | W | — | 9/16/1949 | M | S,U | Peoria |

MENARD

| Name | Race | Age | Date of Execution | Offense | Appeal | County |
|------|------|-----|-------------------|---------|--------|--------|
| Johnson, Merle J. | W | 26 | 10/20/1931 | M | | Coles |
| Johnson, Hazel | B | 23 | 12/11/1931 | M | S | Macon |
| Pannier, Henry | W | 57 | 12/11/1931 | M | | Randolph |
| Green, Willie | B | 31 | 12/11/1931 | M | | St. Clair |
| Jackson, James | B | 25 | 12/11/1935 | M | | St. Clair |
| Gray, Elmer | W | 42 | 8/27/1932 | M | | Wayne |
| Smith, James | B | 25 | 9/23/1932 | M | | St. Clair |
| Shelby, Harry | W | 45 | 12/22/1933 | M | | Jasper |
| Allen, John | W | 26 | 12/22/1933 | M | | Jasper |
| Gray, Martin | B | 28 | 12/22/1933 | M | | Marion |
| Little, Warren | W | 22 | 6/25/1934 | M | | Hamilton |
| Lehne, Thomas J. | W | 42 | 4/23/1935 | M | S | Madison |
| Dedmon, VanBuren | W | 25 | 7/ 9/1935 | M | | St. Clair |
| Balbin, Edward | W | 19 | 7/ 9/1935 | M | | St. Clair |
| Drue, John | W | 21 | 7/ 9/1935 | M | | St. Clair |
| Mitchell, Allen | B | 32 | 2/26/1937 | M | | St. Clair |
| Porter, Marie (Female) | W | 38 | 1/28/1938 | M | | St. Clair |
| Giancola, Angelo | W | 22 | 1/28/1938 | M | | St. Clair |

COOK COUNTY

| Name | Race | Age | Date of Execution | Offense | Appeal | County |
|------|------|-----|-------------------|---------|--------|--------|
| Grecco, Anthony | W | 19 | 2/20/1929 | M | | Cook |
| Walz, Charles | W | 18 | 2/20/1929 | M | | Cook |
| Glover, Napoleon | – | — | 6/20/1929 | M | | Cook |
| Swan, Morgan | – | — | 6/20/1929 | M | | Cook |
| Woodward, Aaron | B | — | 4/11/1930 | M | S | Cook |
| Vogel, August | W | 27 | 5/ 9/1930 | M | | Cook |
| Shadlow, Leonard | B | — | 10/ 3/1930 | M | | Cook |
| Fisher, Lafon | B | — | 10/ 3/1930 | M | S | Cook |
| Brown, Leon | W | — | 11/28/1930 | M | S | Cook |
| Lenhardt, William | – | — | 12/12/1930 | M | S | Cook |
| Jordan, Frank | – | 30 | 10/16/1931 | M | | Cook |
| Rocco, Charles | W | 24 | 10/16/1931 | M | S | Cook |
| Popescue, John | W | 21 | 10/16/1931 | M | S | Cook |
| Sullivan, Richard | W | 35 | 10/16/1931 | M | S | Cook |
| Bell, Frank | W | — | 1/ 8/1932 | M | S | Cook |
| Norsingle, Ben | B | — | 1/15/1932 | M | | Cook |
| Reed, John | B | — | 1/15/1932 | M | | Cook |
| Cohen, Morris | – | 38 | 10/13/1933 | M | | Cook |

| Name | Race | Age | Date of Execution | Offense | Appeal | County |
|------|------|-----|-------------------|---------|--------|--------|
| King, Ross | – | 29 | 10/16/1933 | M | | Cook |
| Scheck, John | W | 21 | 4/20/1934 | M | S | Cook |
| Dale, George | W | 29 | 4/20/1934 | M | S | Cook |
| Francis, Joseph | B | 35 | 4/20/1934 | M | S | Cook |
| McNeil, Alonzo | – | – | 10/12/1934 | M | | Cook |
| Walker, George | – | – | 10/12/1934 | M | | Cook |
| Boulan, Herman | – | 39 | 12/15/1934 | M | | Cook |
| Dittman, Walter | – | 28 | 12/15/1934 | M | | Cook |
| Novak, Chester | – | – | 3/21/1935 | M | | Cook |
| Bogacki, Andrew | W | 25 | 10/21/1936 | M | | Cook |
| Korczykowski, Frank | W | 26 | 10/21/1936 | M | | Cook |
| Swain, Rufo | B | 28 | 2/26/1937 | M | | Cook |
| Rappaport, Joseph | W | 31 | 3/ 2/1937 | M | S | Cook |
| Murawski, Stanley | – | 36 | 4/16/1937 | M | | Cook |
| Whyte, Frank | – | 47 | 4/16/1937 | M | | Cook |
| Schuster, Joseph | – | 30 | 4/16/1937 | M | | Cook |
| Chrisoules, Peter | – | – | 10/15/1937 | M | S | Cook |
| Scott, J.C. | – | – | 4/19/1938 | M | | Cook |
| Seadlund, John Henry | W | 27 | 7/14/1938 | K | F,U | Fed |
| Nixon, Robert | B | 19 | 6/16/1939 | M | S | Cook |
| Cygan, Steve | – | – | 10/13/1939 | M | | Cook |
| Price, Charles | – | – | 10/27/1939 | M | S,U | Cook |
| Poe, Howard | – | – | 4/19/1940 | M | S | Cook |
| Wnukowski, Victor | – | – | 5/17/1940 | M | | Cook |
| Michalowski, Frank | – | – | 5/17/1940 | M | | Cook |
| Schroeder, Robert | – | – | 12/13/1940 | M | | Cook |
| Riley, Edward | – | – | 6/20/1941 | M | S,U | Cook |
| Watson, Orville | – | – | 6/20/1941 | M | S,U | Cook |
| Parks, Earl | B | 26 | 1/15/1942 | M | | Cook |
| Sawicki, Bernard | W | 19 | 1/17/1942 | M | | Cook |
| Pantano, John | W | 35 | 9/18/1942 | M | | Cook |
| Wishon, Ernest | – | – | 11/26/1943 | M | | Cook |
| Williams, Paul | – | – | 3/15/1944 | M | | Cook |
| Krause, Alvin | – | – | 9/15/1944 | M | | Cook |
| Breedlove, Kermit | – | – | 10/19/1945 | M | | Cook |
| Crosby, Charles | – | – | 6/20/1947 | M | | Cook |
| Gaither, Ernest | – | – | 10/24/1947 | M | | Cook |
| Morelli, James | – | – | 11/26/1949 | M | | Cook |
| Varela, Fred | – | – | 4/21/1950 | M | S,U | Cook |
| Najera, Alfonso | – | – | 4/21/1950 | M | S,U | Cook |
| Trulove, Willard | – | – | 11/17/1950 | M | | Cook |
| Jenko, Raymond | W | 20 | 1/25/1952 | M | S | Cook |
| Williams, Harry | B | 22 | 3/14/1952 | M | S | Cook |
| Lindsay, LeRoy | B | 31 | 10/17/1952 | M | S | Cook |
| Davis, Berenice | B | 23 | 10/17/1952 | M | S | Cook |
| Scott, Emanuel | B | 24 | 3/19/1953 | M | S | Cook |
| Carpenter, Richard D. | W | 26 | 12/19/1958 | M | S,U | Cook |
| Ciucci, Vincent | W | 36 | 3/23/1962 | M | S,F,U | Cook |
| Dukes, James | B | 37 | 8/24/1962 | M | S,F,U | Cook |

## INDIANA

*Period of Executions*: 1897–1981
*Total Number*: 74 (includes 1 post-*Furman* execution)
*Method*: Hanging 1897–1907; electrocution 1914–1961
*Other Data*: The execution of one man who was not electrocuted at the state prison but hanged at Indianapolis for the murder of an FBI agent is identified in footnote 1.

| Name | Race | Age | Date of Execution | Offense | Appeal | County |
|------|------|-----|-------------------|---------|--------|--------|
| Jones, Henry | B | 27 | 5/ 7/1897 | M | S | Marion |
| Keith, Joseph | W | 40 | 11/15/1901 | M | S | Gibson |
| Rinkard, John | W | 62 | 1/17/1902 | M | S | Wabash |
| Wheeler, Willis B. | W | 45 | 6/ 6/1902 | M | S | Warrick |
| Russell, Lewis | B | 48 | 9/26/1902 | M | | Gibson |
| Alexander, Matthew | B | 28 | 4/16/1903 | M | | Vigo |
| Copehaver, Ora | W | 26 | 6/12/1903 | M | S | Marion |
| Jackson, William | B | — | 6/12/1903 | M | S | Vanderburgh |
| Hoover, Edward | W | 26 | 11/13/1903 | M | S | Marion |
| Springs, Benjamin | B | 34 | 7/ 1/1904 | M | | Vigo |
| Duggins, Jerry | B | 29 | 7/ 8/1904 | M | | Vigo |
| Smith, Berkeley | B | 30 | 6/30/1905 | M | S | Marion |
| Williams, George | W | 28 | 2/ 8/1907 | M | S | Marion |
| Chirka, John | W | 40 | 2/20/1914 | M | | Lake |
| Rasico, Harry | W | 35 | 2/20/1914 | M | | Vigo |
| Collier, Robert | B | 34 | 10/16/1914 | M | | Vanderburgh |
| Robinson, Kelly | B | 28 | 2/ 1/1916 | M | S | Marion |
| Ray, William | B | 18 | 8/ 5/1920 | M | | Marion |
| Thornton, Will | B | 21 | 12/10/1920 | M | | Lake |
| Donovan, William | W | 35 | 6/ 1/1922 | M | | Montgomery |
| Brooks, Ben | W | 33 | 12/ 1/1922 | M | | Bartholomew |
| Diamond, Harry | W | 25 | 11/14/1924 | M | S | Porter |
| Vergolini, Peter | W | 29 | 1/30/1925 | M | | Lake |
| Koval, John | W | 32 | 10/16/1925 | M | | Lake |
| Stewart, Edward | B | 25 | 1/16/1926 | M | | Marion |
| Jankowski, Peter | W | 26 | 1/22/1926 | M | | Lake |
| Smith, Henry | B | 26 | 3/26/1926 | M | | Porter |
| Hicks, Roosevelt | B | 23 | 7/29/1927 | M | S | Marion |
| Gryzb, John | W | 20 | 4/10/1928 | M | S | Elkhart |
| Britt, James | B | 42 | 3/21/1930 | M | | Lake |
| Saragoza, Ignacio | W | 26 | 6/24/1931 | M | | LaPorte |
| Johnson, Herbert | W | 33 | 2/12/1932 | M | | LaGrange |
| Mcknezzer, Ulysses | B | 29 | 7/ 1/1932 | M | | Porter |
| Moore, John | W | 28 | 3/ 2/1933 | M | | Blackford |
| Shustrom, Glenn | W | 23 | 7/28/1933 | M | S | Lake |
| Witt, Charles | W | 28 | 11/24/1933 | M | S | Boone |
| Edwards, Harley | W | 40 | 3/ 2/1934 | M | | Jackson |
| Hamilton, Louis | W | 27 | 9/28/1934 | M | S | Boone |
| Perkins, Richard | B | 31 | 10/ 1/1934 | M | S | Hancock |
| Coffin, Edward | W | 22 | 10/ 9/1934 | M | | Clark |
| Griggs, Olivett | B | 32 | 6/14/1935 | M | | Lake |
| Chapman, Richard | W | 21 | 11/19/1935 | M | | Lake |

| Name | Race | Age | Date of Execution | Offense | Appeal | County |
|------|------|-----|-------------------|---------|--------|--------|
| Barrett, George W.[1] | W | 55 | 3/24/1936 | M | S | Fed |
| Slaughter, Gaston | B | 35 | 4/17/1936 | M | S | Vigo |
| Thomas, Clarence | W | 31 | 10/19/1936 | M | | Whitley |
| Singer, Harry | W | 25 | 12/26/1936 | M | | Wabash |
| Arkuszewski, Chester | W | 24 | 3/12/1937 | M | | LaPorte |
| Kuhlman, William | W | 28 | 6/10/1937 | M | | Franklin |
| Wiliams, Frank | W | 39 | 6/10/1937 | M | | Franklin |
| Poholsky, John | W | 35 | 6/10/1937 | M | | Franklin |
| Fortune, Raymond | W | 26 | 9/17/1937 | M | S | Huntington |
| Fuller, Willis | W | 28 | 1/14/1938 | M | S | Vigo |
| White, Monroe | B | 32 | 5/ 3/1938 | M | | Newton |
| Hicks, Heber | W | 39 | 5/ 6/1938 | M | S | Franklin |
| Smith, John | W | 22 | 6/ 1/1938 | M | | Whitley |
| Shaw, Robert | W | 29 | 6/28/1938 | M | | LaGrange |
| Marshall, Hugh | W | 19 | 7/ 8/1938 | M | S | Shelby |
| Neal, Vurtis | W | 22 | 7/ 8/1938 | M | S | Shelby |
| Noelke, Henry | W | 32 | 9/30/1938 | M | S | Vanderburgh |
| Dalhover, R. James | W | 32 | 11/17/1938 | M | F,U | Fed |
| Easton, Orelle | W | 25 | 6/ 3/1939 | M | S | LaPorte |
| Swain, James | B | 18 | 6/23/1939 | M | S | Vanderburgh |
| Miller, Adrian | W | 31 | 8/16/1939 | M | | Allen |
| Hawkins, Milton | W | 24 | 11/14/1941 | M | S | Floyd |
| Carter, Virginius | W | 33 | 2/10/1942 | M | | Dearborn |
| Greathouse, Cleveland | B | 64 | 11/26/1945 | M | | Lake |
| Quarles, Frank | B | 44 | 4/ 2/1946 | M | S | Vanderburgh |
| Brown, Robert O. | W | 37 | 2/23/1949 | M | S,U | Jasper |
| Badgley, Frank | W | 49 | 2/23/1949 | M | S,U | Jasper |
| Kallas, Thomas | W | 58 | 3/29/1949 | M | S,U | Lake |
| Click, Franklin | W | 31 | 12/30/1950 | M | S | Allen |
| Watts, Robert A. | B | 27 | 1/16/1951 | M | S,U,NT | Bartholomew |
| Kiefer, Richard Allen | W | 41 | 6/15/1961 | M | S,U,NT | Allen |
| Judy, Steven T. | W | 24 | 3/ 9/1981 | M | S | Marion |

[1]Barrett (3/24/1936) was hanged at Indianapolis for the murder of an FBI agent.

## IOWA

*Period of Executions*: 1894–1963
*Total Number*: 31
*Method*: Hanging
*Period of Abolition*: 1965

| Name | Race | Age | Date of Execution | Offense | Appeal | County |
|------|------|-----|-------------------|---------|--------|--------|
| Dooley, James | W | 18 | 10/19/1894 | M | S | Adams |
| Cumberland, J.K. | W | 48 | 2/ 8/1895 | M | S | Shelby |
| Smith, Joseph C. | B | 44 | 4/20/1906 | M | S | Monroe |
| Junkins, John | B | 24 | 7/29/1910 | M | S | Appanoose |
| Pavey, Ira | W | 31 | 9/ 8/1922 | M | S | Sioux |
| Weeks, Eugene | W | — | 9/15/1922 | M | S | Polk |

| Name | Race | Age | Date of Execution | Offense | Appeal | County |
|------|------|-----|-------------------|---------|--------|--------|
| Cross, Orrie | W | 26 | 11/24/1922 | M | | Polk |
| Throst, Earl | W | — | 3/ 9/1923 | M | S | Allamkee |
| Olander, William | W | 24 | 9/ 7/1923 | M | S,NT | Webster |
| Maupin, Roy | B | 26 | 1/18/1924 | M | S | Polk |
| Burris, Archie | B | 32 | 1/ 2/1925 | M | S,NT | Wapello |
| Simons, Harland | W | 26 | 11/16/1925 | M | | Scott |
| Altringer, J.A.R. | W | — | 11/ 6/1931 | M | | Dubuque |
| Griffin, Pat | W | 36 | 6/ 5/1935 | M | S | Black Hawk |
| Brewer, Elmer | W | — | 6/ 5/1935 | M | S | Black Hawk |
| Tracy, Reginald S. | W | 53 | 11/29/1935 | M | S | Delaware |
| Mercer, John M. | W | 29 | 1/24/1938 | M | S | Cedar |
| Wheaton, Allen B. | W | 20 | 1/24/1938 | M | | Pottawattamie |
| Heinz, Marlo | W | 32 | 4/19/1938 | M | S | Dubuque |
| Jacobsen, Franz A. | W | 30 | 4/19/1938 | M | S | Wapello |
| Rhodes, Walter | W | 32 | 5/ 7/1940 | M | S,U | Johnson |
| Sullivan, Ivan L. | W | 30 | 11/12/1941 | M | S | Lee |
| Kaster, Stanley M. | W | 36 | 12/29/1944 | M | S | Bremer |
| Jarett, William | W | 54 | 2/23/1945 | M | | Webster |
| Heincy, Philip (Father) | W | 72 | 3/29/1946 | M | | Dickinson |
| Heincy, William H. (Son) | W | 45 | 3/29/1946 | M | | Dickinson |
| Bruntlett, Corliss R. | W | 52 | 7/ 6/1949 | M | S | Pottawattamie |
| Beckwith, Edward James | W | 31 | 8/ 4/1952 | M | S,NT | Black Hawk |
| Brown, Charles Noel | W | 29 | 7/24/1962 | M | S | Pottawattamie |
| Kelley, Charles Edwin | W | 21 | 9/ 6/1962 | M | S | Mills |
| Feuger, Victor Harry | W | 27 | 3/15/1963 | K | F,U | Federal |

## KANSAS

*Period of Executions*: 1944–1965
*Total Number*: 15
*Method*: Hanging

| Name | Race | Age | Date of Execution | Offense | Appeal | County |
|------|------|-----|-------------------|---------|--------|--------|
| Hoefgen, Ernest L. | W | 32 | 3/10/1944 | M | | Marion |
| Brady, Fred L. | W | 46 | 4/15/1944 | M | S | Cowley |
| Knox, Clark B. | B | 26 | 4/15/1944 | M | | Wyandotte |
| Tate, Cecil | W | 21 | 7/29/1947 | M | | Kingman |
| Gumtow, George F. | W | 23 | 7/29/1947 | M | | Kingman |
| Miller, George | B | 60 | 5/ 6/1950 | M | S | Miami |
| McBride, Preston | W | 25 | 4/ 6/1951 | M | S | Reno |
| Lammers, James | W | 26 | 1/ 5/1952 | M | S | Donaphin |
| Germany, Nathaniel | B | 30 | 5/21/1954 | M | S,U | Wyandotte |
| Martin, Merle William | W | 45 | 7/16/1954 | M | S | Johnson |
| Andrews, Lowell Lee | W | 22 | 11/30/1962 | M | S,F,U | Wyandotte |
| Hickock, Richard E. | W | 28 | 4/14/1965 | M | S,F,U | Finney |
| Smith, Perry Edward | W | 31 | 4/14/1965 | M | S,F,U | Finney |
| York, George Ronald | W | 23 | 6/22/1965 | M | S,F,U | Russell |
| Latham, James Douglas | W | 23 | 6/22/1965 | M | S,F,U | Russell |

# KENTUCKY

*Period of Executions*: 1911–1962
*Total Number*: 171
*Method*: Electrocution
*Other Data*: In 1920, following the rape and murder of a little girl by Will Lockett (3/11/1920), a law was passed requiring that executions for rape be by hanging in the county jailyards, in the presence of at least fifty witnesses. This law was repealed in 1938. Nine executions imposed under this law are identified in footnote 1.

| Name | Race | Age | Date of Execution | Offense | Appeal | County |
|------|------|-----|-------------------|---------|--------|--------|
| Buckner, James | B | — | 7/ 8/1911 | M | | Marion |
| Penman, Sandy | B | — | 8/ 5/1911 | Ra | | Lincoln |
| Looks, Oliver | B | — | 8/22/1911 | M | | Jefferson |
| Kelly, Matthew | B | — | 9/28/1911 | M | | Jefferson |
| Howard, Charles | B | — | 1/31/1912 | M | | Franklin |
| Richardson, Willard | W | 29 | 4/19/1912 | M | | Carlisle |
| Miracle, Cal | W | — | 8/31/1912 | M | | Bell |
| Smith, Charles | B | — | 9/27/1912 | M | S | Mason |
| Smith, James | B | — | 9/27/1912 | M | S | Mason |
| Ellis, James | B | 28 | 11/22/1912 | M | S | Pulaski |
| Williams, Silas | B | 17 | 3/21/1913 | M | | Woodford |
| Wilson, William | B | — | 3/24/1913 | M | S | Jefferson |
| Bowman, John | W | — | 4/11/1913 | Ra | S | Marion |
| Tolferras, Isom | B | — | 4/18/1913 | Ra | | Todd |
| Brown, Jim | B | — | 4/25/1913 | M | | Clark |
| Martin, Tom | B | — | 6/20/1913 | M | S | Shelby |
| Lawson, Tom | B | — | 6/20/1913 | M | S | Shelby |
| May, General | W | 43 | 6/27/1913 | M | | Laurel |
| Graham, Turner | W | — | 7/30/1915 | M | | Hardin |
| Lane, Will | B | — | 7/30/1915 | M | | Bell |
| Smothers, Wallace | B | — | 9/ 3/1915 | Ra | | Clark |
| Henry, John | B | — | 11/19/1915 | M | | Boyd |
| Garrison, Harry | B | — | 11/17/1916 | Ra | S | Campbell |
| Blue, John H. | B | — | 8/10/1917 | M | S | Jefferson |
| Collins, Melvin | W | — | 7/12/1918 | M | | Carter |
| Lawler, James | W | — | 2/21/1919 | M | S | Kenton |
| Kearney, Pat | W | — | 2/21/1919 | M | S | Kenton |
| Howard, James | B | — | 6/ 6/1919 | M | S | McCracken |
| Holmes, Lennie | B | — | 6/ 6/1919 | M | | Calloway |
| Martin, Lube | B | 34 | 7/25/1919 | M | S | Calloway |
| Music, Charles | W | — | 3/10/1920 | M | S | Boyd |
| Lockett, Will | B | 23 | 3/11/1920 | Ra | | Fayette |
| Ellison, Lee | B | — | 1/31/1921 | M | S | Hopkins |
| Brown, Dave | W | — | 11/16/1922 | M | S | Pike |
| Nichols, Tom | B | — | 1/26/1923 | M | S | Christian |
| Bibbs, Benny | B | — | 1/26/1923 | M | S | Christian |
| Banks, Henry S. | B | — | 5/15/1923 | M | S | Scott |
| Powers, James | W | 23 | 6/18/1923 | M | S | Kenton |
| Chambers, Will | B | 20 | 3/ 7/1924 | M | | Barren |
| Thomas, Frank | W | 71 | 5/ 9/1924 | M | S | Jefferson |

| Name | Race | Age | Date of Execution | Offense | Appeal | County |
|------|------|-----|-------------------|---------|--------|--------|
| Weick, George | W | 51 | 5/ 9/1924 | M | S | Jefferson |
| Miller, Charles | B | 25 | 5/ 9/1924 | M | S | Breckinridge |
| Davis, Sid | B | — | 3/20/1925 | M | S | Fayette |
| Griffin, Leonard | B | — | 3/20/1925 | M | S | Harlan |
| Hall, Elmer | W | — | 6/26/1925 | M | S | Bourbon |
| Newhouse, Richard | W | — | 6/26/1925 | M | S | Bourbon |
| Farrell, George | W | — | 6/26/1925 | M | S | Bourbon |
| Armond, Harry | B | — | 7/ 3/1925 | M | S | Jefferson |
| Ross, Ray[1] | B | 25 | 8/28/1925 | Ra | S | Fayette |
| Harris, Ed[1] | B | 42 | 3/ 5/1926 | Ra |  | Fayette |
| Lake, Edward | W | 32 | 5/28/1926 | M | S | Jefferson |
| Sloan, Elisha | W | 30 | 5/28/1926 | M | S | Perry |
| Baker, John | B | 34 | 5/28/1926 | M | S | Jefferson |
| Brannon, Roger | W | 22 | 12/17/1926 | M | S | Fayette |
| Harris, Smokey | B | — | 12/17/1926 | M |  | Christian |
| Davis, Raymond | W | 28 | 9/16/1927 | M |  | Fayette |
| Bard, Nathan[1] | B | 36 | 11/25/1927 | Ra | S | Hopkins |
| Fleming, Bunyan[1] | B | 32 | 11/25/1927 | Ra | S | Breckenridge |
| Venison, Harold Van[1] | B | 36 | 6/ 3/1928 | Ra | S | Kenton |
| Mitra, Charles P. | W | 23 | 7/13/1928 | M | S | Jefferson |
| Seymour, Orlando | W | 21 | 7/13/1928 | M | S | Jefferson |
| Dockery, Hascue | W | 21 | 7/13/1928 | M | S | Harlan |
| Lawson, Milford | W | 35 | 7/13/1928 | M | S | Knox |
| Moore, Willie | B | 45 | 7/13/1928 | M | S | Jefferson |
| Howard, James | B | — | 7/13/1928 | M | S | Jefferson |
| McQueen, Clarence | B | 38 | 7/13/1928 | M | S | Jefferson |
| Hoard, Carl | W | 22 | 9/13/1929 | M |  | Jefferson |
| Hutsell, Ivan | W | 27 | 9/13/1929 | M | S | Oldham |
| Ratcliffe, Ballard | W | 41 | 6/13/1930 | M | S | Jefferson |
| Edmonds, Richard | B | 36 | 6/13/1930 | M | S | Jefferson |
| Cooksey, A.P. | B | 23 | 4/29/1932 | M | S | Hopkins |
| Rogers, Charles | B | 23 | 4/29/1932 | M | S | Hardin |
| Holmes, Walter | B | 31 | 4/29/1932 | M | S | Hardin |
| Jennings, Sam[1] | B | 36 | 6/17/1932 | Ra | S | Livingston |
| Covington, Jeff | B | 30 | 12/17/1932 | M |  | Madison |
| Carson, Frank | W | 19 | 4/ 7/1933 | M |  | Nelson |
| McGee, Sam | B | 31 | 4/ 7/1933 | M | S | McCracken |
| Pope, Kermit R. | B | — | 4/14/1933 | M | S | Jefferson |
| Gaines, Richard | B | — | 4/14/1933 | M | S | Caldwell |
| Young, John | W | 37 | 4/14/1933 | M | S | Jefferson |
| Waters, William | B | 36 | 11/ 3/1933 | M | S | Montgomery |
| Scott, Ishmael | W | 40 | 11/ 3/1933 | M | S | Floyd |
| Bouton, Harve | W | — | 11/ 3/1933 | M |  | Elliott |
| Dewberry, Walter | B | — | 11/10/1933 | M | S | Hardin |
| Chaney, Will | B | — | 8/24/1934 | M | S | Jefferson |
| Tincher, George W. | W | — | 8/24/1934 | M | S | Scott |
| Glenday, Francis | W | 29 | 12/ 7/1934 | M | S | Scott |
| Graves, Wiley | B | 29 | 2/22/1935 | M | S | Fayette |
| Williams, Charlie | B | — | 3/ 1/1935 | M | S | Christian |
| Smith, James | B | 30 | 5/24/1935 | M | S | Fayette |
| Young, Bill | W | 23 | 6/28/1935 | M | S | Harlan |
| Lotheridge, Eulie | W | 26 | 12/ 6/1935 | M | S | Carroll |

| Name | Race | Age | Date of Execution | Offense | Appeal | County |
|------|------|-----|-------------------|---------|--------|--------|
| Bowman, Neal | W | — | 1/10/1936 | M | S | Mercer |
| Tate, Calvin | W | 21 | 1/17/1936 | M | S | Jefferson |
| Hall, Willard | W | 33 | 1/17/1936 | M | S | Jefferson |
| Matthews, James | W | 19 | 1/31/1936 | M | S | McCreary |
| Lee, Bennie | B | — | 2/21/1936 | M | S | Bell |
| Whitehead, Erleon | W | — | 3/20/1936 | M | S | Barren |
| DeBoe, Willard T.[1] | W | 22 | 4/19/1936 | Ra | S | Livingston |
| Simmons, Roy | B | 22 | 5/15/1936 | M | S | McCracken |
| Drake, Alfred | B | 30 | 5/15/1936 | M | S | Jefferson |
| Woodford, James R. | B | 22 | 5/29/1936 | M | S | Fayette |
| Young, Homer | B | 39 | 6/ 5/1936 | M | S | Bell |
| Bethea, Rainey[1] | B | 22 | 8/14/1936 | Ra | | Davies |
| Underwood, George B. | W | — | 2/19/1937 | M | S | Bullitt |
| Franklin, Sam | B | — | 3/19/1937 | Ro,Arm | S | Jefferson |
| Clift, Arnold | W | 24 | 7/16/1937 | M | S | Laurel |
| Marion, Perry | W | — | 11/12/1937 | M | S | Laurel |
| Montjoy, John "Pete"[1] | B | 24 | 12/17/1937 | Ra | S,U,F | Kenton |
| Triplett, Troy | W | — | 5/20/1938 | M | S | Letcher |
| Denny, Parkie | W | 43 | 9/ 2/1938 | M | S | Madison |
| Mosley, Leonard | B | 43 | 10/28/1938 | Ra | | Meade |
| Warner, Sylvester | W | 29 | 2/10/1939 | M | S | Casey |
| Powell, Arnold | W | — | 3/ 3/1939 | M | S | Estill |
| Griffin, Bonnie | W | — | 3/ 3/1939 | M | S | Estill |
| Waters, Willie | B | — | 3/24/1939 | M | | Jefferson |
| Rice, Arvil | W | — | 7/ 7/1939 | M | S | Bell |
| Smith, Charles H. | W | — | 7/14/1939 | M | S | Lyon |
| Davis, Jack | W | — | 7/21/1939 | M | S | Leslie |
| Higgins, Edward | B | 26 | 7/25/1939 | Ra | | Mercer |
| Phillips, Henry | B | 41 | 7/26/1940 | M | S | Jefferson |
| Houston, Ernest | B | 20 | 8/30/1940 | M | S | Jefferson |
| Richardson, Columbus | B | — | 1/20/1941 | M | S | McCracken |
| Chism, Grover | W | — | 7/ 4/1941 | M | S | Hardin |
| Smiddy, Bill | W | — | 8/29/1941 | M | S | Whitley |
| Satterfield, James | B | 35 | 2/20/1942 | M | S | Jefferson |
| Burnam, Eugene | B | 18 | 3/27/1942 | Ra | S | Fayette |
| Williams, Robert | B | 23 | 6/ 5/1942 | Ra | S | Fayette |
| Robertson, James Lee | B | 26 | 8/ 7/1942 | M | | Fayette |
| Sanders, Jess | B | 56 | 8/28/1942 | M | S | Jefferson |
| Smith, Otis Peter | W | 30 | 8/28/1942 | M | S | Jefferson |
| Combs, McCoy | W | — | 1/15/1943 | M | S | Perry |
| Sexton, Burnett | W | — | 1/15/1943 | M | S | Perry |
| Anderson, Robert | W | — | 2/26/1943 | M | S | Fayette |
| Penny, Tom | W | — | 2/26/1943 | M | S | Fayette |
| Baxter, Raymond S. | W | — | 2/26/1943 | M | S | Fayette |
| Trent, Ernest | W | — | 2/26/1943 | M | S | Breathitt |
| Gray, William Carson | B | 17 | 6/25/1943 | M | S | Fayette |
| Simpson, Archie | B | 20 | 6/25/1943 | M | S | Fayette |
| Nelson, Tommy | W | 35 | 3/16/1945 | M | S,U | Pike |
| Bass, Thomas | B | 25 | 3/16/1945 | M | S,U | Jefferson |
| Fox, Carl | B | — | 4/ 6/1945 | Ra | S | Campbell |
| Hambrick, Ed | B | — | 5/25/1945 | Ra | S | Campbell |
| Adkins, Anderson | W | — | 3/15/1946 | M | S | Pike |

| Name | Race | Age | Date of Execution | Offense | Appeal | County |
|------|------|-----|-------------------|---------|--------|--------|
| Warner, Thomas Earl | B | — | 3/22/1946 | M | S | Mason |
| Jones, Arthur | B | — | 3/22/1946 | M | S | Mason |
| Calhoun, Edward | W | — | 5/24/1946 | M | S | Garrard |
| Tungett, Earl L. | W | — | 7/11/1947 | M | S,U | Lyon |
| Williams, Luther | B | 27 | 2/27/1948 | M | S | Pulaski |
| Nease, Jasper | W | 23 | 7/30/1948 | Ro,Arm | S | Jefferson |
| McPeak, Daniel T. | W | 21 | 11/ 5/1948 | Ro,Arm | S | Jefferson |
| Pool, Charlie | B | — | 1/28/1949 | M | S | Christian |
| Workman, Herbert H. | W | 18 | 3/ 4/1949 | Ro,Arm | S | Jefferson |
| Lightfoot, Lawrence B. | W | — | 6/24/1949 | M | | Campbell |
| Ellison, Raymond | W | 39 | 2/24/1950 | M | S | Muhlenburg |
| Webb, Columbus | W | — | 6/16/1950 | M | S | Martin |
| Shelkels, Albert | B | 20 | 6/ 8/1951 | Ro,Arm | S | Jefferson |
| Robinson, James I. | W | 31 | 1/18/1952 | Ro,Arm | S | Jefferson |
| Bircham, Earl D. | W | 49 | 2/ 1/1952 | Ro,Arm | S,U | Jefferson |
| Quarles, Jessie, Lee | B | 27 | 4/ 4/1952 | M | S | Christian |
| Spears, Roosevelt | B | 47 | 2/27/1953 | M | S | Campbell |
| Read, Thomas William | B | 45 | 6/ 4/1954 | M | S | Jefferson |
| Tarrence, Roy (Father) | W | 49 | 3/18/1955 | M | S,U | Jefferson |
| Tarrence, Leonard (Son) | W | 26 | 3/18/1955 | M | S,U | Jefferson |
| Milam, Ed | B | 25 | 9/16/1955 | M | S,U | Christian |
| Merrifield, Chester | W | 34 | 12/23/1955 | M | S,U | Jefferson |
| Nichols, David | B | 55 | 12/23/1955 | M | S | Jefferson |
| Bowman, James F. | B | 44 | 11/30/1956 | M | S | Jefferson |
| DeBerry, Charles C. | B | 20 | 11/30/1956 | M | S | Jefferson |
| Sheckles, Robert Lee | B | 22 | 11/30/1956 | Ra | S | Jefferson |
| Moss, Kelly | W | 47 | 3/ 2/1962 | M | S,U | Henderson |

[1]Ross (8/28/1925), Harris (3/5/1926), Bard (11/25/1927), Fleming (11/25/1927), Venison (6/3/1928), Jennings (6/17/1932), DeBoe (4/19/1936), Bethea (8/14/1936), and Montjoy (12/17/1937) were hanged in the county jailyards in the presence of at least fifty witnesses.

## LOUISIANA

*Period of Executions*: 1957–1961
*Total Number*: 11
*Method*: Electrocution
*Other Data*: From 1940 to 1956, electrocutions were performed by a portable electric chair which was taken with a generator on a truck from the penitentiary to the county jail.

| Name | Race | Age | Date of Execution | Offense | Appeal | County |
|------|------|-----|-------------------|---------|--------|--------|
| Michaels, John Joseph | B | 27 | 5/31/1957 | Ra | | Orleans |
| Washington, Joseph | B | 34 | 6/21/1957 | M | S | Caddo |
| Bush, James | B | 27 | 6/21/1957 | M | S | Caddo |
| Chinn, Louis | B | 34 | 7/ 5/1957 | M | S | E. Baton Rouge |
| Sheffield, Joseph O. | W | 28 | 8/16/1957 | M | S,F,U,NT | Franklin |
| Edwards, Donald R. | B | 22 | 9/ 6/1957 | Ra | S | Caddo |
| Bailey, D.C. | B | 21 | 10/11/1957 | M | S | Madison |

| Name | Race | Age | Date of Execution | Offense | Appeal | County |
|------|------|-----|-------------------|---------|--------|--------|
| Facianne, Alfred T. | B | 23 | 4/11/1958 | M | S | Tangipahoa |
| McMiller, John G. | B | 44 | 4/11/1958 | M | S | Tangipahoa |
| Brazile, Jasper | B | 43 | 8/15/1958 | M | S,U | Rapides |
| Ferguson, Jesse James | B | 39 | 6/ 9/1961 | M,Ra | S,U | St. Landry |

## MAINE

*Period of Executions*: 1864–1885
*Total Number*: 7
*Method*: Hanging
*Period of Abolition*: 1876–1883, 1887–

| Name | Race | Age | Date of Execution | Offense | Appeal | County |
|------|------|-----|-------------------|---------|--------|--------|
| Spencer, Francis Couillard | W | — | 6/24/1864 | M | | Knox |
| Harris, Clifton | B | 20 | 3/12/1869 | M | | Androscoggin |
| Wagner, Louis H.D. | W | — | 6/25/1875 | M | S | York |
| Gordon, John T. | W | — | 6/25/1875 | M | | Waldo |
| Capone, Raeffaele | W | 27 | 4/17/1885 | M | | Penobscot |
| Santore, Carmine | W | 44 | 4/17/1885 | M | | Penobscot |
| Wilkinson, Daniel | W | 39 | 11/20/1885 | M | S | Sagadhoc |

## MARYLAND

*Period of Executions*: 1923–1961
*Total Number*: 79
*Method*: Hanging; change to lethal gas in 1956

| Name | Race | Age | Date of Execution | Offense | Appeal | County |
|------|------|-----|-------------------|---------|--------|--------|
| Chelton, George | B | 21 | 6/ 8/1923 | Ra | | Somerset |
| Gibson, Carroll | B | 18 | 2/13/1925 | Ra | | Talbot |
| Benson, Isaac | B | 37 | 7/23/1926 | M | | Baltimore Cᵗ |
| Whittemore, Richard Reese | W | 27 | 8/13/1926 | M | S | Baltimore C |
| Simmons, Ottie | B | 19 | 9/ 9/1927 | M | | Frederick |
| Swann, Arthur | B | 20 | 9/ 9/1927 | M | | Frederick |
| Rose, William Henry | B | 23 | 9/ 9/1927 | M | S | Washington |
| Simms, Alfred | B | 19 | 11/11/1927 | Ra | | Pr. George |
| Spragina, Benjamin | W | 28 | 8/ 3/1928 | M | | Baltimore |
| Carey, Charles P. | W | 28 | 8/ 3/1928 | M | S | Baltimore C |
| Watkins, Hopkins | B | 27 | 11/16/1928 | M | S | Baltimore |
| Marsh, John Orestus | W | 51 | 8/ 9/1929 | M | | Caroll |
| Jackson, John | B | 55 | 1/31/1930 | M | | Baltimore C |
| Price, Lorenzo | B | 32 | 6/12/1931 | M | S | Baltimore |
| Blackson, Thomas | B | 42 | 1/15/1932 | M | | Worcester |
| Wright, Walter F. | B | 28 | 4/ 8/1932 | M | | Baltimore |
| Lee, Buel | B | 60 | 10/27/1933 | M | S,U | Baltimore |
| Jupiter, Page | B | 46 | 2/ 2/1934 | M | | Charles |

| Name | Race | Age | Date of Execution | Offense | Appeal | County |
|------|------|-----|-------------------|---------|--------|--------|
| Dent, Gordon | B | 30 | 4/19/1935 | M | | Pr. George |
| Cross, James A. | B | 25 | 4/19/1935 | M | | Pr. George |
| Harold, William | B | 45 | 6/28/1935 | Ra | | Montgomery |
| Poindexter, James | B | 27 | 6/28/1935 | Ra | | Montgomery |
| Perez, Augusto | W | 22 | 6/12/1936 | Ra | | Baltimore C |
| Williams, Willie | B | 25 | 6/12/1936 | M | | Baltimore C |
| Howard, James Irvin | B | 20 | 7/ 9/1937 | M | | Anne Arundel |
| Hammond, Richard | B | 31 | 8/28/1938 | M | S | Baltimore C |
| Turner, James Albert | B | 25 | 8/29/1938 | Ra | | Montgomery |
| Brown, Fred | W | 44 | 3/19/1939 | M | S | Dorchester |
| Sanchez, Thomas C. | W | 40 | 3/15/1940 | Ra | | Talbot |
| Kenton, Alvin | W | 23 | 3/15/1940 | Ra | | Talbot |
| Sorrell, William T. | B | 28 | 5/10/1940 | M | | Baltimore C |
| Harrell, Otis | B | 23 | 5/10/1940 | M | | Baltimore C |
| Williams, Alexander | B | 33 | 6/28/1940 | Ra | S | Anne Arundel |
| Collick, Arthur B. | B | 27 | 9/13/1940 | M | | Baltimore |
| Knott, Wilson | W | 33 | 1/10/1941 | Ra | | Anne Arundel |
| White, French Lee | B | 23 | 6/27/1941 | Ra | | Montgomery |
| Loveless, Earl | W | 22 | 9/26/1941 | M | | Allegany |
| Miller, James Lee | W | 29 | 9/26/1941 | M | | Allegany |
| Baker, James | B | 38 | 12/19/1941 | M | | Dorchester |
| Pritcheet, Wilber | B | 37 | 5/ 8/1942 | Ra | | Dorchester |
| Haywood, Frank | B | 32 | 6/ 5/1942 | Ra | | Pr. George |
| Henry, Andrew | B | 54 | 7/10/1942 | M | | Dorchester |
| Benjamin, Charles J. | B | 23 | 7/24/1942 | M | | Baltimore C |
| Woffard, Edward | B | 27 | 7/24/1942 | M | | Baltimore |
| Gilliam, James | B | 39 | 1/15/1943 | M | | Worcester |
| Ford, James | B | 32 | 3/12/1943 | Ra | S | Baltimore |
| Williams, Frank | B | 23 | 6/ 4/1943 | M | | Baltimore C |
| Holton, Freeman | B | 21 | 6/ 4/1943 | M | | Baltimore C |
| Lampkin, John | B | 19 | 8/13/1943 | Ra | | Baltimore C |
| Holsey, William Charles | B | 33 | 2/25/1944 | M | | Carroll |
| Smith, Martin | B | 20 | 3/31/1944 | Ra | S | Baltimore C |
| Hinton, John | B | 25 | 6/16/1944 | Ra | | Dorchester |
| Watkins, Calvin William | B | 24 | 11/17/1944 | M | | Baltimore C |
| Murphy, Patrick | W | 40 | 7/20/1945 | Ra | S | Pr. George |
| McClam, Luther | B | 28 | 8/17/1945 | M | | Baltimore C |
| Brooks, Donald | W | 31 | 11/30/1945 | M | | Baltimore C |
| Fields, John Henry | B | 38 | 12/28/1945 | M | | Worcester |
| Tasker, William | B | 21 | 1/18/1946 | M | | Anne Arundel |
| Walker, LLoyd | B | 22 | 8/ 9/1946 | Ra | | Baltimore C |
| Peters, Roy Nathan | B | 22 | 10/ 4/1946 | Ra | | Baltimore C |
| Demby, William Daniel | B | 22 | 10/ 4/1946 | Ra | | Baltimore C |
| Barnes, John Lester | B | 25 | 12/13/1946 | Ra | S,U | Pr. George |
| Carmen, Charles Lee | B | 19 | 1/17/1947 | Ra | | Cecil |
| Cooper, William E. | B | 20 | 6/27/1947 | Ra | | Cecil |
| Jones, Weldon Jr. | B | 18 | 8/ 1/1947 | M | S | Wicmico |
| Abbott, Ross J. | W | 24 | 8/ 1/1947 | M | S | Dorchester |
| Smith, Ollie, Jr. | B | 22 | 4/30/1948 | Ra | S | Dorchester |
| Jackson, Henry T. | B | 32 | 4/30/1948 | M | | Worcester |
| Lathco, Roy Lee | W | 39 | 4/30/1948 | Ra | | Baltimore |
| Fram, Howard A. | W | 31 | 7/ 8/1949 | M | | Baltimore C |

| Name | Race | Age | Date of Execution | Offense | Appeal | County |
|------|------|-----|-------------------|---------|--------|--------|
| Knowles, John | B | 26 | 8/12/1949 | M | S | Baltimore C |
| James, Eugene H. | B | 31 | 8/12/1949 | M | S | Baltimore C |
| Glover, Lott | B | 31 | 8/25/1953 | M | S | Pr. George |
| Grammer, George Edward | W | 35 | 6/11/1954 | M | S,U | Baltimore C |
| Thomas, William C. | B | 32 | 6/10/1955 | M | S | Baltimore C |
| Daniels, Eddie Lee | B | — | 6/28/1957 | M | S | Montgomery |
| Kier, Carl Daniel | B | 25 | 1/21/1959 | M | S,NT | Baltimore |
| Shockey, Leonard M. | B | 17 | 4/10/1959 | M | S | Dorchester |
| Lipscomb, Nathaniel | B | 33 | 6/ 9/1961 | M | | Baltimore |

ᴵBaltimore C means the City of Baltimore, a distinct political subdivision of Maryland


## MASSACHUSETTS

*Period of Executions*: 1901–1947
*Total Number*: 65
*Method*: Electrocution
*Other Data*: All executions have taken place at the old prison at Charlestown,
Mass.

| Name | Race | Age | Date of Execution | Offense | Appeal | County |
|------|------|-----|-------------------|---------|--------|--------|
| Storti, Luigi | — | 26 | 12/17/1901 | M | S,F,U | Suffolk |
| Umilian, Franciszek | — | 34 | 12/24/1901 | M | S | Hampshire |
| Cassels, John D. | W | 35 | 5/ 6/1902 | M | | Hampden |
| Best, John C. | — | 37 | 9/ 9/1902 | M | S | Essex |
| Tucker, Charles L. | W | 25 | 6/12/1906 | M | S | Middlesex |
| Schidlofski, John | W | 29 | 7/ 9/1906 | M | | Middlesex |
| Woon, Ham | C | 37 | 10/12/1909 | M | S | Suffolk |
| Sing, Min | C | 31 | 10/12/1909 | M | S | Suffolk |
| Gong, Leon | C | 19 | 10/12/1909 | M | S | Suffolk |
| Rivet, Napoleon J. | — | 32 | 7/28/1910 | M | S | Middlesex |
| Ipson, Andrei | W | 19 | 3/ 7/1911 | M | | Essex |
| Ivankowski, Wassilii | W | 22 | 3/ 7/1911 | M | | Essex |
| Phelps, Silas N. | W | 39 | 1/26/1912 | M | S | Franklin |
| Richeson, Clarence V.T. | W | 36 | 5/21/1912 | M | | Suffolk |
| Marshall, Harry | W | 25 | 6/ 6/1912 | M | S | Plymouth |
| Spencer, Bertram G. | W | 31 | 9/17/1912 | M | S | Hampden |
| Jordan, Chester S. | W | 33 | 9/24/1912 | M | S,U | Middlesex |
| Borasky, Stefan | — | 26 | 6/24/1913 | M | S | Hampden |
| Dorr, William A. | W | 31 | 3/24/1914 | M | S | Essex |
| Falzone, Biago | — | 23 | 5/11/1915 | M | | Middlesex |
| Retkovitz, Anton | W | 37 | 3/16/1916 | M | S | Bristol |
| Ducharme, Francis | W | 27 | 9/11/1917 | M | | Hampden |
| Feci, Francisco | W | 37 | 8/16/1920 | M | S | Middlesex |
| Dascalakis, Paul | — | 30 | 7/14/1923 | M | S | Suffolk |
| Vandenhecke, Cyrille J. | — | 51 | 7/30/1924 | M | S | Essex |
| Stewart, Richard J. | B | 32 | 5/ 5/1926 | M | S | Middlesex |
| Heinlein, Edward J. | W | 26 | 1/ 6/1927 | M | S | Middlesex |
| Deveraux, John J. | W | 25 | 1/ 6/1927 | M | S | Middlesex |

| Name | Race | Age | Date of Execution | Offense | Appeal | County |
|------|------|-----|-------------------|---------|--------|--------|
| McLaughlin, John J. | W | 30 | 1/ 6/1927 | M | S | Middlesex |
| Vanzetti, Bartolomeo | W | 33 | 8/23/1927 | M | S,U | Norfolk |
| Sacco, Nicola | W | 36 | 8/23/1927 | M | S,U | Norfolk |
| Madeiros, Celestino F. | W | 24 | 8/23/1927 | M | | Norfolk |
| Gedzium, Jerry | W | 23 | 2/28/1928 | M | S | Middlesex |
| Gleason, Herbert J. | – | 21 | 3/13/1928 | M | S | Middlesex |
| Desatnick, Nathan | W | 25 | 7/17/1928 | M | S | Worcester |
| Taylor, George E.H. | W | 47 | 3/ 6/1929 | M | S | Essex |
| Knowlton, Frederick Hinman | W | 37 | 5/14/1929 | M | S | Middlesex |
| Trippi, Charles | W | 22 | 12/ 3/1929 | M | S | Worcester |
| Hurley, Paul V. | – | 20 | 9/15/1931 | M | | Norfolk |
| Belenski, Joseph | – | 38 | 10/20/1931 | M | S | Middlesex |
| Fernandes, Sylvester N. | W | 24 | 8/12/1932 | M | | Barnstable |
| Osman, Ahmed | – | 37 | 1/23/1934 | M | S | Norfolk |
| Donnellon, John A. | – | 24 | 2/22/1934 | M | S,F | Middlesex |
| Snyder, Herman | – | 21 | 2/22/1934 | M | S,U | Middlesex |
| Bull, Henry Clay | – | 22 | 2/22/1934 | M | | Franklin |
| Kaminski, Alexander | W | 25 | 2/19/1935 | M | | Hampden |
| Millen, Murton | W | 25 | 6/ 7/1935 | M | S | Norfolk |
| Millen, Irving | W | 22 | 6/ 7/1935 | M | S | Norfolk |
| Faber, Abraham | W | 25 | 6/ 7/1935 | M | S | Norfolk |
| Clark, Miller F. | – | 44 | 1/14/1936 | M | | Suffolk |
| Sherman, Newell P. | W | 27 | 8/ 4/1936 | M | S | Worcester |
| DiStasio, Frank (Father) | W | 52 | 1/18/1938 | M | S | Middlesex |
| Distasio, Anthony (Son) | W | 25 | 1/18/1938 | M | S,U | Middlesex |
| Simpson, Edward | – | 43 | 5/13/1938 | M | S,U | Middlesex |
| Green, Wallace W. | – | 22 | 8/ 2/1939 | M | S | Middlesex |
| St. Saveur, Walter | – | 22 | 8/ 2/1939 | M | S | Middlesex |
| Rousseau, Joseph | – | 29 | 4/22/1941 | M | S | Norfolk |
| Nickerson, James H. | – | 22 | 6/30/1942 | M | S | Middlesex |
| Giacomazza, Paul | – | 19 | 6/30/1942 | M | S | Middlesex |
| Gray, Robert Hayward | – | 34 | 6/25/1943 | M | S | Suffolk |
| Millard, Donald | – | 19 | 6/25/1943 | M | S,U | Plymouth |
| Sheppard, Joseph E. | – | 25 | 6/25/1943 | M | S,U | Plymouth |
| Skopp, Raphael | W | 36 | 8/16/1946 | M | | Suffolk |
| Gertsen, Edward | – | 35 | 5/ 9/1947 | M | | Essex |
| Bellino, Philip R. | W | 32 | 5/ 9/1947 | M | S,U | Essex |

## MISSISSIPPI

*Period of Executions*: 1955–1964
*Total Number*: 31
*Method*: Lethal gas

| Name | Race | Age | Date of Execution | Offense | Appeal | County |
|------|------|-----|-------------------|---------|--------|--------|
| Gallego, Gerald A. | W | 26 | 3/ 3/1955 | M | S | Jackson |
| Donaldson, Allen | B | 28 | 3/ 4/1955 | Ro,Arm | S | Forrest |
| LaFontaine, August | W | 24 | 4/28/1955 | M | S | Hancock |
| Wiggins, John E. | W | 60 | 6/20/1955 | M | S | Jackson |

| Name | Race | Age | Date of Execution | Offense | Appeal | County |
|------|------|-----|-------------------|---------|--------|--------|
| Lewis, Mack C. | B | — | 6/23/1955 | M | S,U | Hancock |
| Johnson, Walter | B | 19 | 8/19/1955 | Ra | S,U | Harrison |
| Gilmore, Murray G. | W | 32 | 12/ 9/1955 | M | S | Monroe |
| Robinson, Mose | B | 21 | 12/18/1955 | Ra | S,U | Humphreys |
| Buchanan, Robert | B | 35 | 1/ 3/1956 | Ra | S | Hinds |
| Keeler, Edgar | B | 38 | 1/27/1956 | M | S | Hinds |
| McNair, O.C. | B | 24 | 2/17/1956 | M | S | Rankin |
| Russell, James | B | 32 | 4/ 5/1956 | M | S | Hinds |
| Townsell, Dewey | B | 26 | 6/22/1956 | M | S | Coahoma |
| Jones, Willie | B | 38 | 7/13/1956 | M | S | DeSoto |
| Drake, Mack | B | 35 | 11/ 7/1956 | Ra | S | Holmes |
| Jackson, Henry | B | 21 | 11/ 8/1956 | M | S | Sharkey |
| Thompson, Joe Louis | B | 21 | 1/11/1957 | M | S | Newton |
| Sorber, Minor | W | 39 | 2/ 8/1957 | M | S,U | Sunflower |
| Wetzell, William A. | W | 32 | 1/17/1958 | M | S,F,U | Sunflower |
| Dean, Allen, Jr. | B | 23 | 4/18/1958 | M | S | Jones |
| Cameron, J.C. | B | 23 | 5/28/1958 | Ra | S | Lincoln |
| Young, Nathaniel | B | 39 | 11/10/1960 | Ra | S | Forrest |
| Stokes, William | B | 27 | 4/21/1961 | M | S | Jones |
| Goldsby, Robert Lee | B | 35 | 5/31/1961 | M | S,F,U | Carroll |
| Simmons, J.W. | B | 28 | 7/14/1961 | M | S | Yazoo |
| Cook, Howard | B | 33 | 12/19/1961 | Ra | S | Coahama |
| Lee, Ellie | B | 31 | 12/20/1961 | Ra | S | Coahama |
| Wilson, Willie | B | 22 | 5/11/1962 | Ra | S | Harrison |
| Slyter, Kenneth M. | W | 28 | 3/29/1963 | M | S | Madison |
| Anderson, Willie J. | B | 21 | 6/14/1963 | M | S | Pike |
| Jackson, Tim | B | 22 | 5/ 1/1964 | M | S | DeSoto |

## MISSOURI

*Period of Executions*: 1938–1965
*Total Number*: 39
*Method*: Lethal gas

| Name | Race | Age | Date of Execution | Offense | Appeal | County |
|------|------|-----|-------------------|---------|--------|--------|
| Wright, William | B | 33 | 3/ 4/1938 | M | S | Jackson |
| Brown, John | B | 34 | 3/ 4/1938 | M | S | Jackson |
| Boyer, Raymond | W | 33 | 3/ 5/1938 | M | S | Jackson |
| Batson, Raymond | B | 33 | 3/30/1938 | M | S | St. Louis City |
| Jones, Johnny | B | 35 | 7/ 5/1938 | Ra | S | New Madrid |
| Richetti, Adam | W | 28 | 10/ 7/1938 | M | S | Jackson |
| Allen, Granville | B | 28 | 10/28/1938 | M | S | Jackson |
| King, Byron E. | W | 28 | 11/ 4/1938 | M | S | St. Louis City |
| Williamson, John J. | W | 63 | 2/15/1939 | M | S | Ste. Genevieve |
| Kenyon, Robert | W | 24 | 4/28/1939 | M | S | Oregon |
| Jackson, Chester | B | 31 | 9/20/1940 | M | S | Jasper |
| West, Robert | B | 25 | 9/20/1940 | M | S | St. Louis City |
| Johnson, Wilburn | B | 40 | 1/ 3/1941 | M | S | Butler |
| Tyler, Ernest | B | 37 | 6/24/1942 | M | | Jackson |

| Name | Race | Age | Date of Execution | Offense | Appeal | County |
|------|------|-----|-------------------|---------|--------|--------|
| Lambus, Allen | B | 73 | 6/16/1944 | M | | Mississippi |
| Thomas, James | B | 21 | 10/19/1944 | Ra | S | St. Louis City |
| Lyles, Leo | B | 22 | 5/25/1945 | M | S | St. Louis City |
| Talbert, William E. | B | 24 | 11/16/1945 | M | S | St. Louis City |
| Sanford, Jesse | B | 37 | 8/16/1946 | M | S,U | Franklin |
| Ellis, Fred | B | 23 | 8/16/1946 | M | S,U | Franklin |
| Ramsey, Van Lee | B | 36 | 1/ 9/1947 | M | S | St. Louis City |
| Perkins, Marshall | B | 59 | 1/24/1947 | Ra | S | Jackson |
| Cochran, Floyd | B | 37 | 9/26/1947 | M | S | Boone |
| Scott, Afton | W | 49 | 11/ 4/1949 | M | S | Wright |
| Bell, George | B | 35 | 12/ 2/1949 | M | S | Jackson |
| Tiedt, Charles | W | 56 | 5/19/1950 | M | S | Buchanan |
| McGee, Claude | W | 39 | 1/ 5/1951 | M | S | Cole |
| Porter, Willie | B | 29 | 10/28/1952 | Ra | | Cole |
| Quilling, Ulas | B | 53 | 5/29/1953 | M | S | Jackson |
| Boyd, Kenneth | B | 23 | 7/10/1953 | M | S | St. Louis City |
| Hall, Carl Austin | W | 34 | 12/18/1953 | K | | Fed |
| Heady, Bonnie Brown (Female) | W | 41 | 12/18/1953 | K | | Fed |
| Booker, Dock | B | 46 | 4/ 1/1955 | M | S | St. Louis City |
| Brown, Arthur Ross | W | 31 | 2/24/1956 | K | | Fed |
| Moore, Thomas J. | B | 42 | 9/13/1957 | M | S | Jackson |
| Tucker, Sammy Aire | W | 26 | 7/26/1963 | M | S,U | Cape Girardeau |
| Odom, Charles Harvey | W | 32 | 3/ 6/1964 | Ra | S,U | Jasper |
| Wolfe, Ronald Lee | W | 34 | 5/ 8/1964 | Ra | | Pike |
| Anderson, Lloyd Leo | B | 22 | 1/26/1965 | M | S,U | St. Louis City |

## NEBRASKA

*Period of Executions*: 1903–1959
*Total Number*: 20
*Method*: Hanging 1903–1913; electrocution 1920–1959

| Name | Race | Age | Date of Execution | Offense | Appeal | County |
|------|------|-----|-------------------|---------|--------|--------|
| Niegenfiend, Gottlieb | W | 28 | 3/13/1903 | M | | Pierce |
| Rhea, William | W | 18 | 7/10/1903 | M | S | Dodge |
| Clark, Harrison | B | 31 | 12/13/1907 | M | S | Douglas |
| Barker, Frank | W | 27 | 1/17/1908 | M | S | Webster |
| Shumway, R. Mead | W | 27 | 3/ 5/1909 | M | S | Gage |
| Taylor, Bert | W | 39 | 10/28/1910 | M | S | Kearney |
| Johnson, Thomas | B | 39 | 5/19/1911 | M | S | Douglas |
| Prince, Albert | B | 24 | 3/21/1913 | M | S | Lancaster |
| Grammer, Allen V. | W | 22 | 12/20/1920 | M | S,F,U | Howard |
| Cole, Allson B. | W | 21 | 12/20/1920 | M | S,U | Howard |
| King, James B. | B | 26 | 6/ 9/1922 | M | S | Lancaster |
| Simmons, Walter R. | W | 24 | 8/11/1925 | M | S,U | Boyd |
| Bartlett, Henry E. | W | 35 | 4/29/1927 | M | S | Kearny |
| Carter, Frank | W | 46 | 6/24/1927 | M | S | Douglas |
| Sharp, Frank E. | W | 49 | 10/19/1928 | M | S | Lancaster |

| Name | Race | Age | Date of Execution | Offense | Appeal | County |
|------|------|-----|-------------------|---------|--------|--------|
| Sherman, Henry | W | 20 | 5/31/1929 | M | S | Dawes |
| MacAvoy, Joseph T. | W | 23 | 3/23/1945 | M | S,U | Clay |
| Iron Bear, Timothy | I | 22 | 12/ 1/1948 | M | S | Sheridan |
| Sundahl, Roland Dean | W | 20 | 4/30/1952 | M | S | Platte |
| Starkweather, Charles | W | 19 | 6/25/1959 | M | S,F,U | Lancaster |

## NEVADA

*Period of Executions*: 1905–1978
*Total Number*: 42 (including 1 post-*Furman* execution)
*Method*: Hanging 1905–1911; shooting 1913; lethal gas 1924–1961
*Other Data*: The Nevada list is complete from Williams, 7/24/1909. John Hancock's case (9/8/1905) was found in a history book and verified by the prison. Sevener (11/17/1905) through Kaiser (5/24/1909) were found and verified by Mr. Espy, who further comments that there may have been other executions in Nevada during the period from September 8, 1905, to July 24, 1909.

| Name | Race | Age | Date of Execution | Offense | Appeal | County |
|------|------|-----|-------------------|---------|--------|--------|
| Hancock, John | – | – | 9/ 8/1905 | M | | Lincoln |
| Sevener, J.P. | – | 48 | 11/17/1905 | M | S | Humboldt |
| Gorman, T.F. | – | 31 | 11/17/1905 | M | S | Humboldt |
| Linderman, Al | – | 27 | 11/17/1905 | M | S | Humboldt |
| Roberts, Fred | – | 18 | 11/17/1905 | M | S | Humboldt |
| Johnny | I | 28 | 12/ 7/1905 | M | S | Elko |
| Ibapah, Joe | I | 24 | 12/ 7/1905 | M | S | Elko |
| Kaiser, Charles | I | – | 5/24/1909 | M | | Douglas |
| Williams, George | I | – | 7/24/1909 | M | S | Esmeralda |
| Casey, Patrick C. | W | – | 8/16/1911 | M | S | Esmeralda |
| Mirkovich, Andrigi | W | – | 5/14/1913 | M | S | Nye |
| Jon, Gee | C | – | 2/ 8/1924 | M | S | Mineral |
| Jukich, Stanko | W | 29 | 5/21/1926 | M | S | White Pine |
| White, Robert H. | – | 41 | 6/ 2/1930 | M | S | Elko |
| Ceja, Luis | M | 28 | 9/ 4/1931 | M | S | Humboldt |
| Hall, John | W | 52 | 11/28/1932 | M | S | Clark |
| Miller, Ray Elmer | – | 34 | 5/ 8/1933 | M | | Clark |
| Behiter, Joseph | W | 56 | 7/13/1934 | M | S | Clark |
| Jones, Luther | – | 33 | 1/26/1937 | M | | Elko |
| Nadal, Domenico | – | 47 | 1/17/1939 | M | | Elko |
| Williamson, Burton F. | – | 43 | 11/21/1939 | M | | Churchill |
| Boyd, Wilson Henry | – | 44 | 5/28/1940 | M | | Elko |
| Kramer, John A. | W | 64 | 8/28/1942 | M | S | White Pine |
| McKinney, Floyd | W | 34 | 11/27/1943 | M | | Churchill |
| Plunkett, Raymond | W | 38 | 6/30/1944 | M | S | White Pine |
| Loveless, Floyd | – | 31 | 9/29/1944 | M | S | Elko |
| Sala, Albert | – | 35 | 8/23/1946 | M | S | Elko |
| Skaug, Paul | W | 26 | 1/10/1947 | M | S,U | Washoe |
| Blackwell, David | – | 18 | 4/22/1949 | M | S,U | Washoe |

| Name | Race | Age | Date of Execution | Offense | Appeal | County |
|------|------|-----|-------------------|---------|--------|--------|
| Varga, Laszlo | – | 24 | 6/ 7/1949 | M | S | Elko |
| Gambetta, Eugene Leo | W | 46 | 10/18/1949 | M | S | Washoe |
| Wiliams, James | – | 32 | 8/24/1950 | M | S | Elko |
| Gregory, Theodore W. | – | 40 | 1/29/1951 | M | S,U | Washoe |
| Arellano, Gregorio | – | 28 | 7/24/1951 | M | S | Washoe |
| Echevarria, Domingo | – | 60 | 11/13/1952 | M | S | Humboldt |
| Fouquette, Clayton | W | 41 | 4/13/1953 | M | S,U | Clark |
| Bourdiais, Ferdinand A. | W | 27 | 4/23/1954 | M | S | Clark |
| Linden, LeRoy L. | – | 47 | 7/15/1954 | M | | Washoe |
| Pedrini, Frank A. | – | 35 | 7/15/1954 | M | | Washoe |
| Steward, Earl Lewis | – | 42 | 2/24/1960 | M | S,U,NT | Elko |
| Archibald, Thayne | W | 22 | 8/23/1961 | M | S | Washoe |
| Bishop, Jesse | W | 46 | 10/23/1978 | M | S | Clark |

## NEW HAMPSHIRE

*Period of Executions*: 1869–1939
*Total Number*: 12
*Method*: Hanging

| Name | Race | Age | Date of Execution | Offense | Appeal | County |
|------|------|-----|-------------------|---------|--------|--------|
| Pike, Josiah L.[1] | W | 31 | 3/ 9/1869 | M | S | Rockingham |
| Evans, Franklin B. | W | 67 | 2/17/1874 | M | | Rockingham |
| Major, Elvin W. | W | 29 | 1/ 5/1877 | M | | Hillsboro |
| Lepage, Joseph | W | — | 3/15/1878 | M | S | Merrimack |
| Pinkham, John Q. | W | — | 3/14/1879 | M | | Stafford |
| Buzzell, Joseph P.[2] | W | 42 | 7/10/1879 | M | S | Carroll |
| Samon, Thomas | W | 36 | 4/17/1885 | M | | Belknap |
| Palmer, James | – | — | 5/ 1/1890 | M | S | Rockingham |
| Almy, Frank C. | W | 36 | 5/16/1893 | M | S | Grafton |
| Comery, Oscar J. | W | 34 | 2/18/1916 | M | S | Hillsboro |
| Small, Frederick L. | W | 50 | 1/15/1918 | M | S | Carroll |
| Long, Howard | W | 32 | 7/14/1939 | M | S | Merrimack |

[1]Pike's case (3/9/1869) was the forerunner of the Durham rule of insanity.
[2]Buzzell (7/10/1879) was acquitted of murder and later tried and convicted on conspiracy to murder.

# NEW JERSEY

*Period of Executions*: 1907–1963
*Total Number*: 161
*Method*: Electrocution
*Other Data*: After New Jersey began electrocuting its condemned felons at the state penitentiary, one man (identified in footnote 1) was hanged under local authority in the county of his conviction at the county seat designated. Mr. Espy comments that there is a "distinct possibility" that there may have been other hangings in New Jersey in the period 1907–March 23, 1909.

| Name | Race | Age | Date of Execution | Offense | Appeal | County |
|------|------|-----|-------------------|---------|--------|--------|
| DiGiovanni, Saverio | W | 31 | 12/11/1907 | M | | Somerset |
| Dorsey, Stephen | B | 26 | 12/17/1907 | M | | Camden |
| Gibson, Charles | B | 31 | 12/17/1907 | M | | Camden |
| Stewart, James | B | 22 | 2/ 4/1908 | M | | Camden |
| Matticks, Gilbert | B | 45 | 2/25/1908 | M | | Cumberland |
| Wilson, George | B | 27 | 3/ 3/1908 | M | | Essex |
| Tomasi, Michael | W | 25 | 3/ 9/1908 | M | S | Hunterdon |
| Ricci, Giancento | W | 35 | 12/22/1908 | M | | Middlesex |
| Montessana, John | W | 50 | 1/11/1909 | M | | Essex |
| Millilio, Sabino | W | 32 | 1/18/1909 | M | S | Hudson |
| Walker, Adolphus | B | 27 | 2/17/1909 | M | | Camden |
| Lang, Frederick[1] | – | – | 3/23/1909 | M | S | New Brunswich |
| Bertchey, Adolph | W | 49 | 8/10/1909 | M | S | Ocean |
| Donegan, Richard | W | 27 | 9/ 7/1909 | M | | Cumberland |
| Ves, George | W | 32 | 1/25/1910 | M | | Middlesex |
| Silverio, Petro | W | 39 | 8/ 9/1910 | M | S | Passaic |
| Rose, Arthur | B | 25 | 8/16/1910 | M | | Passaic |
| Savage, Howard | B | 35 | 8/30/1910 | M | S | Hudson |
| Toft, Gyula | W | 22 | 1/ 3/1911 | M | | Somerset |
| Sears, John | B | 33 | 3/15/1911 | M | | Mercer |
| Buntin, Christopher | B | 34 | 4/18/1911 | M | | Essex |
| Heideman, Frank | W | 27 | 5/23/1911 | M | | Monmouth |
| Luciano, Antonio | W | 28 | 1/16/1912 | M | | Essex |
| Bellini, Mariano | W | 25 | 3/12/1912 | M | | Middlesex |
| Kompovic, Alexander | W | 62 | 11/ 4/1912 | M | | Middlesex |
| Kiviatkowski, Joseph | W | 30 | 1/ 4/1913 | M | S | Hudson |
| Ford, Charles | W | 43 | 2/18/1913 | M | | Camden |
| Sylvanus, Sanders | W | 45 | 6/17/1913 | M | | Hunterdon |
| Diamond, William | B | 21 | 12/ 2/1913 | M | S | Mercer |
| Williams, Edwin | B | 30 | 12/16/1913 | M | | Camden |
| Overton, William | B | 27 | 12/30/1913 | M | S | Essex |
| Fiore, Antonio | W | 34 | 2/10/1914 | M | S | Essex |
| Longo, Raffael | W | 46 | 2/10/1914 | M | | Union |
| Dolan, John | W | 41 | 8/ 8/1914 | M | S | Essex |
| Toth, Joseph | W | 23 | 11/ 2/1914 | M | S | Middlesex |
| Ruggierri, Stefano | W | 17 | 12/22/1914 | M | | Somerset |
| Green, George | B | 24 | 1/ 5/1915 | M | | Monmouth |
| Johnson, Griffin J. | B | 46 | 1/ 5/1915 | M | | Burlington |
| Sparks, Michael | B | 16 | 1/ 5/1915 | M | | Monmouth |
| Kubaszewski, Adolph | W | 30 | 1/26/1915 | M | S | Essex |

| Name | Race | Age | Date of Execution | Offense | Appeal | County |
|------|------|-----|-------------------|---------|--------|--------|
| Martin, August | W | 40 | 2/ 2/1915 | M | | Hudson |
| Haronovick, Tony | W | 26 | 11/30/1915 | M | | Passaic |
| Murphy, Edgar | W | 28 | 12/ 7/1915 | M | S | Burlington |
| Swentain, Emil | W | 30 | 7/ 5/1916 | M | | Monmouth |
| Ashbridge, Wilson | W | 22 | 1/ 2/1917 | M | | Camden |
| Nicolisi, Francesco | W | 23 | 3/27/1917 | M | | Salem |
| Pettito, Calogero | W | 34 | 3/27/1917 | M | | Salem |
| Maywoon, Paul | W | 32 | 8/14/1917 | M | | Hunterdon |
| Iraca, Giovanni | W | 34 | 2/ 9/1918 | M | | Burlington |
| Conway, Thomas | W | 32 | 4/ 9/1918 | M | | Camden |
| Lavieri, Frank | W | 27 | 8/19/1919 | M | S | Middlesex |
| DePalma, Michael | W | 33 | 8/19/1919 | M | S | Middlesex |
| Palmieri, Gennaro | W | 24 | 8/19/1919 | M | S | Middlesex |
| Martin, Camill | W | 25 | 9/14/1920 | M | S | Essex |
| Schilling, Philip | W | 29 | 2/ 1/1921 | M | S | Essex |
| Carrigan, Stephen | W | 35 | 3/15/1921 | M | S | Essex |
| Pierson, Frederick | B | 40 | 7/26/1921 | M | | Warren |
| Lamble, Harold | W | 29 | 8/23/1921 | M | S | Union |
| Fitzsimmons, William | W | 32 | 8/23/1921 | M | | Middlesex |
| Shuck, Raymond | W | 29 | 8/30/1921 | M | S | Camden |
| James, Frank | W | 35 | 8/30/1921 | M | S | Camden |
| Knight, George | B | 26 | 1/17/1922 | M | S | Middlesex |
| Lively, Louis | B | 37 | 1/17/1922 | M | | Burlington |
| Gares, George | W | 56 | 2/ 2/1922 | M | | Middlesex |
| Morehouse, William | W | 57 | 5/31/1922 | M | S | Essex |
| Young, Guilford | W | 28 | 9/ 5/1922 | M | S | Camden |
| Battles, William | B | 19 | 2/13/1923 | M | | Essex |
| Sage, Frank | W | 31 | 1/15/1924 | M | S | Hudson |
| Carlino, Angelino | W | 38 | 1/29/1924 | M | S | Sussex |
| Turco, Antonio | W | 34 | 1/29/1924 | M | S | Sussex |
| Bagdanowitz, Anthony | W | 23 | 7/15/1924 | M | | Camden |
| Briglia, Tony | W | 25 | 7/15/1924 | M | | Gloucester |
| Allen, Edward | W | 25 | 7/15/1924 | M | | Gloucester |
| Taylor, Frank | W | 39 | 7/15/1924 | M | | Gloucester |
| Staub, Anthony | W | 59 | 7/22/1924 | M | | Passaic |
| Genese, Daniel | W | 24 | 12/15/1925 | M | S | Somerset |
| Lynch, James | W | 28 | 11/30/1926 | M | S | Bergen |
| Bruno, Peter | W | 32 | 1/11/1927 | M | | Essex |
| Fuersten, Paul | W | 45 | 5/17/1927 | M | S | Camden |
| Merra, Salvatore | W | 49 | 8/ 5/1927 | M | S | Essex |
| Juliano, Joseph | W | 35 | 11/18/1927 | M | S | Essex |
| Barone, Christopher | W | 21 | 11/18/1927 | M | S | Essex |
| Juliano, Nick Joseph | W | 28 | 11/18/1927 | M | S | Essex |
| Capozzi, Louis | W | 27 | 11/18/1927 | M | S | Essex |
| Yarrow, George | W | 28 | 6/ 1/1928 | M | S | Gloucester |
| Ware, David | B | 49 | 5/31/1929 | M | | Mercer |
| Kudzinkowski, Peter | W | 25 | 12/20/1929 | M | S | Hudson |
| Marrazzo, Joseph | W | 29 | 1/10/1930 | M | | Mercer |
| Pannatiere, Frank | W | 26 | 1/10/1930 | M | | Mercer |
| Close, Henry C. | W | 62 | 4/17/1930 | M | S | Union |
| Murray, John | W | 32 | 7/22/1930 | M | S | Essex |
| Rado, Joseph | W | 27 | 7/22/1930 | M | S | Essex |

| Name | Race | Age | Date of Execution | Offense | Appeal | County |
|---|---|---|---|---|---|---|
| Malanga, Louis | W | 23 | 7/22/1930 | M | S | Essex |
| Giampietro, Victor | W | 24 | 7/22/1930 | M | S | Essex |
| Calabrese, Joseph | W | 24 | 12/29/1930 | M | S | Essex |
| Cort, Arthur | W | 22 | 12/29/1930 | M | S | Essex |
| Gimbel, William | W | 21 | 12/29/1930 | M | S | Essex |
| Grosso, Daniel | W | 32 | 4/10/1931 | M | S | Union |
| Rusnak, Joseph | W | 25 | 7/14/1931 | M | S | Hudson |
| Nardella, Bonaventura | W | 43 | 7/20/1931 | M | S | Passaic |
| Leonar, Vincent Pablo | W | 36 | 7/27/1931 | M | S | Essex |
| Giordano, Peter | W | 20 | 12/30/1931 | M | S | Salem |
| Fithian, Charles | W | 22 | 12/30/1931 | M | S | Salem |
| Frazier, William | W | 31 | 4/ 1/1932 | M | S | Union |
| George, Raymond | B | 22 | 4/25/1932 | M | S | Hudson |
| Compo, Eugene | W | 22 | 6/ 8/1932 | M | S | Essex |
| DiDolce, Guisseppe | W | 43 | 7/20/1932 | M | S | Union |
| Hart, John | B | 32 | 4/ 5/1933 | M |  | Union |
| Fine, Louis | W | 50 | 6/12/1933 | M | S | Atlantic |
| Kumachinsky, Andreacy | W | 52 | 11/ 8/1933 | M |  | Hunterdon |
| Burrell, Melroyal | B | 33 | 3/26/1934 | M | S | Essex |
| Scarpone, Connie | W | 23 | 3/15/1935 | M | S | Mercer |
| Mule, Michael | W | 23 | 3/15/1935 | M | S | Mercer |
| Distefano, George | W | 25 | 3/15/1935 | M | S | Mercer |
| Barth, Kurt | W | 22 | 10/15/1935 | M | S | Essex |
| Favorito, John | W | 25 | 10/15/1935 | M | S | Bergen |
| Johnson, Romaine | B | 32 | 12/30/1935 | M |  | Cumberland |
| Hauptmann, Bruno Richard | W | — | 4/ 3/1936 | M | S,U | Hunterdon |
| Zied, Charles | W | 37 | 6/ 2/1936 | M | S | Camden |
| Metalski, Edward | W | 26 | 8/ 4/1936 | M | S | Middlesex |
| Heathcote, Orby O. | W | 35 | 1/21/1938 | M | S | Mercer |
| Stephan, William J. | W | 29 | 2/ 8/1938 | M | S | Camden |
| Roach, Doran | B | 27 | 3/22/1938 | M | S | Union |
| Faria, Albert | W | 30 | 4/ 1/1938 | M | S | Essex |
| Simmons, Harry | B | 26 | 4/ 1/1938 | M | S | Essex |
| Burrell, Smalley | B | 23 | 8/23/1938 | M | S | Gloucester |
| Brown, William A. | B | 23 | 8/23/1938 | M | S | Gloucester |
| Dworecki, Walter | W | 42 | 3/28/1940 | M | S | Camden |
| Zupkosky, William | W | 31 | 12/ 2/1941 | M | S | Essex |
| Foulds, George | W | 23 | 1/ 6/1942 | M | S | Mercer |
| Cox, Robert | B | 31 | 3/10/1942 | M | S | Camden |
| Swan, John | B | 26 | 2/15/1944 | M | S | Middlesex |
| Jefferson, Howard | B | 30 | 2/29/1944 | M | S | Salem |
| Degroat, Arthur | B | 35 | 11/ 5/1945 | M |  | Bergen |
| Molnar, Daniel | W | 23 | 11/27/1945 | M | S | Middlesex |
| Deegan, Robert | W | 28 | 12/11/1945 | M | S,NT | Bergen |
| Brooks, James | B | 24 | 4/23/1948 | M | S | Essex |
| Hicks, George | B | 22 | 9/28/1948 | M | S,U | Essex |
| Cole, George | B | 24 | 9/28/1948 | M | S,U | Essex |
| Cordasco, Ralph | W | 51 | 6/27/1949 | M | S | Essex |
| Collins, Alfred H. | B | 36 | 8/16/1949 | M | S | Gloucester |
| Tanslmore, Buford | B | 52 | 4/ 4/1950 | M | S | Essex |
| Auld, Howard | W | 26 | 5/27/1951 | M | S,F,U | Camden |

| Name | Race | Age | Date of Execution | Offense | Appeal | County |
|------|------|-----|-------------------|---------|--------|--------|
| Smith, Clarence | W | 38 | 5/13/1952 | M | S | Essex |
| Dunk, Frederick | W | 26 | 5/13/1952 | M | S | Essex |
| Jellison, Robert | W | 23 | 5/13/1952 | M | S | Essex |
| Peterson, Irving Donald | B | 33 | 8/26/1952 | M | S | Monmouth |
| Walker, Theodore | B | 22 | 7/27/1954 | M | S | Mercer |
| Beard, James | B | 40 | 8/17/1954 | M | S | Camden |
| Roscus, Frank J. | W | 34 | 1/ 4/1955 | M | S | Essex |
| Monohan, Eugene | W | 44 | 1/11/1955 | M | S,U | Union |
| Rios, Felipe Nives | P | 27 | 5/ 3/1955 | M | S | Camden |
| Rodriguez, Joaquin | P | 33 | 5/ 3/1955 | M | S | Camden |
| Cruz, Jose | P | 25 | 5/ 3/1955 | M | S | Camden |
| Stokes, Alfred | B | 21 | 9/ 2/1955 | M | S | Union |
| Wise, Harry | B | 22 | 9/ 2/1955 | M | S | Union |
| Wise, Albert | B | 24 | 9/ 2/1955 | M | S | Union |
| Tune, John Henry | B | 24 | 8/21/1956 | M | S,U | Essex |
| Sturdivant, Fred | B | 23 | 7/ 3/1962 | M | S,F,U | Essex |
| Ernst, Joseph | W | 22 | 7/31/1962 | M | S,F,U | Camden |
| Hudson, Ralph James | B | 43 | 1/22/1963 | M | S | Atlantic |

[1]Lang (3/23/1909) was hanged under local authority in the county of his conviction after New Jersey began electrocuting its condemned felons at the state penitentiary.

## NEW MEXICO

*Period of Executions*: 1933–1960
*Total Number*: 8
*Method*: Electrocution 1933–1956; lethal gas 1960
*Period of Abolition*: Capital punishment was abolished June 19, 1969, except for persons convicted of killing police officers or of committing a multiple slaying.

| Name | Race | Age | Date of Execution | Offense | Appeal | County |
|------|------|-----|-------------------|---------|--------|--------|
| Garduno, Santiago | M | — | 7/21/1933 | M | S | Rio Arriba |
| Johnson, Thomas | B | — | 7/21/1933 | M | S | Bernalillo |
| Talamantes, Pete | — | — | 5/10/1946 | M | S | McKinley |
| Young, Louis | B | — | 6/13/1947 | M | S | McKinley |
| Johnson, Arthur F. | — | — | 2/19/1954 | M | S | Chaves |
| Heisler, Frederick W. | W | 33 | 10/29/1954 | M | S | Quay |
| Upton, James L. | — | — | 2/24/1956 | M | S | Bernalillo |
| Nelson, David Cooper | W | — | 2/ 8/1960 | M | S,U,NT | Valencia |

## NEW YORK

*Period of Executions*: 1890–1963
*Total Number*: 695
*Method*: Electrocution
*Period of Abolition*: Capital punishment was abolished June 1, 1965, except for murder of policemen and prison guards.
*Other Data*: Practically all capital cases in New York in recent times have been appealed. There are no opinions on many of them, however. From September 1, 1914, all death sentences were to be executed at Sing Sing. Five cases (identified in footnote 1), executed at Auburn after September 1, 1914, had been sentenced to death before the requirement that executions be performed at Sing Sing.

| Name | Race | Age | Date of Execution | Offense | Appeal | County |
|------|------|-----|-------------------|---------|--------|--------|
| AUBURN | | | | | | |
| Kemmler, William | – | – | 8/ 6/1890 | M | S,U | Erie |
| Tice, Joseph L. | – | 63 | 5/18/1892 | M | S | Monroe |
| Fitzthum, John | W | – | 6/26/1893 | M | S | Erie |
| Taylor, William G. | B | 27 | 7/27/1893 | M | S | Cayuga |
| Johnson, John | B | 39 | 11/14/1893 | M | S | Cayuga |
| Wilson, Charles R. (Lucius) | – | 25 | 5/14/1894 | M | S | Onondaga |
| Lake, William | W | 24 | 4/ 4/1895 | M | S | Orleans |
| Hoch, John | W | 37 | 1/20/1897 | M | S | Lewis |
| Constantino, Giuseppe | W | 31 | 6/22/1897 | M | S | Oneida |
| Powley, Robert G. | W | 35 | 6/29/1897 | M | | Niagara |
| Burgess, Charles | W | 39 | 12/ 7/1897 | M | S | Cayuga |
| Rice, Oscar E. | W | 45 | 8/ 2/1899 | M | S | Chautauqua |
| Kennedy, John | B | 28 | 8/ 2/1899 | M | S | Erie |
| Wennerholm, Frank | W | 28 | 7/16/1901 | M | S | Chautauqua |
| Czolgosz, Leon F. | W | 28 | 10/29/1901 | M | | Erie |
| Krist, Fred | W | 31 | 11/20/1901 | M | S | Tioga |
| Truck, John | W | 43 | 11/18/1902 | M | S | Cortland |
| Egnor, Clarence | W | 26 | 9/14/1903 | M | S | Cayuga |
| White, Frank | B | 22 | 12/29/1903 | M | S | Oswego |
| Giorgio, Antonio | W | 27 | 8/30/1904 | M | | Allegheny |
| Versacia, Guiseppe | W | 21 | 9/ 5/1904 | M | | Allegheny |
| Boggiano, Nelson | W | 23 | 12/13/1904 | M | S | Erie |
| Manzer, Henry Waverly | W | 30 | 9/12/1905 | M | S | Oswego |
| Sexton, Harold (Edward) | W | 36 | 4/16/1907 | M | S | Ontario |
| Giardi, Carlo | W | 37 | 5/21/1907 | M | | Tompkins |
| Bonier, Charles | W | 75 | 7/31/1907 | M | S | Erie |
| Gillette, Chester | W | 23 | 3/30/1908 | M | S | Herkimer |
| DelVermo, Andrea | W | 24 | 11/16/1908 | M | S | Oneida |
| Brasch, William S. | W | 23 | 11/28/1908 | M | S | Monroe |
| Randazzio, Salvatore | W | 22 | 3/16/1909 | M | S | Cattaraugus |
| Farmer, Mary (Female) | W | 29 | 3/29/1909 | M | S | Jefferson |
| Hill, Pacy | W | 41 | 4/26/1909 | M | S | Cattaraugus |
| Scott, William | W | 22 | 6/14/1909 | M | S | Chenango |
| Sanpucci, Guiseppe | W | 23 | 7/ 6/1909 | M | S | Allegheny |
| Rizzio, Teodoro | W | 35 | 11/22/1909 | M | | Oneida |

| Name | Race | Age | Date of Execution | Offense | Appeal | County |
|------|------|-----|-------------------|---------|--------|--------|
| Hill, Earl B. | W | 20 | 4/18/1910 | M | S | Chenango |
| Gilbert, William | B | 29 | 7/ 7/1910 | M | S | Cattaraugus |
| Nesco, Joseph | W | 44 | 5/ 3/1911 | M | S | Seneca |
| Nacco, Joseph | W | 33 | 6/26/1911 | M | S | Niagara |
| Pasquale, Domenico D. | W | 26 | 3/12/1912 | M | S | Monroe |
| Friedman, Ralph | W | 25 | 6/18/1912 | M | S | Monroe |
| Kuhn, Jacob | W | 24 | 6/18/1912 | M | S | Monroe |
| Maruszewski, John | W | 28 | 8/14/1912 | M | S | Erie |
| Williams, James | B | 21 | 9/16/1912 | M | S | Livingston |
| Twiman, William | B | 35 | 3/31/1913 | M | S | Monroe |
| Ciavarella, Raeffaele | W | 30 | 5/21/1913 | M | S | Oswego |
| Goslinski, Michael | W | 22 | 6/ 4/1913 | M | S | Erie |
| Sharpe, Nelson | W | 40 | 12/10/1913 | M | S | Monroe |
| Coyer, George | W | 45 | 8/31/1914 | M | S | Cattaraugus |
| DeGioia, Guisseppi | W | 31 | 8/31/1914 | M | S | Erie |
| Sarzano, Michael | W | 27 | 12/ 9/1914 | M | S | Erie |
| Cino, Guiseppe | W | 23 | 3/22/1915 | M | S | Erie |
| Buoninsegno, Vincenzo | W | 36 | 5/31/1915 | M | S | Oneida |
| Dunn, David | W | 19 | 7/ 2/1915 | M | S | Steuben |
| Sprague, Charles, 2nd | W | 32 | 5/ 1/1916 | M | S | Yates |

## CLINTON

| Name | Race | Age | Date of Execution | Offense | Appeal | County |
|------|------|-----|-------------------|---------|--------|--------|
| Wood, Joseph | W | 37 | 8/ 2/1892 | M | S | Warren |
| Lash, Kornell | – | – | 1/16/1893 | M | S | Schenectady |
| Martello, Sapione | W | – | 6/ 6/1893 | M | S | Saratoga |
| Foy, Martin | – | – | 10/23/1893 | M | S | Saratoga |
| Smith, George H. | – | – | 10/29/1895 | M | S | Albany |
| Davis, Charles N. | – | – | 10/29/1895 | M | S | Albany |
| Shea, Bartholomew | W | 25 | 2/11/1896 | M | S | Rensselaer |
| Zlamel, Joseph | W | 35 | 4/ 4/1896 | M | | Fulton |
| Conroy, Frank | – | – | 8/10/1897 | M | S | St. Lawrence |
| Middleton, C.D. | – | – | 7/29/1902 | M | | Warren |
| Sullivan, James | – | – | 3/24/1903 | M | S | Scoharie |
| O'Connor, William | – | – | 7/ 7/1903 | M | S | Scoharie |
| Van Wormer, Willis | W | 27 | 10/ 1/1903 | M | S | Columbia |
| Van Wormer, Burton | W | 24 | 10/ 1/1903 | M | S | Columbia |
| Van Wormer, Frederick | W | 21 | 10/ 1/1903 | M | S | Columbia |
| Mooney, Allen | – | – | 5/ 3/1904 | M | S | Franklin |
| Combs, Leslie | W | 20 | 2/16/1909 | M | | St. Lawrence |
| Jackson, Frank | B | – | 1/ 5/1910 | M | S | Washington |
| Farnaro, A. | – | – | 6/21/1910 | M | S | Rensselaer |
| Ferrara, Dominico | W | – | 1/ 6/1911 | M | S | Albany |
| Leonardo, Vincent | W | – | 1/ 6/1911 | M | S | Albany |
| Ford, Samuel | – | – | 2/ 1/1911 | M | S | Ulster |
| Green, Charles | – | – | 7/31/1911 | M | S | Albany |
| Caruso, C. | – | – | 3/20/1912 | M | S | Greene |
| Consuli, Nicolo | W | – | 5/28/1912 | M | S | Rensselaer |
| Poulin, Frederick A. | W | – | 2/12/1913 | M | S | Rensselaer |

| Name | Race | Age | Date of Execution | Offense | Appeal | County |
|------|------|-----|-------------------|---------|--------|--------|
| SING SING | | | | | | |
| Smiler, Harris A. | W | 32 | 7/ 7/1891 | M | S,F,U | N.Y. |
| Slocum, James | W | 22 | 7/ 7/1891 | M | S,F,U | N.Y. |
| Wood, Joseph | B | 21 | 7/ 7/1891 | M | S,F,U | N.Y. |
| Jugigo, Subihick | J | 35 | 7/ 7/1891 | M | S,F,U | N.Y. |
| Loppy, Martin D. | W | 51 | 12/ 7/1891 | M | S | N.Y. |
| McElvaine, Charles | W | 20 | 2/ 8/1892 | M | S,F,U | Kings |
| Cotto, Jeremiah | W | 40 | 3/28/1892 | M | S | Kings |
| McGuire, Fred | W | 24 | 12/19/1892 | M | S | Orange |
| Hamilton, James L. | B | 40 | 4/ 3/1893 | M | S | Queens |
| Harris, Carlyle W. | W | 23 | 5/ 8/1893 | M | S | N.Y. |
| Osmond, John L. | W | 30 | 6/12/1893 | M | S | N.Y. |
| Delfino, John | W | 26 | 12/ 4/1893 | M | S | Kings |
| Johnson, Matthew | B | 33 | 2/16/1894 | M | S | N.Y. |
| Hampton, David | B | 27 | 1/28/1895 | M | S | N.Y. |
| Buchanan, Robert W. | W | 31 | 7/ 1/1895 | M | S | N.Y. |
| Leach, Richard | W | 31 | 8/ 5/1895 | M | S | N.Y. |
| Herman, Louis P. | W | 25 | 4/23/1896 | M | S | N.Y. |
| Pustolka, Charles | W | 35 | 4/23/1896 | M | S | N.Y. |
| Feigenbaum, Carl | W | 54 | 4/14/1896 | M | S | N.Y. |
| Mayhew, Arthur | B | 26 | 3/12/1897 | M | S | Queens |
| Scott, Howard A. | B | 30 | 6/14/1897 | M | S | N.Y. |
| Barker, John H. | B | 42 | 7/ 6/1897 | M | S | Westchester |
| Sutherland, Hadley A. | B | 20 | 1/10/1898 | M | S | Kings |
| Thorn, Martin | W | 33 | 8/ 1/1898 | M | S | Queens |
| Decker, Beilor | B | 30 | 1/ 9/1899 | M | S | Richmond |
| Place, Martha (Female) | W | 44 | 3/20/1899 | M | S | Kings |
| Braun, Adrian | W | 38 | 5/29/1899 | M | S | Westchester |
| Fullerson, Lewis | B | 30 | 7/31/1899 | M | S | N.Y. |
| McDonald, Michael | W | 24 | 7/31/1899 | M | S | N.Y. |
| Ferraro, Antonio | W | 37 | 2/26/1900 | M | S | Kings |
| Meyer, Fritz | W | 46 | 5/21/1900 | M | S | N.Y. |
| Mullen, Joseph | W | 30 | 7/23/1900 | M | S | N.Y. |
| Neufeld, William | W | 27 | 1/14/1901 | M | S | N.Y. |
| Priori, Lorenzo | W | 27 | 2/ 6/1901 | M | S | N.Y. |
| Pugh, Benjamin | B | 21 | 8/ 5/1901 | M | S | Kings |
| Zachello, Joseph | W | 28 | 8/29/1901 | M | S | Richmond |
| Hall, Aaron | W | 24 | 8/ 4/1902 | M | S | N.Y. |
| Triola, Antonio | W | 32 | 5/25/1903 | M | S | N.Y. |
| Flannigan, Arthur | W | 27 | 6/ 8/1903 | M | S | N.Y. |
| Turekofski, Toni | W | 32 | 8/ 3/1903 | M | | Kings |
| Conklin, Patrick | W | 31 | 9/ 8/1903 | M | S | N.Y. |
| Gaimari, Carmine | W | 31 | 11/23/1903 | M | S | N.Y. |
| Ennis, William H. | W | 33 | 12/14/1903 | M | S | Kings |
| Tobin, Thomas | W | 38 | 3/14/1904 | M | S | N.Y. |
| Koepping, Albert | W | 22 | 6/13/1904 | M | S | Orange |
| Borgstrom, Oscar | W | 55 | 6/13/1904 | M | S | Westchester |
| Burness, Frank H. | W | 45 | 6/27/1904 | M | S | Kings |
| Spencer, Wiliam | W | 38 | 1/ 9/1905 | M | S | N.Y. |
| Rimieri, Frank | W | 23 | 2/20/1905 | M | S | Kings |
| Koenig, Adolph | W | 23 | 2/20/1905 | M | S | N.Y. |

| Name | Race | Age | Date of Execution | Offense | Appeal | County |
|---|---|---|---|---|---|---|
| Ebelt, Martin[1] | W | 24 | 4/10/1905 | M | S | Westchester |
| Jackson, Charles[1] | B | 31 | 7/17/1905 | M | S | N.Y. |
| Breen, James[1] | W | 24 | 7/17/1905 | M | S | N.Y. |
| Granger, George[1] | W | 20 | 2/25/1907 | M | S | Duchess |
| Furlong, Frank[1] | W | 21 | 3/ 4/1907 | M | S | N.Y. |
| Johnson, John J. | W | 37 | 6/24/1907 | M | S | Westchester |
| Nelson, William | B | 43 | 7/29/1907 | M | S | N.Y. |
| Wenzel, John | W | 33 | 11/18/1907 | M | S | Kings |
| Strollo, Antonio | W | 24 | 3/ 9/1908 | M | S | N.Y. |
| Rogers, Charles H. | W | 38 | 7/20/1908 | M | S | Orange |
| Landiero, Antonio | W | 27 | 7/20/1908 | M | S | N.Y. |
| Governale, Salvatore | W | 25 | 2/ 1/1909 | M | S | N.Y. |
| Jones, William | B | 27 | 3/ 8/1909 | M | S | Nassau |
| Carlin, Bernard | W | 22 | 4/12/1909 | M | S | Kings |
| Hampartjoomian, Bedros | W | 24 | 12/ 6/1909 | M | S | N.Y. |
| Morse, William | B | 25 | 1/ 3/1910 | M | S | Kings |
| Barbuto, John | W | 24 | 1/ 3/1910 | M | S | Orange |
| Giro, Carlo | W | 35 | 2/23/1910 | M | S | Kings |
| Bowser, Charles | B | 38 | 2/28/1910 | M | S | N.Y. |
| Smyth, John | W | 32 | 3/14/1910 | M | S | Kings |
| Coleman, Gilbert | B | — | 5/ 9/1910 | M | S | N.Y. |
| Loose, Carl | W | 57 | 7/25/1910 | M | S | N.Y. |
| Cambaro, Giuseppe | W | 43 | 7/25/1910 | M | S | N.Y. |
| Austin, Samuel | B | 30 | 1/ 3/1911 | M | S | Westchester |
| Gebhart, Fred | W | 39 | 6/12/1911 | M | S | Suffolk |
| Barnes, Thomas | W | 38 | 6/12/1911 | M | S | Kings |
| Serimarco, Giuseppe | W | 27 | 7/17/1911 | M | S | Westchester |
| Wood, Robert F. | W | 47 | 7/17/1911 | M | S | N.Y. |
| Schermerhorn, Frank | W | 23 | 11/20/1911 | M | S | Dutchess |
| Falletta, Peitro | W | 33 | 11/20/1911 | M | S | Westchester |
| Brown, Bert L. | B | 22 | 11/20/1911 | M | S | Westchester |
| Mangano, Philip | W | 53 | 1/ 8/1912 | M | S | N.Y. |
| Wolter, Albert | W | 20 | 1/29/1912 | M | S | N.Y. |
| Swenton, Charles | B | 29 | 2/ 5/1912 | M | S | N.Y. |
| Condido, Salvatore | W | 27 | 5/ 6/1912 | M | S | Rockland |
| Cerelli, Giuseppe | W | 23 | 7/ 8/1912 | M | S | Westchester |
| Wiliams, George | B | 31 | 7/ 8/1912 | M | S | Westchester |
| Zanz, Santo | W | 25 | 7/ 8/1912 | M | | Westchester |
| Collins, John W. | B | 23 | 8/12/1912 | M | S | N.Y. |
| Demarco, Filepo[2] | W | 25 | 8/12/1912 | M | S | Westchester |
| Cona, Vincenzo[2] | W | 22 | 8/12/1912 | M | S | Westchester |
| Giusto, Angelo[2] | W | 22 | 8/12/1912 | M | S | Westchester |
| Cali, Lorenzo L.[2] | W | 26 | 8/12/1912 | M | S | Westchester |
| DeMarco, Salvatore[2] | W | 28 | 8/12/1912 | M | S | Westchester |
| Ferrone, Joseph | W | 30 | 8/12/1912 | M | S | N.Y. |
| Dell'omo, Matteo | W | 33 | 12/16/1912 | M | S | Kings |
| Garfalo, Joseph | W | 38 | 2/10/1913 | M | S | Suffolk |
| Bishop, George | B | 23 | 2/10/1913 | M | S | Kings |
| Cardillo, Donato | W | 22 | 2/10/1913 | M | S | Kings |
| Linglui, William | W | 30 | 5/ 5/1913 | M | S | N.Y. |
| Mulraney, John | W | 31 | 5/19/1913 | M | S | N.Y. |
| Patini, Gregorio | W | 21 | 6/ 2/1913 | M | S | Westchester |

| Name | Race | Age | Date of Execution | Offense | Appeal | County |
|------|------|-----|-------------------|---------|--------|--------|
| Manco, Andrew | W | 28 | 7/ 2/1913 | M | S | Orange |
| Grace, Antonio | W | 25 | 8/ 4/1913 | M | S | Orange |
| Mulchfeldt, Francis W. | W | 31 | 1/19/1914 | M | S | N.Y. |
| Horowitz, Harry[3] | W | 24 | 4/13/1914 | M | S | N.Y. |
| Cirofici, Frank[3] | W | 27 | 4/13/1914 | M | S | N.Y. |
| Seidenschmer, Jacob[3] | W | 21 | 4/13/1914 | M | S | N.Y. |
| Rosenberg, Louis[3] | W | 24 | 4/13/1914 | M | S | N.Y. |
| Robacci, Pietro | W | 29 | 6/22/1914 | M | S | Westchester |
| Bressen, William | W | 27 | 9/ 2/1914 | M | S | Kings |
| McKenna, Joseph J. | W | 33 | 9/ 2/1914 | M | S | N.Y. |
| Hing, Eng | C | 20 | 2/ 5/1915 | M | S | N.Y. |
| Dock, Lee | C | 30 | 2/ 5/1915 | M | S | N.Y. |
| Kane, Robert | W | 28 | 2/26/1915 | M | S | Kings |
| Campanelli, Vincenzo | W | 36 | 2/26/1915 | M | S | N.Y. |
| Vogt, Oscar | W | 37 | 2/26/1915 | M | S | N.Y. |
| Ferri, Joseph | W | 26 | 6/30/1915 | M | S | Nassau |
| Beycker, Charles | W | 43 | 7/30/1915 | M | S | N.Y. |
| Haynes, Samuel | B | 52 | 7/30/1915 | M | S | Putnam |
| Draniewicz, Karol | W | 23 | 8/27/1915 | M | S | N.Y. |
| Trapey, Thomas | W | 42 | 9/ 3/1915 | M | S | Kings |
| Venditi, Pasquale | W | 47 | 9/ 3/1915 | M | S | Kings |
| Salemne, Antonio | W | 26 | 9/ 3/1915 | M | S | Monroe |
| Roach, Louis M. | W | 40 | 9/ 3/1915 | M | S | Montgomery |
| Perry, William | B | 27 | 9/ 3/1915 | M | S | N.Y. |
| Tolley, Worthy | W | 49 | 12/17/1915 | M | S | Greene |
| Marquardt, Ludwig | W | 58 | 12/17/1915 | M | S | Ulster |
| Ponton, Antonio | W | 28 | 1/ 7/1916 | M | S | Schenectady |
| Marendi, Giuseppe | W | 28 | 2/ 4/1916 | M | S | Kings |
| Schmidt, Hans | W | 33 | 2/18/1916 | M | S | N.Y. |
| Watson, Walter | W | 41 | 3/ 3/1916 | M | S | Kings |
| Champlain, Roy | W | 30 | 6/ 2/1916 | M | S | Allegheny |
| Supe, Giovanni | W | 31 | 6/ 2/1916 | M | S | Westchester |
| Shillitoni, Oreste[4] | W | 23 | 6/30/1916 | M | S | N.Y. |
| Bradford, Allen | B | 29 | 8/ 4/1916 | M | S | N.Y. |
| Hanel, Joseph | W | 36 | 9/ 1/1916 | M | S | Kings |
| Trybus, Jan | W | 33 | 9/ 1/1916 | M | S | Genesee |
| Bambrick, Thomas | W | 26 | 10/ 7/1916 | M | S | N.Y. |
| Kumrow, Charles | W | 20 | 12/19/1916 | M | S | Erie |
| Millstein, Stanley J. | W | 19 | 12/19/1916 | M | S | Oneida |
| Vun der Corput, Petrius C.[5] | W | 25 | 4/21/1917 | M | S | N.Y. |
| Impoluzzo, Antonio | W | 20 | 5/17/1917 | M | S | N.Y. |
| Waite, Arthur Warren | W | 29 | 5/24/1917 | M | S | N.Y. |
| Waldeman, Arthur | W | 24 | 7/12/1917 | M | S | N.Y. |
| Mulholland, Joseph A. | W | 29 | 8/30/1917 | M | S | N.Y. |
| Schuster, Alex | W | 25 | 8/30/1917 | M | S | N.Y. |
| Kushnieruk, John | W | 20 | 5/23/1918 | M | S | Essex |
| Lischuk, Stephen | W | — | 6/13/1918 | M | S | Essex |
| Briggs, Alvah | W | 25 | 6/13/1918 | M | S | St. Lawrence |
| Ostransky, Hyman | W | 38 | 6/13/1918 | M | S | N.Y. |
| Berg, Johann | W | 45 | 7/18/1918 | M | S | Kings |
| Roberto, Guisseppe | W | 23 | 8/30/1918 | M | S | Erie |
| Van Poueke, C.E. | W | 49 | 10/ 3/1918 | M | S | Bronx |

| Name | Race | Age | Date of Execution | Offense | Appeal | County |
|------|------|-----|-------------------|---------|--------|--------|
| Cohen, Jacob | W | 28 | 12/19/1918 | M | S | Kings |
| Cleveland, Alton | W | 36 | 1/ 9/1919 | M | S | Kings |
| Ferraro, Giovanni | W | 36 | 3/21/1919 | M | S | Cattaraugus |
| Esposito, Vincenzo | W | 31 | 1/ 8/1920 | M | S | Schenectady |
| Hamby, Gordon Fawcett | W | 27 | 1/29/1920 | M | S | Kings |
| Harrison, Richard | W | 26 | 5/13/1920 | M | S | N.Y. |
| Cantine, Chester | W | 21 | 5/13/1920 | M | S | Dutchess |
| Jankowski, Leo | W | 26 | 5/28/1920 | M | S | Clinton |
| Levandowski, Walter | W | 25 | 5/28/1920 | M | S | Clinton |
| Byrd, James N. | B | 26 | 7/22/1920 | M | S | Ulster |
| Hyatt, Elmer | W | 19 | 7/29/1920 | M | S | Monroe |
| Egan, John P. | W | 25 | 8/27/1920 | M | S | Bronx |
| Kelley, Frank | W | 40 | 8/27/1920 | M | S | Kings |
| Bojanowski, Walter | W | 26 | 9/ 9/1920 | M | S | Erie |
| Baker, Howard | W | 20 | 12/ 9/1920 | M | S | Wayne |
| Usefof, Joseph | W | 23 | 12/ 9/1920 | M | S | Bronx |
| Milano, Joseph | W | 22 | 12/ 9/1920 | M | S | Bronx |
| McLaughlin, Charles W. | W | 23 | 12/ 9/1920 | M | S | Bronx |
| Cassidy, James P. | W | 27 | 12/ 9/1920 | M | S | Bronx |
| Garcia, Henry | W | 38 | 1/27/1921 | M | S | Cattaraugus |
| Sanchez, A.L. | W | 33 | 1/27/1921 | M | S | Cattaraugus |
| Walker, Jesse | W | 20 | 2/10/1921 | M | S | Kings |
| Nichols, Guy | W | 25 | 3/13/1921 | M | S | Kings |
| Odell, James L. | W | 24 | 4/29/1921 | M | S | Monroe |
| Cassalano, Michael | W | 29 | 5/ 5/1921 | M | S | Queens |
| Bulge, John P. | B | 27 | 7/21/1921 | M | S | Kings |
| Giordano, Angelo | W | 42 | 9/ 1/1921 | M | S | N.Y. |
| Van Reed, Harry B. | W | 36 | 9/ 1/1921 | M | S | N.Y. |
| McNally, Edward J. | W | 30 | 9/15/1921 | M | S | Richmond |
| Brazee, George | W | 59 | 12/15/1921 | M | S | Otsego |
| Marweg, William J. | W | 41 | 1/12/1922 | M | S | Erie |
| Persons, Edward | W | 41 | 1/12/1922 | M | S | Chautauqua |
| Mulford, Raymond F. | W | 29 | 1/12/1922 | M | S | Erie |
| Givner, Harry | W | 27 | 2/ 2/1922 | M | S | Westchester |
| Slover, Floyd E. | W | 21 | 2/ 2/1922 | M | S | Erie |
| McCormick, George F. | W | 22 | 3/ 2/1922 | M | S | N.Y. |
| Kubel, Lawrence | W | 37 | 3/23/1922 | M | S | Nassau |
| Torrence, Lawrence | W | 29 | 4/20/1922 | M | S | Erie |
| Ebanista, Luigi | W | 23 | 6/ 8/1922 | M | S | Rockland |
| Librero, Albert | W | 24 | 6/ 8/1922 | M | S | Rockland |
| Rosenwasser, Julius | W | 26 | 6/ 8/1922 | M | S | N.Y. |
| Bell, William | B | 27 | 6/15/1922 | M | S | Queens |
| Rossi, Michael | W | 65 | 6/29/1922 | M | S | Westchester |
| Taizo, Saito | O | 23 | 7/20/1922 | M | S | N.Y. |
| Nunziato, Peter | W | 28 | 7/20/1922 | M | S | Queens |
| Smith, Herbert W. | W | 33 | 8/31/1922 | M | S | Chenango |
| Boddy, Luther | B | 22 | 8/31/1922 | M | S | N.Y. |
| Brown, Henry | B | 23 | 1/25/1923 | M | S | Bronx |
| Zampelli, Joseph | W | 25 | 2/15/1923 | M | S | Queens |
| Westling, A.J. | W | 38 | 2/15/1923 | M | S | Bronx |
| Rabasvotch, A. | W | 34 | 3/ 1/1923 | M | S | Kings |
| Evans, William J. | W | 24 | 4/19/1923 | M | S | Richmond |

| Name | Race | Age | Date of Execution | Offense | Appeal | County |
|------|------|-----|-------------------|---------|--------|--------|
| Fradiano, Michael | W | 50 | 4/26/1923 | M | S | Bronx |
| Alfano, Joseph | W | 24 | 4/26/1923 | M | S | Queens |
| Kindlon, Thomas | W | 21 | 6/ 7/1923 | M | S | Albany |
| Lester, Thomas | W | 23 | 6/ 7/1923 | M | S | Albany |
| Smith, Key P. | W | 37 | 6/22/1923 | M | S | Kings |
| Blackstone, Robert J. | B | 27 | 7/12/1923 | M | S | Bronx |
| Amendola, Raeffaele | W | 34 | 8/30/1923 | M | S | Oneida |
| Semione, Emilio | W | 38 | 12/ 6/1923 | M | S | Erie |
| Becker, Abraham | W | 35 | 13/13/1923 | M | S | Bronx |
| Hacker, George W. | W | 34 | 12/13/1923 | M | S | Broome |
| Santanello, Harry | W | 29 | 12/13/1923 | M | S | Broome |
| Viandante, Antonio | W | 41 | 4/10/1924 | M | S | Onondaga |
| Norkin, Reuben | W | 32 | 4/17/1924 | M | S | Bronx |
| Mastrota, Alberigo | W | 32 | 6/12/1924 | M | S | Queens |
| Lozado, Eulogia | F | 26 | 7/24/1924 | M | S | N.Y. |
| Emieleta, John | W | 23 | 1/ 8/1925 | M | S | Suffolk |
| Rys, John | W | 19 | 1/ 8/1925 | M | S | Suffolk |
| Smith, Edward | W | 37 | 1/15/1925 | M | S | Erie |
| Geary, Ambrose | W | 38 | 1/15/1925 | M | S | Erie |
| Malcolm, Harry | W | 34 | 1/15/1925 | M | S | Erie |
| Ferranti, Nick | W | 44 | 1/22/1925 | M | S | Broome |
| Lerma, Florencio | W | 26 | 1/22/1925 | M | S | Erie |
| Leonard, John T. | W | 23 | 1/22/1925 | M | S | Bronx |
| Murphy, Patrick | W | 30 | 3/12/1925 | M | S | Erie |
| Minnick, Frank H. | W | 34 | 3/12/1925 | M | S | Erie |
| Diamond, Joseph | W | 22 | 4/30/1925 | M | S | Kings |
| Diamond, Morris | W | 28 | 4/30/1925 | M | S | Kings |
| Farina, John | W | 23 | 4/30/1925 | M | S | Kings |
| Durkin, John | W | 25 | 8/27/1925 | M | S | Bronx |
| Miller, Julius | B | 44 | 9/17/1925 | M | S | N.Y. |
| Rapito, Luigi | W | 34 | 1/29/1926 | M | S | Cayuga |
| Klatt, Emil | W | 35 | 1/29/1926 | M | S | Westchester |
| Wasser, Matthew | W | 27 | 2/ 4/1926 | M | S | Niagara |
| Mimms, Ernest T. | B | 29 | 2/ 4/1926 | M | S | Bronx |
| Daley, Frank A. | W | 21 | 6/24/1926 | M | S | Westchester |
| Wing, Sam | C | 19 | 7/15/1926 | M | S | Kings |
| Hoyer, William W. | B | 26 | 8/19/1926 | M | S | N.Y. |
| Demaio, David | W | 34 | 8/19/1926 | M | S | Westchester |
| Garguila, John | W | 19 | 8/26/1926 | M | S | N.Y. |
| Brescia, Cosimo | W | 19 | 8/26/1926 | M | S | Kings |
| Brennan, John J. | W | 28 | 12/ 2/1926 | M | S | Kings |
| Barszyouk, Kasimir | W | 21 | 12/ 9/1926 | M | S | Kings |
| Barszyouk, William | W | 28 | 12/ 9/1926 | M | S | Kings |
| Maxwell, John | W | 21 | 12/ 9/1926 | M | S | Kings |
| Williams, George | B | 27 | 1/ 6/1927 | M | S | N.Y. |
| Humes, Edgar | B | 23 | 1/ 6/1927 | M | S | N.Y. |
| Goldson, Charles | B | 23 | 1/ 6/1927 | M | S | N.Y. |
| Bradley, Ben | B | 28 | 1/13/1927 | M | S | N.Y. |
| Kosmowski, Mike | W | 36 | 1/20/1927 | M | S | Erie |
| Hilton, Paul E. | W | 27 | 2/17/1927 | M | S | Queens |
| Paretti, Tony | W | 35 | 2/17/1927 | M | S | Kings |
| Frlia, Giuseppe | W | 33 | 3/17/1927 | M | S | Monroe |

| Name | Race | Age | Date of Execution | Offense | Appeal | County |
|------|------|-----|-------------------|---------|--------|--------|
| Provenzano, Giuseppe | W | 24 | 3/17/1927 | M | S | Monroe |
| Wagner, William | W | 24 | 7/14/1927 | M | S | Kings |
| Heslin, Peter | W | 28 | 7/21/1927 | M | S | N.Y. |
| Albrecht, Charles | W | 33 | 9/29/1927 | M | S | N.Y. |
| Seiler, Peter A. | W | 22 | 12/16/1927 | M | S | N.Y. |
| Ricci, George A. | W | 33 | 12/16/1927 | M | S | Kings |
| Mason, Louis | B | 24 | 1/ 5/1928 | M | S | Erie |
| Doran, Charles J. | W | 25 | 1/ 5/1928 | M | S | Albany |
| Snyder, Ruth Brown (Female) | W | 33 | 1/12/1928 | M | S | Queens |
| Gray, H. Judd | W | 36 | 1/12/1928 | M | S | Queens |
| Ecker, Philip | W | 21 | 3/ 1/1928 | M | S | N.Y. |
| Baldwin, Frank | B | 21 | 4/ 6/1928 | M | S | Seneca |
| Wagner, William L. | W | 24 | 6/21/1928 | M | S | Erie |
| Lefkowitz, Joseph | W | 30 | 7/19/1928 | M | S | Kings |
| Lie, Ludwig H. | W | 39 | 8/ 2/1928 | M | S | Kings |
| Kalinowski, Alexander | W | 50 | 8/ 9/1928 | M | S | Cayuga |
| Graham, Daniel J. | W | 26 | 8/ 9/1928 | M | S | N.Y. |
| Appel, George | W | 41 | 8/ 9/1928 | M | S | Queens |
| Miller, Martin | B | 32 | 8/30/1928 | M | S | Kings |
| Moran, Thomas | W | 20 | 12/14/1928 | M | S | Kings |
| Fisher, Israel | W | 19 | 1/24/1929 | M | S | Kings |
| Helfant, Isidore | W | 21 | 1/24/1929 | M | S | Kings |
| Dreitzer, Harry | W | 23 | 1/24/1929 | M | S | Kings |
| Fabri, John | W | 31 | 8/29/1929 | M | S | Onondaga |
| Kowalski, Frank | W | 25 | 1/ 2/1930 | M | S | Erie |
| Brown, Arthur | W | 34 | 1/ 2/1930 | M | S | Erie |
| Schlager, John E. | W | 32 | 1/ 9/1930 | M | S | Erie |
| Plaia, Frank | W | 20 | 1/30/1930 | M | S | Nassau |
| Sclafonia, Michael | W | 20 | 1/30/1930 | M | S | Nassau |
| Ziolowski, Stephen | W | 24 | 5/29/1930 | M | S | Erie |
| Grzechowiak, Stephen | W | 29 | 7/17/1930 | M | S | Erie |
| Rybarczyk, Max | W | 31 | 7/17/1930 | M | S | Erie |
| Bogdanoff, Alex | W | 35 | 7/17/1930 | M | S | Erie |
| Force, William | W | 28 | 8/28/1930 | M | S | Cayuga |
| Udwin, Claud | W | 29 | 8/28/1930 | M | S | Cayuga |
| Thomas, Jesse | W | 20 | 8/28/1930 | M | S | Cayuga |
| Bolger, James | W | 19 | 12/12/1930 | M | S | Nassau |
| Butler, James R. | W | 20 | 12/12/1930 | M | S | Nassau |
| Ferdinandi, Italo | W | 22 | 12/12/1930 | M | S | Nassau |
| Velluchio, Anthony | W | 40 | 2/26/1931 | M | S | Montgomery |
| Luciano, Anthony | W | 36 | 2/26/1931 | M | S | Montgomery |
| Turner, Haywood | B | 29 | 6/25/1931 | M | S | Bronx |
| Innes, Fred | B | 38 | 6/25/1931 | M | S | Bronx |
| Carmosino, Fred | W | 19 | 7/ 2/1931 | M | S | Bronx |
| Mangiamele, Ferdinand | W | 24 | 7/ 2/1931 | M | S | Bronx |
| Leonelli, Nicholas | W | 23 | 7/ 2/1931 | M | S | Bronx |
| Metelski, Andrew P. | W | 21 | 7/23/1931 | M | S | Erie |
| Johnson, Herbert | B | 19 | 7/23/1931 | M | S | Scoharie |
| Lipschitz, Harry | W | 25 | 8/27/1931 | M | S | Westchester |
| Seaton, Maurice | B | 42 | 9/ 4/1931 | M | S | N.Y. |
| Duringer, Rudolph | W | 26 | 12/10/1931 | M | S | Bronx |
| Carrato, Alphonse | W | 41 | 1/ 7/1932 | M | S | Westchester |

| Name | Race | Age | Date of Execution | Offense | Appeal | County |
|------|------|-----|-------------------|---------|--------|--------|
| Caricari, Giuseppe | W | 27 | 1/ 7/1932 | M | S | Westchester |
| Senna, Joseph | W | 32 | 1/14/1932 | M | S | Bronx |
| Crowley, Francis | W | 19 | 1/21/1932 | M | S | Nassau |
| Delmiar, Gavino | F | 32 | 1/28/1932 | M | S | Kings |
| Sardini, Peter | W | 28 | 3/31/1932 | M | S | Kings |
| Scifo, Dominic | W | 24 | 3/31/1932 | M | S | Queens |
| Rodrick, Michael | W | 20 | 3/31/1932 | M | S | Queens |
| Borowsky, Walter | W | 24 | 3/31/1932 | M | S | Queens |
| Dawson, John | B | 35 | 6/ 9/1932 | M | S | N.Y. |
| Giordano, Frank | W | 32 | 7/ 2/1932 | M | S | Bronx |
| Odierno, Dominick | W | 20 | 7/ 2/1932 | M | S | Bronx |
| Corbellini, Alfred | W | 21 | 7/15/1932 | M | S | N.Y. |
| Cozzi, Alfred | W | 20 | 7/15/1932 | M | S | N.Y. |
| Raffa, Luigi | W | 36 | 7/22/1932 | M | S | Bronx |
| Katoff, Louis | W | 27 | 7/22/1932 | M | S | Bronx |
| Mayo, Frank | W | 29 | 7/22/1932 | M | S | Bronx |
| Harris, George | W | 35 | 9/ 2/1932 | M | S | N.Y. |
| Markowitz, Charles | W | 21 | 12/10/1932 | M | S | N.Y. |
| Brown, Joseph | W | 20 | 12/10/1932 | M | S | N.Y. |
| Harris, Peter | W | 21 | 1/12/1933 | M | S | Cattaraugus |
| Carpenter, Thomas | B | 19 | 1/12/1933 | M | S | Bronx |
| Bates, Charles | B | 19 | 1/12/1933 | M | S | Bronx |
| Nunes, Alexander | W | 44 | 1/19/1933 | M | S | Westchester |
| Turner, William | W | 22 | 2/ 2/1933 | M | S | N.Y. |
| Polowicz, Bruno | W | 36 | 4/20/1933 | M | S | Niagara |
| Kasprzcak, Alex | W | 39 | 4/20/1933 | M | S | Niagara |
| Lopez, Antonio | W | 26 | 5/25/1933 | M | S | N.Y. |
| Jackson, William H. | B | 40 | 6/ 1/1933 | M | S | Niagara |
| Covington, Nathaniel | B | 28 | 7/13/1933 | M | S | N.Y. |
| Witherell, Stephen R. | W | 30 | 8/17/1933 | M | S | St. Lawrence |
| Jordan, John | W | 33 | 8/17/1933 | M | S | Queens |
| Swan, George | W | 21 | 8/17/1933 | M | S | Queens |
| Carrion, Alex | W | 27 | 8/24/1933 | M | S | Bronx |
| Negron, Frank | W | 25 | 8/24/1933 | M | S | Bronx |
| Edmonds, Harry | B | 50 | 9/ 1/1933 | M | S | Bronx |
| Tinsley, John | B | 25 | 9/ 1/1933 | M | S | Bronx |
| McKinney, John | B | 42 | 9/ 1/1933 | M | S | Suffolk |
| Owens, Winston C. | B | 34 | 1/11/1934 | M | S | N.Y. |
| Willis, Joseph | B | 24 | 1/11/1934 | M | S | N.Y. |
| Cunningham, Herman | B | 23 | 1/11/1934 | M | S | N.Y. |
| Price, Lloyd | B | 22 | 3/ 1/1934 | M | S | Kings |
| Pasqua, Frank | W | 24 | 6/ 7/1934 | M | S | Bronx |
| Marino, Anthony | W | 27 | 6/ 7/1934 | M | S | Bronx |
| Kriesberg, Daniel | W | 29 | 6/ 7/1934 | M | S | Bronx |
| Vogel, William | W | 26 | 6/14/1934 | M | S | N.Y. |
| Caccamise, Ross | W | 24 | 6/14/1934 | M | S | Monroe |
| Murphy, Joseph | W | 27 | 7/ 5/1934 | M | S | Bronx |
| Canora, Frank | W | 51 | 7/12/1934 | M | S | Rockland |
| Antonio, Anna (Female) | W | 27 | 8/ 9/1934 | M | S | Albany |
| Faraci, Sam | W | 42 | 8/ 9/1934 | M | S | Albany |
| Saeta, Vincent | W | 33 | 8/ 9/1934 | M | S | Albany |
| Brengard, Alphonse | W | 29 | 9/ 6/1934 | M | S | Nassau |

| Name | Race | Age | Date of Execution | Offense | Appeal | County |
|------|------|-----|-------------------|---------|--------|--------|
| Seaman, Harold | W | 21 | 1/10/1935 | M | S | Kings |
| Walsh, Vincent | W | 21 | 1/10/1935 | M | S | N.Y. |
| Mitchell, Frank | W | 26 | 1/17/1935 | M | S | N.Y. |
| Leonti, Giuseppe | W | 43 | 1/24/1935 | M | S | N.Y. |
| Paskowitz, William | W | 26 | 2/ 7/1935 | M | S | Bronx |
| Crotty, Peter | W | 26 | 2/ 7/1935 | M | S | Bronx |
| Giallarenzi, Alfred | W | 30 | 2/ 7/1935 | M | S | Onondaga |
| DeLeo, Vincent | W | 29 | 2/21/1935 | M | S | Clinton |
| Salek, Bruno | W | 20 | 4/25/1935 | M | S | Erie |
| Pluzdrak, Stanley | W | 17 | 4/25/1935 | M | S | Erie |
| Coo, Eva (Female) | W | 41 | 6/27/1935 | M | S | Otsego |
| Scarnici, Leonard | W | 27 | 6/27/1935 | M | S | Schoharie |
| Downey, Patrick | W | 31 | 7/11/1935 | M | S | Suffolk |
| Lindsay, Alfred G. | W | 29 | 8/29/1935 | M | S | Cattaraugus |
| Morris, Percy | B | 29 | 12/ 5/1935 | M | S | Bronx |
| Brown, Jeff | B | 22 | 12/ 5/1935 | M | S | Bronx |
| Raymond, Newman | W | 22 | 1/ 9/1936 | M | S | N.Y. |
| Angelini, Amerigo | W | 23 | 1/ 9/1936 | M | S | N.Y. |
| Rooney, Thomas | W | 23 | 1/ 9/1936 | M | S | N.Y. |
| Orley, Ray | W | 22 | 1/ 9/1936 | M | S | N.Y. |
| Smith, John | B | 41 | 1/16/1936 | M | S | Bronx |
| Fish, Albert H. | W | 66 | 1/16/1936 | M | S | Westchester |
| Flynn, Francis A. | W | 39 | 2/27/1936 | M | S | Queens |
| Mohlsick, Peter | W | 20 | 4/16/1936 | M | S | Westchester |
| Bickler, Howard | W | 21 | 4/16/1936 | M | S | Westchester |
| Buckvich, Nick | W | 42 | 4/23/1936 | M | S | Monroe |
| Kropowitz, Charles | W | 22 | 5/28/1936 | M | S | Kings |
| Rosenberg, George | W | 22 | 5/28/1936 | M | S | Kings |
| Russo, Frank | W | 24 | 5/28/1936 | M | S | Kings |
| DeMartino, Vincent | W | 27 | 5/28/1936 | M | S | Kings |
| Consentino, Damiano | W | 39 | 6/ 4/1936 | M | S | Kings |
| Collins, John | W | 26 | 7/ 9/1936 | M | S | Queens |
| Creighton, Frances Q. (Female) | W | 36 | 7/16/1936 | M | S | Nassau |
| Appelgate, Everett C. | W | 36 | 7/16/1936 | M | S | Nassau |
| Flores, Raymond | W | 26 | 7/23/1936 | M | S | N.Y. |
| McFarland, Theodore | W | 38 | 8/20/1936 | M | S | Kings |
| Rogas, Charles | W | 35 | 8/27/1936 | M | S | Kings |
| DiDionne, Theodore | W | 31 | 1/ 7/1937 | M | S | Kings |
| Bolognia, Joseph | W | 24 | 1/14/1937 | M | S | Kings |
| Lazar, Louis | W | 29 | 1/14/1937 | M | S | Kings |
| Ham, Charles | B | 19 | 1/21/1937 | M | S | Kings |
| Fowler, Frederick | B | 18 | 1/21/1937 | M | S | Kings |
| White, Chester | B | 33 | 1/21/1937 | M | S | Nassau |
| Fiorenza, John | W | 25 | 1/21/1937 | M | S | N.Y. |
| Volkmann, Alfred D. | W | 20 | 2/11/1937 | M | S | Greene |
| Wing, Chew | C | 32 | 6/10/1937 | M | S | N.Y. |
| Eisenberg, Harry | W | 43 | 7/ 1/1937 | M | S | Kings |
| Edwards, Watson | W | 25 | 7/ 1/1937 | M | S | Kings |
| Garlaus, Anthony | W | 33 | 7/ 1/1937 | M | S | Kings |
| Green, Major | B | 33 | 8/19/1937 | M | S | Queens |
| Apicello, Louis | W | 40 | 8/26/1937 | M | S | Kings |

| Name | Race | Age | Date of Execution | Offense | Appeal | County |
|------|------|-----|-------------------|---------|--------|--------|
| Ossido, Salvatore | W | 27 | 1/ 6/1938 | M | S | Kings |
| Brown, James | B | 30 | 2/24/1938 | M | S | Ulster |
| Roberts, Terence | W | 30 | 5/26/1938 | M | S | N.Y. |
| Marks, Lawrence | W | 50 | 6/ 2/1938 | M | S | Kings |
| Lewis, George | W | 25 | 8/11/1938 | M | S,N.T. | Kings |
| Cummings, Felix J. | W | 27 | 8/11/1938 | M | S,N.T. | Kings |
| Rylowicz, John | W | 39 | 8/18/1938 | M | S | Nassau |
| Lucas, David | B | 29 | 1/ 5/1939 | M | S | Niagara |
| Gatti, Salvatore | W | 29 | 1/ 5/1939 | M | S | N.Y. |
| Sberna, Charles | W | 29 | 1/ 5/1939 | M | S | N.Y. |
| Forte, Vincente | W | 19 | 1/12/1939 | M | S | Kings |
| Friedman, Arthur | W | 21 | 1/26/1939 | M | S | N.Y. |
| Guariglia, Dominick | W | 18 | 1/26/1939 | M | S | N.Y. |
| O'Laughlin, Joseph H. | W | 23 | 1/26/1939 | M | S | N.Y. |
| Gilmore, Thomas K. | W | 42 | 2/ 9/1939 | M | S | Orange |
| Hermanowski, Michael | W | 24 | 2/16/1939 | M | S | Suffolk |
| Bohan, Thomas | W | 34 | 2/16/1939 | M | S | N.Y. |
| Alex, Michael | W | 28 | 2/23/1939 | M | S | N.Y. |
| Perry, Arthur | B | 24 | 8/24/1939 | M | S | Queens |
| Maselkiewicz, Theodore | W | 53 | 12/21/1939 | M | S | Erie |
| McDonald, Everett | B | 40 | 12/21/1939 | M | S | N.Y. |
| Myslivec, Anton | W | 54 | 12/21/1939 | M | S | Suffolk |
| Abreu, Anselmo | W | 41 | 1/ 4/1940 | M | S | Bronx |
| Sacoda, Joseph S. | W | 28 | 1/11/1940 | K | S | N.Y. |
| Gula, Demetrius | W | 27 | 1/11/1940 | K | S | N.Y. |
| Markham, Sidney | W | 21 | 1/18/1940 | M | S | Kings |
| Jenner, Frank | W | 21 | 2/15/1940 | M | S | Onondaga |
| Kulka, John | W | 24 | 2/15/1940 | M | S | N.Y. |
| Thingstead, Bertal | W | 29 | 2/15/1940 | M | S | N.Y. |
| Schweinberger, Gus | W | 30 | 4/25/1940 | M | S | Westchester |
| Alridge, Oliver R. | B | 47 | 7/11/1940 | M | S | Cattaraugus |
| Pryor, James | B | 23 | 7/11/1940 | M | S | N.Y. |
| Wheelock, Norman | W | 27 | 8/ 1/1940 | M | S | Steuben |
| Ertrel, Benjamin | W | 25 | 9/12/1940 | M | S | N.Y. |
| Blazek, Frank | W | 30 | 9/12/1940 | M | S | Bronx |
| Greenfield, Major | B | 33 | 1/ 9/1941 | M | S | Bronx |
| Williams, Norman | B | 32 | 2/ 6/1941 | M | S | N.Y. |
| Brown, Eugene | B | 26 | 2/ 6/1941 | M | S | N.Y. |
| D'Agosto, Arcangelo | W | 27 | 2/13/1941 | M | S | Kings |
| Bowling, Walter | W | 40 | 2/13/1941 | M | S | Kings |
| Dolny, George | W | 22 | 2/13/1941 | M | S | Kings |
| Garosella, Joseph P. | W | 26 | 2/20/1941 | M | S | Nassau |
| Balatniecov, Hyman | W | 28 | 2/20/1941 | M | S | N.Y. |
| Adler, David | W | 26 | 2/20/1941 | M | S | N.Y. |
| Salemi, David | W | 33 | 6/ 5/1941 | M | S | Kings |
| Goldstein, Martin[6] | W | 35 | 6/12/1941 | M | S | Kings |
| Strauss, Harry[6] | W | 31 | 6/12/1941 | M | S | Kings |
| Garrett, Dewey | B | 21 | 7/10/1941 | M | S | N.Y. |
| Cole, Stanley | W | 35 | 7/10/1941 | M | S | N.Y. |
| Zeitz, George | W | 25 | 9/18/1941 | M | S | Kings |
| Richardson, Isaac | B | 28 | 1/ 8/1942 | M | S | N.Y. |
| Jones, Ralph G. | B | 35 | 1/15/1942 | M | S | N.Y. |
| Anerum, Henry | B | 31 | 1/15/1942 | M | S | N.Y. |

| Name | Race | Age | Date of Execution | Offense | Appeal | County |
|------|------|-----|-------------------|---------|--------|--------|
| Renna, Arthur | W | 36 | 1/22/1942 | M | S | Bronx |
| Conroy, Thomas | W | 39 | 1/29/1942 | M | S | Bronx |
| Abbendando, Frank[6] | W | 31 | 2/19/1942 | M | S | Kings |
| Maione, Harry[6] | W | 32 | 2/19/1942 | M | S | Kings |
| Cvek, George | W | 24 | 2/26/1942 | M | S | Bronx |
| Mardavich, Morris | W | 24 | 3/ 5/1942 | M | S | N.Y. |
| Esposito, Anthony | W | 36 | 3/12/1942 | M | S | N.Y. |
| Esposito, William | W | 29 | 3/12/1942 | M | S | N.Y. |
| Riordan, Joseph | W | 26 | 6/11/1942 | M | S | Westchester |
| McGale, Charles | W | 45 | 6/11/1942 | M | S | Westchester |
| Barone, Carlo | W | 27 | 9/10/1942 | M | S | Kings |
| Hicks, Edward | B | 21 | 9/10/1942 | M | S | Kings |
| Edwards, Lawrence | B | 18 | 9/17/1942 | M | S | N.Y. |
| Jacinto, Manuel | W | 23 | 9/17/1942 | M | S | Orange |
| Clark, James | B | 21 | 9/17/1942 | M | S | N.Y. |
| Sileo, Edmund | W | 27 | 1/14/1943 | M | S | Kings |
| Sonsky, Joseph | W | 32 | 1/14/1943 | M | S | N.Y. |
| Castellano, Frank | W | 26 | 1/21/1943 | M | S | N.Y. |
| Mendez, Angelo | W | 30 | 1/21/1943 | M | S | N.Y. |
| Elling, Harold J. | W | 20 | 3/ 4/1943 | M | S | N.Y. |
| Shonbrun, Eli E. | W | 33 | 4/29/1943 | M | S | N.Y. |
| Cullen, John | W | 45 | 4/29/1943 | M | S | N.Y. |
| Dejesus, Benitez | B | 18 | 7/ 8/1943 | M | S | N.Y. |
| Haight, Edward | W | 17 | 7/ 8/1943 | M | S | Westchester |
| Diaz, William | B | 18 | 7/ 8/1943 | M | S | N.Y. |
| Haynes, Alfred | B | 26 | 7/15/1943 | M | S | Kings |
| Almodovar, Anibal | W | 21 | 9/16/1943 | M | S | N.Y. |
| Mascari, Joseph C. | W | 32 | 1/ 6/1944 | M | S | Madison |
| Lewis, Herbert | B | 35 | 1/13/1944 | M | S | Kings |
| Valle, Louis | W | 43 | 1/21/1944 | M | S | Nassau |
| Regan, John | W | 33 | 2/10/1944 | M | S | N.Y. |
| Palmer, Joseph | W | 27 | 3/ 2/1944 | M | S | Kings |
| Soollami, Vincent | W | 26 | 3/ 2/1944 | M | S | Kings |
| Capone, Louis[6] | W | 48 | 3/ 4/1944 | M | S,F,U | Kings |
| Weiss, Emanuel[6] | W | 38 | 3/ 4/1944 | M | S,F,U | Kings |
| Buchalter, Louis "Lepke" | W | 47 | 3/ 4/1944 | M | S,F,U | Kings |
| Ranford, John | B | 40 | 5/25/1944 | M | S | Nassau |
| Parisi, Louis | W | 24 | 6/ 3/1944 | M | S | N.Y. |
| Sealy, Winston A. | B | 21 | 6/22/1944 | M | S | Kings |
| Cooke, Gordon | B | 19 | 6/22/1944 | M | S | Kings |
| Dimaria, Frank | W | 23 | 6/29/1944 | M | S | N.Y. |
| Bellomo, Alex | W | 25 | 6/29/1944 | M | S | N.Y. |
| DeLutro, Peter | W | 23 | 6/29/1944 | M | S | N.Y. |
| Bing, Lew York | C | 18 | 8/31/1944 | M | S | N.Y. |
| Li, Yun Tieh | C | 24 | 8/31/1944 | M | S | N.Y. |
| Fowler, Helen (Female) | B | 37 | 11/16/1944 | M | S | Niagara |
| Knight, George | B | 26 | 11/16/1944 | M | S | Niagara |
| Little, Oliver | B | 22 | 1/17/1946 | M | S | N.Y. |
| Donaldson, George W. | W | 48 | 3/ 7/1946 | M | S | Rensselaer |
| Gold, Abraham | W | 44 | 4/25/1946 | M | S | Kings |
| Brookins, Louis | W | 21 | 9/12/1946 | M | S | Monroe |
| Suckow, Henry Paul | W | 24 | 3/ 6/1947 | M | S | Queens |
| Koberski, Edward E. | W | 22 | 3/ 6/1947 | M | S | Queens |

| Name | Race | Age | Date of Execution | Offense | Appeal | County |
|------|------|-----|-------------------|---------|--------|--------|
| Kahkoska, Edward | W | 22 | 3/ 6/1947 | M | S | Queens |
| Johnson, Arthur | B | 21 | 4/17/1947 | M | S | Kings |
| Washington, William | B | 28 | 4/17/1947 | M | S | Kings |
| Caraway, Ward Beecher | B | 22 | 7/ 3/1947 | M | S | Nassau |
| Di Cristofaro, Salvatore | W | 36 | 7/10/1947 | M | S | Erie |
| Jones, Edward | B | 23 | 7/10/1947 | M | S | Kings |
| Sims, Arnold | B | 23 | 7/10/1947 | M | S | Kings |
| Thomas, William | B | 20 | 7/10/1947 | M | S | N.Y. |
| Daniel, Webster | B | 37 | 8/21/1947 | M | S | N.Y. |
| Bussey, Enix | B | 31 | 12/ 4/1947 | M | S | N.Y. |
| Jackson, Jauvham | B | 18 | 1/ 8/1948 | M | S | Kings |
| Papa, Anthony R. | W | 27 | 7/ 1/1948 | M | S | Nassau |
| Haughton, Lester | B | 24 | 7/22/1948 | M | S,U | Bronx |
| Moore, George C. | B | 34 | 7/22/1948 | M | S,U | Bronx |
| Shaket, Milton | W | 34 | 9/16/1948 | M | S | N.Y. |
| Reilly, John | W | 32 | 9/16/1948 | M | S | N.Y. |
| Gray, Harris | B | 18 | 1/ 6/1949 | M | S | N.Y. |
| Smiley, Louis | B | 19 | 1/13/1949 | M | S | N.Y. |
| Pannell, Eugene | B | 27 | 1/20/1949 | M | S | N.Y. |
| Grant, Wilie | B | 24 | 1/20/1949 | M | S | N.Y. |
| Monge, George L. | B | 23 | 1/20/1949 | M | S | N.Y. |
| Bretagna, Santo | W | 27 | 3/ 3/1949 | M | S | N.Y. |
| Rosenberg, William | W | 42 | 3/ 3/1949 | M | S | N.Y. |
| Dupree, Herman | B | 32 | 6/30/1949 | M | S | N.Y. |
| Dupree, Harold | B | 27 | 6/30/1949 | M | S | N.Y. |
| Dunn, John M. | W | 36 | 7/ 7/1949 | M | S,U | N.Y. |
| Sheridan, Andrew | W | 56 | 7/ 7/1949 | M | S,U | N.Y. |
| Jackson, William M. | B | 23 | 9/ 1/1949 | M | S | N.Y. |
| Arrington, Floyd | B | 22 | 9/ 1/1949 | M | S | N.Y. |
| Davis, Walter | B | 21 | 9/ 8/1949 | M | S | Kings |
| Bruno, Frank | W | 31 | 1/ 5/1950 | M | S | Kings |
| Reeh, George Peter | W | 31 | 1/12/1950 | M | S | N.Y. |
| Perez, Julio Ramirez | W | 36 | 5/25/1950 | M | S | N.Y. |
| LaMarr, Harley G. | I | 19 | 1/11/1951 | M | S | Erie |
| Bunch, William W. | B | 21 | 2/15/1951 | M | S | Nassau |
| Walker, Gilberto C. | B | 26 | 3/ 1/1951 | M | S | N.Y. |
| King, John Joseph | W | 21 | 3/ 8/1951 | M | S | Queens |
| Power, Richard J.J. | W | 21 | 3/ 8/1951 | M | S | Queens |
| Fernandez, Raymond M. | W | 34 | 3/ 8/1951 | M | S | Bronx |
| Beck, Martha Jule (Female) | W | 29 | 3/ 8/1951 | M | S | Bronx |
| Sain, John | W | 38 | 4/12/1951 | M | S | Bronx |
| Stein, Bernard | W | 35 | 3/ 6/1952 | M | S | N.Y. |
| Ford, Wallace, Jr. | B | 31 | 10/30/1952 | M | S | Genesee |
| Kelly, Edward H. | W | 53 | 10/30/1952 | M | S | Ulster |
| Paonessa, Joseph L. | W | 42 | 1/15/1953 | M | S | Dutchess |
| Lewis, Stephen D. | W | 42 | 1/22/1953 | M | S | Genesee |
| Wojcik, Frank | W | 56 | 4/16/1953 | M | S | Wyoming |
| Rosenberg, Julius | W | 37 | 6/19/1953 | E | S,F,U | Fed |
| Rosenberg, Ethel (Female) | W | 35 | 6/19/1953 | E | S | Fed |
| Snyder, Donald H. | W | 26 | 7/16/1953 | M | S | Putnam |
| Draper, William H. | W | 34 | 1/ 7/1953 | M | S | Monroe |
| O'Dell, Maurice | W | 28 | 1/ 7/1954 | M | S | Erie |

| Name | Race | Age | Date of Execution | Offense | Appeal | County |
|------|------|-----|-------------------|---------|--------|--------|
| Griffin, Walter | W | 26 | 1/ 7/1954 | M | S | Erie |
| Martin, John | B | 29 | 3/11/1954 | M | S | Kings |
| Allen, Henry Louis | B | 19 | 3/11/1954 | M | S | Kings |
| Scott, Emile Hendricka | B | 21 | 7/15/1954 | M | S | N.Y. |
| Vanderwyde, William | W | 40 | 7/22/1954 | M | S,U | N.Y. |
| Puff, Gerhard A. | W | 40 | 8/12/1954 | M | S,F,U | Fed |
| Green, John Dale | B | 24 | 8/26/1954 | M | S | Bronx |
| Jacobs, Barry | W | 22 | 8/26/1954 | M | S | Bronx |
| Matthews, Henry | W | 18 | 2/10/1955 | M | S | N.Y. |
| Rosario, Romulo | W | 38 | 2/17/1955 | M | S | N.Y. |
| Wissner, Nathan | W | 43 | 7/ 9/1955 | M | S,F,U | Westchester |
| Stein, Harry A. | W | 57 | 7/ 9/1955 | M | S,F,U | Westchester |
| Cooper, Calman | W | 47 | 7/ 9/1955 | M | S,F,U | Westchester |
| Reed, Clarence M. | W | 32 | 9/ 8/1955 | M | S | N.Y. |
| Nichols, Edward J. | B | 28 | 9/ 8/1955 | M | S | N.Y. |
| Byers, William | W | 19 | 1/12/1956 | M | S | N.Y. |
| Roye, Norman | B | 17 | 1/19/1956 | M | S | N.Y. |
| Roche, John Francis | W | 28 | 1/26/1956 | M | S | N.Y. |
| Edwards, Ernest Lee | W | 22 | 6/28/1956 | M | S | Kings |
| Newman, Frank J. | W | 51 | 8/23/1956 | M | S | Nassau |
| Reade, Joseph | W | 27 | 8/30/1956 | M | S | Chautauqua |
| Salemi, Leonardo | W | 44 | 2/28/1957 | M | S | N.Y. |
| Browne, MacDonald F. | W | 31 | 3/14/1957 | M | S | Bronx |
| Santiago, Miguel | W | 29 | 8/15/1957 | M | S | N.Y. |
| Taylor, David | B | 44 | 11/21/1957 | M | S | Bronx |
| Burke, Elmer Francis | W | 40 | 1/ 9/1958 | M | S | N.Y. |
| Dan, Nicholas, Jr. | B | 20 | 7/ 3/1958 | M | S | Niagara |
| LaMarca, Angelo John | W | 33 | 8/ 7/1958 | M | S | Nassau |
| Richardson, Virgil | B | 29 | 11/20/1958 | M | S | Queens |
| Eckwerth, Edward | W | 31 | 5/22/1959 | M | S,U | Westchester |
| Turner, Jackson, Jr. | B | 23 | 7/16/1959 | M | S | Queens |
| Dawkins, Ralph | B | 22 | 7/16/1959 | M | S | Queens |
| Keith, Leroy | B | 52 | 7/23/1959 | M | S | Bronx |
| Mason, Ivory | B | 40 | 1/14/1960 | M | S | N.Y. |
| Vargas, Pablo | W | 35 | 5/12/1960 | M | S,U | N.Y. |
| Green, Walter T. | B | 33 | 5/19/1960 | M | S | Erie |
| Flakes, Henry | B | 33 | 5/19/1960 | M | S | Erie |
| Phillips, Willard H. | B | 44 | 6/23/1960 | M | S | Nassau |
| Chapman, Ronald | B | 20 | 12/ 1/1960 | M | S | N.Y. |
| Downs, Ralph | B | 28 | 1/ 5/1961 | M | S | Bronx |
| Miller, Woodrow | B | 32 | 6/ 8/1961 | M | S | Kings |
| Wood, Frederick Charles | W | 51 | 3/21/1963 | M | S,U | Queens |
| Mays, Eddie Lee | B | 34 | 8/15/1963 | M | S | N.Y. |

[1]Ebelt (4/10/1905) through Furlong (3/4/1907) were executed at Auburn since they had been sentenced to death before the requirement that executions be performed at Sing Sing.
[2]Crime partners.
[3]"Gyp the Blood," "Dago Frank," "Whitey Lewis," and "Lefty Louis," respectively. All were involved in the murder of gambler Herman Rosenthal on July 15, 1912. A police lieutenant hired the four to kill Rosenthal.
[4]On June 21, 1916, Shillitoni killed a guard (McCarthy) and escaped for three hours.
[5]Von der Corput helped build the death-house.
[6]Murder, Inc.

## NORTH CAROLINA

*Period of Executions*: 1901–1961
*Total Number*: 362
*Method*: Electrocution 1910–1936; lethal gas 1936–1961
*Other Data*: Those who were sentenced to death before the lethal gas law was passed in 1946 were electrocuted.

| Name | Race | Age | Date of Execution | Offense | Appeal | County |
|------|------|-----|-------------------|---------|--------|--------|
| Morrison, Walter | B | 37 | 3/18/1910 | Ra | | Robeson |
| Mills, Philip | B | — | 2/10/1911 | M | | Transylvania |
| Montague, Nathan | B | — | 2/15/1911 | M | | Granville |
| Allison, James B. | W | 51 | 2/24/1911 | M | S | Buncombe |
| West, Lewis | B | 24 | 5/ 5/1911 | M | | Wilson |
| Lewis, Norman | B | — | 5/12/1911 | M | S | Nash |
| Marshall, Novell, Jr. | B | 31 | 10/27/1911 | Ra | | Warren |
| French, Ross | I | — | 11/24/1911 | M | | Swain |
| Love, Taylor | B | — | 12/ 1/1911 | M | | Haywood |
| Sandling, L.M. | W | — | 12/29/1911 | M | S | New Hanover |
| Bagley, Brad | B | — | 5/17/1912 | M | S | Martin |
| Wilkins, G.C. | B | — | 6/21/1912 | M | S | Nash |
| Cobb, R.W. | W | 23 | 3/ 6/1914 | M | S | Halifax |
| Finger, Sidney T. | B | — | 6/19/1914 | M | | Rowan |
| Lane, Grady | B | — | 8/21/1914 | M | S | Moore |
| Cameron, Jim | B | — | 8/28/1914 | M | | Moore |
| Gannaway, Harvey | B | — | 10/16/1914 | M | | Forsyth |
| Craig, Howard | B | — | 12/ 4/1914 | Ra | | Stanly |
| Bell, Willie | B | — | 7/ 8/1915 | M | | Durham |
| Trull, Charles E. | W | — | 9/ 3/1915 | M | S | Mecklenburg |
| Walker, Ed | B | — | 1/28/1916 | M | S | Guilford |
| Dorset, Jeff | B | — | 1/28/1916 | M | | Guilford |
| Cooper, Jim | B | — | 2/11/1916 | M | S | Rowan |
| Poston, George | B | 23 | 2/25/1916 | M | | Gaston |
| Lowry, Ernest | B | — | 2/25/1916 | M | S | Gaston |
| Swinson, Lawrence | B | 23 | 7/ 7/1916 | B | | New Hanover |
| Black, Willie | B | 16 | 7/21/1916 | Ra | | Greene |
| Smith, Arthur | B | 26 | 8/ 1/1916 | M | | Cumberland |
| Savage, John | B | 51 | 8/ 4/1916 | M | | Washington |
| Maske, Bunk | B | 24 | 5/25/1917 | M | | Union |
| Williams, Charles | B | 60 | 9/25/1917 | M | | Iredell |
| Perkins, Lee | B | — | 10/10/1917 | B | | Craven |
| Terry, J.A. | W | 60 | 11/ 9/1917 | M | S | Guilford |
| Nevils, Earl | B | 24 | 3/15/1918 | Ra | S | Wake |
| Williams, Willie | B | — | 4/26/1918 | Ra | | Buncombe |
| Moore, Frank | B | — | 5/24/1918 | M | | Duplin |
| Perry, Herbert | B | — | 5/25/1918 | Ra | S | Granville |
| Council, Lonnie | B | — | 6/ 7/1918 | M | | Durham |
| Cain, Baxter | B | 33 | 9/13/1918 | M | S | Rowan |
| Spencer, Napoleon | B | — | 12/20/1918 | M | S | Surry |
| Warren, Jim Henry | B | — | 4/26/1919 | M | | Greene |
| Gwynn, Tom | B | — | 6/27/1919 | Ra | | Catawba |
| Dupree, Aaron | B | 34 | 11/14/1919 | M | | Hoke |

| Name | Race | Age | Date of Execution | Offense | Appeal | County |
|------|------|-----|-------------------|---------|--------|--------|
| Godly, C.L. | W | — | 1/16/1920 | Ra | | Johnston |
| Cain, Joe | W | 39 | 3/ 5/1920 | M | S | Surry |
| Cain, Gardner | W | 43 | 3/ 5/1920 | M | S | Surry |
| Connor, Ralph | B | — | 9/20/1920 | M | S | Iredell |
| Jackson, Andrew | B | — | 11/ 5/1920 | Ra | | Lincoln |
| McDowell, Arthur | B | — | 12/ 3/1920 | Ra | | Davidson |
| Johnson, Tom | B | — | 12/ 3/1920 | Ra | S | Guilford |
| Hopkins, William | B | — | 3/21/1921 | M | | Sampson |
| Frazier, Luke | B | — | 5/27/1921 | M | | Craven |
| Henderson, Frank | B | — | 10/10/1921 | M | S | Madison |
| Harris, J.T. | W | — | 10/20/1921 | M | S | Buncombe |
| Coldwell, Henry | B | — | 10/31/1921 | M | S | Wayne |
| Westmoreland, W.Y. | W | — | 11/21/1921 | M | S | Iredell |
| Morehead, Claude | B | — | 11/30/1921 | M | | Guilford |
| Murphy, Angus | B | — | 9/15/1922 | Ra | | Moore |
| Thomas, Jasper | B | — | 9/15/1922 | Ra | | Moore |
| Burnette, McIver | B | 16 | 10/12/1922 | M | S | Wake |
| Williams, Robert | B | — | 3/ 1/1923 | M | S | Columbus |
| Hardison, Wilie | B | — | 4/27/1923 | M | | Onslow |
| Perry, Wiley | B | — | 5/ 9/1923 | M | | Granville |
| Nobles, D.M. | W | — | 6/26/1923 | M | | Columbus |
| Dill, Ed | B | — | 6/28/1923 | Ra | S | Beaufort |
| Miller, Jim | B | — | 10/ 5/1923 | M | S | Lenoir |
| Goss, John | B | — | 12/ 7/1923 | Ra | | Mitchell |
| Washington, Lee | B | 20 | 12/28/1923 | Ra | | Nash |
| Morgan, Vance | B | — | 11/28/1924 | M | | Union |
| Leak, John | B | — | 1/ 5/1925 | M | S | Davidson |
| Hale, Kenneth | B | 17 | 1/ 5/1925 | M | S | Davidson |
| Jones, David | B | — | 2/18/1925 | M | | Chowan |
| Stewart, C.W. (Father) | W | 51 | 4/17/1925 | M | S | Brunswick |
| Stewart, Elmer (Son) | W | 23 | 4/17/1925 | M | S | Brunswick |
| Walton, Leon | B | — | 4/21/1925 | M | S | Hoke |
| Singleton, William H. | B | — | 5/ 8/1925 | M | | Craven |
| Collins, Jim | B | 19 | 6/ 5/1925 | M | S | Anson |
| Williams, Will | B | — | 6/12/1925 | M | S | Scotland |
| Love, George | B | — | 6/19/1925 | M | S | Haywood |
| McMillan, John | B | — | 10/ 2/1925 | Ra | | Moore |
| Robinson, Thomas | B | — | 10/ 2/1925 | Ra | | New Hanover |
| Dawkins, John Wesley | B | — | 1/ 8/1926 | M | S | Forsyth |
| Montague, Arthur | B | 22 | 1/22/1926 | Ra | S | Burke |
| Jones, Fred | B | 24 | 6/11/1926 | M | S | Forsyth |
| Williams, John | B | — | 9/21/1926 | M | | Halifax |
| Lumpkin, Robert | B | — | 3/11/1927 | M | | Robeson |
| Walker, Ernest P. | B | — | 4/22/1927 | M | S | Durham |
| Mitchell, Pearl | B | — | 6/10/1927 | M | S | Chatham |
| Bazemore, George F. | B | — | 9/23/1927 | M | S | Greene |
| Graham, Hector | B | — | 12/ 9/1927 | M | S | Hoke |
| Devlin, David | B | 22 | 2/17/1928 | M | | Rowan |
| Thomas, Clarence | B | — | 4/27/1928 | M | S | Forsyth |
| Clyburn, John | B | — | 5/25/1928 | M | S | Mecklenburg |
| Newsome, Larry | B | 22 | 9/28/1928 | M | S | Wayne |
| McGurrie, Leo | B | 28 | 4/26/1929 | M | | Gaston |

| Name | Race | Age | Date of Execution | Offense | Appeal | County |
|------|------|-----|-------------------|---------|--------|--------|
| Willey, Freddie | B | 17 | 6/28/1929 | Ra | | Randolph |
| Buckner, Willie | W | 28 | 9/12/1929 | Ra | | Craven |
| Fox, Ernest | B | — | 11/22/1929 | M | S | Edgecombe |
| Evans, Ray | B | — | 3/14/1930 | M | S | Richmond |
| Macon, John Buddy | B | — | 4/ 4/1930 | M | S | Warren |
| Mangum, Robert | B | — | 4/17/1930 | Ra | | Franklin |
| Brumfield, James | B | 23 | 5/ 9/1930 | B | | Union |
| Spivey, James | W | — | 5/23/1930 | M | S | Lee |
| Sharp, Aaron | B | — | 9/26/1930 | M | | Wilson |
| Richardson, Berry | B | — | 9/26/1930 | M | | Wilson |
| Lawrence, Henry | B | — | 10/10/1930 | B | S | Hertford |
| Massey, Willie | B | — | 11/ 7/1930 | M | S | Durham |
| Sloan, Will | B | — | 11/ 7/1930 | M | S | Person |
| Gattis, Sidney M. | B | 49 | 1/23/1931 | M | | Durham |
| McRae, Dave | B | — | 2/13/1931 | M | S | Scotland |
| Borden, Thomas H. | B | — | 2/13/1931 | B | | Vance |
| Autrey, Wilson | B | 19 | 8/10/1931 | Ra | | Union |
| Goldston, Ben | B | 36 | 8/21/1931 | M | | Chatham |
| Ballard, J.W. | B | 17 | 12/11/1931 | M | S | Rowan |
| Matthews, Bernice | B | 20 | 12/11/1931 | M | S | Rowan |
| Herring, Chevis | B | — | 12/18/1931 | M | S | Sampson |
| Respus, Asbury | B | 56 | 1/ 8/1932 | M | | Guilford |
| Myers, John Robert | B | — | 3/25/1932 | M | S | Pitt |
| Moore, Dudlay | B | 19 | 4/29/1932 | M | S | Davidson |
| Edney, Plato | W | 34 | 7/15/1932 | M | S | Henderson |
| Donnell, Noel | B | 24 | 8/26/1932 | M | S | Guilford |
| Lee, Leroy | B | 24 | 10/14/1932 | M | S | Guilford |
| Greer, Alec | B | 22 | 12/16/1932 | M | | Gaston |
| Wallace, Harvey | B | 31 | 12/16/1932 | M | S | Lee |
| Avent, Hezzie | W | — | 1/27/1933 | M | S | Scotland |
| McNair, Dave | B | 23 | 5/19/1933 | M | S | Guilford |
| Fogleman, Clay | W | 30 | 8/ 4/1933 | M | S | Rockingham |
| Stone, Bryant | W | 44 | 9/ 8/1933 | M | S | Wilkes |
| Lee, Johnny | B | — | 9/15/1933 | M | S | Harnett |
| Thaxton, Walter | B | — | 2/23/1934 | M | S | Person |
| Brooks, Jesse | B | 46 | 3/16/1934 | M | S | Durham |
| Johnson, James | B | 26 | 3/16/1934 | M | S | Hoke |
| Cooper, Theodore | B | — | 4/27/1934 | M | S | Durham |
| Stefanoff, Mike | W | — | 5/18/1934 | M | S | Alexander |
| Sheffield, James | W | 47 | 5/18/1934 | M | S | Haywood |
| Smith, Ossie | B | — | 6/15/1934 | M | | Northampton |
| Dalton, Joe E. | W | — | 6/22/1934 | M | S | Henderson |
| Edwards, James L. | B | 17 | 7/ 6/1934 | M | S | Mecklenburg |
| Ferrell, Clyde | W | — | 7/ 6/1934 | M | S | Durham |
| Keaton, George | B | — | 9/21/1934 | M | S | Forsyth |
| Crocket, Willie | B | — | 9/28/1934 | M | S | Forsyth |
| Bittings, Emanuel | B | — | 9/28/1934 | M | S | Person |
| Johnson, Tom | B | — | 11/16/1934 | M | S | Sampson |
| Hart, Johnny | B | — | 11/16/1934 | M | S | Sampson |
| Howard, Preston | B | — | 11/16/1934 | M | S | Sampson |
| Green, B.G. (Father) | W | 48 | 12/ 7/1934 | M | S | Alexander |
| Green, Lester (Son) | W | 25 | 12/ 7/1934 | M | S | Alexander |

| Name | Race | Age | Date of Execution | Offense | Appeal | County |
|------|------|-----|-------------------|---------|--------|--------|
| Black, R.E. | W | 25 | 12/ 7/1934 | M | S | Alexander |
| Satterfield, Rufus | W | 44 | 12/13/1934 | M | S | Wayne |
| Etheridge, Sidney | W | — | 3/15/1935 | M | S | Onslow |
| Sentelle, Louis | W | — | 7/12/1935 | M | | Cleveland |
| Whitfield, George | B | 21 | 7/12/1935 | Ra | S,U | Guilford |
| Williams, Taft | B | — | 8/ 2/1935 | M | S | Columbus |
| Waller, Dortch | B | 43 | 8/ 2/1935 | M | S | Granville |
| McMillan, Houston | B | — | 8/ 9/1935 | M | S | Cumberland |
| Glover, Vander | B | — | 8/ 9/1935 | M | S | Cumberland |
| Miller, Caesar | B | 18 | 9/ 6/1935 | M | S | Craven |
| Gosnell, Arthur | W | 18 | 10/ 4/1935 | M | S | Madison |
| Gunter, Oris | W | 20 | 10/ 4/1935 | M | S | Madison |
| Thomas, Robert | W | 23 | 10/ 4/1935 | M | S | Madison |
| Dunlap, Robert | W | 26 | 1/17/1936 | M | S | Buncombe |
| Foster, Allen | W | 20 | 1/24/1936 | M | | Hoke |
| Jenkins, Ed | W | 40 | 1/31/1936 | Ra | | Gaston |
| Long, William[1] | B | 19 | 2/ 7/1936 | M | S | Alamance |
| Watson, Thomas | B | 32 | 2/ 7/1936 | M | | Durham |
| Sanford, J.T. | B | 30 | 2/ 7/1936 | M | | Durham |
| Johnson, Jake | B | 36 | 3/19/1936 | Ra | S | Rockingham |
| Hester, Ed | W | 19 | 3/20/1936 | M | S | Wake |
| Bufkin, Bright | W | 43 | 3/27/1936 | M | S | Columbus |
| Dingle, Lawrence | B | 32 | 5/ 8/1936 | M | S | Forsyth |
| Williams, Germie | B | 23 | 5/ 8/1936 | M | S | Forsyth |
| Batten, Marvin | W | 29 | 5/29/1936 | M | | Johnston |
| Horne, John | W | 37 | 6/19/1936 | M | S | Chowan |
| Grier, Henry[1] | B | 43 | 7/10/1936 | M | S | Forsyth |
| Hodgin, William A. | B | 36 | 7/17/1936 | M | S | Forsyth |
| Galman, Willie Lee | B | 21 | 8/21/1936 | M | S | Forsyth |
| Kinyon, John | B | 75 | 8/21/1936 | Ra | S | Granville |
| Carden, J.B.[1] | W | — | 9/ 4/1936 | M | S,U | Durham |
| Alston, George | B | 21 | 9/ 4/1936 | M | S | Orange |
| Pressley, John | B | 43 | 11/13/1936 | M | S | Gaston |
| Tate, Willie | B | 29 | 11/20/1936 | M | S | Pitt |
| Macklin, Evans | B | 20 | 11/20/1936 | M | S | Halifax |
| Moore, Martin | B | 23 | 12/11/1936 | M | S | Buncombe |
| Brown, Robert Glenn | B | 18 | 7/ 9/1937 | M | | Craven |
| Steele, Fred | B | 22 | 7/16/1937 | M | S | Mecklenburg |
| Jones, Sam | B | 21 | 7/16/1937 | M | S | Mecklenburg |
| Grey, Fred | B | 26 | 7/23/1937 | M | | Onslow |
| Winchester, Hunter | B | 24 | 7/23/1937 | M | S | Guilford |
| Watson, A.W. | W | 20 | 7/30/1937 | M | S | Martin |
| Perry, Thomas | B | 23 | 7/30/1937 | Ra | S | Wake |
| Exum, George | B | 22 | 8/ 6/1937 | M | | Wayne |
| McNeill, James | B | 21 | 8/13/1937 | M | S | Harnett |
| McNeill, Leroy | B | 17 | 8/13/1937 | M | S | Robeson |
| Perry, William | B | 18 | 12/10/1937 | M | S | Chatham |
| Caldwell, Walter | B | 37 | 12/10/1937 | Ra | S | Iredell |
| Sermons, James | B | 29 | 1/21/1938 | M | S | Forsyth |
| Marshall, James | B | 30 | 2/ 4/1938 | B | | Wayne |
| Smoak, E.L. | W | 40 | 2/18/1938 | M | S | New Hanover |
| Exum, Milford | W | 39 | 2/18/1938 | M | S | Wayne |

| Name | Race | Age | Date of Execution | Offense | Appeal | County |
|------|------|-----|-------------------|---------|--------|--------|
| Outlaw, Sylvester | B | 32 | 4/29/1938 | Ra | S | Duplin |
| Hadley, Waddell | B | 22 | 4/29/1938 | Ra | S | Sampson |
| Baldwin, Empire | B | 25 | 6/10/1938 | Ra | S | Columbus |
| Outlaw, Apsom | B | 29 | 6/17/1938 | Ra | S | Duplin |
| Gardner, Lonnie | B | 27 | 6/17/1938 | Ra | S | Duplin |
| Brice, Wiley | B | 35 | 7/ 1/1938 | M | | Alamance |
| Payne, Bill | W | 41 | 7/ 1/1938 | M | S | Buncombe |
| Turner, Wash | W | 36 | 7/ 1/1938 | M | S | Buncombe |
| Linney, Tom | B | 32 | 9/23/1938 | M | S | Forsyth |
| Jefferson, L.J. | B | 17 | 9/23/1938 | M | S | Forsyth |
| Ford, George | B | 20 | 9/30/1938 | M | | Scotland |
| Robinson, Ed | B | 33 | 11/18/1938 | Ra | S | Iredell |
| Hawie, John Ernest | B | 29 | 12/ 2/1938 | Ra | S | Forsyth |
| Parnell, Baxter | W | 33 | 12/ 9/1938 | M | S | Cabarrus |
| Stovall, King Solomon | B | 26 | 1/20/1939 | M | S | Granville |
| De Journette, Bat | B | 43 | 4/ 7/1939 | M | S | Guilford |
| Braceley, Clarence | B | 24 | 4/ 7/1939 | M | S | Vance |
| Dixon, James | B | 38 | 5/ 5/1939 | M | S | Cabarrus |
| Mattocks, Edward Lee | B | 21 | 5/26/1939 | M | | Onslow |
| Burney, Dave | B | 47 | 6/ 9/1939 | M | S | Jones |
| Alston, Ed | B | — | 6/16/1939 | M | S | Durham |
| Henderson, James | B | 21 | 7/ 7/1939 | M | S | New Hanover |
| Capers, Alfred | B | 23 | 7/ 7/1939 | M | S | Robeson |
| Hammond, Bricey | B | 24 | 7/ 7/1939 | M | S | Robeson |
| Morris, Arthur | B | 25 | 9/ 1/1939 | B | S | Wake |
| Godwin, James F. | W | 20 | 9/22/1939 | M | S | Guilford |
| Fain, Charles | B | 26 | 10/ 6/1939 | Ra,B | S | Cherokee |
| Richardson, Willie | B | 19 | 10/27/1939 | B | S | Nash |
| Bowser, Claude, Jr. | B | 22 | 10/28/1939 | M | S | Halifax |
| Williams, Raymond | B | 20 | 11/24/1939 | M | S | Sampson |
| Maxwell, Glenn | B | 50 | 1/19/1940 | M | S | Alleghany |
| Rogers, Clarence | B | 26 | 1/19/1940 | M | S | Durham |
| Bryant, Nathaniel | B | 17 | 2/16/1940 | M,B | S | Hoke |
| Young, William | B | 22 | 2/16/1940 | M,B | S | Hoke |
| Williams, Robert | B | 20 | 3/15/1940 | Ra | S | Cumberland |
| Page, Zeb | B | 29 | 4/ 5/1940 | Ra | S | Johnston |
| Gibson, Simon Cooley | B | 23 | 5/24/1940 | Ra | S | New Hanover |
| Hopkins, Charlie | B | 64 | 6/14/1940 | M | S | Rutherford |
| Flynn, Lee | W | 44 | 6/28/1940 | M | S | McDowell |
| Smith, Zedekiel | B | 29 | 12/ 6/1940 | M | S | Sampson |
| Hudson, Dollie | B | 27 | 4/18/1940 | M | S | Northampton |
| Woodard, Sylvester | B | 33 | 5/ 2/1941 | M | S | Wayne |
| Shaw, James | B | — | 5/23/1941 | M | S | Columbus |
| Wall, Fleet Jack | B | 33 | 6/ 6/1941 | M | S | Anson |
| Cureton, Noah | B | 51 | 6/13/1941 | M | S | Mecklenburg |
| Cash, Hubert Y. | W | 40 | 8/22/1941 | M | S | Durham |
| Melvin, Tom | B | 42 | 9/ 5/1941 | M | S | Wayne |
| Peele, George | B | — | 10/10/1941 | M | S | Bertie |
| Morrow, Luther | B | 26 | 12/12/1941 | M | S | Union |
| Westcott, Roland | W | 21 | 1/ 9/1942 | M | S | New Hanover |
| Sturdivant, Robert | B | 29 | 2/13/1942 | M | S | Bladen |
| Gibson, Arthur | B | 32 | 8/ 7/1942 | Ra | S | Buncombe |

| Name | Race | Age | Date of Execution | Offense | Appeal | County |
|------|------|-----|-------------------|---------|--------|--------|
| Smith, Walter | W | 63 | 8/21/1942 | M | S | Wayne |
| Allen, Herman | W | 35 | 10/30/1942 | M | S | Johnston |
| Harris, Otis | B | 17 | 10/30/1942 | Ra | S | Bertie |
| Long, William | B | 31 | 11/13/1942 | M | | Pitt |
| Phillips, Daniel | B | 29 | 1/ 1/1943 | M | S | Durham |
| Phillips, Rosanna (Female) | B | 25 | 1/ 1/1943 | M | S | Durham |
| Hairston, Sam | B | 22 | 1/29/1943 | Ra | S | Forsyth |
| Heares, Palmer | W | 35 | 2/19/1943 | M | | Robeson |
| Lee, John Henry | B | 19 | 4/16/1943 | Ra | S | Camden |
| Moody, Lewis | B | 26 | 5/21/1943 | M | S | Northampton |
| Bryant, Bill | W | 39 | 6/ 4/1943 | M | S | McDowell |
| Smith, Percell | I | 22 | 6/ 4/1943 | Ra | S | Robeson |
| Hunt, Harvey | I | 21 | 6/ 4/1943 | Ra | S | Robeson |
| Utley, James | B | 24 | 6/18/1943 | M | S | Montgomery |
| Poole, William Henry | B | 29 | 10/ 8/1943 | M | S | Pasquotank |
| Smith, Willie | B | 47 | 10/29/1943 | M | S | Wake |
| Redfern, John Willie | B | 40 | 11/26/1943 | M | S | Warren |
| Grass, Clyde | W | 31 | 12/10/1943 | M | S | Cabarrus |
| Harris, Alex | W | 48 | 1/28/1944 | M | S | Hoke |
| Farrell, Andrew W. | W | 24 | 2/18/1944 | Ra | S | Durham |
| Grainger, Wayman | B | 19 | 2/25/1944 | M | S | Columbus |
| Taylor, James | B | 20 | 11/ 3/1944 | M | S | Wake |
| Alexander, Charles | B | 23 | 11/17/1944 | Ra | S | Halifax |
| Buchanan, James | B | 19 | 11/24/1944 | Ra | S | Mecklenburg |
| Brooks, George W. | B | 20 | 11/24/1944 | Ra | S | Mecklenburg |
| Wade, Melvin | B | 24 | 12/29/1944 | Ra | S | Scotland |
| Thompson, Ralph | B | 18 | 12/29/1944 | M | S | Mecklenburg |
| Williams, Bessie Mae (Female) | W | — | 12/29/1944 | M | S | Mecklenburg |
| Biggs, William Dalton | W | 21 | 3/ 9/1945 | M | S | Guilford |
| Messer, John Edgar | W | 21 | 3/ 9/1945 | M | S | Guilford |
| Biggs, Elmer Hardy | W | 23 | 3/ 9/1945 | M | S | Guilford |
| Hill, Horis | W | — | 5/25/1945 | M | | Jones |
| McDaniel, Lacy | B | 34 | 6/ 6/1945 | Ra | | Guilford |
| French, Henry | B | 35 | 6/22/1945 | M | S | Montgomery |
| Jones, William H. | B | — | 6/22/1945 | M | S | Wake |
| Williams, Burnett | B | — | 10/26/1945 | Ra | S | Lee |
| Mays, Edward | B | — | 11/ 2/1945 | M | S | Lee |
| Hightower, Walter | B | 32 | 2/15/1946 | M | | Wilkes |
| King, Alligood | B | — | 4/26/1946 | M | S | Lenoir |
| Hart, Thomas B. | B | — | 5/ 4/1946 | M | S | Halifax |
| Herring, Gurney | B | — | 5/24/1946 | Ra | S | Wayne |
| Walker, George | B | 23 | 6/21/1946 | Ra | S | Harnett |
| Deaton, Fred | W | 39 | 6/28/1946 | M | S | Gaston |
| Stewart, Fab | B | — | 6/28/1946 | M | S | Wake |
| Floyd, Edward W. | W | — | 10/25/1946 | M | S | Northampton |
| Nash, Robert L. | W | — | 11/ 1/1946 | M | S | Wake |
| Johnson, Wilbert | B | — | 11/22/1946 | Ra | S | Wake |
| Primus, Charles, Jr. | B | — | 11/22/1946 | Ra | S | Wake |
| Williams, Calvin C. | B | — | 12/13/1946 | M | | Sampson |
| Mathews, Herman | B | — | 12/13/1946 | M | | Sampson |
| Ragland, Otis | B | — | 3/14/1947 | Ra | S | Martin |

| Name | Race | Age | Date of Execution | Offense | Appeal | County |
|------|------|-----|-------------------|---------|--------|--------|
| Montgomery, Bennie | B | — | 3/28/1947 | M | S | Union |
| Horton, Richard | B | — | 4/ 4/1947 | M | S | Wilkes |
| Martin, Eunice | B | — | 4/11/1947 | M | S | Forsyth |
| McLeod, Ben Frank | B | — | 5/23/1947 | M | S | Scotland |
| Sanders, Albert | B | — | 6/ 6/1947 | M | S | Johnson |
| Farmer, James Marvin | B | — | 6/ 6/1947 | M | S | Johnson |
| Artis, Moses | B | — | 6/27/1947 | M | S | Duplin |
| Brown, Woodrow | B | — | 6/27/1947 | Ra | S | Wake |
| Kirpsey, Roy | B | — | 6/27/1947 | M | S | Columbus |
| McCain, Richard | B | — | 10/ 3/1947 | M | S | Mecklenburg |
| Lumpkins, Jethro | B | — | 10/ 3/1947 | M | S | Mecklenburg |
| Messer, Robert | W | — | 10/ 3/1947 | M | S | Jackson |
| O'Dear, Earl | W | — | 10/ 3/1947 | M | S | Jackson |
| Cherry, Wilie | B | 25 | 10/ 3/1947 | M,Ra | S | Northampton |
| Douglas, Oscar | B | 40 | 10/10/1947 | Ra | S | Davis |
| Stanley, Lester | B | — | 10/31/1947 | M | S | Edgecombe |
| Brooks, J.C. | B | — | 10/31/1947 | M | S | Henderson |
| Nunn, Thurman | B | — | 10/31/1947 | M | S | Henderson |
| Brown, Grady | B | — | 10/31/1947 | M | S | Henderson |
| Little, William | B | — | 11/14/1947 | Ra | S | Wake |
| Letters, Ralph V. | W | — | 11/14/1947 | Ra | S | Wilkes |
| Bell, Marvin C. | W | — | 11/14/1947 | Ra | S | Wilkes |
| Black, Frank | B | — | 1/ 2/1948 | M | | Lenoir |
| Breeze, John H. | B | — | 1/16/1948 | M | S | Orange |
| Anderson, Booker T. | B | — | 4/23/1948 | M,Ar | S | Pitt |
| Hooks, Buster | B | — | 4/23/1948 | Ra | S | Randolph |
| Jackson, James L. | B | 50 | 5/ 7/1948 | M | S | Burke |
| Hammonds, George | B | 30 | 6/ 4/1948 | M | S | Davidson |
| Wilson, Henderson | B | 27 | 6/ 4/1948 | M | S | Davidson |
| West, James Pete | B | 20 | 11/19/1948 | M | S | Duplin |
| Creech, James | W | 37 | 1/28/1949 | M | S | Johnston |
| Garner, Emmett | W | — | 3/18/1949 | M | S | Harnett |
| Cockrell, Roy | W | 42 | 3/25/1949 | M | S | Nash |
| Lewis, James E. | B | 26 | 6/17/1949 | M | S | Robeson |
| Reid, Allen T. | B | 29 | 12/ 9/1949 | B | S,U | Wilson |
| Brown, Audie Lee | B | 27 | 12/ 9/1949 | M | S | Randolph |
| Medlin, Monroe | B | 23 | 12/ 9/1949 | M | S | Mecklenburg |
| Jones, Uzelle | B | 35 | 12/16/1949 | M | S | Hoke |
| Chavis, Hector | I | 28 | 12/30/1949 | M | S | Robeson |
| Jacobs, Lelander | I | 29 | 12/30/1949 | M | S | Robeson |
| Heller, Lee | B | 47 | 1/ 6/1950 | M | S | Catawba |
| Bridges, Jack | W | — | 5/19/1950 | M | S | Wake |
| Shackleford, Claude E. | W | 34 | 7/21/1950 | Ra | S | Guilford |
| Lamm, Covey Connor | W | — | 11/10/1950 | M | S | Wilson |
| Lyles, Ernest | B | 33 | 11/24/1950 | Ra | | Franklin |
| Shedd, Curtis | W | 29 | 3/23/1951 | M | S | Macon |
| Hall, James Richard | W | 36 | 3/29/1951 | M | S | Jackson |
| Rogers, John Henry | B | — | 4/27/1951 | M | S | Sampson |
| Roman, John Andrew | B | 28 | 6/ 6/1952 | M | S | Davidson |
| Miller, Lafayette | B | 22 | 5/ 1/1953 | M | S | Beaufort |
| Spiller, Raleigh | B | — | 5/29/1953 | Ra | S,F,U | Bertie |
| Brown, Clyde | B | — | 5/29/1953 | Ra | S,F,U | Forsyth |

| Name | Race | Age | Date of Execution | Offense | Appeal | County |
|------|------|-----|-------------------|---------|--------|--------|
| Daniels, Lloyd Ray | B | — | 11/ 6/1953 | M | S,F,U | Pitt |
| Daniels, Bennie | B | — | 11/ 6/1953 | M | S,F,U | Pitt |
| Scales, Richard | B | 29 | 7/15/1955 | M | S | Guilford |
| Conner, Robert S. | B | — | 7/13/1956 | B | S | Forsyth |
| McAfee, Ross | B | 42 | 11/22/1957 | M | | Alexander |
| Bunton, Julius | B | 21 | 2/28/1958 | B | S | Guilford |
| Bass, Matthew P. | B | 43 | 12/ 5/1958 | Ra | | Wake |
| Boykin, Theodore | B | 32 | 10/27/1961 | M,Ra | | Duplin |

'These men were electrocuted because they were sentenced to death before the lethal gas law was passed.

## NORTH DAKOTA

*Period of Executions*: 1905
*Total Number*: 1
*Method*: Hanging
*Period of Abolition*: Capital punishment was abolished in 1915 except for treason and first-degree murder committed by a prisoner serving a life sentence for first-degree murder.

| Name | Race | Age | Date of Execution | Offense | Appeal | County |
|------|------|-----|-------------------|---------|--------|--------|
| Rooney, John | – | — | 10/17/1905 | M | S,U | Cass |

## OHIO

*Period of Executions*: 1885–1963
*Total Number*: 344
*Method*: Hanging 1885–1896; electrocution 1897–1963
*Other Data*: In regard to appeals, all cases in Ohio are decided by the Court of Appeals in each county. These decisions are not reported. An appeal to the Ohio Supreme Court can only be taken on a question of the state constitution; therefore, no appeals are listed in that column. After the state of Ohio began executing its condemned felons at the state penitentiary, one man (identified in footnote 1) was hanged under local authority in the county of his conviction at the county seat designated.

| Name | Race | Age | Date of Execution | Offense | Appeal | County |
|------|------|-----|-------------------|---------|--------|--------|
| Wagner, Valentine | W | 56 | 7/31/1885 | M | S | Morrow |
| Hartnett, Patrick | W | 38 | 9/30/1885 | M | S | Hamilton |
| Grenier, Frederick[1] | W | 27 | 10/17/1885 | M | | Columbus |
| Grover, Arthur J. | W | 33 | 5/14/1886 | M | S | Wood |
| Terrell, Josiah | W | 27 | 9/ 2/1887 | M | | Meigs |
| George, William | W | 23 | 5/18/1888 | M | | Muskingum |
| Stanyard, Ebenezer | W | 24 | 7/13/1888 | M | | Mahoning |
| Morgan, Charles | W | 53 | 8/ 3/1888 | M | | Portage |

| Name | Race | Age | Date of Execution | Offense | Appeal | County |
|------|------|-----|-------------------|---------|--------|--------|
| Lueth, Otto | W | 16 | 8/29/1890 | M | S | Cuyahoga |
| Smith, John | W | 30 | 8/29/1890 | M | | Hamilton |
| Miller, Ellis | W | 40 | 12/ 2/1890 | M | S | Union |
| Sharkey, Elmer | W | 23 | 12/19/1890 | M | | Preble |
| Popp, Henry | W | 31 | 12/19/1890 | M | | Stark |
| Blair, Edward | W | 26 | 8/21/1891 | M | S | Putnam |
| Fitzgerald, William | W | 24 | 12/18/1891 | M | | Mahoning |
| Harvey, Jacob | W | 26 | 6/24/1892 | M | | Montgomery |
| Craig, Charles | B | 37 | 9/ 9/1892 | M | | Hamilton |
| McCarthy, Edward | W | 25 | 9/ 9/1892 | M | | Hamilton |
| Van Loon, Frank A. | W | 22 | 8/ 4/1893 | M | | Putnam |
| Whaley, William | B | 18 | 6/22/1894 | M | | Greene |
| Hart, Charles | W | 18 | 4/12/1895 | M | | Paulding |
| Geschwelm, George | W | 32 | 4/26/1895 | M | | Franklin |
| Prince, Lafayette | W | 48 | 5/29/1895 | M | | Cuyahoga |
| Molnar, John | W | 22 | 6/26/1895 | M | | Cuyahoga |
| McDonough, Michael | W | 59 | 6/28/1895 | M | | Hardin |
| Taylor, William | B | 18 | 7/26/1895 | M | | Franklin |
| Edwards, Isaac L. | W | 44 | 9/17/1895 | M | | Hocking |
| Adams, Martin | W | 29 | 9/27/1895 | M | | Hamilton |
| Paul, William | W | 33 | 4/29/1896 | M | | Brown |
| Haas, William | W | 17 | 4/21/1897 | M | | Hamilton |
| Wiley, William | W | 38 | 4/21/1897 | M | | Hamilton |
| Miller, Frank | W | 27 | 9/ 3/1897 | M | | Franklin |
| Frantz, Albert | W | 21 | 11/19/1897 | M | | Montgomery |
| Early, Frank | B | 33 | 5/14/1898 | M | | Hamilton |
| Nelson, Charles | B | 22 | 11/ 4/1898 | M | | Wood |
| Kirves, Bruno | W | 47 | 8/17/1899 | M | | Montgomery |
| Gardner, Richard | B | 25 | 11/ 9/1900 | M | | Ross |
| Ferell, Rosslyn | B | 22 | 3/ 1/1901 | M | | Union |
| Ruthven, Ed | W | 30 | 6/28/1901 | M | | Cuyahoga |
| Bennett, John | B | 26 | 4/15/1904 | M | | Lorain |
| Berg, Carl | W | 19 | 6/ 3/1904 | M | | Fulton |
| Schiller, Michael G. | W | 39 | 6/17/1904 | M | | Mahoning |
| Johnson, Moses | B | 28 | 6/18/1904 | M | | Scioto |
| Wade, Albert | W | 42 | 7/14/1904 | M | | Lucas |
| Wade, Benjamin | W | 29 | 7/14/1904 | M | | Lucas |
| Stimmel, Charles | W | 26 | 7/22/1904 | M | | Montgomery |
| Knapp, Alfred A. | W | 41 | 9/19/1904 | M | | Butler |
| Fisher, Albert | W | 45 | 10/ 7/1904 | M | | Lucas |
| Harmon, Lewis | W | 27 | 10/28/1904 | M | | Franklin |
| Loveland, Otis | W | 38 | 11/25/1904 | M | | Franklin |
| Nichols, William | W | 67 | 12/ 9/1904 | M | | Hardin |
| Hamilton, Herman | B | 19 | 3/24/1905 | M | | Scioto |
| Styles, Butler | B | 33 | 9/21/1906 | M | | Franklin |
| Castor, Frank | W | 28 | 2/15/1907 | M | S | Franklin |
| Haugh, Oliver Crook | W | 35 | 4/19/1907 | M | | Montgomery |
| Cornelius, James W. | W | 36 | 6/28/1907 | M | | Stark |
| White, Henry | B | 25 | 7/19/1907 | M | | Warren |
| Davis, Albert | B | 41 | 10/25/1907 | M | | Clark |
| Fowler, Royal | W | 26 | 11/ 1/1907 | M | | Montgomery |
| Earl, Frank A. | W | 28 | 12/20/1907 | M | | Shelby |

| Name | Race | Age | Date of Execution | Offense | Appeal | County |
|------|------|-----|-------------------|---------|--------|--------|
| Crooks, Harry Edward | W | 45 | 10/29/1909 | M | | Montgomery |
| Rife, Harry | W | 38 | 1/19/1910 | M | | Preble |
| Kilpatrick, John | B | 26 | 2/ 5/1910 | M | | Jefferson |
| Davis, Charles | B | 27 | 3/11/1910 | M | | Lawrence |
| Swan, William T. | B | 25 | 9/ 2/1910 | M | | Ross |
| Willman, Cletus A. | W | 29 | 7/28/1911 | M | | Stark |
| Justice, Charles | W | 42 | 10/27/1911 | M | | Greene |
| Scott, Steve | B | 32 | 11/ 3/1911 | M | | Miami |
| Davis, Thomas | B | 26 | 12/15/1911 | M | | Pickaway |
| Klawetch, Rocco | W | 46 | 11/15/1912 | M | | Erie |
| Selvaggio, Dominic | W | 35 | 11/22/1912 | M | | Erie |
| Kinney, Frank | W | 55 | 12/12/1913 | M | | Cuyahoga |
| Jenkins, Wesley | B | 30 | 12/ 4/1914 | M | | Montgomery |
| Beard, Harley | W | 18 | 12/ 4/1914 | M | | Lawrence |
| Ellis, Reuben | B | 26 | 2/ 6/1917 | M | | Hamilton |
| Clark, Albert | W | 28 | 6/22/1917 | M | | Miami |
| Snoufer, Blaine | W | 26 | 12/12/1917 | M | | Franklin |
| Burnetti, Charles | W | 35 | 2/ 1/1918 | M | | Stark |
| Washington, Aaron G. | B | 21 | 7/26/1918 | M | | Montgomery |
| Wright, William | B | 37 | 9/20/1918 | M | | Franklin |
| Biondo, Pasquale | W | 27 | 10/ 4/1918 | M | | Summit |
| Spillman, Brazil | B | 35 | 10/18/1918 | M | | Hamilton |
| Mazzano, Frank | W | 19 | 2/21/1919 | M | | Summit |
| Borgio, Rosario | W | 24 | 2/21/1919 | M | | Summit |
| Chivaro, Paul | W | 30 | 7/24/1919 | M | | Summit |
| Morgan, James | B | 52 | 9/26/1919 | M | | Williams |
| Seinich, Frank | W | 30 | 10/17/1919 | M | | Tuscarawas |
| Ness, Edward | W | 35 | 3/ 9/1920 | M | | Hamilton |
| Edinger, Jacob | W | 25 | 3/ 9/1920 | M | | Hamilton |
| Damico, Vincent | W | 24 | 3/31/1920 | M | | Summit |
| Dell, Joseph | W | 25 | 1/ 7/1921 | M | | Cuyahoga |
| O'Neil, Robert | B | 26 | 1/ 7/1921 | M | | Cuyahoga |
| Gross, Charles | B | 27 | 1/20/1921 | M | | Cuyahoga |
| Rehfeld, Charles | W | 43 | 5/28/1921 | M | | Sandusky |
| Howell, Dick | W | 42 | 6/ 2/1921 | M | | Stark |
| Richardson, Royce | B | 32 | 7/ 1/1921 | M | | Lucas |
| Motto, Frank | W | 26 | 8/29/1921 | M | | Cuyahoga |
| Brown, Sylvester | B | 27 | 9/ 9/1921 | M | | Mahoning |
| Davy, Andy | W | 38 | 9/20/1921 | M | | Franklin |
| Cooper, John | B | 42 | 9/30/1921 | M | | Franklin |
| Harding, Arthur | B | 38 | 2/24/1922 | M | | Lucas |
| Bland, Harry | W | 27 | 3/ 1/1922 | M | | Meigs |
| Wright, Walter | W | 28 | 3/ 1/1922 | M | | Jefferson |
| McGuire, John | W | 30 | 3/ 3/1922 | M | | Lucas |
| Tyler, LeRoy | B | 34 | 3/ 3/1922 | M | | Mahoning |
| Champlin, Roy | W | 27 | 3/24/1922 | M | | Scioto |
| Bush, George | B | 41 | 5/ 5/1922 | M | | Mahoning |
| Vaiden, John | B | 26 | 5/ 5/1922 | M | | Franklin |
| Purpera, Samuel | W | 17 | 5/ 9/1922 | M | | Cuyahoga |
| Benigno, Dominick | W | 26 | 6/14/1922 | M | | Cuyahoga |
| Gackenbach, John | B | 21 | 6/20/1922 | M | | Marion |
| Myeskie, Steve | W | 22 | 6/23/1922 | M | | Mahoning |

| Name | Race | Age | Date of Execution | Offense | Appeal | County |
|------|------|-----|-------------------|---------|--------|--------|
| Shelton, Ludie C. | B | 24 | 1/26/1923 | M | | Hamilton |
| Habig, Charles | W | 32 | 2/16/1923 | M | | Cuyahoga |
| White, Henry | B | 41 | 3/ 2/1923 | M | | Franklin |
| Arnold, Charles | W | 64 | 3/ 2/1923 | M | | Franklin |
| Forbes, Stanley | W | 27 | 4/13/1923 | M | | Franklin |
| Holt, Noble | W | 27 | 4/27/1923 | M | | Hamilton |
| Wellions, James | B | 40 | 7/13/1923 | M | | Franklin |
| Roberts, Adam Logan | B | 41 | 9/ 6/1921 | M | | Franklin |
| Layer, Irvin | W | 38 | 11/ 2/1923 | M | | Montgomery |
| Karayians, John | W | 33 | 12/ 7/1923 | M | | Trumbull |
| Long, Edward | W | 23 | 1/ 4/1924 | M | | Belmont |
| Nelson, John | B | 28 | 2/ 1/1924 | M | | Clark |
| Sipcich, Mike | W | 56 | 2/ 8/1924 | M | | Hamilton |
| Hollis, Bill | B | 24 | 3/28/1924 | M | | Mahoning |
| Head, Clem | B | 31 | 4/15/1924 | M | | Mahoning |
| Brooks, Charles | B | 52 | 4/28/1924 | M | | Perry |
| Rossi, Louis | W | 35 | 4/29/1924 | M | | Mahoning |
| Caparra, Vincenzo | W | 33 | 6/25/1924 | M | | Jefferson |
| Avant, James | B | 41 | 12/ 5/1924 | M | | Mahoning |
| Kuszik, Alex | W | 19 | 12/12/1924 | M | | Summit |
| Kane, Joseph | W | 21 | 1/ 9/1925 | M | | Mahoning |
| Highwarden, Bert | B | 49 | 2/ 9/1925 | M | | Champaign |
| Brown, Henry | B | 54 | 2/20/1925 | M | | Hamilton |
| Thomas, Charles | B | 24 | 3/27/1925 | M | | Franklin |
| Prymas, Joseph | W | 24 | 4/24/1925 | M | | Cuyahoga |
| Adkins, Jason | W | 30 | 5/ 1/1925 | M | | Scioto |
| Ward, Fred | W | 30 | 5/16/1925 | M | | Belmont |
| Gwodenknow, Kondat | W | 37 | 6/12/1925 | M | | Belmont |
| Traylor, Lenzey | W | 21 | 8/ 7/1925 | M | | Scioto |
| Ferranto, Cosmo | W | 45 | 9/ 4/1925 | M | S | Cuyahoga |
| Walters, Calvin | B | 28 | 9/18/1925 | M | | Perry |
| Tudor, Bucur | W | 39 | 11/20/1925 | M | S | Cuyahoga |
| Little, Robert | B | 40 | 11/20/1925 | M | | Hamilton |
| Henry, James | B | 37 | 1/ 9/1926 | M | | Hamilton |
| Liska, Frank | W | 42 | 6/25/1926 | M | S | Cuyahoga |
| Clark, William | W | 19 | 7/ 8/1926 | M | S | Sandusky |
| Bryant, John | B | 40 | 9/ 2/1926 | M | | Meigs |
| Rhodes, Richard | W | 29 | 9/ 2/1923 | M | | Meigs |
| Hedrick, John | W | 30 | 9/ 2/1926 | M | | Meigs |
| Ross, Emanuel | B | 17 | 11/26/1926 | M | S | Cuyahoga |
| Thompson, Robert F. | W | 54 | 1/ 8/1927 | M | | Coshocton |
| Workman, Scott | W | 40 | 3/31/1927 | M | | Clermont |
| Leyon, James D. | W | 27 | 4/ 8/1927 | M | | Huron |
| Thoma, George W. | W | 23 | 4/ 8/1927 | M | | Richland |
| Hickman, John | W | 30 | 6/10/1927 | M | | Ross |
| Wargo, George | W | 60 | 6/10/1927 | M | S | Lake |
| Halterman, Leo | W | 27 | 6/17/1927 | M | | Fayette |
| Orleck, Philip | W | 21 | 7/18/1927 | M | | Richland |
| Hewitt, Floyd | W | 16 | 1/ 6/1928 | M | | Ashtabula |
| Coverson, John | B | 18 | 1/ 9/1928 | M | | Hamilton |
| Peppers, Eddie | B | 21 | 3/15/1928 | M | | Gallia |
| Wilson, W.H. | B | 19 | 7/ 5/1928 | M | | Scioto |

| Name | Race | Age | Date of Execution | Offense | Appeal | County |
|---|---|---|---|---|---|---|
| Coleman, James | B | 18 | 7/ 5/1928 | M | | Scioto |
| Rucker, John | B | 46 | 11/30/1928 | M | | Hamilton |
| Hoppe, Stanley | W | 26 | 11/30/1928 | M | | Lucas |
| Bradshaw, John | B | 51 | 1/11/1929 | M | | Franklin |
| Koon, Everett | W | 29 | 2/15/1929 | M | | Marion |
| Nevins, James | W | 40 | 7/ 1/1929 | M | | Cuyahoga |
| Ford, Rodney | W | 28 | 7/19/1929 | M | | Hamilton |
| Maul, Arthur J. | W | 24 | 11/ 1/1929 | M | | Summit |
| Snook, James H. | W | 49 | 2/28/1930 | M | | Franklin |
| Richardson, John | W | 22 | 5/26/1930 | M | | Summit |
| Akers, Lee | W | 17 | 6/13/1930 | M | | Cuyahoga |
| Litteral, John | B | 42 | 6/20/1930 | M | | Athens |
| Williams, George | W | 68 | 6/28/1930 | M | | Cuyahoga |
| Dull, Lawrence | W | 25 | 7/11/1930 | M | | Seneca |
| Cramer, Charles | W | 31 | 11/10/1930 | M | | Brown |
| Walker, Bert | W | 42 | 11/10/1930 | M | | Summit |
| Massa, Fred | W | 26 | 1/30/1931 | M | | Crawford |
| McCartney, Kenneth | W | 25 | 1/30/1931 | M | | Crawford |
| Sites, Earl | W | 27 | 1/30/1931 | M | | Crawford |
| Hamilton, Arthur | W | 41 | 4/ 7/1931 | M | | Logan |
| King, Charles | W | 39 | 4/30/1931 | M | | Butler |
| Williams, John | B | 39 | 5/21/1931 | M | | Butler |
| Romeo, James | W | 29 | 5/25/1931 | M | | Stark |
| Ralls, Walter | B | 31 | 11/13/1931 | M | | Crawford |
| Ralls, Blanton | B | 19 | 11/13/1931 | M | | Crawford |
| Smith, Tilby | W | 26 | 11/20/1931 | M | | Ashtabula |
| Tangules, Gust | W | 37 | 1/ 8/1932 | M | | Summit |
| Hunt, Dan | W | 58 | 3/11/1932 | M | | Putnam |
| Glasscock, John | W | 35 | 4/22/1932 | M | | Cuyahoga |
| Brown, Walker | B | 24 | 6/ 3/1932 | M | | Pickaway |
| Loudermilk, Henry | W | 47 | 6/ 3/1932 | M | | Pickaway |
| Adams, Lacey | B | 38 | 6/10/1932 | M | | Pickaway |
| Little, Arthur | B | 39 | 7/22/1932 | M | | Pickaway |
| Enzulus, William | W | 22 | 1/ 7/1933 | M | | Cuyahoga |
| Downing, John | W | 43 | 3/10/1933 | M | | Franklin |
| Brown, Athay | B | 26 | 3/10/1933 | M | | Cuyahoga |
| Meeker, Herbert | W | 23 | 3/22/1933 | M | | Holmes |
| Rotunno, Tony | W | 31 | 4/28/1933 | M | | Trumbull |
| Atterholt, Ralph | W | 30 | 4/28/1933 | M | | Trumbull |
| Murphy, James | B | 22 | 8/14/1933 | M | | Hamilton |
| Murphy, Joseph | B | 18 | 8/14/1933 | M | | Hamilton |
| Probaski, Chester | W | 25 | 11/24/1933 | M | | Richland |
| Chandler, Merrill E. | B | 22 | 11/24/1933 | M | | Richland |
| Vacchiano, Frank | W | 22 | 12/29/1933 | M | | Lucas |
| Bruno, Albert | W | 27 | 2/ 6/1934 | M | | Lucas |
| Kittrells, Irmel | B | 26 | 6/25/1934 | M | | Highland |
| Miller, Edward | W | 28 | 10/15/1934 | M | | Stark |
| Pierpont, Harry | W | 31 | 10/17/1934 | M | | Allen |
| Thacker, Herbert | W | 21 | 11/22/1934 | M | | Jackson |
| Freeman, Ray | W | 25 | 11/22/1934 | M | | Jackson |
| Mosley, Isaac | B | 23 | 11/23/1934 | M | | Hamilton |
| Pennell, Hampton | B | 37 | 1/ 4/1935 | M | | Franklin |

| Name | Race | Age | Date of Execution | Offense | Appeal | County |
|------|------|-----|-------------------|---------|--------|--------|
| Wright, William | B | 39 | 4/ 9/1935 | M | | Franklin |
| Treadway, Peter | W | 38 | 6/ 1/1935 | M | | Cuyahoga |
| Swiger, Russell | W | 21 | 7/22/1935 | M | | Muskingum |
| Smith, Roy | W | 29 | 8/ 9/1935 | M | | Van Wert |
| Walters, Willard | B | 25 | 9/27/1935 | M | | Franklin |
| Davis, George | B | 24 | 10/17/1935 | M | | Mahoning |
| Blackam, Theo | B | 19 | 10/23/1935 | M | | Hamilton |
| Lamphier, Ethol B. | W | 45 | 11/ 1/1935 | M | | Huron |
| Peacock, Norman | W | 22 | 3/11/1936 | M | | Hamilton |
| Thompson, James | W | 27 | 4/25/1936 | M | | Lawrence |
| Eberle, Donald | W | 30 | 6/23/1936 | M | | Cuyahoga |
| Keller, Richard | W | 30 | 7/ 1/1936 | M | | Hamilton |
| Player, John | W | 30 | 8/ 5/1936 | M | | Cuyahoga |
| Brown, James | B | 26 | 12/ 4/1936 | M | | Cuyahoga |
| Kotowicz, Steve | W | 23 | 5/19/1937 | M | | Lucas |
| Thompson, J.H. | B | 67 | 12/17/1937 | M | | Highland |
| Gardner, William H. | W | 35 | 1/17/1938 | M | S | Franklin |
| Hines, Charles | W | 25 | 1/17/1938 | M | | Hamilton |
| Jones, Everett | W | 33 | 3/25/1938 | M | | Fayette |
| Williams, Thomas | B | 19 | 6/27/1938 | M | | Jefferson |
| Hobbs, William | W | 32 | 7/ 6/1938 | M | | Butler |
| Snow, Robert | W | 27 | 7/13/1938 | M | S | Summit |
| Peters, William | B | 43 | 9/26/1938 | M | | Cuyahoga |
| Thomas, Sam | B | 23 | 10/26/1938 | M | | Hamilton |
| Ferrito, Carl | W | 20 | 11/ 3/1938 | M | S | Cuyahoga |
| Mosley, Fred | W | 47 | 11/30/1938 | M | | Knox |
| Hahn, Anna Marie (Female) | W | 31 | 12/ 7/1938 | M | | Hamilton |
| Figuli, Stephen | W | 20 | 12/21/1938 | M | | Franklin |
| Cline, John W. | W | 25 | 2/ 1/1939 | M | | Butler |
| Tracy, Frank | W | 32 | 3/ 3/1939 | M | | Franklin |
| Chapman, Harry | W | 36 | 4/19/1939 | M | | Clark |
| Dingledine, Henry (Son) | W | 28 | 4/19/1939 | M | | Clark |
| Dingledine, Harry (Father) | W | 55 | 4/19/1939 | M | | Clark |
| Roush, Harvey L. | W | 47 | 4/26/1939 | M | | Marion |
| Babich, Nick | W | 54 | 5/ 9/1939 | M | | Trumbull |
| Caldwell, Willie | B | 23 | 6/14/1939 | M | | Cuyahoga |
| Young, Pang | B | 18 | 7/12/1939 | M | | Hamilton |
| Williams, Lafe | W | 47 | 10/25/1939 | M | | Butler |
| Bohannon, Monroe | B | 33 | 7/10/1940 | M | | Hamilton |
| Harris, Eugene | B | 24 | 10/23/1940 | M | | Montgomery |
| Dimarco, Joseph | W | 23 | 1/14/1941 | M | | Cuyahoga |
| Cirasole, Anthony | W | 29 | 1/14/1941 | M | | Cuyahoga |
| Sevastis, Bill | W | 54 | 2/25/1941 | M | | Belmont |
| Williams, Thomas | B | 37 | 12/19/1941 | M | | Lucas |
| Thompson, Wayne | W | 24 | 1/21/1942 | M | | Franklin |
| Doney, Buffert | W | 48 | 7/22/1942 | M | | Stark |
| Jennings, William P. | B | 22 | 3/31/1943 | M | | Mahoning |
| Lock, Henry | B | 43 | 4/26/1943 | M | | Franklin |
| Treat, Anthony | W | 58 | 6/30/1943 | M | | Hamilton |
| Griffin, Erwin | B | 19 | 9/15/1943 | M | | Franklin |
| Ralph, Edward J. | W | 32 | 10/ 4/1943 | M | | Cuyahoga |
| Hand, Louis V. | W | 17 | 1/14/1944 | M | | Mercer |

| Name | Race | Age | Date of Execution | Offense | Appeal | County |
|------|------|-----|-------------------|---------|--------|--------|
| Johnson, Willie | B | 57 | 3/10/1944 | M | | Cuyahoga |
| Brown, James W. | B | 28 | 4/ 6/1945 | M | | Hamilton |
| Jenkins, Cook | B | 24 | 4/ 6/1945 | M | | Hamilton |
| Collett, James W. | W | 61 | 4/20/1945 | M | S | Fayette |
| Johnson, Elder | B | 52 | 9/ 8/1945 | M | | Franklin |
| Hagert, Henry W. | W | 19 | 10/ 3/1945 | M | S | Cuyahoga |
| Stewart, Charles | B | 30 | 10/10/1945 | M | | Summit |
| Carter, Frank D. | W | 25 | 11/ 8/1945 | M | | Hamilton |
| Brown, Ralph | W | 32 | 2/ 9/1946 | M | | Lorain |
| Naiberg, Frank | W | 45 | 2/ 9/1946 | M | | Lorain |
| Koons, Russell E. | W | 23 | 4/ 2/1947 | M | | Clark |
| Wormack, Fred, Jr. | B | 22 | 4/16/1947 | M | | Hamilton |
| Freeman, Nathaniel | B | 24 | 8/ 5/1947 | M | | Cuyahoga |
| Britton, Robert | B | 22 | 11/11/1947 | M | | Cuyahoga |
| Griffin, James | B | 26 | 11/22/1947 | M | | Cuyahoga |
| Sexton, George M. | B | 21 | 1/30/1948 | M | | Erie |
| Dace, Floyd | B | 21 | 3/12/1948 | M | | Cuyahoga |
| Salter, Kenneth | W | 32 | 4/23/1948 | M | S | Lucas |
| Gayles, Clifford | B | 34 | 7/ 2/1948 | M | | Butler |
| Curnutt, Elmer | W | 21 | 7/16/1948 | M | S | Hamilton |
| Frohner, Donald | W | 16 | 8/20/1948 | M | | Mahoning |
| Strain, Nathaniel | B | 26 | 10/25/1948 | M | S | Franklin |
| Daniels, Robert Murl | W | 24 | 1/ 3/1949 | M | | Richland |
| Beach, Harold | W | 23 | 2/ 2/1949 | M | | Cuyahoga |
| Thomas, John | B | 34 | 2/ 4/1949 | M | | Franklin |
| Payton, Howard M. | B | 30 | 2/28/1949 | M | | Stark |
| Nichols, Lester | W | 43 | 3/ 4/1949 | M | | Allen |
| Adams, Asbell | W | 19 | 4/ 8/1949 | M | | Hamilton |
| Williams, Roger | W | 34 | 4/11/1949 | M | | Logan |
| Berry, Andrew | W | 44 | 4/29/1949 | M | | Lucas |
| Reed, Ralph | W | 27 | 5/ 4/1949 | M | S | Cuyahoga |
| Milhouse, Frank | B | 23 | 5/25/1949 | M | | Cuyahoga |
| Burson, John | W | 33 | 5/27/1949 | M | | Stark |
| Davis, Barney | B | 22 | 6/23/1949 | M | S | Cuyahoga |
| Osinski, John C. | W | 40 | 7/22/1949 | M | | Lucas |
| Wisecup, Mahlon | W | 49 | 7/25/1949 | M | | Highland |
| Buchanan, James | B | 25 | 10/26/1949 | M | | Cuyahoga |
| Dodds, Harry | W | 21 | 2/24/1950 | M | | Athens |
| McClure, Ted R. | B | 24 | 5/10/1950 | M | | Cuyahoga |
| Spencer, Delbert | W | 52 | 7/21/1950 | M | | Athens |
| Yankey, Cecil H. | W | 41 | 9/12/1950 | M | | Highland |
| Tudor, Dwight D. | W | 29 | 1/26/1951 | M | | Clark |
| Doty, George E. | W | 28 | 2/ 9/1951 | M | | Belmont |
| Eakins, Morzell | B | 32 | 4/27/1951 | M | | Hamilton |
| Amerman, Max | W | 27 | 11/15/1951 | M | | Medina |
| Stevenson, Lon | B | 19 | 1/18/1952 | M | | Cuyahoga |
| Tiller, George | B | 43 | 2/29/1952 | M | | Hamilton |
| Edwards, James C. | B | 31 | 5/ 9/1952 | M | | Stark |
| Gregg, Chester | W | 57 | 7/11/1952 | M | | Hardin |
| Ross, George F. | W | 28 | 1/16/1953 | M | | Cuyahoga |
| Angel, Louis A. | W | 19 | 1/23/1953 | M | | Licking |
| Lucear, Marvin | B | 38 | 2/20/1953 | M | S | Cuyahoga |

| Name | Race | Age | Date of Execution | Offense | Appeal | County |
|------|------|-----|-------------------|---------|--------|--------|
| Gemmell, Robert | W | 29 | 7/10/1953 | M | | Franklin |
| Dean, Dovie (Female) | W | 55 | 1/15/1954 | M | | Clermont |
| Butler, Betty (Female) | B | 25 | 6/12/1954 | M | | Hamilton |
| Muskus, Russell | W | 33 | 7/ 9/1954 | M | | Stark |
| Nettles, Sam B. | W | 31 | 8/ 6/1954 | M | | Lucas |
| Schrieber, Bernard | W | 19 | 3/15/1956 | M | | Lucas |
| Wilson, Walter | B | 30 | 7/13/1956 | M | | Cuyahoga |
| Allen, Joseph | B | 59 | 9/20/1956 | M | | Cuyahoga |
| Tannyhill, Samuel W. | W | 26 | 11/26/1956 | M | | Sandusky |
| Shackleford, Harold | B | 32 | 6/24/1957 | M | | Licking |
| Walker, Norman | W | 33 | 1/ 3/1958 | M | | Cuyahoga |
| Morhaus, Robert V. | W | 22 | 1/10/1958 | M | | Hamilton |
| Vaughn, James | B | 30 | 2/28/1958 | M | | Cuyahoga |
| Jackson, Robert | B | 40 | 7/ 7/1958 | M | | Hamilton |
| Trotter, Sam | B | 20 | 7/ 7/1958 | M | S | Hamilton |
| Collins, Bennie | B | 54 | 12/19/1958 | M | | Lucas |
| Byomin, Walter J. | W | 41 | 7/ 3/1959 | M | | Lorain |
| Lyons, Robert L. | B | 29 | 2/19/1960 | M | | Cuyahoga |
| Cosby, Joseph | B | 23 | 9/30/1960 | M | | Cuyahoga |
| Penelton, H.B. | B | 30 | 3/17/1961 | M | | Richland |
| Fenton, Ronald G. | W | 29 | 6/ 1/1962 | M | | Summit |
| Buck, James Rodney | W | 24 | 6/22/1962 | M | | Summit |
| Griffin, Robert | B | 44 | 2/15/1963 | M | S | Cuyahoga |
| Reinbolt, Donald L. | W | 29 | 3/15/1963 | M | | Franklin |

[1]Grenier (10/17/1885) was hanged under local authority in the county of his conviction after Ohio began executing its condemned felons at the state penitentiary.

## OKLAHOMA

*Period of Executions*: 1915–1966
*Total Number*: 83
*Method*: Electrocution

| Name | Race | Age | Date of Execution | Offense | Appeal | County |
|------|------|-----|-------------------|---------|--------|--------|
| Bookman, Henry | B | 28 | 12/10/1915 | M | | McIntosh |
| Towery, Cecil | B | 22 | 11/ 6/1916 | M | S | McIntosh |
| Williams, Willie | B | 34 | 4/13/1917 | M | S | Muskogee |
| Young, Charley | B | 26 | 4/13/1917 | M | | Tillman |
| Taylor, Chester | B | 44 | 4/13/1917 | M | | Creek |
| Prather, John | B | 25 | 5/ 3/1918 | M | S | Pittsburg |
| Brown, James | B | 33 | 11/ 8/1918 | M | S | Muskogee |
| Braught, T.R. | W | 27 | 5/23/1919 | M | S | Creek |
| Betterton, Monroe | W | 47 | 7/ 9/1920 | M | S | Craig |
| Blakely, Robert | W | 39 | 2/25/1921 | M | | Muskogee |
| Ledbetter, John | I | 31 | 2/25/1921 | M | S | Muskogee |
| Thomas, Eli | B | 21 | 7/15/1921 | M | S | LeFlore |
| Sabo, Steve | W | 50 | 3/17/1922 | M | | Coal |
| Watkins, Sam | W | 39 | 5/ 5/1922 | M | S | Atoka |
| Harvey, Aaron | W | 21 | 1/13/1924 | M | S | McCurtain |

| Name | Race | Age | Date of Execution | Offense | Appeal | County |
|------|------|-----|-------------------|---------|--------|--------|
| Pope, Jack | W | 45 | 1/13/1924 | M | S | McCurtain |
| Birkes, Richard | W | 29 | 9/ 5/1924 | M | S | Craig |
| Scott, Leroy | B | 21 | 5/29/1925 | M | S | Pittsburg |
| Washington, Johnnie | B | 28 | 12/ 4/1925 | M | | Jackson |
| O'Neal, Willie | B | 25 | 6/29/1928 | M | | Oklahoma |
| Wigger, Walter | W | 30 | 6/29/1928 | M | S | Ottawa |
| Bruster, Theodore | B | 20 | 6/29/1928 | M | S | Muskogee |
| Guest, Tom | W | 48 | 7/17/1930 | M | S | Pottawatomie |
| Forrest, James | B | 23 | 7/17/1930 | Ra | S | Stephens |
| Hembree, E.S. | I | 32 | 4/17/1931 | Ra | S | Stephens |
| Cole, Paul | W | 33 | 7/10/1931 | M | S | Seminole |
| Nichols, Bennie | B | 31 | 8/21/1931 | M | S | Ponotoc |
| Lovett, Henry | W | 39 | 9/25/1931 | M | S | Canadian |
| Kenney, Martin | W | 48 | 3/11/1932 | M | S | Oklahoma |
| Harris, A.M. | W | 49 | 6/17/1932 | M | S | Oklahoma |
| Davis, Charles | B | 41 | 8/19/1932 | M | S | Blaine |
| Alder, I.J. | W | 50 | 8/19/1932 | M | S | Blaine |
| Covington, Ivory | B | 25 | 1/27/1933 | M | S | Choctaw |
| Rightsell, Nathan | W | 26 | 2/24/1933 | M | S | Choctaw |
| Lattimer, Charlie | W | 29 | 3/24/1933 | M | S | Comanche |
| McDonald, Proctor | W | 23 | 5/ 5/1933 | M | S | Creek |
| Martin, Joe | W | 53 | 5/ 5/1933 | M | S | Noble |
| Ellis, Albert | W | 25 | 5/ 5/1933 | Ro | S | Carter |
| Nichols, Luke | W | 43 | 5/19/1933 | M | | Alfalfa |
| Oliver, George | W | 18 | 8/25/1933 | M | S | Murray |
| Oliver, Claude | W | 28 | 8/25/1933 | M | S | Murray |
| Dumas, Charley | B | 28 | 10/20/1933 | Ra | S | Coal |
| Patton, Ted | W | 25 | 10/20/1933 | M | S | Sequoyah |
| Johnson, William | B | 28 | 11/10/1933 | M | S | Muskogee |
| Quinn, Earl | W | 29 | 11/24/1933 | M | S | Garfield |
| Morris, Tom | B | 40 | 11/24/1933 | M | S | Pittsburg |
| Clark, Frank | B | 60 | 10/19/1934 | M | S | McCurtain |
| Oglesby, Ernest | W | 26 | 1/ 4/1935 | M | S | Oklahoma |
| Cargo, Robert | W | 21 | 5/24/1935 | M | S | Oklahoma |
| Barrett, Chester | W | 37 | 9/20/1935 | M | S | Creek |
| Riley, Bun | W | 29 | 9/20/1935 | M | S | Pittsburg |
| Rowan, Alfred | B | 29 | 9/20/1935 | M | S | Jackson |
| Guyton, Roy | B | 24 | 3/20/1936 | M | S | Oklahoma |
| Hargus, James | W | 24 | 4/24/1936 | M | S | Tulsa |
| Gooch, Arthur[1] | W | 27 | 6/19/1936 | K | F,U | Fed |
| Sands, Charlie | B | 21 | 6/11/1937 | M | S | Comanche |
| Siler, Leon | W | 22 | 6/11/1937 | M | S | Comanche |
| Mannon, Roy | W | 38 | 3/ 1/1940 | M | S | Wagoner |
| Cunningham, Roger | W | 35 | 11/15/1940 | M | S | Oklahoma |
| Abby, Warren | W | 58 | 8/29/1941 | M | S | Custer |
| Tuggle, J.D. | W | 23 | 2/ 9/1942 | M | S | Garvin |
| Porter, Finley | B | 38 | 4/16/1943 | M | S | Pittsburg |
| Prather, Hiram | W | 35 | 7/14/1943 | M | S | Pittsburg |
| Johnson, Amon | B | 29 | 3/23/1945 | M | S | Lincoln |
| Norman, Cliff | B | 29 | 11/ 9/1945 | Ra | S | Murray |
| Bingham, Alfred | W | 40 | 5/31/1946 | M | S | Tulsa |
| Johnson, Mose | I | 32 | 1/30/1946 | M | S | Pittsburg |

| Name | Race | Age | Date of Execution | Offense | Appeal | County |
|------|------|-----|-------------------|---------|--------|--------|
| Broyles, Harlin | W | 32 | 1/30/1947 | M | S,U | Seminole |
| Grayson, Lewis | B | 28 | 5/25/1948 | Ra | S | Muskogee |
| Gould, Gen | B | 40 | 9/27/1948 | M | S | Atoka |
| Kletke, Max | W | 23 | 1/ 6/1951 | M | S,U | Oklahoma |
| Hathcox, Jearell | W | 38 | 7/27/1951 | M | S,U | Oklahoma |
| Mott, Milburn | W | 33 | 9/21/1951 | M | S,U | Tulsa |
| DeWolf, Carl | W | 33 | 11/17/1953 | M | S,U | Tulsa |
| Fairris, Hurbie | W | 22 | 1/18/1956 | M | S | Oklahoma |
| Loel, Otto | W | 46 | 1/11/1957 | M | S,U | Oklahoma |
| Hendricks, Robert | W | 66 | 2/ 5/1957 | M | S,U | Craig |
| Williams, Edward | W | 30 | 7/28/1960 | K | S,U | Tulsa |
| Spence, James | W | 31 | 8/31/1960 | M | S,U | Cotton |
| Young, Ray Allen | W | 34 | 12/15/1960 | M | S,U | Jackson |
| Doggett, Shelby | W | 23 | 10/ 1/1962 | M | S,U | Comanche |
| Dare, Richard | W | 30 | 6/ 1/1963 | M | S,U | Oklahoma |
| French, James Donald | W | 30 | 8/10/1966 | M | S | Pittsburg |

[1]Arthur Gooch (6/19/1936) was sentenced by the U.S. District Court for kidnapping with bodily harm, and the death penalty was mandatory. Unlike state prisoners, who were electrocuted, he was sentenced to be hung. It was felt by the U.S. Marshal that the state penitentiary provided the securest detention facilities for Gooch, so the grounds were rented from the state for the hanging.

## OREGON

*Period of Executions*: 1904–1962
*Total Number*: 60
*Method*: Unknown 1904–1931; lethal gas 1939–1964
*Period of Abolition*: 1914–1920, 1964
*Other Data*: After the state of Oregon began executing its condemned felons at the state penitentiary, two men (identified in footnote 1) were hanged under local authority in the counties of their convictions at the county seats designated.

| Name | Race | Age | Date of Execution | Offense | Appeal | County |
|------|------|-----|-------------------|---------|--------|--------|
| Armstrong, Pleasant[1] | W | — | 1/22/1904 | M | | Baker |
| Egbert, Harry D. | W | 22 | 1/29/1904 | M | | Harney |
| Guglielmo, Frank | W | 23 | 5/ 5/1905 | M | S | Multnomah |
| Lauth, George W. | W | 25 | 7/13/1905 | M | S | Clackamas |
| Williams, Norman[1] | W | 55 | 7/21/1905 | M | | Wasco |
| Barnes, John C. | W | — | 9/18/1906 | M | S | Douglas |
| Shepherd, Fred A. | W | 23 | 11/30/1906 | M | | Crook |
| Hose, Henry | W | 32 | 12/21/1906 | M | | Multnomah |
| Megorden, Holliver | W | — | 6/28/1907 | M | S | Malheur |
| Johnson, Walter M. | W | 23 | 2/ 5/1909 | M | | Washington |
| Timmons, C.Y. | W | 37 | 2/26/1909 | M | | Marion |
| Nordstrom, Adolph M. | W | 28 | 6/18/1909 | M | | Tillamock |
| Anderson, Joseph | W | — | 7/ 2/1909 | M | S | Multnomah |
| Jancigaj, Math | W | 28 | 10/22/1909 | M | S | Clackamas |
| Finch, James | W | — | 11/12/1909 | M | S | Multnomah |

| Name | Race | Age | Date of Execution | Offense | Appeal | County |
|------|------|-----|-------------------|---------|--------|--------|
| Roselair, John D. | W | 47 | 9/ 8/1910 | M | S | Washington |
| Harrell, Isaac N. | W | 48 | 9/ 9/1910 | M | | Lake |
| Morgan, Mike | W | — | 12/13/1912 | M | | Josephine |
| Garrison, Frank | W | — | 12/13/1912 | M | S | Coos |
| Faulder, Noble | W | — | 12/13/1912 | M | | Klamath |
| Roberts, H.E. | W | — | 12/13/1912 | M | | Multnomah |
| Humphrey, Charles | W | — | 3/22/1913 | M | S | Benton |
| Humphrey, George | W | — | 3/22/1913 | M | S | Benton |
| Spanos, Mike | W | 22 | 10/31/1913 | M | S | Jackson |
| Seymour, Frank | W | — | 10/31/1913 | M | S | Jackson |
| Hansel, Oswald C. | W | 55 | 11/17/1913 | M | | Clatsop |
| Bancroft, Emmet | W | — | 11/ 5/1920 | M | | Umatilla |
| Kirby, Elvie D. | W | — | 7/ 7/1922 | M | S | Umatilla |
| Rathie, John L. | W | — | 7/ 7/1922 | M | S | Umatilla |
| Howard, George | W | — | 9/ 8/1922 | M | S | Malheur |
| Walters, Husted | W | 23 | 3/ 9/1923 | M | S | Multnomah |
| Casey, Dan | W | — | 8/24/1923 | M | S | Multnomah |
| Parker, George | W | 32 | 1/ 4/1924 | M | | Linn |
| Peare, L.W. | W | 70 | 5/22/1925 | M | S | Coos |
| Covell, Arthur | W | — | 5/22/1925 | M | S | Coos |
| Lloyd, W.R. | W | 27 | 11/30/1925 | M | | Polk |
| Cody, Archie | W | 44 | 4/16/1926 | M | | Malheur |
| Brownlee, Albert | W | 27 | 5/17/1927 | M | S | Lane |
| Butchek, John | W | 45 | 6/10/1927 | M | S | Multnomah |
| Kelley, Ellsworth | W | — | 4/20/1928 | M | S,U | Marion |
| Willos, James | W | — | 4/20/1928 | M | S,U | Marion |
| Kingsley, James E. | W | 25 | 10/30/1931 | M | S | Jackson |
| McCarthy, LeRoy H. | W | 26 | 1/20/1939 | M | S | Multnomah |
| Cline, Claude E. | W | — | 7/26/1940 | M | | Wheeler |
| Thomas, James H. | W | 19 | 10/30/1941 | M | | Gilliam |
| Soto, John A. | W | 17 | 3/20/1942 | M | | Umatilla |
| Wallace, William E. | W | 54 | 2/26/1943 | M | S | Multnomah |
| Cunningham, Harvey | B | 38 | 3/ 6/1944 | M | S | Multnomah |
| Layton, Richard H. | W | 36 | 12/ 8/1944 | M | S,U | Polk |
| Folkes, Robert E. Lee | B | 24 | 1/ 5/1945 | M | S,U | Linn |
| Merten, Henry W. | W | — | 1/15/1945 | M | S | Clackamas |
| Higgins, Walter | W | — | 1/15/1945 | M | S | Clackamas |
| Dennis, Andrew W. | W | 45 | 2/ 2/1946 | M | S | Multnomah |
| Bailey, Kenneth Wm. | W | — | 9/13/1946 | M | S | Malheur |
| Henderson, Wardell H. | B | 27 | 1/23/1948 | M | S | Multnomah |
| Long, Wayne LeRoy | W | 26 | 8/ 8/1952 | M | S | Clackamas |
| Leland, Morris | W | 22 | 1/ 9/1953 | M | S,U | Multnomah |
| Payne, Frank O. | W | 52 | 1/ 9/1953 | M | S | Multnomah |
| Karnes, Albert | W | 24 | 1/30/1953 | M | | Marion |
| McGahuey, Leeroy S. | W | — | 8/20/1962 | M | S | Jackson |

[1]Armstrong (1/22/1904) and Williams (7/21/1905) were hanged under local authority in the counties of their convictions after Oregon began executing its condemned felons at the state penitentiary.

## PENNSYLVANIA

*Period of Executions*: 1915–1962
*Total Number*: 351
*Method*: Electrocution
*Other Data*: After the state of Pennsylvania began electrocuting its condemned felons at the state penitentiary, one man (identified in footnote 1) was hanged under local authority in the county of his conviction at the county seat designated.

| Name | Race | Age | Date of Execution | Offense | Appeal | County |
|------|------|-----|-------------------|---------|--------|--------|
| Talap, John | W | — | 2/23/1915 | M | | Montgomery |
| Tassone, Rocco | W | — | 3/ 8/1915 | M | S | Lancaster |
| Mondolo, Nicola | W | — | 4/ 5/1915 | M | S | Fayette |
| Plewka, Andreas | W | — | 7/12/1915 | M | | Bucks |
| Pennington, Roland S. | W | — | 2/21/1916 | M | S | Delaware |
| March, Gerald H. | W | — | 2/21/1916 | M | S | Delaware |
| Kristan, Martin | W | 40 | 3/20/1916 | M | | Allegheny |
| Louisa, Mike | W | — | 4/10/1916 | M | | Schuylkill |
| Reilly, James[1] | – | — | 4/25/1916 | M | | Philadelphia |
| Webb, Henry J.H. | B | — | 5/ 1/1916 | M | S | Allegheny |
| Douglas, Charles | B | — | 5/22/1916 | M | | Westmoreland |
| Marturanto, Gaspar | W | — | 6/26/1916 | M | | Cambria |
| Chichirella, Thomas | W | — | 6/26/1916 | M | | Cambria |
| Becze, Andrew | W | — | 7/10/1916 | M | | Westmoreland |
| Miller, Jacob | W | — | 7/17/1916 | M | S | Philadelphia |
| Filler, H.E. | W | — | 9/27/1916 | M | S,U | Westmoreland |
| Woceshoski. Stanislof | W | — | 12/ 4/1916 | M | | Beaver |
| Digiso, Dominick | W | — | 12/ 4/1916 | M | S | Schuylkill |
| O'Brian, Joseph W. | W | — | 12/11/1916 | M | | Montgomery |
| Brobst, Jonas | W | — | 1/ 8/1917 | M | | Lehigh |
| Nelson, John | B | — | 7/10/1917 | M | | Wyoming |
| Gallery, Patrick | W | — | 7/10/1917 | M | | Northampton |
| Sheppard, Cornelius | B | — | 7/23/1917 | M | | Dauphin |
| Robinson, John | B | — | 9/17/1917 | M | | Dauphin |
| Wilson, Elwood | B | — | 9/17/1917 | M | | Dauphin |
| Kotur, Nickolo | W | — | 10/ 1/1917 | M | | Dauphin |
| Lacie, John | B | — | 11/ 5/1917 | M | S | Cambria |
| Anthony, James | B | — | 11/12/1917 | M | S | Cumberland |
| Miller, Archie | B | — | 11/12/1917 | M | S | Cumberland |
| Wendt, Frank Alfred | W | — | 12/ 3/1917 | M | S | Blair |
| Uptic, Mike | W | — | 4/ 8/1918 | M | | Westmoreland |
| Edwards, Samuel | B | 30 | 4/15/1918 | M | | Somerset |
| Warren, William | B | — | 5/20/1918 | M | | Chester |
| Polito, Guisseppi | W | — | 5/27/1918 | M | | Westmoreland |
| Obric, Illio | W | 34 | 5/27/1918 | M | | Lebanon |
| Christley, John O. | W | — | 6/10/1918 | M | | Dauphin |
| Kyler, Charles | B | — | 10/14/1918 | M | | Dauphin |
| Carey, Andrew | B | — | 10/14/1918 | M | | Dauphin |
| Salladay, Henry Martin | W | — | 10/21/1918 | M | | Northumberland |
| Salladay, Jacob | W | — | 10/21/1918 | M | | Northumberland |
| Cutlip, Herven Lee | W | — | 10/28/1918 | M | | Allegheny |

| Name | Race | Age | Date of Execution | Offense | Appeal | County |
|------|------|-----|-------------------|---------|--------|--------|
| Patterson, Albert | W | — | 10/28/1918 | M | | Allegheny |
| Ressler, Frank | W | — | 11/18/1918 | M | | Westmoreland |
| Dantine, John Baptist | W | — | 11/18/1918 | M | S | Beaver |
| Zec, Lazar | W | — | 12/ 9/1918 | M | S | Lancaster |
| Garner, Samuel | W | — | 12/16/1918 | M | | Lancaster |
| McMiller, William | B | — | 12/16/1918 | M | | Allegheny |
| Barcons, Sam | W | — | 1/13/1919 | M | | Dauphin |
| Dickerson, Hardy | — | — | 4/28/1919 | M | | Fayette |
| Medio, Patsy | W | — | 5/19/1919 | M | | Somerset |
| Moon, Franklin Bertie | W | 27 | 6/ 2/1919 | M | S | Northumberland |
| Smolleck, Peter | W | — | 6/16/1919 | M | | Lehigh |
| Brown, William | B | — | 6/16/1919 | M | | Clearfield |
| Mulferno, Tony | W | — | 10/20/1919 | M | S | Clarion |
| Evans, William | — | — | 10/27/1919 | M | | Dauphin |
| Sandoe, John | W | — | 10/27/1919 | M | | Lancaster |
| Psaros, Gregory | W | — | 10/27/1919 | M | | Lancaster |
| Bednorciki, Bronoslaw | W | — | 12/22/1919 | M | S | Beaver |
| Brown, Robert Henry | B | — | 1/ 5/1920 | M | S | Allegheny |
| Hiter, William | B | — | 2/ 9/1920 | M | | Lancaster |
| Brown, Lawrence | B | — | 2/ 9/1920 | M | S | Dauphin |
| Draskovich, Boza | W | 24 | 3/ 1/1920 | M | | Lawrence |
| Bollin, Lazarus | B | 19 | 3/11/1920 | M | | Lawrence |
| Green, Frank | B | — | 3/29/1920 | M | | Allegheny |
| Dunmore, Buck | B | — | 4/27/1920 | M | | Allegheny |
| Dolish, Sam | W | — | 5/ 3/1920 | M | | Allegheny |
| Rowland, Bennie | B | — | 6/ 1/1920 | M | | Allegheny |
| Russell, William | B | — | 6/ 1/1920 | M | | Allegheny |
| Brown, Edward | B | — | 6/ 1/1920 | M | S | Philadelphia |
| Morrison, John | W | — | 11/ 1/1920 | M | S | Allegheny |
| Coles, Samuel | B | — | 11/ 1/1920 | M | S | Allegheny |
| Johnson, William | B | — | 12/13/1920 | M | S | Erie |
| Sansone, Jennaro | — | | 12/13/1920 | M | S | Erie |
| Moore, Lindsey | B | — | 12/20/1920 | M | S | Westmoreland |
| Davis, James | B | — | 2/28/1921 | M | S | Allegheny |
| Insano, Antonio | W | — | 4/18/1921 | M | S | Jefferson |
| Collins, Clarence | W | 22 | 4/25/1921 | M | S | Adams |
| Reinecker, Charles Clinton | W | 20 | 4/25/1921 | M | S | Adams |
| Byrd, Charles | B | — | 5/16/1921 | M | S | Dauphin |
| Green, Timothy | B | — | 5/16/1921 | M | S | Dauphin |
| Curry, John | B | 24 | 5/23/1921 | M | | Somerset |
| Tompkins, George | W | — | 5/23/1921 | M | S | Blair |
| Hudson, Milton | B | — | 6/20/1921 | M | S | Erie |
| Stragin, William | B | — | 6/20/1921 | M | S | Erie |
| Schlop, Steve | W | — | 6/20/1921 | M | S | Erie |
| Trammel, Robert | B | — | 6/20/1921 | M | | Erie |
| Allen, Joseph | — | — | 7/25/1921 | M | | Wyoming |
| Knight, William | B | — | 9/26/1921 | M | | Chester |
| Wilson, Love | B | — | 10/ 3/1921 | M | | Dauphin |
| Diaco, Dominico | W | 32 | 10/24/1921 | M | S | Delaware |
| Palma, Frank | W | — | 11/28/1921 | M | S | Lackawanna |
| Tao, Chung | C | — | 1/ 3/1922 | M | | Berks |
| Tillman, Marshall | B | 32 | 4/16/1922 | M | | Cambria |

| Name | Race | Age | Date of Execution | Offense | Appeal | County |
|------|------|-----|-------------------|---------|--------|--------|
| Lewis, Walter A. | B | — | 1/23/1922 | M | | Delaware |
| Mason, John | B | — | 1/23/1922 | M | | Allegheny |
| Marano, Michael | W | — | 2/27/1922 | M | | Philadelphia |
| White, Albert | W | — | 3/20/1922 | M | S | Lawrence |
| McAnaney, Bernard | W | — | 3/27/1922 | M | | Allegheny |
| Shurilla, John | W | — | 3/27/1922 | M | | Fayette |
| Patterson, Archie Adolph | B | — | 4/ 3/1922 | M | S | Northampton |
| Carter, Earl | B | — | 5/15/1922 | M | S | Philadelphia |
| Steward, George | B | — | 5/22/1922 | M | | Fayette |
| Lisowski, Henry K. | W | — | 6/19/1922 | M | S | Schuylkill |
| Di Stefano, James | W | — | 6/26/1922 | M | | Blair |
| Ebersole, Jonas | W | 33 | 7/17/1922 | M | | Bedford |
| Dreher, Joseph | B | — | 7/17/1922 | M | S | Philadelphia |
| McCloskey, Gilbert | W | — | 7/24/1922 | M | S | Blair |
| Emery, Perley J. | W | — | 7/31/1922 | M | S | Philadelphia |
| Erico, Peter | W | — | 9/25/1922 | M | S | Luzerne |
| Puntariao, Antonio | W | — | 9/25/1922 | M | S | Luzerne |
| Blakeley, H.A. | W | 42 | 10/22/1922 | M | S | Butler |
| Disalvo, James | W | — | 10/30/1922 | M | S | Clarion |
| Ryhall, Thomas Vernon | W | 36 | 10/30/1922 | M | S | Lawrence |
| Sipple, Curtis | W | 21 | 10/30/1922 | M | | York |
| Kerr, Fred L. | W | — | 11/ 6/1922 | M | S | Beaver |
| Troy, Walter | W | — | 12/ 4/1922 | M | S | Allegheny |
| Way, Harry | B | — | 12/ 4/1922 | M | | Lancaster |
| Thomas, Joseph | B | — | 12/11/1922 | M | S | Allegheny |
| Smith, Floyd | – | — | 3/ 5/1923 | M | | Bradford |
| Newson, Clarence | B | — | 5/21/1923 | M | S | Philadelphia |
| Newman, Marcus W. | W | — | 7/22/1923 | M | S | Allegheny |
| Fragassa, Angelo | W | — | 12/10/1923 | M | S | Washington |
| Daniele, Marcantonio | W | — | 12/10/1923 | M | S | Washington |
| Ingram, Chester | – | — | 12/31/1923 | M | | Fayette |
| Roberts, Lawrence | W | — | 1/28/1924 | M | | Venango |
| Ware, George | B | — | 2/25/1924 | M | S | Philadelphia |
| Delfino, Dominick | W | 34 | 3/10/1924 | M | S | Lackawanna |
| Bland, George | B | — | 3/17/1924 | M | | Dauphin |
| Savage, Lorenzo | B | — | 3/31/1924 | M | | Allegheny |
| Morgan, Willie N. | W | — | 4/28/1924 | M | S | Philadelphia |
| Platt, Albert | W | — | 4/28/1924 | M | | Crawford |
| Myma, John F. | W | 27 | 5/ 5/1924 | M | S | Lackawanna |
| Grymkowski, Walter | W | 35 | 6/23/1924 | M | | Carbon |
| Matlovski, Martin | W | 33 | 6/23/1924 | M | | Carbon |
| Trinkle, Joseph | W | — | 6/30/1924 | M | S | Philadelphia |
| Daily, John A. | W | — | 7/ 7/1924 | M | S | Allegheny |
| Jackson, Henry | B | — | 3/30/1925 | M | | Allegheny |
| Osfinger, Charles | W | — | 4/ 6/1925 | M | | Philadelphia |
| Adams, Grant | W | 22 | 4/ 6/1925 | M | | Berks |
| Gelfi, Angelo | W | — | 4/20/1925 | M | S | Westmoreland |
| Soos, Michael | W | — | 4/27/1925 | M | S | Cambria |
| Meleski, John | W | 34 | 5/25/1925 | M | S | Cambria |
| Burchanti, John | W | — | 6/ 1/1925 | M | S | Lackawanna |
| Torti, John | W | — | 6/ 1/1925 | M | S | Lackawanna |
| Edwards, Henry | B | — | 6/29/1925 | M | | Allegheny |

| Name | Race | Age | Date of Execution | Offense | Appeal | County |
|------|------|-----|-------------------|---------|--------|--------|
| Bassi, Michael | W | — | 9/21/1925 | M | S | Cambria |
| Pezzi, Tony | W | — | 9/21/1925 | M | S | Cambria |
| Branhan, Julius McKinley | B | — | 9/28/1925 | M | S | Philadelphia |
| Walker, John | B | — | 9/28/1925 | M | S | Philadelphia |
| Lyons, William | B | — | 10/ 5/1925 | M | S | Philadelphia |
| Stevenson, Edward | B | — | 10/12/1925 | M | | Fayette |
| Scott, James | B | — | 10/19/1925 | M | S | Westmoreland |
| Wichrowski, Anthony | W | — | 10/19/1925 | M | | Berks |
| Girsch, John | W | — | 10/26/1925 | M | S | Mercer |
| Weiss, Michael | W | — | 10/26/1925 | M | S | Mercer |
| Hartman, Philip A. | W | 24 | 11/30/1925 | M | | Adams |
| Grinage, Irvin | B | — | 1/25/1926 | M | | Berks |
| Crocker, Leamon | B | — | 1/25/1926 | M | | Berks |
| Brue, Robert | B | — | 1/25/1926 | M | S | Berks |
| Legins, Thomas | B | — | 3/ 1/1926 | M | S | Philadelphia |
| Prescott, George H. | W | — | 3/29/1926 | M | S | Allegheny |
| Dorst, Milo D. | W | — | 5/24/1926 | M | S | Allegheny |
| Steel, Charles | W | — | 6/ 1/1926 | M | | Allegheny |
| Cicere, Angelo | W | — | 6/28/1926 | M | S | Westmoreland |
| Musztuk, John | W | — | 7/12/1926 | M | | Crawford |
| Orlakowski. Paul | W | 28 | 12/27/1926 | M | S | Allegheny |
| Fasci, Paul | W | 25 | 12/27/1926 | M | S | Lackawanna |
| Webb, Walter Francis | B | 28 | 2/28/1927 | M | | Delaware |
| Wilson, Amos | B | 25 | 2/28/1927 | M | | Delaware |
| Curry, Joseph | W | — | 3/ 7/1927 | M | S | Philadelphia |
| Bentley, Harry | W | — | 3/ 7/1927 | M | S | Philadelphia |
| Juliano, William | W | — | 3/ 7/1927 | M | S | Philadelphia |
| Doris, Frank | W | — | 3/ 7/1927 | M | S | Philadelphia |
| Nolly, Carl | B | — | 9/26/1927 | M | S | Philadelphia |
| Weeks, Jerry | B | — | 11/21/1927 | M | | Fayette |
| Winter, Raymond | W | — | 1/ 9/1928 | M | S | Allegheny |
| Meyers, William | W | — | 1/ 9/1928 | M | S | Philadelphia |
| Scovem, Leon | W | — | 1/23/1928 | M | S | Northumberland |
| Arnold, Frank | B | — | 2/20/1928 | M | S | Philadelphia |
| Lockett, Frank Edward | B | — | 2/20/1928 | M | S | Philadelphia |
| Matakovich, Marko | W | — | 4/23/1928 | M | | Washington |
| Loftus, Rodger | W | — | 4/23/1928 | M | S | Philadelphia |
| Kameniski, Joseph | W | 20 | 7/30/1928 | M | | Lackawanna |
| Phillips, William R. | W | 34 | 10/ 1/1928 | M | | Delaware |
| Parker, Jesse G. | W | 20 | 10/ 1/1928 | M | | Delaware |
| Lovell, Charles | W | — | 11/26/1928 | M | S | Huntingdon |
| Dilsworth, Rogers | B | — | 12/ 3/1928 | M | S | Philadelphia |
| Wormsley, Wray | B | — | 12/31/1928 | M | S | Washington |
| Luccitti, Tony | W | — | 1/14/1929 | M | S | Washington |
| Danarowicz, Benjamin | W | 32 | 1/14/1929 | M | S | Philadelphia |
| Mellor, Charles F. | W | — | 1/14/1929 | M | S | Philadelphia |
| Jawarski, Paul | W | 30 | 1/21/1929 | M | S | Allegheny |
| James, Calvin D. | W | — | 1/21/1929 | M | S | Bucks |
| Parker, James | B | — | 3/ 4/1929 | M | S | Erie |
| Parker, Raymond | B | — | 3/ 4/1929 | M | S | Erie |
| Wilson, John H. | B | — | 3/ 4/1929 | M | S | Erie |
| Miquel, Elverez | — | 28 | 3/25/1929 | M | | Schuylkill |

| Name | Race | Age | Date of Execution | Offense | Appeal | County |
|------|------|-----|-------------------|---------|--------|--------|
| Lazzarini, Angelo | W | — | 6/24/1929 | M | | Beaver |
| Weston, William Jr. | B | — | 9/30/1929 | M | S | Philadelphia |
| Guida, Guisseppa | W | 37 | 2/ 3/1930 | M | S | Bucks |
| Sloat, Ralph Russell | W | 29 | 3/31/1930 | M | S | Lackawanna |
| Pierce, John | B | 31 | 6/23/1930 | M | | Delaware |
| Avery, Martin | B | — | 6/30/1930 | M | | Allegheny |
| Sled, William Henry | B | — | 6/30/1930 | M | | Allegheny |
| Tauza, Frank | W | — | 6/30/1930 | M | S | Luzerne |
| Flori, James | W | — | 7/ 7/1930 | M | S | Philadelphia |
| Winder, Arthur, alias Albert Wilson (Slim) | B | 27 | 9/22/1930 | M | | Delaware |
| Coon, Harry | W | 27 | 11/17/1930 | M | | Potter |
| Schroeder, Irene (Female) | W | — | 2/23/1931 | M | S | Lawrence |
| Dague, W. Glenn | W | — | 2/23/1931 | M | S | Lawrence |
| Martin, Thomas F. | W | 26 | 3/ 2/1931 | M | S | Philadelphia |
| Watkins, William | B | 25 | 4/20/1931 | M | S | Chester |
| Szachewicz, Sigismund | W | — | 5/25/1931 | M | S | Luzerne |
| Nafus, John | W | — | 5/25/1931 | M | S | Luzerne |
| Williams, Alexander | B | 18 | 6/ 8/1931 | M | S | Delaware |
| Peterson, Cleo | B | — | 6/22/1931 | M | S | Allegheny |
| Williams, Clarence | B | — | 6/22/1931 | M | S | Allegheny |
| Spirellis, Peter | W | — | 6/29/1931 | M | | Schuylkill |
| Powell, Frank | W | — | 8/17/1931 | M | S | Cambria |
| Cantilla, Frank | W | — | 8/17/1931 | M | S | Cambria |
| Parse, Joseph | W | — | 8/17/1931 | M | S | Cambria |
| Crow, Carl | W | — | 8/17/1931 | M | S | Cambria |
| Snipes, C. William | W | — | 9/28/1931 | M | | Bucks |
| Starchok, Harry | W | 29 | 11/30/1931 | M | | Cambria |
| Kosh, Joseph | W | 27 | 2/ 1/1932 | M | S | Lackawanna |
| Roman, Joseph | W | — | 2/29/1932 | M | S | Cambria |
| Wallandz, Quincy | B | 24 | 3/28/1932 | M | | Philadelphia |
| Collins, Fred | B | 37 | 5/16/1932 | M | | Centre |
| De Grasse, William | W | 22 | 6/27/1932 | M | | Delaware |
| Hudock, Joseph E. | W | — | 1/ 5/1933 | M | | Luzerne |
| Kurutz, John | W | — | 6/26/1933 | M | S | Northampton |
| Lilly, Robert Roland | B | — | 9/18/1933 | M | | Philadelphia |
| Stabinski, Frank | W | — | 1/ 8/1934 | M | S | Luzerne |
| Tretosky, Anthony | W | 19 | 1/ 8/1934 | M | S | Luzerne |
| Sterling, Joseph | B | — | 2/26/1934 | M | S | Philadelphia |
| Harris, Robert | B | — | 2/26/1934 | M | S | Philadelphia |
| Skawinski, Wallace | W | 23 | 3/ 5/1934 | M | S | Lackawanna |
| Riggs, James Joseph | W | 24 | 3/ 5/1934 | M | S | Lackawanna |
| Bach, Richard C. | W | 25 | 4/ 9/1934 | M | S | Philadelphia |
| Walker, Charles | B | — | 5/28/1934 | M | S | Philadelphia |
| Talarico, William | W | — | 4/ 8/1935 | M | S | Philadelphia |
| Mika, Walter | W | — | 4/ 8/1935 | M | S | Philadelphia |
| Edwards, Robert Allen | W | 21 | 5/ 6/1935 | M | S | Luzerne |
| Deni, William | W | — | 7/ 3/1935 | M | S | Philadelphia |
| Strawser, Sherman L. | W | 29 | 7/22/1935 | M | | Snyder |
| Iacobino, Dominick | W | 50 | 9/ 9/1935 | M | S | Lackawanna |
| Kozier, John | W | 33 | 9/30/1935 | M | | Fayette |
| Farrell, Martin | W | — | 12/ 2/1935 | M | S | Bucks |

| Name | Race | Age | Date of Execution | Offense | Appeal | County |
|------|------|-----|-------------------|---------|--------|--------|
| Wiley, Francis | W | — | 12/ 2/1935 | M | S | Bucks |
| Jordan, John Davis | W | — | 12/ 9/1935 | M | | Chester |
| Thompson, Clarence | B | 35 | 5/25/1936 | M | S | Delaware |
| Gable, Jacob | W | 21 | 1/ 4/1937 | M | S | Cambria |
| Dreamer, Robert | W | 30 | 2/ 1/1937 | M | S | Washington |
| Yacas, Andy | — | — | 5/ 3/1937 | M | | Indiana |
| England, Marcus | B | 39 | 5/10/1937 | M | S | Berks |
| Shawell, Edward | B | 36 | 5/10/1937 | M | S | Berks |
| Crittenton, Roy | B | 36 | 6/28/1937 | M | S | Delaware |
| Meyer, Alexander | W | 20 | 7/12/1937 | M | | Chester |
| Becker, John | W | 37 | 7/26/1937 | M | S | Jefferson |
| Strantz, Walter | — | — | 2/ 7/1938 | M | S | Northumberland |
| Sullivan, Martin | W | 72 | 3/21/1938 | M | | Allegheny |
| Hawk, Ralph E. | W | 20 | 3/28/1938 | M | | Franklin |
| Reibaldi, Fred | W | 28 | 3/28/1938 | M | | Philadelphia |
| Gregg, Albert | — | — | 3/28/1938 | M | | Philadelphia |
| Rose, Edward | W | 21 | 4/25/1938 | M | S | Delaware |
| Dumniak, Theodore | W | 20 | 4/25/1938 | M | S | Delaware |
| Oreszak, John | W | 21 | 4/25/1938 | M | S | Delaware |
| Bowers, Wendell Forrest | W | 20 | 6/13/1938 | M | | Montgomery |
| Fugmann, Michael | W | — | 7/18/1938 | M | S | Luzerne |
| Mitchell, Fred Holland | — | — | 10/10/1938 | M | | Somerset |
| Peronace, Antonio | — | — | 10/31/1938 | M | S | Northumberland |
| Blackwell, William McKinley | B | 40 | 2/27/1939 | M | | Allegheny |
| Lockard, Roy | — | — | 3/27/1939 | M | S | Blair |
| Hipple, Ernest M. | — | 21 | 4/24/1939 | M | S | Sullivan |
| Ferry, Paul | — | — | 10/23/1939 | M | S | Erie |
| Bailey, Willie | — | — | 10/23/1939 | M | | Philadelphia |
| Redmon, Ira Bob | — | — | 10/23/1939 | M | | Philadelphia |
| Golden, Charles Edward | — | — | 10/30/1939 | M | | Philadelphia |
| Tankard, Walter | — | — | 10/30/1939 | M | | Philadelphia |
| Fuller, James | — | — | 12/18/1939 | M | S | Philadelphia |
| Legrand, Walter | — | — | 12/18/1939 | M | S | Philadelphia |
| Ginyard, Benjamin | — | — | 1/29/1940 | M | | Allegheny |
| Schurtz, Andrew | — | — | 2/26/1940 | M | S | Northumberland |
| Kelly, William | — | — | 2/26/1940 | M | S | Philadelphia |
| Howell, George | B | 22 | 7/15/1940 | M | S | Philadelphia |
| Petrillo, Paul | W | 49 | 3/31/1941 | M | S | Philadelphia |
| Petrillo, Herman | W | — | 10/20/1941 | M | S | Philadelphia |
| Ernest, William Joseph | W | 36 | 10/27/1941 | M | | Montgomery |
| Jones, Willie | — | — | 11/24/1941 | M | S | Allegheny |
| Frizbie, Harold | — | — | 11/24/1941 | M | S | Sullivan |
| Wilson, William | — | — | 8/10/1942 | M | | Allegheny |
| Childers, John | B | 33 | 3/29/1943 | M | S | Philadelphia |
| Green, Herbert | B | 41 | 4/26/1943 | M | | Philadelphia |
| Musto, Michael | — | — | 3/20/1944 | M | S | Blair |
| Gatling, George Nelson | B | 37 | 9/25/1944 | M | | Philadelphia |
| Elliott, Thomas Hayes | — | — | 11/27/1944 | M | S | Dauphin |
| McKeithen, Shellie | — | — | 1/ 7/1946 | M | | Allegheny |
| West, John Darius | W | 27 | 3/25/1946 | M | S | Erie |

| Name | Race | Age | Date of Execution | Offense | Appeal | County |
|------|------|-----|-------------------|---------|--------|--------|
| Pepperman, Robert William | W | 29 | 3/25/1946 | M | S | Erie |
| Sykes, Corinne (Female) | B | 22 | 10/14/1946 | M | S,U | Philadelphia |
| Morris, Frederick | W | 24 | 10/28/1946 | M | | Delaware |
| Ewell, Peter J. | B | 24 | 2/24/1947 | M | | Philadelphia |
| Black, Allen W. | – | 29 | 2/24/1947 | M | | Montgomery |
| Jones, Samuel H. | B | 42 | 3/ 3/1947 | M | S | Philadelphia |
| Brooks, David | B | 22 | 4/28/1947 | M | S | Philadelphia |
| Wooding, Albert | – | – | 4/28/1947 | M | S | Philadelphia |
| Beatty, Joshua Elwood | – | 47 | 9/29/1947 | M | | Dauphin |
| Moyer, Charles Frederick | W | 25 | 10/ 6/1947 | M | S | Delaware |
| Byron, William Paul | – | – | 10/ 6/1947 | M | S | Delaware |
| Bubna, Mike | W | 37 | 10/20/1947 | M | | Erie |
| Brown, Lawrence | B | 19 | 10/27/1947 | M | | Philadelphia |
| Chavis, William | B | 22 | 12/ 8/1947 | M | S,U | Philadelphia |
| Holley, Grant | B | 48 | 7/12/1948 | M | S | Philadelphia |
| Rumage, William | W | 30 | 10/11/1948 | M | S | Philadelphia |
| Taranow, Daniel Peter | W | 23 | 11/ 8/1948 | M | S | Delaware |
| Keller, Rufus E. | W | – | 7/11/1949 | M | | Lehigh |
| Neill, George A. | W | 24 | 9/26/1949 | M | S | Philadelphia |
| Simmons, Ray H. | W | 26 | 1/ 9/1950 | M | S,U | Adams |
| Di Pofi, Edward E. | W | 24 | 1/ 9/1950 | M | S,U | Allegheny |
| Minoff, George | W | 51 | 2/27/1950 | M | S | Dauphin |
| Givens, John William | W | 52 | 2/27/1950 | M | S | Beaver |
| Niemi, Alexander | W | 30 | 9/25/1950 | M | S | Delaware |
| Maloney, Walter, Jr. | W | 41 | 9/25/1950 | M | S | Delaware |
| Shupp, Robert Clement | – | – | 1/ 8/1951 | M | S | Lehigh |
| Agoston, Alexander | W | – | 1/ 9/1951 | M | S,U | Columbia |
| Gibbs, Edward Lester | W | 25 | 4/23/1951 | M | S | Lancaster |
| Chambers, Joseph | B | 28 | 2/25/1952 | M | S | Philadelphia |
| Bryant, Edward | B | 28 | 2/25/1952 | M | S | Philadelphia |
| Daversa, Dominick | – | – | 3/30/1953 | M | S | Westmoreland |
| Phillips, Joseph Stevenson | – | – | 3/30/1953 | M | S | Westmoreland |
| Carey, Ollie | – | – | 5/18/1953 | M | S | Montgomery |
| Homeyer, Charles E. | W | 54 | 5/18/1953 | M | S | Wyoming |
| McGrew, Oscar | – | – | 3/15/1954 | M | S | Erie |
| Ensminger, Clyde Vernon | – | – | 3/29/1954 | M | | Cumberland |
| Patskin, William | W | 46 | 4/ 5/1954 | M | S | Lackawanna |
| Bibalo, Joseph | W | 23 | 5/17/1954 | M | S | Susquehanna |
| Edwards, Grover Cleveland | W | 36 | 4/25/1955 | M | S | Philadelphia |
| Robinson, Benjamin F. | – | – | 4/25/1955 | M | | Delaware |
| Maxwell, William | B | 27 | 7/11/1955 | M | | Delaware |
| Lance, Patrick Alexander | W | 30 | 7/25/1955 | M | S | Beaver |
| Thompson, Elijah, Jr. | B | 22 | 7/25/1955 | M | S | Beaver |
| Capps, George | W | 22 | 9/26/1955 | M | S | Bucks |
| Wable, John Wesley | W | 24 | 9/26/1955 | M | S | Westmoreland |
| Cole, William Durant | – | – | 5/13/1956 | M | S | Allegheny |
| Gossard, Harry | W | 39 | 6/ 4/1956 | M | S | Cambria |
| Graves, Lester | – | 25 | 4/13/1959 | M | S | Philadelphia |
| Thompson, Cleveland | – | – | 5/ 4/1959 | M | S,F,U | Allegheny |
| Williams, Robert L. | B | 22 | 10/28/1959 | M | S | Philadelphia |
| Schuk, Arthur Grover | W | 44 | 10/23/1961 | M | S | Beaver |

| Name | Race | Age | Date of Execution | Offense | Appeal | County |
|------|------|-----|-------------------|---------|--------|--------|
| McCoy, Frank | W | 36 | 1/29/1962 | M | S | Philadelphia |
| Smith, Elmo | W | 41 | 4/ 2/1962 | M | S | Montgomery |

¹Reilly (4/25/1916) was hanged under local authority in the county of his conviction after Pennsylvania began electrocuting its condemned felons at the state penitentiary.

## SOUTH CAROLINA

*Period of Executions*: 1912–1962
*Total Number*: 241
*Method*: Electrocution

| Name | Race | Age | Date of Execution | Offense | Appeal | County |
|------|------|-----|-------------------|---------|--------|--------|
| Reed, William | B | — | 8/ 6/1912 | Awira | | Anderson |
| Weldon, Alex | B | 55 | 8/13/1912 | M | S | Florence |
| Cole, John | B | — | 8/22/1912 | M | | Charleston |
| Alexander, Edward | B | — | 9/20/1912 | Awira | | Winnsboro |
| Hyde, Samuel N. | W | 27 | 10/ 1/1912 | M | S | Anderson |
| Glover, Clinyon | B | — | 11/12/1912 | Awira | S | Dorchester |
| Boozer, Sam | B | — | 1/ 2/1913 | M | S | Newberry |
| Green, Frank | B | 18 | 4/ 4/1913 | Awira | | Bennettsville |
| Rushing, C.P. | W | 40 | 4/18/1913 | M | | Chesterfield |
| Dukes, Sam | B | 25 | 7/ 1/1913 | M | | Florence |
| Garrett, M.L. | W | — | 7/14/1913 | M | | Lee |
| Kelley, Herman | B | 23 | 8/ 8/1913 | Awira | S | Florence |
| Mullivee, Ernest | B | — | 8/18/1913 | M | S | Walhalla |
| Reynolds, David | B | — | 9/ 4/1913 | M,Con | | Beaufort |
| Green, Joseph | B | — | 9/ 4/1913 | M,Con | | Beaufort |
| Madison, Scott | B | — | 12/22/1913 | M | | Barnwell |
| Canty, Albert | B | — | 1/ 3/1914 | M | | Charleston |
| Thompson, Harry | B | — | 1/ 3/1914 | M | | Charleston |
| Hill, Buck | B | — | 2/ 9/1915 | Ra | | Richland |
| McCullum, Floyd | B | — | 2/ 6/1915 | Ra | | Pickens |
| Haile, Durant | B | — | 3/17/1915 | M | | Camden |
| Grice, Tommie | B | — | 8/ 4/1915 | Ra | | Florence |
| McNeil, Jessie | B | — | 9/ 2/1915 | M | | Bennettsville |
| Griffin, Meeks | B | — | 9/29/1915 | M | S | Chester |
| Griffin, Tom | B | — | 9/29/1915 | M | S | Chester |
| Crosby, John | B | — | 9/29/1915 | M | S | Chester |
| Price, Nelson | B | — | 9/29/1915 | M | S | Chester |
| Malloy, Joe | B | — | 9/29/1915 | M | S | Bennettsville |
| Logan, Charley | B | — | 10/15/1915 | M | | Abbeville |
| Hamilton, Peter | B | — | 2/ 4/1916 | Awira | | Pickens |
| Good, Israel | B | — | 2/25/1916 | Ra | | York |
| Bailey, Slabo | B | — | 4/28/1916 | M | | Laurens |
| Collins, Monroe | B | — | 5/15/1916 | Awira | | Greenville |
| Grant, Joe | B | — | 5/15/1916 | M | | Edgefield |
| Johnston, Ellis | B | — | 9/15/1916 | Awira | | Edgefield |
| Johnson, John | B | — | 10/23/1917 | M | S | Dillon |

| Name | Race | Age | Date of Execution | Offense | Appeal | County |
|------|------|-----|-------------------|---------|--------|--------|
| Palucca, Mockey | B | — | 10/12/1917 | M | | Orangeburg |
| Gardner, John | B | — | 1/25/1918 | M | | Beaufort |
| Furgerson, William | B | — | 5/10/1918 | Awira | | Barnwell |
| Holliware, Sam | B | — | 7/19/1918 | Awira | S | Walterboro |
| Johnson, Samuel | B | — | 1/10/1919 | Awira | S | York |
| Walker, Aaron | B | — | 3/18/1919 | Awira | | Greenwood |
| Johnson, George | B | — | 7/11/1919 | Awira | S | Lancaster |
| Witherspoon, Moser | B | — | 11/14/1919 | M | | Lancaster |
| Maxwell, John | B | — | 8/ 6/1920 | M | | Charleston |
| Washington, James | B | — | 9/24/1920 | Ra | | Greenville |
| Butler, Grover | B | — | 12/14/1920 | Awira | S | Spartanburg |
| Lomax, Will | B | — | 2/ 4/1921 | M | | Greenville |
| Griffin, Adam | B | — | 3/ 4/1921 | M | | Sumter |
| Fogle, Freddie | B | — | 3/25/1921 | M | | St. Matthews |
| Littlejohn, Ivey | B | — | 2/18/1921 | M | | Spartanburg |
| Wilson, Albert | B | — | 5/ 3/1921 | M | S | Richland |
| Griffin, Pink | B | — | 9/ 2/1921 | M | S | Greenwood |
| Whaley, Harvey | B | — | 11/ 4/1921 | M | S | St. Matthews |
| Choice, Tillmans | B | — | 12/ 2/1921 | Ra | | Spartanburg |
| Franklin, Curtis | B | — | 2/ 3/1922 | Ra | | Aiken |
| Harrison, Iva | W | — | 2/16/1922 | M | S | Richland |
| Hood, Will | B | — | 4/ 7/1922 | M | | Greenville |
| Fox, C.O. | W | — | 6/16/1922 | M | | Lexington |
| Gappins, Jesse | W | — | 6/16/1922 | M | | Lexington |
| Kirby, S.J. | W | — | 6/16/1922 | M | | Lexington |
| Jeffords, Frank | W | — | 12/22/1922 | M | S | Richland |
| Johnson, Thomas | B | 16 | 2/ 2/1923 | M | | Bamberg |
| Harrison, Ira | W | 22 | 2/16/1923 | M | S | Richland |
| Terry, Jake | B | — | 3/16/1923 | M | | Hampton |
| Adams, Eugene | B | 20 | 6/22/1923 | M | | Orangeburg |
| Allen, George | B | — | 7/20/1923 | M | | Anderson |
| Gaines, Frank | B | — | 12/21/1923 | M | | Beaufort |
| Garvin, Julius | B | — | 12/22/1923 | M | | Beaufort |
| Chandler, Jeff | W | — | 2/ 1/1924 | M | S | Greenville |
| Simuel, Charlie | B | — | 6/20/1924 | Awira | | Spartanburg |
| Robinson, Rubin | B | — | 11/ 7/1924 | M | | Chester |
| King, Mostimes | W | 25 | 12/ 5/1924 | M | | Chesterfield |
| Harrell, Frank | W | 24 | 12/ 5/1924 | M | | Chesterfield |
| Orr, Carroll | B | — | 1/ 5/1925 | M | S | Charleston |
| Jeffries, Draper | B | — | 8/28/1925 | M | | Spartanburg |
| Cooper, John | B | 43 | 8/27/1926 | M | | Charleston |
| Thompson, McKinley | B | — | 8/12/1927 | M | | York |
| Robinson, Charlie | B | 23 | 4/19/1929 | M | S | Charleston |
| Palmer, George | B | — | 1/ 4/1929 | M | | Charleston |
| Brown, John | B | — | 1/ 4/1929 | M | | Charleston |
| Truesdale, Eli | B | — | 4/29/1930 | M | | Lee |
| Moore, Ossie | B | — | 5/16/1930 | M | | Allendale |
| Washington, George | B | — | 5/16/1930 | M | | Allendale |
| Johnson, Paul | W | — | 6/24/1930 | M | S | Spartanburg |
| Coleman, Ray | W | — | 6/24/1930 | M | S | Spartanburg |
| Poozer, Tillman | B | — | 2/27/1931 | M | S | Lexington |
| Thomas, Earnest | B | — | 2/27/1931 | M | S | Lexington |

| Name | Race | Age | Date of Execution | Offense | Appeal | County |
|------|------|-----|-------------------|---------|--------|--------|
| Cantrell, John | B | — | 2/27/1931 | M | S | Lexington |
| Bird, George | B | — | 2/27/1931 | M | S | Lexington |
| Eldridge, Robert | B | — | 2/27/1931 | M | S | Lexington |
| Huckman, James | B | — | 2/27/1931 | M | S | Lexington |
| Blakely, Sonnau | B | — | 5/26/1931 | M | S | Greenville |
| Moore, J.P. | B | — | 6/12/1931 | Awira | | Cherokee |
| Floyd, Albert | W | 25 | 7/10/1931 | M | S | Aiken |
| Dean, Richard | B | — | 1/ 8/1932 | M | S | Spartanburg |
| King, David | B | — | 1/ 8/1932 | M | S | Spartanburg |
| Studevant, James | B | — | 1/ 8/1932 | Ra | | Horry |
| Jones, Roy | B | — | 4/29/1932 | M | S | Spartanburg |
| Williams, Hilton | B | — | 7/15/1932 | M | S | Bennettsville |
| Tucker, Buster | B | 25 | 7/29/1932 | M | | Walterboro |
| Copeland, B.T. | B | — | 7/29/1932 | M | | Walterboro |
| Woods, Ebans | B | — | 7/29/1932 | M | | Darlington |
| Howell, O.E. | W | 42 | 12/16/1932 | M | S | Sumter |
| Dicks, James | B | — | 3/ 3/1933 | M | | Aiken |
| Jones, James | B | — | 3/ 3/1933 | M | | Aiken |
| Sanders, William | B | — | 3/ 3/1933 | M | | York |
| Smith, Ronnie | B | 21 | 7/21/1933 | Ra | S | Laurens |
| Wardlaw, Tom | B | 53 | 12/ 4/1933 | M | S | Newberry |
| Holmes, James | B | 26 | 12/ 4/1933 | M | S | Sumter |
| Wiles, Robert | W | 49 | 3/12/1934 | M | | Richland |
| Watkins, John | B | 24 | 4/13/1934 | M | | Fairfield |
| Ellis, John | B | 18 | 4/27/1934 | M | | Charleston |
| Kinlock, James | B | 20 | 4/27/1934 | M | | Charleston |
| Lee, Eddie | B | — | 6/ 6/1934 | M | | Georgetown |
| Richardson, Tom | B | — | 6/ 6/1934 | M | | Georgetown |
| Brown, Payton | W | 22 | 7/13/1934 | M | | Darlington |
| Jones, Reuben | B | 18 | 7/20/1934 | M | S | Lancaster |
| Pugh, Eaver | B | 24 | 10/12/1934 | M | | Sumter |
| Cunningham, Joe | B | 19 | 11/30/1934 | M | | Richland |
| Floyd, Clarence | B | 20 | 1/ 4/1935 | Ra | S | Lexington |
| Williams, Curtis | B | — | 5/24/1935 | M | S | Greenville |
| Harris, Thurman | B | 24 | 6/ 7/1935 | Awira | | Barnwell |
| Emanuel, Ransome | B | 65 | 7/26/1935 | M | | Florence |
| Stewart, Monroe | B | 22 | 7/26/1935 | M | | Calhoun |
| Blanden, D.M. | B | 19 | 8/16/1935 | M | S | Spartanburg |
| Luster, Cornell | B | — | 12/20/1935 | M | S | Greenville |
| Hill, Harry | B | — | 12/20/1935 | M | S | Greenville |
| Ashley, Robert | B | 17 | 6/26/1936 | M | | Richland |
| Desseseau, Wash | B | 25 | 7/24/1936 | M | | Lee |
| Mixon, James | B | 20 | 7/24/1936 | M | | Lee |
| Anderson, Sam | W | — | 12/11/1936 | M | S | Anderson |
| Powell, Sam | W | — | 12/11/1936 | M | S | Anderson |
| McDuffy, George | B | — | 4/ 9/1937 | M | | Lee |
| McDonald, Furman | W | — | 8/20/1937 | M | S | Winnsboro |
| Gaines, Earnest | B | 25 | 4/13/1938 | M | | Saluda |
| Rivers, Benjamin | B | 46 | 4/29/1938 | M | S | Charleston |
| Goodman, L.O. | B | — | 7/29/1938 | M | | Florence |
| Gates, George | B | — | 12/ 9/1938 | Ra | | Darlington |
| Woods, William | W | 25 | 3/24/1939 | M | S | Richland |

| Name | Race | Age | Date of Execution | Offense | Appeal | County |
|------|------|-----|-------------------|---------|--------|--------|
| Suttles, Roy | W | 29 | 3/24/1939 | M | S | Richland |
| Bair, J.V. | W | 28 | 3/24/1939 | M | S | Richland |
| Moorman, Herbert | W | 42 | 3/24/1939 | M | S | Richland |
| Crans, Clayton | W | 29 | 3/24/1939 | M | S | Richland |
| Wingard, George | W | 23 | 3/24/1939 | M | S | Richland |
| Humphries, Edward | W | — | 4/11/1939 | M | | Dillon |
| Broughton, Joseph | B | — | 6/23/1939 | M | | Berkeley |
| McGill, Otis | W | 31 | 7/28/1939 | M | S | Greenville |
| Odom, Grover | W | — | 10/24/1939 | M | | York |
| Dash, Frank | B | 18 | 1/19/1940 | M | | McCormick |
| Bibbs, Press | B | 26 | 3/29/1940 | M | S | Calhoun |
| Lowery, Will | B | — | 6/14/1940 | Ra | | York |
| Lansing, Frank | B | — | 7/27/1940 | M | | Horry |
| Abney, George | B | 38 | 9/ 6/1940 | M | | Saluda |
| Woodward, Josiah | B | 21 | 1/31/1941 | Awira | | Aiken |
| Hann, J.C. | W | 27 | 2/ 7/1941 | M | S | Pickens |
| Evans, Hugh | W | 22 | 2/ 7/1941 | Ra | | Richland |
| Evans, Willie | W | 20 | 2/ 7/1941 | Ra | | Richland |
| Lee, Hampton | W | 26 | 2/ 7/1941 | Ra | | Richland |
| Hood, Will | B | — | 4/11/1941 | M | | Winnsboro |
| Daniels, Heyward | B | — | 7/11/1941 | Awira | | Orangeburg |
| Heyward, Ben | B | — | 8/15/1941 | M | S | Beaufort |
| Long, Roy | B | 27 | 11/21/1941 | Ra | | Pickens |
| Thomas, George | B | 30 | 2/20/1942 | Ra | S | Georgetown |
| Bounds, Monroe | B | — | 3/13/1942 | M | | Florence |
| Pickney, Cyrus | B | — | 7/10/1942 | Awira | | Berkeley |
| Gamon, Richard | B | 22 | 8/ 7/1942 | Awira | | Manning |
| Grant, Alchrist | B | — | 9/11/1942 | Awira | S,U | Berkeley |
| Robinson, John | W | — | 12/11/1942 | M | | Spartanburg |
| Frazier, Johnny | B | — | 12/11/1942 | M | | Darlington |
| Logue, Sue (Female) | W | — | 1/15/1943 | M,Acc | S | Lexington |
| Bagwell, Clarence | W | — | 1/15/1943 | M | S | Lexington |
| Logue, George | W | — | 1/15/1943 | M,Acc | S | Lexington |
| Jones, Jesse | B | — | 4/ 2/1943 | M | S | Spartanburg |
| McKinney, Sylvester | B | — | 7/16/1943 | M | | Spartanburg |
| Sims, Johnny | B | — | 7/16/1943 | M | | Spartanburg |
| Osbourne, Sammy | B | 20 | 11/19/1943 | M | S,U | Barnwell |
| Timmons, Frank | B | 20 | 5/12/1944 | Awira | | Horry |
| Stinney, George | B | 14 | 6/16/1944 | M | | Manning |
| Hamilton, Bruce | B | 22 | 6/16/1944 | Awira | | Greenville |
| Jones, Hurley | B | — | 11/ 3/1944 | Ra | | Greenville |
| Gilstrap, Charles | W | — | 2/ 9/1945 | Ra | S | Greenville |
| Carter, George | B | — | 12/ 4/1945 | M | | Greenville |
| Pringle, Wash | B | — | 1/25/1946 | M | | Sumter |
| Judge, Junius | B | 25 | 7/12/1946 | M | S | Charleston |
| Gatlin, L.C. | B | 20 | 7/19/1946 | M | S | Charleston |
| Smith, Charlie | B | — | 11/29/1946 | M | | Berkeley |
| Scott, Louis | B | — | 12/20/1946 | M | S | Williamsburg |
| Covington, Cleve | B | — | 1/ 3/1947 | M | | Marion |
| Stinette, Rosa M. (Female) | B | — | 1/17/1947 | M | | Florence |
| Jordon, Robert | B | — | 2/14/1947 | M | S | Florence |
| Haggins, Talmadge | B | — | 4/18/1947 | M | | Lancaster |

| Name | Race | Age | Date of Execution | Offense | Appeal | County |
|------|------|-----|-------------------|---------|--------|--------|
| Jones, Freddie | B | 19 | 4/25/1947 | M | S | Chester |
| Dickerson, John | B | 35 | 5/ 2/1947 | M | | Charleston |
| Davis, William A. | B | — | 6/20/1947 | Ra | S | Sumter |
| Sims, J.C. | B | — | 7/11/1947 | M | | Anderson |
| Junior, Bert G. | B | — | 7/25/1947 | Ra | | Darlington |
| Pooler, William | B | — | 8/ 1/1947 | Ra | | Darlington |
| Pringle, Leonard | B | — | 8/15/1947 | M | | Chester |
| Willis, Earnest | B | — | 8/15/1947 | M | | Chester |
| Miller, Roosevelt | B | — | 12/12/1947 | Ra | S | Greenville |
| Howard, Earnest | B | 25 | 1/ 2/1948 | Awira | | Chesterfield |
| Gidron, Willie | B | 19 | 1/ 9/1948 | M | S | Calhoun |
| Davis, Lawrence | B | 29 | 9/17/1948 | M | | Marlboro |
| Jamison, Matthew | B | 18 | 12/ 3/1948 | Ra | | Lexington |
| Troy, Leroy | B | 22 | 12/31/1948 | Ra | | Horry |
| Lincoln, Willie | B | 26 | 2/ 4/1949 | M | S | Orangeburg |
| Talbot, Willie | B | — | 10/28/1949 | Ra | | Greenwood |
| Butler, Charles W. | B | — | 6/ 2/1950 | M | | Marlboro |
| Preylow, E.T. | B | — | 6/30/1950 | M | | Saluda |
| Elmore, Larry | B | — | 8/ 4/1950 | M | | Laurens |
| Gantt, Carroll | B | — | 11/16/1951 | M | | Orangeburg |
| Harvey, Smith | B | 40 | 1/25/1952 | M | S | Beaufort |
| Cox, Frank | W | — | 2/15/1952 | M | S | Spartanburg |
| Blassingame, William P. | W | — | 4/18/1952 | M | S | Spartanburg |
| Priester, John | B | — | 4/18/1952 | M | | Beaufort |
| Priester, J.P. | B | — | 4/18/1952 | M | | Beaufort |
| Wyatt, Roland | B | — | 6/13/1952 | Ra | S | Spartanburg |
| Gantt, Landy R. | W | — | 3/ 5/1954 | M | S,U | Horry |
| Gainey, Sheldon | W | — | 3/ 5/1954 | M | S,U | Horry |
| Glenn, Otis | B | — | 3/12/1954 | M | | Orangeburg |
| Carney, Raymond | B | 37 | 5/ 7/1954 | M | | Florence |
| Hayden, Willie | B | — | 8/27/1954 | M | | Lancaster |
| Waitus, Arthur | B | 37 | 4/15/1955 | M | S | Georgetown |
| Chasteen, Marvin | W | — | 10/ 7/1955 | M | S | McCormick |
| Daniels, Clay | B | 26 | 12/ 2/1955 | Ra | | Lee |
| Daniels, Junior | B | 24 | 12/ 2/1955 | Ra | | Lee |
| Wright, Samuel | B | 21 | 1/13/1956 | M | S | Orangeburg |
| Boone, Henry Lee | B | — | 2/20/1956 | M | S | Cherokee |
| Fuller, Raymond | B | — | 7/27/1956 | M | S | Spartanburg |
| Byrd, Harold | B | 24 | 8/31/1956 | M | | Spartanburg |
| Daniels, Willie M. | B | — | 6/ 7/1957 | Ra | | Allendale |
| Smith, James E. | B | — | 7/ 5/1957 | Awira | | Abbeville |
| Johnson, Robert | B | — | 5/31/1960 | Ra | S | Orangeburg |
| Bullock, Quincy | B | 46 | 4/28/1961 | M | S,U | Dillon |
| Robinson, Charlie | B | — | 5/26/1961 | Ra | S,U | Orangeburg |
| Britt, Otis | W | — | 6/19/1961 | M | S,U | Orangeburg |
| Westbury, Douglas | W | — | 6/19/1961 | M | S,U | Orangeburg |
| Outen, Walter J. | B | 31 | 7/14/1961 | Ra | S | Richland |
| Thorne, Douglas | W | — | 4/20/1962 | Ra | S,U | Greenville |
| Young, Ray Landy | B | — | 4/20/1962 | M | S,U | Greenville |

## SOUTH DAKOTA

*Period of Executions*: 1947
*Total Number*: 1
*Method*: Electrocution
*Other Data*: During World War II it was impossible to get materials for an
electric chair, and several death sentences had to be commuted for that reason.

| Name | Race | Age | Date of Execution | Offense | Appeal | County |
|------|------|-----|-------------------|---------|--------|--------|
| Stitts, George | W | 33 | 4/ 8/1947 | M | S | Lawrence |

## TENNESSEE

*Period of Executions*: 1909–1960
*Total Number*: 134
*Method*: Electrocution
*Other Data*: Not all appeals in the state of Tennessee appear to be reported
in the lawbooks. Therefore, Teeters listed none. Espy has subsequently identified 6 appeals, which are indicated. In 1909, the Tennessee legislature passed
and the governor signed into law a bill providing that future executions in that
state be carried out at the state prison instead of the county of conviction. The
method of execution remained hanging and this was the law until the brief
period of abolition (1915–1916). 1912 is the only year in this period for which
much research has been done. When capital punishment was reinstated, the
method became electrocution. The listing of executions 1909–1915 is probably
incomplete and the exact number of executions is unknown. (Nine executions
have been identified thus far by Mr. Espy. These are indicated in footnote 1.)

| Name | Race | Age | Date of Execution | Offense | Appeal | County |
|------|------|-----|-------------------|---------|--------|--------|
| Mitchell, William[1] | W | 42 | 10/ 1/1909 | M | | Rutherford |
| Palmer, Cecil[1] | B | — | 10/ 1/1909 | Ra | | Wilson |
| Byrom, C.F.[1] | W | 53 | 3/15/1911 | M | | Wilson |
| Kinnon, Tom[1] | B | — | 1/13/1912 | Ra | | Haywood |
| Bailey, John[1] | W | — | 7/26/1912 | M | | Decatur |
| Shelton, George[1] | W | — | 7/26/1912 | M | | Decatur |
| Rose, George[1] | W | 70 | 8/26/1912 | M | | McMinn |
| Dunlap, Sidney[1] | B | — | 9/ 4/1912 | Ra | | Fayette |
| Temples, Leo[1] | B | 17 | 12/19/1912 | Ra | | Shelby |
| Morgan, Julius | B | — | 7/16/1916 | Ra | | Dyer |
| Williams, J.D. | B | — | 7/ 8/1918 | Ra | | Giles |
| Alsup, Eddie | B | — | 7/ 8/1918 | Ra | | Giles |
| Ewing, Frank | B | — | 5/21/1919 | Ra | | Davidson |
| Walker, Winifred | B | — | 1/ 8/1920 | Ra | | Jefferson |
| Young, Lorenzo | B | — | 9/ 3/1920 | M | | Shelby |
| Jackson, Cyrenus | B | 18 | 8/ 3/1921 | M | | Hamilton |
| Neal, Taylor | B | 19 | 8/ 3/1921 | M | | Hamilton |
| Graham, Chesley | B | — | 8/17/1921 | M | | Hardin |
| Allen, Will | B | — | 8/17/1921 | M | | Hardin |

| Name | Race | Age | Date of Execution | Offense | Appeal | County |
|------|------|-----|-------------------|---------|--------|--------|
| Goshton, Hamp | B | — | 8/17/1921 | M | | Shelby |
| Green, John | W | — | 2/17/1922 | M | | Washington |
| Fields, Asbury | W | 47 | 2/18/1922 | M | | Bradley |
| Stephens, Otto | W | — | 3/ 1/1922 | M | | Anderson |
| Petree, Charles | W | 23 | 3/ 1/1922 | M | | Anderson |
| McClure, John B. | W | 26 | 3/ 1/1922 | M | | Anderson |
| Christmas, Tom | W | 26 | 3/ 1/1922 | M | | Anderson |
| Mays, Maurice | B | — | 3/15/1922 | M | | Knox |
| Bunch, Granville | W | — | 4/11/1922 | M | | Anderson |
| Dwight, William | B | 18 | 7/25/1922 | M | | Hamilton |
| McElroy, Jim | W | — | 8/15/1922 | M | | Roane |
| Harris, Austin | B | — | 1/14/1922 | M | | Madison |
| Burchfield, Ben | W | 44 | 1/14/1925 | M | | Sullivan |
| Tate, Robert | W | 26 | 11/ 5/1925 | M | | Marion |
| Barr, Charley | B | 26 | 11/ 5/1926 | M | | Marion |
| Webb, John Franklin | B | — | 5/20/1927 | Ra | | Shelby |
| Wallace, John Henry | B | 37 | 5/25/1927 | M | | Rutherford |
| Coggins, Herman | W | 29 | 11/10/1927 | Ra | | Davidson |
| Fowler, Ben | B | — | 1/25/1928 | M | | Scott |
| Terrell, Will | B | 22 | 6/19/1928 | Ra | | Davidson |
| Brown, Henry | B | — | 8/22/1928 | Ra | | Davidson |
| Jones, John | B | — | 2/14/1930 | M | | Roane |
| Gunn, Carey | B | 21 | 2/14/1930 | Ra | | Hardeman |
| Harris, Theodore J. | B | 22 | 1/27/1931 | M | | Knox |
| Shaw, John T. | B | — | 7/ 3/1933 | M | | Davidson |
| Bevins, Oscar | B | 25 | 9/ 7/1933 | Ra | | Hamilton |
| Wilcoxen, Andrew | B | 26 | 9/ 7/1933 | Ra | | Hamilton |
| Jones, Willie | B | 24 | 10/30/1933 | M | | Shelby |
| Emory, Joe | B | 39 | 2/ 5/1934 | M | | Knox |
| Swann, James | B | 20 | 2/ 5/1934 | M | | Knox |
| Allen, Jim | B | 21 | 1/ 5/1934 | M | | Knox |
| Fain, Lewis | B | — | 2/26/1934 | M | | Knox |
| Smith, Percy | B | — | 4/ 4/1934 | Ra | | Shelby |
| Graham, Jasper | B | — | 4/ 4/1934 | Ra | | Shelby |
| Mays, Frank | B | — | 4/ 4/1934 | Ra | | Shelby |
| Deal, John | B | 31 | 9/15/1934 | M | | Shelby |
| Pillow, James | B | — | 9/15/1934 | M | | Shelby |
| Lee, Bill | W | 24 | 1/21/1936 | M | | Monroe |
| Kennedy, Walter | W | 18 | 1/21/1936 | M | | Anderson |
| Willis, Louis | B | 27 | 1/28/1936 | M | | Davidson |
| Womack, Ernest | B | 18 | 4/10/1936 | M | | Warren |
| Smith, James | B | 27 | 8/14/1936 | M | | Lincoln |
| Ballard, Curley | B | 56 | 8/14/1936 | M | | Sullivan |
| Clark, James | B | 23 | 8/14/1936 | M | | Shelby |
| Harris, Ernest K. | B | 23 | 5/22/1936 | Ra | | Bedford |
| Barrett, Elmer | B | 22 | 11/18/1936 | M | | Knox |
| Taylor, James | B | 25 | 3/15/1937 | Ra | | Davidson |
| Berry, Anderson | B | — | 3/17/1937 | M | | Lincoln |
| Franklin, Tom | B | 20 | 3/18/1937 | M | | Davidson |
| McCoig, Gus | W | 25 | 4/ 8/1937 | M | | Union |
| Eatmon, Ray W. | W | 24 | 4/16/1937 | M | | Shelby |
| Dunn, Howard | W | 22 | 4/30/1937 | M | | Davidson |

| Name | Race | Age | Date of Execution | Offense | Appeal | County |
|------|------|-----|-------------------|---------|--------|--------|
| Farmer, William | W | 19 | 4/30/1937 | M | | Davidson |
| Turner, James | B | 25 | 8/ 5/1937 | M | | Shelby |
| Parrish, Jimmie Lee | B | 35 | 8/ 9/1937 | Awira | | Davidson |
| Ritchie, Fred | W | 32 | 9/10/1937 | Awira | | Davidson |
| McKinney, Gus | B | 19 | 4/15/1938 | M | | Shelby |
| Mosby, Arthur | B | — | 7/25/1938 | M | | Shelby |
| Stanley, Ernest | B | — | 1/10/1939 | M | | Morgan |
| Tollett, White Miller | W | 28 | 1/11/1939 | M | S | Carter |
| Johnson, Herman | B | 22 | 3/28/1939 | M | | Davidson |
| Murray, Frank | B | 19 | 3/28/1939 | M | | Davidson |
| Evans, Harley | W | — | 3/28/1939 | M | | Fentress |
| Harris, Hubert | B | 22 | 4/ 4/1939 | M | | Davidson |
| Martin, J.O. | W | 43 | 4/10/1939 | M | | Shelby |
| McKay, Joe | B | — | 4/10/1939 | M | | Shelby |
| Smith, Willie James | B | — | 4/10/1939 | M | | Shelby |
| Williams, Willie | B | 33 | 4/15/1939 | M | | Davidson |
| Wills, Clyde | W | 29 | 1/10/1940 | Ra | | Knox |
| Mobley, C.C. | B | 35 | 3/15/1940 | Ra | | Shelby |
| Nelson, William Henry Clay | W | 44 | 9/ 4/1940 | M | | Dyer |
| Goodin, James | B | — | 9/ 4/1940 | M | | Shelby |
| Gilmore, Van | B | 31 | 4/18/1941 | Ra | | Shelby |
| Reed, Walter | B | 55 | 7/18/1941 | M | | Hamilton |
| Cole, Carl | B | 19 | 7/24/1941 | M | | Madison |
| Porter, Lee Willie | B | 21 | 7/24/1941 | M | | Madison |
| West, Lawrence | B | — | 7/30/1941 | M | | Montgomery |
| Walden, Roy | W | 36 | 2/13/1942 | Ra | S | Knox |
| Dixon, Ernest | W | 23 | 2/14/1942 | Ra | | Knox |
| Dockery, John | W | 20 | 2/14/1942 | Ra | | Knox |
| Goode, John Henry | B | — | 3/20/1942 | M | | Shelby |
| May, Clarence | W | 33 | 3/20/1942 | M | | Polk |
| Hedden, William | W | 44 | 3/30/1943 | M | | Polk |
| Cannon, Robert | B | 27 | 3/30/1943 | M | | Shelby |
| Spigner, Marshall | W | 40 | 7/15/1943 | M | | Shelby |
| Tucker, James F. | W | 29 | 7/15/1943 | M | | Davidson |
| Arwood, Clyde | W | 24 | 8/14/1943 | M | | Fed |
| Hall, Robert | B | 50 | 12/15/1943 | M | | Hamilton |
| Hambrick, George | B | — | 4/24/1945 | M | | Davidson |
| Dixon, Billy | B | — | 7/18/1945 | Ra | | Montgomery |
| Walker, Thomas | B | 33 | 3/ 1/1946 | M | | Shelby |
| Outlaw, Johnnie | B | 27 | 3/ 1/1946 | M | | Shelby |
| Douglas, George | B | 20 | 7/ 5/1946 | Ra | | Shelby |
| Luffman, John H. | W | — | 8/30/1946 | M | | Stewart |
| Hicks, Alvin | W | 21 | 8/30/1946 | M | | Stewart |
| Duboise, Albert | W | — | 4/11/1947 | M | | Rutherford |
| Hodge, John, Jr. | B | 28 | 6/19/1947 | Ra | | Davidson |
| Jackson, Fred | B | 18 | 8/11/1947 | M | | Shelby |
| Sandusky, James | W | 20 | 4/22/1948 | M | | Hickman |
| Kelley, John | W | 21 | 4/22/1948 | M | | Hickman |
| Turner, W.J.C. | B | 21 | 8/31/1948 | Ra | | Davidson |
| Scribner, James | B | 25 | 8/31/1948 | Ra | | Davidson |
| Taylor, Tommy Howard | B | — | 8/31/1948 | Ra | | Davidson |

| Name | Race | Age | Date of Execution | Offense | Appeal | County |
|------|------|-----|-------------------|---------|--------|--------|
| Thompson, Barney | B | 29 | 2/17/1949 | M | | Bradley |
| Watson, Bruce E. | B | 25 | 6/10/1949 | Ra | | Shelby |
| Lacy, Paul | B | 28 | 11/15/1949 | M | | Maury |
| Steele, Clyde | B | 21 | 1/24/1950 | Ra | S | Knox |
| Voss, Samuel T. | B | 29 | 4/15/1955 | M | S | Davidson |
| Kirkendall, Harry | B | — | 8/ 1/1955 | M | | Wilson |
| Sullins, Charlie | W | 34 | 8/ 1/1955 | M | | Wilson |
| Crenshaw, Robert | B | 41 | 9/15/1955 | Ra | | Davidson |
| Gibbs, Billy Thomas | W | — | 5/ 6/1957 | M | S | Coffee |
| Allen, Jimmy | B | 36 | 3/15/1957 | M | | Davidson |
| Rutledge, Tom | W | — | 6/15/1959 | M | | Warren |
| Tines, William | B | — | 11/ 7/1960 | Ra | S | Knox |

¹Mitchell (10/1/1909) through Temples (12/19/1912) were hanged in their counties of conviction after Tennessee passed the law to execute condemned felons at the state prison.

## TEXAS

*Period of Executions*: 1924–1982
*Total Number*: 362 (including 1 post-*Furman* execution)
*Method*: Electrocution, 1924–1964; lethal injection, 1982

| Name | Race | Age | Date of Execution | Offense | Appeal | County |
|------|------|-----|-------------------|---------|--------|--------|
| Matthews, Mack | B | — | 2/ 8/1924 | M | S | Tyler |
| Washington, George | B | — | 2/ 8/1924 | M | S | Newton |
| Johnson, Melvin | B | — | 2/ 8/1924 | M | S | Liberty |
| Morris, Ewell | B | — | 2/ 8/1924 | M | S | Liberty |
| Reynolds, Charles | B | — | 2/ 8/1924 | M | S | Red River |
| Dyer, Blaine | B | — | 3/28/1924 | M | S | Dallas |
| Lawson, Earnest | B | — | 3/28/1924 | M | S | Dallas |
| Williams, Booker J. | B | — | 4/ 4/1924 | M | S | Angelina |
| Curry, Tommie | B | — | 4/17/1924 | M | S | Smith |
| Humphreys, Harle | B | — | 5/22/1924 | M | S | Falls |
| Cadena, Frank | B | — | 5/23/1924 | M | S | Bexar |
| Henderson, Ed | B | — | 6/ 9/1924 | Ra | S | Polk |
| Kirby, Ed | B | — | 10/10/1924 | M | S | Colorado |
| Welk, Sidney | W | 31 | 4/ 3/1925 | M | S | Dallas |
| Twitty, La Vannie | B | — | 6/ 5/1925 | M | S | Dallas |
| Noel, Frank | B | — | 7/ 3/1925 | Ra | | Dallas |
| Noel, Lorenzo | B | — | 7/ 3/1925 | Ra | | Dallas |
| Rushing, Edwin | B | — | 7/17/1925 | M | | Anderson |
| Gray, George C. | W | — | 8/ 7/1925 | M | S | Titus |
| Carr, Melton | B | — | 1/ 1/1926 | Ra | S | Walker |
| Rueda, Agapito | B | 29 | 1/ 9/1926 | M | | El Paso |
| Vaughn, Willie | B | 23 | 3/12/1926 | Ra | | Bexar |
| Robinson, S.A. | B | — | 4/ 6/1926 | M | | Dallas |
| Robinson, Forest | B | — | 4/ 6/1926 | M | | Dallas |
| Smith, John | B | 23 | 4/16/1926 | M | S | Brown |
| Harris, T. | B | — | 5/ 3/1926 | M | S | Harris |

| Name | Race | Age | Date of Execution | Offense | Appeal | County |
|------|------|-----|-------------------|---------|--------|--------|
| Phillips, Sam | B | 32 | 5/14/1926 | M | S | Ft. Bend |
| Tilford, Fred L. | B | — | 7/ 9/1926 | M | | Navarro |
| Bains, F.D. | B | — | 2/18/1927 | M | S | Bexar |
| Satchell, Bryant | B | — | 3/17/1927 | M | | McLennan |
| Briscoe, Matthew | B | 38 | 5/20/1927 | Ra | S | Bexar |
| Snow, F.M. | W | 65 | 8/12/1927 | M | S | Erath |
| Joshlin, Ed | B | 19 | 8/22/1927 | Ra | | Victoria |
| Robinson, Willie | B | — | 9/23/1927 | M | S | Denton |
| Sparks, Tillman | B | — | 9/26/1927 | M | | Bexar |
| Millikin, A.V. | W | — | 11/ 5/1927 | M | S | Caldwell |
| Hassell, George J. | W | — | 2/10/1928 | M | S | Parmer |
| Benton, Robert Lee | B | — | 2/10/1928 | M | S | Crosby |
| Fisher, Willie | B | — | 4/12/1928 | M | S | Harris |
| Davenport, Lawrence | B | — | 6/ 1/1928 | M | S | Harris |
| Thomas, Garrett | B | 28 | 8/ 3/1928 | M | S | Live Oak |
| Servina, Esquell | B | 21 | 9/ 7/1928 | Ra | S | Bexar |
| Rodriguez, Clemento | B | 22 | 9/ 7/1928 | Ra | | Bexar |
| Ross, Tom | B | — | 9/28/1928 | M | S | Nacogdoches |
| Alexander, O.T. | B | 37 | 9/28/1928 | M | S | Harris |
| Byrnes, Floyd Newton | W | 25 | 1/11/1929 | M | S | Tom Green |
| Wilborn, Wade | B | — | 4/12/1929 | M | S | Titus |
| Blake, Robert F. | W | 26 | 4/19/1929 | M | S | Swisher |
| Sanders, Mathis | B | — | 4/27/1929 | Ra | | Brazos |
| Jarman, Silas | B | 17 | 5/24/1929 | Ro,Fr | S | Grayson |
| Wells, O.C. | W | — | 6/20/1929 | M | S | Coleman |
| Grady, Willie | B | 22 | 7/26/1929 | Ra | S | Hunt |
| Leahy, H.J. | W | — | 9/ 2/1929 | M | S | Williamson |
| Helms, Henry | W | 33 | 9/ 6/1929 | Ro,Fr | S | Eastland |
| Merriman, Lee Roy | W | 29 | 11/29/1929 | Ra | S | Dallas |
| Aldridge, Ben | W | 26 | 12/19/1929 | Ra | S | Dallas |
| Adams, Bishop | B | — | 3/13/1930 | M | S | Travis |
| Scott, Jordan | B | — | 5/22/1930 | M | S | McLennan |
| Pruitt, William | W | 22 | 6/ 6/1930 | M | S | Dallas |
| Williams, Rainey | B | 38 | 8/ 8/1930 | Ra | S | Jefferson |
| Davis, Lee | B | 26 | 8/22/1930 | M | S | Brazoria |
| Washington, Jesse Lee | B | — | 9/12/1930 | M | S | Roberts |
| Smith, Bill | W | — | 10/17/1930 | M | S | Jones |
| Arcos, Lus G. | M | 29 | 11/ 7/1930 | M | S | Medina |
| Maples, J.J. | W | 34 | 11/28/1930 | M | | Harris |
| Twitty, Marcuso | W | — | 4/24/1931 | Ra | S | Gray |
| Herrera, Ofilio | M | — | 6/19/1931 | M | S | Mason |
| Riles, Joshua | B | 31 | 7/24/1931 | Ra | S | Galveston |
| Jenkins, Will | B | 46 | 7/28/1931 | Ra | S | Harris |
| Shield, Joe | W | 36 | 8/14/1931 | M | S | Brown |
| Munoz, Nicando | M | 26 | 10/30/1931 | M | S | Hidalgo |
| Rodriguez, Victor | M | 20 | 10/30/1931 | M | S | Hidalgo |
| Wing, Red | I | — | 11/30/1931 | M | | Comal |
| Fritts, Will | W | 38 | 12/18/1931 | M | S | Kent |
| Ross, Bonnie Lee | B | — | 12/18/1931 | Ra | | Morris |
| Jackson, Alfred | B | — | 1/ 8/1932 | M | S | Bexar |
| McKee, Ira | W | 32 | 1/ 8/1932 | M | S | Dawson |
| White, Jake | B | 32 | 4/ 1/1932 | M | | Dallas |

| Name | Race | Age | Date of Execution | Offense | Appeal | County |
|------|------|-----|-------------------|---------|--------|--------|
| Williams, James | B | — | 4/20/1932 | M | S | Hunt |
| Johnson, Earnest | B | 20 | 6/ 5/1932 | M | S | Caldwell |
| Lopez, Estamisado | M | — | 6/10/1932 | M | S | Willacy |
| Grogans, Charlie | B | 33 | 7/28/1932 | Ra | | Jefferson |
| Green, John L. | B | 18 | 8/ 5/1932 | M | S | Medina |
| Johnson, Richard | B | 35 | 8/10/1932 | M | S | Wichita |
| Brown, Richard | B | 19 | 8/10/1932 | M | S | Young |
| Haskins, Walter | B | — | 4/ 7/1933 | M | | Ellis |
| Bennett, R.T. | B | 25 | 8/18/1933 | M | S | Dallas |
| Williams, Marshall | B | 24 | 11/20/1933 | M | S | Walker |
| Ortiz, Pantaleon | M | 34 | 12/12/1933 | M | S | Refugio |
| Thomas, Clarence | B | 18 | 12/15/1933 | M | S | Hunt |
| Cook, Tom | B | 34 | 12/19/1933 | M | S | Harris |
| Booker, Clarence | B | 25 | 12/29/1933 | M | S | Travis |
| Stewart, Carl | B | 23 | 12/29/1933 | M | S | Travis |
| Hunt, Dewey R. | W | 27 | 12/29/1933 | M | S,U | Dallas |
| Kelly, Ira | W | 38 | 1/18/1934 | Ra | S | Harris |
| Flours, Frank | B | 33 | 2/ 2/1934 | M | | McLennan |
| Burkley, Thurman | B | 19 | 2/ 9/1934 | M | S | Dallas |
| Burkley, Bluit | B | 20 | 2/ 9/1934 | M | S | Dallas |
| Mott, Jesse | B | 34 | 2/ 9/1934 | M | S | Dallas |
| Jackson, Sack | B | 45 | 4/ 6/1934 | Ra | | Rusk |
| Outlaw, Charlie | W | 58 | 4/27/1934 | M | S | Angelina |
| Williams, Johnnie | B | 31 | 5/ 1/1934 | M | S | Harris |
| Brooks, Nathan | W | — | 6/ 1/1934 | M | S | Harris |
| Stanton, Ed | W | — | 9/28/1934 | M | S | Swisher |
| Jackson, Jack | B | — | 11/19/1934 | M | S | Liberty |
| Woolfolk, June | B | 36 | 11/23/1934 | M | S | Bexar |
| Lane, LeRoy | W | 24 | 1/25/1935 | M | | Dallas |
| Dobbins, C.B. | W | 35 | 2/ 1/1935 | M | S | Harris |
| Burns, Leonard | W | 41 | 2/15/1935 | M | S | Bowie |
| Smith, Cabe | B | 25 | 3/19/1935 | M | S | Harris |
| Rector, Ira | B | — | 4/ 2/1935 | M | S | Grimes |
| Arnold, Doyl | W | — | 4/19/1935 | M | S | Callahan |
| Palmer, Joe | W | — | 5/10/1935 | M | S | Grimes |
| Hamilton, Raymond | W | 22 | 5/10/1935 | Ra | S | Walker |
| Carr, Albert | B | 35 | 6/ 7/1935 | Ra | S | Harris |
| Willis, John B. | W | 42 | 6/12/1935 | Ra | S | Smith |
| Stewart, Elijah | W | 28 | 6/12/1935 | M | S | Harris |
| Cernoch, Lewis | W | 39 | 7/12/1935 | M | S | Williamson |
| Trapper, John | B | — | 8/14/1935 | M | S | Uvalde |
| Dade, Johnnie | B | — | 8/16/1935 | M | S | Brazoria |
| Coume, Bernard | W | — | 8/23/1935 | M | S | Angelina |
| Boyd, Ben | B | — | 8/30/1935 | M | S | Wharton |
| May, W.D. | W | 39 | 9/ 6/1935 | M | S | Tarrant |
| Hildreth, W.R. | W | — | 11/25/1935 | M | S | Howard |
| Cantrell, Pierson | W | — | 12/ 6/1935 | M | S | Wood |
| James, C.B. | W | 32 | 12/31/1935 | M | S | Tyler |
| Carr, Henry | B | — | 1/ 3/1936 | M | S | Tyler |
| Hill, Fred | B | 23 | 1/10/1936 | M | S | Travis |
| Stalcup, Virgil | W | 27 | 5/ 4/1936 | Ra | S | Lubbock |
| Dickerson, Willie | B | 22 | 5/29/1936 | M | S | Cass |

| Name | Race | Age | Date of Execution | Offense | Appeal | County |
|------|------|-----|-------------------|---------|--------|--------|
| Tance, Arla | B | — | 5/30/1936 | M | | Harris |
| Davis, William R. | B | — | 6/ 5/1936 | M | | Travis |
| McCallister, James D. | W | — | 6/ 5/1936 | Ra | S | Hidalgo |
| Rivera, Juan | M | 25 | 6/23/1936 | M | S | Bastrop |
| Warren, Grady | W | — | 7/10/1936 | M | S | Upshur |
| Brown, Oscar | B | — | 7/10/1936 | M | S | Refugio |
| Brown, Mack Coupie | B | — | 7/10/1936 | M | S | Refugio |
| Warren, Glenn | W | — | 7/20/1936 | M | S | Angelina |
| Carrasco, Antonio | M | 41 | 10/23/1936 | M | S | Hudspeth |
| Banks, Elmo | B | — | 10/23/1936 | M | S | Lynn |
| Joiner, Lonnie | W | — | 5/28/1937 | M | | Newton |
| Pruitt, Elmer | B | 24 | 5/30/1937 | M | S | Henderson |
| Beard, Dwight | W | 27 | 6/ 4/1937 | M | S | Dallas |
| Ellison, Wisie | B | — | 6/ 4/1937 | M | | Caldwell |
| Matura, C. | W | 66 | 7/ 2/1937 | M | S | Stonewall |
| McCarty, Earnest | B | 20 | 7/ 9/1937 | M | | Tarrant |
| Patton, George | W | 50 | 7/30/1937 | M | S | Ellis |
| Trammel, Luke | W | — | 8/20/1937 | M | S | Brazoria |
| Hemphill, Albert Lee | B | 23 | 1/14/1938 | M | S | Dallas |
| Kelly, LeRoy | B | — | 3/15/1938 | M | | Lamb |
| Terrell, Virgil | B | — | 3/31/1938 | Ra | | Gregg |
| Banks, Johnnie | B | — | 4/29/1938 | M | S | Brazoria |
| Vaughn, John W. | W | 32 | 4/30/1938 | M | S | Bexar |
| Young, Roscoe | B | — | 5/ 6/1938 | Ro | S | Harrison |
| Young, Henderson | B | — | 5/ 6/1938 | Ra | S | Harrison |
| Layes, Paul | W | 33 | 5/10/1938 | M | S | Hays |
| Brooks, Charlie | B | — | 5/31/1938 | M | S | Cass |
| Moore, Tommie | B | — | 6/ 3/1938 | M | S | Limestone |
| Calhoun, Mark Henry | B | 18 | 6/17/1938 | Ra | S | Dallas |
| Wells, Tommie | B | 25 | 6/17/1938 | Ra | S | Bowie |
| Grays, Tobie | B | — | 7/29/1938 | M | S | Wharton |
| Boss, Vince | W | 22 | 8/ 2/1938 | M | S | Caldwell |
| Morgan, Callo H. | W | 38 | 8/19/1938 | M | S | El Paso |
| Polanco, Jesse | M | 22 | 8/19/1938 | M | S | Bexar |
| Canedo, Salinas | M | 26 | 10/28/1938 | M | | Bexar |
| Norman, Morris | B | — | 12/16/1938 | Ra | S | Donley |
| Williams, Wenzell | B | 19 | 3/ 6/1939 | M | S | Dallas |
| Nealy, Harvey T. | B | 21 | 4/10/1939 | M | S | Dallas |
| Herrera, Jesus | M | 49 | 4/15/1939 | M | S | Wilson |
| Lugo, Gennaro | M | — | 4/23/1939 | M | S | San Patricio |
| Miles, James C. | B | 23 | 4/23/1939 | Ra | S | Dallas |
| Randall, Bennie | B | 26 | 5/ 7/1939 | Ra | S | Colorado |
| Ervin, James | B | 29 | 5/19/1939 | Ra | S | Tarrant |
| Caesar, Johnny | B | 32 | 5/21/1939 | M | S | Dallas |
| Rhodes, Ladell | B | — | 6/26/1939 | M | S | Harrison |
| Walker, Lee | B | — | 6/30/1939 | Ra | S | Freestone |
| Salazer, Frank | M | 23 | 12/16/1939 | M | S | Nolan |
| Lacy, Harry | B | — | 12/19/1939 | M | S | Montgomery |
| Rickman, J.W. | W | 22 | 3/18/1940 | M | | Collin |
| Hampton, Bluitt | B | — | 3/31/1940 | M | S | Dallas |
| Walker, Robert Ballard | W | 27 | 4/19/1940 | M | S | Dallas |
| Lyons, Webster | B | — | 4/28/1940 | M | S | Bexar |

| Name | Race | Age | Date of Execution | Offense | Appeal | County |
|------|------|-----|-------------------|---------|--------|--------|
| Manning, Robert | B | 21 | 4/28/1940 | M | S | Bexar |
| Franks, Burton | W | 22 | 6/ 7/1940 | M | S | Ellis |
| Handez, Placido | M | — | 6/ 9/1940 | M |  | Hidalgo |
| Murphy, Florence L. | B | 26 | 8/30/1940 | Ra | S | Kaufman |
| Martinez, Ascension | M | — | 2/21/1941 | M | S | Hidalgo |
| Muldrow, Theodia | B | 19 | 2/21/1941 | Ra |  | Dallas |
| Griffin, George | B | — | 4/20/1941 | Ra | S | Nueces |
| Harris, Tommie | B | 24 | 6/ 6/1941 | M | S | Tarrant |
| Reese, Arlin F. | W | — | 8/24/1941 | M | S | Limestone |
| Wesley, Albert, Jr. | B | 20 | 12/28/1941 | Ra | S | Dallas |
| Glover, Nehemiah | B | 28 | 1/28/1942 | M | S,U | Harris |
| Robinson, Richard | B | 38 | 2/15/1942 | Ra | S | Harris |
| Goldsby, Charlie | B | 36 | 2/22/1942 | Ra |  | Jefferson |
| King, Rogers Lee | B | 20 | 3/22/1942 | M | S | Johnson |
| Alford, James | W | 26 | 5/ 8/1942 | M | S | Bexar |
| Morris, McKinley | B | 30 | 5/16/1942 | M | S,U | Wilson |
| Brown, Orrin J. | W | — | 6/15/1942 | M | S | Hansford |
| Hill, Luther | B | — | 7/ 5/1942 | M | S | Panola |
| Hart, Edward, Jr. | B | 25 | 7/29/1942 | Ra | S | Dallas |
| Walker, Ben | B | — | 8/ 1/1942 | Ra | S | Harrison |
| Benevidez, Emiliano | M | — | 8/ 8/1942 | M |  | Schleicher |
| Turner, C.L. | B | — | 9/ 2/1942 | M | S | Dallas |
| Lera, Leo | W | 33 | 2/19/1943 | M | S | Ft. Bend |
| Wilson, Arthur Lee | B | 24 | 7/21/1943 | M | S | Dallas |
| Beard, Rex | W | 19 | 9/ 3/1943 | M | S | Fisher |
| Quiroz, Dolores | M | — | 10/29/1943 | M |  | Jeff Davis |
| Jordan, Bruce Elton | W | — | 4/16/1944 | M |  | Colorado |
| Gutierrez, Juan | M | — | 5/ 2/1944 | M | S | Hidalgo |
| Williams, David | B | 17 | 7/ 9/1944 | Ra | S | Travis |
| Johnson, Bennie | B | — | 7/ 9/1944 | M | S | Chambers |
| Whittle, Clay | W | — | 7/30/1944 | M | S | Houston |
| Johnson, Willie | B | 36 | 8/27/1944 | M | S | Fayette |
| Johnson, George | B | — | 8/27/1944 | M | S | Bowie |
| Stephens, J.B. | W | 38 | 12/19/1944 | M | S | Ellis |
| Murray, Allen | B | 32 | 12/31/1944 | Ra | S | Denton |
| Williams, Henry | B | — | 3/ 4/1945 | M | S | Gonzales |
| Holloway, Robert J. | B | 24 | 3/25/1945 | M | S | McLennan |
| Harper, Julius | B | 19 | 7/ 7/1945 | M | S | Harris |
| Oglesby, Joseph W. | B | — | 9/ 2/1945 | Ra |  | Reeves |
| Elliott, Jarvin R. | B | — | 1/18/1946 | M | S | Bowie |
| Gamble, Richard | B | 32 | 6/28/1946 | M | S | Tarrant |
| Newman, L.C. | B | — | 7/19/1946 | M | S | Polk |
| Moore, Clyde | B | — | 8/ 8/1946 | Ra |  | Henderson |
| Leza, Joe G. | M | 32 | 9/ 1/1946 | M |  | Bexar |
| Palm, Harold Lee | B | 32 | 9/ 1/1946 | Ra | S | Bexar |
| Henderson, L.D. | B | — | 3/21/1947 | M | S | Grimes |
| Zachary, P.H. | B | — | 4/ 1/1947 | M | S | Williamson |
| Wilson, Huie | B | 36 | 5/ 2/1947 | M | S | Harris |
| Allen, Oscar | B | 45 | 5/29/1947 | M | S | Dallas |
| Jones, Louis | B | — | 6/ 2/1947 | M | S | Gonzales |
| Norris, William A. | B | — | 6/ 7/1947 | M | S | Hudspeth |
| Allen, Charlie | B | 57 | 6/26/1947 | M | S | Dallas |

| Name | Race | Age | Date of Execution | Offense | Appeal | County |
|------|------|-----|-------------------|---------|--------|--------|
| Adams, Arthur | B | 38 | 9/ 5/1947 | M | S | Tarrant |
| Pearson, Elijah | B | 46 | 9/12/1947 | M | S | Harris |
| Davis, Raymond | B | — | 10/ 5/1947 | M | S | Newton |
| Cline, Lonnie Harvey | W | 27 | 1/ 2/1948 | M | S | Dallas |
| West, Nolan | W | 25 | 2/ 4/1948 | M | S | Harris |
| Johnson, Bennie | B | 26 | 3/28/1948 | Ra | S | Ft. Bend |
| Rushing, Clayton | W | — | 3/28/1948 | M | S | Jasper |
| Sims, Willie | B | 36 | 4/25/1948 | Ra | S | Harris |
| Saulter, Joseph Lee | W | 34 | 7/ 9/1948 | M | S | Galveston |
| Coleman, John Amos | B | — | 7/18/1948 | Ra | S | Gregg |
| Brown, Henry | B | — | 8/ 1/1948 | M | S | Harrison |
| McCane, Riley B. | W | — | 8/20/1948 | M | | Jefferson |
| Smith, Cleo | B | — | 8/24/1948 | Ra | S | Bowie |
| Hill, Andrew | B | — | 10/ 3/1948 | M | S | Bowie |
| Moore, Wilson | B | 29 | 2/ 1/1949 | Ra | | Harris |
| Williams, Thurman | B | 23 | 2/13/1949 | M | S | Harris |
| Larkin, Thomas | B | — | 2/21/1949 | M | S | Harrison |
| Northern, Buster | W | 20 | 4/16/1949 | M | S | Dallas |
| Jones, W. Fred | W | — | 8/10/1949 | M | S | Crosby |
| Kerzee, General | B | 57 | 8/10/1949 | M | | Dallas |
| McLendon, F.M. | B | — | 8/14/1949 | M | S | Lee |
| Stovall, Cleveland, Jr. | B | — | 9/11/1949 | Ra | S | Tarrant |
| Gibson, Samuel B. | B | — | 1/29/1950 | M | S | Howard |
| Wilson, William, Jr. | B | 31 | 2/ 5/1950 | Ra | S,U | Harris |
| Morrow, J.W. | W | 29 | 2/ 9/1950 | M | S | Harris |
| Blackmon, James Willis | B | — | 4/ 5/1950 | M | | Harris |
| Smith, William, Jr. | B | — | 4/ 5/1950 | M | S | Harris |
| Bunn, Lee Everett | B | 27 | 5/ 3/1950 | M | S | McLennan |
| Ray, William | W | 34 | 6/ 9/1950 | Ra | S | Navarro |
| Edwards, Nathaniel | B | 27 | 5/17/1950 | Ra | | Harris |
| White, Dan | W | — | 6/ 2/1950 | M | S | Palo Pinto |
| Henderson, Porter | B | 41 | 6/14/1950 | M | S | Harris |
| Lewis, Felix | W | — | 6/21/1950 | Ra | S | Live Oak |
| McFarland, Eugene | B | 26 | 6/30/1950 | Ra | S | Harris |
| Johnson, Edward Exnoal | B | 30 | 12/29/1950 | Ra | S | Harris |
| Pickett, Ben | B | 35 | 1/13/1951 | Ra | S,U | Harris |
| Price, Thomas Jefferson | W | 30 | 2/ 1/1951 | M | S | Dallas |
| Patterson, J.B. | W | 44 | 3/14/1951 | M | S | Harris |
| Williams, Allen Conway | W | 39 | 3/21/1951 | Ra | S | Harris |
| Bessard, Morris | B | 23 | 6/27/1951 | Ra | S | Harris |
| Williams, Sam | B | 53 | 7/ 3/1951 | M | S | Harris |
| Robinson, Y.B. | B | 32 | 7/16/1951 | M | S | Wichita |
| Adair, Fred Felix, Jr. | W | 27 | 9/ 5/1951 | Ra | S | Dallas |
| Matthews, Allen | B | 26 | 9/ 5/1951 | Ra | S | Harris |
| Sims, L.C. | B | 26 | 9/ 5/1951 | Ra | S | Collin |
| Mitchell, Steve | W | 39 | 9/25/1951 | M | S | Harris |
| Edwards, Albert | W | 47 | 10/ 9/1951 | M | S | Harris |
| Mouton, Abbie | B | 31 | 12/ 8/1951 | M | S | Jefferson |
| McMurrin, Richard S. | B | — | 1/ 8/1952 | Ra | S,U | Galveston |
| Johnson, Robert Lee | W | 31 | 3/12/1952 | M | S | Dallas |
| Johnson, Marvin Eugene | W | 21 | 4/ 9/1952 | M | S | Brown |
| Jones, William K. | W | — | 4/26/1952 | M | S | Jones |

| Name | Race | Age | Date of Execution | Offense | Appeal | County |
|------|------|-----|-------------------|---------|--------|--------|
| Savage, Henry | B | — | 4/30/1952 | Ra | S | Grimes |
| Ross, Herman Lee | B | — | 6/ 4/1952 | M | S,U,NT | Galveston |
| Haley, Thomas | W | 27 | 7/10/1952 | Ra | S | Tarrant |
| Preston, Major | B | — | 8/ 8/1952 | Ra | S,U,NT | Trinity |
| Reed, Booker T. | B | — | 10/28/1952 | M | S | Dallas |
| Paris, Alton | B | 60 | 12/ 2/1952 | M | S,U | Anderson |
| Goleman, Darious | W | 35 | 2/ 4/1953 | M | S | Liberty |
| Hulen, R.J. | W | 43 | 2/ 6/1953 | M | S | Potter |
| Gasway, Samuel James | W | 35 | 3/21/1953 | Ra | S,U | Potter |
| Farmer, Frank | W | 51 | 6/10/1953 | M | S | Floyd |
| Allison, Louis | B | 22 | 10/ 7/1953 | Ra | S | Harris |
| Green, Walter Collins | W | 24 | 2/19/1954 | M | S | Culberson |
| Klinedinst, Charles E.M. | W | — | 3/19/1954 | Ra | S | Dallas |
| Clark, Charles D. | W | 43 | 3/25/1954 | M | S | Tom Green |
| Gage, Willie Lee | B | 42 | 4/23/1954 | Ra | S | Tarrant |
| Richardson, Jimmy | B | — | 6/24/1954 | Ra | S | Freestone |
| Barnes, Charles W. | B | 24 | 7/14/1954 | M | S | Harris |
| Rayson, Marvin | B | 28 | 7/17/1954 | M | S | Palo Pinto |
| Whitaker, Walter E., Jr. | W | 21 | 9/ 1/1954 | M | S | Wilbarger |
| Sampson, Maurice | B | 20 | 9/29/1954 | M | S | Harris |
| Brown, Donald Hawkins | W | — | 1/12/1955 | M | S,U | Dallas |
| Butcher, Harry F. | W | 26 | 5/20/1955 | Ra | S | Midland |
| Meyer, Henry William | W | 63 | 6/ 8/1955 | M | S | Harris |
| Jackson, Floyd Ray | B | — | 8/18/1955 | Ra | S | Dallas |
| Farrar, Carrol | W | 36 | 1/ 4/1956 | M | S | Harris |
| Gordon, Johnnie Elwood | B | — | 1/24/1956 | Ra | S | Harris |
| Walker, Tommie Lee | B | 19 | 5/12/1956 | M | S | Dallas |
| Washington, Marion A. | B | 26 | 6/ 8/1956 | M | S | McLennan |
| Fite, Flandell | B | — | 8/23/1956 | Ra | | Dallas |
| Pierce, Timothy | B | — | 8/30/1956 | Ra | | Dallas |
| Bingham, Leonard Lionel | W | — | 10/30/1956 | M | S | Pecos |
| McHenry, John Edward | B | 25 | 1/ 3/1957 | Ra | S | Harris |
| Webb, Leslie | B | 34 | 1/ 4/1957 | M | S | Wood |
| Ellisor, Merle Wayne | W | 34 | 4/ 4/1957 | M | S,F,U | Harris |
| McGowan, Yancey A. | W | 64 | 4/14/1957 | M | S | Harris |
| Hall, Wilburn Monroe | W | 30 | 8/21/1957 | M | | Harris |
| Wright, John | B | — | 9/14/1957 | M | S | Bell |
| White, Charlie | W | 42 | 2/ 6/1958 | M | S | Travis |
| Mack, John Wayne | B | — | 3/ 6/1958 | Ra | S | Dallas |
| Blankenship, Alvin Charles | B | 28 | 6/11/1958 | Ro,Fr | S | Harris |
| Thompson, Theodore | B | — | 6/20/1958 | Ra | S | Dallas |
| Shaver, Jimmie N. | W | 33 | 7/25/1958 | M | S | Bell |
| Lamkin, Marshall | B | — | 9/19/1958 | M | S | Caldwell |
| Slater, Philip | B | 36 | 2/ 4/1959 | M | S | Montgomery |
| Williams, Milton | B | 28 | 5/28/1959 | Ra | | Lee |
| Smith, Jessie Doffies | B | 42 | 8/ 4/1959 | M | | Harris |
| Williams, Junior Lee | B | — | 3/ 5/1960 | Ra | | Wharton |
| Moon, Nearvel | W | 19 | 4/28/1960 | M | S | Harris |
| Draper, Howard, Jr. | B | — | 5/26/1960 | Ra | S | Dallas |
| Wiliams, George | B | 30 | 7/ 8/1960 | M | S | Williamson |
| Philpot, Willie Edward | B | 27 | 7/15/1960 | M | S | Gregg |
| Moses, George | B | 28 | 8/12/1960 | M | S | Harris |

| Name | Race | Age | Date of Execution | Offense | Appeal | County |
|------|------|-----|-------------------|---------|--------|--------|
| Martinez, Eusebio Regalado | M | 24 | 8/27/1960 | M | | Midland |
| Holmes, Samuel M. | B | 20 | 11/30/1960 | Ra | S | Travis |
| Williams, Charles E. | B | 19 | 6/ 3/1961 | Ra | S | Houston |
| Edwards, James | B | — | 6/23/1961 | Ra | S | Dallas |
| Leath, Fred Thomas | W | 40 | 11/ 9/1961 | M | S | Tarrant |
| Forgey, Charles Louis | W | 23 | 1/10/1962 | Ra | S | Dallas |
| Wiley, Roosevelt | B | — | 1/11/1962 | M | S | Johnson |
| Wilson, Donald Ray | W | 20 | 3/20/1962 | M | S,U | Johnson |
| Johnson, Adrian | B | 19 | 4/19/1962 | M | S | Harris |
| Bradley, Herbert Lemuel | B | 20 | 5/16/1962 | Ro,Fr | S | Dallas |
| Stickney, Howard B. | W | 24 | 5/23/1962 | M | S,F,U | Harris |
| Mosley, Walter Henry | W | 26 | 7/18/1962 | M | S | Harris |
| Stein, Bobby Louis | B | 29 | 9/ 5/1962 | M | S | Harris |
| Gibson, Roscoe | B | 38 | 10/ 6/1962 | Ra | S | Harris |
| Sneed, Joe D. | B | — | 1/ 3/1963 | Ra | S | Dallas |
| McIntyre, Bennie Lee | B | — | 1/20/1963 | Ra | S | Lynn |
| Luton, Leo Daniel | W | 33 | 2/20/1963 | M | S,F,U | Dallas |
| Lavan, John | B | 23 | 3/31/1963 | M | S | Harris |
| Parker, Jesse Earl | B | — | 2/12/1964 | Ra | S | Dallas |
| Bradford, Bobby Clyde | B | 31 | 3/11/1964 | M | S | Harris |
| O'Connor, Lawrence | B | 24 | 4/26/1964 | Ra | S | Harris |
| Echols, James Andrew | B | 19 | 5/ 7/1964 | Ra | S | Harris |
| Johnson, Joseph | B | 27 | 7/30/1964 | M | S | Harris |
| Brooks, Charlie, Jr. | B | 40 | 12/7/1982 | M | S | Tarrant |

## UTAH

*Period of Executions*: 1903–1977
*Total Number*: 32 (including 1 post-*Furman* execution)
*Method*: Shooting, except Morris (4/30/1912) and Kirkham (6/7/1958) were hanged.

| Name | Race | Age | Date of Execution | Offense | Appeal | County |
|------|------|-----|-------------------|---------|--------|--------|
| Mortensen, Peter | W | 39 | 11/20/1903 | M | S | Salt Lake |
| Rose, Frank | W | 30 | 4/22/1904 | M | | Salt Lake |
| Morris, J.J. | W | 44 | 4/30/1912 | M | S | Salt Lake |
| Zirmay, Jules | W | 33 | 5/22/1912 | M | S | Salt Lake |
| Thorne, Harry | W | 24 | 9/26/1912 | M | S | Salt Lake |
| Riley, Thomas | W | 27 | 10/24/1912 | M | | Salt Lake |
| Romero, Frank | W | 28 | 2/20/1913 | M. | S | Carbon |
| Hillstrom, Joseph | W | 33 | 11/19/1915 | M | S,U | Salt Lake |
| DeWeese, Howard | W | 33 | 5/24/1918 | M | S | Salt Lake |
| Borrich, John | W | 33 | 12/20/1919 | M | | Tooele |
| Maslich, Steve | W | 36 | 1/20/1922 | M | S | Salt Lake |
| Oblizalo, Nick | W | 33 | 6/ 9/1922 | M | S | Salt Lake |
| Gardner, George H. | W | 37 | 9/31/1923 | M | S | Salt Lake |
| Woods, Omer R. | W | 48 | 1/18/1924 | M | S | Salt Lake |
| Allen, George | W | 20 | 2/20/1925 | M | | Salt Lake |

| Name | Race | Age | Date of Execution | Offense | Appeal | County |
|------|------|-----|-------------------|---------|--------|--------|
| Cano, Pedro | M | 28 | 5/15/1925 | M | S | Summit |
| Seybolt, Ralph W. | W | 26 | 1/15/1926 | M | S | Salt Lake |
| McGowan, Edward | B | 51 | 2/ 5/1926 | M | S | Carbon |
| Green, Delbert | W | 27 | 7/10/1936 | M | S,U | Davis |
| Deering, John W. | W | 40 | 10/31/1938 | M | | Salt Lake |
| Condit, Donald W. | W | 26 | 7/30/1942 | M | S | Iron |
| Avery, Wallace R. | W | 35 | 2/ 5/1943 | M | S | Weber |
| Cox, Austin | W | 40 | 6/19/1944 | M | S | Weber |
| Roedel, James J. | W | 28 | 7/13/1945 | M | S | Uintah |
| Mares, Elisio J. | M | 25 | 9/10/1951 | M | S,F,U | Summit |
| Gardner, Ray Dempsey | W | 30 | 9/29/1951 | M | S,U | Weber |
| Neal, Don Jesse | W | 36 | 7/ 1/1955 | M | S,U | Salt Lake |
| Braasch, Vern A. | W | 28 | 5/11/1956 | M | S,F,U | Iron |
| Sullivan, Melvin L. | W | 26 | 5/11/1956 | M | S,F,U | Iron |
| Kirkham, Barton Kay | W | 22 | 6/ 7/1958 | M | S | Salt Lake |
| Rogers, James W. | W | 50 | 3/30/1960 | M | S,U | San Juan |
| Gilmore, Gary Mark | W | 36 | 1/17/1977 | M | S | Utah |

## VERMONT

*Period of Executions*: 1864–1954
*Total Number*: 21
*Method*: Hanging 1864–1914; electrocution 1919–1954
*Period of Abolition*: Capital punishment was abolished in 1965 except for the murder of policemen and prison guards or second unrelated murder.

| Name | Race | Age | Date of Execution | Offense | Appeal | County |
|------|------|-----|-------------------|---------|--------|--------|
| Kavanagh, Sandy | W | 61 | 1/20/1864 | M | | Chittenden |
| Barnette, William | W | 58 | 1/20/1864 | M | | Chittenden |
| Ward, John | W | 25 | 3/20/1868 | M | S | Chittenden |
| Miller, Hiram | W | 32 | 6/25/1869 | M | | Windsor |
| Welcome, Henry | W | 18 | 1/20/1871 | M | | Chittenden |
| Gravelin, Henry | W | 48 | 3/14/1879 | M | | Windsor |
| Phair, John P. | W | 38 | 4/10/1879 | M | S | Rutland |
| Magoon, Asa | W | 57 | 11/28/1879 | M | S | Washington |
| Tatro, Edward | W | 21 | 4/ 2/1880 | M | S | Franklin |
| Haydon, Edwin | – | 29 | 2/25/1881 | M | S | Orleans |
| Carr, Royal S. | W | 44 | 4/29/1881 | M | S | Washington |
| Meaker, Emeline (Female) | W | 44 | 3/30/1883 | M | S | Washington |
| Bell, Sylvester H. | – | 56 | 1/ 1/1892 | M | S | Franklin |
| Rogers, Mary M. (Female) | W | 21 | 12/ 8/1905 | M | S | Bennington |
| Kent, Elroy | W | 35 | 1/ 5/1912 | M | S | Washington |
| Bosworth, Arthur | – | 27 | 1/ 2/1914 | M | S | Orange |
| Warner, George E. | W | 47 | 7/12/1919 | M | S | Windsor |
| Stacey, Bert | – | – | 7/ 7/1932 | M | S | Washington |
| Watson, Ronald | – | – | 1/ 2/1947 | M | S | Rutland |
| Blair, Francis | W | 31 | 2/ 8/1954 | M | S | Windsor |
| Demag, Donald | W | 29 | 12/ 8/1954 | M | S | Windsor |

# VIRGINIA

*Period of Executions*: 1908–1982
*Total Number*: 238 (including 1 post-*Furman* execution)
*Method*: Electrocution
*Other Data*: After the state of Virginia began electrocuting its condemned felons at the state penitentiary, one man (identified by footnote 1) was hanged under local authority in the county of his conviction at the county seat designated.

| Name | Race | Age | Date of Execution | Offense | Appeal | County |
|------|------|-----|-------------------|---------|--------|--------|
| Smith, Henry | B | 22 | 10/13/1908 | Ra | | Norfolk |
| Green, Winston | B | 17 | 10/30/1908 | Ra,Att | | Chesterfield |
| Davenport, Frank | B | 23 | 1/ 4/1909 | M | | Norfolk |
| Gillespie, Charles | B | 24 | 2/18/1909 | Ra,Att | | Richmond |
| Gilbert, Benjamin | W | 19 | 3/19/1909 | M | | Norfolk City |
| Christian, Arthrlius | B | 17 | 3/22/1909 | M | | Botetourt |
| Smith, James | B | 24 | 4/ 8/1909 | M | | Henrico |
| Payne, Joel[1] | B | — | 4/ 9/1909 | M | | Bedford |
| Seaborne, Barry | B | 22 | 4/16/1909 | Ra | | Greenville |
| Brown, John (Father) | B | 57 | 4/30/1909 | M | | Powhatan |
| Brown, William (Son) | B | 33 | 4/30/1909 | M | | Powhatan |
| Taylor, Joe (Brother) | B | 34 | 5/ 5/1909 | M | | Powhatan |
| Taylor, Isham (Brother) | B | 32 | 5/ 5/1909 | M | | Powhatan |
| Jenkins, Lewis | B | 40 | 5/ 7/1909 | M | | Powhatan |
| Flemming, John | B | 27 | 7/30/1909 | M | | Lunenberg |
| Wise, William H. | B | 29 | 8/27/1909 | M | | Petersburg City |
| Bragg, Howard H. | W | 24 | 9/24/1909 | M | | Rockbridge |
| Traynham, Jack | B | 24 | 11/12/1909 | M | | Lynchburg City |
| Robinson, Harry | B | 23 | 12/ 9/1909 | M | | Warren |
| Breckinbridge, Clifton | B | 20 | 12/17/1909 | Ra,Att | | Staunton City |
| Spinher, Thurman | B | 18 | 1/14/1910 | M | | Bedford |
| Parker, W.P. | B | 25 | 1/25/1910 | M | | Norfolk City |
| Goins, William | B | 28 | 1/28/1910 | M | | Roanoke |
| Little, Howard | W | 38 | 2/11/1910 | M | | Buchanan |
| Blake, Willie | B | 23 | 2/11/1910 | Ra | | Norfolk |
| Rouse, Elijah | B | 28 | 4/25/1910 | M | | Norfolk |
| Smith, Henry | B | 45 | 6/ 3/1910 | M · | | Alexandria City |
| Noel, Thomas | B | — | 6/10/1910 | M | | Norfolk |
| Hamilton, Angelo S. | W | 27 | 7/ 1/1910 | M | | Lynchburg City |
| Brown, Arch | W | 32 | 9/22/1910 | M | | Augusta |
| Barbour, Pink | B | 22 | 9/23/1910 | M | | Rockingham |
| Eccles, John | B | 17 | 11/11/1910 | M | | Henry |
| Coles, Waverley | B | 20 | 11/25/1910 | M | | Richmond City |
| Smyth, J.J. | W | 34 | 12/16/1910 | M | | Norfolk City |
| Sitlington, Harry | B | 17 | 12/16/1910 | M | | Rockbridge |
| Biggs, Richard H. | B | 28 | 1/ 7/1911 | M | | Newport News City |
| Holloman, Alex | B | 24 | 6/ 2/1911 | M | | Princess Anne |
| Beattie, Henry Clay | W | 26 | 11/24/1911 | M | | Chesterfield |
| Williamson, John | B | 20 | 3/15/1912 | M | | Halifax |
| Ferby, John | B | 20 | 6/14/1912 | M | | Chesterfield |

| Name | Race | Age | Date of Execution | Offense | Appeal | County |
|------|------|-----|-------------------|---------|--------|--------|
| Price, William | B | 20 | 6/14/1912 | M | | Chesterfield |
| Nixon, Clarence | B | 24 | 6/21/1912 | Ra | | Norfolk |
| Jackson, Byrd | B | 18 | 6/21/1912 | Ro | S | Caroline |
| Christian, Virginia (Female) | B | 17 | 8/16/1912 | M | | Elizabeth City |
| Peyton, Herbert | B | 20 | 11/ 8/1912 | M | | King George |
| Quarles, Richard T. | B | 29 | 1/ 3/1913 | Ra | | Hanover |
| Sullivan, Roy M. | W | 32 | 2/28/1913 | M | | Pittsylvania |
| Allen, Floyd (Father) | W | 56 | 3/28/1913 | M | S | Wythe |
| Allen, Claude (Son) | W | 23 | 3/28/1913 | M | S | Wythe |
| Goode, James | B | 28 | 5/ 2/1913 | M | | Newport News City |
| Wright, Alfred | B | 21 | 5/16/1913 | Ra | S | Appomattox |
| Hargrove, F.L. | B | 39 | 6/20/1913 | M | | Spottsylvania |
| Carter, Nelson V. | W | 47 | 6/27/1913 | M | | Spottsylvania |
| Goggin, Owen | B | 36 | 6/27/1913 | Ra,Att | | Bedford |
| Bailey, Benjamin | B | 21 | 8/ 8/1913 | Ra | | Fairfax |
| Glinn, William | B | 26 | 8/16/1913 | M | | Norfolk City |
| Collins, Minnie | B | 20 | 10/31/1913 | Ra,Att | | Northamoton |
| Walker, Newell | W | 29 | 12/ 5/1913 | M | | Charles City |
| Archer, Lee | B | 22 | 12/ 5/1913 | Ra | | Princess Anne |
| Moore, Charlton | B | 54 | 1/16/1914 | M | | King William |
| Rhodes, Wilie | B | 27 | 1/30/1914 | M | | Charlotte |
| Lee, Marion | B | 30 | 3/19/1914 | M | | Williamsburg City[2] |
| Boyd, Walter | B | 24 | 3/27/1914 | M | | Richmond City |
| Woods, George | B | 32 | 5/22/1914 | M | | Danville City |
| Calloway, Will | B | 48 | 7/10/1914 | M | | Lee |
| Puryear, Willie | B | 19 | 8/ 7/1914 | Ra,Att | | Mecklenburg |
| Coach, Henry | B | 33 | 8/21/1914 | Ro,Hwy | | Nottaway |
| Edmunds, John | B | 27 | 12/18/1914 | M | | Prince Edward |
| Neale, Arthur | B | 19 | 1/ 8/1915 | Ro,Hwy | | King William |
| Miller, Charles | B | 29 | 3/26/1915 | M | | Halifax |
| Caple, Herbert | B | 24 | 4/30/1915 | Ro | | Sussex |
| Sydner, Skipwith | B | 25 | 5/21/1915 | M | | Halifax |
| Cole, Thomas | B | 22 | 6/ 4/1915 | Ra | | Mecklenburg |
| Jones, Lem | B | 19 | 6/10/1915 | M | | Norfolk City |
| Canter, Luther | W | 24 | 6/11/1915 | M | | Washington |
| Rollins, John Lewis | B | 31 | 8/20/1915 | Ra,Att | | Caroline |
| Matthews, George | B | 32 | 8/20/1915 | Ra | | Caroline |
| Pryor, Ed | B | 27 | 9/10/1915 | Ro | | Surry |
| Stanfield, Sherman | B | 18 | 9/17/1915 | Ra,Att | | Pittsylvania |
| Ellis, Percy | B | 16 | 3/15/1916 | M | | Norfolk City |
| Lee, Joe | B | 83 | 4/21/1916 | M | | Caroline |
| Williams, John Henry | B | 23 | 5/28/1916 | Ra | | Nottaway |
| Maloy, Milton | B | 19 | 7/ 7/1916 | Ra | | Wise |
| Green, Richard | B | 19 | 8/25/1916 | M | S | Charlotte |
| Hickens, Clifford | B | 19 | 8/25/1916 | M | | Roanoke City |
| Lewis, Henry | B | 23 | 9/ 8/1916 | M | | Lynchburg City |
| Harris, Minzer | B | 19 | 10/ 2/1916 | Ra | | Buckingham |
| Corbett, James | B | 22 | 10/ 2/1916 | M | | Norfolk City |
| Warren, Hansom | B | 23 | 6/15/1917 | M | | Isle of Wight |

| Name | Race | Age | Date of Execution | Offense | Appeal | County |
|------|------|-----|-------------------|---------|--------|--------|
| Cosby, Hamilton | B | 25 | 6/20/1917 | M | | Charlottesville City |
| Jones, Robert | B | 32 | 6/20/1917 | M | S | Charlottesville City |
| Barrett, Albert | B | 35 | 8/31/1917 | M | | Charlotte |
| Burgess, William | B | 29 | 10/26/1917 | Ra | | Fairfax |
| Langhorne, Paul | B | 39 | 6/ 7/1918 | M | | Newport News City |
| Nixon, Guy | B | 19 | 7/ 2/1918 | M | | Norfolk City |
| Bailey, Tolson | B | 17 | 7/ 2/1918 | M | | Norfolk City |
| Williams, Horace | B | 21 | 3/26/1919 | M | S | Culpeper |
| Stuart, Harvey | B | 36 | 3/26/1919 | M | | Buena Vista City |
| Warren, Jerry | B | 29 | 6/27/1919 | M | | Northampton |
| Jacobs, Erper | B | 29 | 10/30/1919 | M | S | Portsmouth City |
| Williams, Robert | B | 23 | 11/13/1920 | M | S | Lynchburg City |
| Williams, John H. | B | 27 | 3/ 5/1921 | M | | Lynchburg City |
| Sydner, Giles | B | 23 | 4/ 8/1921 | Ra | | Halifax |
| Haskins, Raleigh | B | 18 | 9/30/1921 | M | | Dinwiddie |
| Griffith, Judge | B | 22 | 9/30/1921 | M | | Dinwiddie |
| Hadley, Wilbur Amos | W | 39 | 12/ 9/1921 | M | | Henrico |
| Hart, Harry | B | — | 1/23/1922 | Ra,Att | S | Augusta |
| Thompson, Edmund | B | 23 | 2/ 7/1922 | M | S | Botetourt |
| Lockett, Henry | B | 34 | 2/23/1922 | M | | Albemarle |
| Sparks, Thomas | B | 26 | 2/24/1922 | M | | Albemarle |
| Elmoe, Will | B | 29 | 3/31/1922 | M | S | Richmond City |
| Barnes, Henry | B | 32 | 4/ 4/1922 | M | | Orange |
| Brown, Ernest | B | 20 | 5/26/1922 | M | S | Orange |
| Clayton, Willie E. | B | 23 | 1/ 5/1923 | M | S | Henrico |
| Harris, Alvin W. | B | 22 | 2/ 6/1923 | M | S | Prince William |
| Wriggins, George | B | 31 | 3/ 2/1923 | M | | Petersburg City |
| Riddick, Sam | B | 32 | 6/25/1923 | M | S | Warwick |
| Corbett, Robert | B | 35 | 9/28/1923 | M | | Roanoke City |
| Lewis, Fritz | B | 17 | 9/12/1924 | M | | Caroline |
| Clear, Otto | B | 18 | 9/12/1924 | M | | Caroline |
| Cooper, Isaac I. | B | 39 | 3/ 6/1925 | M | S | Roanoke |
| Dandridge, Prince | B | 33 | 3/12/1925 | M | | Henrico |
| Carter, James | B | 30 | 4/17/1925 | Ra | | Prince Edward |
| Lee, Percy | B | 34 | 5/ 1/1925 | Ra,Att | S | Henrico |
| Hoke, Rodney | W | 19 | 7/10/1925 | M | | Alleghany |
| Allen, Horace | B | 45 | 7/17/1925 | M | | Isle of Wight |
| Perman, Henry | B | 28 | 9/29/1925 | Ra | | Norfolk |
| McMillan, Doc Earl | B | 30 | 10/ 9/1925 | M | | Norfolk City |
| Spencer, William | B | 28 | 1/22/1926 | M | S | Lee |
| Disse, Rudolph E. | W | 20 | 2/19/1926 | M | | Richmond City |
| Watkins, Louis | B | 28 | 3/19/1926 | M | | Richmond City |
| Patterson, James | B | 37 | 8/27/1926 | M | S,U | Petersburg City |
| Satchell, James | B | 25 | 9/24/1926 | M | | Northampton |
| Gee, William | B | 21 | 1/14/1927 | Ra | | Warwick |
| Perfey, Henry | B | 21 | 4/15/1927 | M | | Norfolk |
| Thomas, William | B | 23 | 4/15/1927 | Ra,Att | | Madison |
| Boersig, Louis P. | W | 44 | 7/ 7/1927 | M | | Fairfax |
| Nelson, William | B | 25 | 11/15/1927 | Ra,Att | S | Hopewell City |

| Name | Race | Age | Date of Execution | Offense | Appeal | County |
|------|------|-----|-------------------|---------|--------|--------|
| Winningham, Shirely | B | 25 | 1/25/1928 | M | | Richmond City |
| Gray, Burn V. | B | 36 | 5/18/1928 | M | | Petersburg City |
| Washington, James | B | 19 | 7/27/1928 | Ra | | Loudon |
| Jones, Henry | B | 20 | 3/29/1929 | Ra | | Mecklenburg |
| Moten, Henry | B | 27 | 5/17/1929 | M | | Norfolk City |
| Haskins, Sam | B | 32 | 9/ 6/1929 | M | | Powhatan |
| Clayborn, Luther | B | 35 | 11/29/1929 | M | | Roanoke City |
| Fields, John | B | 23 | 2/20/1930 | M | | Gloucester |
| Payne, Elwood | B | 33 | 9/19/1930 | M | | Fauquier |
| Bellamy, Alphonso | B | 19 | 10/31/1930 | M | | Newport News City |
| Dorson, Ollie | B | 40 | 2/ 3/1931 | M | | Princess Anne |
| Groome, Calvin | B | 18 | 6/26/1931 | Ra | | Amherst |
| Pannell, Sam | B | 18 | 5/20/1932 | Ra | | Halifax |
| Cox, Randolph G. | B | 41 | 6/ 3/1932 | M | S | Richmond |
| Mann, Frank | B | 38 | 10/ 6/1933 | M | | Nansemond |
| Mais, Robert | W | 29 | 2/ 2/1935 | M | | Richmond City |
| Legenza, Walter | W | 42 | 2/ 2/1935 | M | | Richmond City |
| Jones, Philip | B | 25 | 3/11/1935 | M | | Botetourt |
| Daugherty, John | W | 44 | 2/ 7/1936 | M | | Fluvanna |
| Shell, John | B | 30 | 2/21/1936 | M | | Spotsylvania |
| Jackson, Joe | B | 23 | 2/21/1936 | M | | Spotsylvania |
| Watson, Isaac Frank | B | 54 | 7/ 3/1936 | M | | Halifax |
| Hart, Thomas Cole | W | 29 | 7/24/1936 | M | | Scott |
| Wyche, Lawrence | B | 30 | 8/20/1937 | M | | Greensville |
| Leake, Willie | B | 30 | 8/20/1937 | M | | Greensville |
| Winsor, John | B | 25 | 12/31/1937 | M | | Loudon |
| McNeill, Jasper | B | 24 | 3/25/1938 | M | | Amherst |
| Jackson, James | B | 28 | 3/25/1938 | M | | Elizabeth City |
| Martin, Joe | B | 31 | 4/ 8/1938 | M | | Lynchburg City |
| Cypress, Otis | B | 32 | 11/25/1938 | M | | Surry |
| Pingley, George W. | W | 44 | 11/25/1938 | M | | Frederick |
| Brooks, Irving | B | 23 | 1/20/1939 | Ro | | King William |
| Anderson, John | B | 27 | 2/10/1939 | Ra | | Loudon |
| Williams, Harry | B | 20 | 4/ 7/1939 | M | S | Greene |
| Swanson, Sam | B | 27 | 12/15/1939 | M | | Pittsylvania |
| Abdell, J.C. | W | 42 | 1/ 5/1940 | M | | Norfolk City |
| McCann, John Henry | B | 63 | 1/26/1940 | M | | Norfolk City |
| Bradshaw, Willie | B | 65 | 4/12/1940 | Ra,Att | S | Halifax |
| Davis, Wilmer | B | 25 | 4/26/1940 | M | | Southampton |
| Brown, Charlie | B | 26 | 9/26/1941 | Ra | | Isle of Wight |
| Johnson, Charles T., Jr. | B | 19 | 1/16/1942 | M | | Nelson |
| Diggs, William Henry | B | 24 | 1/16/1942 | M | | Nelson |
| Waller, Odell | B | 25 | 7/ 2/1942 | M | S,U | Pittsylvania |
| Mooring, James, Jr. | B | 22 | 3/19/1943 | M | | Norfolk City |
| Farris, Harry Edward | W | 28 | 10/15/1943 | M | | Richmond City |
| Woodall, Raymond | W | 36 | 3/ 3/1944 | M | | Pittsylvania |
| Walker, Howard | B | 27 | 5/26/1944 | Ra | | Winchester City |
| Clatterbuck, Thomas W. | W | 34 | 6/16/1944 | M | | Loudon |
| Jones, Willie Rodgers | B | 29 | 2/ 2/1945 | Ra | | Norfolk City |
| Thomas, Holman B. | B | 41 | 3/ 1/1945 | M | S | Lunenburg |
| McDaniel, Raymond | W | 30 | 3/ 2/1945 | M | S | Campbell |

| Name | Race | Age | Date of Execution | Offense | Appeal | County |
|------|------|-----|-------------------|---------|--------|--------|
| Christian, Mancy | B | 27 | 5/ 1/1945 | Ra | | Nansemond |
| Pearson, Lonnie | B | 31 | 8/ 3/1945 | Ra,Ro | | Norfolk |
| Holloman, Andrew J. | B | 31 | 1/11/1946 | Ra | | Norfolk |
| Fagan, Ernest Edward | B | 30 | 2/15/1946 | M | | Norfolk City |
| Cross, Nelson | B | 33 | 4/15/1946 | M | | Danville City |
| Harrison, Thomas E. | W | 19 | 5/20/1946 | M | | Roanoke |
| Grissett, George | B | 33 | 6/21/1946 | M | S | Princess Anne |
| Hough, James | B | 29 | 6/21/1946 | M | S | Princess Anne |
| Johnson, Arthur | B | 22 | 6/21/1946 | M | S | Princess Anne |
| Fletcher, James Lee | B | 24 | 9/13/1946 | M | S | Accomack |
| Holland, Robert | B | 22 | 9/13/1946 | M | S | Accomack |
| Gusler, Amon J. | W | 52 | 1/ 3/1947 | M | | Henry |
| Thomas, Ephream | B | 27 | 5/23/1947 | M | S | Nansamont |
| Davis, William | B | 43 | 7/18/1947 | M | | Fauguier |
| Morton, Buford Russel | B | 30 | 10/17/1947 | Ra | | Danville City |
| Laurence, Raymond | B | 30 | 10/24/1947 | | | Newport News City |
| Baldwin, Sam | B | 35 | 1/23/1948 | M | | Accomack |
| Brooks, John Major | B | 20 | 4/23/1948 | | | Halifax |
| James, Johnnie | B | 30 | 10/29/1948 | Ra | | Newport News City |
| Rayfield, Alfred | B | 35 | 11/17/1950 | M | | Accomack |
| Fuller, Ben Franklin | B | 42 | 12/ 8/1950 | | S | Mecklenburg |
| Hailey, George Thomas | W | 24 | 2/ 2/1951 | M | | Halifax |
| Hampton, Joe Henry | B | 21 | 2/ 2/1951 | Ra | F | Martinville City |
| Hairston, Howard Lee | B | 20 | 2/ 2/1951 | Ra | F | Martinville City |
| Millmer, Booker T. | B | 22 | 2/ 2/1951 | Ra | F | Martinville City |
| Hairston, Frank J. | B | 20 | 2/ 2/1951 | Ra | F | Martinville City |
| Taylor, John Clabon | B | 23 | 2/ 5/1951 | Ra | F | Martinville City |
| Hairston, James Luther | B | 22 | 2/ 5/1951 | Ra | F | Martinville City |
| Grayson, Francis De Salles | B | 38 | 2/ 5/1951 | Ra | F | Martinville City |
| Jones, Ulysses | B | 32 | 7/13/1951 | | | Nansemond |
| Joyner, Floyd, Jr. | B | 39 | 12/12/1951 | | S | Roanoke |
| Jackson, Albert, Jr. | B | 24 | 8/25/1952 | Ra | S | Charlottesville C. |
| Kensinger, John Clay | W | 29 | 5/26/1954 | M | | Arlington |
| Groom, John Sterling | B | 48 | 10/14/1954 | M | | Culpeper |
| Russell, Alonzo | B | 41 | 7/14/1955 | | | Rockbridge |
| Gregory, John Lewis | B | 23 | 6/ 4/1957 | | | Norfolk City |
| Dobie, Lloyd Junius | B | 26 | 7/12/1957 | Ra | S | South Hampton |
| McGray, Jeremiah | B | 24 | 4/18/1958 | | | Caroline |
| Sherod, E.J. | B | 24 | 6/ 6/1958 | | | Richmond City |
| Dabney, Clarence Sparrow | B | 25 | 11/21/1958 | | S | Lynchburg City |
| Brown, William | B | 56 | 4/24/1959 | | | Caroline |
| Boyd, Willy Dameron | B | 24 | 4/24/1959 | M | | Goochland |
| Fuller, Harry Eugene | B | 31 | 6/30/1960 | | S | Alexandria City |
| Burch, Linwood | B | 23 | 2/17/1961 | Ra | | Newport News City |
| Lucas, Grover Earl | W | 51 | 3/10/1961 | M | S | Roanoke City |
| Hart, Claude Leon, Jr. | W | 32 | 11/17/1961 | | | Norfolk City |
| Cobbs, Jim | B | 46 | 12/ 8/1961 | | | Halifax |

| Name | Race | Age | Date of Execution | Offense | Appeal | County |
|------|------|-----|-------------------|---------|--------|--------|
| Garland, Carroll L. | B | 27 | 3/ 2/1962 | | | Lynchburg City |
| Coppola, Frank J. | W | 38 | 8/10/1982 | M | S | Newport News |

[1]Payne (4/9/1909) was hanged under local authority in the county of his conviction after Virginia began electrocuting its condemned felons at the state penitentiary.
[2]Williamsburg City and James City County have concurrent jurisdiction.

## WASHINGTON

*Period of Executions*: 1904–1963
*Total Number*: 73
*Method*: Hanging
*Period of Abolition*: 1913–1919
*Other Data*: Capital punishment, which was first abolished in 1913, was restored in 1919 if the jury specifically recommended it. The death penalty was mandatory until 1909, then was left to the discretion of the judge.

| Name | Race | Age | Date of Execution | Offense | Appeal | County |
|------|------|-----|-------------------|---------|--------|--------|
| Champoux, James | W | 29 | 5/ 6/1904 | M | S | King |
| Clark, Charles C. | W | 26 | 9/ 2/1904 | M | S | Thurston |
| Arao, Henry | J | 28 | 6/ 3/1905 | M | | Spokane |
| Pasquale, Frank | W | 28 | 9/15/1905 | M | S | Pierce |
| McPhail, Angus J. | W | 45 | 12/ 8/1905 | M | S | Snohomish |
| White, William ("Kid") | W | 18 | 3/ 2/1906 | M | S | King |
| Brooks, Simon | W | 46 | 5/13/1906 | M | | Clark |
| Armstrong, A.A. | W | 53 | 6/ 8/1906 | M | S,NT | Chehalis |
| Miller, Fred | W | 25 | 3/22/1907 | M | | Cowlitz |
| Niculas, Juan | F | 22 | 4/16/1909 | M | | Kitsap |
| Gauvette, Joseph M. | W | 44 | 8/27/1909 | M | S | Spokane |
| Barnes, Hezekiah W. ("Bud") | W | 26 | 11/12/1909 | M | S | Walla Walla |
| Quinn, Richard | W | 32 | 5/13/1910 | M | S | Snohomish |
| Barkar, Frank J. | W | 23 | 6/20/1910 | M | S | Spokane |
| Jahns, Frederick Wm. | W | 63 | 4/21/1911 | M | S | Stevens |
| Smith, John | W | 26 | 4/ 1/1924 | M | | King |
| Mahoney, James E. | W | 38 | 12/ 1/1922 | M | S | King |
| Whitfield, George E. | W | 22 | 6/13/1924 | M | S | Clark |
| Waller, Ralph | W | 34 | 6/27/1924 | M | | Garfield |
| Walton, Thomas | W | 39 | 12/12/1924 | M | S | Walla Walla |
| Moseley, L.E. | B | 45 | 2/19/1926 | M | S | King |
| Winters, Alfred A. | B | 30 | 5/27/1927 | M | S | Cowlitz |
| Lopez, Manuel | M | 41 | 2/15/1928 | M | | Whitman |
| Bailey, Emmett | W | 39 | 8/10/1928 | M | S | Lewis |
| Gaines, Wallace C. | W | 48 | 8/31/1928 | M | S,U | King |
| Baker, Luther | W | 61 | 3/29/1929 | M | S | Clark |
| Clark, Preston R. | W | 39 | 7/11/1930 | M | S | Walla Walla |
| Wilkins, Robert Lee | W | 44 | 8/15/1930 | M | S | Walla Walla |
| Schaffer, Arthur | W | 29 | 8/29/1930 | M | S | Mason |
| Moock, Archie Frank | W | 33 | 9/12/1930 | M | S | Spokane |

| Name | Race | Age | Date of Execution | Offense | Appeal | County |
|------|------|-----|-------------------|---------|--------|--------|
| Miller, George J. | W | 48 | 12/18/1931 | M | S | Spokane |
| Carpenter, Harold | W | 31 | 4/15/1932 | M | S | Thurston |
| Dubuc, Walter | W | 17 | 4/15/1932 | M | S | Thurston |
| Stratton, Ollie Lee | W | 24 | 7/28/1933 | M | S | Jefferson |
| Bradley, Ted | W | 26 | 5/11/1934 | M | S | King |
| Miller, Byron | W | 42 | 10/ 3/1934 | M | S | Yakima |
| Yick, Hong | C | 44 | 7/19/1935 | M | | King |
| Flemming, Barney | B | 29 | 4/ 3/1936 | M | | King |
| Stringer, Glenn R. | W | 24 | 5/29/1936 | M | | Clark |
| Hall, Leo | W | 34 | 9/11/1936 | M | S | Kitsap |
| Hawkins, Clifford | W | 25 | 2/23/1938 | M | | Skagit |
| Ryan, Claude H. | W | 34 | 2/25/1938 | M | S | Lewis |
| Knapp, Stanley | W | 21 | 8/ 5/1938 | M | S | Spokane |
| O'Donnell, Joseph R. | W | 40 | 11/21/1938 | M | S,NT | King |
| Leuch, Bernard R. | W | 41 | 8/ 4/1939 | M | S | Mason |
| Buttry, Paul | W | 39 | 9/15/1939 | M | S | Grays Harbor |
| Talbott, Earl | W | 19 | 9/18/1939 | M | S | Walla Walla |
| Wright, Roy | W | 19 | 10/ 6/1939 | M | S | Yakima |
| Carson, Ralph | W | 54 | 12/ 8/1939 | M | | Clallam |
| Bouchard, Edward L. | W | 46 | 9/ 6/1940 | M | | Snohomish |
| Marable, Jack | W | 40 | 10/ 4/1940 | K | S | Thurston |
| Lewis, Arley Ovoyd | W | 29 | 1/30/1941 | M | | Clark |
| Davis, Denzel | W | 24 | 3/24/1941 | M | S | King |
| Anderson, John Bruce | W | 58 | 11/14/1941 | M | S | Spokane |
| Montgomery, Chester | B | 29 | 3/19/1943 | M | S | Spokane |
| Jacobs, Roy Willard | W | 41 | 4/ 6/1943 | M | | Pierce |
| Williams, Persia | B | 38 | 9/ 8/1944 | M | | King |
| Heberling, Edward | W | 32 | 12/ 8/1944 | M | | King |
| Bill, Joe | E | 30 | 9/ 7/1945 | M | | King |
| Wessel, Joseph B. | W | 44 | 1/18/1946 | M | | Pierce |
| Clark, Woodrow Wilson | W | 30 | 2/ 5/1946 | M | S,U | Spokane |
| Clark, John Henry | B | 26 | 1/ 7/1947 | M | S | King |
| Bird, Jake | B | 47 | 7/15/1949 | M | S,F,U | Pierce |
| Perkins, Arthur B. | W | 24 | 11/ 4/1949 | M | S,F,U | Thurston |
| Williams, Wayne L. | W | 33 | 11/18/1949 | M | S | Snohomish |
| Odell, Wayne W. | W | 23 | 6/18/1951 | M | S | Whitman |
| Rio, Grant E. | W | 29 | 12/10/1951 | M | S,U | Whitman |
| Wilson, Turman G. | W | 26 | 1/ 3/1953 | M | S,F,U | Clark |
| Wilson, Utah E. | W | 22 | 1/ 3/1953 | M | S,F,U | Clark |
| Farley, Artell J. | W | 27 | 12/15/1956 | M | S,U | Pierce |
| Collins, Harvey John | W | 32 | 12/ 3/1957 | M | S,U | Pierce |
| Broderson, John R. | W | 34 | 6/25/1960 | M | | Clark |
| Self, Joseph Chester | W | 32 | 6/20/1963 | M | S,U | King |

## WEST VIRGINIA

*Period of Executions*: 1899–1959
*Total Number*: 94
*Method*: Hanging 1899–1941; electrocution 1951–1959
*Period of Abolition*: Capital punishment was abolished in 1965.

| Name | Race | Age | Date of Execution | Offense | Appeal | County |
|------|------|-----|-------------------|---------|--------|--------|
| Caldwell, Shep | B | — | 10/10/1899 | M | | McDowell |
| Broadsnax, Frank | B | — | 11/ 9/1899 | M | | McDowell |
| Walker, Frank | B | — | 12/15/1899 | M | | Fayette |
| Carter, George | B | — | 3/21/1902 | M | S | Kanawha |
| Young, Louis | B | — | 5/ 1/1902 | M | S | McDowell |
| Mooney, John | W | — | 5/ 9/1902 | M | S | Ohio |
| Fridak, Frank | W | — | 5/ 9/1902 | M | | Ohio |
| Christian, Perry | W | — | 6/13/1902 | M | | Fayette |
| Henry, State | B | — | 10/24/1902 | M | S | Wetzel |
| Davis, Wilfred | W | — | 6/ 5/1903 | M | S | Randolph |
| Williams, George | B | — | 9/ 9/1904 | Ra | S | Jefferson |
| Johnson, Frank | B | — | 7/17/1908 | M | | Harrison |
| Brown, Arthur | B | — | 8/27/1909 | M | S | McDowell |
| Wayne, Thomas | B | 45 | 12/23/1910 | M | | Fayette |
| Stevenson, Frank | B | — | 2/17/1911 | M | S | Mercer |
| Cook, Jesse | W | — | 3/10/1911 | M | S | McDowell |
| Furbish, William | B | 28 | 3/17/1911 | Ra | | Harrison |
| Williams, James | B | — | 4/ 4/1913 | M | | McDowell |
| Marshall, John | B | — | 4/11/1913 | M | | McDowell |
| Sterling, Henry | B | — | 6/ 6/1913 | M | | McDowell |
| Bix, John | W | — | 6/ 6/1913 | M | | McDowell |
| Green, Henry | B | — | 3/ 6/1914 | M | | Mingo |
| Jones, Silas | B | — | 7/10/1914 | M | | Cabell |
| Stuart, Will | B | — | 7/ 2/1915 | M | S | Greenbrier |
| Thomas, Will | B | — | 7/ 2/1915 | M | | Ohio |
| Jarrell, Nat | W | — | 7/ 9/1915 | M | S | Kanawha |
| Forest, Charles | B | — | 9/10/1915 | M | | McDowell |
| Hetton, William | W | — | 8/ 4/1916 | M | | Randolph |
| Lay, James | B | — | 9/ 1/1916 | M | | McDowell |
| Ferguson, Hugh | B | — | 8/ 6/1919 | M | | Morgan |
| Bragg, Hugh | W | — | 4/30/1920 | M | | Webster |
| Lutz, Jacob | W | — | 7/22/1921 | M | S | Taylor |
| Green, Hobart | W | — | 8/ 5/1921 | M | | Brooks |
| Harbor, Henry | B | — | 10/ 7/1921 | M | | McDowell |
| Williams, Leroy | B | — | 3/ 3/1922 | Ra | S | Kanawha |
| Payton, Monroe | B | — | 5/ 4/1922 | Ra | | Berkeley |
| Banhage, George | W | — | 11/ 2/1923 | M | | Brooke |
| Ferri, Richard | W | 26 | 1/ 4/1924 | M | | Harrison |
| Connizzaro, Philip | W | 26 | 1/ 4/1924 | M | | Harrison |
| Salamante, Nick | W | 33 | 1/ 4/1924 | M | | Harrison |
| Muratore, Sam | W | — | 2/15/1924 | M | | Harrison |
| McCoy, Tiny | W | 23 | 9/12/1924 | M | S | Pocahontas |
| Ford, Robert | B | 25 | 1/29/1926 | M | S | Harrison |
| Sawyer, Harry | B | 24 | 4/19/1926 | Ra | | Mingo |

| Name | Race | Age | Date of Execution | Offense | Appeal | County |
|---|---|---|---|---|---|---|
| Euman, Philip | B | 19 | 8/20/1926 | M | | Harrison |
| Jackson, Henry | B | 44 | 9/10/1926 | M | | Marshall |
| Jefferies, Pierce | B | — | 2/18/1927 | Ra | | Greenbrier |
| Swain, Wesley | W | — | 2/ 3/1928 | Ra | | Wood |
| Brady, Andrew | B | 37 | 3/30/1928 | Ra | S | Hardy |
| Pike, Lawrence | W | 31 | 8/10/1928 | M | | Preston |
| Grogan, Henry | B | 20 | 2/ 8/1929 | Ra | | Raleigh |
| Carr, Theodore | W | — | 6/14/1929 | M | | Pocahontas |
| Morrison, Willard | W | — | 9/13/1929 | M | | Kanawha |
| Wilmot, Walter | W | — | 9/13/1929 | M | | Kanawha |
| Crabtree, Walter | W | 35 | 5/ 9/1930 | M | | Hampshire |
| Darnell, Roosevelt | W | 25 | 11/14/1930 | M | | Greenbrier |
| Stephens, Emory | W | — | 2/20/1931 | M | | Mingo |
| Adams, Will | W | 35 | 2/20/1931 | M | | Mingo |
| Myer, Frank | W | — | 6/19/1931 | M | | Pocahontas |
| Powers, Harry | W | — | 3/18/1932 | M | | Harrison |
| Blount, James | B | — | 5/12/1932 | M | | Greenbrier |
| Brill, Omer | W | — | 8/10/1933 | M | | Hardy |
| Fraser, Leo | W | — | 11/24/1933 | M | | Jackson |
| Corey, Joe | W | — | 12/ 8/1933 | M | S | Kanawha |
| Blankenship, Greely | W | — | 1/ 7/1935 | M | | Mingo |
| Branch, Robert | B | 39 | 7/13/1935 | M | | Ohio |
| Pramera, Frank | W | — | 4/13/1937 | M | | Brooks |
| Becker, Willie | W | — | 6/25/1937 | M | | Kanawha |
| Brown, Mervin | B | — | 9/10/1937 | M | | Mercer |
| Read, William | W | 25 | 11/ 5/1937 | M | | Braxton |
| Styres, Raymond | W | — | 3/13/1938 | M | | Ohio |
| Booth, Arnett Dillon | W | 46 | 3/21/1938 | K | | Cabell |
| Travis, John | W | 25 | 3/21/1938 | K | | Cabell |
| Adkins, Orville | W | 25 | 3/21/1938 | K | | Cabell |
| Hartman, Byzantine | W | — | 6/28/1940 | M | | Upshur |
| Tross, Paul | B | — | 12/ 6/1940 | Ra | | Mineral |
| Chambers, James | B | — | 3/30/1945 | M | | Randolph |
| Turner, William | W | 29 | 12/28/1945 | M | | Preston |
| Collins, Richard | W | — | 10/11/1946 | M | | Kanawha |
| Gordon, William | W | 21 | 1/ 3/1947 | M | | Mercer |
| Burton, Paul | W | 33 | 1/ 2/1948 | M | | Logan |
| McCauley, Mark | W | — | 1/30/1948 | M | S | Mineral |
| Perison, Mathew O. | B | — | 9/23/1948 | M | | Logan |
| Steed, Lemuel | B | 28 | 10/15/1948 | M | | Fayette |
| Peterson, Bud | B | — | 2/25/1949 | M | S | Logan |
| Painter, Fred | W | — | 3/26/1951 | M | S | Kanawha |
| Burdette, Harry | W | — | 3/26/1951 | M | S | Kanawha |
| Hewlett, James | W | 21 | 4/10/1951 | M | | Cabell |
| Gardner, Gahel | W | — | 4/17/1953 | M | | Mason |
| Ingham, Tom | B | — | 3/27/1954 | M | | McDowell |
| Hopkins, Robert | W | 27 | 9/ 7/1956 | M | | Kanawha |
| Linger, Eugene | W | — | 6/ 5/1958 | M | | Upshur |
| Fudge, Larry | W | 26 | 7/ 1/1958 | M | | Cabell |
| Bruner, Elmer | W | 40 | 4/ 3/1959 | M | S | Cabell |

## WYOMING

*Period of Executions*: 1912–1965
*Total Number*: 14
*Method*: Hanging 1912–1933; lethal gas 1937–1965

| Name | Race | Age | Date of Execution | Offense | Appeal | County |
|------|------|-----|-------------------|---------|--------|--------|
| Seng, Joseph | C | — | 5/12/1912 | M | S | Uinta |
| Jenkins, J. Warren | W | 28 | 11/14/1913 | M | S | Laramie |
| Flanders, Willard | W | — | 6/16/1916 | M | S | Sheridan |
| Palmer, Wilmer P. | W | 32 | 8/11/1916 | M | S | Natrona |
| White, Orange W. | W | — | 10/20/1916 | M | S,U | Natrona |
| Geow, Yee | C | 18 | 3/11/1921 | M | | Laramie |
| Brownfield, George | – | — | 3/10/1930 | M | | Crook |
| Aragon, Charles | I | — | 5/14/1930 | M | S | Fremont |
| Taylor, Talton | W | 33 | 5/11/1933 | M | | Johnson |
| Carroll, Perry H. | W | 36 | 8/13/1937 | M | S | Laramie |
| Lantzer, Stanley S. | W | 38 | 4/19/1940 | M | S | Laramie |
| Brown, Cleveland, Jr. | B | 27 | 11/17/1944 | M | S | Lincoln |
| Ruhl, Henry | W | 35 | 4/27/1945 | M | S,U | Fed |
| Pixley, Andrew | M | 22 | 12/10/1965 | M | | Washakie |

# APPENDIX B

LEGISLATIVE AND JUDICIAL
ACTIONS ON CAPITAL
PUNISHMENT SINCE *FURMAN*:
AN INVENTORY

This appendix provides a state-by-state history of the availability of capital punishment in the post-*Furman* era through an inventory of the legislative and judicial actions that have specified the nature and conditions of its use. The information identifies statutory sections that define the procedures required for the imposition of a death sentence by a judge or jury and for its review by the state appellate courts. Other matters, such as appointment of counsel, rules of evidence, severability of sections, and classification of capital crimes, are not included (unless covered in those explicitly selected sections). Also excluded are matters pertaining to method of execution and procedures attendant thereon.

Information is provided in the following specific areas: *Enactment* of the original legislation establishing the death penalty after *Furman*; *Invalidation* by the judicial action of a state or federal appellate court, ruling against the constitutionality of the particular death penalty statute; *Revision* by the judicial action of a state supreme court interpreting a statute so as to keep it in force as law, or altering it to the same effect (for example, by severing unconstitutional portions); *Reenactment* by a state legislature, typically reworking the statute so as to comply with Supreme Court directives (reenactments usually but do not necessarily follow judicial invalidations or revisions—for instance, when the statute in question is clearly flawed); *Amendment* by leg-

islative action, which is considerably less far-reaching than reenactment (amendments include minor additions to or alterations of statutory
aggravating circumstances).

Finally, each entry provides the effective date of the law, U.S.
citations on federal cases, citations to the regional reporter on state
cases, and citations to the specific publisher on state statutes.

| Action | Date | Cite | Comments |
|---|---|---|---|
| *Alabama* | | | |
| ENACTED | 3/7/76 | ALA. CODE ss13-11-1 to 13-11-9 | |
| INVALIDATED | 6/20/80 | *Beck* v. *Alabama*, 447 U.S. 625 | |
| JUDICIALLY REVISED | 12/19/80 | *Beck* v. *State*, 396 So. 2d. 645 | To comply with *Beck* v. *Alabama* |
| REENACTED | 7/1/81 | 1981 Ala. Acts No. 81-178 | |
| *Arizona* | | | |
| ENACTED | 8/8/73 | ARIZ. REV. STAT. ANN. s13-454 | |
| INVALIDATED | 4/21/78 | *Richmond* v. *Cardwell*, 450 F. Supp. 519 | |
| | and 7/3/78 | *Jordan* v. *Arizona*, 438 U.S. 911 | |
| JUDICIALLY REVISED | 7/20/78 | *State* v. *Watson*, 586 P. 2d 1253 | |
| REENACTED | 5/1/79 | ARIZ. REV. STAT. ANN. s13-703 | |
| *Arkansas* | | | |
| ENACTED | 7/24/73 | ARK. STAT. ANN. ss41-4710 to 41-4714 | |
| REENACTED | 1/1/76 | ARK. STAT. ANN. ss41-1301 to 41-1309 | |
| AMENDED | 3/17/77 | ARK. STAT. ANN. s41-1302 | Weight of evidence standards as to aggravating and mitigating circumstances added |
| *California* | | | |
| ENACTED | 1/1/74 | CAL. PENAL CODE ss190 to 190.3 (West) | |
| INVALIDATED | 12/7/76 | *Rockwell* v. *Superior Court of Ventura County*, 556 P.2d 1101 | |
| REENACTED | 8/11/77 | CAL. PENAL CODE ss190.1 to 190.6 (West) | |
| AMENDED (by referendum) | 11/7/78 | CAL. PENAL CODE ss190.1 to 190.6 (West) | Crime eligibility expanded by initiative measure |

## Colorado

| | | | |
|---|---|---|---|
| ENACTED | 1/1/75 | COLO. REV. STAT. s16-11-103 | |
| INVALIDATED | 10/23/78 | *People* v. *District Court*, 586 P.2d 31 | |
| REENACTED | 7/1/79 | COLO. REV. STAT. s16-11-103 | |

## Connecticut

| | | | |
|---|---|---|---|
| ENACTED | 10/1/73 | CONN. GEN. STAT. ANN. ss53a-46a, 53a-46b (West) | |
| REENACTED | 7/1/81 | 1980 Conn. Pub. Acts No. 80-332 (House Bill No. 5058) | Limitations on mitigating circumstances removed. |

## Delaware

| | | | |
|---|---|---|---|
| ENACTED | 3/29/74 | DEL. CODE tit. 11 s4209 | |
| INVALIDATED | 10/22/76 | *State* v. *Spence*, 367 A. 2d 983 | |
| REENACTED | 4/14/77 | DEL. CODE tit. 11 s4209 | |

## Florida

| | | | |
|---|---|---|---|
| ENACTED | 12/8/72 | FLA. STAT. ANN. s921.141 (West) | |
| AMENDED | 7/3/79 | FLA. STAT. ANN. s921.141 (West) | Limitation on mitigating circumstances removed. |

## Georgia

| | | | |
|---|---|---|---|
| ENACTED | 3/28/73 | GA. CODE ANN. ss26-3102, 27-2534.1, 27-2537 | |

## Idaho

| | | | |
|---|---|---|---|
| ENACTED | 3/27/73 | IDAHO CODE ss19-2515, 19-2527 | |
| REENACTED | 3/28/77 | IDAHO CODE ss19-2515, 19-2827 | |

## Illinois

| | | | |
|---|---|---|---|
| ENACTED | 7/1/74 | ILL. REV. STAT. ch. 38, s1005-8-1A | |
| INVALIDATED | 9/29/75 | *People Ex. Rel Rice* v. *Cunningham*, 336 N.E. 2d 1 | |
| REENACTED | 6/21/77 | ILL. ANN. STAT. ch. 38, s9-1 (Smith-Hurd) | |

## Indiana

| | | | |
|---|---|---|---|
| ENACTED | 4/24/73 | IND. CODE s35-13-4-1 (Burns 1975) | |
| INVALIDATED | 4/6/77 | *French* v. *State*, 362 N.E. 2d 834 | |
| REENACTED | 10/1/77 | IND. CODE ANN. s35-50-2-9 (Burns) | |

*Kentucky*

| ENACTED | 1/1/75 | KY. REV. STAT. ANN. s532.030 (Baldwin) | |
|---|---|---|---|
| REENACTED | 12/22/76 | KY. REV. STAT. ANN. ss532.025, 532.035, 532.075 (Baldwin) | |

*Louisiana*

| ENACTED | 7/2/73 | LA. REV. STAT. ANN. s14:30 (West) | |
|---|---|---|---|
| INVALIDATED | 7/2/76 | *Roberts* v. *Louisiana*, 428 U.S. 325 | |
| REENACTED | 10/2/76 | LA. CODE CRIM. PRO. ANN. arts. 905 to 905.9 (West) | |

*Maryland*

| ENACTED | 7/1/75 | MD. ANN. CODE art. 27 s413 | |
|---|---|---|---|
| INVALIDATED | 11/9/76 | *Blackwell* v. *State*, 365 A.2d 545 | |
| REENACTED | 7/1/78 | MD. ANN. CODE art. 27 ss413, 414 | |
| AMENDED | 7/1/79 | MD. ANN. CODE art. 27 ss413, 414 | Limitation on mitigating circumstances removed |

*Massachusetts*

| INVALIDATED | 12/22/75 | *Commonwealth* v. *O'Neal*, 330 N.E. 2d 676 | Remaining mandatory provision (for rape-murder) of pre-*Furman* statute invalidated |
|---|---|---|---|
| ENACTED | 11/13/79 | MASS. ANN. LAWS ch. 265 s2, ch. 279 s53–56 (Michie/Law Co-op) | |
| INVALIDATED | 10/28/80 | *D.A. for the Suffolk District* v. *Watson*, 411 N.E. 2d 1274 | |
| REENACTED (by referendum) | 12/22/82 | MASS. ANN. LAWS ch. 279 s57–71 | State constitutional amendment re-establishing statute enacted 11/13/79 |

*Mississippi*

| ENACTED | 4/23/74 | MISS. CODE ANN. ss97-3-65(1), 97-3-19(2), 97-25-55(1) | |
|---|---|---|---|
| JUDICIALLY REVISED | 10/5/76 | *Jackson* v. *State*, 337 So.2d 1242 | To comply with *Gregg* et al. |
| REENACTED | 4/13/77 | MISS. CODE ANN. ss99-19-101, 99-19-103, 99-19-105 | |

*Missouri*

| ENACTED | 9/28/75 | MO. ANN. STAT. ss559.005, 559.009 (Vernon) | |
|---|---|---|---|
| INVALIDATED | 3/15/77 | *State* v. *Duren*, 547 S.W.2d 476 | |
| REENACTED | 5/26/77 | MO. ANN. STAT. ss565.012, 565.014 | |
| AMENDED | 5/20/80 | MO. ANN. STAT. s565.012 | Two aggravating circumstances added |

*Montana*

| ENACTED | 1/1/74 | MONT. REV. CODES ANN. s94-5-105, 304, 305 | |
| REENACTED | 4/8/77 | MONT. REV. CODES ANN. ss95-2206.6 to 95-2206.15 | |

*Nebraska*

| ENACTED | 4/20/73 | NEB. REV. STAT. ss29-2522,29-2523 | |
| AMENDED | 4/19/78 | NEB. REV. STAT. ss29-2521.01, 29-2521.02, 29-2521.03, 29-2521.04 | Legislative findings and standards of review added. |

*Nevada*

| ENACTED | 7/1/73 | NEV. REV. STAT. s200.030 | |
| AMENDED | 7/1/77 | NEV. REV. STAT. ss200.033, 200.035 | Mandatory provision deleted, aggravating and mitigating circumstances added. |

*New Hampshire*

| ENACTED | 4/15/74 | N.H. REV. STAT. ANN. s630.1 | |
| AMENDED | 9/3/77 | N.H. REV. STAT. ANN. ss630.1, 630.5 | Mandatory provision deleted; mitigating and aggravating circumstances added. |

*New Jersey*

| ENACTED | 8/6/82 | NJSA 2A:165-1 et seq. | |

*New Mexico*

| ENACTED | 3/23/73 | N.M. STAT. ANN. s40A-29-2 | |
| INVALIDATED | 8/20/76 | *State* v. *Rondeau*, 553 P.2d 688 | |
| REENACTED | 7/1/79 | N.M. STAT. ANN. ss31-20A-1 to 31-20A-6 | |
| AMENDED | 3/17/81 | N.M. STAT. ANN. ss31-20A-1 to 31-20A-6 | One aggravating circumstance added. |

*New York*

| ENACTED | 9/1/74 | N.Y. PENAL LAW (Consol) ss125.27, 60.06 | |
| INVALIDATED | 11/15/77 | *People* v. *Davis*, 371 N.E.2d 456 | Homicide by defendant under life sentence excepted. |

*North Carolina*

| JUDICIALLY REVISED | 1/18/73 | *State* v. *Waddell*, 194 S.E.2d 19 | Discretionary provision deleted (to comply with *Furman*) |
| ENACTED | 4/8/74 | N.C. GEN. STAT. ss14-17, 14-21 | |

## North Carolina (cont.)

| | | | |
|---|---|---|---|
| INVALIDATED | 7/2/76 | *Woodson* v. *North Carolina,* 428 U.S. 280 | |
| REENACTED | 6/1/77 | N.C. GEN. STAT. s15A-2000 | |
| AMENDED | 5/14/79 and 1/1/80 | N.C. GEN. STAT. s15A-2000 | Each added one aggravating circumstance |

## Ohio

| | | |
|---|---|---|
| ENACTED | 1/1/74 | OHIO REV. CODE ANN. s2929.04 (Page) |
| INVALIDATED | 7/3/78 | *Lockett* v. *Ohio,* 438 U.S. 586 |
| REENACTED | 10/19/81 | OHIO REV. CODE ANN. s2929.04 |

## Oklahoma

| | | | |
|---|---|---|---|
| ENACTED | 5/17/73 | OKLA. STAT. ANN. tit.21 ss701.3, 701.5, 701.6 (West) | |
| REENACTED | 7/24/76 | OKLA. STAT. ANN. tit.21 ss701.9 to 701.15 (West) | |
| AMENDED | 5/8/81 | OKLA. STAT. ANN. tit.21 s701.12A (West) | Aggravating and mitigating circumstances added. |

## Oregon

| | | |
|---|---|---|
| ENACTED | 12/7/78 | OR. REV. STAT. s163.116 |
| INVALIDATED | 1/20/81 | *Quinn* v. *State,* 623 P.2d 630 |

## Pennsylvania

| | | | |
|---|---|---|---|
| ENACTED | 3/26/74 | PA. CONS. STAT. ANN. s1311 (Purdon) | |
| INVALIDATED | 11/30/77 | *Com.* v. *Moody,* 382 A.2d 442 | |
| REENACTED | 9/13/78 | PA. CONS. STAT. ANN. s1311 (Purdon) | |
| TRANSFERRED | 12/4/80 | PA. CONS. STAT. ANN. s1311 (Purdon) | From Chapter 13 of Title 18 to Chapter 97 of Title 42 (PA. CONS. STAT. ANN. s9711 [Purdon]) |

## Rhode Island

| | | |
|---|---|---|
| ENACTED | 6/26/73 | R.I. GEN. LAWS s11-23-2 |
| INVALIDATED | 2/19/79 | *State* v. *Cline,* 397 A.2d 1309 |

## South Carolina

| | | | |
|---|---|---|---|
| ENACTED | 7/2/74 | S.C. CODE s16-3-20 | |
| INVALIDATED | 7/21/76 | *State* v. *Rumsey,* 226 S.E.2d 894 | |
| REENACTED | 6/8/77 | S.C. CODE ss16-3-20, 16-3-25 | |
| AMENDED | 6/31/78 | S.C. CODE ss16-3-20, 16-3-25 | One aggravating circumstance added |

*South Dakota*

| | | |
|---|---|---|
| ENACTED | 2/27/79 | S. D. COD. LAWS ss23A-27A-1 to 6, 23A-27A-9 to 13 |

*Tennessee*

| | | | |
|---|---|---|---|
| ENACTED | 2/27/74 | TENN. CODE ANN. s39-2406 | |
| INVALIDATED | 1/24/77 | *Collins* v. *State*, 550 S.W. 2d 643, cert. denied 434 U.S. 905, rehearing denied 434 U.S. 977 | |
| REENACTED | 4/11/77 | TENN. CODE ANN. ss39-2404, 39-2406 | |
| AMENDED | 3/19/81 | TENN. CODE ANN. ss39-2404, 39-2406 | One aggravating circumstance added |

*Texas*

| | | |
|---|---|---|
| ENACTED | 6/14/73 | TEX. CODE CRIM. PROC. ANN. art. 37.071 (Vernon) |

*Utah*

| | | | |
|---|---|---|---|
| ENACTED | 7/1/73 | UTAH CODE ANN. ss76-3-206, 76-3-207 | |
| AMENDED | 5/10/77 | UTAH CODE ANN. s76-3-206 | Review process expedited |

*Virginia*

| | | |
|---|---|---|
| ENACTED | 10/1/75 | VA. CODE ss18-2-31, 18-2-10 |
| AMENDED | 7/1/77 | VA. CODE ss17-110.1 and 19.2-264.2 to 19.2-264.5 |

*Washington*

| | | | |
|---|---|---|---|
| ENACTED | 11/4/75 | WASH. REV. CODE ANN. s9A.32.046 | |
| REENACTED | 6/10/77 | WASH. REV. CODE ANN. ss9A.32.046, 9A.32.045 | To comply with *Gregg* |
| INVALIDATED | 4/16/81 | *State* v. *Frampton*, 627 P.2d 922 | 1977 enactment invalidated |
| REENACTED | 5/14/81 | 1981 Wash. Legis. Serv. Chapter 138 (House Bill No. 76) | |

*Wyoming*

| | | |
|---|---|---|
| ENACTED | 2/24/73 | WYO. STAT. ANN. s6-54 |
| INVALIDATED | 1/27/77 | *Kennedy* v. *State*, 559 P. 2d 1014 |
| REENACTED | 2/28/77 | WYO. STAT. ANN. ss6-4-102, 6-4-103 |

# APPENDIX C

## BIBLIOGRAPHY

Abramowitz, E., and D. Paget. 1964. "Executive Clemency in Capital Cases." *N. Y. U. L. Rev.* 39:136.

Acta Juridica. 1971. "Contempt of Court? The Trial of Barend Van Dyk Van Niekerk." *Acta Juridica*:77.

Adams, C. D. 1956. "Benefit of Clergy in Fayette County." *K. S. B. J.* 20:129.

Adams, J. K. 1973. "Mandatory Death: *State* v. *Waddell.*" *North Carolina Central L. J.* 4:292.

Adams, W. 1970. "Capital Punishment in Imperial and Soviet Criminal Law." *Am. J. of Comp. L.* 18:575.

Adelstein, R. P. 1979. "Informational Paradox and the Pricing of Crime: Capital Sentencing Standards in Economic Perspective." *J. of Crim. L.* 70:281.

Aden, M. 1972. "Bygone Forms of Capital Punishment." *Codicillus* 13 (October):20.

Adler, S. 1981. "Florida's Zealous Prosecutors: Death Specialists." *American Lawyer* 3 (September):35.

*Aikens* v. *California.* 1972. 406 U.S. 813.

Akman, D. D. 1966. "Homicides and Assaults in Canadian Penitentiaries." *Canadian J. of Correction* 8:284.

Akron Law Review. 1974. "Legislative Response to *Furman* v. *Georgia* (92 Sup. Ct. 2726) —Ohio Restores the Death Penalty." *Akron L. Rev.* 8:149.

A large part of this bibliography appeared in *Executions in America* (1974) and was compiled by Douglas B. Lyons. Additional references, through 1983, have been added. All entries are listed alphabetically by author, except for unauthored documents and articles, which are listed by responsible government agency or journal title, and court cases, which are listed by plaintiff's name.

Akron Law Review. 1978. "Criminal Law—Death Penalty—Cruel and Unusual Punishment—Individualized Sentencing Determination." *Akron L. Rev.* 12:360.

Alabama Law Review. 1980. "Statutory Construction: Criminal Law and Procedure (Alabama Law Survey)." *Alab. L. Rev.* 31:714.

Alabama Law Review. 1982. "Criminal Law and Procedure" (Section VI, Part E of 1980–1981 Survey of Developments in Alabama Law). *Alab. L. Rev.* 33 (Spring):662.

Albany Law Review. 1973. "The Death Penalty—The Alternatives Left After *Furman* v. *Georgia.*" *Albany L. Rev.* 37:344.

Albinsky, H. S. 1963. "British Constitution and the Capital Punishment Controversy." *J. of Public L.* 12:193.

Alcock, T. 1752. *Observations on the Defects of the Poor Law and on the Causes and Consequences of the Great Increase and Burden of the Poor.* London: R. Baldwin.

Alexander, M. 1966. "The Abolition of Capital Punishment." *Proceedings of the Am. Corr. Assoc.* 96:16.

Ali, S. 1978. "Zia Survives the Backlash." *Far Eastern Econ. Rev.* 100 (August):9.

Allen, E. J. 1960. "Capital Punishment: Your Protection and Mine." *The Police Chief* 27. Reprinted in Bedau (1967b), p. 135, and McCafferty (1972), p. 117.

Allredge, E. P. 1942. "Why the South Leads the Nation in Murder and Manslaughter." *The Quarterly Rev.* 2:123.

Almond, G. A., and J. S. Coleman, eds. 1960. *The Politics of Developing Areas.* Princeton, N.J.: Princeton University Press.

Alston, J. P. 1976. "Japanese and American Attitudes Toward the Abolition of Capital Punishment." *Criminology* 14 (August):271.

American Bar Association. 1959. "Proceedings of the Section of Criminal Law." *American Bar Association, Section on Criminal Law*:5.

American Bar Association Journal. 1962. "Time Lapse Between Sentence and Execution: The United States and Canada Compared." *A. B. A. J.* 48:1043.

American Bar Association Journal. 1981. "Juror Selection . . . Capital Cases." *A. B. A. J.* 67 (January):100.

American Bar Association Journal. 1982. "E.R.A., Handgun Control, and the Death Penalty." *A. B. A. J.* 68 (March):266.

American Criminal Law Review. 1979. "New Direction for Capital Sentencing or an About-Face for the Supreme Court?" *Am. Crim. L. Rev.* 16:317.

American Digest System. n.d. *Decennial Digest.* St. Paul, Minn.: West Publishing Company.

American Journal of Criminal Law. 1972. "Sentencing Procedure—Due Process Does Not Require that a Defendant Charged with a Capital Offense Receive a Hearing for Sentencing Purposes Separate from the Hearing to Ascertain Guilt, or that the Jury Have Legislative Standards to Guide It in Determining His Sentence." *Am. J. of Crim. L.* 1:109.

American Journal of Criminal Law. 1977. "Death Penalty in the Soviet Union." *Am. J. of Crim. L.* 5 (May):225.

American Journal of Criminal Law. 1978. "Capital Punishment—Rape—Death Held to Be Cruel and Unusual Punishment for the Crime of Rape of an Adult Woman." *Am. J. of Crim. L.* 6 (January):107.

American Journal of Criminal Law. 1979. "Eighth Amendment Proportionality." *Am. J. of Crim. L.* 7 (July):253.

American Law Reports. 1920. "Abolition of Death Penalty as Affecting Right to Bail of One Charged with Murder in First Degree." *A. L. R.* 8:1352.

American Law Reports. 1933. "Constitutionality of Statute which Makes Specified Punishment or Penalty Mandatory and Permits No Exercise of Discretion on Part of Court or Jury." *A. L. R.* 83:1362.

American Law Reports. 1942. "Recommendation of Mercy in Capital Case." *A. L. R.* 138:1230.

American Law Reports. 1956. "Beliefs Regarding Capital Punishment as Disqualifying Juror in Capital Case for Cause." *A. L. R.* 2d, 48:560.

American Law Reports. 1963. "Upon Whom Rests Burden of Proof Where Bail Is Sought Before Judgment, but After Indictment in Capital Case, as to Whether Proof is Evident or the Presumption Great." *A. L. R.* 2d, 89:355.

American Law Reports. 1965. "Unanimity as to Punishment in Criminal Cases Where Jury Can Recommend Lesser Penalty." *A. L. R.* 3d, 1:1461.

American Law Reports. 1971. "Comment Note: Beliefs Regarding Capital Punishment as Disqualifying Juror in Capital Case—Post-*Witherspoon* Cases." *A. L. R.* 3d, 39:550.

American Review of Reviews. 1909. "Does Capital Punishment Prevent Convictions?" *Am. Rev. of Reviews* 40:219.

Amir, M. 1971. *Patterns in Forcible Rape.* Chicago: University of Chicago Press.

Amnesty International Publications. 1974. *Amnesty International.* Chile: Amnesty International Publications.

Amnesty International Publications. 1979. *The Death Penalty.* Chile: Amnesty International Publications.

Amsterdam, A. G. 1971a. "The Case Against the Death Penalty." *Juris Doctor* (November):11.

Amsterdam, A. G. 1971b. "Comment: Racism in Capital Punishment: Impact of *McGautha* v. *California.*" *Black L. J.* 1:185.

Amsterdam, A. G. 1972. Testimony, in Hart-Celler Hearings, p. 46.

Ancel, M. 1962. *The Death Penalty in European Countries.* The Council of Europe.

Ancel, M. 1964. "The Problem of the Death Penalty." Authorized translation in the *Revue de Droit Pénal et de Criminologie,* 44th Year (1963-1964):373. Reprinted in Sellin (1967a), p. 3.

Andenaes, J. 1966. "General Preventive Effects of Punishment." *U. Penn. L. Rev.* 114:949.

Andenaes, J. 1968. "Does Punishment Deter Crime?" *Crim. L. Quarterly* 11:76.

Andenaes, J. 1970. "The Morality of Deterrence." *U. Chicago L. Rev.* 37:649.

Andenaes, J. 1971. "Deterrence and Specific Offenses." *U. Chicago L. Rev.* 38:537.

Annals of the American Academy of Political and Social Science. 1907. "Crime and Capital Punishment: A Symposium. Garner, Crime and Judicial Inefficiency (601); Barrows, Legislative Tendencies as to Capital Punishment (618); Cutler, Capital Punishment and Lynching (622); Shipley, Homicide and the Death Penalty in Mexico (625)." *The Annals* 29:601.

Annual Survey of American Criminal Law. 1977. "Criminal Law—Capital Punishment. Entrapment." *Annual Survey of Am. L.* 1977:365.

Anttila, I. 1967. "The Death Penalty in Finland." *Pena de Morte* 1:173.

Archbold, E. 1848. "Abolition of Capital Punishment." *Western L. J.* 5:421.

Archer, D., and R. Gartner. 1976. "Violent Acts and Violent Times: A Comparative Approach to Postwar Homicide Rates." *Am. Socio. Rev.* (December):937.

Arizona Law Review. 1972a. "Appellate Review of Sentences in Arizona Supreme Court." *Ariz. L. Rev.* 14:477.

Arizona Law Review. 1972b. "Criminal Law—Procedure—The Death Qualified Jury (in Arizona Supreme Court)." *Ariz. L. Rev.* 14:467.

Arizona State Law Journal. 1974. "Resurrection of the Death Penalty: The Validity of Arizona's Response to *Furman* v. *Georgia* (92 Sup. Ct. 2726)." *Ariz. State L. J.* 1974:257.

Arkansas Law Review. 1969. "Constitutional Law—Challenge for Cause on the Ground of Conscientious Scruples Against Capital Punishment." *Ark. L. Rev.* 23:108.

Arkansas Law Review. 1972. "Jury Discretion and the Unitary Trial Procedure in Capital Cases." *Ark. L. Rev.* 26:33.

Arkansas Law Review. 1978. "*Collins* v. *State* [(Ark.)548 S.W. 2d. 106]: Arkansas' Death Penalty Gets New Life." *Ark. L. Rev.* 31:719.

Arkin, S. D. 1980. "Discrimination and Arbitrariness in Capital Punishment: An Analysis of Post-*Furman* Murder Cases in Dade County, Florida, 1973–1976." *Stanford L. Rev.* 33 (November):75.

Arnold, J. C. 1952. "Royal Commission on Capital Punishment." *Sol. J.* 18:280; 19:21.

Arnold, J. C. 1954. "Report on Capital Punishment." *Sol. J.* 20:263; 21:5.

Arnold, W. R. 1971. "Race and Ethnicity Relative to Other Factors in Juvenile Court Dispositions." *Am. J. of Sociol.* 77:211.

Arteaga, D. 1980. *The Death Penalty Versus Thou Shalt Not Kill.* New York: Vantage.

Atkinson, M. 1972. "Punishment as Assurance." *University of Tasmania L. Rev.* 4:45.

Avio, K. L. 1979. "Capital Punishment in Canada: A Time-Series Analysis of the Deterrent Hypothesis." *Canadian Journal of Economics* 12 (November):647.

Bailey, R. 1962. "Facing Death, A New Life Perhaps Too Late." *Life* 53 (July):28. Reprinted in Bedau (1967b), p. 556, as "Rehabilitation on Death Row."

Bailey, W. C., and R. W. Smith. 1972. "Punishment: Its Severity and Certainty." *J. C. L. C. & P. S.* 63:530.

Bailey, W. C. 1974. "Murder and the Death Penalty." *J. C. L. C.* 65 (September):416.

Bailey, W. C. 1975. "Murder and Capital Punishment: Some Further Evidence." *Am. J. of Orthopsychiatry* 45 (July):669.

Bailey, W. C. 1976. "Reply with Rejoinder." *Crime and Delinquency* 22 (January):31.

Bailey, W. C. 1977. "Imprisonment v. The Death Penalty as a Deterrent to Murder." *Law and Human Behavior* 1:239.

Bailey, W. C. 1978a "Deterrence and the Death Penalty for Murder in Utah: A Time Series Analysis." *J. Cont. L.* 5:1.

Bailey, W. C. 1978b. "Analysis of the Deterrent Effect of the Death Penalty in North Carolina." *N. C. Central L. J.* 10:29.

Bailey, W. C. 1979a. "Deterrent Effect of the Death Penalty for Murder in California." *S. Calif. L. Rev.* 52 (March):743.

Bailey, W. C. 1979b. "Deterrence and the Death Penalty for Murder in Oregon." *Willamette L. Rev.* 16:67.

Bailey, W. C. 1979c. "Deterrent Effect of the Death Penalty for Murder in Ohio: A Time Series Analysis." *Cleveland St. L. Rev.* 28:51.

Bailey, W. C. 1980a. "Multivariate Cross-Sectional Analysis of the Deterrent Effect of the Death Penalty." *Sociology and Social Research* 64 (January):183.

Bailey, W. C. 1980b. "Deterrence and the Celerity of the Death Penalty: A Neglected Question in Deterrence Research." *Social Forces* 58 (June):1308.

Bailey, W. C. 1982. "Capital Punishment and Lethal Assaults Against Police." *Criminology* 19 (February):608.

Baldus, D. C., and J. W. L. Cole. 1975. "Statistical Evidence on the Deterrent Effect of Capital Punishment: A Comparison of the Work of Thorsten Sellin and Isaac Ehrlich on the Deterrent Effect of Capital Punishment." *Yale L. J.* 85 (December–January):164.

Baldus, D. C., C. A. Pulaski, Jr., G. Woodworth, and F. D. Kyle. 1980. "Identifying Comparatively Excessive Sentences of Death: A Quantitative Approach." *Stanford L. Rev.* 33 (November):1.

Baldus, D. C., G. Woodworth, and C. A. Pulaski, Jr. 1982a. "The Impact of Procedural Reform on Excessiveness, Differential Treatment along Racial Lines and Arbitrariness in Death Sentencing: The Georgia Experience before and after *Furman* v. *Georgia.*" Draft Report to the National Institute of Justice. Center for Interdisciplinary Studies, College of Law, Syracuse University.

Baldus, D. C., G. Woodworth, and C. A. Pulaski, Jr. 1982b. "Proportionality Review of Death Sentences: An Empirical Study of the Georgia Experience." Draft Report to the National Institute of Justice. Center for Interdisciplinary Studies, College of Law, Syracuse University.

Ball, F. J., Jr. 1962. "Death in Two Chapters." *The Alabama Lawyer* 23:385.

Ball, J. C. 1955. "Deterrence Concept in Criminology and Law." *J. C. L. C. & P. S.* 46:347.

Balough, J. K., and J. D. Green. 1966. "Capital Punishment: Some Reflections." *Fed. Prob.* 30 (December):24.

Baltimore Law Review. 1971. "Capital Punishment . . . On the Way Out?" *Baltimore L. Rev.* 1:28.

Banks, A. S. 1971. *Cross-Polity Time-Series Data.* Cambridge, Mass.: M.I.T. Press.

Banks, A. S., and R. B. Textor. 1963. *A Cross-Polity Survey.* Cambridge, Mass.: M.I.T. Press.

Barber, R. N., and R. D. Wilson. 1968. "Deterrent Aspects of Capital Punishment and Its Effects on Conviction Rates: The Queensland Experience." *Australia & New Zealand J. of Crime* 1:101.

Barbour, W. T. 1919. "Efforts to Abolish the Death Penalty in Illinois." *J. C. L. C.* 9:500.

*Barefoot v. Estelle.* 1983. 51 LW 5189.

Barkaw, I., and J. O. Lofberg. 1979. *Sycophancy in Athens* and *Capital Punishment in Ancient Athens.* New York: Arno Press.

Barnes, H. E., and N. Teeters. 1943. *New Horizons in Criminology.* Englewood Cliffs, N.J.: Prentice-Hall.

Barnhill, D. S. 1982. "Administering the Death Penalty." *Wash. & Lee L. Rev.* 39 (Winter):101.

Barrett, E. L., Jr. 1972. "Anderson and the Judicial Function." *S. Calif. L. Rev.* 45:739.

Barrows, S. J. 1907. "Legislative Tendencies as to Capital Punishment (in *Crime and Capital Punishment: A Symposium*). *The Annals* 29:601, 618.

Barry, J. V. W. 1958. " . . . Hanged by the Neck Until . . . " *Sydney L. Rev.* 2:401.

Barzun, J. 1962. "In Favor of Capital Punishment." *The American Scholar* 31:181. Reprinted in Bedau (1967b), p. 154, and McCafferty (1972), p. 89.

Baylor Law Review. 1969. "Unlawful Discrimination in Jury Selection: *Witherspoon* and Related Cases." *Baylor L. Rev.* 21:72.

Baylor Law Review. 1971. "The Survival of the Death Penalty." *Baylor L. Rev.* 23:499.

Baylor Law Review. 1974. "Is the Death Penalty Dead?" *Baylor L. Rev.* 26:114.

Beal, R. 1969. "There Should Be No Capital Punishment." *The Arizona Advocate* (March):5.

Bean, F. D., and R. G. Cushing. 1971. "Criminal Homicide, Punishment, and Deterrence: Methodological and Substantive Reconsiderations." *Soc. Sci. Quarterly* 52:277.

Beasley, N. B. 1927. "Aren't We All Killers—An Interview with Henry Ford." *Collier's* (June):7.

Beccaria, C. di 1963. *On Crimes and Punishment* (1764) (tr. H. Paolucci). Indianapolis: Bobbs-Merrill Co.

Bedau, H. A. 1958a. "A Bibliography of Capital Punishment and Related Topics, 1948–1958a." *Prison Journal* 38:41.

Bedau, H. A. 1958b. "Survey of the Debate on Capital Punishment in Canada, England, and the United States, 1948–1958." *Prison Journal* 38:35.

Bedau, H. A. 1959a. "Capital Punishment in America, Review and Forecast." *Friends Journal* 5:102.

Bedau, H. A. 1959b. "The Case Against the Death Penalty." *The New Leader* (August 17–24):19.

Bedau, H. A. 1959c. "The Death Penalty Today." *The Christian Century* 76:320.

Bedau, H. A. 1959d. "A Note on the Hauptmann Case and on the Argument for Deterrence." *N. J. S. B. J.* 2:255.

Bedau, H. A. 1959e. "The Right to Kill." *The Progressive* 23:50.

Bedau, H. A. 1960. "Capital Punishment in the United States." *Howard L. J.* 10:225.

Bedau, H. A. 1962. "The Struggle for Law Reform." *N. J. S. B. J.* 5:718.

Bedau, H. A. 1964. "Death Sentences in New Jersey 1907–1960." *Rutgers L. Rev.* 19:1.

Bedau, H. A. 1965. "Capital Punishment in Oregon, 1903–1964." *Ore. L. Rev.* 45:1.

Bedau, H. A. 1967a. "A Social Philosopher Looks at the Death Penalty." *Am. J. of Psychiatry* 123:1361.

Bedau, H. A., ed. 1967b. *The Death Penalty in America.* New York: Anchor Press.

Bedau, H. A. 1967c. "The Issue of Capital Punishment." *Current History*, No. 312.

Bedau, H. A. 1968. "The Courts, the Constitution, and Capital Punishment." *Utah L. Rev.* 1968:201.

Bedau, H. A. 1970. "Deterrence and the Death Penalty: A Reconsideration." *J. C. L. C. & P. S.* 61:539.

Bedau, H. A. 1971a. "The Death Penalty in America: Review and Forecast." *Fed. Prob.* 35 (June):32. Reprinted in Hart–Celler Hearings.

Bedau, H. A. 1971b. "The Politics of Death." *Boston After Dark* (November 2):6.

Bedau, H. A. 1972a. "Capital Punishment and the Supreme Court." *The Jewish Advocate* (August 10).

Bedau, H. A. 1972b. "The Politics of Death." *Trial* 8 (March–April):44.

Bedau, H. A. 1972c. "Supreme Court Challenged by 8th Amendment Death Penalty Pleas." *The Jewish Advocate* (February 3).

Bedau, H. A. 1972d. Testimony, in Hart-Celler Hearings, p. 192.

Bedau, H. A. 1973a. *The Case Against the Death Penalty.* American Civil Liberties Union (Pamphlet).

Bedau, H. A. 1973b. "The Nixon Administration and the Deterrent Effect of the Death Penalty." *U. Pitt. L. Rev.* 34:557.

Bedau, H. A. 1974. "A Trial Interview: S. Caswell." *Trial* 10 (May–June):47.

Bedau, H. A. 1976. "Felony Murder Rape and the Mandatory Death Penalty: A Study in Discretionary Justice." *Suffolk U. L. Rev.* 10:493.

Bedau, H. A. 1977a. *The Courts, the Constitution, and Capital Punishment.* Lexington, Mass.: D.C. Heath.

Bedau, H. A. 1977b. "Death Penalty: Social Policy and Social Justice." *Ariz. State L. J.* 1977:767.

Bedau, H. A. 1978. Statement Submitted to the Committee on the Judiciary, 95th Congress, Second Session, on s1382, April 27 and May 11, 1978.

Bedau, H. A. 1980. "The 1964 Death Penalty Referendum in Oregon." *Crime and Delinquency* 26 (October):528.

Bedau, H. A., ed. 1982. *The Death Penalty in America*, 3rd ed. New York: Oxford University Press.

Bedau, H. A., and C. M. Pierce, eds. 1976. *Capital Punishment in the United States*. New York: AMS Press.

Beichman, A. 1963. "The First Electrocution." *Commentary* 35 (May):410.

Belser, C. H., Jr. 1968. "Criminal Procedure—South Carolina Death Penalty Statutes—Guilty Pleas— Sentencing by the Jury." *South Carolina Law Review*. 20:841.

Bennett, J. V. 1958. "Historic Move: Delaware Abolishes Capital Punishment." *A. B. A. J.* 44:1053.

Bennett, J. V. 1966. "Our Penal System: Does It Deter Violence?" *Am. Crim. L. Q.* 4:68.

Bensing, R. C., and O. Schroeder, Jr. 1960. *Homicide in an Urban Community*. Springfield, Ill.: Thomas.

Benson, D. H. 1982a. "Texas Capital Sentencing Procedure after *Eddings* (*Eddings* v. *Oklahoma*, 102 Sup. Ct. 869): Some Questions Regarding Constitutional Validity." *Southern Texas L. J.* 23:315.

Benson, D. H. 1982b. "Constitutionality of Ohio's New Death Penalty Statute." *Univ. of Toledo L. Rev.* 14 (Fall):103.

Bentham, J. 1976. "Hanging Question." *New Statesman* 92 (November 26):743.

Berger, R. 1982. *Death Penalties: The Supreme Court's Obstacle Course*. Cambridge, Mass.: Harvard University Press.

Berger, S. 1978. "Application of the Cruel and Unusual Punishment Clause under the Canadian Bill of Rights." *McGill L. J.* 24:161.

Beristain, A. 1977. "Capital Punishment and Catholicism." *Int. J. of Crim. & Pen.* 5 (November):321.

Berkowitz, L., and J. McCauley. 1971. "The Contagion of Criminal Violence." *Sociometry* 34, 2:238.

Berman, D. M. 1959. "The Case Against Capital Punishment." *N. J. S. B. J.* 2:180.

Berns, W. 1979. *For Capital Punishment: Crime and the Morality of the Death Penalty*. New York: Basic Books.

Berns. W. 1980. "Defending the Death Penalty." *Crime and Delinquency* 26 (October):503.

Bernstein, T. 1973. "A Grand Success." *I.E.E.E. Spectrum* (February):54.

Berriault, G. 1966. "The Last Firing Squad, Executioners of Utah." *Esquire* (June):88.

Berry, J. (H. S. Ward, ed.). 1892. *My Experience as an Executioner* (reprint). Detroit: Gale Research Co.

Berry, R. M. 1982. "Death-Qualification and the 'Fireside Induction.' " *Univ. of Arkansas at Little Rock L. J.* 5:1.

Beyleveld, D. 1982. "Ehrlich's Analysis of Deterrence." *British J. of Criminology* 22 (April):101.

Bhutto, Z. A. 1979. *If I Am Assassinated*. Ghaziabad, India: Vikas Publishing House.

Bice, S. H. 1972. "*Anderson* and the Adequate State Ground." *S. Calif. L. Rev.* 45:750.

Bickel, A. M. 1967. "Death Penalty Litigation." *The New Republic* (August 19):13.

Biddle, W. C. 1969. "A Legislative Study of the Effectiveness of Criminal Penalties." *Crime and Delinquency* 15:354.

Black, C. L., Jr. 1971. "The Crisis in Capital Punishment." *Md. L. Rev.* 231:289. Reprinted in Hart-Celler Hearings, p. 435.

Black, C. L., Jr. 1974. *Capital Punishment: The Inevitability of Caprice and Mistake*. New York: Norton.

Black, C. L., Jr. 1976. "Due Process for Death: *Jurek* v. *Texas* (96 Sup. Ct. 2950) and Companion Cases." *Catholic U. L. Rev.* 26:1.

Black, C. L., Jr. 1977. "Death Penalty Now." *Tulane L. Rev.* 51 (April):429.

Black, C. L., Jr. 1978. "Reflections on Opposing the Penalty of Death." *St. Mary's L. J.* 10:1.

Black, C. L., Jr. 1980. "Objections to S1382, A Bill to Establish Rational Criteria for the Imposition of Capital Punishment." *Crime and Delinquency* 26 (October):441.

Black, C. L., Jr. 1981. *Capital Punishment: The Inevitability of Caprice and Mistake*, rev. ed. New York: W. W. Norton.

Black, E. 1981. *Why Men Play God: The Case Against Capital Punishment*. San Francisco: Cragmont Publications.

Black, T., and T. Orsagh. 1978. "New Evidence on the Efficacy of Sanctions as a Deterrent to Homicide." *Soc. Sci. Quarterly* 58 (March):616.

Bleakley, H. 1977. *The Hangmen of England* (reprint of 1929 edition). Charlestown, Mass.: Charles River Books.

Blease, C. 1959. "Abolition of the Death Penalty in California." *Lawyers' Guild Rev.* 19:58.

Block, E. B. 1962. *And May God Have Mercy . . . The Case Against Capital Punishment*. San Francisco: Fearon.

Blom-Cooper, L. J., ed. 1969. *The Hanging Question*. London: Duckworth and Company.

Blom-Cooper, L. J. 1973. "The Penalty for Murder." *British J. of Criminology* 13:188.

Bluestone, H., and C. L. McGahee. 1962. "Reaction to Extreme Stress: Impending Death by Execution." *Am. J. of Psychiatry* 119:393.

Board of Christian Service of the General Conference Mennonite Church. 1963. *Church, the State, and the Offender*. Newton, Kan.: Faith and Life.

Bonnie, R. J. 1980. "Psychiatry and the Death Penalty: Emerging Problems in Virginia (Survey of Virginia Law, 1978–1979)." *Va. L. Rev.* 66 (March):167.

Borchard, E. M., and F. L. Sanville. 1932. "When Justice Goes Astray" (from "Convicting the Innocent"). *Prison Journal* 12:16.

Boris, S. B. 1979. "Stereotypes and Dispositions for Criminal Homicide." *Criminology* 1979 (August):139.

Bork, R. H., J. C. Keeney, A. R. Randolph, Jr., F. H. Easterbrook, J. M. Feit, and H. M. Stone. 1974 (see *Fowler* v. *North Carolina*).

Borowitz, A. I. 1978. "Under Sentence of Death." *A. B. A. J.* 64 (August):1259.

Boston University Law Review. 1974. "Supreme Judicial Court and the Death Penalty: The Effects of Judicial Choice on the Legislative Options." *Boston U. L. Rev.* 54 (January):158.

Boston University Law Review. 1979. "Escape from Cruel and Unusual Punishment: A Theory of Constitutional Necessity." *Boston U. L. Rev.* 59 (March):334.

Bowers, W. J. 1972. "A Causal Framework for the Analysis of Deterrence and Related Processes." Paper Presented at Meetings of the American Society of Criminology (Caracas, Venezuela).

Bowers, W. J. 1973. "Competing Functions of the Criminal Sanctions: Deterrence, Retribution and Repression." Paper Presented at Meetings of the American Political Science Association (New Orleans).

Bowers, W. J. 1974. *Executions in America*. Lexington, Mass.: D.C. Heath.

Bowers, W. J. 1983a. "The Illusion of Deterrence in David Phillips's Research on Executions." Center for Applied Social Research, Northeastern University.

Bowers, W. J. 1983b. "Discrimination in Capital Punishment: Kleck's Data Versus his Claims." Center for Applied Social Research, Northeastern University.

Bowers, W. J., J. F. McDevitt, and A. Diana. 1983. "Proportionality Review by the Georgia Supreme Court: Evaluation or Rationalization?" Center for Applied Social Research, Northeastern University.

Bowers, W. J., and G. L. Pierce. 1975a. "Deterrence, Brutalization or Nonsense: A Critique of Isaac Ehrlich's Research on Capital Punishment." Center for Applied Social Research, Northeastern University.

Bowers, W. J., and G. L. Pierce. 1975b. "The Illusion of Deterrence in Isaac Ehrlich's Research on Capital Punishment." *Yale L. J.* 85 (December–January).

Bowers, W. J., and G. L. Pierce. 1978. "Preliminary Tabulations of the Death Sentence in Florida and Georgia." Center for Applied Social Research, Northeastern University.

Bowers, W. J., and G. L. Pierce. 1979a. "Preliminary Tabulations of Imposition of the Death Sentence in Florida, Georgia, and Texas." Center for Applied Social Research, Northeastern University.

Bowers, W. J., and G. L. Pierce. 1979b. "Preliminary Tabulations Reflecting Arbitrariness and Discrimination under Post-*Furman* Capital Statutes." Center for Applied Social Research, Northeastern University.

Bowers, W. J., and G. L. Pierce. 1979c. "Capital Punishment as a Case Study in the Incremental Evaluation of Guided Discretion." Center for Applied Social Research, Northeastern University.

Bowers, W. J., and G. L. Pierce. 1980. "Arbitrariness and Discrimination under Post-*Furman* Capital Statutes." *Crime and Delinquency* 26 (October):563.

Bowers, W. J., and R. Salem. 1972. "Severity of Formal Sanctions as a Repressive Response to Deviant Behavior." *L. S. Rev.* 6:427.

Boyd, J. A., Jr., and J. J. Logue. 1980. "Developments in the Application of Florida's Capital Felony Sentencing Law." *U. Miami L. Rev.* 34 (May):441.

Bradford, K. 1977. *Miracle on Death Row.* Lincoln, Va.: Chosen Books Publications.

Bradford, W. 1968. "Enquiry How Far the Punishment of Death Is Necessary in Pennsylvania (in 1793)." *Am. J. of Legal History* 12:122, 245.

Braithwaite, J. W. 1965. "Executive Clemency in California: A Case Study in Interpretation of Criminal Responsibility." *Issues in Criminology* 1:77.

Brasfield, P., and J. M. Elliot. 1982. *Deathman Pass Me By: Two Years on Death Row.* San Bernardino, Ca.: Borgo Press.

Brearly, H. C. 1932. *Homicide in the United States.* Chapel Hill: University of North Carolina Press.

Brennan, M. V. 1982. "Capital Representation in the State of Florida." Draft report prepared for the Florida Justice Institute (Miami, Florida).

Brimmell, G. P. 1973. "Death Penalty—Canada's Five Years of Limited Abolition Fail to Settle Issue." *National Observer* (January):7.

British Journal of Crime and Delinquency. 1954. "A Symposium on the Report of the Royal Commission on Capital Punishment, 1949–1953." *British Journal of Crime and Delinquency* 4, 3:158.

Bronson, E. J. 1970. "On the Conviction-Proneness and Representativeness of the Death Qualified Jury: An Empirical Study of Colorado Veniremen." *U. Colorado L. Rev.* 42:1.

Broocks, L. 1977. "Texas Penal Code Section 12–31(b) and *Witherspoon*: An Irreconcilable Pair?" *Am. J. of Crim. L.* 5 (October):313.

Brooker, F. 1972. "The Deterrent Effect of Punishment." *Criminology* 9:469.

Brooklyn Law Review. 1963. "Penal Law—Elimination of the Mandatory Death Penalty (in New York)." *Brooklyn L. Rev.* (1963):96.

Brooklyn Law Review. 1968. "Constitutional Law: Capital Punishment Clause of the Federal Kidnaping Act Is Unconstitutional as It Imposes a Chilling Effect on the Right to Demand a Jury Trial." *Brooklyn L. Rev.* 35:122.

Brooklyn Law Review. 1978. "Disinterment of an Ancient Law: An Eye for an Eye, No Death for Rape." *Brooklyn L. Rev.* 44:622.

*Brooks v. Estelle.* 1982. 697 F. 2d 586 (5th Cir.).

*Brooks v. Francis.* 1981. No. 83-8028 (S.D. GA) Petitioner's Brief.

*Brooks v. Zant.* 1981(see *Brooks v. Francis*).

*Brown v. Board of Education.* 1954. 347 U.S. 483.

Brown, H. P. 1889. "The New Instrument of Execution." *North American Review* 149:586.

Brown, W. 1963. *Women Who Died in the Chair.* New York: Collier.

Browning, J. R. 1974. "New Death Penalty Statutes: Perpetuating a Costly Myth." *Gonzaga L. Rev.* 9:651.

Brudner, A. 1980. "Retributivism and the Death Penalty." *U. Toronto L. J.* 30:337.

Buchman, R. L. 1980. "The Final Sentence: Nebraska's Death Penalty" (7th Annual Survey of Nebraska Law). *Creighton L. Rev.* 14:256.

Buffalo Law Review. 1975. "Eighth Amendment, Beccaria, and the Enlightenment: An Historical Justification for the *Weems* v. *United States* Excessive Punishment Doctrine." *Buffalo L. Rev.* 24:783.

Buffum, P. C. 1975. "Prison Killings and Death Penalty Legislation." *Prison Journal* 53:49.

Burbey, L. H. 1938. "History of Execution in What Is Now the State of Michigan." *Mich. Hist. Mag.* 22:443.

Bureau of the Census. 1937. *Mortality Statistics* (Annual, prior to 1937). U.S. Department of Commerce.

Bureau of the Census. 1943. *Vital Statistics Rates in the United States: 1900–1940.* U.S. Department of Commerce.

Bureau of the Census. 1960. *Historical Statistics of the United States, from Colonial Times to 1957.* U.S. Department of Commerce.

Bureau of the Census. 1969. *Census of the Governments.* U.S. Department of Commerce.

Bureau of the Census. 1971. *Census of the Populations.* Washington, D.C.: U.S. Government Printing Office.

Bureau of the Census. 1971. *Governmental Finances in 1969–1970.* U.S. Department of Commerce.

Bureau of the Census. Annual. *Current Population Reports: Population Estimates and Projections.* U.S. Department of Commerce.

Bureau of the Census. Annual. *Statistical Abstracts of the United States.* U.S. Department of Commerce.

Bureau of the Census. Annual. *Vital Statistics of the United States.* U.S. Department of Commerce.

Bureau of the Census. *Annual Current Population Reports: Population Estimates and Projections.* U.S. Department of Commerce.

Bureau of Labor Statistics. 1971. "Employment and Earnings." U.S. Department of Labor.

Burns, C. L. 1962. *Tait Case.* Forest Grove, Ore.: International Scholarly Book Service.

Burr, C. B. 1971. "Appellate Review as a Means of Controlling Criminal Sentencing Discretion—A Workable Alternative?" *U. Pitt. L. Rev.* 33:1.

Burrill, D. 1973. "The Immorality of the Death Penalty." *The Christian Century* (January 24):99.

Butler, M. T. 1973. "Comment—Constitutional Law—Capital Punishment—*Furman* v. *Georgia* and Georgia's Statutory Response." *Mercer L. Rev.* 24:891.

Buxton, R. J. 1973. "The Politics of Criminal Law Reform: England: Capital Punishment." *Am. J. of Comp. L.* 21:230, 239.

Bye, R. T. 1919. *Capital Punishment in the United States.* Philadelphia: The Committee of Philanthropic Labor of Philadelphia Yearly Meeting of Friends.

Bye, R. T. 1926. "Recent History and Present Status of Capital Punishment in the United States." *J. C. L. C.* 17:234.

Caldwell, O. J. 1952. "Why Is the Death Penalty Retained?" *The Annals* 264:45.

California Assembly Committee on Criminal Procedure. 1968. "Deterrent Effects of Criminal Sanctions."

California Assembly Subcommittee of the Judiciary Committee. 1957. "Report of the Subcommittee of the Judiciary Committee on Capital Punishment."

California Governor's Office, E. G. Brown. 1963. "Statement . . . On Capital Punishment" (January 31, 1963).

California Journal. 1972. "State Supreme Court Rules Death Penalty Unconstitutional in California." *California Journal* 3 (February):51.

California Law Review. 1964. "The California Penalty Trial." *Calif. L. Rev.* 52:386.

California Law Review. 1967. "Governor Reagan and Executive Clemency." *Calif. L. Rev.* 55:407.

California Law Review. 1970. "Criminal Procedure, Death Penalty." *Calif. L. Rev.* 58:229.

Calvert, E. R. 1932. "The Problem of Capital Punishment." *Prison Journal* 12:25.

Calvert, E. R. 1973. *Capital Punishment in the Twentieth Century*, fifth edition revised (1936); and *The Death Penalty Inquiry* (1931). Montclair, N.J.: Patterson Smith.

Cambanis, C. 1975. *The Execution*. Austin, Tex.: Thorp Springs.

Campion, D. 1955. "The State Police and the Death Penalty." Minutes of the Proceedings and Evidence, app. F, part II, no. 20, Joint Committee of the Senate and the House of Commons on Capital Punishment and Lotteries. Canada: Queens Printer.

Campion, D. R. 1973. "Of Many Things." *America* (April 7):inside cover.

Camus, A. 1960. "Reflections on the Guillotine." *Evergreen Rev.* 3:5. Reprinted in A. Camus, *Resistance, Rebellion and Death*, 1960, p.175.

Canada, Department of Justice. 1965. "Capital Punishment: Materials Relating to Its Purpose and Value."

Canada, Joint Committee of the Senate and House of Commons on Capital and Corporal Punishments and Lotteries. 1956. "Report."

Canada and the World. 1972. "Hanging: Should It Be Restored?" *Canada and the World* (November):3.

Canadian Bar Review. 1954. "Abolition of Capital Punishment—A Symposium." *Canadian B. Rev.* 32:485.

Canadian Criminology and Corrections Association. 1972. "The Death Penalty, An Official Statement of Policy of the Canadian Criminology and Corrections Association." Canadian Criminology and Corrections Association (November 1972).

Capital University Law Review. 1976. "*Gregg* v. *Georgia* (96 Sup. Ct. 2909), *Proffitt* v. *Florida* (96 Sup. Ct. 2960), and *Jurek* v. *Texas* (96 Sup. Ct. 2950): Burden of Proof in Capital Cases Past, Present, and Future." *Capital U. L. Rev.* 6:155.

Capote, T. 1968. "Death Row, U.S.A." *Esquire* (October):194.

Cardarelli, A. P. 1968. "An Analysis of Police Killed by Criminal Action, 1961–1963." *J. C. L. C. & P. S.* 59:447.

Carnes, E. 1981. "Alabama's 1981 Capital Punishment Statute." *Alabama Lawyer* 42 (July):456.

Carney, F. J., and A. L. Fuller. 1969. "A Study of Plea Bargaining in Murder Cases in Massachusetts." *Suffolk U. L. Rev.* 3:292.

Carrington, F. G. 1972. Testimony, in Hart-Celler Hearings, p. 222.

Carrington, F. G. 1978. *Neither Cruel Nor Unusual*. Westport, Conn.: Arlington House.

Carrington, F. G. 1982. "Deterrence, Death, and the Victims of Crime: A Common Sense Approach" (Symposium: The Crisis in the Criminal Justice System: Myth or Reality?) *Van. L. Rev.* 35 (April):587.

Carroll, J. M. 1974. "Death Penalty Provision of the New Penal Code." *KY. B. J.* 38 (October):15.

Carter, R. M. 1965. "The Johnny Cain Story: A Composite of the Men Executed in California." *Issues in Criminology* 1:60.

Carter, R. M., and K. L. Smith. 1969. "The Death Penalty in California: A Statistical and Composite Portrait." *Crime and Delinquency* 15:62.

Casey, D. A. 1980. "*Grigsby* v. *Mabry* (483 F. Supp. 1372): A New Look at Death-Qualified Juries." *Am. Crim. L. Rev.* 18:145.

Casey, O. J. 1975. "Governor Lee Cruce, White Supremacy and Capital Punishment, 1911–1915." *Chronicles of Oklahoma* 52:456.

Castelli, J. 1973. "Theology Shifting on Death Penalty." *National Catholic Reporter* (April 6):1.

Caswell, S. 1974. "Capital Punishment: Cementing a Fragile Victory." *Trial* 10 (May–June):47.

Catherwood, R. H. 1973. "Why the Volte-Face, Mr. Diefenbaker?" *The Financial Post* (March 10):6.

Catholic Lawyer. 1960. "Capital Punishment: The Issues and the Evidence." *Catholic Lawyer* 6:269.

Catholic University Law Review. 1953. "Cruel and Unusual Punishments." *Cath. U. L. Rev.* 3:117.

Catholic University Law Review. 1973. "The *Furman* Case: What Life Is Left in the Death Penalty?" *Cath. U. L. Rev.* 22,3 (Spring):651.

Ceylon, Commission of Inquiry on Capital Punishment, Sessional Paper XIV-1959. 1962. The Congressional Record (March 1, 1962):3019.

Chambliss, W. J. 1966. "The Deterrent Influence of Punishment." *Crime and Delinquency* 12:70.

Chambliss, W. J. 1967. "Types of Deviance and the Effectiveness of Legal Sanctions." *Wisc. L. Rev.* 1967:703.

Chandler, D. B. 1976. *Capital Punishment in Canada*. Toronto: McClelland & Stewart.

Chappell, D., G. Geis, and R. Hardt. 1972. "Explorations in Deterrence and Criminal Justice." *Crim. L. B.* 8:514.

Chicago-Kent Law Review. 1978. "1977 Illinois Death Penalty Statute: Does It Comply with Constitutional Standards?" *Chicago-Kent L. Rev.* 54:869.

Childs, R. W. 1960. "Keep Capital Punishment." *Penn. B. A. Q.* 31:337.

Chipman, E. N., Jr. 1981. "The Indiana Death Penalty: An Exercise in Constitutional Futility." *Valparaiso U. L. Rev.* 15:409.

Chiricos, T. G., and G. P. Waldo. 1970. "Punishment and Crime: An Examination of Some Empirical Evidence." *Social Problems* 18:200.

Chiricos, T. G., P. D. Jackson, and G. P. Waldo. 1972. "Inequality in the Imposition of a Criminal Label." *Social Problems* 19:533.

Christian Century. 1936a. "Kentucky Puts on a (Public) Hanging." *Christian Century* (August 26):1124.

Christian Century. 1936b. "Capital Punishment." *Christian Century* (April 22):591.

Christian Century. 1973. "Genesis and Capital Punishment." *Christian Century* (March 28):355.

Christoph, J. B. 1962. *Capital Punishment and British Politics*. Chicago: University of Chicago Press.

Clark, C. E. 1927. "The Death Penalty in Illinois." *Proceedings of the Illinois State Bar Association*:173.

Clark, R. 1979. "Rush to Death: Spenkelink's Last Appeal." *The Nation* 229:335.

*Clark v. Louisiana State Penitentiary*. 1983. 694 F. 2d 75 (5th Cir. *modified* 697 F. 2d 699).

Cleveland State Law Review. 1974. "Response to *Furman* (*Furman* v. *Georgia*, 92 Sup. Ct. 2726): Can Legislators Breathe Life Back into Death?" *Cleveland S. L. Rev.* 23:172.

Coakley, J. F. 1963. "Capital Punishment." *Am. Crim. L. Q.* 1:27.

Cobin, H. L. 1961. "Citizen Action for Abolishing Capital Punishment." *J. C. L. C. & P. S.* 52:90.

Cobin, H. L. 1967. "Abolition and Restoration of the Death Penalty in Delaware." In Bedau, 1967b, p.359.

Coburn, D. R. 1970. "Disparity in Sentences and Appellate Review of Sentencing." *Rutgers L. Rev.* 25:207.

Cohen, B. L. 1970a. "The Penology of the Talmud." *Israel L. Rev.* 5:53.

Cohen, B. L. 1970b. *Law Without Order: Capital Punishment and the Liberals*. Westport, Conn.: Arlington House.

Cohen, B. L. 1972a. "Crime and the New Liberalism." *Canada Month* 12, 5:9.

Cohen, B. L. 1972b. "The Need for Capital Punishment." *Chitty's L. J.* 20:86.

Cohen, F. 1970. "Comments on the Scrupled-Juror Problem." *J. Legal Education* 23:21.

Cohen, H. A. 1974. "The Constitutional Status of the Death Penalty in New Jersey." *Criminal Justice Quarterly* 2:5.

Cohen, J. A. 1968. "The Death Penalty in Red China," in *The Criminal Process in the People's Republic of China, 1949–1963*, J. A. Cohen, ed., 1968, p.535. Cambridge, Mass.: Harvard University Press.

Cohen, S. B. 1968. "Psychiatrists Look at Capital Punishment." *Psychiatric Digest* 29:45.

Cohen, Y. A. 1969. "Ends and Means in Political Control: State Organization and the Punishment of Adultery, Incest, and Violation of Celibacy." *The American Anthropologist* 71:658.

*Coker* v. *Georgia.* 1977. 433 U.S. 584, 97 Sup. Ct. 2861.

Colquitt, J. A. 1982. "The Death Penalty Laws of Alabama." *Alab. L. Rev.* 35 (Winter):213.

Columbia Law Review. 1945. "Federal Kidnaping Act—Imposition of Death Penalty." *Columbia L. Rev.* 45:797.

Columbia Law Review. 1978. "*Coker* v. *Georgia* (97 Sup. Ct. 2861): Disproportionate Punishment and the Death Penalty for Rape." *Columbia L. Rev.* 78 (December):1714.

Colussi, A. 1981–1982. "Unconstitutionality of Death Qualifying a Jury prior to the Determination of Guilt: The Fair Cross-section Requirement in Capital Cases." *Creighton L. Rev.* 15:595.

Combs, M. W. 1980. "Supreme Court and Capital Punishment: Uncertainty, Ambiguity, and Judicial Control." *Southern University L. Rev.* 7 (Fall):1.

*Commonwealth* v. *O'Neal.* 1975. 339 N.E. 2d 676.

Congressional Digest. 1973a. "Pro and Con Discussion, Should Capital Punishment be Abolished in the United States, Pro: Lunsford (p.10); Sellin (p.26); Lyons (p.12); Lowery (p.16); Amsterdam (p.20); Con: Wyman (p.11); Petersen (p.13); King (p.15); Carrington (p.21); van den Haag (p.25)." *Congressional Digest* 52 (January):1.

Congressional Digest. 1973b. "Past Efforts to Abolish Capital Punishment." *Congressional Digest* 52 (January):2.

Congressional Digest. 1973c. "Excerpts from the Supreme Court's 1972 Capital Punishment Decision." *Congressional Digest* 52 (January):6.

Congressional Digest. 1973d. "Developments Since the Supreme Court Decision." *Congressional Digest* 52 (January):8.

Connecticut Bar Journal. 1966. "Constitutional Law—Eighth Amendment: Cruel and Unusual Punishment: A Vehicle for Reappraising the Application of the Criminal Law to the Individual." *Ct. B. J.* 40:521.

Connecticut Bar Journal. 1971. "Constitutionality of the Connecticut Penal Code (Title 53a) Guilty Plea/Capital Punishment Provisions." *Ct. B. J.* 45:441.

Connecticut, Office of Legislative Research, Connecticut General Assembly. 1973. "Capital Punishment in Connecticut After *Furman* v. *Georgia*" (March 1973).

Conners, C. S. 1982. "The Death Penalty in Military Courts: Constitutionally Imposed?" *UCLA L. Rev.* 30 (December):366.

Connor, P. S. 1980. "Death Penalty (Survey of Virginia Law, 1978–1979)." *Va. L. Rev.* 66 (March):264.

Conway, D. A. 1974. "Capital Punishment and Deterrence: Some Considerations in Dialogue Form." *Philosophy and Public Affairs* 3:431.

Coody, D. W. 1982. "Fifth and Sixth Amendments—Privilege Against Self-Incrimination and Right to Counsel—Compelled Competency Examination in Capital Punishment Cases (Case Note), *Estelle* v. *Smith* 101 Sup. Ct. 1866 (1981)." *Am. J. of Crim. L.* 10 (March):65.

Cook, F. J. 1956. "Capital Punishment: Does It Prevent Crime?" *The Nation* (March 10):194.

Cook, J. G. 1980. "Punishment" (Criminal Law in Tennessee in 1979—A Critical Survey). *Tenn. L. Rev.* 48:47.

Cooper, D. D. 1974. *The Lesson of the Scaffold: The Public Execution Controversy in Victorian England.* Athens, Ohio: Ohio University Press.

Cornelius, B. G. 1981. "California's Death Penalty Statute: Dead or Alive?" *Criminal Justice Journal* 4 (Spring):525.

Cornell Law Review. 1969. "*United States* v. *Jackson*: Guilty Pleas and Replacement of Capital Punishment Provisions." *Cornell L. Rev.* 54:448.

Costello, M. 1973a. "Death Penalty Revival." *Editorial Research Reports* (January 10):23.

Costello, M. 1973b. "Society's Views of Criminal Justice." *Editorial Research Reports* (January 10):29.

Costello, M. 1973c. "Early American Views and Use of Ultimate Penalty." *Editorial Research Reports* (January 10):30.

Costello, M. 1973d. "Trend Toward Fewer Executions in the United States." *Editorial Research Reports* (January 10):32.

Costello, M. 1973e. "Status of Capital Punishment in Other Countries." *Editorial Research Reports* (January 10):35.

Cowan, C., W. Thompson, and P. C. Ellsworth. 1983. "The Effects of Death Qualification on Jurors' Predisposition to Convict and on the Quality of Deliberation." To be published in *Crime and Delinquency.*

Cozart, R. 1959. "Clemency under the Federal System." *Fed. Prob.* 23 (September):3.

Craig, J. M. 1981. "Capital Punishment in North Carolina: The 1977 Death Penalty Statute and the North Carolina Supreme Court." *N. C. L. Rev.* 59 (June):911.

Crime and Delinquency. 1964. "Policy Statement on Capital Punishment." National Council on Crime and Delinquency, Board of Trustees. *Crime and Delinquency* 10:105.

Crime and Delinquency. 1973. "La Guillotine in 20th Century." *Crime and Delinquency* 19:290.

Crime and Delinquency. 1980. "Capital Punishment in the United States" (Symposium). *Crime and Delinquency* 26 (October):441.

Criminal Law Bulletin. 1972. "Recent Decisions, Decisions of the United States Supreme Court, Cruel and Unusual Punishment—Death Penalty." *Crim. L. B.* 8:700.

Criminal Law Review. 1969. "Capital Punishment." *Crim. L. Rev.* (1969):621.

Cronin, J. D. 1981. "Constitutional Law—Capital Punishment." *Massachusetts L. Rev.* 66 (Spring):100.

Cucinotta, G. B. 1969. "*Witherspoon*—Will the Due Process Clause Further Regulate the Imposition of the Death Penalty?" *Duquesne L. Rev.* 7:414.

Curran, W. J., and W. Cascells. 1980. "The Ethics of Medical Participation in Capital Punishment by Intravenous Drug Injection." *N. E. J. of Med.* 302 (January):1980.

Current History. 1971. *"McGautha* v. *California." Current History* (July):40.

Curvant, B. A., and F. N. Waldrop. 1952. "The Murderer in the Mental Institution." *The Annals* 284:35.

Cutler, J. E. 1907. "Capital Punishment and Lynching." *The Annals* 29:622.

Daniels, W. J. 1977. "Non Occides: Thurgood Marshall and the Death Penalty." *Texas So. U. L. Rev.* 4:243.

Dann, R. H. 1935. "The Deterrent Effect of Capital Punishment." *Friends Social Service Series* 29:1.

Dann, R. H. 1952. "Capital Punishment in Oregon." *The Annals* 284:110. Reprinted in Bedau (1967b), p. 327, as "Abolition and Restoration of the Death Penalty in Oregon."

Darrow, C. 1939. "Capital Punishment." In Johnson, 1939, p. 94.

Darrow, C., and R. L. Calder. 1928. "Is Capital Punishment Right? A Debate." *The Forum* 80 (September):327.

Davidow, R. P., and G. D. Lowe. 1979. "Attitudes of Potential and Present Members of the Legal Profession Toward Capital Punishment—A Survey and Analysis." *Mercer L. Rev.* 30:585.

Davis, C. 1980. *Waiting For It.* New York: Harper & Row.

Davis, D. B. 1955. "Murder in New Hampshire." *New England Quarterly* 28:147.

Davis, D. B. 1957. "Movements to Abolish Capital Punishment in America, 1787–1861." *Am. Hist. Rev.* 63:23.

Davis, P. C. 1978a. "Texas Capital Sentencing Procedures: The Role of the Jury and the Restraining Hand of the Expert." *J. Crim. L.* 69:300.

Davis, P. C. 1978b. "The Death Penalty and the Current State of the Law." *Crim. L. B.* 14 (January–February):5.

Davis, R. A. 1975. "Capital Punishment and the Pennsylvania Prison Society." *Prison Journal* 53:72.

Davis, R. P. 1974. *The Tasmanian Gallows.* Hobart, Tasmania: Cat & Fiddle Press.

Dawson, M. 1980. "Is the Death Penalty in the Military Cruel and Unusual?" *J.A.S.J.* 31:53.

Dawtry, F. 1966. "The Abolition of the Death Penalty in Britain." *British J. of Criminology* 6:183.

Dawtry, F. 1967. "Criminal Statistics." *Justice of the Peace and Local Government Review* (September 2):543.

Day. 1971a. "Kill Me Now!" *The Intermountain Observer* (May):1.

Day. 1971b. "Raymond Allen Snowden." *The Intermountain Observer* (May):15.

Death Penalty Conference. 1977. Howard University, Washington, D.C. Jointly sponsored by the NAACP Legal Defense Fund and the Center for Studies in Criminology and Criminal Justice, University of Pennsylvania.

Decker, D. H. 1982. "When Does Double Jeopardy Preclude the Imposition of a Harsher Sentence at a Retrial? (Case Note), *Bullington* v. *Missouri* 101 Sup. Ct. 1852 (1981)." *Southern Texas L. J.* 23 (Winter):241.

Deets, L. E. 1948. "Changes in Capital Punishment Policy Since 1939." *J. C. L. C.* 38:584.

DeMent, I. 1968. "A Plea for the Condemned." *The Alabama Lawyer* 29:440.

Department of Commerce. 1966. *The National Income and Product Accounts of the United States, 1929–1965 Statistical Tables.* U.S. Department of Commerce.

Department of Commerce. Annual. *Survey of Current Business.* U.S. Department of Commerce.

DePaul Law Review. 1960. "Review of Legal But Excessive Sentences in the Federal Courts." *DePaul L. Rev.* 10:104.

DePaul Law Review. 1972. "Constitutional Law—The Remains of the Death Penalty: *Furman* v. *Georgia.*" *DePaul L. Rev.* 22:481.

DePaul Law Review. 1979. "Evolution of the Eighth Amendment and the Standards for the Imposition of the Death Penalty." *DePaul L. Rev.* 28:351.

DePaul Law Review. 1981. "Constitutional Procedure for the Imposition of the Death Penalty—*Godfrey* v. *Georgia* (100 Sup. Ct. 1759)." *DePaul L. Rev.* 30 (Spring):721.

Derryberry, L. 1973. "Cruel and Unusual Punishment." *Texas Police J.* 21 (October):10.

Desky, R. M. 1963. "Should Capital Punishment Be Abolished in California?" *The Commonwealth* 39 (November 11):19.

Dession, G. H. 1954. "Gowers Report and Capital Punishment." *N. Y. U. L. Rev.* 29:1061.

Detroit College Law Review. 1976. "*Gregg* v. *Georgia* (96 Sup. Ct. 2909): The Search for the Civilized Standard." *Detroit College L. Rev.* 1976:645.

DeWolf, L. H. 1973. "The Death Penalty: Cruel, Unusual, Unethical, and Futile." *Religion in Life* 42:37.

Diamond, B. L. 1975. "Murder and the Death Penalty: A Case Report." *Am. J. of Orthopsychiatry* 45 (July):712.

Dickens, C. 1850. "Capital Punishment, Execution of the Mannings." *Western L. J.* 7:351.

Dickinson Law Review. 1977. "Resurrection of Capital Punishment—The 1976 Death Penalty Cases." *Dickinson L. Rev.* 81:543.

Dikijian, A. 1969. "Capital Punishment—A Selected Bibliography, 1940–1968." *Crime and Delinquency* 15:162.

Dillon, R. G. 1980. "Capital Punishment in Egalitarian Society: The Meta' Case." *Journal of Anthropological Research* 36 (Winter):437.

DiSalle, M. V. 1959. "Special Message on Capital Punishment." *Ohio S. Senate J.* (February 10):5.

DiSalle, M. V. 1964. "Comments on Capital Punishment and Clemency." *Ohio State L. J.* 25:71.

DiSalle, M. V. (with L. G. Bochman). 1965. *The Power of Life or Death.* New York: Random House.

DiSalle, M. V. 1967a. "Capital Punishment: Deterrent to Crime—Or to Justice." *Industrial Union Department Agenda* (A.F.L.–C.I.O.) (May):20.

DiSalle, M. V. 1967b. "Justice, the Law, and Capital Punishment." *Am. J. of Psychiatry* 123 (May):11.

DiSalle, M. V. 1968. Testimony, in Hart Hearings, p. 8.

DiSalle, M. V. 1969. "Trends in the Abolition of Capital Punishment." *U. Toledo L. Rev.*:1.

*District Attorney of Suffolk County* v. *James Watson and Others.* 1980. 411 N.E. 2d 1274.

Dix, G. E. 1977a. "Death Penalty, 'Dangerousness,' Psychiatric Testimony, and Professional Ethics." *Am. J. of Crim. L.* 5 (May):151.

Dix, G. E. 1977b. "Administration of the Texas Death Penalty Statute: Constitutional Infirmities Related to the Prediction of Dangerousness." *Texas L. Rev.* 55 (November):1343.

Dix, G. E. 1979. "Appellate Review of the Decision to Impose Death." *Georgetown L. J.* 68 (October):97.

Dix, G. E. 1980. "Constitutional Validity of the Texas Capital Murder Scheme: A Continuing Question." *Texas B. J.* 43 (July):627.

Dix, G. E. 1981. "Expert Prediction Testimony in Capital Sentencing: Evidentiary and Constitutional Considerations." *Am. Crim. L. Rev.* 19 (Summer):1.

Doleschal, E. D. 1969. "The Deterrent Effect of Legal Punishment." *Information Rev. on Crime & Del.* 1,7 (June).

Donnelly, R. C. 1952. "Unconvicting the Innocent." *Vanderbilt L. Rev.* 6:20.

Donnelly, R. C., and C. W. Brewster. 1961. "Capital Punishment in Connecticut." *Ct. B. J.* 35:39.

Donnelly, S. J. M. 1978. "Theory of Justice, Judicial Methodology, and the Constitutionality of Capital Punishment: Rawls, Dworkin, and a Theory of Criminal Responsibility." *Syracuse L. Rev.* 29:1109.

Donohue, J. J. III. 1980. "*Godfrey* v. *Georgia* (100 Sup. Ct. 1759): Creative Federalism, the Eighth Amendment, and the Evolving Law of Death." *Catholic U. L. Rev.* 30:13.

Dorin, D. D. 1981. "Two Different Worlds: Criminologists, Justices and Racial Determination in the Imposition of Capital Punishment in Rape Cases." *J. Crim. L.* 72 (Winter):1667.

Douglas, C. H. 1977. "Death Penalty: Chinese Style." *Trial* 13 (February):44.

Dressler, J. 1979. "Jurisprudence of Death by Another: Accessories and Capital Punishment." *U. Colorado L. Rev.* 51:17.

Drewery, G. 1974. "Parliament and Hanging: Further Episodes in an Undying Saga." *Parliamentary Affairs* 27:251.

Drinan, R. F. 1952. "The State and Insane Condemned Criminals." *Jurist* 12:92.

Duff, C. 1955. *A New Handbook on Hanging.* Chicago: Henry Regnery.

Duff, C. 1974. *A Handbook on Hanging* (reprint of 1961 edition). Totowa, N.J.: Rowman & Littlefield.

Duff, L. B. 1949. *The County Kerchief.* Toronto: Ryerson Press.

Duffy, C. R., and A. Hirshberg. 1962. *88 Men and 2 Women.* New York: Doubleday.

Duffy, C. R., and A. Hirshberg. 1968. Testimony, in Hart Hearings, p. 19.

Duke Law Journal. 1968. "Jury Challenges, Capital Punishment, and *Labat* v. *Bennett*: A Reconciliation." *Duke L. J.* (1968):283.

Duquesne Law Review. 1981. "Constitutional Law—Eighth Amendment—Capital Punishment—State Death Penalty Statutes—Procedural Safeguards." *Duquesne L. Rev.* 19 (Spring):539.

Durant, W. 1927. "Abolish Capital Punishment, Yes." American League to Abolish Capital Punishment. Reprinted from the *N.Y. Telegram* (May 6, 1927).

Durant, W. 1939. "Abolish the Death Penalty." In Johnson, 1939, p. 106.

Durham, B. T. 1980. "Constitutional Law—Broader Protection Provided by the Ex-Post Facto Provision of the Tennessee Constitution than by the Federal Constitution (Case Note), *Miller* v. *State* 584 S.W. 2d 6758 (Tenn. 1979)." *Memphis S. U. L. Rev.* 10:378.

Durick, J. A. 1973. "Death Penalty Unchristian." *National Catholic Reporter* (March 16):1.

Durkheim, E. 1933. *The Division of Labor in Society.* Translated by G. Simpson. New York: Macmillan.

Eastern Africa Law Review. 1970. "Uganda and Kondos (Aggravated Robbers): The Capital Punishment Revisited." *E. Africa L. Rev.* 3:83.

Edison, M. 1970. "The Empirical Assault on Capital Punishment." *J. Legal Education* 23:2.

Ehrenzweig, A. A. 1965. "A Psychoanalysis of the Insanity Plea—Clues to the Problems of Criminal Responsibility and Insanity in the Death Cell." *Crim. L. B.* 1:3.

Ehrhardt, C. W., P. A. Hubbart, L. H. Levinson, W. M. Smiley, and T. A. Wills. 1973a. "The Aftermath of *Furman*: The Florida Experience, I. The Future of Capital Punishment in Florida: Analysis and Recommendations." *J. C. L. C.* 64:2.

Ehrhardt, C. W., and L. H. Levinson. 1973b. "The Aftermath of *Furman*: The Florida Experience, II. Florida's Legislative Response to *Furman*: An Exercise in Futility?" *J. C. L. C.* 64:10.

Ehrlich, I. 1972. "Deterrent Effect of Criminal Law Enforcement." *J. Legal Studies* 1:259.

Ehrlich, I. 1973. "The Deterrent Effect of Capital Punishment: A Question of Life and Death." (Working Paper # 18). National Bureau of Economic Research.

Ehrlich, I. 1975a. "The Deterrent Effect of Capital Punishment: A Question of Life and Death." *Am. Ec. Rev.* 65 (June):397.

Ehrlich, I. 1975b. "Data Sources." (Unpublished memorandum on file with the *Yale L. J.*)

Ehrlich, I. 1975c. "Deterrence: Evidence and Inference." *Yale L. J.* 85 (December–January):209.

Ehrlich, I. 1975d. "Rejoinder." *Yale L. J.* 85 (December–January):368.

Ehrlich, I. 1977. "Capital Punishment and Deterrence: Some Further Thoughts and Additional Evidence." *J. Pol. Econ.* 85 (August):741.

Ehrlich, I. 1982. "Of Positive Methodology, Ethics, and Polemics in Deterrence Research." *British J. of Criminology* 22 (April):124.

Ehrlich, I., and J. C. Gibbons. 1977. "On the Measurement of the Deterrent

Effect of Capital Punishment and the Theory of Deterrence." *J. Legal Studies* 6 (January):35.

Ehrmann, H. B. 1952. "The Death Penalty and the Administration of Justice." *The Annals* 284:73. Reprinted in Bedau (1967b), p. 415, and Sellin (1967a), p. 189.

Ehrmann, H. B. 1969. *The Case That Will Not Die:* Commonwealth v. Sacco and Vanzetti. Boston: Little, Brown.

Ehrmann, S. R. 1961. "Capital Punishment Today—Why?" In Herbert Bloch, ed., *Crime in America*, pp.81,91. New York: Philosophical Library, Inc.

Ehrmann, S. R. 1962. "For Whom the Chair Waits." *Fed. Prob.* 26 (March):14. Reprinted in Bedau (1967b), p. 492, as "The Human Side of Capital Punishment," and in McCafferty (1972), p. 187.

Einstadter, W. J. 1965. "The Hangman's Fear." *Issues in Criminology* 1:124.

Eisenberg, H. 1978. "Team Defense—The Holistic Approach: An Interview with Millard Farmer." *NLADA Briefcase* 36 (March):16.

Elkins, S. M. 1968. *Slavery*. Chicago: University of Chicago Press.

Ellis, H. D., Jr. 1981. "Constitutional Law: The Death Penalty: A Critique of the Philosophical Bases Held to Satisfy the Eighth Amendment Requirements for its Justification." *Okla. L. Rev.* 34 (Summer):567.

Ellsworth, P. C., and L. Ross. 1983. "Public Opinion and Capital Punishment: A Close Examination of the Views of the Abolitionists and Retentionists." *Crime and Delinquency* 29, 1:116.

England, J. C. 1977. "Capital Punishment in the Light of Constitutional Evolution: An Analysis of Distinctions Between *Furman* and *Gregg* (*Gregg* v. *Georgia*, 96 Sup. Ct. 2909)." *Notre Dame Lawyer* 52 (April):596.

England, Royal Commission on Capital Punishment. 1953. "Report." H.M.S.O.

England, Select Committee on Capital Punishment." 1931. "Report."

*Enmund* v. *Florida*. 1982. 73. L. 2d 1140, 102 Sup. Ct. 3368.

Enslin, M. S. 1972. "Capital Punishment—Cruel and Unusual?" *Religion in Life* 41:254.

Erez, E. 1981. "Thou Shalt not Execute: Hebrew Law Perspective on Capital Punishment." *Criminology* 19 (May):25.

Erickson, W. H. 1982. "Pronouncements of the U.S. Supreme Court Relating to the Criminal Law Field: 1981–1982." *Colorado Lawyer* 11 (September):2327.

Erikson, K. T. 1966. *The Wayward Puritans*. New York: John Wiley.

Erskine, H. 1970. "The Polls: Capital Punishment." *Public Opinion Quarterly* 34:290.

Eshelman, B. E., and F. Riley. 1972. *Death Row Chaplain*. Englewood Cliffs, N.J.: Prentice-Hall.

Espy, M. W., Jr. 1980. "Capital Punishment and Deterrence: What the Statisics Cannot Show." *Crime and Delinqency* 26 (October):537.

Europe, The Council of Europe, European Committee on Crime Problems. 1967. "The Effectiveness of Punishment and Other Measures of Treatment."

Evjen, V. H. 1968. "Let's Abolish Capital Punishment." *Lutheran Women* (March). Reprinted in McCafferty, p. 218.

Ewer, P. A. 1980. "Eighth Amendment—The Death Penalty (Case Note), *Godfrey v. Georgia* 100 Sup. Ct. 1759 (1980)." *J. C. L. C.* 71:538.

Ewing, C. P. 1982. "Psychologists and Psychiatrists in Capital Sentencing Proceedings: Experts or Executioners?" *Social Action and the Law* 8 (July/August):67.

Existential Psychiatry. 1966. "Capital Punishment." *Existential Psychiatry* 1:7.

Faia, M. A. 1982. "Willful, Deliberate, Premeditated and Irrational: Reflections on the Futility of Executions." State Government 55, 1:14.

Fair, R. C. 1970. "The Estimation of Simultaneous Equation Models with Lagged Endogenous Variables and First Order Serially Correlated Errors." *Econometrics* 38:507.

Farrell, R. A., and V. L. Swigert. 1978. "Legal Disposition of Inter-Group and Intra-Group Homicides." *Sociological Quarterly* 19, 22:565.

Fattah, E. A. 1972. *A Study of the Deterrent Effect of Capital Punishment with Special Reference to the Canadian Situation.* Department of the Solicitor General, Canada.

Fattah, E. A. 1981. "Is Capital Punishment a Unique Deterrent? A Dispassionate Review of Old and New Evidence." *Canadian J. of Criminology* 23 (July):291.

Federal Bureau of Investigation. 1976. *Uniform Crime Reporting Handbook.* Washington, D.C.: U.S. Government Printing Office.

Federal Bureau of Investigation. Annual. *Uniform Crime Reports for the United States.* U.S. Department of Justice.

Federal Bureau of Prisons. 1958. "Executions." *National Prisoner Statistics*, Bulletin no. 20. U.S. Department of Justice.

Federal Bureau of Prisons. 1971. "Capital Punishment 1930–1970." *National Prisoner Statistics*, Bulletin no. 46. U.S. Department of Justice.

Feierabend, I. K., R. L. Feierabend, and B. A. Nesvold. 1969. "Social Change and Political Violence: Cross National Patterns." In H. D. Graham and T. R. Gurr, eds., *Violence in America*, p. 497. Government Printing Office.

Felson, R. B., and H. J. Steadman. 1979. "Situations and Processes Leading to Criminal Violence." New York State Department of Mental Hygiene.

Feltham, J. D. 1969. "Common Law and the Execution of Insane Criminals." *Melbourne U. L. Rev.* 4:434.

Ferrer, J. F. 1972. "The Plot to Kill Capital Punishment." *World* (November 7):19.

Feuer, L. 1959. *Marx and Engels: Basic Writing in Politics and Philosophy.* New York: Doubleday.

*Fikes* v. *Alabama.* 1961. 352 U.S. 191.

Filler, L. 1952. "Movements to Abolish the Death Penalty in the United States." *The Annals* 284:124. Reprinted in Sellin (1967a), p. 22.

Finkel, R. H. 1967. "A Survey of Capital Offenses." In Sellin, 1967a, p. 22.

Fitzgerald, R., and P. C. Ellsworth. 1983. "Due Process vs. Crime Control: Death Qualification and Jury Attitudes." To be published in *Crime and Delinquency*.

Fitzroy, H. W. K. 1936. "The Punishment of Crime in Provincial Pennsylvania." *Penn. Mag. of History of Biographies* 60:242.

Flammang, C. J. 1974. "The Issue of Capital Punishment." *Law and Order* 22 (July):28.

Florida Civil Liberties Union. 1964. "Rape: Selective Electrocution Based on Race" (pamphlet).

Florida, Governor's Committee. 1972. "A Final Report of the Governor's Committee to Study Capital Punishment" (November 17, 1972).

Florida, Special Commission for the Study of Abolition of Death Penalty in Capital Cases. 1965. Report.

Florida State University Law Review. 1974. "Florida's Legislative and Judicial Responses to *Furman* v. *Georgia* (92 Sup. Ct. 2726): An Analysis and Criticism." *Florida State U. L. Rev.* 2:108.

Florida State University Law Review. 1978. "Step Toward Uniformity: Review of Life Sentences in Capital Cases." *Florida State U. L. Rev.* 6:1015.

Fogelson, R. M., ed. 1974. *Capital Punishment: Nineteenth-Century Arguments*. New York: Arno Press.

Foley, L. A., and R. S. Powell. 1982. "The Discretion of Prosecutors, Judges and Jurists in Capital Cases." *Criminal Justice Rev.* 7(2):16.

Fordham Law Review. 1968. "Criminal Procedure—Jury Selection—Jury's Imposition of Death Penalty Held Unconstitutional Where Procedure for Choosing Jurors Eliminated Those with Scruples Against Capital Punishment Not Amounting to Absolute Opposition." *Fordham L. Rev.* 37:129.

Fordham Law Review. 1973. "Constitutional Law—Capital Punishment—Death Penalty as Presently Administered Held Unconstitutional." *Fordham L. Rev.* 41:671.

Forman, W. H., Jr. 1970. "De Facto Abolition of the Death Penalty in Louisiana?" *La. B. J.* 18:199.

Forst, B. E. 1977. "Deterrent Effect of Capital Punishment: A Cross-State Analysis of the 1960s." *Minn. L. Rev.* 61 (May):743.

Fortas, A. 1977. "The Case Against Capital Punishment." *The New York Times Magazine* (January 23):8.

Forucci, G. D., R. Richard, and N. K. Stalcup. 1982. "The 'Briggs Instruction' Violates Due Process (California Supreme Court Survey: January–June, 1982) (Case Note), *People* v. *Haskett* 640 P. 2d 776 (Cal. 1982)." *Pepperdine L. Rev.* 10 (December):212.

*Fowler* v. *North Carolina*. 1975. 420 U.S. 969. Brief for the United States as *Amicus Curiae* in *Fowler* v. *North Carolina*.

Frank, J., and B. Frank. 1957. *Not Guilty*. New York: Doubleday.

Frankel, D. S. 1980. "Constitutionality of the Mandatory Death Penalty for Life-Term Prisoners Who Murder." *N. Y. U. Law Rev.* 55 (October):636.

Frankel, M. E. 1972. "Lawlessness in Sentencing." *U. Cincinnati L. Rev.* 41:1.

Frazier, S. H. 1974. "Murder—Single and Multiple." In *Aggression* 52 (res. pub.,

Association for Research in Nervous and Mental Health Disease, 1974), ch. 16.

Fridman, G. H. L. 1955. "Royal Commission on Capital Punishment—Death and Deterrence" *Solicitor's J.* 22:80.

Friedman, L. R. 1960. "Life or Death." *California S. B. J.* 35:534.

Friedman, L. S. 1975. "The Use of Multiple Regression Analysis to Test for a Deterrent Effect of Capital Punishment: Prospects and Problems" (Working Paper No. 38, revised). Graduate School of Public Policy, University of California, Berkeley.

Frink, D. M. 1980. "Constitutional Law—Mandatory Death Penalty Declared Unconstitutional for Failure to Permit Consideration of Any Mitigating Circumstances (Case Note), *State* v. *Cline* 397 A. 2d 1309 (R.I. 1979)." *Suffolk U. L. Rev.* 14:578.

Fruman, N. 1973. "The Guillotine—France Still Uses It Today." *Canada and the World* (March):17.

*Furman* v. *Georgia.* 1972. 408 U.S. 238, 92 Sup. Ct. 2726.

Galifianakas, N., and R. V. Dellums. 1972. "Should the Death Penalty Be Retained? Galifianakas, Yes; Dellums, No." *The American Legion Magazine* (November):16.

Gallemore, J. L., and E. K. Panton. 1972. "Inmate Responses to Lengthy Death Row Confinement." *Am. J. of Psychiatry* 129 (August):2.

Gardner, G. 1959. "Criminal Law: Capital Punishment in Britain." *A. B. A. J.* 45:259.

Gardner, M. R. 1978. "Executions and Indignities—An Eighth Amendment Assessment of Methods of Inflicting Capital Punishment." *Ohio State L. J.* 39:96.

Gardner, M. R. 1979. "Illicit Legislative Motivation as a Sufficient Condition for Unconstitutionality under the Establishment Clause—A Case for Consideration: The Utah Firing Squad." *Wash. U. L. Quarterly* 1979:435.

Gardner, R. L. 1978. "Capital Punishment: The Philosophers and the Court." *Syracuse L. Rev.* 29:1175.

Garfinkel, H. 1949. "Research Note on Inter- and Intra-Racial Homicides." *Social Forces* 27:369.

Garner, J. W. 1907. "Crime and Judicial Inefficiency." *The Annals*:29.

Garrett, S. M. 1982. "Applying the Frye Test to Psychiatric Predictions of Dangerousness in Capital Cases (Case Note), *People* v. *Murtishaw* 631 P. 2d 446 (Cal. 1981)." *Calif. L. Rev.* 70 (July):1069.

Gastil, R. 1971. "Homicide and the Regional Culture of Violence." *Am. Sociol. Rev.* 36:412.

Gayle, M. E. 1976. "S.1 and the Death Penalty: The Persistence of Discretion." *Loyola L. A. L. Rev.* 9 (March):251.

Gaylord, C. L. 1977. "Capital Punishment in Ancient United States: A Legal-Anthropological Perspective from 12,000 A.D." *Case and Comment* 82 (January–February):3.

Geiger, A. L., and S. Selbach. 1982. "S.B. 1: Ohio Enacts Death Penalty Statute." *Univ. of Dayton L. Rev.* 7 (Spring):532.

Geis, G. 1953. "The Death Penalty in Oklahoma." *Proceedings of the Oklahoma Academy of Science* 34:191.

Gelber, S. 1966. "Swinging Is for Squares." *Police* 10 (July–August):41.

Gelles, R. J. 1975. "Family Experience and Public Support of the Death Penalty." *Am. J. of Orthopsychiatry* 45 (July):596.

George, B. J. 1981a. "Sentencing and Offender Treatment: Criminal Procedure." *N. Y. Law School L. Rev.* 26 (Winter):169.

George, B. J. 1981b. "United States Supreme Court 1980–1981 Term: Criminal Law Decisions." *N. Y. Law School L. Rev.* 27 (Winter):1.

George Washington Law Review. 1971. "Constitutional Law—The Eighth Amendment's Proscription of Cruel and Unusual Punishment Precludes Imposition of the Death Sentence for Rape When the Victim's Life Is Neither Taken Nor Endangered." *George Washington L. Rev.* 40:161.

Georgia Law Review. 1968. "Constitutional Law—Jury—Imposition of Death Penalty by Jury from which Jurors Are Disqualified for General Objections to Capital Punishment Violates the Constitutional Guarantee of Trial by an Impartial Jury." *GA. L. Rev.* 3:234.

Gerber, R. J. 1974. "Death Penalty We Can Live With." *Notre Dame Lawyer* 50 (December):251.

Gerber, R. J., and P. D. McAnany. 1967. "Punishment: Current Survey of Philosphy and Law." *St. Louis L. Rev.* 11:491.

Gernet, M. 1915. *Smertnaia Kasn* (Capital Punishment). Moscow.

Gerry, E. T. 1889. "Capital Punishment by Electricity." *North American Rev.* 149:21.

Gerstein, R. M. 1960. "A Prosecutor Looks at Capital Punishment." *J. C. L. C. & P. S.* 51:525. Reprinted in McCafferty (1972), p. 129.

Gerstein, R. S. 1974. "Capital Punishment—'Cruel and Unusual': A Retributivist Response." *Ethics* 85 (October):75.

Gertz, E. 1972. "The Making of the Illinois Constitution of 1970." *John Marshall J. of Prac. & Proc.* 5:215.

Gettinger, S. H. 1979. *Sentenced to Die*. New York: Macmillan.

Giardini, G. I., and R. G. Farrow. 1952. "The Paroling of Capital Offenders." *The Annals* 284:45. Reprinted in Sellin (1967a), p. 169.

Gibbs, J. P. 1968. "Crime, Punishment, and Deterrence." *S.W. Soc. Sci. Quarterly* 48:515.

Gibbs, J. P. 1978a. "Death Penalty, Retribution, and Penal Policy." *J. C. L. C.* 69:291.

Gibbs, J. P. 1978b. "Preventive Effects of Capital Punishment Other Than Deterrence." *Crim. L. B.* 14 (January–February):34.

Gibson, J. L. 1978. "Race as a Determinant of Criminal Sentences: A Methodological Critique and Case Study." *L. S. Rev.* 1978:455.

Gillers, S. 1980. "Deciding Who Dies." *U. Penn. L. Rev.* 129 (November):1.

Gilloon, T. J. 1981. "Capital Punishment and the Burden of Proof: The Sentencing Decision." *Calif. W. L. Rev.* 17:316.

Ginsberg, W. R. 1953. "Punishment of Capital Offenders—A Critical Examination of the Connecticut Statute." *Ct. B. J.* 27:273.

Girsh, F. J. 1978. "*Witherspoon* Question: The Social Science and the Evidence." *NLADA Briefcase* 35:99.

Glaser, D. 1979. "Capital Punishment—Deterrent or Stimulus to Murder? Our Unexamined Deaths and Penalties." *U. Toledo L. Rev.* 10:317.

Glaser, D., and M. S. Ziegler. 1973. "You May Kill, but You Must Promise Not to Use Discretion: *Furman* v. *Georgia* (92 Sup. Ct. 2726)." *Loyola L. A. L. Rev.* 6 (September):526.

Glaser, D., and M. S. Ziegler. 1974. "Use of the Death Penalty v. Outrage at Murder." *Crime and Delinquency* 20 (October):333.

Glendale Law Review. 1977. "California's Death Penalty: Did the Legislature Do Its Job?" *Glendale L. Rev.* 2,1:1.

Glenn, D. A. 1981. "*Witherspoon* Revived (Case Note), *Adams* v. *Texas* 448 U.S. 38 (1980)." *Houston L. Rev.* 18 (May):931.

Glover, E. 1954. "Psychiatric Aspects of the Report on Capital Punishment." *Modern L. Rev.* 17:329.

Glover, J. 1977. *Causing Death & Saving Lives.* New York: Penguin.

Glueck, S., and E. Glueck. 1967. "Beyond Capital Punishment." *Pena de Morte* 1:265.

*Godfrey* v. *Georgia*. 1980. 446 U.S. 420.

Goetz, R. J. 1961. "Should Ohio Abolish Capital Punishment?" *Cleveland-Marshall L. Rev.* 10:365.

Goins, C. 1942. "The Travelling Executioner." *American Mercury* 54:93.

Gold, L. H. 1961. "A Psychiatric Review of Capital Punishment." *J. Forensic Sci.* 6:465.

Goldberg, A. 1972. "Supreme Court Review, 1972, Foreword: The Burger Court, 1971 Term: One Step Forward, Two Steps Backward?" *J. C. L. C. & P. S.* 63:463.

Goldberg, A., and A. M. Dershowitz. 1970. "Declaring the Death Penalty Unconstitutional." *Harv. L. Rev.* 83:1773.

Goldberg, A. J. 1973. "Death Penalty and the Supreme Court." *Ariz. L. Rev.* 15:355.

Goldberg, A. J. 1978a. "Death Penalty for Rape." *Hastings Const. L. Quarterly* 5:1.

Goldberg, A. J. 1978b. "Death Penalty for Rape—Cruel and Unusual Punishment." *La. L. Rev.* 38:868.

Goldberg, F. 1969. "Toward Expansion of *Witherspoon*, Capital Scruples, Jury Bias, and the Use of Psychological Data to Raise Presumptions in the Law." *Harv. C. R.–C. L. L. Rev.* 5:53.

Goldberg, S. 1974. "On Capital Punishment." *Ethics* 85 (October):67.

Golub, D. S. 1980. "Human Rights Commentator (Mexican–American Prisoner Treaties: Capital Punishment: Medicaid Abortions)." *CT. B. J.* 54 (April):156.

Gomes, O. 1980. "Death Penalty for Murder" (India). *Crim. L. J.* 86 (May):20.

Gonciarz, E. F. 1982. "No Blanket Exemption under the Eighth Amendment for Juveniles on Death Row (Case Note), *Eddings* v. *Oklahoma* 50 U.S.L.W. 4161 (1982)." *Capital U. L. Rev.* 11 (Summer):785.

Gonzaga Law Review. 1982. "Refinement of Washington Death Penalty Act." *Gonzaga L. Rev.* 17:715.

Good, E. M. 1967. "Capital Punishment and Its Alternatives in Ancient Near Eastern Law." *Stanford L. Rev.* 19:947.

Goodman, L. H., T. Miller, and P. DeForrest. 1966. *A Study of the Deterrent Value of Crime Prevention Measures as Perceived by Criminal Offenders.* Institute for Defense Analyses, Bureau of Social Science Research.

Goolrick, F. H. 1981. "Counsel for the Condemned." *Student Lawyer* 9 (February):24(7).

Gordon, S. E. 1973. "The Death Penalty: Should Capital Punishment Be Retained or Abolished?" *Canada and the World* (March):18.

Gottlieb, G. H. 1967a. "Testing the Death Penalty." *S. Calif. L. Rev.* 34:268. Reprinted in Bedau (1967b), p. 194, as "Is the Death Penalty Unconstitutional?"

Gottlieb, G. H. 1967b. *Capital Punishment.* Santa Barbara, Calif.: Center for the Study of Democratic Institutions.

Gottlieb, G. H. 1969. "Capital Punishment." *Crime and Delinquency* 15:1.

Goyer, Jean-Pierre. 1972. "Capital Punishment. New Material: 1965–1972." Department of the Solicitor General.

Granucci, A. F. 1969. "Nor Cruel and Unusual Punishment Inflicted—The Original Meaning." *Calif. L. Rev.* 57:839.

Grassberger, R. 1958. "Der Ruf Nach Der Todesstrafe." *Juristiche Blatter* 80:436.

Graves, W. F. 1956. "A Doctor Looks at Capital Punishment." *J. of the Loma Linda U. School of Med.* 10:137. Reprinted in Bedau (1967b), p. 322, as "The Deterrent Effect of Capital Punishment in California."

Gray, L. N., and J. D. Martin. 1969. "Punishment and Deterrence: Another Analysis of Gibbs' Data." *Soc. Sci. Quarterly* 50:389.

Great Britain, Royal Commission on Capital Punishment (1949–1953). 1980. Report. Westport, Conn.: Greenwood Press.

Green, W. M. 1929. "An Ancient Debate on Capital Punishment." *Classical Journal* 241:267.

Greenberg, J. 1972. Testimony, in Hart-Celler Hearings, p. 69.

Greenberg, J. 1977. "Death Penalty—Where Do We Go From Here?" *NLADA Briefcase* 34 (December–January):55.

Greenberg, J. 1982. "Capital Punishment as a System." *Yale L. J.* 91 (April):908.

Greenberg, J., and J. Himmelstein. 1969. "Varieties of Attack on the Death Penalty." *Crime and Delinquency* 15:112. Reprinted in McCafferty (1972), p. 231.

Greene, E. 1982. "Double Jeopardy and Resentencing in Bifurcated Criminal Proceedings (Case Note), *Bullington* v. *Missouri* 101 Sup. Ct. 1852 (1982)." *Brigham Young Univ. L. Rev.* (Winter):192.

*Gregg* v. *Georgia.* 1976. 428 U.S. 153, 96 Sup. Ct. 2909.

Griffiths, O. 1970. "Capital Punishment in South Australia, 1936–1964." *Australia and New Zealand J. of Crime* 3:214.

Grisez, G. G. 1970. "Toward a Consistent Natural-Law Ethics of Killing." *Am. J. of Jurisprudence* (1970):64.

Gross, S., and R. Mauro. 1983. "Patterns of Death: An Analysis of Racial Disparities in Capital Sentencing and Homicide Victimization." Stanford Law School, Stanford University.

Grunhut, M. 1952. "Murder and the Death Penalty in England." *The Annals* 284:158.

Guillot, E. E. 1952. "Abolition and Restoration of the Death Penalty in Missouri." *The Annals* 284:105. Reprinted in Bedau (1967b), p. 351, and Sellin (1967a), p. 124.

Gurr, T. R. 1969a. "New Error-Compensated Measures for Comparing Nations: Some Correlates of Civil Strife." Princeton University Research Monograph No. 25. Princeton, N.J.: Center of International Studies.

Gurr, T. R. 1969b. "A Comparative Study of Civil Strife." In Graham and Gurr, eds., *Violence in America*, vol. 2 of a Staff Report of the National Commission on the Causes and Prevention of Violence. Beverly Hills, Ca.: Sage Publications.

Hadley, Lord Carr of, and D. Burnham. 1980. "The Capital Punishment Debate 1979: A Review." *J. Crim. L.* 44 (May):111.

Hahlo, H. R. 1971. "Scandalizing Justice: The Van Niekerk Story." *U. Toronto L. Rev.* 21:378.

Hale, L. 1961. *Hanged in Error.* Hamondsworth, England: Penguin.

*Hamilton* v. *Alabama.* 1961. 368 U.S. 52.

Hamilton, L., ed. 1854. *Memoirs, Speeches and Writings of Robert Rantoul, Jr.* Boston: John P. Jewett.

Hamilton, V., and L. Rotkin. 1979. "The Capital Punishment Debate; Public Perceptions of Crime and Punishment." *J. App. Soc. Psy.* 9 (July–August):350.

Hammer, R. 1969a. *Between Life and Death.* New York: Macmillan.

Hammer, R. 1969b. "The Case that Could End Capital Punishment, *Maxwell* v. *Bishop.*" *New York Times Magazine* (October 12):46.

*Hance* v. *Zant.* 1983. 696 F. 2d 940 (11th Cir.).

Hancock, C. 1979. "Perils of Calibrating the Death Penalty Through Special Definitions of Murder." *Tulane L. Rev.* 53 (April):828.

Haney, C. 1980. "Juries and the Death Penalty: Readdressing the *Witherspoon* Question." *Crime and Delinquency* 26 (October):512.

Hardman, D. G. 1977. "Notes at an Unfinished Lunch." *Crime and Delinquency* 23 (October):365.

Hare, J. H. 1981. "The Death Penalty" (Annual Survey of South Carolina Law, 1980). *S. C. L. Rev.* 33 (August):53.

Harriman, W. A. 1958. "Mercy Is a Lonely Business." *Saturday Evening Post* (March 22):24.

Harrington, D. C., and J. Dempsey. 1969. "Psychological Factors in Jury Selection." *Tenn. L. Rev.* 37:173.

Harrison, E., and A. V. J. Prather. 1973. *No Time for Dying.* Englewood Cliffs, N.J.: Prentice Hall.

Hart-Celler Hearings. 1972. "Hearings Before Subcommittee No. 3 of the Committee on the Judiciary, House of Representatives, 92nd Cong. 2nd Sess., on H.R. 8414, H.R. 9486: *To Suspend the Death Penalty for Two Years*, H.R. 3243, H.R. 193, H.R. 11797: *To Abolish the Death Penalty under All Laws of the United States, and for Other Purposes*, and H.R. 12217: *To Abolish the Death Penalty under All Laws of the United States, and Authorize the Imposition of Life Imprisonment in Lieu Thereof, and for Other Purposes*, Serial No. 29."

Hart Hearings. 1968. "Hearings Before the Subcommittee on Criminal Laws and Procedures of the Committee on the Judiciary, United States Senate, 90th Cong., 2nd Sess., on S. 1760. *A Bill to Abolish the Death Penalty under All Laws of the United States, and for Other Purposes* (1968)."

Hart, H. L. A. 1957. "Murder and the Principles of Punishment: England and the United States." *N. W. U. L. Rev.* 52:433.

Hartmann, R. 1923. "The Use of Lethal Gas in Nevada Executions." *St. Louis L. Rev.* 8:164.

Hartness, J. 1981. "Proposals to Balance Interests of the Defendant and State in the Selection of Capital Juries: A *Witherspoon* Qualification." *N. C. L. Rev.* 59 (April):767.

Hartung, F. E. 1952. "Trends in the Use of Capital Punishment." *The Annals* 284:8.

Harvard Law Review. 1966. "The Cruel and Unusual Punishment Clause and the Substantive Criminal Law." *Harv. L. Rev.* 79:635.

Harvard Law Review. 1968. "Imposition of Death Penalty by Jury (in Supreme Court, 1967 Term)." *Harv. L. Rev.* 82:156.

Harvard Law Review. 1971. "The Supreme Court, 1970 Term: Standardless Jury Sentencing and Unitary Trials in Capital Cases." *Harv. L. Rev.* 85:282.

Harvard Law Review. 1972. "Cruel and Unusual Punishments (in The Supreme Court, 1971 Term)." *Harv. L. Rev.* 86:76.

Harvard Law Review. 1974. "Discretion and the Constitutionality of the New Death Penalty Statutes." *Harv. L. Rev.* 87 (June):1690.

Harvey, W. B. 1982. "Fifth Amendment Privilege in Bifurcated Capital Trials" (Annual Survey of South Carolina Law, 1981). *S. C. L. Rev.* 34 (August):112.

Haskins, G. L. 1956. "The Capitall Lawes of New England." *Harv. L. S. Bull.* 7:10.

Hastings Law Journal. 1962. "Trial Courts' Power to Reduce Punishments Fixed by Juries in First Degree Murder Trials." *Hastings L. J.* 13:474.

Hastings Law Journal. 1969. "The Jury: A Reflection of the Prejudices of the Community." *Hastings L. J.* 20:1417.

Hausknecht, M. 1979. "Metaphors of Life and Death." *Dissent* 26:331.

Hawkins, G. E. 1969. "Punishment and Deterrence: The Educative, Moralizing and Habituative Effects." *Wisc. L. Rev.* (1969):550.

Hayner, N. S., and J. R. Cranor. 1952. "The Death Penalty in Washington State." *The Annals* 284:105.

Hazard, G. C., Jr., and D. W. Louisell. 1962a. "Death, the State, and the Insane." *UCLA L. Rev.* 9:381.

Hazard, G. C., Jr., and D. W. Louisell. 1962b. "Insanity as a Defense: The Bifurcated Trial." *Calif. L. Rev.* 49:805.

Hearings before the Committee on the Judiciary, 86th Congr., 2nd Sess., House of Representatives, on H.R. 870: *To Abolish the Death Penalty* (1960).

Hearings before the Subcommittee on Criminal Laws and Procedures of the Senate Committee on the Judiciary, 90th Cong., 2nd Sess., on s1760: *To Abolish the Death Penalty* (1970).

Hearings before the Subcommittee on Criminal Laws and Procedures of the Committee on the Judiciary, U.S. Senate, 92nd Cong., 2nd Sess., Reform of the Federal Criminal Laws, Staff Report: *State Experience with Bifurcated Trial in Capital Cases.* Part III, Subpart A (1972): 1156.

Heline, T. 1965. *Capital Punishment: Trends Toward Abolition.* Los Angeles: New Age.

Hellwig, L. G. 1982. "The Death Penalty in Washington: An Historical Perspective." *Wash. L. Rev.* 57 (July):525.

Henry, J. W., Jr. 1960. "*Tennessee v. Wash Jones*: The Closing Argument for the Defense." *A. B. A. J.* 46:52.

Henson, R. G. 1971. "Utilitarianism and the Wrongness of Killing." *Philosophical Rev.* 80:320.

Herman, A. 1964. "An Acerbic Look at the Death Penalty in Ohio." *Western Reserve L. Rev.* 15:512.

Hermann, P. J. 1969. "Occupations of Jurors as an Influence on Their Verdict." *Forum* 5:150.

Hertel, J. R. 1972. "Can a Christian Defend Capital Punishment?" *America* (October 7):262.

Hertz, R., and R. Weisberg. 1981. "In Mitigation of the Penalty of Death: *Lockett* v. *Ohio* and the Capital Defendant's Right to Consideration of Mitigating Circumstances." *Calif. L. Rev.* 69 (March):317.

Hewlings, D. 1972. "The Treatment of Murderers." *Howard J. of Pen. C. P.* 13:96.

Higgins, T. J. 1973. "Why the Death Penalty?" *Triumph* (February):20.

Hill, S. 1967. "The Abolition of Capital Punishment in England." *Women Lawyers J.* 53:7.

Hinds, L. S. 1976. "Death Penalty: Continuing Threat to America's Poor." *Freedomways* 16, 1:39.

Hirschi, T., and H. C. Selvin. 1967. *Delinquency Research: An Appraisal of Analytic Methods.* New York: The Free Press.

Hitchens, C. 1974. "Quare Fellows." *New Statesman* 87 (June 28):917.

Hochkammer, W. O., Jr. 1969. "The Capital Punishment Controversy." *J. C. L. C. & P. S.* 60:360.

Hoenack, S. A., and W. C. Weiler. 1980. "A Structural Model of Murder Behavior and the Criminal Justice System." *Am. Ec. Rev.* 70 (June):327.

Hofstra Law Review. 1974. "*Furman* v. *Georgia* (92 Sup. Ct. 2726): Will the Death of Capital Punishment Mean a New Life for Bail?" *Hofstra L. Rev.* 2:432.

Hogan, B. 1974. "Killing Ground: 1964–73." *Crim. L. Rev.* 1974 (July):387.

Hogan, B. 1980. "Reform of the Law of Homicide." *Univ. of New Brunswick L. J.* 29:9.

Hogan, J. 1955. "Story on Capital Punishment." *Calif. L. Rev.* 43:76.

Hogan, J. 1961. "Murder by Perjury." *Fordham L. Rev.* 30:285.

Holloway, A. 1967. *The Death Penalty in Ohio.* Barnesville, Oh.: Religious Society of Friends.

Hook, S. 1967. "The Death Sentence." Reprinted in Bedau (1967b), p. 146.

Hoover, J. E. 1960. "Statements in Favor of the Death Penalty." *FBI L. Enforcement Bull. and Uniform Crime Reports* 29:30.

Hornum, F. 1956. "Two Debates: France, 1791, England, 1956." In Sellin, 1967a, p.55.

Horwitz, E. L. 1973. *Capital Punishment, U.S.A.* Philadelphia: Lippincott.

Houchins, P. 1971. "Racial Discrimination in Punishment for Crime." *A. L. R.* 3, 40:227.

*House* v. *Balkcom.* 1979. C78-1471A (N.D. GA.).

Houston Law Review. 1967. "The Federal Kidnaping Act Is Unconstitutional in that It Impairs the Free Exercise of the Sixth Amendment Right to Trial by Jury [U.S.D.C.]." *Houston L. Rev.* 5:166.

Houston Law Review. 1971a. "The Imposition of the Death Penalty for Rape Where the Victim's Life Has Been Neither Taken nor Endangered Constitutes Cruel and Unusual Punishment under the Eighth Amendment." *Houston L. Rev.* 8:795.

Houston Law Review. 1971b. "Where It Is Doubtful Whether a Prospective Juror Has Absolute Conscientious Scruples Against, and Could Never Vote For, the Death Sentence, the Trial Court Cannot Resolve That Doubt to Exclude Even One Venireman." *Houston L. Rev.* 8:967.

Houston Law Review. 1974. "House Bill 200: The Legislative Attempt to Reinstate Capital Punishment in Texas." *Houston L. Rev.* 11 (January):410.

Houston Law Review. 1978. "Constitutionality of Imposing the Death Penalty for Felony Murder." *Houston L. Rev.* 15 (January):356.

Howard Law Journal. 1977. "Constitutional Law—State Statute Allowing Jury Discretion in Imposing the Death Sentence which is Not Arbitrary and Capricious and Does Not Violate the Eighth and Fourteenth Amendments." *Howard L. J.* 20:500.

Howard Law Journal. 1978. "Criminal Law—Death as a Punishment for Rape—Disproportional, Cruel, and Unusual Punishment." *Howard L. J.* 29:955.

Howard Law Journal. 1979. "*Furman* to *Gregg*: The Judicial and Legislative History." *Howard L. J.* 22:53.

Howard League for Penal Reform. 1925. *The Abolition of the Death Penalty in Denmark, Holland, Norway, and Sweden.* London: The Howard League for Penal Reform.

Hubbard, F. P., et al. 1982. "A 'Meaningful' Basis for the Death Penalty: The Practice, Constitutionality, and Justice of Capital Punishment in South Carolina." *S. C. L. Rev.* 34 (December):391.

Hughes, G. 1979. "License to Kill." *The New York Review of Books* 26 (II) (June 28):22.

Hughes, T. P. 1965. "Harold P. Brown and the Executioner's Current: An Incident in the AC–DC Controversy." *Publications in the Humanities* 70:143.

Huie, W. B. 1971. *The Execution of Private Slovik*. New York: Delacorte.

Hull, R. 1971. "Death as Proper Punishment: The Public Debate Hides Much." *Canada Month* 12, 6:13.

Idaho Law Review. 1972. "Sentencing for Murder." *Idaho L. Rev.* 8:284.

Idaho Law Review. 1978. "*State* v. *Creech* [(Idaho)—P. 2d—] and *State* v. *Lindquist* [(Idaho)—P. 2d—]; Retroactive Capital Punishment in Idaho." *Idaho L. Rev.* 14:493.

Illinois, Department of Public Welfare. 1930. "Tenth (Eleventh and Twelfth) Report of the Department of Public Welfare" (1928, 1929, 1930).

Illinois, Legislative Council. 1951. "Bills to Abolish the Death Penalty in Illinois."

Illinois, Legislative Council. 1954. "Capital Punishment for Serious Sex Offenses." Bulletin 2–130.

Illinois, Legislative Council. 1972. "Reinstatement of the Death Penalty."

Ingram, T. R., ed. 1963. *Essays on the Death Penalty*. Houston, Tex.: St. Thomas.

International Commission of Jurists Bulletin. 1961. "History of the Death Penalty in the U.S.S.R." *Int. Comm. of Jurists Bull.* 12:55.

International Human Rights Law Group. 1980. "Complaint Alleging a Violation of Human Rights in the United States of America" (submitted to the Inter-American Commission on Human Rights by Nicholas Ulmer, Esq.).

International Review of Criminal Policy. 1974. "Capital Punishment: Report of the Secretary-General." *Int. Rev. of Criminal Policy* 31:91.

Intramural Law Review of Wake Forest. 1968. "Status of the Death Penalty: Constitutional Restrictions on the Imposition of Capital Punishment." *Intramural L. Rev. of Wake Forest* 5:183.

Iowa Law Review. 1960. "Criminal Law—Judicial Review, Appellate Modification of Excessive Sentence (*Smith* v. *U.S.*)." *Iowa L. Rev.* 46:159.

Iowa Law Review. 1972. "Mental Suffering under Sentence of Death: A Cruel and Unusual Punishment." *Iowa L. Rev.* 57:814.

Irish Law Times. 1877. "The Abolition of Capital Punishment in Maine." *Irish Law Times* 11:278.

Jackson, B., and D. Christian. 1980. *Death Row*. Boston: Beacon Press.

Jacoby, J. E., and R. Paternoster. 1982. "Sentencing Disparity and Jury Packaging: Further Challenges to the Death Penalty." *J. C. L. C.* 73,1 (Spring):379.

James, A. 1977. *Capital Punishment*. New York: Belmont-Tower.

James, W. E. 1974. "Capital Punishment, an Overview: California, the United States and the Appellate Courts." *The Attorney General's L. J.* [Calif.] 1974:1.

Jayewardene, C. H. S. 1961. "The Death Penalty in Ceylon." *Ceylon J. of History and Social Studies* 3:166.

Jayewardene, C. H. S. 1972. "The Canadian Movement Against the Death Penalty." *Canadian J. of Crime and Correction* 14:366.

Jayewardene, C. H. S. 1973. "The Death Penalty and the Safety of Canadian Policeman." *Canadian J. of Criminolgy and Corrections* 15 (October):356.

Jayewardene, C. H. S. 1977. *Penalty of Death: The Canadian Experiment.* Lexington, Mass.: D.C. Heath.

Jayewardene, C. H. S., and H. Jayewardene. 1980. "The Public Opinion Argument in the Death Penalty Debate." *Canadian J. of Criminology and Corrections* 22 (October):404.

Jeffery, C. R. 1965. "Criminal Behavior and Learning Theory." *J. C. L. C. & P. S.* 56:294.

Jessup, L. K. 1958. "The Abolition of Capital Punishment, a Summary of the Debates During the Twelfth Session of the General Assembly of the United Nations." Quaker Program at the United Nations.

Jewel, H. H. 1961. "The Death Penalty." *Calif. S. B. J.* 36:228.

Johanson, B. O. 1971. "Capital Punishment." *Tydskrif vir Hedendaagse Romeins-Hollandse Reg* 34:350.

Johnson, E. H. 1957. "Selective Factors in Capital Punishment." *Social Forces* 36:165.

Johnson, G. B. 1941. "The Negro and Crime." *Annals* 271:93.

Johnson, J. E., ed. 1939. *Capital Punishment.* New York: H. W. Wilson Co.

Johnson, K. L. 1981. "The Death Row Right to Die: Suicide or Intimate Decision?" *S. Calif. L. Rev.* 54 (March):575.

Johnson, M. D. 1982. "Capital Sentencing Review under Supreme Court Rule 28." *La. L. Rev.* 42 (Spring):1100.

Johnson, R. 1980. "Warehousing for Death: Observations on the Human Environment on Death Row." *Crime and Delinquency* 26 (October):545.

Johnston, J. 1972. *Econometric Models*, 2nd edition. New York: McGraw-Hill Book Company.

Jones, E. 1965. *The Last Two to Hang.* New York: Stein and Day.

Jones, H., and N. Potter. 1981. "Deterrence, Retribution, Denunciation, and the Death Penalty." *UMKC L. Rev.* 49:158.

Joseph, C. C. 1982. "Postconviction Procedure" (Symposium: Developments in the Law, 1980–1981). *La. L. Rev.* 42 (Winter):693.

Josephson, B. R. 1979. *Humane Reciprocity: The Moral Necessity of the Capital Penalty.* Ann Arbor, Mich.: Ann Arbor Books.

Journal of California Law Enforcement. 1972a. "California District Attorneys File Separate Petition for Rehearing on Death Penalty Decision." *J. Calif. Law Enforcement* 6 (April):176.

Journal of California Law Enforcement. 1972b. "Attorney General Younger Petitions California Supreme Court for Rehearing on Death Penalty Decision." *J. Calif. Law Enforcement* 6 (April):167.

Journal of Criminal Law. 1973. "Capital Punishment After *Furman* (*Furman v. Georgia*, 92 Sup. Ct. 2726)." *J. Crim. L.* 64 (September):281.

Journal of Criminal Law. 1978. "Capital Punishment: Death for Murder Only." *J. Crim. L.* 69:179.

Journal of Criminal Law. 1979. "Deterrence and the Death Penalty: A Temporal Cross-Sectional Approach." *J. Crim. L.* 70:235.

Journal of Criminal Law. 1980. "Eighth Amendment—The Death Penalty." *J. Crim. L.* 71:538.

Journal of Criminal Law. 1981. "Death Penalty for Trafficking" *J. Crim. L.* 45 (February):29.

Journal of Criminal Law, Criminology, and Police Science. 1972. "Cruel and Unusual Punishment, the Death Penalty Cases, *Furman, Jackson, Branch,* (in Supreme Court Review)." *J. C. L. C. & P. S.* 63:484.

Journal of Urban Law. 1976. "Criminal Procedure—Jury Selection—A Prospective Juror Who Has Personal Doubts About Capital Punishment and Cannot State that He Will Be Able to Pass Impartially Upon the Guilt of a First Degree Murder Defendant Facing a Mandatory Death Penalty Upon Conviction Can Be Challenged for Cause by the Prosecution." *J. Urban L.* 53 (February):557.

Joyce, J. A. 1961. *Capital Punishment: A World View.* Nashville: Thomas Nelson and Sons.

Judson, C. J., et al. 1969. "A Study of the California Penalty Jury in First Degree Murder Cases." *Stanford L. Rev.* 21:1297.

Junker, J. M. 1972. "The Death Penalty Cases: A Preliminary Comment." *Wash. L. Rev.* 48:95.

*Jurek* v. *Estelle.* 1979. Cert. denied. 593 F. 2d 672 (5th Cir.).

*Jurek* v. *Texas.* 1976. 428 U.S. 262.

Juris Doctor. 1973. "Capital Punishment, 1973: Just as Cruel and More Usual Every Day." *Juris Doctor* 3 (December):12.

Jurow, G. L. 1971. "New Data on the Effect of a 'Death Qualified' Jury on the Guilt Determination Process." *Harv. L. Rev.* 84:567.

Justice of the Peace. 1953. "Capital Punishment in the Case of Women and Adolescents." *Justice of the Peace* 117:669.

Kahn, E. 1970. "The Death Penalty in South Africa." *Tydskrif Vir Hedendaagse Romeins-Hollandse Reg* 18:108.

Kalven, H., Jr., and H. Zeisel. 1966. *The American Jury.* Boston: Little, Brown.

Kalven, H., Jr., and H. Zeisel. 1966a. "The American Jury and the Death Penalty." *U. Chicago L. Rev.* 33:769.

Kansas, Office of the Director of Penal Institutions. 1963. "Capital Punishment in Kansas."

Kanter, S. 1979a. "Dealing with Death: The Constitutionality of Capital Punishment in Oregon." *Willamette L. Rev.* 16:1.

Kanter, S. 1979b. "Deterrence and the Death Penalty: A Temporal Cross-Sectional Approach." *J. Crim. L.* 70:235.

Kanter, S. 1981. "Brief Against Death: More on the Constitutionality of Capital Punishment in Oregon." *Willamette L. J.* 17 (Summer):629.

Kaplan, E. A. 1969. "Guilty Pleas, Jury Trial, and Capital Punishment—the Effects of *United States* v. *Jackson.*" *La. L. Rev.* 29:389.

Karge, S. W. 1976. "Capital Punishment." *J. C. L. C.* 67 (December):437.

Karge, S. W. 1978. "Capital Punishment: Death for Murder Only." *J. C. L. C.* 69:179.

Karni, E. 1971. "The Value of Time and the Demand for Money." University of Chicago (unpublished doctoral dissertation).

Kassell, C. 1924. "Recent Death Orgies: A Study of Capital Punishment." *South Atlantic Quarterly* 23:295.

Kassell, C. 1925. "Recent Death Orgies: A Study of Capital Punishment." *American L. Rev.* 59:126.

Kastenmeier, R. W., and J. Dowdy. 1966. "Should Capital Punishment Be Abolished for Federal Crimes? Kastenmeier, Yes; Dowdy, No." *The American Legion Magazine* October:20.

Kazis, I. J. 1959. "Judaism and the Death Penalty." In *Man's Right to Life*, Ruth Leigh, ed., 1959. Reprinted in Bedau (1967b), p. 171.

Keating, P. J. 1981. "Constitutional Law—Fifth Amendment—Double Jeopardy in Capital Sentencing (Case Note), *Bullington* v. *Missouri* 101 Sup. Ct. 1852 (1981)." *Akron L. Rev.* 15 (Fall):398.

Keedy, E. R. 1949. "History of the Pennsylvania Statute Creating Degrees of Murder." *U. Penn. L. Rev.* 97:759.

Kelegian, H. H., and W. E. Oates. 1974. *Introduction to Econometrics: Principles and Applications.* New York: Harper & Row.

Kelling, G. L., T. Pate, D. Dieckman, and C. E. Brown. 1974. *The Kansas City Preventive Patrol Experiment.* Washington, D.C.: Police Foundation.

Kendall, D. E. 1975. "Constitutional Attacks on the Death Penalty." *NLADA Briefcase* 32 (January–February):120.

Kennedy, L. 1971. *Ten Rillington Place.* New York: Avon.

Kent, S. 1977. "A Review of Capital Punishment in the United States." *Albertus Magnus* 1:8.

Kentucky Bench and Bar. 1981. "Death Penalty: Cruel and Unusual Punishment When Imposed Upon Juveniles." *Ky. Bench & Bar* 45 (April):16.

Kentucky Law Journal. 1966. "In Defense of Capital Punishment." *Ky. L. J.* 54:742.

Kentucky Law Journal. 1968a. "Personality Tests for Prospective Jurors." *Ky. L. J.* 56:832.

Kentucky Law Journal. 1968b. "Capital Punishment: A Model for Reform." *Ky. L. J.* 57:508.

Kentucky Law Journal. 1974. "Eighth Amendment and Kentucky's New Capital Punishment Provisions—Waiting for the Other Shoe to Drop." *Ky. L. J.* 63:399.

Kentucky, Legislative Research Commission. 1965. "Capital Punishment."

Kerans, P. 1977. "Distributive and Retributive Justice in Canada." *Dalhousie L. J.* 4 (October):76.

Keubler, J. 1963. "Punishment by Death." *Editorial Research Reports* 2,3 (July 17).

Kim, C., and T. R. LeBlang. 1975. "Death Penalty in Traditional China." *Ga. J. of Int. & Comp. L.* 5:77.

Kim, R. C. C. 1965. "Capital Punishment: Time for a Stand." *J. of Church and State* 7, 2:226.

King, D. R. 1978. "The Brutalization Effect: Execution Publicity and the Incidence of Homicide in South Carolina." *Social Forces* 57 (December):683.

King, F. A. 1958. "Thirteenpence–Halfpenny for the Hangman." *Justice of the Peace* 122:216.

Kingsley, R. 1957. "The Case Against Capital Punishment." *L. A. B. Bull.* 32:195.

Kingsley, R. 1960. "Life or Death: Another View." *Calif. S. B. J.* 35:549.

Kinney, R. R. 1966. "In Defense of Capital Punishment." *Ky. L. J.* 54:742.

Kinsolving, L. 1956. "Capital Punishment: A Reaction from a Member of the Clergy." *A. B. A. J.* 42:850.

Kirk, R. 1980. "Criminal Character and Mercy." *Modern Age* 24:338.

Kitchen, R. 1973. "Abolish Capital Punishment?" *The Lamp* (June):2.

Klare, H. 1969. "Capital Punishment." *The Criminologist* 4:75.

Klare, H. 1970. "Post Mortem on Hanging." *British J. of Criminology* 10:186.

Kleck, G. 1979. "Capital Punishment, Gun Ownership, and Homicide." *Am. J. of Sociol.* 84 (January):882.

Kleck, G. 1981. "Racial Discrimination in Criminal Sentencing: A Critical Evaluation of the Evidence with Additional Evidence on the Death Penalty." *Am. Sociol. Rev.* 46 (December):783.

Klein, E. 1972. "Capital Punishment, Crime and Morality." *J. Beverly Hills B. A.* 6 (September):64.

Klein, L. R., B. E. Forst, and V. Filatov. 1978. "The Deterrent Effect of Capital Punishment: An Assessment of the Estimates," in *Deterrence and Incapacitation: Estimating the Effects of Criminal Sanctions on Crime Rates*, A. Blumstein, J. Cohen, and D. Nagin, eds. Washington, D.C.: National Academy of Sciences.

Knell, B. E. F. 1965. "Capital Punishment: Its Administration in Relation to Juvenile Offenders in the Nineteenth Century and Its Possible Administration in the Eighteenth." *British J. of Criminology* 5:198.

Knorr, S. J. 1979. "Deterrence and the Death Penalty: A Temporal Cross-Sectional Approach." *J. C. L. C.* 70:235.

Knowlton, R. E. 1953. "Problems of Jury Discretion in Capital Cases." *U. Penn. L. Rev.* 101:1099.

Koenig, D. M. 1982. "Capital Punishment and Crimes of Murder" (Criminal Sentencing Symposium, *Enmund* v. *Florida* 102 Sup. Ct. 3368 (1982)). *Loyola U. L. J.* 13 (Summer):817.

Koeninger, R. C. 1969. "Capital Punishment in Texas, 1924–1968." *Crime and Delinquency* 15:132.

Koestler, A. 1957. *Reflections on Hanging.* New York: Macmillan.

Koestler, A., and C. H. Rolph. 1960. *Hanged by the Neck.* Hamondsworth, England: Penguin.

Kofoed, A. 1982. "Who Shall Live and Who Shall Die?: *State* v. *Osborn* and the Idaho Death Penalty (Case Note), *State* v. *Osborn* 631 P. 2d 187 (Id. 1981)." *Idaho L. Rev.* 18 (Spring):195.

Kohlberg, L. 1975. "The Development of Moral Judgments Concerning Capital Punishment." *Am. J. of Orthopsychiatry* 45 (July):614.

Kohn, A. C. 1966. "Capital Punishment in Missouri." *J. Mo. B.* 22:53.

Kohn, M. G. 1972. "Constitutional Law—Eighth Amendment—The Death Penalty as Presently Administered under Discretionary Sentencing Statutes Is Cruel and Unusual, *Furman* v. *Georgia*." *Seton Hall L. Rev.* 4:244.

Korn, R. R., and L. W. McCorkle. 1959. *Criminology and Penology.* New York: Holt, Rinehart and Winston.

Kuh, R. H. 1965. "The Death Penalty: An Enforcement View Urging Retention." *Nat. D. A. Assoc. J.* 1:76.

Kuh, R. H. 1970. "Comments on the Scrupled-Juror Problem." *J. Legal Education* 23:16.

Kurland, P., ed. 1977. *The Supreme Court Review.* Chicago: University of Chicago Press.

Land and Water Law Review. 1974. "Bastard or Legitimate Child of *Furman* (*Furman* v. *Georgia*, 92 Sup. Ct. 2726)? An Analysis of Wyoming's New Capital Punishment Law." *L. W. L. Rev.* 9:209.

Landerer, L. E. 1971. "Capital Punishment as a Human Rights Issue before the United Nations." *Revue des Droits de L'Homme* 4:2, 511.

Lanza-Kaduce, L. 1982. "Formality, Neutrality, and Goal-Rationality: The Legacy of Weber in Analyzing Legal Thought." *J. C. L. C.* 73 (Summer):533.

Larkin, P. J. 1980. "Eighth Amendment and the Execution of the Presently Incompetent." *Stanford L. Rev.* 32 (April):765.

Lasky, I. I. 1974. "Paradigm of Religion, Medicine, and Capital Punishment." *Medicine, Science, and the Law* 14 (January):26.

Lassers, W. J. 1967. "Proof of Guilt in Capital Cases—An Unscience." *J. C. L. C. & P. S.* 58:310.

Lassers, W. J. 1971. "Death Takes a Holiday." *Trans-Action* 1971 (January):10.

Lavinsky, M. B. 1965. "Executive Clemency: A Study of a Decisional Problem Arising in the Terminal Stages of the Criminal Process." *Chicago-Kent L. Rev.* 42:13.

Law Journal. 1953. "Royal Commission on Capital Punishment." *L. J.* 103:713.

Law Notes. 1930. "Manner of Inflicting Death Penalty as Cruel and Unusual Punishment." *Law Notes* 34:104.

Law Reporter. 1846. "Capital Punishment in the United States." *L. Reporter* (March):487.

Law Times. 1866. "Capital Punishment [in Switzerland]." *Law Times* 41:151.

Law Times. 1934. "General Intelligence: Capital Punishment." *Law Times* 171:59.

Law Times. 1953. "Capital Punishment, Royal Commission's Report." *Law Times* 216:505.

Lawes, L. 1932. *Twenty Thousand Years in Sing Sing.* New York: Long.

Lawes, L. 1939. "A Brief History of States without the Death Penalty: Capital Crimes in the United States; Capital Punishment Abroad." In Johnson, 1939, p.14.

Lawes, L. 1969. *Man's Judgment of Death* (reprint of 1924 edition). Montclair, N.J.: Patterson Smith.

Lawrence, J. 1960. *A History of Capital Punishment.* New York: Citadel.

Leary, M. E. 1972. "California Views the Death Penalty." *America* (August 5):55.

Leary, M. E. 1973. "Is the Death Penalty Dead?" *America* (February 3):95.

Leavy, D. 1981. "A Matter of Life and Death: Due Process Protection in Capital Clemency Proceedings." *Yale L. J.* 90 (March):889.

Ledewitz, B. S. 1982. "The Requirement of Death: Mandatory Language in the Pennsylvania Death Penalty Statute." *Duquesne L. Rev.* 21 (Fall):103.

Lehtinen, M. W. 1977. "Value of Life: An Argument for the Death Penalty [with Reply by G. W. Smith]." *Crime and Delinquency* 23 (July):237.

Leitch, D. 1972. "Return of the Guillotine." *The New Statesman* (December 1):800.

Lejins, P. P. 1952. "The Death Penalty Abroad." *The Annals* 284:137.

Lempert, R. 1980. "Desert and Deterrence: An Evaluation of the Moral Bases for Capital Punishment." *Michigan Law Review* 79 (May):177.

Lempert, R. 1983. "The Effect of Executions on Homicides: A New Look in an Old Light." *Crime and Delinquency* 29, 1:88.

Leon, J. S. 1978. "Cruel and Unusual Punishment: Sociological Jurisprudence and the Canadian Bill of Rights." *U. Toronto Fac. L. Rev.* 36:222.

Leopold, N. 1958. *Life Plus 99 Years.* New York: Doubleday.

Lester, D. 1979a. "Executions as a Deterrent to Homicide." *Psychological Reports* 44 (April):562.

Lester, D. 1979b. "Deterring Effect of Executions on Murder as a Function of Number and Proportion of Executions." *Psychological Reports* 45 (October):598.

Lester, D. 1980. "Effect of Gary Gilmore's Execution on Homicidal Behavior." *Psychological Reporter* 47 (December, 2):1262.

Levie, G. J. 1980. "Death Penalty Jurors: Who's the Fairest of Them All?" *L. A. Lawyer* 2 (January):34.

Levine, S. 1972. *Death Row: An Affirmation of Life.* New York: Ballantine.

Lewis, C. S., et al. 1978. *Essays on the Death Penalty,* 3rd edition. Houston, Tex.: St. Thomas.

Lewis, P. W. 1979. "Killing the Killers: A Post-*Furman* Profile of Florida's Condemned: A Personal Account." *Crime and Delinquency* 25 (April):200.

Library of Congress, Legislative Reference Service. 1966. *Capital Punishment: Pro and Con Arguments* (1966). Reprinted in Hearings Before the Subcommittee on Criminal Laws and Procedures of the Committee on the Judiciary, United States Senate, 92nd Cong., 2nd Sess., *Reform of the Federal Criminal Laws,* Part III, Subpart A.P. 1057(1972).

Liebman, J. S., and M. J. Shepard. 1978. "Guiding Capital Sentencing Discretion Beyond the 'Boiler Plate': Mental Disorder as a Mitigating Factor." *Ga. L. J.* 66 (February):757.

Lindquist, C. A. 1967. "An Analysis of Juror Selection Procedures in the U.S. District Courts." *Temple L. Quarterly* 41:32.

Lipset, S. M., M. Trow, and J. Coleman. 1956. *Union Democracy.* New York: The Free Press.

Lipson, L. 1962. "Crime and Punishment, Execution: Hallmark of 'Socialist Legality'." *Problems in Communism* 11 (September–October):21.

Literary Digest. 1936. "Legal Infants in the Electric Chair." *Literary Digest* (March 7):18.

*Lockett* v. *Ohio*. 1978. 438 U.S. 586.

Loeb, R. H. 1978. *Crime and Capital Punishment*. New York: Franklin Watts.

Logan, C. H. 1972. "General Deterrent Effect of Imprisonment." *Social Forces* 5 (September):64.

Long, T. A. 1973. "Capital Punishment—'Cruel and Unusual'?" *Ethics* 83:214.

Lopez-Rey, M. 1980. "General Overview of Capital Punishment as a Legal Sanction." *Fed. Prob.* 44 (March):18.

Lord, C. G. 1979. "Biased Assimilation and Attitude Polarization: The Effects of Prior Theories on Subsequently Considered Evidence." *J. P. S. P.* 37 (November):2098.

Louisiana Law Review. 1945. "Sentence—Method of Execution (State ex rel. *Pierre* v. *Jones*)." *La. L. Rev.* 6:298.

Louisiana Law Review. 1969a. "Prospective Jurors and Capital Punishment." *La. L. Rev.* 29:381.

Louisiana Law Review. 1969b. "A Case for the Abolition of Capital Punishment." *La. L. Rev.* 29:393.

Louisiana Law Review. 1970. "Disposition of *Witherspoon*-Type Cases." *La. L. Rev.* 30:502.

Louisiana Law Review. 1977. "Disclosure of Presentence Reports in Capital Cases." *La. L. Rev.* 38:226.

Loyola Law Review. 1968. "Criminal Procedure—Jury Selection in Capital Cases." *Loyola L. Review* 15:128.

Loyola Law Review. 1977. "Conscientious Objectors to the Death Penalty— Can They Be Excluded from the Jury?" *Loyola L. Review* 23:604.

Loyola Law Review. 1978a. "Unconstitutionality of the Death Penalty for Rape: A Life Only for a Life." *Loyola L. Review* 24:314.

Loyola Law Review. 1978b. "First-Degree Murder Statutes and Capital Sentencing Procedures: An Analysis and Comparison of Statutory Systems for the Imposition of the Death Penalty in Georgia, Florida, Texas, and Louisiana." *Loyola L. Review* 24:709.

Loyola University Law Journal. 1974. "New Illinois Death Penalty: Double Constitutional Trouble." *Loyola U. L. J.* 5:351.

Luckenbill, D. 1977. "Criminal Homicide as a Situated Transaction." *Social Problems* 1977 (December):176.

Lunden, W. A. 1961. "The Death Penalty." *Police* 5 (July–August):34.

Lunden, W. A. 1962. "Death Penalty Delays." *A. B. A. J.* 48:1043. Reprinted in *Police* 7 (July–August 1963):18.

Lyons, D. B. 1972a. Testimony, in Hart-Celler Hearings, p. 243.

Lyons, D. B. 1972b. "Capital Punishment—A Selected Bibliography." *Crim. L. B.* 8:783.

MacDonald, C. F. 1892. "The Infliction of the Death Penalty by Means of

Electricity: Being a Report of Seven Cases." *Transactions of the Med. Soc. of the State of N. Y.*:400.

Mackey, P. E. 1972a. "Capital Punishment in New Netherland [New York]. *Halve Maen* 47 (July):7.

Mackey, P. E. 1972b. "Reverend George Barrell Cheever: Yankee Reformer as Champion of the Gallows." *Proceedings of the Am. Antiq. Soc.* (October):323.

Mackey, P. E. 1973. "Edward Livingston on the Punishment of Death." *Tulane L. Rev.* 48 (December):25.

Mackey, P. E. 1974. "Mandatory Capital Punishment? The Inutility of Mandatory Capital Punishment: An Historical Note." *Boston U. L. Rev.* 54 (January):30.

Mackey, P. E. 1982. *Hanging in the Balance: The Anti-Capital Punishment Movement in New York State, 1776–1861.* New York: Garland.

Mackey, P. E., ed. 1977. *Voices Against Death: American Opposition to Capital Punishment.* New York: Burt Franklin.

MacNamara, D. E. J. 1962. "A Survey of Recent Literature on Capital Punishment." *Am. J. of Corrections* 24:16.

Maestro, M. 1973. "Pioneer for the Abolition of Capital Punishment: Cesare Beccaria." *J. History of Ideas* 34 (July):463.

Maestro, M. 1980. "Death Penalty Viewed as an Act of Self-Defense by Two Italian Jurists in the Eighteenth Century." *American Philosophical Society Proceedings* 124 (February):52.

Maher, T. K. 1981. "Constitutional Law: Are Death-qualified Juries no Longer Qualified to Assess Guilt? (Case Note), *Grigsby* v. *Mabry* 483 F. Supp. 1372 (E. D. Ark. 1980)." *N. C. L. Rev.* 59 (April):792.

Maheshwari, C. L. 1965. "Death Penalty in India." *J. of Corrections Work* 12:78.

Mailer, N. 1979. *The Executioner's Song.* Boston: Little, Brown.

Malinvaud, E. 1970. *Statistical Methods of Econometrics.* New York: Elsevier North-Holland.

Malone, P. 1979. "Death Row and the Medical Model." *Hastings Center Rep.* 9 (October):5.

Mangum, C. S. 1940. *The Legal Status of the Negro.* Chapel Hill: University of North Carolina Press.

Mangum, G. C. 1980. "Vague and Overlapping Guidelines: A Study of North Carolina's Capital Sentencing Statute." *Wake Forest L. Rev.* 16 (October):765.

Manheim, K. M. 1978. "Capital Punishment Cases: A Criticism of Judicial Method." *Loyola U. L. Rev.* (L.A.) 12 (December):85.

Marshall, G. 1961. "Parliament and the Prerogative of Mercy." *Public Law*:8.

Marshall, H., and R. Purdy. 1972. "Hidden Deviance and the Labelling Approach: The Case for Drinking and Driving." *Social Problems* 19:541.

Marshall, R. T. 1972. "In the Wake of the Death Penalty Decisions . . . A Texas Dilemma." *Voice for the Defense* 1,3:3.

Martin, J. B. 1960a. "Death, The Poor Man's Penalty." *American Weekly* (May 15):9.

Martin, J. B. 1960b. "Crime of Passion." *Saturday Evening Post* (July 30). Reprinted (with omissions) in Bedau (1967b), p. 519.

Martin, J. B. 1960c. "The Question of Identity." *Saturday Evening Post* (August 13):34.

Maryland, Legislative Council, Committee on Capital Punishment. 1962. "Report" (October 3, 1962). Legislative Council of Maryland.

Mason, D. 1977. "Death Row—Rhodesian Style." *New Statesman* 94 (August 12):202.

Massachusetts, Department of Corrections. 1968. "An Analysis of Convicted Murderers in Massachusetts: 1943–1966."

Massachusetts, Special Commission Established for the Purpose of Investigating and Studying the Abolition of the Death Penalty in Capital Cases. 1958. "Report and Recommendations."

Massie, R. L. 1971. "Death by Degrees." *Esquire* (April):179.

Mather, P. B. 1965. "Death Penalty Abolished." *The Christian Century* (March 24):382.

Mattick, H. W. 1972. *The Unexamined Death*. Chicago: John Howard Associates.

Maxfield, J. R. 1982. "Constitutional Law—Is the Current Test of the Constitutionality of Capital Punishment Proper? (Case Note), *Hopkinson* v. *State* 632 P. 2d 79 (Wyo. 1981)." *L. W. L. Rev.* 17:681.

*Maxwell* v. *Bishop*. 1970. 398 U.S. 262.

Mazor, L. J. 1975. "On Death in the Criminal Law." *J. Cont. L.* 1:246.

McCafferty, J. A. 1954. "Capital Punishment in the United States: 1930 to 1952." M.A. thesis, Ohio State University.

McCafferty, J. A. 1961. "The Death Sentence and Then What?" *Crime and Delinquency* 7:363. Reprinted in Bedau (1967b), p. 90, as "The Death Sentence, 1960."

McCafferty, J. A. 1963. "Major Trends in the Use of Capital Punishment." *Fed. Prob.* 25 (September):15. Reprinted in *Crim. L. Quarterly* 1 (1963), p.9.

McCafferty, J. A., ed. 1972. *Capital Punishment*. New York: Random House.

McCaffrey, J. P. 1936. "Mass Executions." *Commonwealth* 25 (December 11):176.

McCall, D. J. 1978. "Evolution of Capital Punishment in Wyoming: A Reconciliation of Social Retribution and Humane Concern?" *L. W. L. Rev.* 13:865.

McClellan, D. D., and M. Rokeach. 1969. "Dogmatism and the Death Penalty: A Reinterpretation of the Duquesne Poll Data." *Duquesne L. Rev.* 8:125.

McClellan, G. S., ed. 1961. *Capital Punishment*. New York: H. W. Wilson Company.

McClelland, L. R. 1959. "Conscientious Scruples Against the Death Penalty in Pennsylvania." *Penn. B. A. Q.* 30:252.

*McCorquodale* v. *Balkcom*. 1981. 525 F. Supp. 431 (N.D. GA).

McDonald, L. 1972. "Capital Punishment in South Carolina: The End of an Era." *S. C. L. Rev.* 24:762.

McGaan, D. 1981. "The Right to a Lesser Included Offense Instruction in Capital Cases (Case Note), *Beck* v. *Alabama* 447 U.S. 625 (1980)." *Wisc. L. Rev.* (Summer):560.

McGahey, R. 1980. "Dr. Ehrlich's Magic Bullet: Economic Theory, Econometrics, and the Death Penalty." *Crime and Delinquency* 26 (October):485.

*McGautha* v. *California*. 1971. 402 U.S. 183.

McGee, R. A. 1964. "Capital Punishment as Seen by a Correctional Administrator." *Fed. Prob.* 28 (June):11. Reprinted in McCafferty (1972), p. 161.

McGrath, W. T. 1973. "The Death Penalty." *Canadian J. of Criminology and Corrections* 15 (January):118.

McIntyre, D. M. 1960. "Delays in the Execution of Death Sentences." A.B.F. Research Memorandum Series Report #24.

McKee, D. L., and M. L. Sesnowitz. 1976. "Welfare Economic Aspects of Capital Punishment." *Am. J. of Ec. and Sociol.* 35 (January):41.

McLean, R. 1980. "Reconstruction of Arizona's Death Penalty Statute under *Watson*." *Ariz. L. Rev.* 22 (Winter):1037.

McMahon, D. F. 1973. "Capital Punishment." *FBI L. Enforcement Bull.* 42 (February):20.

McMahon, D. P. 1982. "Rape, Recidivism, and Capital Punishment: Time for the Supreme Court to Re-examine its Interpretation of the Eighth Amendment." *Ohio N. U. L. Rev.* 9 (January):99.

Mead, G. H. 1918. "The Psychology of Punitive Justice." *Am. J. of Sociol.* (March):585.

Meador, R. 1975. *Capital Revenge.* Ardmore, Pa.: Dorrance.

Medico-Legal Journal. 1926. "League for the Abolition of Capital Punishment." *Medico-Legal J.* 43:66.

Meehan, J. J. 1974a. "The Death Penalty in California." *The Attorney General's L. J.* [Calif.] 1974:30.

Meehan, J. J. 1974b. "Charging the Death Penalty in California." *The Attorney General's L. J.* [Calif.] 1974:14.

Meinz, J. R., and M. Schuster. 1981. "Mitigation under the Illinois Death Penalty Act." *Illinois Bar J.* 69 (June):606.

Meltsner, M. 1971. "Capital Punishment: The Moment of Truth." *Juris Doctor* (November):4.

Meltsner, M. 1973a. *Cruel and Unusual: The Supreme Court and Capital Punishment.* New York: Random House.

Meltsner, M. 1973b. "Capital Punishment." *The New Republic* (July 21):12.

Meltsner, M. 1973c. "Litigating Against the Death Penalty: The Strategy Behind *Furman*." *Yale L. J.* 82:1111.

Melville, K. 1973. "Capitol [sic] Punishment." *The Sciences* (May):20.

Memphis State University Law Review. 1977. "Death Penalty in Tennessee—Recent Developments." *Memphis S. U. L. Rev.* 8:107.

Mengden, W. 1978. "The Death Penalty? Part 1. Pro: A Just and Moral Deterrent." *Police Journal* 26, 1 (February):7.

Meyer, H. H. B. 1912. *Select List of References on Capital Punishment.* Washington, D.C.: Library of Congress.

Meyer, J. 1968. "Reflections on Some Theories of Punishment." *J. C. L. C. & P. S.* 59:595.

Michigan, Legislative Research Bureau. 1957. "History of Capital Punishment in the State of Michigan."

Michigan State Bar Journal. 1928. "Report of Committee on Capital Punishment." *Mich. S. B. J.* 8:278.

Midgley, J. 1974. "Public Opinion and the Death Penalty in South Africa." *British J. of Criminology* 14 (October):345.

Miller, A. H. 1978. "The Ultimate Silencer." *The Nassau Lawyer* 25 (May):403.

Millet, C. H., and T. I. Waine. 1981. "Voir Dire Examinations (California Supreme Court Survey: July–November 1980), *Hovey* v. *Superior Court of Alameda County,* 616 P. 2d 130 (Calif. 1980)." *Pepperdine L. Rev.* 8 (January):504.

Milligan, C. S. 1967. "A Protestant's View of the Death Penalty." In Bedau, 1967b, p.175.

Milton, J. R. L. 1971. "A Cloistered Virtue?" *So. Africa L. J.* 87:424.

Minnesota Law Review. 1969. "Criminal Procedure: Selecting a Jury to Determine Capital Punishment." *Minn. L. Rev.* 53:838.

Minnesota Law Review. 1971. "Constitutional Law—Capital Punishment for Rape Constitutes Cruel and Unusual Punishment When No Life Is Taken or Endangered." *Minn. L. Rev.* 56:95.

Miranda, J. J. 1980. "Death Sentence for Murder in India." *Crim. L. J.* 86 (September):35.

Mironenko, Y. P. 1959. "The Campaign to Extend the Death Penalty." *Institute for the Study of the USSR* 6, Bulletin 25.

Misner, R. L. 1979. "Resentencing to Death under *State* v. *Watson* [(Ariz.) 586 P. 2d 1253]: A Denial of the Right to a Speedy Trial." *Ariz. State L. J.* 1979:137.

Missouri Law Review. 1979. "Sentencer Must Have Some Discretion in Imposing Capital Punishment: Another Retreat from *Furman* v. *Georgia.*" *Mo. L. Rev.* 44:359.

*Mitchell* v. *Hopper.* 1982. 538 F. Supp. 77 (S.D. GA).

Modern Law Review. 1954. "Report of the Royal Commission on Capital Punishment 1949–1953." *Modern L. Rev.* 17:57.

Momboisse, R. M. 1962. "Early California Justice: First Murder Trial." *Calif. S. B. J.* 37:736.

Montana Law Review. 1977. "Montana's Death Penalty After *State* v. *McKenzie* [33 St. Rptr. 1043 (1976)]." *Montana L. Rev.* 38:209.

Moore, M. 1975. "Attitude Toward Capital Punishment: Scale Validation [Thurstone's Scale]" *Psychological Reports* 37 (August):21.

*Moore* v. *Balkcom.* 1981. 513 F. Supp. 772, 803 (S.D. GA).

Morris, A. 1960. "Thoughts on Capital Punishment." *Wash. L. Rev.* 35:335.

Morris, N. 1967. "Two Studies on Capital Punishment." *Pena de Morte* 2:411.

Morris, N. 1979. "Hans Mattick and the Death Penalty: Sentimental Notes on Two Topics." *U. of Toledo L. Rev.* 10:299.

Morris, N., and F. E. Zimring. 1969. "Deterrence and Corrections." *The Annals* 381:137.

Morrison, D. E., and R. E. Henkel. 1969. *The Significance Test Controversy.* Chicago: Aldine.

Morrison, W. A. 1973. "Criminal Homicide and the Death Penalty in Canada: Time for Reassessment and New Directions: Toward a Typology of Homicide." *Canadian J. of Criminology and Corrections* 15 (October):367.

Morsbach, H., and G. Morsbach. 1967. "Attitudes Towards Capital Punishment in South Africa." *British J. of Criminology* 7:394.

Mortimer, P. 1979. "Death by Ceremonial." *New Statesman* 97 (March 30):434.

Moschizisker, M. von. 1949. "Capital Punishment in the Pennsylvania Courts." *Penn. B. A. Q.* 20:174.

Mosk, S. 1968. "Eighth Amendment Rediscovered." *Loyola L. A. L. Rev.* 1:4.

Mueller, G. O. W. 1962. "Penology on Appeal: Appellate Review of Legal But Excessive Sentences." *Van. L. Rev.* 15:671.

Mueller, G. O. W. 1967. "From Death to Life." *Pena de Morte* 2:187.

Mueller, G. O. W., and D. J. Besharov. 1969. "Bifurcation: The Two-Phase System of Criminal Procedure in the United States." *Wayne L. Rev.* 15:613.

Mulligan, W. H. 1978. "Crystal-balling Death?" *Baylor L. Rev.* 30:35.

Mulligan, W. H. 1979. "Cruel and Unusual Punishments: The Proportionality Rule." *Fordham L. Rev.* 47 (April):639.

Mullin, C. 1980. "The Jury System in Death Penalty Cases: A Symbolic Gesture." *L. C. P.* 43:137.

Mulvihill, D., and M. M. Tumin. 1969. *Crimes of Violence,* Vol. 11. National Commission on the Causes and Prevention of Violence.

Murchison, K. M. 1978. "Toward a Perspective on the Death Penalty Cases." *Emory L. J.* 27:469.

Murdy, R. G. 1961. "A Moderate View of Capital Punishment." *Fed. Prob.* 25 (September):11.

Murton, T. 1969. "Treatment of Condemned Prisoners." *Crime and Delinquency* 15:94.

Myrdal, G. 1944. *An American Dilemma.* New York: Harper and Brothers.

NAACP Legal Defense and Educational Fund, Inc. 1971a. Brief for Petitioner in *Aikens* v. *California,* O.T. 1971, No. 68-5027.

NAACP Legal Defense and Educational Fund, Inc. 1971b. Brief for Petitioner in *Furman* v. *Georgia,* O.T. 1971, No. 69-5003.

NAACP Legal Defense and Educational Fund, Inc. 1971c. Brief for Petitioner in *Jackson* v. *Georgia,* O.T. 1971, No. 69-5030.

NAACP Legal Defense and Educational Fund, Inc. 1973. Memorandum on Mandatory and Discretionary Capital Statutes, by N. Garin.

NAACP Legal Defense and Educational Fund, Inc. *Death Row USA.* Bimonthly Newsletter. New York: NAACP Legal Defense and Educational Fund.

Nakell, B. 1978. "The Cost of the Death Penalty." *Crim. L. Bull.* 14 (January–February):69.

Nathanson, J., et al. 1969. "Mr. Barzun and Capital Punishment." *Crime and Delinquency* 15:28.

National Center for Health Statistics. 1967. *Homicide in the United States, 1950–1964.* U.S. Department of Health, Education and Welfare.

National Commission on the Causes and Prevention of Violence, H. D. Graham and T. R. Gurr. 1969. *Crimes of Violence,* Vol. 2 of a staff report.

National Commission on the Causes and Prevention of Violence, D. J. Mulvihill and M. M. Tumin. 1969. *Crimes of Violence,* Vol. 9 of a staff report.

National Commission on Reform of Federal Criminal Laws. 1970. "Working Papers," 2:1350.

National Criminal Justice Information and Statistics Service. 1978. "Capital Punishment." U.S. Department of Justice.

National Criminal Justice Information and Statistics Service. 1979a. *Capital Punishment.* Washington, D.C.: U.S. Government Printing Office.

National Criminal Justice Information and Statistics Service. 1979b. *Sourcebook of Criminal Justice Statistics 1978.* U.S. Department of Justice.

National Criminal Justice Information and Statistics Service. 1980. *Capital Punishment.* Washington, D.C.: U.S. Government Printing Office.

Nelson, A. 1973. "The Politics of Criminal Law Reform: Sweden." *Am. J. of Comp. L.* 21:269,278.

Nelson, H. 1978. "The Swinging Index: Capital Punishment and British and Australian Administrations in Papua and New Guinea, 1888–1945." *J. Pacific History* 13,3–4:130.

Nelson, M., and P. Petrakis. 1972. "To Qualify Their Death Penalty Initiative—The Law Enforcement Officials from Governor Reagan and Attorney General Younger on Down Stretched and Broke the Law." *The San Francisco Bay Guardian* (October 4):3.

New Hampshire Bar Journal. 1967. "Results of Membership Poll as to Abolishment of Capital Punishment." *N. H. B. J.* 9:171.

New Jersey. 1972. "Public Hearings Before Assembly Judiciary Committee on Senate Bill No. 799 and Assembly Bills 556 & 1318 (Death Penalty)."

New Jersey, Commission to Study Capital Punishment. 1964. "Report."

New Statesman. 1975. "Keeping A Cool Head." *New Statesman* 90 (December 5):697.

New York, Commission on Capital Punishment. 1888. "Report."

New York, Temporary Commission on Revision of the Penal Law and Criminal Code. 1965. "Special Report on Capital Punishment."

New York City Bar Association. 1972. "Committee Reports, Legislation to Suspend Capital Punishment," by the Committee on Federal Legislation (of the Association of the Bar of the City of New York), 27 Record of the Assoc. of the B. of the City of N.Y. 390. Also in Hart-Celler Hearings, p. 88.

New York Law School Law Review. 1981. "Constitutional Law—Eighth Amendment—Violations by Federal Officials—Money Damages Remedy—*Carlson* v. *Green* (100 Sup. Ct. 1468)." *N. Y. Law School L. Rev.* 27:240.

New York University Law Review. 1954. "Criminal Procedure—'King's Evidence'—Cooperation With Prosecution as a Basis for Pardon." *N. Y. U. L. Rev.* 29:1021.

New York University Law Review. 1961. "Effectiveness of the Eighth Amendment: An Appraisal of Cruel and Unusual Punishment." *N. Y. U. L. Rev.* 36:846.

New York University Law Review. 1964. "The Two-Trial System in Capital Cases." *N. Y. U. L. Rev.* 39:50.

New York University Legal Forum. 1961. "Symposium on Capital Punishment." *N. Y. U. Legal Forum* 7:248.

New York University Legal Forum. 1968. "Constitutional Law—Jury Selection—Exclusion Due to Conscientious Scruples Against Death Penalty Held Unconstitutional." *N. Y. U. Legal Forum* 14:373.

New Zealand. 1968. *Crime in New Zealand.* Department of Justice.

New Zealand Law Journal. 1950. "Proposed Restoration of Capital Punishment." *New Zealand L. J.* 26:177.

Newman, F., et al. 1982. "First Panel Discussion: Sources of International Human Rights Law and Some Applications" (Proceedings: Conference on International Human Rights Law in State and Federal Courts). *U. S. F. L. Rev.* 17 (Fall):17.

Newsday. 1972. "A Five-Part Special Report on the U.S. Supreme Court's Historic Rulings of June 29 Ending Capital Punishment." [Including Clark, Ramsey, "The Spirit of the Law Has Been Preserved"(p. 5); Reagan, Ronald, "Man Should Be Held Accountable for His Deeds"(p. 6); Kamisar, "Will Capital Punishment Live Again?" (p. 7).] 1972 Special Reprint (July 17–21).

Nietzel, M. T., and R. C. Dillehay. 1982. "The Effects of Variations in Voir Dire Procedures in Capital Murder Trials." *Law and Human Behavior* 6 (Winter):1.

Nordin, J. M. 1981. "Criminal Procedure: Creating Great Risk of Death to More than One Person as an Aggravating Circumstance." *Okla. L. Rev.* 34 (Spring):325.

Normandeau, A. 1970. "Pioneers in Criminology: Charles Lucas—Opponent of Capital Punishment." *J. C. L. C. & P. S.* 61:218.

North Carolina Central Law Journal. 1976. "Historical Analysis of Mandatory Capital Punishment." *North Carolina Central L. J.* 57:306.

North Carolina Law Review. 1964. "Constitutional Law—Cruel and Unusual—Capital Punishment." *N. C. L. Rev.* 42:909.

North Carolina Law Review. 1969. "Criminal Law—*United States* v. *Jackson* and Its Impact Upon State Capital Punishment Legislation." *N. C. L. Rev.* 47:421.

North Carolina Law Review. 1971. "Criminal Procedure: Capital Sentencing by a Standardless Jury." *N. C. L. Rev.* 50:118.

North Carolina Law Review. 1973. "Criminal Procedure—Eighth Amendment Proportionality Analysis in Its Infancy." *N. C. L. Rev.* 52 (December):442.

North Carolina Law Review. 1974. "Criminal Procedure—Judicial Legislation of Capital Punishment. *State* v. *Waddell* [(NC) 194 S.E. 2d 19]" *N. C. L. Rev.* 52 (March):875.

North Carolina State Board of Charities and Public Welfare. 1929. "Capital Punishment in North Carolina: Special Bulletin Number 10."

Northwestern University Law Review. 1971. "Criminal Law: The *Witherspoon* Test in Illinois (in Illinois Supreme Court Review)." *N. W. U. L. Rev.* 65:963.

Northwestern University Law Review. 1971. "Due Process and Bifurcated Trials: A Double-Edged Sword." *N. W. U. L. Rev.* 66:327.

Notre Dame Lawyer. 1976. "Capital Punishment: A Review of Recent Supreme Court Decisions." *Notre Dame Lawyer* 52 (December): 261.

O'Halloran, A. 1965. "Capital Punishment." *Fed. Prob.* 29 (June):33.

O'Neill, P., and D. E. Levings. 1979. "Inducing Biased Scanning in a Group Setting to Change Attitudes Toward Bilingualism and Capital Punishment." *J. P. S. P.* 37 (August):1432.

O'Quinn, M. A. 1982. "Appellate Review of the Death Sentence in Nebraska" (Survey of Nebraska Law: June 1, 1980–May 31, 1981). *Creighton L. Rev.* 15 (Winter):248.

O'Sullivan, J. L. 1974. "Report in Favor of the Abolition of the Punishment of Death by Law, Made to Legislature of the State of New York, April 14, 1841" (facsimile ed.). New York: Arno Press.

Oberer, W. E. 1961. "Does Disqualification of Jurors for Scruples Against Capital Punishment Constitute Denial of Fair Trial on the Issue of Guilt?" *Texas L. Rev.* 39:759.

Oberer, W. E. 1964. "The Death Penalty and Fair Trial." *The Nation* (April 6):342. Reprinted in Sellin (1967a), p. 226.

Occhino, L. 1981. "Constitutional Procedure for the Imposition of the Death Penalty (Case Note), *Godfrey* v. *Georgia* 446 U.S. 420 (1980)." *DePaul L. Rev.* 30 (Spring):721.

Ohio Legislative Service Commission. 1961. "Capital Punishment." Staff Research Report no. 46.

Ohio Legislative Service Commission. 1972. "Capital Punishment—Legislative Implications of U.S. Supreme Court Decision in *Furman* v. *Georgia*." Staff Research Report No. 107.

Ohio North Law Review. 1977. "*Gregg* v. *Georgia* (96 Sup. Ct. 2909): Will the Ohio Death Penalty Survive?" *Ohio N. L. Rev.* 4:441.

Ohio North Law Review. 1978. "*Gardner* v. *Florida* (97 Sup. Ct. 1197): Presentence Reports in Capital Sentencing Procedures." *Ohio N. L. Rev.* 5 (January):175.

Ohio State Law Journal. 1969. "Jury—Challenge for Cause to Capital Punishment Objectors." *Ohio State L. J.* 30:421.

Ohio State Law Journal. 1972. "Reflections on the Proposed Ohio Law of Homicide." *Ohio State L. J.* 33:422.

Ohio State Law Journal. 1974. "Capital Punishment Statutes After *Furman* (*Furman* v. *Georgia*, 92 Sup. Ct. 2726)." *Ohio State L. J.* 35:651.

Ohio State Law Journal. 1977. "Constitutionality of Ohio's Death Penalty." *Ohio State L. J.* 38:617.

Oklahoma Law Review. 1980. "Criminal Law: Oklahoma's Death Penalty Statutes Reviewed." *Okla. L. Rev.* 33:448.

Oklahoma Law Review. 1981. "Constitutional Law: The Death Penalty: A Critique of the Philosophical Bases Held to Satisfy the Eighth Amendment Requirements for its Justification." *Okla. L. Rev.* 34 (Summer):567.

Opalinski, C. R. 1980. "Evolving Standards of Decency: The Constitutionality of North Carolina's Capital Punishment Statute (Case Note), *State* v. *Barfield*, 259 S.E. 2d 510 (N.C. 1979)." *Wake Forest L. Rev.* 16 (October):737.

Ortved, W. N. 1971. "Reform of the Law Relating to Capital Punishment: A Study in the Operation of Parliamentary Institutions." *Fac. of L. Rev.* 29:73.

Osborne, T. M., and R. E. Crowe. 1925. "The Death Penalty: A Debate; Osborne, Thou Shalt Not Kill; Crowe, Capital Punishment Protects Society." *The Forum* 73 (February):156.

Packer, H. L. 1964. "Making the Punishment Fit the Crime." *Harv. L. Rev.* 77:1071.

Paine, D. F. 1962. "Capital Punishment." *Tenn. L. Rev.* 29:534.

Palmer, L. I. 1979. "Two Perspectives on Structuring Discretion: Justices Stewart and White on the Death Penalty." *J. Crim. L.* 70:194.

Pangburn, C. H. 1982. "Constitutional Law—The Eighth Amendment Prohibits the Penalty of Death for One Who neither Took Life, Attempted or Intended to Take life, nor Contemplated that Life Would Be Taken (Case Note), *Enmund* v. *Florida* 102 Sup. Ct. 3368." *Vill. L. Rev.* 28 (November):173.

Panick, D. 1982. *Judicial Review of the Death Penalty*. White Plains, NY: Sheridan.

Parker, R. 1972. "Florida Statute 775.082: Ex Post Facto, Bill of Attainder, and Policy Aspects of a Sentence of No Parole—Life Imprisonment." *U. Pitt. L. Rev.* 34:290.

Partington, D. H. 1965. "The Incidence of the Death Penalty for Rape in Virginia." *Wash. & Lee L. Rev.* 22:43.

Passell, P. 1975. "The Deterrent Effect of the Death Penalty: A Statistical Test." *Stanford L. Rev.* 28:61.

Passell, P., and J. B. Taylor. 1975. "The Deterrent Effect of Capital Punishment: A Comment" (Discussion Paper #74-7509). Department of Economics, Columbia University.

Passell, P., and J. B. Taylor. 1976. "The Deterrence Controversy: A Reconsideration of the Time Series Evidence." In Bedau and Pierce, eds., 1976.

Passell, P., and J. B. Taylor. 1977. "Reply With Rejoinder." *Am. Ec. Rev.* 67 (June):445.

Paternoster, R. 1983. "Race of Victim and Location of Crime: The Decision to Seek the Death Penalty in South Carolina" (A Multi-Disciplinary Symposium on Current Death Penalty Issues). *J. C. L. C.* 74 (3).

Patil, V. 1981. "Capital Punishment." *Crim. L. J.* 87 (June):29.

Paton, J. I. 1968. *Is Capital Punishment Christian?* Lincoln, Neb.: Back to the Bible Broadcast.

Patrick, C. H. 1965. "The Status of Capital Punishment: A World Perspective." *J. C. L. C. & P. S.* 56:397.

Patrick, C. H. 1970. "Capital Punishment and Life Imprisonment in North Carolina, 1946 to 1968: Implications for Abolition of the Death Penalty." *Intramural L. Rev. of Wake Forest* 6:417.

*Patton* v. *Mississippi.* 1947. 332 U.S. 463.

Peck, J. K. 1975. "The Deterrent Effect of Capital Punishment: Ehrlich and His Critics." *Yale L. J.* 85 (December–January):359.

Pena de Morte. 1967. *Pena de Morte,* 2 volumes. Faculdade de Direito da Universidade de Coimbra (Portugal).

Pennell, L. T. 1967. "Capital Punishment." *Alberta L. Rev.* 5:176.

Pennsylvania Bar Association Quarterly. 1959. "Capital Punishment and the Pennsylvania Courts." *Penn. B. A. Q.* 20:174.

Pennsylvania, Joint Legislative Committee on Capital Punishment. 1961. "Report."

*People* v. *Anderson.* 1972. 6 Cal. 3d 628, 100 Cal. Rptr. 152, 493 P. 2d 8.

Phelps, H. A. 1928a. "Effectiveness of Life Imprisonment as a Repressive Measure Against Murder in Rhode Island." *J. of the American Statistical Assn.* 23, 161A (March):174.

Phelps, H. A. 1928b. "Rhode Island's Threat Against Murder." *J. C. L. C.* 18:552.

Philippines, Laurel Report on Penal Reforms. 1969. "The State of Philippine Penal Institutions and Penology." Senator Salvador H. Laurel, Chairman, Committee on Justice, Senate of the Philippines, Chapter XI. *Death Penalty*:185.

Phillips, D. P. 1974. "The Influence of Suggestion on Suicide: Substantive and Theoretical Implications of the Werther Effect." *American Sociol. Rev.* 39 (June):340.

Phillips, D. P. 1980. "The Deterrent Effect of Capital Punishment: New Evidence on an Old Controversy." *Am. J. of Sociol.* 86 (July):139.

Phillips, D. P. 1981. "Strong and Weak Research Designs for Detecting the Impact of Capital Punishment on Homicide." *Rutgers L. Rev.* 33 (Spring):790.

Phillips, L., and H. L. Votey. 1972. "An Economic Analysis of the Deterrent Effect of Law Enforcement on Criminal Activity." *J. C. L. C. & P. S.* 63:330.

Pierrepoint, A. 1974. *Executioner, Pierrepoint.* London: Harrap.

Piliavin, I., and S. Briar. 1964. "Police Encounters with Juveniles." *Am. J. of Sociol.* 70:206.

*Plessy* v. *Ferguson.* 1897. 163 U.S. 537.

Podgers, J. 1980. "The Psychiatrist's Role in Death Penalty Debated." *A. B. A. J.* 66 (December):1509.

Poe, D. A. 1969. "Capital Punishment Statutes in the Wake of *United States* v. *Jackson*: Some Unresolved Questions." *George Washington L. Rev.* 37:448.

Police. 1967. "Some Crimes Demand the Death Penalty." *Police* 11 (March–April):4.

Pollak, O. 1952. "The Errors of Justice." *The Annals* 284:115. Reprinted in Sellin (1967a), p. 207.

Pollak, S. R. 1972. Testimony, in Hart-Celler Hearings, p.134.

Polsby, D. D. 1973. "The Death of Capital Punishment?—*Furman* v. *Georgia.*" In P. B. Kurland, *The Supreme Court Review.* Chicago: University of Chicago Press.

Porth, R. K. 1982. "Limitation on Scope of Examination; Multiple Aggravating Circumstances; Arbitrary Factors Influencing a Death Sentence" (Annual Survey of South Carolina law, 1981). *S. C. L. Rev.* 34 (August):118.

Posey, F. A. 1981. "Texas Law Requiring Veniremen's Oath that the Death Penalty Will Not Affect their Deliberations Is Unconstitutional as Applied (Case Note), *Adams* v. *Texas* 100 Sup. Ct. 2521 (1980)." *Texas Tech L. Rev.* 12 (May):764.

Post, A. 1944. "Early Efforts to Abolish Capital Punishment in Pennsylvania." *Penn. Mag. of History and Biography* 68:48.

Post, A. 1945. "The Anti-Gallows Movement in Ohio." *Ohio S. Arch. & Hist. Rev.* 54:109.

Potratz, W. G. 1980. "The Prosecutor's Discretionary Power to Initiate the Death Sentencing Hearing." *DePaul L. Rev.* 29:1097.

Potter, C. F. 1938. "I Saw a Man Electrocuted." *Reader's Digest* (February 24):170.

Potter, J. D. 1969. *The Art of Hanging.* South Brunswick, N.J.: A. S. Barnes and Company.

Poulton, T. P. 1979. "Viewpoint: End the Death Penalty." *Flor. B. J.* 53 (July–August):448.

*Powell* v. *Alabama.* 1932. 287 U.S. 45.

Powers, E. 1966. *Crime and Punishment in Early Massachusetts: A Documentary History.* Boston: Beacon Press.

Powers, E. 1981. "Legal History of Capital Punishment in Massachusetts." *Fed. Prob.* 45 (September):15.

President's Commission on Law Enforcement and Administration of Justice. 1967a. "Report: The Challenge of Crime in a Free Society."

President's Commission on Law Enforcement and Administration of Justice. 1967b. "Report: Crime and Its Impact: An Assessment."

Prettyman, B., Jr. 1961. *Death and the Supreme Court.* New York: Harcourt, Brace, Jovanovich.

Prevezer, S. 1957. "The English Homicide Act [of 1957]: A New Attempt to Revise the Law of Murder." *Columbia L. Rev.* 57:624.

Priddy, S. V. 1981. "*Godfrey* v. *Georgia*: Possible Effects on Virginia's Death Penalty Law (Case Note), *Godfrey* v. *Georgia* 446 U.S. 420 (1980)." *U. Richmond L. Rev.* 15 (Summer):951.

Prison Journal. 1932a. "Bibliography." *Prison Journal* 12 (October):28.

Prison Journal. 1932b. "Other Countries in Which the Death Penalty Has Been Abolished or Abrogated." *Prison Journal* 12:20.

Prison Journal. 1958. "Pennsylvania Criminal Homicide and Execution Statistics." *Prison Journal* 38:74.

Prison Journal. 1959. "Pardon and Commutation." *Prison Journal* 38:1.

*Proffitt* v. *Florida*. 1976. 428 U.S. 242.

*Proffitt* v. *Wainwright*. 1982. 685 F. 2d. 1227 (11th Cir.).

Prosecutor, The. 1972. "Death Penalty Voided." *The Prosecutor* 8:243,350.

Public Health Service. Annual. *Vital Statistics Rates in the United States.* U.S. Department of Health, Education, and Welfare.

Public Law. 1982. "Fundamental Rights in the Privy Council." *Public Law* (Autumn):344.

Pugh, G. W., and M. H. Carver. 1970. "Due Process and Sentencing: From *Mapp* to *Mempa* to *McGautha*." *Texas L. Rev.* 49:25.

Pugsley, R. A. 1981. "Retributivist Argument Against Capital Punishment." *Hofstra L. Rev.* 9 (Summer):1501.

Quinn, J. R. 1972. "Homicides under the Colorado Criminal Code." *Denver L. J.* 49:137.

Radelet, M. L. 1981. "Racial Characteristics and the Imposition of the Death Penalty." *Am. Sociol. Rev.* 46 (December):918.

Radelet, M. L., and G. L. Pierce. 1983. "Race and Prosecutorial Discretion in Homicide Cases." Paper presented at the 1983 meeting of the American Sociological Association in Detroit.

Radelet, M. L., and M. Vandiver. 1983. "The Florida Supreme Court and Death Penalty Appeals." To be published in *J. C. L. C.*

Radin, M. J. 1978. "Jurisprudence of Death: Evolving Standards for the Cruel and Unusual Punishments Clause." *U. Penn. L. Rev.* 126 (May):989.

Radin, M. J. 1980. "Cruel Punishment and Respect for Persons: Super Due Process for Death." *S. Calif. L. Rev.* 53 (May):1143.

Radzinowicz, L. 1948. *A History of English Criminal Law and Its Administration From 1750.* London: Stevens and Sons Limited (vol. 2 & 3, 1956; vol. 4, 1968).

Ramabrahmam, K. 1980. "Death Penalty" (India). *Crim. L. J.* 86 (December):49.

Ramundo, B. A. 1963. "Capital Punishment in the Building of Communism." *A. B. A. J.* Section on International and Comparative Law:215.

Randall, W. S. 1969. "Under Sentence of Death." *The Philadelphia Bulletin* (November 2, 3, 4).

Rankin, J. H. 1979. "Changing Attitudes Toward Capital Punishment." *Social Forces* 58:194.

Raper, A. F. 1933. *The Tragedy of Lynching.* Chapel Hill: University of North Carolina Press.

Rappaport, J., R. M. Sorenson, and K. D. Smith. 1982. "A Trial Judge's Discretion to Waive the Operation of Special Circumstances under the Death Penalty Statute (California Supreme Court Survey: July 1981–December 1981) (Case Note), *People* v. *Williams* 637 P. 2d 1029 (Cal. 1981)." *Pepperdine L.Rev.* 9 (May):968.

Ray, J. J. 1982. "Attitude to the Death Penalty in South Africa—with some International Comparisons." *Journal of Social Psychology* 116 (April):287.

Reagan, R. 1972. "Excerpts of Remarks by Governor Ronald Reagan to the

California Peace Officers Association, Anaheim, California, May 22, 1972." *J. Calif. L. Enforcement* (July):1.

Reckless, W. C. 1969. "Use of the Death Penalty." *Crime and Delinquency* 15:43. Reprinted in McCafferty (1972), p. 38.

Redman, S. T. 1981. "Constitutional Law—Eighth Amendment—Capital Punishment—State Death Penalty Statutes—Procedural Safeguards—The Supreme Court of the United States Has Held that the Alabama Death Penalty Statute which Prohibited a Jury Instruction of Lesser Included Offenses in a Capital Case is Unconstitutional Because it Diminishes the Reliability of the Guilt Determination Process, Leading to an Arbitrary and Irrational Imposition of the Death Penalty (Case Note), *Beck* v. *Alabama* 447 U.S. 625 (1980)." *Duquesne L. Rev.* 19 (Spring):539.

Reed, L. M. T. 1973. "*Furman* v. *Georgia* and Kentucky Statutory Law." Kentucky Bar Journal 37 (January):25.

Reeves, E. R., and P. M. Sabalis. 1980. "South Carolina Death Penalty Law (Survey of South Carolina Law), *Furman* v. *Georgia* 408 U.S. 238 (1972)." *S. C. L. Rev.* 32 (August):81.

Reichert, W. O. 1959. "Capital Punishment Reconsidered." *Kentucky L. Rev.* 47:397.

Reid, C. G. 1964. "Phone Call." *Harper's* (April):164.

Reid, D., and J. K. Gurwell. 1973. *Eyewitness*. Houston: Cordovan Press.

Reifsnyder, R. 1955. "Capital Crimes in the States." *J. C. L. C. & P. S.* 45:690.

Reik, T. 1959. "Freud's Views on Capital Punishment," in *The Compulsion to Confess*. New York: John Wiley, p. 469.

Reilly, P. 1973. "Parliament's Agony Over Capital Punishment." *Saturday Night* (March):15.

Renda, E. A. 1982. "The Bitter Fruit of *McGautha*: *Eddings* v. *Oklahoma* and the Need for Weighing Method Articulation in Capital Sentencing." *Am. Crim. L. Rev.* 20 (Summer):63.

Review of The Int. Comm. of Jurists. 1969. "Capital Punishment in the Second Half of the Twentieth Century." *Review of the Int. Comm. of Jurists* 2:33.

Reynolds, M. O. 1977. "Reply With Rejoinder." *Am. J. of Ec. and Sociol.* 36 (January):105.

Rice, P. J. 1969. "Constitutional Law—Right to Trial by Jury—The Effect on State Statute Where Similar Federal Statute Held Unconsitutional." *Mercer L. Rev.* 20:309.

Richards, R. C., and S. C. Hoffman. 1981. "Death among the Shifting Standards: Capital Punishment after *Furman*." *S. Dak. L. Rev.* (Spring):243.

Richardson, B. W. 1890. "The Execution by Electricity." *Scientific American* (September 27):200.

Riddell, W. R. 1929a. "The First Legal Execution for Crime in Upper Canada." *L. Q. R.* 46:122.

Riddell, W. R. 1929b. "Judicial Execution by Burning at the Stake in New York." *A. B. A. J.* 15:373.

Riddell, W. R. 1930. "Post-Reformation Burning at the Stake of Heretics." *J. C. L. C.* 21:254.

Riedel, M. 1965. "The Poor and Capital Punishment." *Prison Journal* 45:24.

Riedel, M. 1976. "Discrimination in the Imposition of the Death Penalty: A Comparison of the Characteristics of Offenders Sentenced Pre-*Furman* and Post-*Furman* (*Furman* v. *Georgia*, 92 Sup. Ct. 2726)." *Temple L. Quarterly* 49:261.

Riedel, M., and J. P. McCloskey. 1975. "The Governor's Study Commission on Capital Punishment: A Content Analysis of the Testimony of Expert Witnesses." *Prison Journal* 53:19.

Riga, P. J. 1981. "Capital Punishment and the Right to Life: Some Reflections on the Human Right as Absolute." *Univ. of Puget Sound L. Rev.* (Fall):23.

Riley, K. W. 1981. "The Death Penalty in Georgia: An Aggravating Circumstance." *American Univ. L. Rev.* 30 (Spring):835.

Riley, T. J. 1960. "The Right of the State to Inflict Capital Punishment." *Catholic Lawyer* 6:279.

Ringold, S. M. 1966. "The Dynamics of Executive Clemency." *A. B. A. J.* 52:240. Reprinted in Sellin (1967a), p. 226.

*Roberts* v. *Louisiana*. 1976. 96 Sup. Ct. 3001.

Robertson, G. 1974. "Michael X on Death Row." *New Statesman* 87 (January 11):40.

Robin, G. D. 1964. "The Executioner: His Place in English Society." *British J. of Sociology* (1964):234.

Roche, P. Q. 1958. "A Psychiatrist Looks at the Death Penalty." *Prison Journal* 38:46.

Rockefeller, W. 1971. "Executive Clemency and the Death Penalty." *Catholic U. L. Rev.* 21:94.

Rogers, R. R. 1976. "Death Penalty." *NLADA Briefcase* 34 (October):1.

Rogers, R. R. 1978. "Death Penalty and Guilty Pleas: Ohio Rule 11(c)(3)—A Constitutional Answer to a Capital Defendant's Dilemma." *Ohio N. L. Rev.* 5:687.

Rosenberg, D., and K. Levy. 1978. "Capital Punishment: Coming to Grips with the Dignity of Man." *Calif. W. L. Rev.* 14:275.

Rosenberg, W. S. 1948. "America's Greatest Mass Execution." *American Mercury* 67:565.

Rosett, A. 1972. "Discretion, Severity, and Legality in Criminal Justice." *Southern Calif. L. Rev.* 46:12.

Ross, S., and H. Kupferberg. 1969. "The Longest Week in One Man's Life." *Parade* (May 4):4.

Ross, W. E. 1905. "The Death Penalty—Reasons for Its Abolition." *Va. L. Register* 11:625.

Roucek, J. S. 1971. "The Capital Punishment in Its Legal and Social Aspects." *Int. J. of Legal Research* 6 (December):49.

Roucek, J. S. 1979. "Capital Punishment in the USSR." *Ukranian Quarterly* 30:166.

Rubin, S. 1969. "Supreme Court, Cruel and Unusual Punishment, and the Death Penalty." *Crime and Delinquency* 15:121. Reprinted in McCafferty, p. 245.

Rubin, S. 1973. "Developments in Correctional Law: From Abolition of the Death Penalty to Abolition of Prisons." *Crime and Delinquency* 19:241.

*Rudolph* v. *Alabama*. 1963. Cert. denied 375 U.S. 889.

Rush, B. 1792. *Considerations on the Injustice and Impolicy of Punishing Murder by Death.* Philadelphia: M. Carey.

Rutgers Law Review. 1967. "*United States* v. *Jackson*: The Possible Consequences of Impairing the Right to Trial by Jury [U.S.D.C.]." *Rutgers L. Rev.* 22:167.

Rutgers Law Review. 1969. "*State* v. *Laws*: Appellate Power to Reduce Jury Determined Death Sentences." *Rutgers L. Rev.* 23:490.

Ryan, S. 1969. "Capital Punishment in Canada." *British J. of Crime* 9:80.

Salem, R., and W. J. Bowers. 1970. "Severity of Formal Sanctions as a Deterrent to Deviant Behavior." *L. S. Review* 5:21.

Samaha, J. B. 1978. "Hanging for Felony—Rule of Law in Elizabethan Colchester." *Historical Journal* 21 (December):763.

Samuelson, G. W. 1968. "The Effect of the Abolition of the Death Penalty in Delaware During 1956 to 1966." In Hart Hearings, p. 112.

Samuelson, G. W. 1969. "Why Was Capital Punishment Restored in Delaware?" *J. C. L. C. & P. S.* 60:148.

San Diego Law Review. 1973. "Footnote to *Furman*: Failing Justification for the Capital Case Exception to the Right to Bail After Abolition of the Death Penalty." *San Diego L. Rev.* 10:349.

San Diego Law Review. 1975. "Cruel or Unusual Punishments in California: New Problems in Fitting Punishment to Crimes." *San Diego L. Rev.* 12 (March):359.

Sarat, A. 1977. "Deterrence and the Constitution: On the Limits of Capital Punishment." *Journal of Behavioral Economics* 6:311.

Sarat, A., and N. Vidmar. 1976. "Public Opinion, the Death Penalty, and the Eighth Amendment: Testing the Marshall Hypothesis." *Wisc. L. Rev.* 1976:171.

Satlow, B. 1971. "Witness at an Execution." *Juris Doctor* (November):13.

Savitz, L. 1955. "Capital Crimes as Defined in American Statutory Law." *J. C. L. C. & P. S.* 46:355.

Savitz, L. 1958a. "A Brief History of Capital Punishment in Pennsylvania." *Prison Journal* 38:50.

Savitz, L. 1958b. "A Study in Capital Punishment." *J. C. L. C. & P. S.* (November–December):338.

Schardt, A. 1973. "Death Penalty." *Civil Liberties* (July):4.

Schedler, G. 1976. "Capital Punishment and Its Deterrent Effect." *Social Theory and Practice* 4:47.

Schilder, P. 1936. "The Attitude of Murderers Towards Death." *J. Abn. & Soc. Psych.* 31:348.

Schuessler, K. F. 1952. "The Deterrent Influence of the Death Penalty." *The Annals* 284:54.

Scientific American. 1890. "Execution by Electricity." *Scientific American* (March 1):131.

Scientific American. 1890. "The First Electrical Executions." *Scientific American* (August 16):96.

Scientific American. 1895. "Electrocution." *Scientific American* (July 13):28.

Scofield, G. R. 1980. "Due Process in the United States Supreme Court and the Death of the Texas Capital Murder Statute." *Am. J. of Crim. Law* 8 (March):1.

Scott, A. W. 1952. "The Pardoning Power." *The Annals* 284:95.

Scott, B. B. 1968. "Discriminatory Sentencing and Unitary Trial: Two Areas for Application of the *United States* v. *Jackson* Rationale." *U. Pitt. L. Rev.* 31:118.

Scott, G. R. 1950. *The History of Capital Punishment.* Ann Arbor, Mich.: Finch Press Reprints.

Seabury Press. 1979. *The Death Penalty and Torture.* New York: Seabury Press.

Sellin, T. 1932. "Common Sense and the Death Penalty." *Prison Journal* 12:10.

Sellin, T. 1950a. "A Note on Capital Executions in the United States." *British J. of Delinquency* 1:6.

Sellin, T. 1950b. "The Death Penalty and Police Safety." From Second Session, Twenty-second Parliament, 1955; Appendix F of the Minutes of Proceedings and Evidence, No. 20, of the Joint Committee of the Senate and the House of Commons on Capital and Corporal Punishment and Lotteries: 718–728. Canada: Queens Printers.

Sellin, T. 1955. "Philadelphia Gibbet Iron." *J. C. L. C. & P. S.* 46:11.

Sellin, T., ed. 1959. *The Death Penalty.* Philadelphia: The American Law Institute.

Sellin, T. 1961. "Capital Punishment." *Fed. Prob.* 25 (September):3.

Sellin, T. 1965a. "Capital Punishment." *Crim. L. Quarterly* 8:36.

Sellin, T. 1965b. "Homicides and Assaults in American Prisons: 1964." *Acta Criminologiae et Medicinae Legalis Japonica* 31:139.

Sellin, T. 1965c. "The Inevitable End of Capital Punishment." *Crim. L. Quarterly* 8:36. Reprinted in Sellin (1967b), p. 122.

Sellin, T. 1966. "Homicides and Serious Assaults in Prisons." Aristotelian University of Thessaloniki, *Annual of the School of Law and Economics* 14:139.

Sellin, T. 1967a. *Capital Punishment.* New York: Harper & Row.

Sellin, T. 1967b. "The Death Penalty in the United States." *Pena de Morte* 1:153.

Sellin, T. 1968. Testimony, in Hart Hearings, p. 80.

Sellin, T. 1972. Testimony, in Hart-Celler Hearings, p. 162.

Sellin, T. 1980. *The Penalty of Death.* Beverly Hills, Calif.: Sage Publications.

Sellin, T., and M. E. Wolfgang. 1964. *The Measurement of Delinquency.* New York: John Wiley.

Shane, S. M. 1962. "Window on a Gas Chamber." *The Nation* (February 24):170.

Sharpe, T. G., Jr. 1978. "Death Penalty Punishment Hearing: Preserving the Constitutional Questions Relating to Self-Incrimination and Lack of Standing in Psychiatric Testing." *Texas B. J.* 41 (March):253.

*Shaw* v. *Martin*. 1980. 613 F. 2d. 487 (4th Cir.).

Shawcross, W. 1973. "Nixon and the Death Penalty." *New Statesman* 87 (March 16):366.

Sheehan, T. M. 1965. "Administrative Review and Capital Punishment: The Canadian Concept." *Am. J. of Corrections* 27:2.

Shell, B. T. 1981. "Criminal Procedure: *Godfrey* v. *Georgia* (100 Sup. Ct. 1759) and the 'Especially Heinous, Atrocious, or Cruel' Murder." *Okla. L. Rev.* 34 (Spring):337.

*Sheperd* v. *Florida* 1951. 341 U.S. 50.

Sherman, P. R. 1968. ". . . Nor Cruel and Unusual Punishments Inflicted." *Crime and Delinquency* 14:73.

Shin, K. 1978. *Death Penalty and Crime: Empirical Studies.* Fairfax, Va.: George Mason University, Center for Economic Analysis.

Shipley, M. 1905a. "Abolition of Capital Punishment in Switzerland." *American L. Rev.* 39:734.

Shipley, M. 1905b. "Results of the Practical Abolition of Capital Punishment in Belgium." *Publications of the American Statistical An.* 9:307.

Shipley, M. 1906. "The Abolition of Capital Punishment in Italy and San Marino." *American L. Rev.* 40:240.

Shipley, M. 1907a. "The Abolition of Capital Punishment in France." *American L. Rev.* 41:561.

Shipley, M. 1907b. "Homicide and the Death Penalty in Mexico." (In *Crime and Capital Punishment: A Symposium*) *The Annals* 29:601,625.

Shipley, M. 1909. "Does Capital Punishment Prevent Convictions?" *American L. Rev.* 43:321.

Silver, I. 1972. "Death and the Judges: Cruel and Unusual Punishment?" *Commonweal* (April 4):136.

Silver, R. M. 1981. "Constitutionality of the New Mexico Capital Punishment Statute." *New Mexico L. Rev.* 11 (Summer):269.

Sindel, R. 1982. "Commentary on *Bullington* v. *Missouri*" (Criminal Sentencing Symposium). *Loyola U. L. J.* 13 (Summer):841.

Singer, B. F. 1970. "Psychological Studies of Punishment." *Calif. L. Rev.* 58:405.

Singh, A., and C. H. S. Jayewardene. 1978. "A Research Note—Conservatism and Toughmindedness as Determinant of the Attitudes Toward Capital Punishment." *Canadian J. of Criminology* 20 (April):191.

Skolnick, J. 1969. *The Politics of Protest.* New York: Simon and Schuster.

Slobogin, C. 1982. "*Estelle* v. *Smith*: The Constitutional Contours of the Forensic Evaluation." *Emory L. J.* 31 (Winter):71.

Slovenko, R. 1964. "And the Penalty Is (Sometimes) Death." *Antioch Rev.* 24:351.

Smith, A. L., and R. M. Carter. 1969. "Count Down for Death." *Crime and Delinquency* 15:77.

Smith, D. B. 1981. "Death Penalty—California Statute Upheld: *People* v. *Jackson*, 28 Cal. 3d 264,618P. 2d 149 (1980)." *American J. of Trial Advocacy* 5 (Summer):175.

Smith, D. J. 1957. "The Case for the Death Penalty." *L. A. B. Bull.* 32:195.

Smith, E. 1968. *Brief Against Death.* New York: Knopf.

Smith, U. 1893. "Gasocutions." *Scientific American* (December 9):370.

*Smith* v. *Balkcom.* 1981. 660 F. 2d 573 (5th Cir.).

*Smith* v. *Balkcom.* 1982. 677 F. 2d 20 (5th Cir.).

*Smith* v. *Balkcom.* 1982. 74 L. Ed 2 148 cert. denied Oct. 4, 1982.

Snortum, J. R., and V. H. Ashear. 1972. "Prejudice, Punitiveness, and Personality." *J. of Personality Assessment* 36 (June):291.

Snow, J. S. 1981. "Criminal Procedure—Capital Punishment—Admission of Compelled Psychiatric Testimony at Sentencing Phase Violates Defendant's Fifth and Sixth Amendment Rights (Case Note), *Estelle* v. *Smith* 101 Sup. Ct. 1866 (1981)." *St. Mary's L. J.* 3 (Winter):391.

Snyder, O. C. 1961. "Capital Punishment: The Moral Issue." *West Va. L. Rev.* 63:99.

Social Service Review. 1931. "Sir Samuel Romilly and the Abolition of Capital Punishment." *Social Service Rev.* 5:276.

Social Service Review. 1972. "The Road Up from Barbarism." *Social Service Rev.* 46:431.

Social Service Review. 1973. "On Capital Punishment." *Social Service Rev.* 47 (September):426.

Soelling, K. 1959. "Capital Punishment." *Chitty's L. J.* 8:146.

Solomon, G. F. 1975. "Capital Punishment as Suicide and as Murder." *Am. J. of Orthopsychiatry* 45 (July):701.

Sorokin, P. A. 1937. *Social and Cultural Dynamics.* New York: Bedminster Press.

South Africa Law Journal. 1971. "Statement by the Council of the Society of University Teachers of Law." *So. Africa L. J.* 87:467.

South Carolina Law Review. 1968. "Criminal Procedure—Empaneling Jurors— Death Sentence Invalidated When Veniremen Excluded for Voicing Scruples Against Imposition of Capital Punishment." *S. C. L. Rev.* 20:833.

South Carolina Law Review. 1970. "Criminal Procedure—Empaneling Jurors— Use of Challenges for Exclusion of Veniremen Who Oppose Imposition of Capital Punishment." *S. C. L. Rev.* 22:98.

South Carolina Law Review. 1980. "South Carolina Death Penalty Law" (Survey of South Carolina Law). *S. C. L. Rev.* 32 (August):81.

South Dakota Law Review. 1970. "Voir Dire Examination in Capital Cases: The Prosecutor's Burden." *S. Dak. L. Rev.* 15:412.

Southern California Law Review. 1950. "Criminal Law—Constitutional Law— Execution of Insane Persons (*Phyle* v. *Duffy*)." *S. Calif. L. Rev.* 23:246.

Southern California Law Review. 1952. "Commutation of Sentence—Effect of Conditions Attached by Governor (*Green* v. *Gordon*)." *S. Calif. L. Rev.* 26:92.

Southern California Law Review. 1958. "Recent Changes in California Law Regarding Jury's Discretion in Selecting First Degree Murder Penalty." *S. Calif. L. Rev.* 31:200.

Southern California Law Review. 1969. "Towards Assuring Fair Trials in Capital Cases: Some Reflections on *Witherspoon*." *S. Calif. L. Rev.* 42:329.

Southwestern Law Journal. 1968. "Criminal Law—Death Penalty Imposed by Jury, but Not by Judge, Unconstitutional." *S. W. L. J.* 22:544.

Southwestern Law Journal. 1969. "*Pittman* v. *State*, The Death Penalty and Texas Jurors." *S. W. L. J.* 23:405.

Southwestern Law Journal. 1973. "Death Penalty—A Cruel and Unusual Punishment." *S. W. L. J.* 27 (May):298.

Southwestern Law Review. 1972. "Recent Case, *People* v. *Anderson*." *Southwestern L. Rev.* 4:343.

Spangler, J. A. 1969. "California's Death Penalty Dilemma." *Crime and Delinquency* 15:142.

Speaker, F. 1975. "Capital Punishment: Ineffective, Unjust, Unconstitutional." *Prison Journal* 53:36.

Spear, C. 1844. *Essays on the Punishment of Death*. Boston: by the author. London: John Green.

*Spenkelink* v. *Wainwright*. 1978. 578 F. 2d 582 CA5.

St. John's Law Review. 1972. "*Furman* v. *Georgia*: Deathknell for Capital Punishment?" *St. John's L. Rev.* 47:107.

St. Louis Law Journal. 1970. "The Supreme Court and Capital Punishment: From *Wilkerson* to *Witherspoon* and Beyond." *St. Louis L. J.* 14:463.

St. Louis University Law Review. 1972. "Appellate Review of Sentences: A Survey." *St. Louis U. L. Rev.* 17:221.

St. Mary's Law Journal. 1975. "Constitutional Law—Death Penalty—Texas Death Penalty Statutes Comply with the Discretion Requirements of the United States Supreme Court." *St. Mary's L. J.* 7:454.

St. Mary's Law Journal. 1977a. "Criminal Procedure—Capital Punishment—Texas Statutes Amended to Provide for Execution by Intravenous Injection of a Lethal Substance. Tex. Laws 1977, ch. 138, arts. 43.14 and 43.18 at 287.88." *St. Mary's L. J.* 9:359.

St. Mary's Law Journal. 1977b. "Death-Prone Jurors: The Disintegration of the *Witherspoon* Rule in Texas." *St. Mary's L. J.* 9:288.

Stanford Law Review. 1958. "Post-Conviction Remedies in California Death Penalty Cases." *Stanford L. Rev.* 11:94.

Stanford Law Review. 1964. "Revival of the Eighth Amendment: Development of Cruel Punishment Doctrine by the Supreme Court." *Stanford L. Rev.* 16:996.

Stanford Law Review. 1969. "A Study of the California Penalty Jury in First Degree Murder Cases." *Stanford L. Rev.* 21:1297.

Stanford Law Review. 1980. "Discrimination and Arbitrariness in Capital Punishment: An Analysis of Post-*Furman* Murder Cases in Dade County, Florida 1973–1976." *Stanford L. Rev.* 33 (November):75.

Stanton, J. M. 1969. "Murderers on Parole." *Crime and Delinquency* 15:149.

Staples, M. H. 1966. "Capital Punishment: A Retentionist's View." *Chitty's L. J.* (1966):338.

Starrs, J. E. 1967. "The Forbidding Fruits of Capital Punishment." *Catholic World* 205:286.

Start, R. R., and T. D. McBride. 1960. "Abolish the Death Penalty." *Penn. B. A. Q.* 31:408.

State Government News. 1973. "Thirteen States Restore Death Penalty." *State Government News* 16:2.

Stein, J. 1980. "Specialty Reporters (Reflections on the Death Penalty Reporter)." *Case and Comment* 85 (November–December):33.

Stevens, G. 1971. "Above and Beyond Capital Punishment." *Saturday Review* (September 25):28.

Stout, J. K. 1959. "Executive Clemency in Pennsylvania." *The Shingle* 22:111.

Strauss, F. 1970. *Where Did Justice Go?* Boston: Gambit.

Styron, W. 1962a. "Death in Life of Benjamin Reid." *Esquire* (February):114.

Styron, W. 1962b. "The Aftermath of Benjamin Reid." *Esquire* (November):79.

Suffolk University Law Review. 1967. "Constitutional Law—Kidnaping—Capital Punishment—*United States* v. *Jackson* [U.S.D.C.]." *Suffolk U. L. Rev.* 1:130.

Suffolk University Law Review. 1968a. "Criminal Law—Kidnaping—*United States* v. *Jackson.*" *Suffolk U. L. Rev.* 3:203.

Suffolk University Law Review. 1968b. "Constitutional Law—Jury Selection—*Witherspoon* v. *State of Illinois.*" *Suffolk U. L. Rev.* 3:210.

Suffolk University Law Review. 1969. "Note: The Eighth Amendment and Our Evolving Standards of Decency: A Time for Reevaluation." *Suffolk U. L. Rev.* 3:616.

Suffolk University Law Review. 1971. "Constitutional Law—Cruel and Unusual Punishment." *Suffolk U. L. Rev.* 5:504.

Suffolk University Law Review. 1972. "Constitutional Law—Cruel or Unusual Punishment: The Death Penalty, *People* v. *Anderson.*" *Suffolk U. L. Rev.* 6:1045.

Suffolk University Law Review. 1974. "Death Penalty in Massachusetts." *Suffolk U. L. Rev.* 8:632.

Sultan, A. 1965. "Recent Judicial Concepts of 'Cruel and Unusual Punishment'." *Vill. L. Rev.* 10:271.

Summerfield, L. D. 1960. "For the Death Penalty." *Nev. S. B. J.* 25:105.

Suni, E. Y. 1982. "Recent Developments in Missouri: Criminal Law: Homicide." *UMKC L. Rev.* 50 (Summer):440.

Survey. 1915. "Why the People of Arizona Voted to Keep Their Public Hangman." *Survey* 33:585.

Sutherland, E. H. 1925. "Murder and the Death Penalty." *J. C. L. C.* 15:522.

Sutherland, E. H., and D. R. Cressey. 1966. *Principles of Criminology*, 7th edition. Philadelphia: Lippincott.

Suzuki, Y. 1973. "The Politics of Criminal Law Reform: Japan: Capital Punishment." *Am. J. of Comp. L.* 21:287, 299.

Swigert, V. L., and R. A. Farrell. 1976. *Murder, Inequality, and the Law: Differential Treatment in the Legal Process.* Lexington, Mass.: D. C. Heath.

Swigert, V. L., and R. A. Farrell. 1977. "Normal Homicides and the Law." *Am. Sociol. Rev.* 42:16.

Syracuse Law Review. 1968. "Constitutional Law:—State May Not Constitutionally Impose Death Penalty Pursuant to Verdict of Jury from Which Those with Conscientious Scruples Against Capital Punishment Were Excluded." *Syracuse L. Rev.* 20:93.

Syracuse Law Review. 1979. "Impact of a Sliding-Scale Approach to Due Process of Capital Punishment Litigation." *Syracuse L. Rev.* 30:675.

Syracuse Law Review. 1981. "*Rummel* v. *Estelle* (100 Sup. Ct. 1133): Sentencing Without a Rational Basis." *Syracuse L. Rev.* 32 (Summer):803.

Tao, L. S. 1976. "Beyond *Furman* v. *Georgia* (92 Sup. Ct. 2726): The Need for a Morally-Based Decision on Capital Punishment." *Notre Dame Lawyer* 51 (April):722.

Tao, L. S. 1977. "Constitutional Status of Capital Punishment: An Analysis of *Gregg* (*Gregg* v. *Georgia*, 96 Sup. Ct. 2909), *Jurek* (*Jurek* v. *Texas*, 96 Sup. Ct. 2950), *Roberts* (*Roberts* v. *Louisiana*, 96 Sup. Ct. 3001), and *Woodson* (*Woodson* v. *North Carolina*, 96 Sup. Ct. 2978)." *U. Detroit J. of Urban L.* 54:345.

Tarde, G. 1912. *Penal Philosophy*. Boston: Little, Brown.

Tarnopolsky, W. S. 1978. "Just Deserts or Cruel and Unusual Treatment or Punishment? Where Do We Look for Guidance?" *Ottawa L. J.* 10:1.

Tasker, R. 1978. "Long Shadow of the Gallows." *Far Eastern Econ. Rev.* 101 (September):23.

Taylor, C. L., and M. C. Hudson. 1972. *World Handbook of Political and Social Indicators*, 2nd ed. New Haven: Yale University Press.

Teeters, N. K. 1958. "Public Executions in Philadelphia." *Prison Journal* 38:63.

Teeters, N. K. 1960. "Public Executions in Pennsylvania, 1682 to 1834." *J. of the Lancaster County Historical Society* 64:85.

Teeters, N. K., and J. H. Hedblom. 1967. *Hang by the Neck*. Springfield, Ill.: Thomas.

Teeters, N. K., and C. J. Zibulka. n.d. "Executions under State Authority." Reprinted in part in U.S. Senate, Committee on the Judicial, "Hearings Before the Subcommittee on Criminal Laws and Procedures." 90th Congress, 2nd Session, on s1760, March 21, 22, and July 2, 1968 (1970:209–236)).

Teeven, J. J. 1972. "Deterrent Effects of Punishment: The Canadian Case." *Canadian J. of Criminology and Corrections* 14:68.

Temple Law Quarterly. 1932. "The Penalty in Pennsylvania for Murder in the First Degree." *Temple L. Quarterly* 7:330.

Temple Law Quarterly. 1969. "The Unanimity Requirement of a Jury's Determination and the *Witherspoon* Exclusionary Rule." *Temple L. Quarterly* 43:46.

Temple Law Quarterly. 1972. "Capital Sentencing—Effect of *McGautha* and *Furman*." *Temple L. Quarterly* 45:619.

Texas, Department of Corrections. 1972. "A Synopsis of Offenders Receiving the Death Sentence in Texas." Research Report no. 8, Division of Research, Texas Department of Corrections.

Texas Tech Law Review. 1975. "Criminal Law—Capital Punishment—The Texas Statutes Authorizing the Death Penalty Do Not Violate the Eighth Amendment's Prohibition of Cruel and Unusual Punishment." *Texas Tech L. Rev.* 7:170.

Texas Tech Law Review. 1976. "Constitutional Law—The Death Penalty for the Crime of Murder Does Not Violate the Eighth Amendment." *Texas Tech L. Rev.* 8:515.

*Texas v. Loudres.* 1980. 614 S.W. 2d 407.

Thomas, C. A. 1975. "A Sociological Perspective on Public Support for Capital Punishment." *Am. J. of Orthopsychiatry* 45 (July):641.

Thomas, C. W. 1977. "Eighth Amendment Challenges to the Death Penalty: The Relevance of Informed Public Opinion." *Van. L. Rev.* 30 (October):1005.

Thomas, P. A. 1957. "Murder and the Death Penalty." *Am. J. of Corrections* 19:16,30. Reprinted in Bedau (1967b), p. 242, as "Attitudes of Wardens Toward the Death Penalty."

Thomas, T. 1969. *This Life We Take.* San Francisco: Friends Committee on Legislation.

Thompson, W. C., C. L. Cowan, P. C. Ellsworth, and J. C. Harrington. 1983. "Death Penalty Attitudes and Conviction Proneness: The Translation of Attitudes into Verdicts." To be published in *Crime and Delinquency.*

Timaeus, D. 1981. "Fourteenth Amendment—Due Process—Texas Penal Code Section 12.31(b) Unconstitutionally Permits the Exclusion for Cause of Jurors Who have General Objections to, or Religious or Moral Scruples Against, the Death Penalty (Case Note), *Adams* v. *Texas* 448 U.S. 38 (1980)." *Am. J. of Crim. L.* 9 (July):252.

Tingler, R. A. 1970. "Unconstitutional Punishment." *Crim. L. Bull.* 6:311.

Tisdale, D. E. W. 1959. "Capital Punishment—A Practical Viewpoint." *Canadian Bar J.* 2:255.

Tittle, C. R. 1969. "Crime Rates and Legal Sanctions." *Social Problems* 16:409.

Toby, J. 1964. "Is Punishment Necessary?" *J. C. L. C. & P. S.* 55:332.

Tolstoy, L. 1908. "Government by Execution." *Living Age* 258 (August 8):349.

Tomkinson, C. 1972. "The Weekly Editor: [Don Reid] Witnessed 189 Executions." *Editor and Publisher* (September 16):30.

Topping, C. W. 1952. "The Death Penalty in Canada." The Annals 284:147.

Treadwell, C. A. L. 1944. "Capital Punishment: Is Its Abolition Justifiable?" *New Zealand L. J.* 20:215.

Triche, C. W. 1979. *Capital Punishment Dilemma, 1950–1977: A Subject Bibliography.* Troy, N. Y.: Whitston Publishing Co.

Trogolo, R. E. 1974. "Capital Punishment under the UCMJ After *Furman* (*Furman* v. *Georgia*, 92 Sup. Ct. 2726)." *Air Force L. Rev.* 16:86.

Tulane Law Review. 1973. "Constitutional Law—Eighth Amendment—Death Penalty as Currently Administered Constitutes Cruel and Unusual Punishment." *Tulane L. Rev.* 47 (June):1167.

Tulane Law Review. 1977. "Constitutional Law—Capital Punishment and the Eighth Amendment." *Tulane L. Rev.* 51 (February):360.

Tulane Law Review. 1979. "Constitutional Criminal Law—The Role of Mitigating Circumstances in Considering the Death Penalty." *Tulane L. Rev.* 53 (February):608.

Tullock, G. 1974. "Does Punishment Deter Crime?" *The Public Interest* 36:108.

Turffs, R. 1981. "Capital Punishment—Lesser Included Offenses—Penalty Enhancement." *American J. of Trial Advocacy* 4 (Spring):730.

Turkington, R. C. 1967. "Unconstitutionally Excessive Punishments: An Examination of the Eighth Amendment and the *Weems* Principle." *Crim. L. Bull.* 3:145.

Turnbull, C. 1979. "Death by Decree." *NLADA Briefcase* 36 (March):12.

Turner, J. 1980. "Cruel and Unusual Punishment (Tenth Annual Review of Criminal Procedure: United States Supreme Court and Courts of Appeals 1979–1980)." *Georgetown L. J.* 69 (December):524.

Tuttle, E. P. 1961. *The Crusade Against Capital Punishment in Great Britain.* New York: Times Books.

Tyler, S. 1965. "Electrocution as a Spectator Sport." *Fact* (March–April):47.

Tyler, T. R., and R. Weber. 1982. "Support for the Death Penalty: Instrumental Response to Crime, or Symbolic Attitude?" *Law and Sociology Rev.* 17 (November):21.

Ulmer, N. 1980. "Complaint Alleging a Validation of Human Rights in the United States of America." International Human Rights Law Group. Submitted to the Inter-American Commission on Human Rights.

UMKC Law Review. 1974. "Finding the Death Penalty Cruel and Unusual." *UMKC L. Rev.* 43:162.

UMKC Law Review. 1976. "Missouri's Unconstitutional Death Penalty: A Proposal for Reform." *UMKC L. Rev.* 45:223.

United Nations, Department of Economic and Social Affairs. 1960. "Capital Punishment, Report."

United Nations, Economic and Social Council. 1971a. "Capital Punishment, Italy, Norway, United Kingdom of Great Britain and Northern Ireland and Uruguay: Draft Resolution." E/AC.7/L.578 (April 2, 1971).

United Nations, Economic and Social Council. 1971b. "Capital Punishment." Note by the Secretary-General, E/4947 (February 23, 1971).

United Nations, Economic and Social Council. 1971c. Resolution Adopted by the Economic and Social Council, 1574(L). "Capital Punishment." E/RES/1574(L) (May 2, 1971).

United Nations, Economic and Social Council. 1973a. "Capital Punishment." Report of the Social Committee, E/5298 (April 24, 1973).

United Nations, Economic and Social Council. 1973b. "Capital Punishment." Report to the Secretary-General, E/5242 (February 23, 1973).

United Nations, Economic and Social Council, Commission on Human Rights. 1969. "Capital Punishment in the Republic of South Africa." E/CN.4/AC22/20:15.

United Nations Monthly. 1966. "U.N. and the Issue of Capital Punishment." *United Nations Monthly* (February):53.

United Nations, Publications. 1968. "Capital Punishment." Report, Developments, 1961–1965.

University of California at Los Angeles Law Review. 1971. "Punishment Rationale for Diminished Capacity." *UCLA L. Rev.* 18:561.

University of California at Los Angeles Law Review. 1972a. "Sentencing under the Proposed California Criminal Code." *UCLA L. Rev.* 19:526.

University of California at Los Angeles Law Review. 1972b. "Murder Under the Proposed California Criminal Code." *UCLA L. Rev.* 19:622.

University of Chicago Law School. 1970. *A Selected International Bibliography on Capital Punishment.* University of Chicago Law School, the Center for Studies in Criminal Justice.

University of Cincinnati Law Review. 1971. "Criminal Law—Rape—Death Penalty—Eighth Amendment Prohibition Against Cruel and Unusual Punishments Forbids Execution When the Victim's Life Was Neither Taken Nor Endangered." *U. Cincinnati L. Rev.* 40:396.

University of Cincinnati Law Review. 1973. "Constitutional Law—Cruel and Unusual Punishments—The Imposition and Carrying Out of the Death Penalty under Current Discretionary Sentencing Statutes Constitutes Cruel and Unusual Punishment in Violation of the Eighth and Fourteenth Amendments." *U. Cincinnati L. Rev.* 42:172.

University of Florida Law Review. 1968. "Jurors: Conscientious Scruples Against Capital Punishment Will Not Automatically Give Rise to Dismissal of Juror for Cause." *U. Florida L. Rev.* 21:262.

University of Florida Law Review. 1971. "Bifurcating Florida's Capital Trials: Two Steps Are Better Than One." *U. Florida L. Rev.* 24:127.

University of Kansas City Law Review. 1960. "Comment—Criminal Law—Capital Punishment." *U. K. C. L. Rev.* 28:170.

University of Miami Law Review. 1969. "Constitutional Law—Capital Punishment and the Challenge for Cause." *U. Miami L. Rev.* 23:631.

University of Miami Law Review. 1974. "Florida Death Penalty: A Lack of Discretion?" *U. Miami L. Rev.* 28:723.

University of Pennsylvania Law Review. 1960. "Criminal Procedure—Scope of Appellate Review of Sentences in Capital Cases." *U. Penn. L. Rev.* 108:434.

University of Pennsylvania Law Review. 1961. "Criminal Procedure—Federal Court of Appeals Vacates Sentence on Grounds of Severity and Remands to District Court for Resentencing (*U.S.* v. *Wiley*)." *U. Penn. L. Rev.* 109:422.

University of Richmond Law Review. 1971. "Cruel and Unusual Punishment: Constitutionality of the Death Penalty for Rape Where Victim's Life Neither Taken Nor Endangered." *U. Richmond L. Rev.* 5:392.

University of Richmond Law Review. 1972. "Criminal Procedure—Virginia's Limited Use of a Two-Trial System—*Snider* v. *Cox*." *U. Richmond L. Rev.* 6:386.

University of Richmond Law Review. 1976. "Capital Punishment: Constitutional Parameters for the Ultimate Penalty." *U. Richmond L. Rev.* 11:101.

University of San Fernando Valley Law Review. 1968. "The Death Oriented Jury Shall Live." *U. San Fernando V. L. Rev.* 1:253.

University of San Fernando Valley Law Review. 1974. "Death—California Style: Reviewing the Constitutionality of the State's New Capital Punishment Law." *U. San Fernando V. L. Rev.* 3:145.

University of San Francisco Law Review. 1976. "Prohibiting Cruel or Unusual Punishment: California's Requirement of Proportionate Sentencing after *Wingo* [*People* v. *Wingo* (Cal.) 534 P. 2d 1001] and *Rodriquez* [*Rodriquez*, In re (Cal) 537 P. 2d 384]." *U. S. F. L. Rev.* 10:524.

U.S. Congress, House of Representatives. 1979. Hearings before the Subcommittee on Criminal Justice on H.R. 13360, 95th Congress, 2nd Session (July 19, 1978).

U.S. Congress, Senate Judiciary Committee. 1973. Hearings before the Subcommittee on Criminal Laws and Procedures on s1401, 93rd Congress, 1st Session (June 13, July 26, 1973).

U.S. Congress, Senate Judiciary Committee. 1974. "To Establish Rational Criteria for the Imposition of Capital Punishment." 93rd Congress, 2nd Session.

U.S. Congress, Senate Judiciary Committee. 1975. Hearings before the Subcommittee on Criminal Laws and Procedures, on the Criminal Justice Reform Act of 1975 (including s1), 94th Congress, 1st Session (April 17, 18, 1975).

U.S. Congress, Senate Judiciary Committee. 1977. Hearings before the Subcommittee on Criminal Laws and Procedures on s1382, 95th Congress, 1st Session (May 18, 1977).

U.S. Congress, Senate Judiciary Committee. 1978. Hearings before the Subcommittee on Criminal Laws and Procedures on s1382 (April 27, May 11, 1978).

U.S. Congress, Senate Judiciary Committee. 1980. "Establishing Constitutional Procedures for the Imposition of Capital Punishment," on s114, 96th Congress, 2nd Session (January 17, 1980).

U.S. Senate, Committee on the Judiciary. 1981. Capital Punishment Hearings, April 10–May 1, 1981, on s114, "Bill to Establish Constitutional Procedures for the Imposition of the Sentence of Death, and for Other Purposes," 97th Congress, 1st Session.

Utah Law Review. 1969. "Due Process Standard of Jury Impartiality Precludes Death-Qualification of Jurors in Capital Case." *Utah L. Rev.* (1969):154.

van den Haag, E. 1969. "On Deterrence and the Death Penalty." *J. C. L. C. & P. S.* 60:141. Reprinted in McCafferty, p. 102; also in Hart-Celler Hearings, p. 127.

van den Haag, E. 1977a. "A Response to Bedau." *Ariz. State L. J.* 1977:767.

van den Haag, E. 1977b. "Death Penalty Statutes: A Post-*Gregg* v. *Georgia* (96 Sup. Ct. 2909) Survey and Discussion of Eighth Amendment Safeguards." *Washburn L. J.* 16:497.

van den Haag, E. 1978a. "In Defense of the Death Penalty: A Legal-Practical-Moral Analysis." *Crim. L. B.* 14 (January–February):51.

van den Haag, E. 1978b. "The Collapse of the Case Against Capital Punishment." *National Rev.* 30 (March):395.

Van Hoomissen, G. 1965. "The Death Penalty: Reformation or Vindictive Justice?" *Nat. D. A. Assoc. J.* 1:80.

Van Niekerk, S. V. 1970. "Hang by the Neck." *So. Africa L. J.* 86:475.

Van Niekerk, S. V. 1971. "Name Not a Rope in His House That Hang'd Himself." *So. Africa L. J.* 87:465.

Vance, C. J. 1973. "The Death Penalty after *Furman.*" *The Notre Dame Lawyer* 48:850.

Vanderbilt Law Review. 1969. "Criminal Law—Exclusion for Cause of Prospective Jurors with Scruples Against Death Penalty Violates Due Process." *Van. L. Rev.* 21:864.

Vanderbilt Law Review. 1977. "*Gardner* v. *Florida* (97 Sup. Ct. 1197): The Application of Due Process to Sentencing Procedures." *Van. L. Rev.* 63 (November):1281.

Victor, D. 1972. "*Furman* v. *Georgia*: The Burger Court Looks at Judicial Review." *Law and Social Order*:393.

Vidmar, N., and T. Dittenhofer. 1981. "Informed Public Opinion and Death Penalty Attitudes." *Canadian J. of Criminology* 23 (January):43.

Vidmar, N., and P. Ellsworth. 1974. "Public Opinion and the Death Penalty." *Stanford L. Rev.* 26 (June):1245.

Villanova Law Review. 1962. "Criminal Procedure—Determination of Accused's Right to Bail in Capital Cases." *Vill. L. Rev.* 7:438.

Villanova Law Review. 1968. "Constitutional Law:—Criminal Procedure—Voir Dire Examination of Jurors in Capital Cases—Dismissal for Cause of Jurors Who Voice Only General Objections to Death Penalty Held Unconstitutional as Violative of Due Process." *Vill. L. Rev.* 14:125.

Villenga, J. J. 1959. "Is Capital Punishment Wrong?" *Christianity Today* 4:7. Reprinted in Bedau (1967b), p. 123, as "Christianity and the Death Penalty."

Virginia Law Review. 1956. "Criminal Law: Jury Entitled to Know Length of Maximum Sentence and Possibility of Parole When Determining Whether Death Penalty Should Be Imposed." *Va. L. Rev.* 42:1144.

Virginia Law Review. 1964. "Criminal Law: Double Jeopardy—Sentence of Life Imprisonment in Initial Trial Precludes Death Sentence for Same Offense in Trial on Remand." *Va. L. Rev.* 50:559.

Virginia Law Review. 1966. "Note—The Congress, the Court, and Jury Selection: A Critique of Titles I and II of the Civil Rights Bill of 1966." *Va. L. Rev.* 52:1069.

Virginia Law Review. 1972. "Capital Punishment in Virginia." *Va. L. Rev.* 58:97.

Vold, G. B. 1932. "Can the Death Penalty Prevent Crime?" *Prison Journal* 12:4.

Vold, G. B. 1952. "Extent and Trend of Capital Crimes in the United States." *The Annals* 284:2.

Von Hentig, H. 1947. *Crime: Causes and Conditions.* New York: McGraw-Hill.

Von Mittermaier, C. J. 1980. *Capital Punishment* (reprint of 1865 edition, J. M. Moir, ed.). Westport, Conn.: Hyperion.

Wake Forest Law Review. 1971. "Criminal Law—The Limited Application of the Eighth Amendment's Cruel and Unusual Punishment Clause to the Death Penalty." *Wake Forest L. Rev.* 7:494.

Waldo, G. P. 1970. "The Criminality Level of Incarcerated Murderers and Non-Murderers." *J. C. L. C. & P. S.* 61:60.

Walker, C. E. 1981. "The Cloning of the Prosecutorial Apple (Double Jeopardy and Capital Punishment) (Case Note)." *Northern Illinois Univ. L. Rev.* 2 (Winter):119.

Walker, L. 1973. "The Legal Eye—The Black Death Penalty." *Essence* (March):28.

Wall, B. 1972. "Recent Developments, Jury Assessment of the Death Penalty." *Military L. Rev.* 55:247.

Warren, D. I. 1970. "Justice in Recorder's Court: An Analysis of Misdemeanor Cases in Detroit." Unpublished.

Washburn Law Journal. 1969. "Competency of Jurors Who Have Conscientious Scruples Against Capital Punishment." *Washburn L. J.* 8:352.

Washburn Law Journal. 1977. "Death Penalty Statutes: A Post-*Gregg* v. *Georgia* (96 Sup. Ct. 2909) Survey and Discussion of Eighth Amendment Safeguards." *Washburn L. J.* 16:497.

Washington, H. A., ed. 1859. *The Writings of Thomas Jefferson*, Vol. 8. New York: J. C. Riker.

Washington Law Review. 1982. "Death Penalty in Washington: An Historical Perspective." *Wash. L. Rev.* 57 (July):525.

Washington Research Project. 1971. *The Case Against Capital Punishment.* Washington, D.C.: Washington Research Project.

Washington University Law Quarterly. 1960. "Judicial Limitations on the Constitutional Protection Against Cruel and Unusual Punishment." *Wash. U. L. Quarterly* (1960):160.

Washington University Law Quarterly. 1977. "Defendants' Right to Disclosure of Presentence Investigation Reports in Capital Cases." *Wash. U. L. Quarterly* (1977):728.

Washington University Law Review. 1972. "The Constitutionality of the Death Penalty for Non-Aggravated Rape, 1972." *Wash. U. L. Rev.* (1972):170.

Waugh, A. 1974. "Not to Worry." *New Statesman* 87 (March 29):442.

Wayne Law Review. 1969. "Constitutional Law—Cruel and Unusual Punishment—Eighth Amendment Applied to Sentence Within Valid Statutory Limits." *Wayne L. Rev.* 15:882.

Wayne Law Review. 1979. "Criminal Law—Death Penalty—Right of a Defendant to Have Any Relevant Aspect of His Character and Circumstances of Offense Used as Factors in Mitigating a Death Sentence." *Wayne L. Rev.* 25 (July):1147.

Webster, P. P. 1982. "*Estelle* v. *Smith* (101 Sup. Ct. 1866): Extending the Privilege Against Self-Incrimination to Use of Psychiatric Examinations in Texas Death Penalty Proceedings (Case Note)." *Southern Texas Law Journal* 22:355.

Wechsler, H. 1960. "Five Major Issues." *Life* 48 (May 9):46. Reprinted in McClellan (1961), p. 53.

Weigel, S. A. 1968. "Appellate Revision of Sentences: To Make the Punishment Fit the Crime." *Stanford L. Rev.* 20:405.

Weihofen, H. 1979. *The Urge to Punish.* Westport, Conn.: Greenwood Press.

Weiland, S. C., and G. Jones. 1972. "Federal Procedural Implications of *Furman* v. *Georgia*: What Rights for the Formerly Capital Offender?" *Am. J. of Crim. L.* 1:317.

Weissbrodt, M. H., and D. S. Marcus. 1968. "The Death Penalty Cases." *Calif. L. Rev.* 56:1268.

Weissman, J. C. 1982. "Sentencing Due Process: Evolving Constitutional Principles." *Wake Forest L. Rev.* 18 (June):523.

Welch, R. C. 1972. "Life on Death Row." *Military Life* (October):3.

Welling, B., and L. A. Hipfner. 1976. "Cruel and Unusual? Capital Punishment in Canada." *U. Toronto L. J.* 20:55.

West, L. J. 1968. "A Psychiatrist Looks at the Death Penalty." In Hart Hearings, p. 123.

West, L. J. 1975. "Psychiatric Reflections on the Death Penalty." *Am. J. of Orthopsychiatry* 45 (July):689.

Wheeler, M. E. 1972. "Toward a Theory of Limited Punishment: An Examination of the Eighth Amendment." *Stanford L. Rev.* 24:838.

White, W. S. 1973. "Constitutional Invalidity of Convictions Imposed by Death-Qualified Juries." *Cornell L. Rev.* 58 (July):1176.

White, W. S. 1974. "The Role of the Social Sciences in Determining the Constitutionality of Capital Punishment." *Duquesne L. Rev.* 13:279.

White, W. S. 1976a. "Disproportionality and the Death Penalty: Death as a Punishment for Rape." *U. Pitt. L. Rev.* 38:145.

White, W. S. 1976b. "*Witherspoon* Revisited: Exploring the Tension Between *Witherspoon* and *Furman*." *U. Cincinnati L. Rev.* 45:19.

White, W. S. 1980. "Death-Qualified Juries: The 'Prosecution-Proneness' Argument Reexamined." *U. Pitt. L. Rev.* 41:353.

White, W. S. 1981. "Waiver and the Death Penalty: The Implications of *Estelle* v. *Smith* (101 Sup. Ct. 1866)." *J. Crim. L.* 72 (Winter):1522.

Widener, R. L. 1982. "Doctrine of Applied Acquittal and Capital Sentencing" (Annual Survey of South Carolina Law, 1981). *S. C. L. Rev.* 34 (August):114.

William and Mary Law Review. 1971. "Constitutional Law—Death Penalty as Cruel and Unusual Punishment for Rape." *William and Mary L. Rev.* 12:682.

Williams, F. H. 1960. "The Death Penalty and the Negro." *The Crisis* 67:501.

Wingersky, M. F. 1954. "Report of the Royal Commission on Capital Punishment (1949–1953), A Review." *J. C. L. C. & P. S.* 44:695.

Winick, B. J. 1982. "Prosecutorial Peremptory Challenge Practices in Capital Cases: An Empirical Study and a Constitutional Analysis." *Michigan L. Rev.* 81 (November):1.

Wisconsin Law Review. 1976. "Constitutional Law—Eighth Amendment—Appellate Sentence Review." *Wisc. L. Rev.* 1976:655.

Wisconsin Law review. 1978. "Constitutional Law—Criminal Law—Eighth

Amendment—Death as a Punishment for Rape is Cruel and Unusual Punishment." *Wisc. L. Rev.* 1978:253.

Wisconsin Law Review. 1981. *"Beck* v. *Alabama* (100 Sup. Ct. 2382): The Right to a Lesser Included Offense Instruction in Capital Cases." *Wisc. L. Rev.*:560.

Wisconsin, Legislative Reference Library. 1962. "Capital Punishment in the States with Special Reference to Wisconsin." Information Bulletin no. 210.

*Witherspoon* v. *Illinois.* 1968. 391 U.S. 510.

Wolf, B. H. 1973. *Pileup on Death Row.* New York: Doubleday.

Wolf, E. D. 1964. "Analysis of Jury Sentencing in Capital Cases: New Jersey 1937–1961." *Rutgers L. Rev.* 19:56.

Wolfgang, M. E. 1958. *Patterns in Criminal Homicide.* Philadelphia: University of Pennsylvania Press.

Wolfgang, M. E. 1959. "Murder, the Pardon Board, and Recommendations by Judges and District Attorneys." *J. C. L. C. & P. S.* 50:4.

Wolfgang, M. E. 1961. "A Sociological Analysis of Criminal Homicide." *Fed. Prob.* 25 (March):48. Reprinted in Bedau (1967b), p. 74.

Wolfgang, M. E. 1972. Testimony, in Hart-Celler Hearings.

Wolfgang, M. E. 1978. "The Death Penalty: Social Philosophy and Social Science Research." *Crim. L. B.* 14 (January–February).

Wolfgang, M. E., and B. Cohen. 1970. *Crime and Race Conceptions and Misconceptions.* New York: Institute of Human Relations Press.

Wolfgang, M. E., A. Kelly, and H. C. Nolde. 1962. "Comparison of the Executed and the Commuted Among Admissions to Death Row." *J. C. L. C. & P. S.* 53:301. Reprinted in Bedau (1967b), p. 464, as "Executions and Commutations in Pennsylvania."

Wolfgang, M. E., and M. Riedel. 1973. "Race, Judicial Discretion, and the Death Penalty." *The Annals* 407:119.

Wolfgang, M. E., and M. Riedel. 1975. "Rape, Race and Death Penalty in Georgia." *Am. J. of Orthopsychiatry* 45:658.

Wollan, L. A., Jr. 1973. "Death Penalty After *Furman* (*Furman* v. *Georgia*, 92 Sup. Ct. 2726)." *Loyola U. L. J.* 4:339.

Wolpin, K. I. 1978. "Capital Punishment and Homicide in England: A Summary of Results with Reply by A. M. Polinsky." *Am. Ec. Rev.*, Papers and Proceedings 68 (May):422, 435.

Wonacott, J., and R. Wonacott. 1972. *Econometrics.* New York: John Wiley.

Wood, A. L. 1952. "The Alternatives to the Death Penalty." *The Annals* 284:63.

Woods, B. A. 1982. "Sixth Amendment—Trial by an Impartial Jury—the Breadth of the Basis for Excluding Veniremen under the *Witherspoon* Doctrine (Case Note), *Adams* v. *Texas* 448 U.S. 38 (1980)." *Am. J. of Crim. L.* 10 (March):47.

*Woodson* v. *North Carolina.* 1976. 96 Sup. Ct. 2978.

Wordsworth, W. 1842. "Sonnets on the Punishment of Death." *U.S. Mag. & Democ. Rev.* 10 (March):272.

Worley, F. 1956. "Bill to Abolish Capital Punishment in Pennsylvania." *Dickinson L. Rev.* 60:167.

Wright, D. R. 1972. "The Role of the Judiciary: From *Marbury* to *Anderson*." *Calif. L. Rev.* 60:1262.

Wright, J. De P. 1980. "Capital Punishment in Ontario." *Law and Society Gazette* 14 (June):203.

Yager, T. C. 1958. "Executive Clemency." *Calif. S. B. J.* 33:221.

Yale Law Journal. 1975. "Strategies of Abolition." *Yale L. J.* 84 (July):1769.

Yale Law Journal. 1981. "Matter of Life and Death: Due Process Protection in Capital Clemency Proceedings." *Yale L. J.* 90 (March):889.

Yetter, J. F. 1978a. "Florida Death Penalty—Is It Unconstitutional under State Law ?" *Flor. B. J.* 52 (May):372.

Yetter, J. F. 1978b. "*Gardner* v. *Florida* (97 Sup. Ct. 1197): Pre-Sentence Reports in Capital Sentencing Procedures." *Ohio N. L. Rev.* 5 (January):175.

Yoder, J. H. 1961. *Christian and Capital Punishment.* Newton, Kan.: Faith and Life.

Young, H. J. 1966. "Treason and Its Punishment in Revolutionary Pennsylvania." *Penn. Mag. of History and Biography* 90:287.

Young, R. L. 1971. "No Standards Required to Guide Death-Penalty Jury." *A. B. A. J.* 57:808.

Young, R. L. 1980a. "Capital Punishment . . . Lesser Offenses." *A. B. A. J.* 66 (October):1280.

Young, R. L. 1980b. "Capital Punishment . . . Jurors' Scruples." *A. B. A. J.* 66 (October):1280.

Young, R. L. 1981. "Capital Punishment . . . Sentences." *A. B. A. J.* 67 (September):1184.

Young, R. L. 1982a. "Capital Punishment . . . Mitigating Factors." *A. B. A. J.* 68 (March):345.

Young, R. L. 1982b. "Capital Punishment . . . Aggravating Circumstances." *A. B. A. J.* 68 (July):846.

Young, R. L. 1982c. "Capital Punishment . . . Lesser Offenses." *A. B. A. J.* 68 (July):848.

Young, R. L. 1982d. "Criminal Law . . . Felony Murder." *A. B. A. J.* 68 (October):1298.

Younger, I. 1980. "Three Footnotes to Legal History." *Cornell L. J.* 7 (June):15.

Yunker, J. A. 1982a. "The Relevance of the Identification Problem to Statistical Research on Capital Punishment." *Crime and Delinquency* 28 (January):96.

Yunker, J. A. 1982b. "Testing the Deterrent Effect of Capital Punishment: A Reduced Form Approach." *Criminology* 19 (February):626.

Zanger, J. 1965. "Crime and Punishment in Early Massachusetts." *Wm. & Mary Q.* 2, 3:471.

Zeisel, H. 1968. "Some Data on Juror Attitudes Toward Capital Punishment." Center for Studies in Criminal Justice, University of Chicago Law School.

Zeisel, H. 1976. "Deterrent Effect of the Death Penalty: Facts v. Faiths." *Supreme Court Rev.* 1976:317.

Zeisel, H. 1981. "Race Bias in the Administration of the Death Penalty: The Florida Experience." *Harv. L. Rev.* 95 (December):456.

Zelmanowits, J. 1961. "Is There Such a Thing as Capital Punishment?" *British J. of Criminology* 2:78.

Ziferstein, I. 1967. "A Psychiatrist Looks at Capital Punishment." *Frontier* 8:5.

Zimmerman, I. 1963. *Punishment Without Crime.* New York: Clarkson Potter.

Zimring, F. E. 1971. *Perspectives on Deterrence.* Washington, D.C.: Government Printing Office (National Clearinghouse of Mental Health, Center for Studies of Crime and Delinquency (January)).

Zimring, F. E. 1972. "The Medium Is the Message: Firearm Caliber as a Determinant of Death from Assault." *J. Legal Studies* 1:97.

Zimring, F. E., J. Eigen, and S. O'Malley. 1976. "Punishing Homicide in Philadelphia: Perspectives on the Death Penalty." *U. Chicago L. Rev.* 43:227.

Zimring, F. E., and G. Hawkins. 1968. "Deterrence and Marginal Groups." *J. of Research in Crime and Delinquency* 5:100.

Zimring, F. E., and G. Hawkins. 1973. *Deterrence: The Legal Threat in Crime Control.* Chicago: University of Chicago Press.

# INDEX